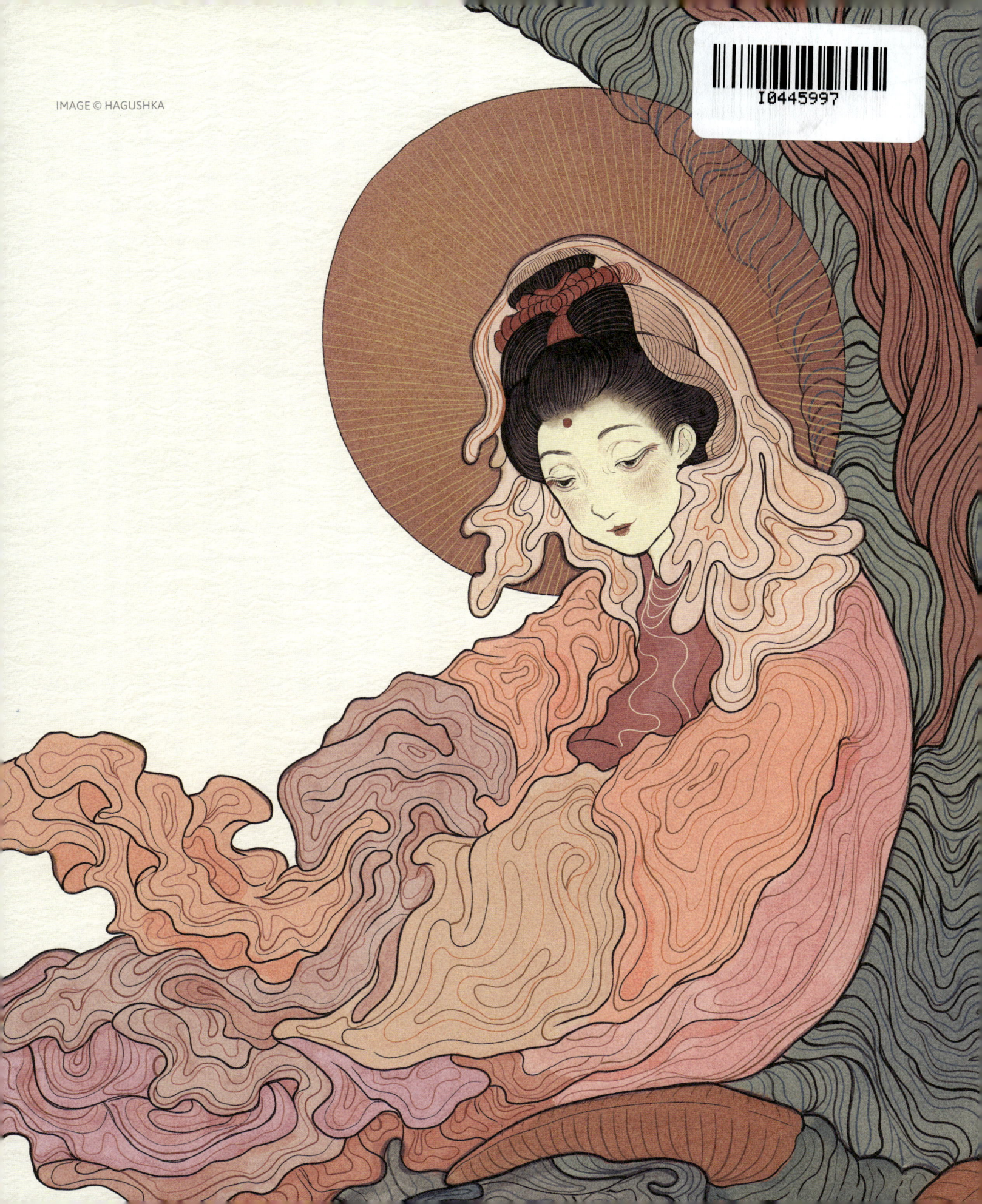

IMAGE © HAGUSHKA

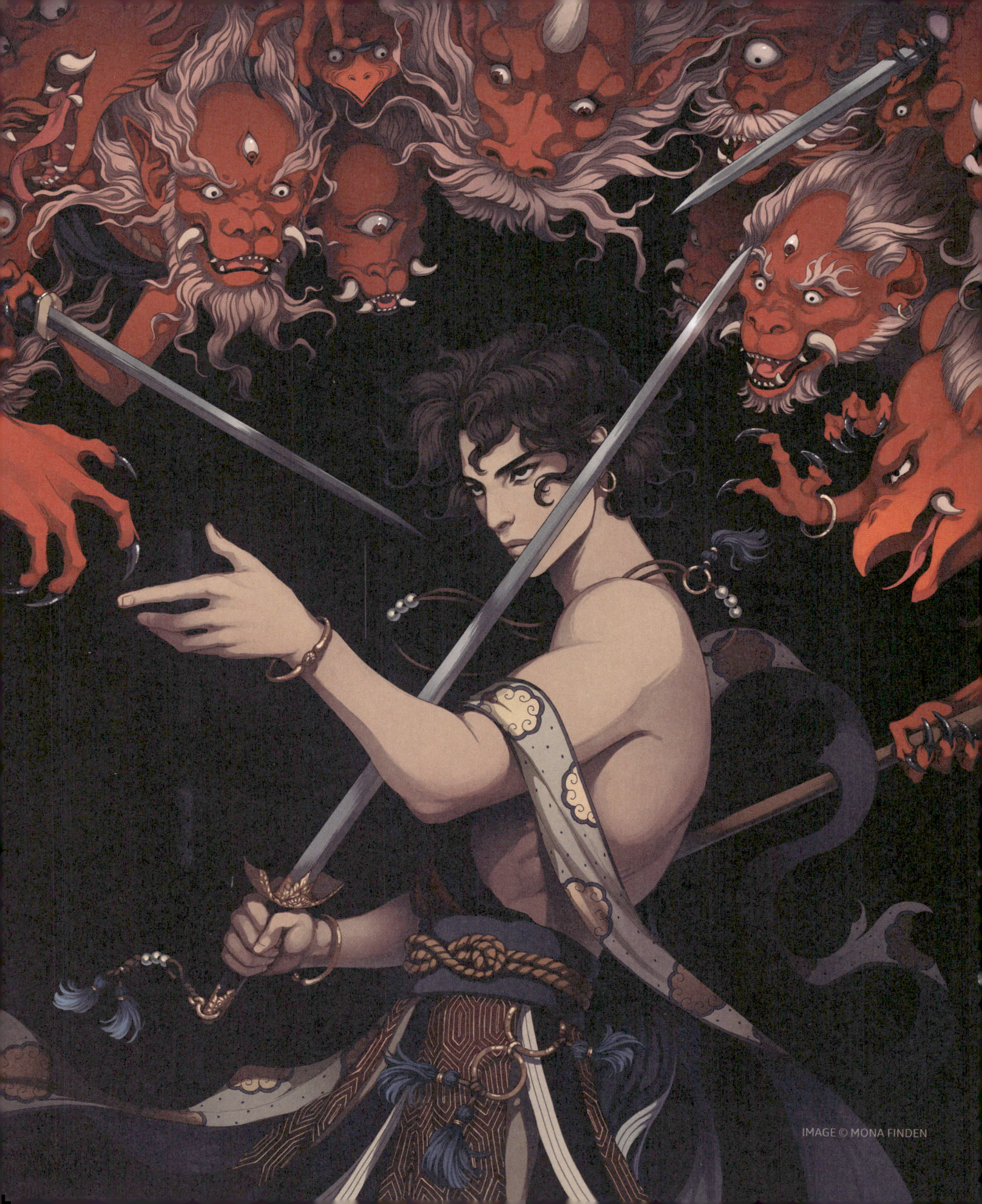

IMAGE © MONA FINDEN

HOKUSAI

AN ARTISTS' TRIBUTE

3dtotal Publishing

3dtotalPublishing

Correspondence: **publishing@3dtotal.com**
Website: **store.3dtotal.com**

Every effort has been made to ensure the credits and contact information listed are present and correct. In the case of any errors that have occurred, the publisher respectfully directs readers to **store.3dtotal.com/pages/information** for any updated information and corrections.

First published in the United Kingdom, 2025, by 3dtotal Publishing.

Address: 3dtotal.com Ltd,
29 Foregate Street, Worcester,
WR1 1DS, United Kingdom.

Hard cover ISBN: 978-1-915992-14-7

Printed and bound in China
by C&C Offset Printing Co., Ltd

Visit **store.3dtotal.com** for a complete list of available book titles.

Editorial Project Manager: Rhiannon Joseph
Lead Editor: Samantha Rigby
Lead Designer: Joseph Cartwright
Studio Manager: Simon Morse
Managing Director: Tom Greenway

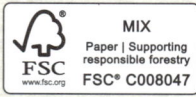

IMAGE © JOHANNA FORSTER

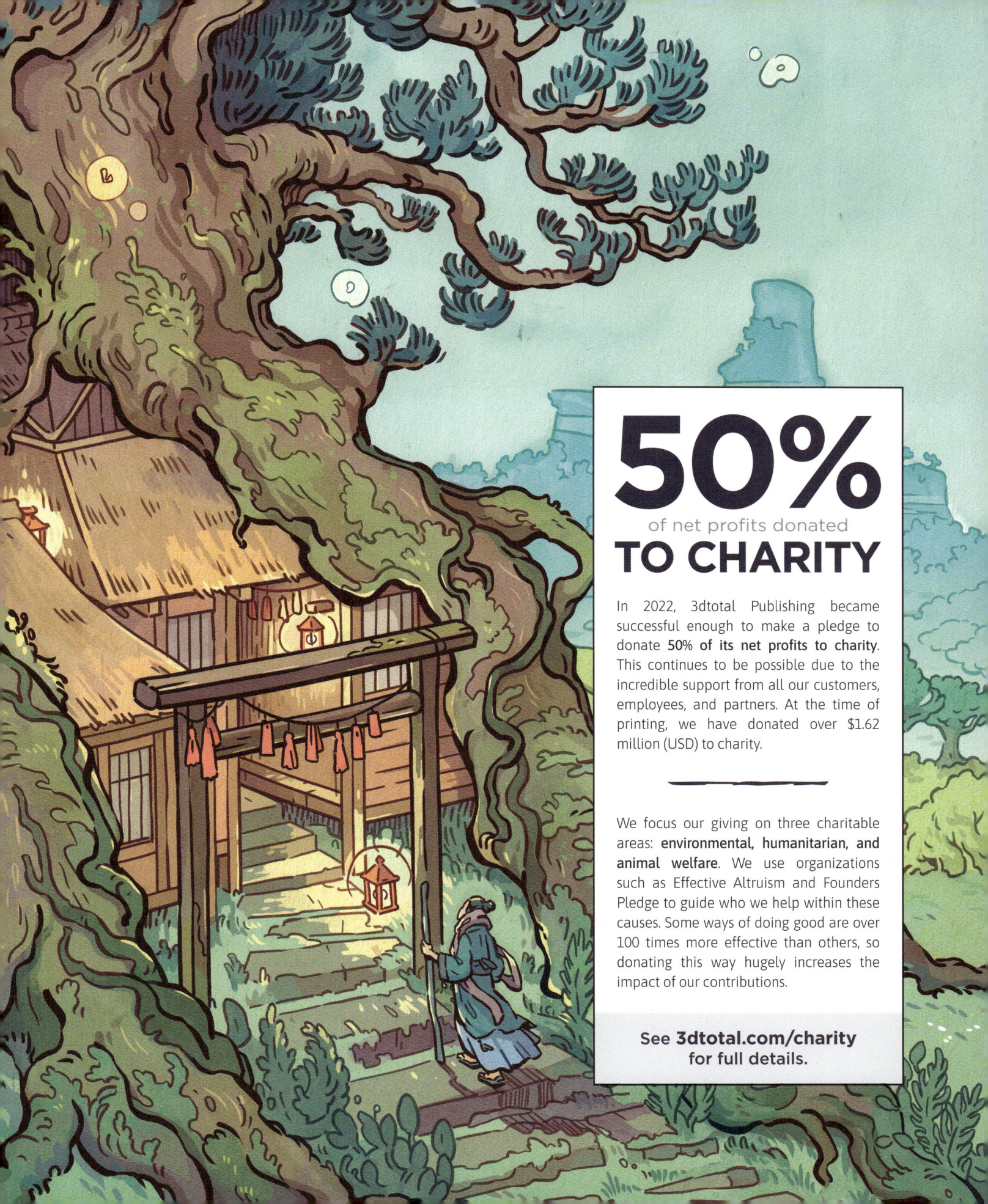

50%
of net profits donated
TO CHARITY

In 2022, 3dtotal Publishing became successful enough to make a pledge to donate **50% of its net profits to charity**. This continues to be possible due to the incredible support from all our customers, employees, and partners. At the time of printing, we have donated over $1.62 million (USD) to charity.

We focus our giving on three charitable areas: **environmental, humanitarian, and animal welfare**. We use organizations such as Effective Altruism and Founders Pledge to guide who we help within these causes. Some ways of doing good are over 100 times more effective than others, so donating this way hugely increases the impact of our contributions.

See **3dtotal.com/charity**
for full details.

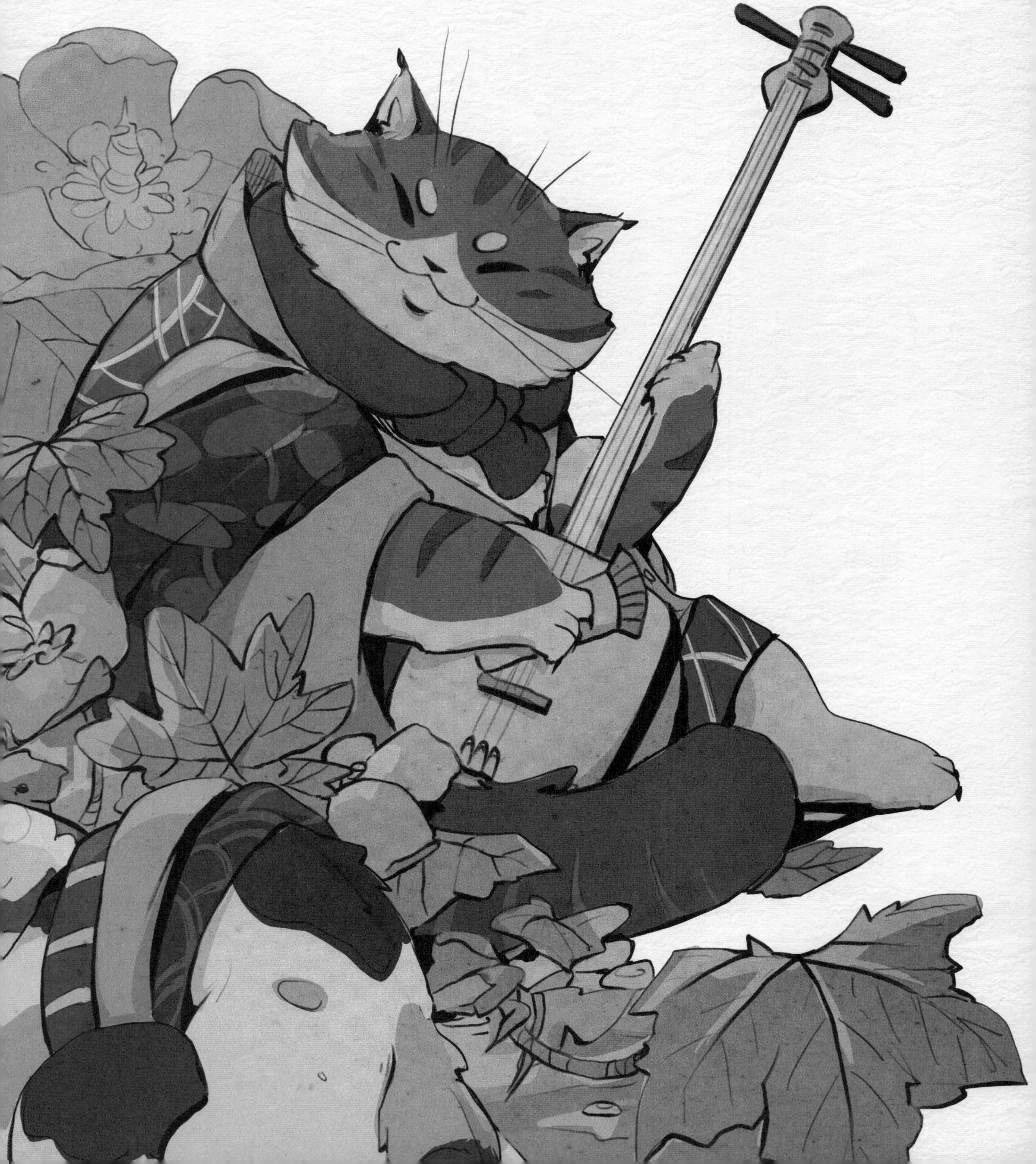

CONTENTS

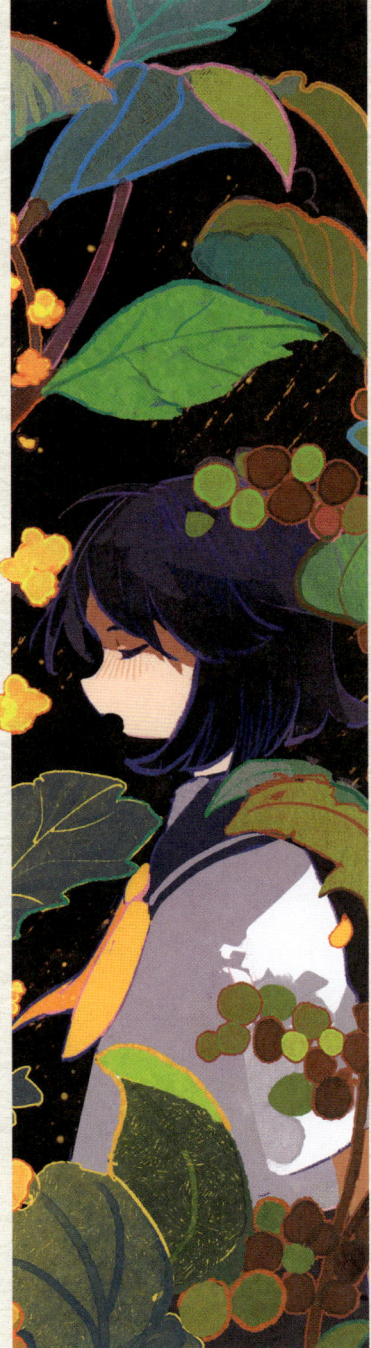

IMAGE © MENGXUAN LI

Hokusai is a force to be reckoned with. Imagine asking someone in 1830s Edo (present-day Tokyo) about Katsushika Hokusai. They would most likely cite the name of one of his famous prints, either his series of views of Mount Fuji, his images of ghost stories, or one of his hugely famous books, like his influential *Hokusai manga* (literally *Hokusai's Doodles*) or his goofy guide to self-taught dancing, *Odori hitorigeiko* (*Dancing on your Own*). During his own time already, Hokusai was celebrated as one of the most famous artists of the late Edo period. In a sense, it is hard to imagine a time when Hokusai was not famous. From an early age, he apprenticed in a printmaker's studio and engaged in the physical act of making the kinds of Japanese artworks he would eventually become most known for. Hard work, talent, and an acute understanding of the art business enabled the emergence of the global event that is Hokusai.

The artist's fame is rooted in many aspects coalescing around a sweet spot, like a perfect equation where each variable contributes to an exact final outcome. For one, although Hokusai made many bespoke paintings – art objects that were unique and required significant expense to make and buy – his main output is in the thousands of prints he designed. Available for the price of a bowl of noodles – a lunch – pretty much anyone could own a Hokusai. All it took was an empty stomach. This affordability – in a sense, the democratic nature of Hokusai's prints – has changed dramatically, especially in recent years, when the art market made an impression of his *Great Wave*, the most expensive Japanese print ever sold.

Hokusai himself had a part in the creation of his own phenomenon. Like many of his Edo-period artist peers, Hokusai was adept at promoting his own image and actively encouraging others to copy his style – while at the same time complaining that competitors did not match up to his aptitude. The many books that Hokusai designed served in implicit and explicit ways to disseminate his method into the broader ecosystem of art-making and art-buying during his time. *Hokusai manga*, published first in ten successive volumes between 1814 and 1819, effectively functioned as a guidebook to Hokusai's style. Paired with his lifetime fame along with the thousands of prints he made and, to some degree, his paintings, books like these helped embed his name in the popular realm. Hokusai made himself a new mainstream.

The self-promotion worked; he is still everywhere. In 1883, the French art critic, Louis Gonse, in his *L'art japonais*, sang Hokusai's praises and, in many ways, cemented his fame by declaring that he was, 'One of the greatest and most ingenious painters of his nation.' Hokusai's work went viral before the concept of 'viral' even existed. As Gonse attests, after his death in 1849, his prints took on a life of their own. They were transmitted from Japan to Europe and eventually made their way to America. On both sides of the Atlantic, and really across the world, Hokusai impacted artists and continues to do so today. Naturally, he was not the only Japanese artist making waves at the time – Hiroshige and Utamaro were savoured for their innovative techniques. But Hokusai stood out. While Hiroshige and Utamaro's works existed in the elite world of Paris's art and culture, over time Hokusai came to touch people across social strata and arrested their attention for nearly 200 years since his death. Think about how inspirational his prints must have been for European artists who had never seen anything like his use of space and colour, his combination of solemnity and humour. Vincent van Gogh was particularly smitten with Hiroshige's work, but it was Hokusai's brushwork that really affected people across the world. Hokusai's visual language is Japanese and international at the same time; it is local and border-transcending. His work is raw and confident; it is traditional and completely fresh.

While plenty of artists fade into obscurity, Hokusai's star has only become brighter. When Japan started opening up to the world during the Meiji era – changing the relatively hermetic island nation of Hokusai's own time into a geopolitical power that helped extend Hokusai's status onto the international stage – he became something of Japan's cultural ambassador. He also became a catalyst for contemporary culture, ranging from Studio Ghibli to the official entry stamps for tourists coming to Japan. Even today, he serves equally as a representation of traditional Japan and as a global influencer.

Hokusai's legacy is really solidified by the depth by which his work has become woven into Japan's (and the world's) shared cultural fabric. His prints, especially, are not just museum pieces; they are part of how Japan sees itself and how the world sees Japan. It is remarkable when you think about it: a guy who spent his days making woodblock prints in Edo-period Japan ended up creating images that would speak to people across centuries and continents. Every time someone puts the *Great Wave* on a phone case or a T-shirt, they are adding to Hokusai's larger-than-life persona in a way he probably never imagined – or perhaps he did.

Just consider the design of the new Japanese 1,000-yen bill issued in 2024, which has the *Great Wave* on its back. Anyone travelling with a Japanese passport is carrying Hokusai with them; every page of the document has an image of his series, *Thirty-six Views of Mount Fuji (Fugaku sanjūrokkei)* on them. Even your smartphone carries Hokusai's fingerprints. Try typing 'wave' and you will see an emoji that is based on this most iconic of prints.

I felt the wave of Hokusai just as I am writing these words, when a New Year's card reached me from a major Japanese corporation. It had Hokusai's *Great Wave* on the cover. The governor of Tokyo made the same choice for her season's greetings card. Hokusai lives!

FRANK FELTENS
CURATOR OF JAPANESE ART
SMITHSONIAN'S NATIONAL MUSEUM OF ASIAN ART

INTRODUCTION

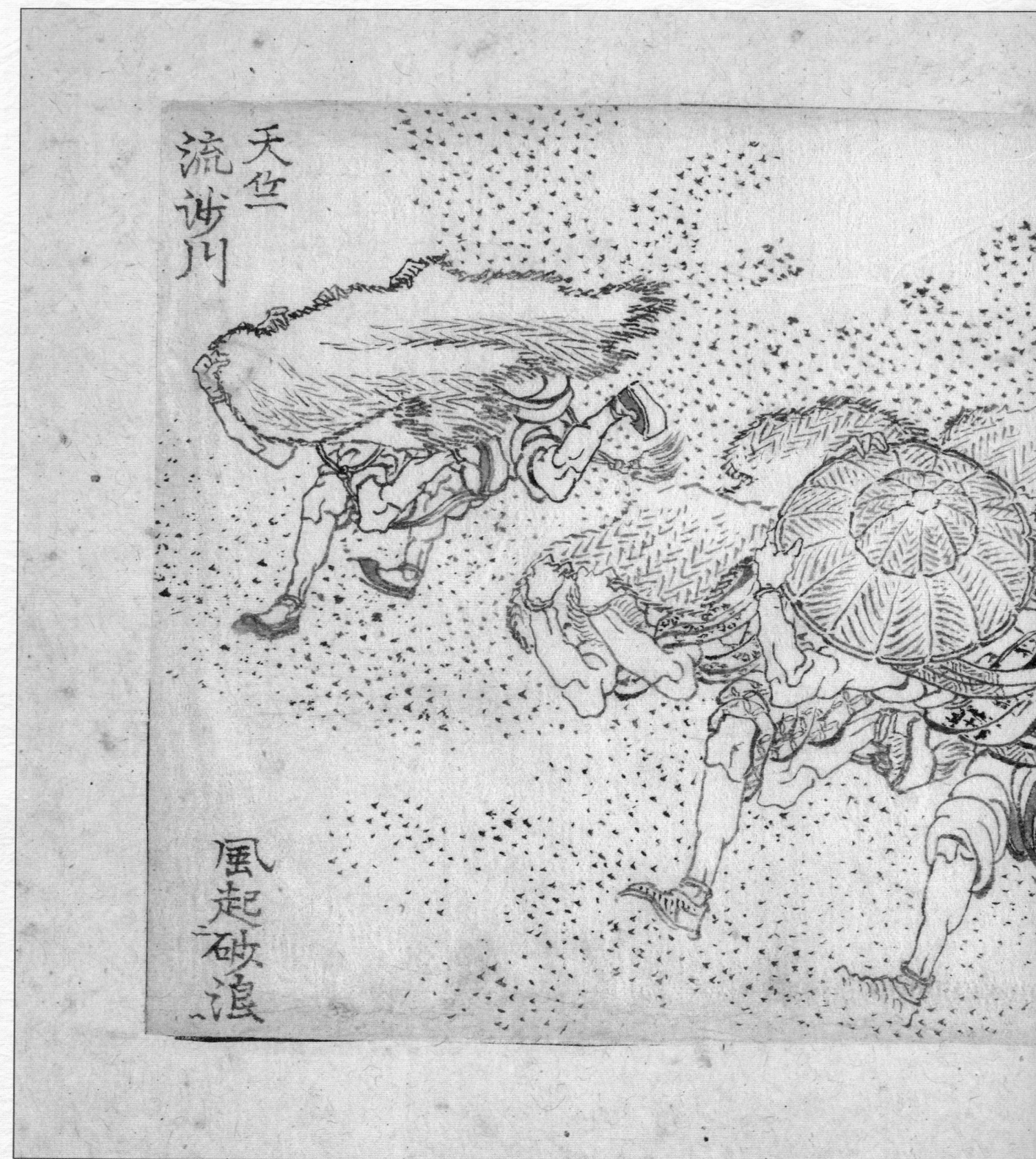

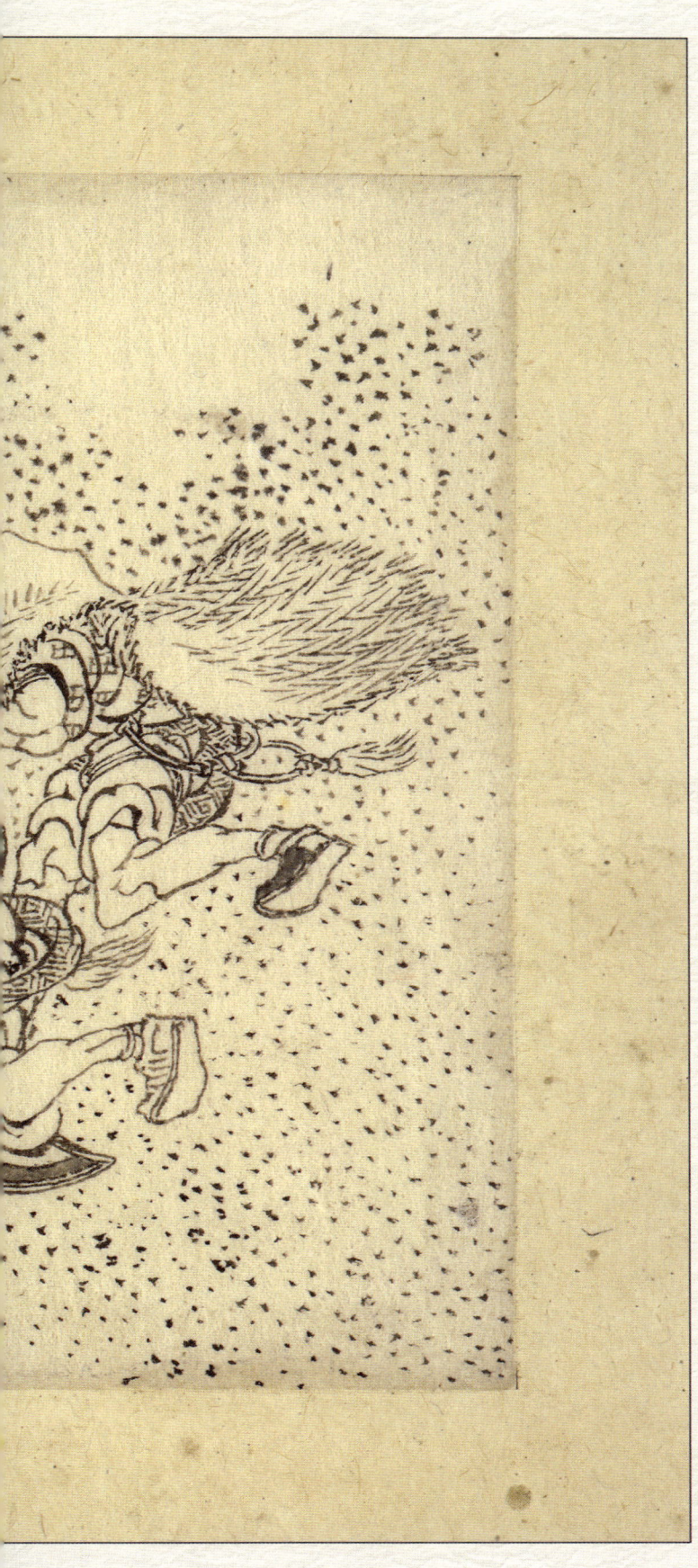

RECREATIONS

THE GODDESS NÜWA RE
PRECIOUS STONES TO R
THAT SEPARATE HEAVEN

BY LOLLOCO

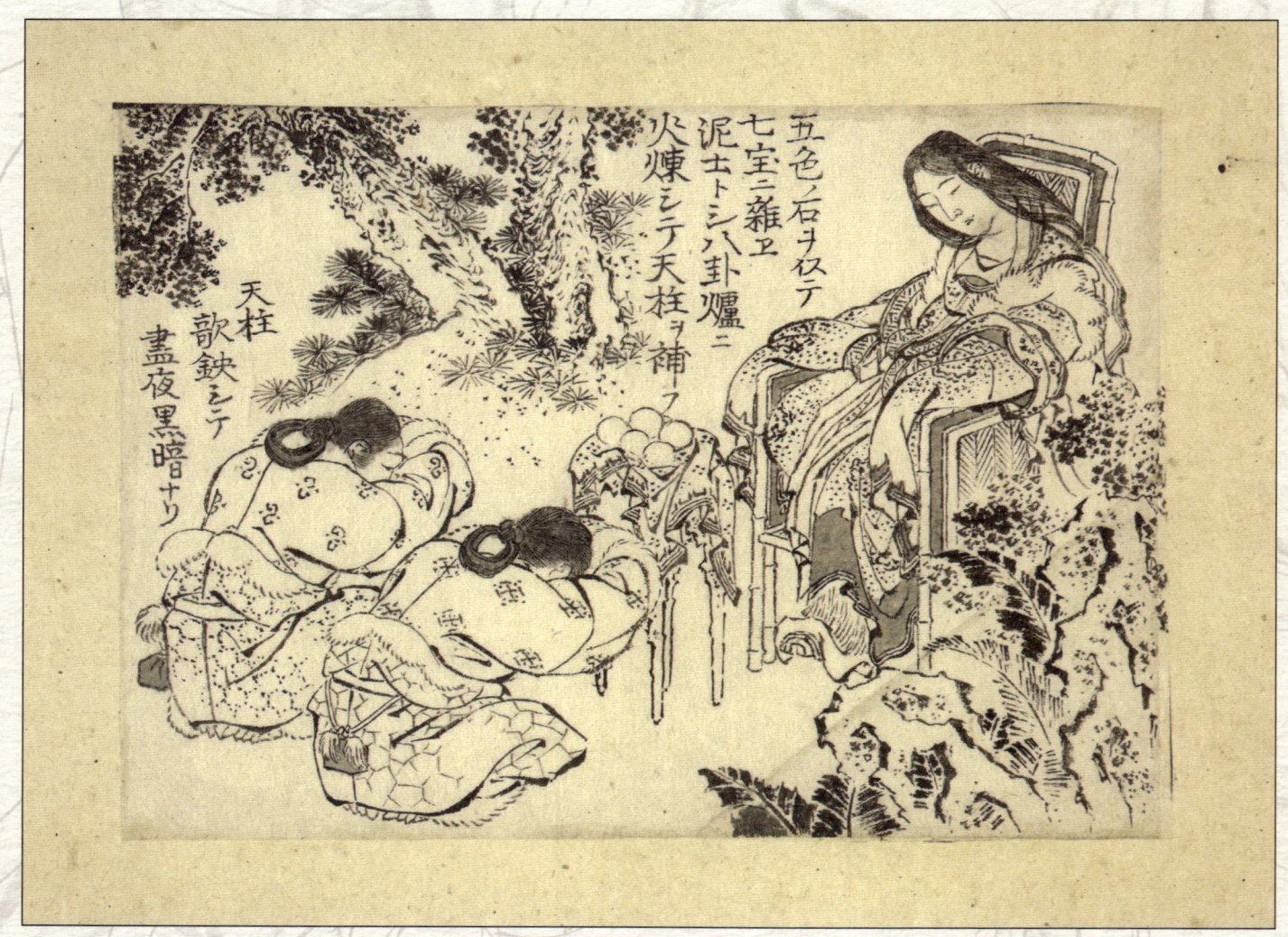

CEIVES
PAIR THE PILLARS
AND EARTH

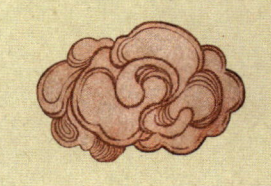

DISCOVERING HOKUSAI

Like many artists fortunate enough to discover their passion for art at an early age, I have wanted to express my feelings and ideas through visual storytelling for as long as I can remember. Whether I am inspired by a book or a beautiful sunset on a warm, summer evening, every meaningful experience has drawn me back to art and the desire to capture what I see. When I first started my art journey, I didn't know much about art techniques, but that never stopped me from practising and honing my skills. I wanted art to be my calling, not just a passion.

For all the various art movements, styles, and revolutionary artists, three have completely captured my heart: Alphonse Mucha, Qiu Ying (仇英), and, of course, Katsushika Hokusai (葛飾北齋). Although they come from different cultures and periods, and even have different styles, they share an affinity for intricate brushwork, defined lines, and harmonious yet striking colour palettes. However, before I discovered their works, I had two first loves: manga for its detailed line work, and anime for its expert use of cel shading, colour grading, and visual narratives.

They still continue to be major sources of inspiration for my artworks, specifically the works of manga duo Adachitoka (Adachi and Tokashiki) who wrote and illustrated *Noragami: Stray God* (ノラガミ), as well as the exceptional Hayao Miyazaki (宮崎駿) of Studio Ghibli.

All of my love and appreciation for the above leads back to Hokusai and his mesmerizing works. In my opinion, the most distinctive thing about his art is his control over negative space and line weight to draw the viewer's attention to specific elements. He also masterfully combines colours to create harmonious gradients, which, as a result, makes his pieces have an epic, theatrical feel while retaining a sense of soul through clear symbolism. His illustration *The goddess Nüwa receives precious stones to repair the pillars that separate heaven and earth* has deeply resonated with me and prompted me to learn more about the legend that first inspired it. While I am unable to recreate his work, I hope to attain a similar sense of drama and soul in my interpretation, using his original as inspiration.

01 ROUGH SKETCH

I always start with a rough sketch to capture the overall compositional flow and make notes of the components I want to incorporate. For this recreation, I already have an image and story I want to convey, so at this stage, my goal is to capture it as swiftly and easily as possible.

First, I take note of the original composition and the intentional distance between the goddess Nüwa and the two human girls offering precious stones needed to repair the pillars and save the human world. Though the goddess takes the central stage, the maidens play crucial roles for delivering the narrative. The goal is to make all the other elements in the artwork lead back to them. Inspired by Hokusai's other works, I want to add a few other elements to the background such as mountains, waves, and so on.

SKETCHING WITHOUT OVERTHINKING –
ALLOW YOUR VISION TO COME TO LIFE AND
YOUR BRUSHSTROKES TO FLOW EFFORTLESSLY

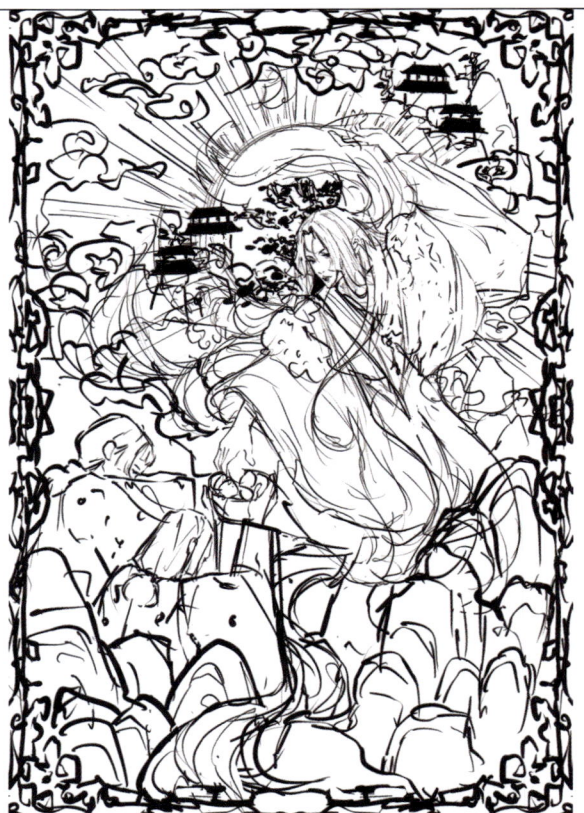

02 CLEAN SKETCH

Once the composition is established and I understand the direction in which the narrative is headed, I take my time refining my lines and defining the sketch. While I am not being too meticulous with keeping each line sharp and perfect, I pay close attention to their flow and how effectively I can transfer the shapes. Creating a clean sketch is essential for me because it forms the foundation for the line work to follow. Since I want the clothes and hair to be the primary focal points of the artwork, I focus much of my attention on portraying their movement.

CLEANING THE SKETCH AND
DEFINING FOCAL POINTS

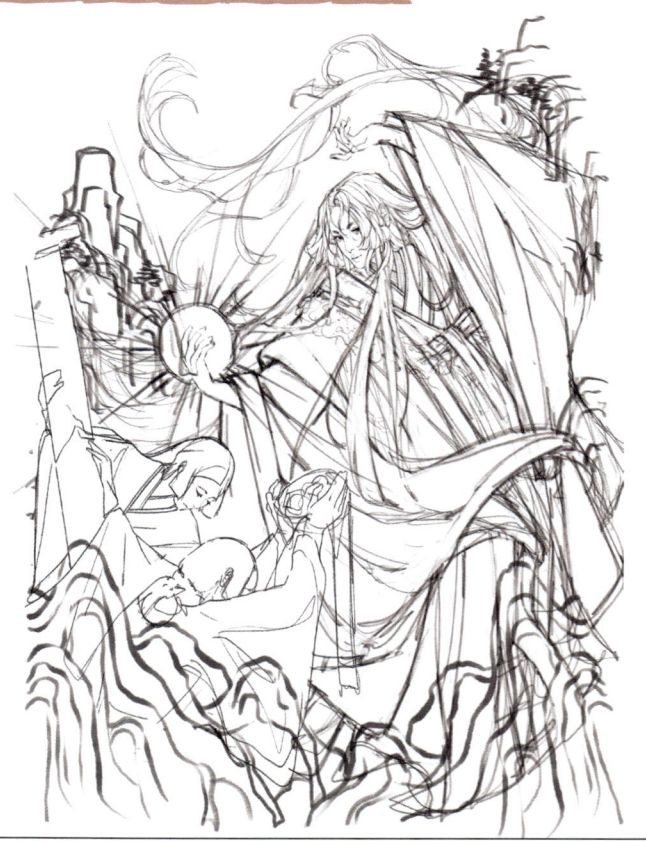

03 LINE WORK: DEFINING HAIR

I begin my line art by refining the main character's face and hair, the latter of which is one of the most important parts of my illustrations. While keeping the hairstyle close to its original look (Heian-style, long and loose with straight-cut strands around the face), I want to add more volume and flow in order to highlight Nüwa's magnificence, while adding more dynamism to the overall composition. The fluidity of water and fire serves as inspiration for the intertwined hair strands. I work on each strand deliberately, using confident and intentional brushstrokes.

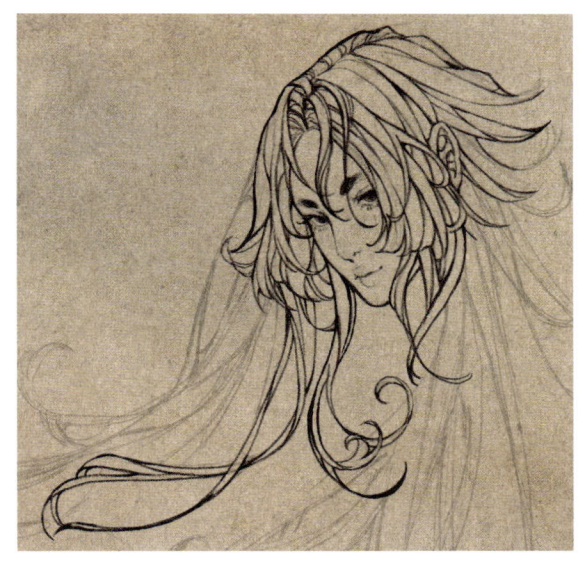

REFINING THE HAIR AND KEEPING EACH BRUSHSTROKE INTENTIONAL

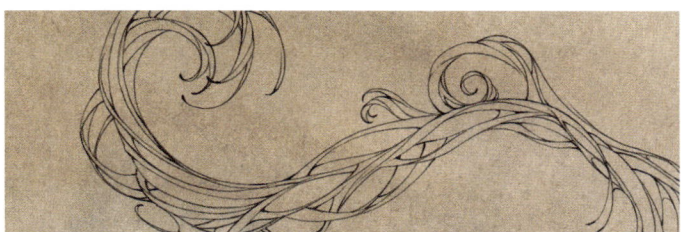

04 LINE WORK: SHAPES & WEIGHT

Since line art is the primary means of visual expression in my work process, I always pay attention to line weight and shape language, specifically when drawing clothes. Inspired by the Heian period's jūnihitoe (twelve-layered kimono), I add large, angular sleeves and multiple layers to give Nüwa a grand feel. The kimonos on the two human girls are simpler, but still layered. I add softer curves inside the folds and sharper angular shapes along the corners and edges of the fabric. Combining this with thin and thick brushstroke variations gives my lines a subtle contrast within the overlapping shapes.

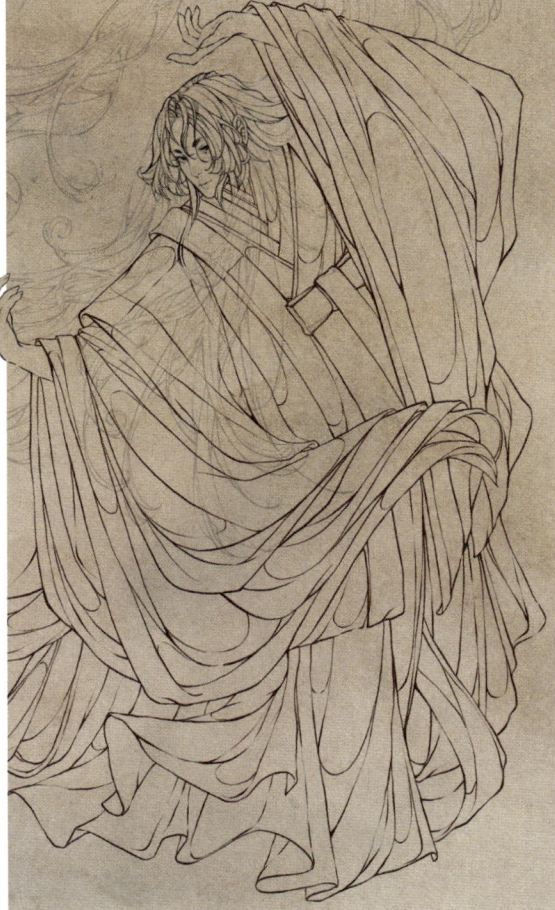

USING SHAPES AND LINE WEIGHT TO STYLIZE FABRIC

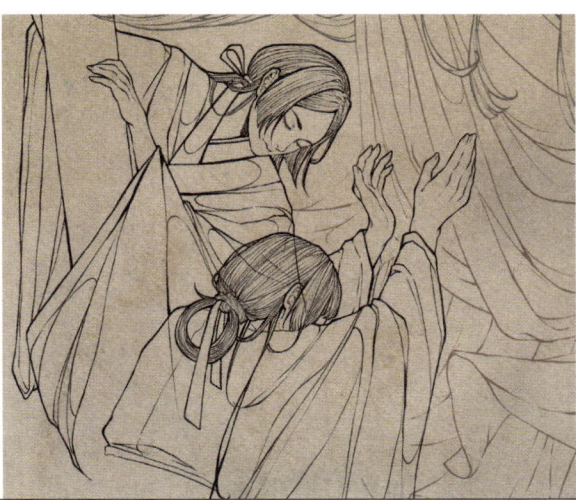

05 SKETCHING WITH COLOUR

Once I lay down the line work for my primary subjects (and I am satisfied with how everything is positioned), I make another version using colours and textured brushes. This step helps me to define the shapes in the landscape and settle on a colour palette. It also allows me an opportunity to reconsider things and make any necessary compositional changes before finalizing the line art. I realize I like the combination of green and red – a complementary colour palette; green is the primary, low-saturated colour, while red is more of a vibrant accent colour.

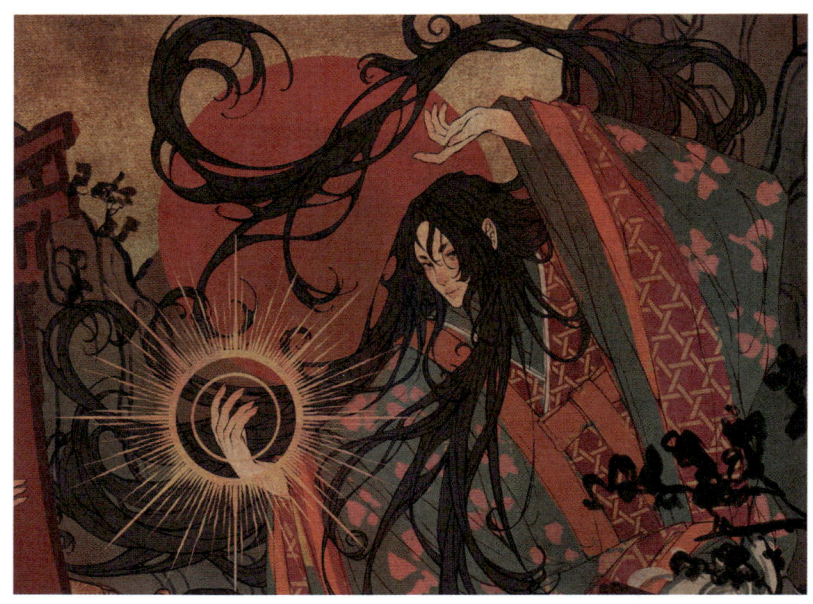

USING TEXTURED BRUSHES TO EXPERIMENT WITH SHAPES AND COLOURS

06 ADDING LINE CONTRAST

When approaching the landscape, I like to have a combination of thinner and thicker lines to help differentiate the elements. In the original artwork, Hokusai uses the traditional ukiyo-e brushstroke technique to add details to the tree and plants. Inspired by the inky, flowing feeling of those lines, I attempt to add volume and flow to my lines using a pressure-sensitive ink brush, gradually building mountain shapes and creating an interesting contrast between the lines. These thicker brushstrokes give the mountains an instant sense of solidity and weight.

USING A PRESSURE-SENSITIVE INK BRUSH TO VARY THICKNESS AND ADD CONTRAST TO LINE WORK

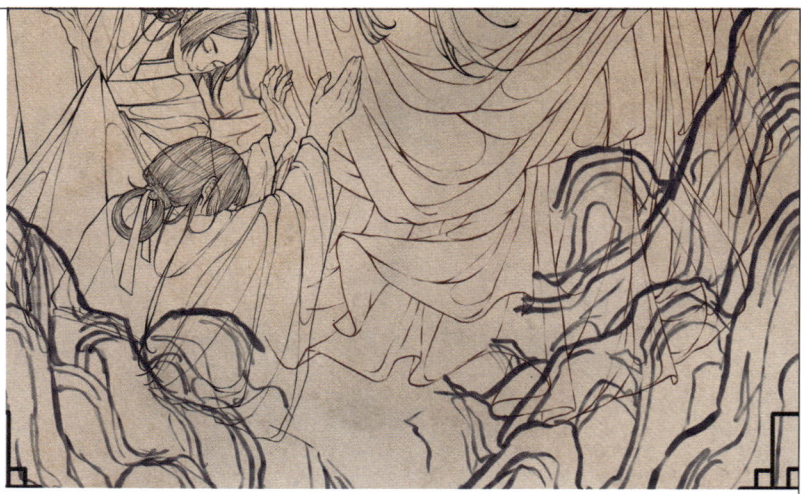

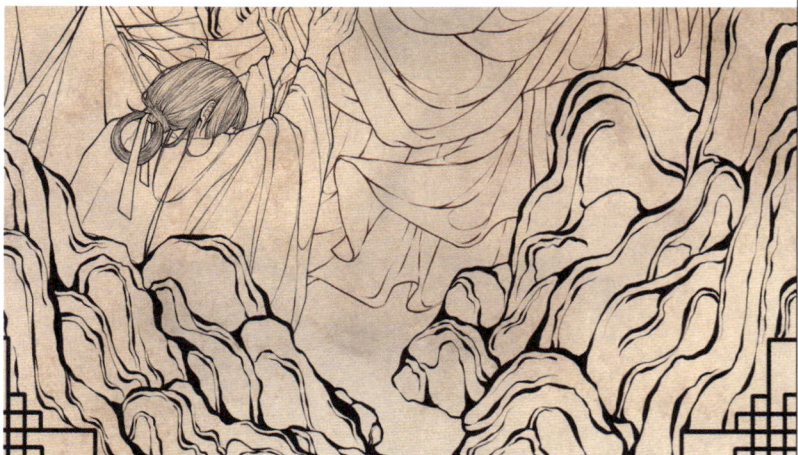

07

DELICATE BRUSHSTROKES

To strike a balance with the bold line work I used for the mountains in the previous step, I use thinner, softer lines for the pillars to give a delicate impression. For the waves, I want to achieve a traditional Japanese aesthetic, inspired by Hokusai's famous illustration, *The Great Wave*. My aim is to attain comparable stylization, keeping my lines thin and loose while allowing my strokes to curve and swirl, creating an interesting pattern. The pillar design follows the traditional patterns found on many Japanese shrines. I plan to add more wooden details later.

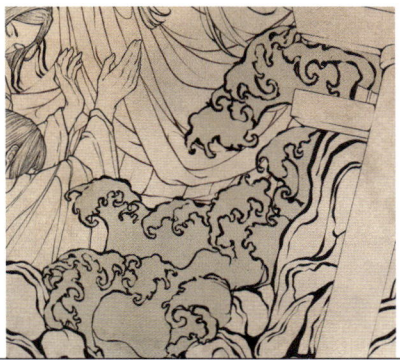
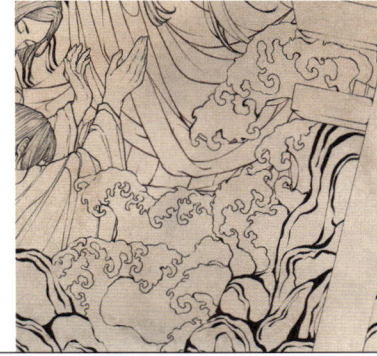
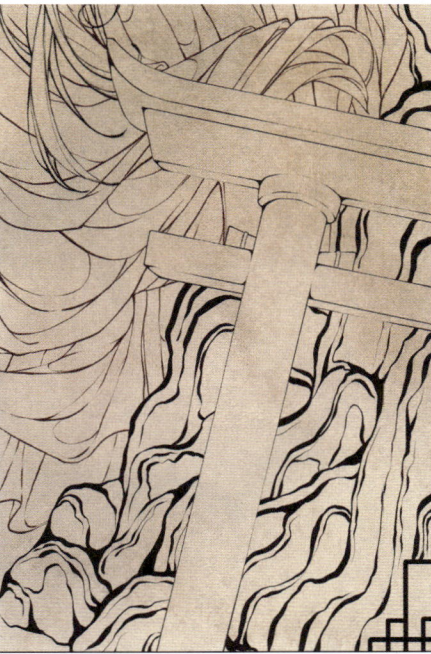

08

LAYING DOWN FOUNDATIONS

Once my line art is perfected and all the main elements work well with each other, it's time to layer in my flat colours as the base for the next crucial phase. I find that layer separation makes it much easier to make changes and stay organized, especially when dealing with complex and highly detailed compositions. Each colour has its own layer and belongs to its own group. Using a flat brush, I fill in areas with colour, using my colour sketch as a guide. Greens and blues take up the majority of the canvas, with reds and oranges reserved to emphasize focal points and create contrast.

LAYERING BASE COLOURS AND KEEPING EVERYTHING ORGANIZED

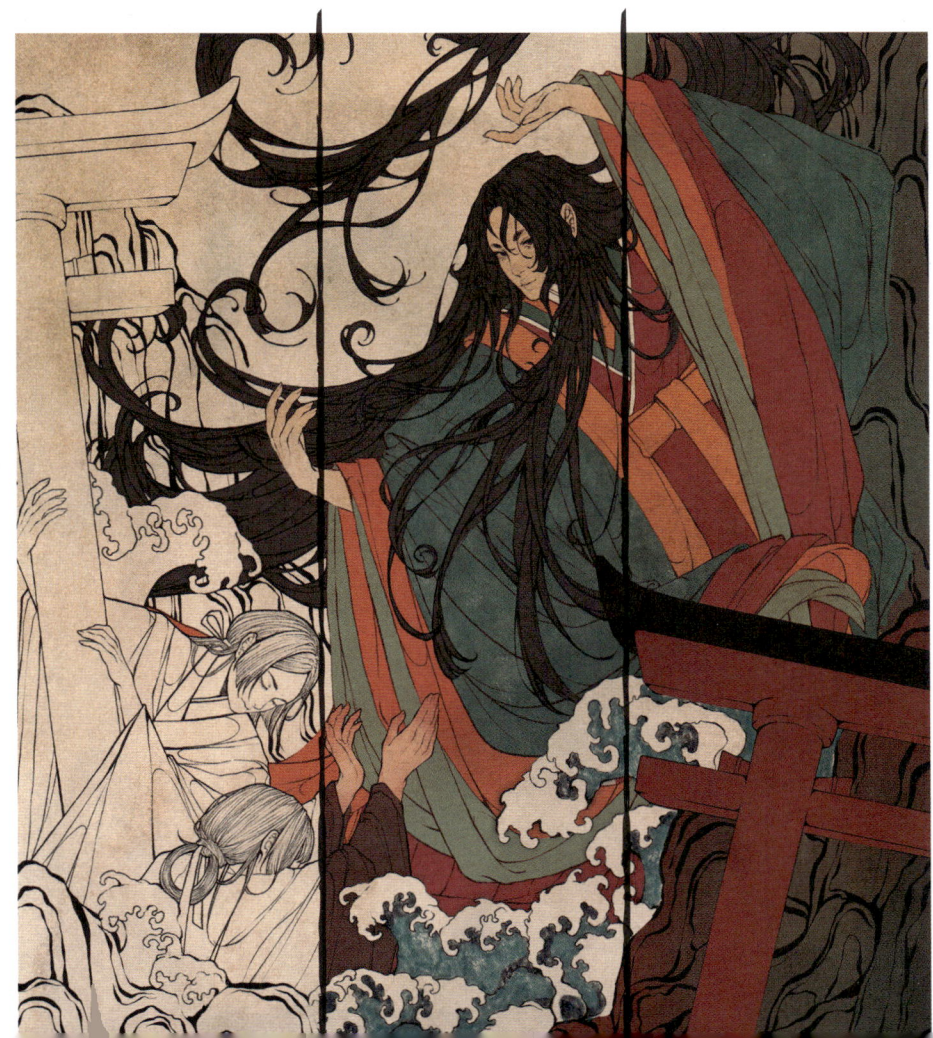

09 ADDING DETAILS: WAVES

At this stage, I work progressively on each group of elements, applying gradients for vibrancy, texture for depth, and different shades for contrast. I add a pattern inside the waves, following the traditional Hokusai wave design, giving it a little twist of my own. As I work digitally, I take full advantage of my medium and experiment with different opacities and blending modes on each layer. The goal is to make the illustration interesting but not too overpowering. I use a colour-picker tool to sample different shades from the colour sketch I made in Step 05.

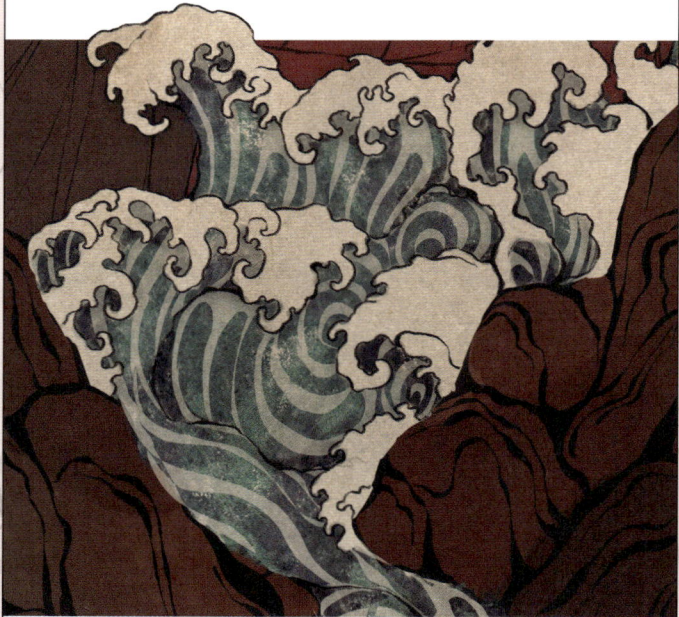

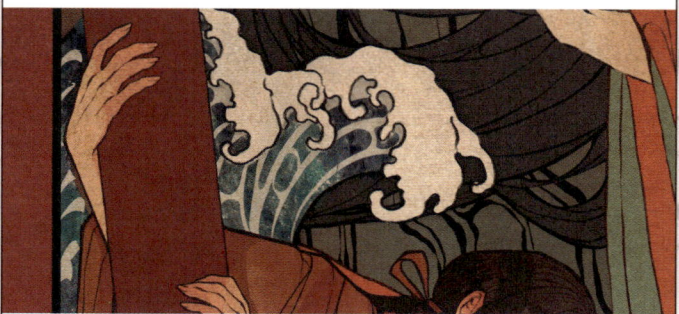

ADDING GRADIENTS AND PLAYING WITH
TEXTURES AND BLENDING MODES

10 PATTERNS & PRINTS

Inspired by the beauty of Japanese patterns found in traditional clothing, I add them to my artwork, mindful of their meanings and cultural symbolism. I use Asanoha and Same-komon patterns for the kimonos on the two human girls, which represent resilience and protection, respectively. For Nüwa's kimono pattern, I use Rokkaku-kagome (Ami), which is often associated with water-related visuals and warding off evil. I embellish the long sleeves with a flower pattern inspired by the customary designs found on the Heian period's jūnihitoe kimonos.

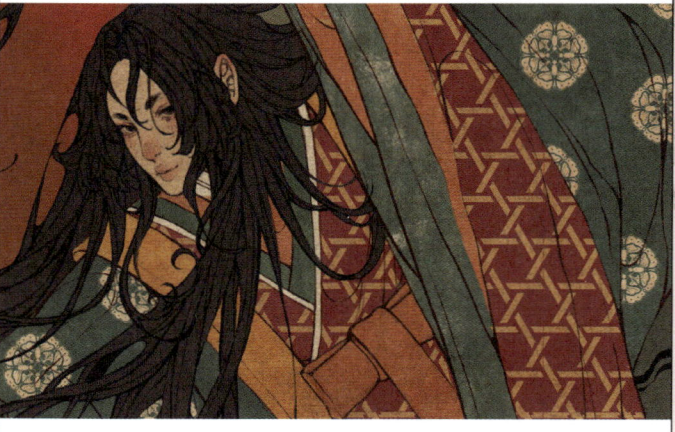

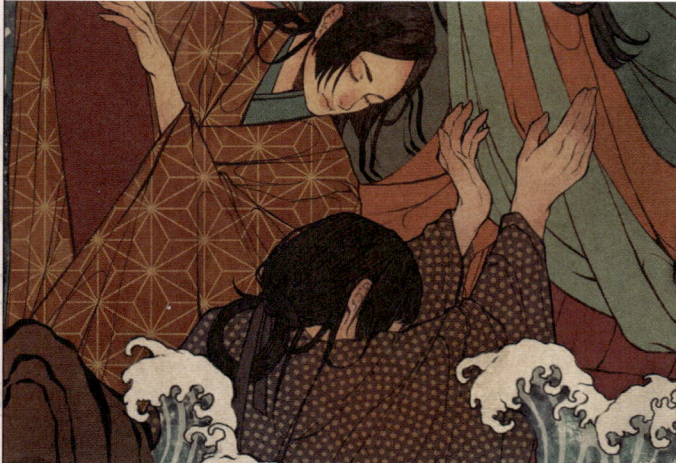

INCORPORATING TRADITIONAL
PATTERN DESIGNS TO THE KIMONOS

11 ADDING DETAILS: MOUNTAINS

Similar to how I added gradients and textures to the waves, I add several different layers of textures and gradients on top of the mountain's base colours. I focus on adding more vibrancy to the contrast by using saturated blue and purple hues. I notice this technique is used a lot in both Hokusai's landscapes and other traditional Japanese artworks where mountains appear to have a bright-blue gradient. In accordance with the rules of atmospheric perspective, the mountains that are closer to the viewer have darker, more saturated values, while those further back appear softer, giving the subtle impression of distance.

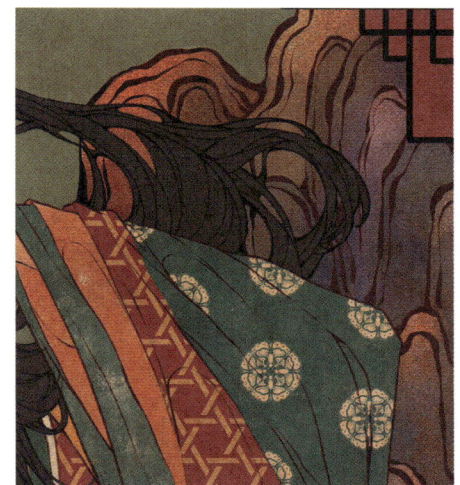

BLENDING IN MORE VIBRANT TEXTURES AND GRADIENTS TO THE LANDSCAPE

12 RENDERING WITH PENCIL

One of my favourite parts of the rendering process is adding small, intricate details using a textured pencil brush. Combining digital art with the charm of traditional pencil-drawing techniques, I apply different strokes, varying the pressure on my stylus and gradually building a wooden pattern over the pillars. Next, I use a lighter sketch-like brush to add shading to areas for additional texture, mimicking the look of real pencil shading. I take my time rendering the hair with the pencil, drawing singular brushstrokes through each strand's entire length, giving the hair more definition and depth.

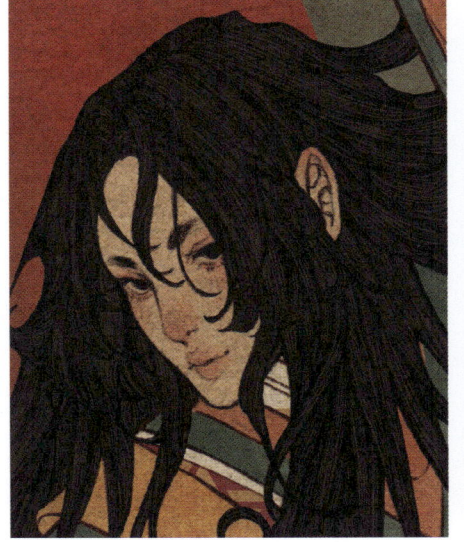

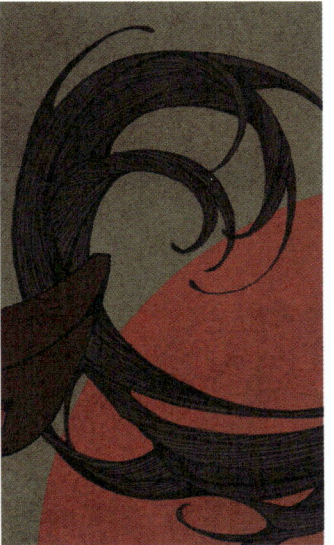

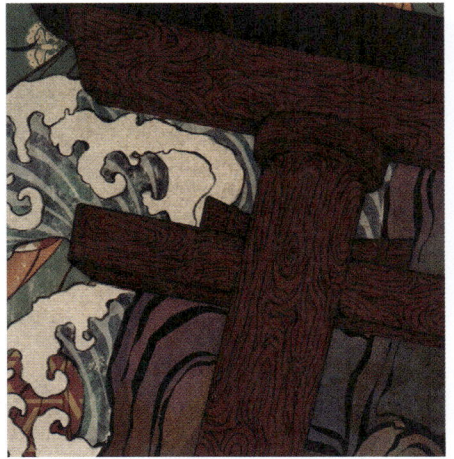

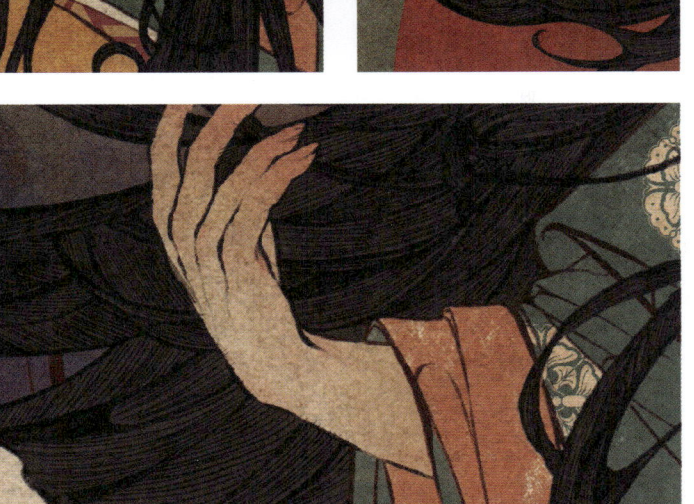

SHADING AREAS TO CREATE MORE DEPTH AND BUILDING DETAILS WITH THE PENCIL

Lolloco

13 BLOCKING OUT SHADOWS

To retain a flatter look, I prefer to block my shadows by using a cel-shading technique. I use a textured scatter brush and the Lasso tool to create interesting curves and shapes. Though it's a technique often used in animation and manga, I really like incorporating it into my illustrations. At this stage, I can see everything slowly coming together. I make notes of other minor things I can add to complement the composition.

USING CEL-SHADING TECHNIQUE TO ADD SHADOWS IN INTERESTING SHAPES

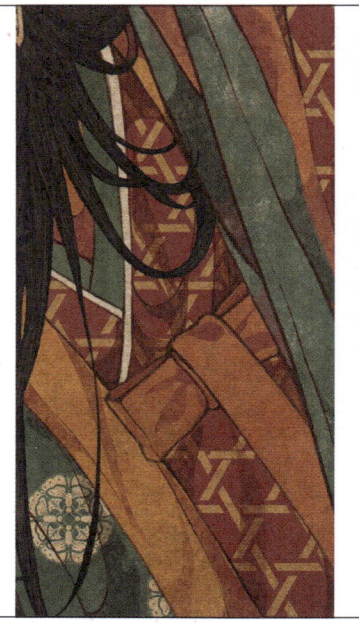
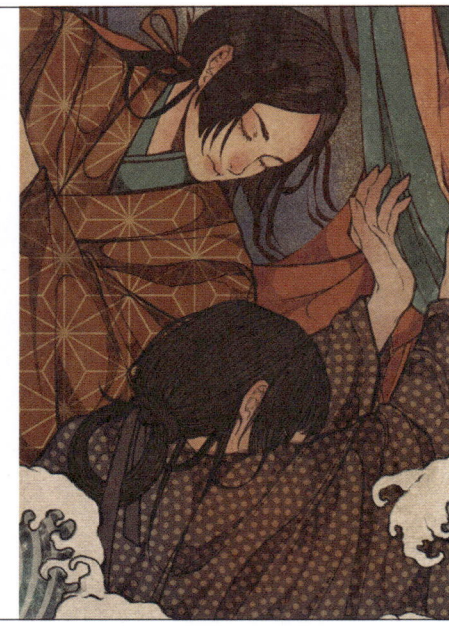

14 FINAL DETAILS & PERFECTING THE COMPOSITION

Once all the core elements are laid out, I add in a few last details, starting with the precious stones. Each one symbolizes a different natural element. I am inspired by the symbolism associated with the phrase 'the circle of life', and decide to add a sun motif that emits a golden light from the stone in Nüwa's hand. The stone shines brightly, casting a warm light upon the mountains. I also decide to add in a few stylized swirls, focusing on the top and bottom of the composition and softly wrapping around the focal points. I believe this creates a sense of togetherness and makes the scene feel more dynamic.

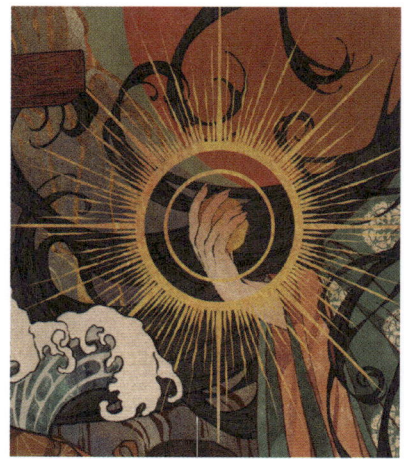
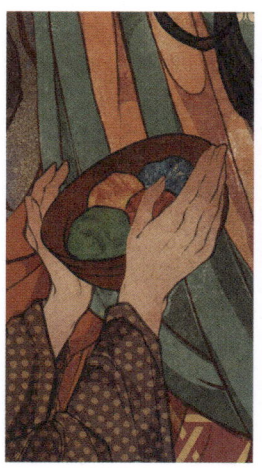
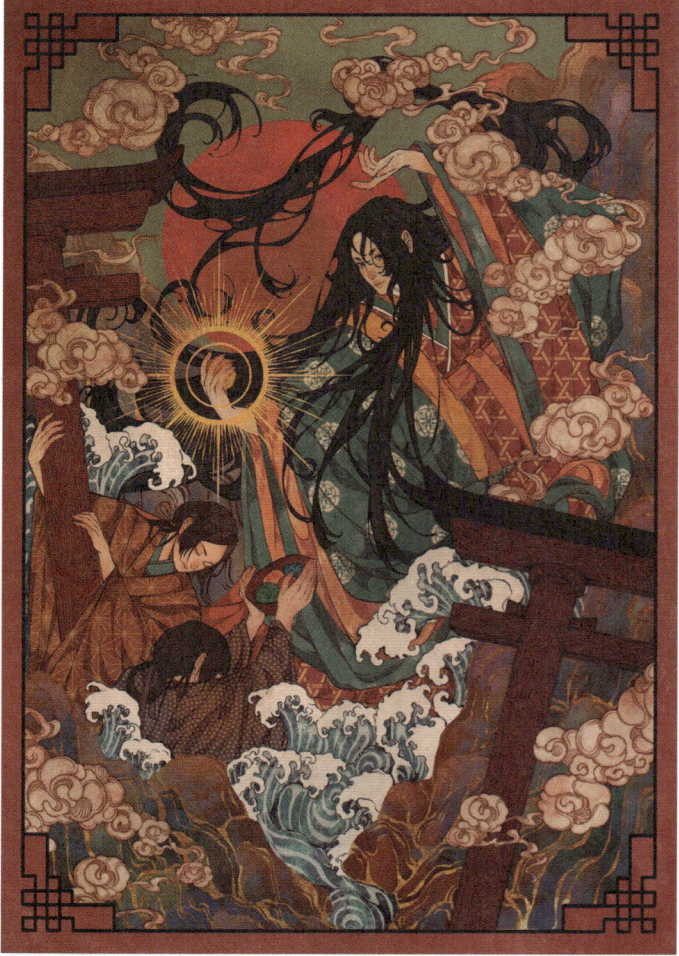

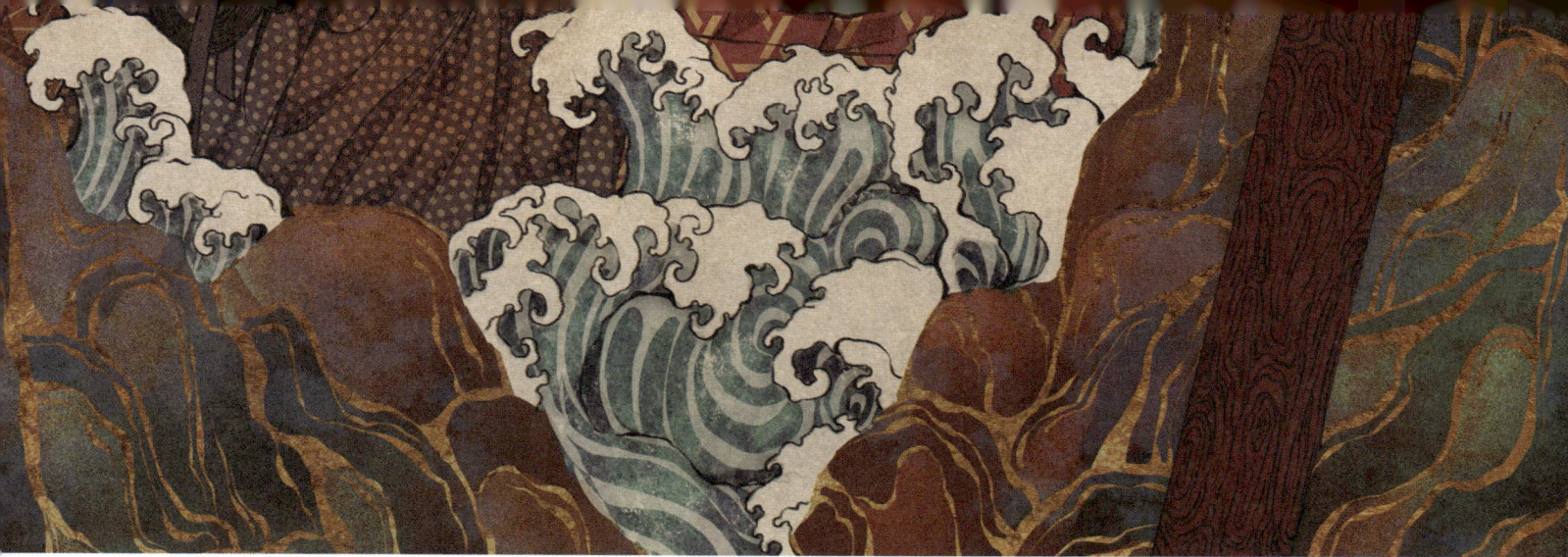

15 FINAL REFINEMENTS

As a last step, I focus on perfecting and balancing my colours by using the Colour Adjustments tool. In a new layer set to Overlay and at low opacity, I use a semi-transparent wash brush to add light splashes of blue and pink to the canvas. This balances the colours and brings a sense of unity to both cold and warm tones. To give everything a bit more depth and to bring out focal elements, I add blurred shadows beneath each layer. Lastly, as the cherry on top, I cover the entire canvas with watercolour-paper texture and grungy bristle brushstrokes to make the illustration feel like a traditional piece.

THERE CAN NEVER BE TOO
MUCH TEXTURE AND DEPTH

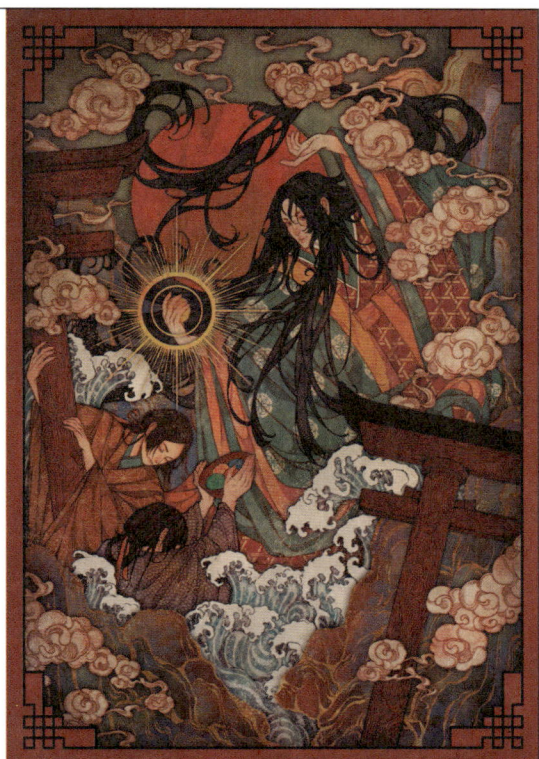

CONCLUSION

I can say with the utmost confidence that working on this project has been one of the most exciting experiences of my artistic journey so far. Not only was I able to honour such a legendary artist with my humble interpretation of his work, I was also given an opportunity to work with an art style that has inspired me for the majority of my life. I enjoyed every minute I spent bringing this piece together. Learning new techniques, widening my cultural understanding, and exploring the limits of my own style has been a wonderful experience.

Lolloco

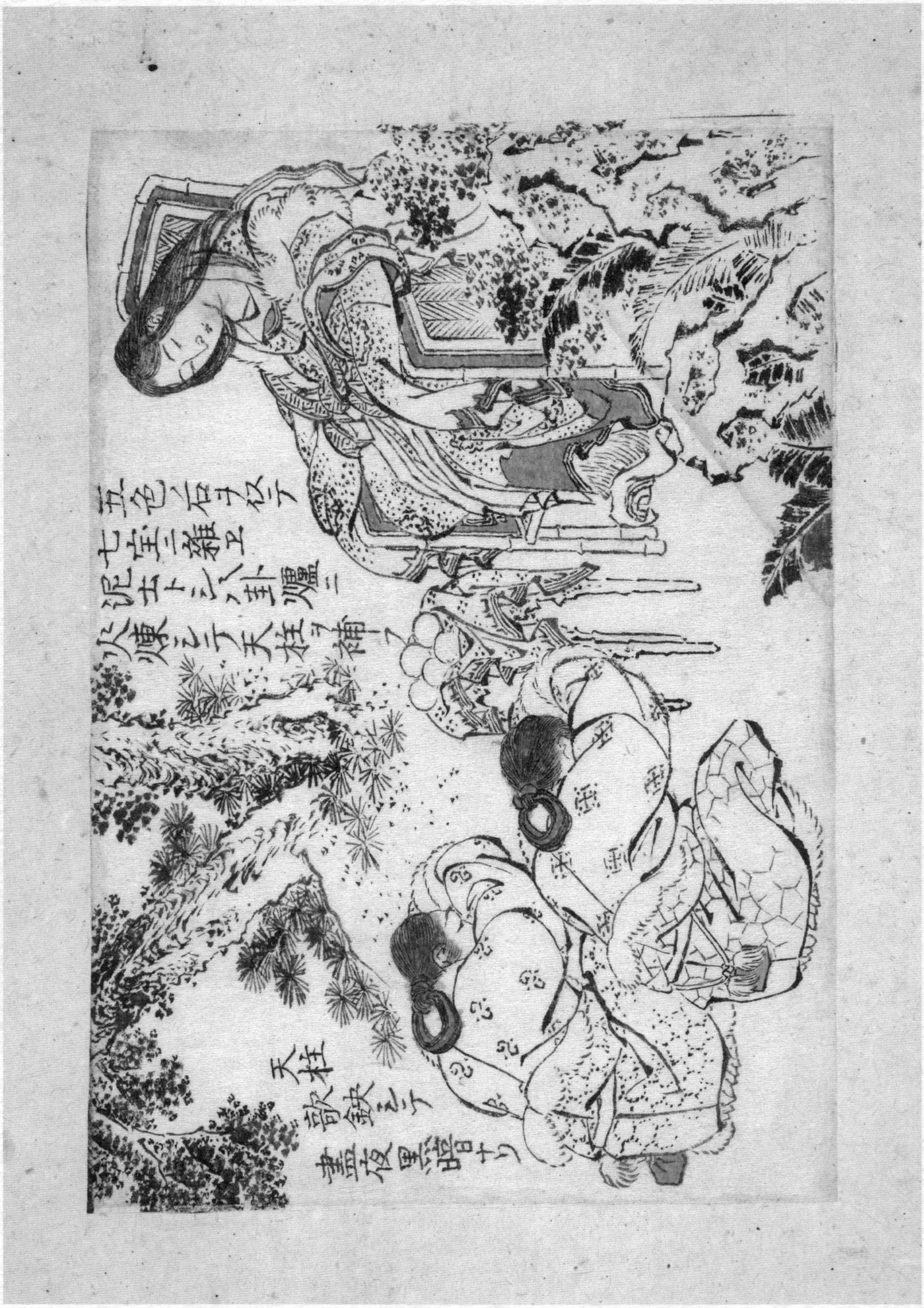
五色ノ石ヲ以テ
七宝ニ雑ヱ
泥土トシテ以テ爐ニ
火煉シテ天柱ヲ補フ
天柱
欹缺シテ
昼夜冥暗ナリ

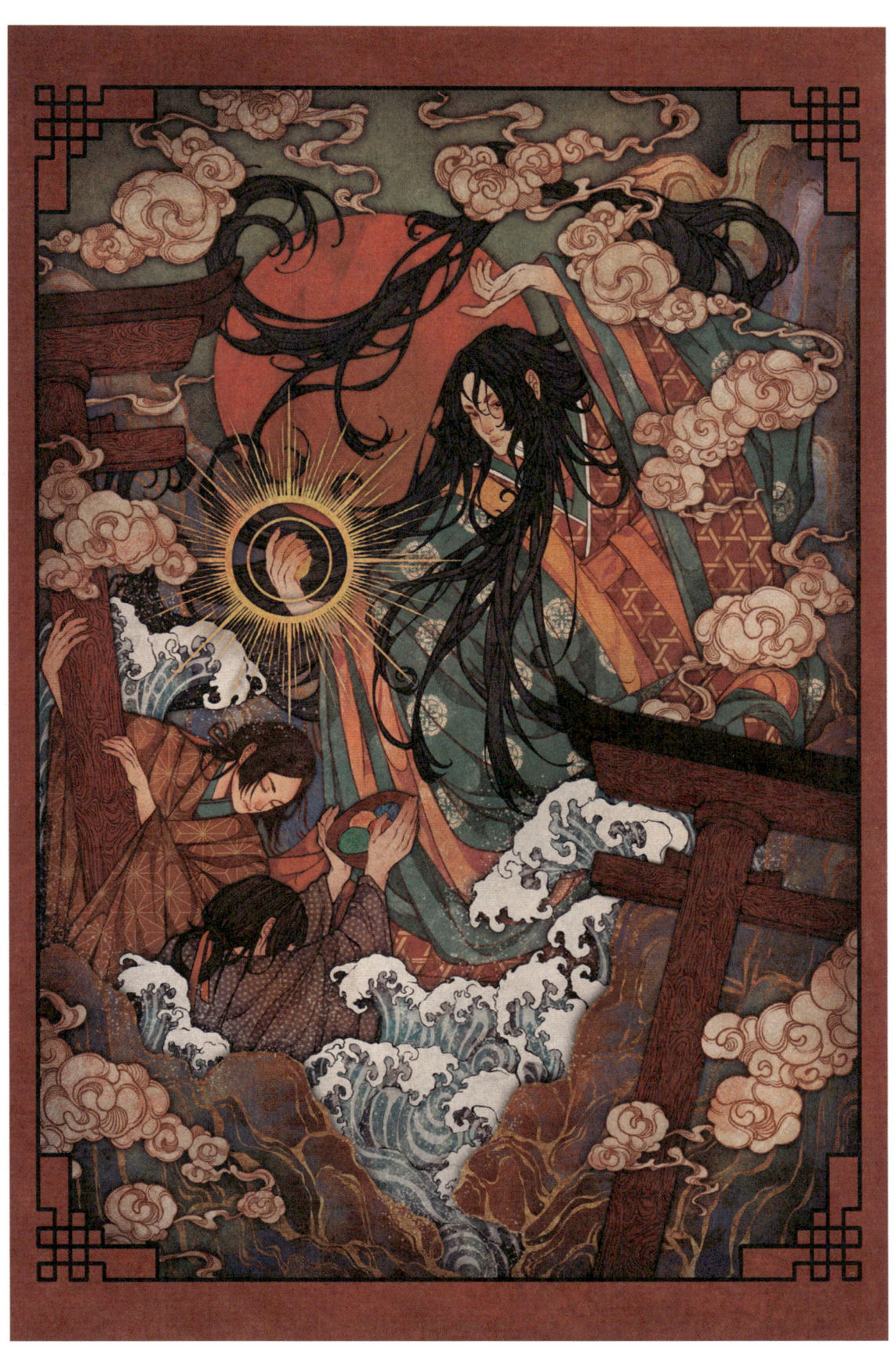

THE GODDESS NÜWA RECEIVES PRECIOUS STONES TO
REPAIR THE PILLARS THAT SEPARATE HEAVEN AND EARTH

LOLLOCO

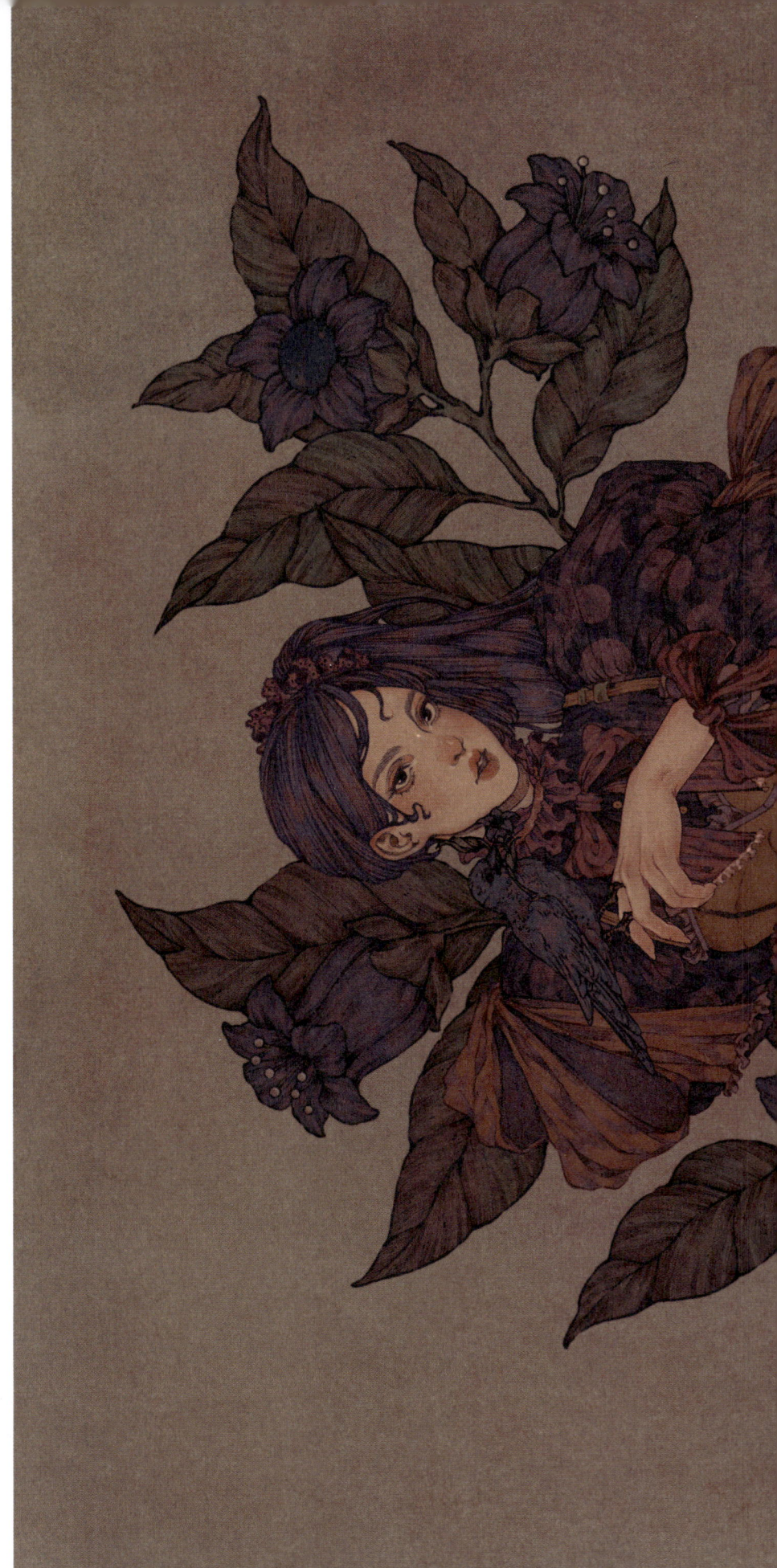

GALLERY: LOLLOCO

Belladonna
The beautiful lady in purple –
she who devours the nightmares

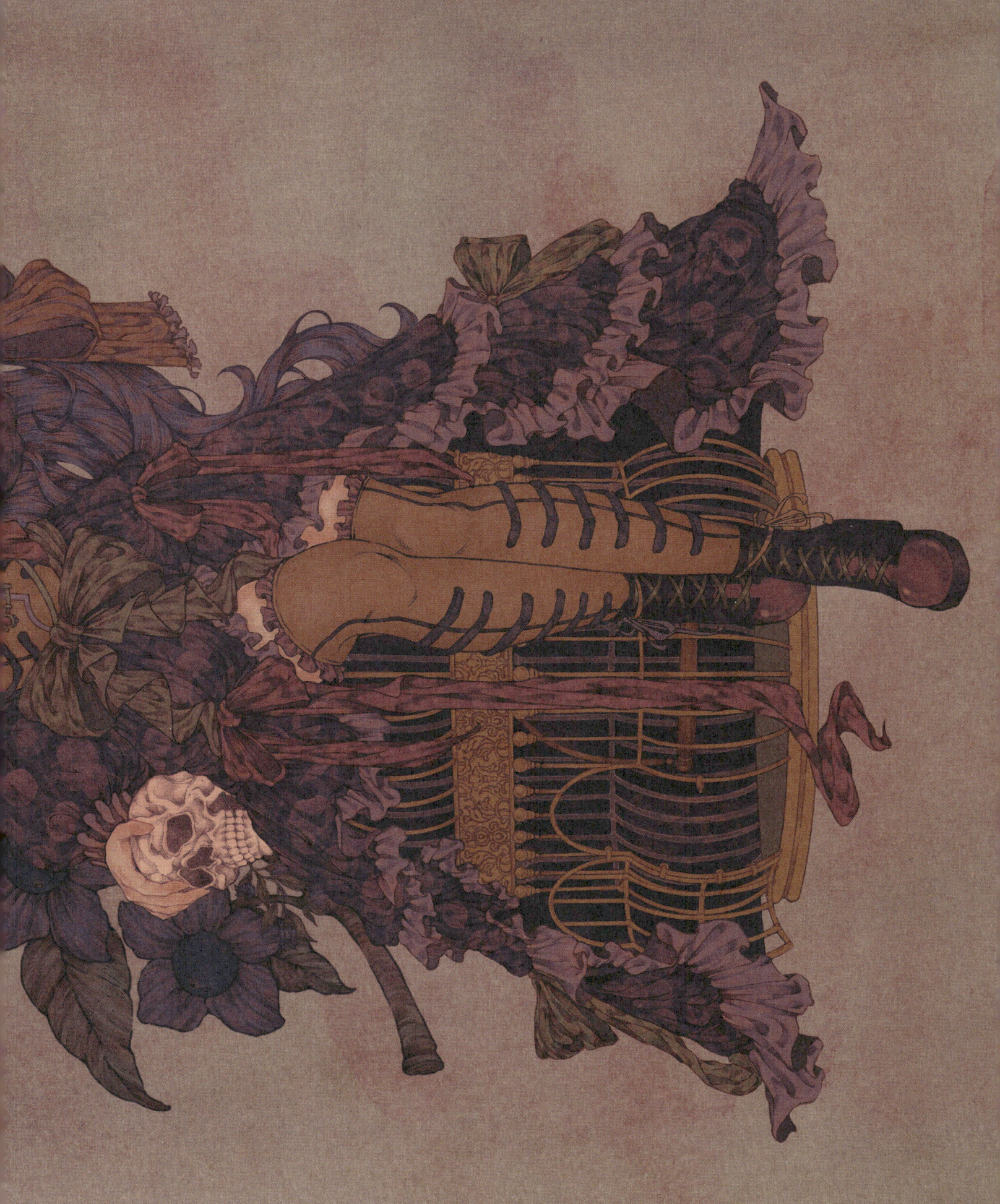

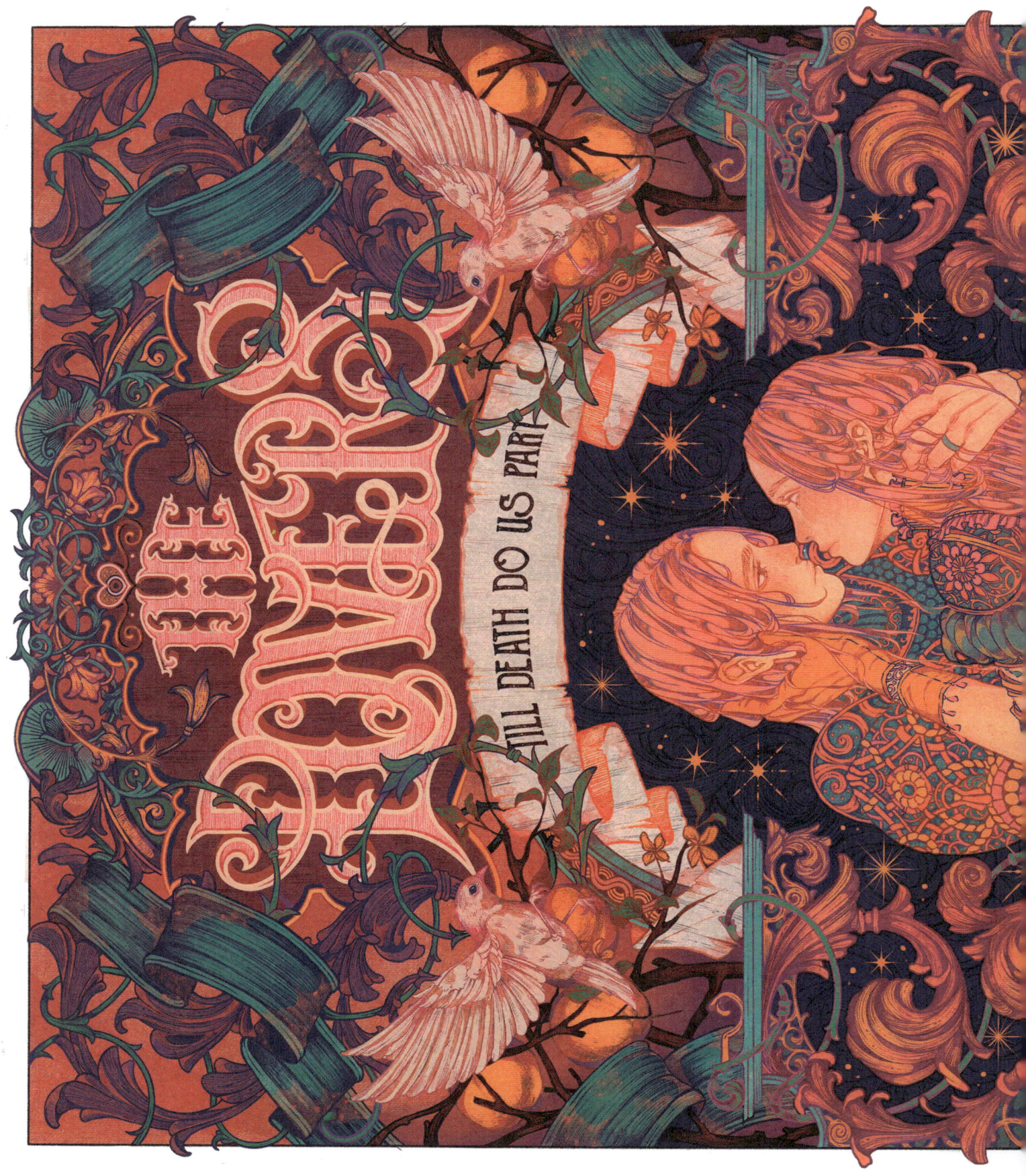

THE LOVERS

TILL DEATH DO US PART

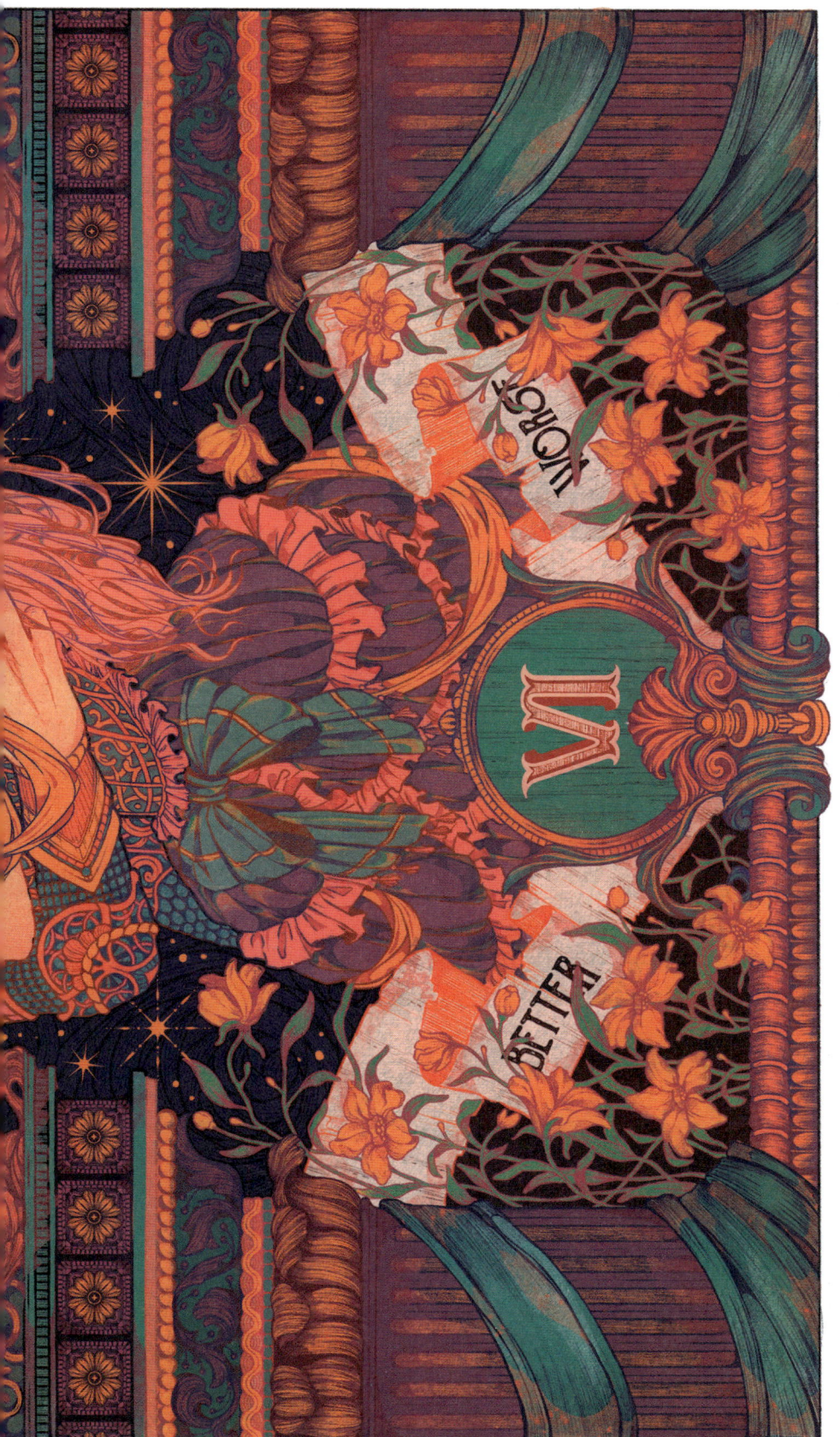

NEXT SPREAD, LEFT: *A Lucid Dream*
I wanted to capture the concept of a
beautiful lie that we sell to ourselves;
an illusion that comes with a heavy
price that we are still willing to pay

NEXT SPREAD, RIGHT: *Falling Star by
Jasmine Romero*
Soulmates means a soul
searches a lifetime for its second half

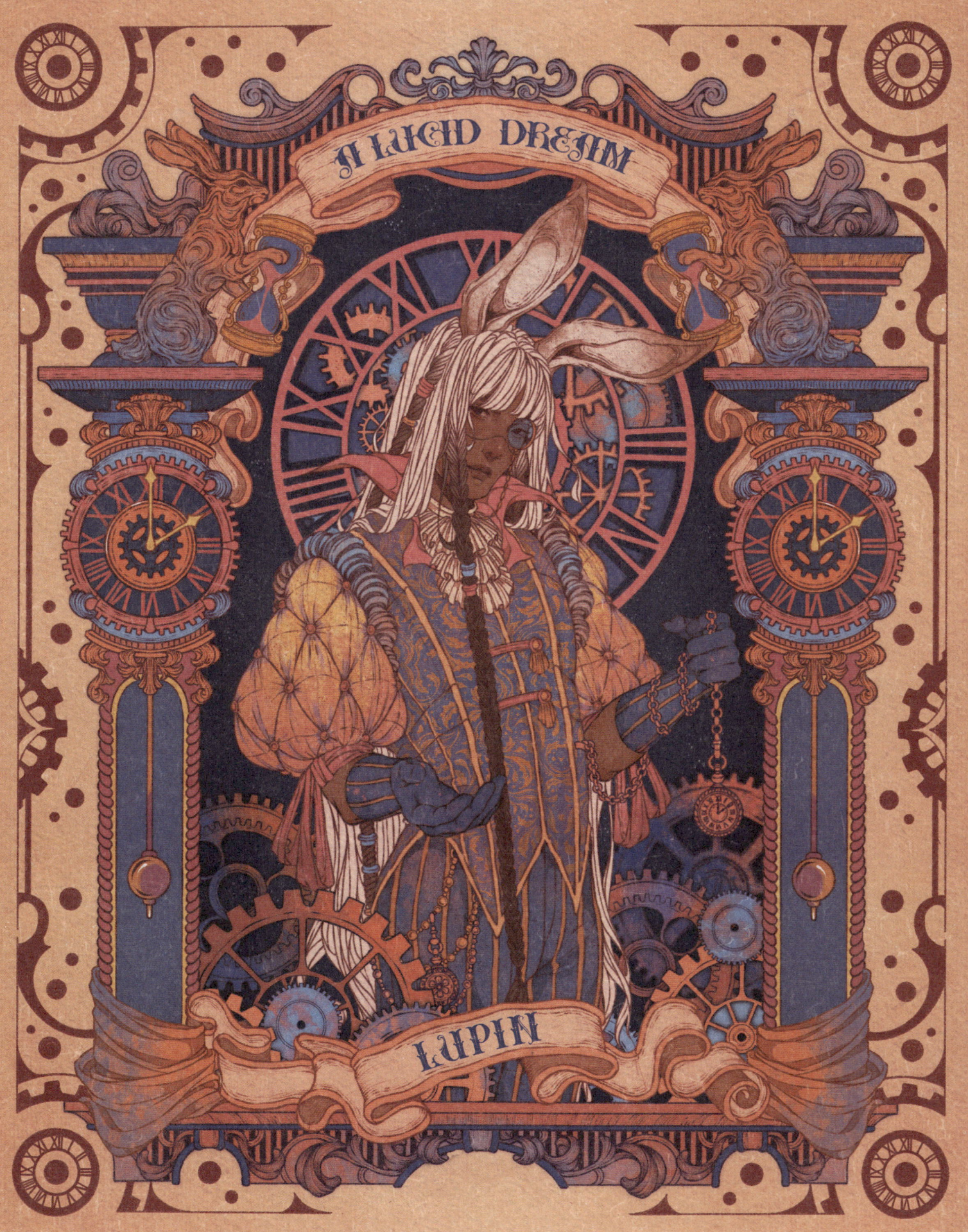

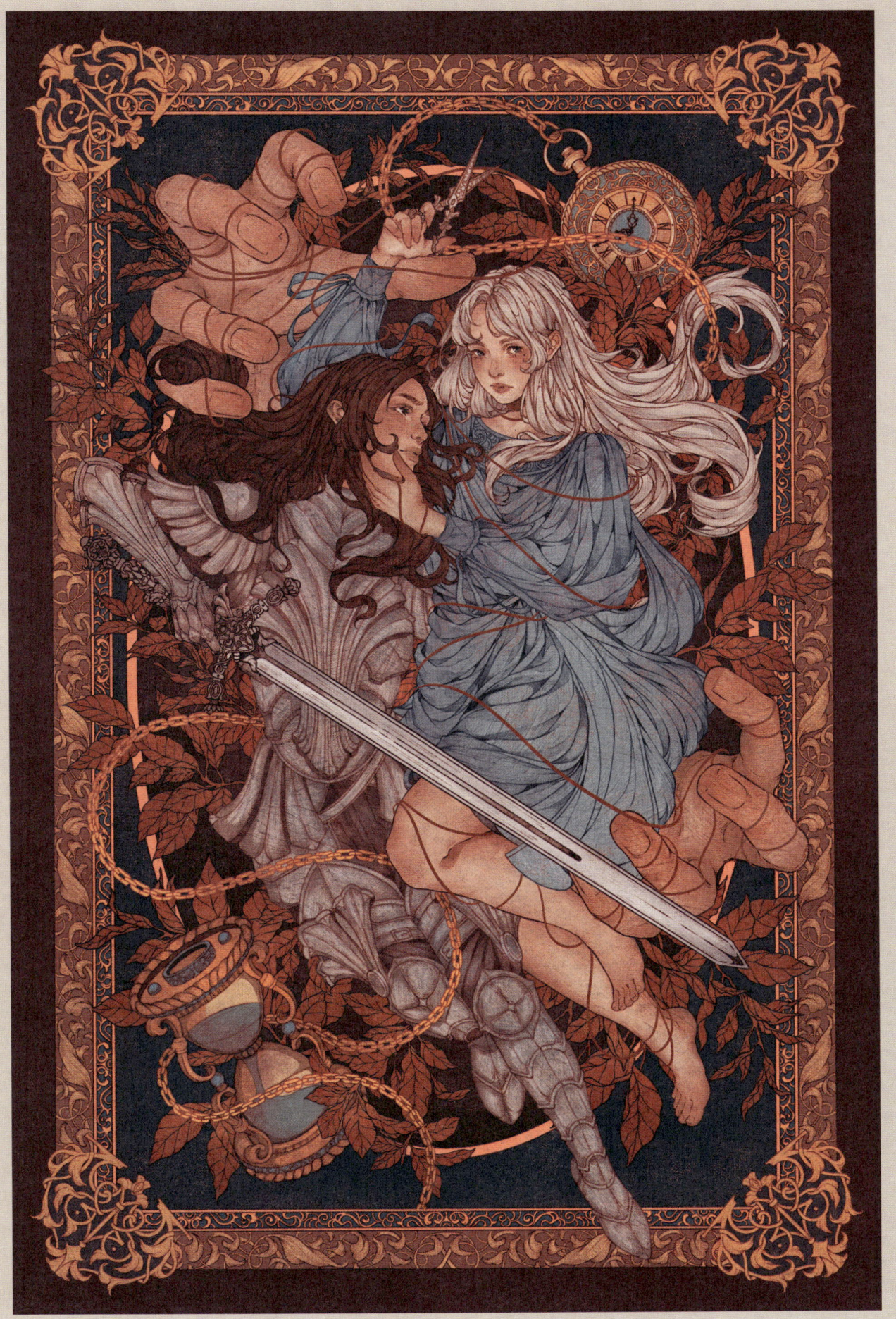

DAOIST MASTER ZHOU S
A CLOUD-LADDER TO TH

BY KELOGSLOOPS

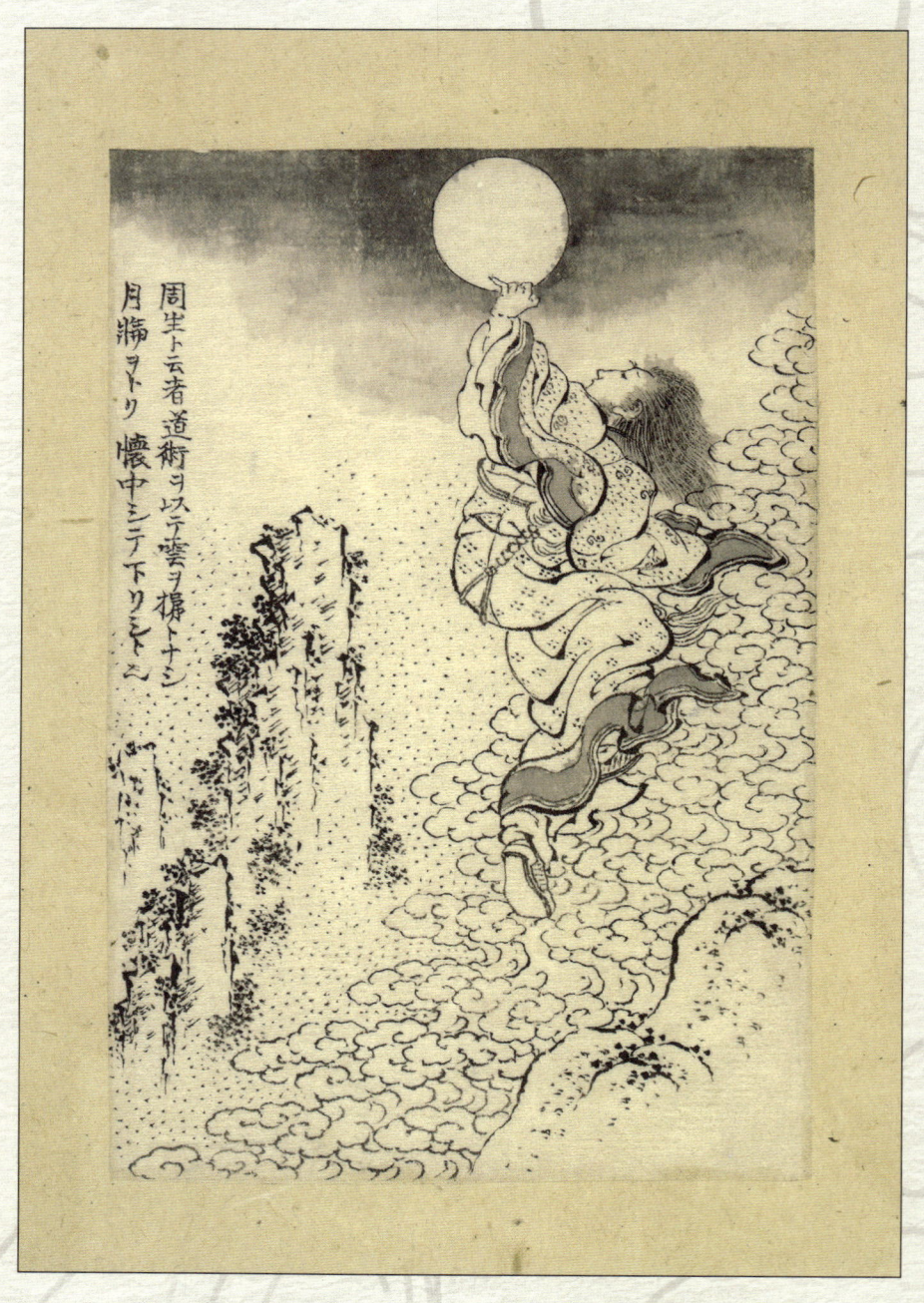

⁄ENG ASCENDS
MOON

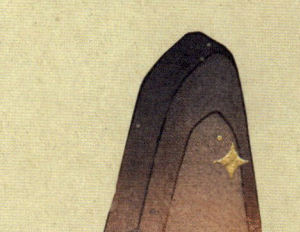

DISCOVERING
HOKUSAI

I often paint female portraiture and have found joy in experimenting with the wonderful world of watercolour. Much like Hokusai, I can find inspiration for my works in just about anything: a colour combination, poetry, lyrics, patterns on a piece of tile, or even something more complex like the feelings of grief or loss.

My first clear memory of creating art was when I learned to draw Sailor Moon, a character from a popular anime show in the 1990s. From then on, I became obsessed with drawing characters from anime shows, manga series, and video games, which have all influenced my current artistic style. Whether or not I was aware of it growing up, I was drawn to the large, cute, stylized eyes, the crazy colourful hairstyles, the heroic and powerful characters, and the magical, action-packed fantasy stories these shows, games, and books

often told. It wasn't until much later, in my late teens and early adulthood, that I began to step away from the anime and manga styles that I adored to try to find my own artistic voice. I delved into topics and genres of interest like realism, comic superheroes, chibi, and even graffiti illustrations. But despite all my experimentations, I always found that my work held traits reminiscent of my early drawing roots – anime and manga.

In my current era, I am focusing a lot on trying to let the storytelling aspect of my work shine through. My compositions are much quieter, poised to let the narrative sing, and I believe that was also one of Hokusai's best traits. His composition and storytelling is top notch. Everything is composed in a way that emanates that stillness, making his pieces feel so calm and peaceful. The viewer can just lose themselves in determining the story of each work's characters.

01 INITIAL DIGITAL SKETCH

I always start by doing some loose sketches to get a sense of composition, flow, and movement. In this stage, I don't focus on any details at all and just try to capture a feeling. Since I am recreating an existing work, there isn't too much room for composition exploration as I want to keep it relatively the same: a figure ascending a ladder of clouds (atop mountains) to reach the moon.

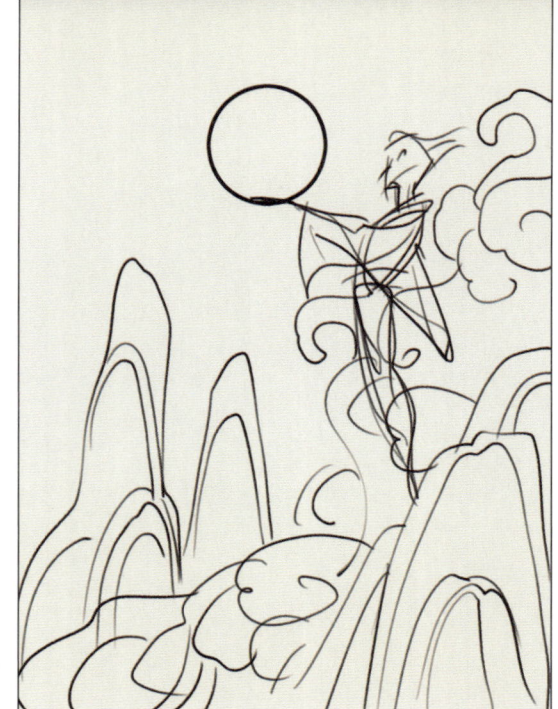

FIRST CONCEPT SKETCH, DRAWN DIGITALLY USING ADOBE PHOTOSHOP

02 DIGITAL REFINEMENT & COLOUR MOCK-UP

I further refine the sketch to focus a bit more on the anatomy and details of the figure, clouds, and mountains. I think shape language and silhouettes are really important for creating an interesting composition, so I try to focus on that and plan it out with intention. At the same time, I also start mocking up possible colour palettes. I settle on a dreamy twilight skyscape and colour palette using oranges with warm purples and dusky blues.

REFINED CONCEPT SKETCH, CLEANED UP AND COLOURIZED IN ADOBE PHOTOSHOP

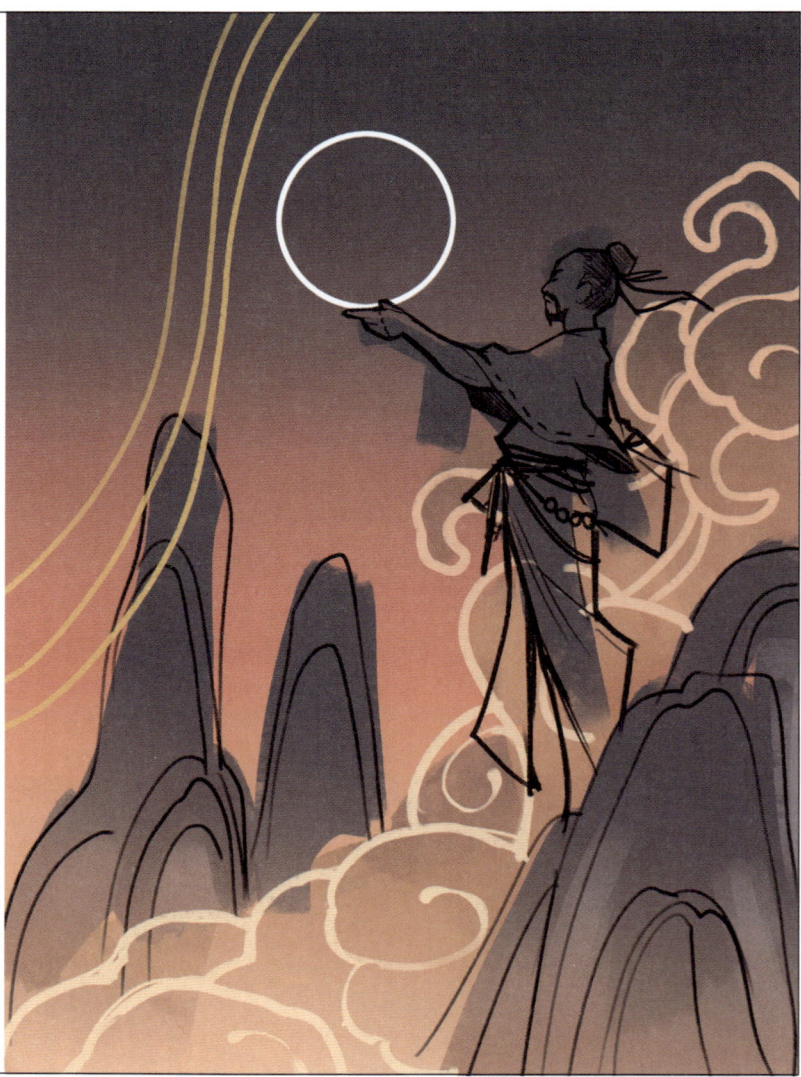

03 WATERCOLOUR TRIALS & COLOUR SKETCH

Before I start the actual painting, I trial different watercolour swatches and combinations by painting a little composition sketch. Each watercolour pigment has different and unique qualities, so I test all kinds to find colours that I feel will be useful. It's also helpful to see the colours against one another to make sure there is a sense of harmony. For example, a non-staining, granulating purple wouldn't be useful for this concept since I want things to be very deep, smooth, and even.

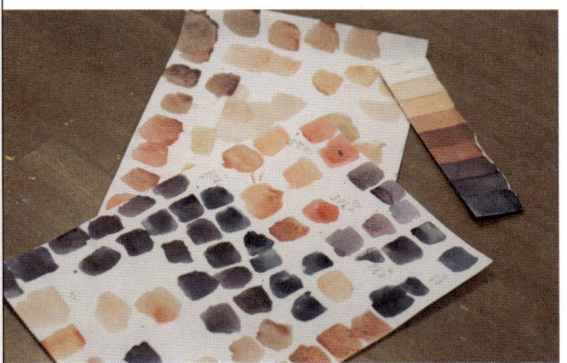
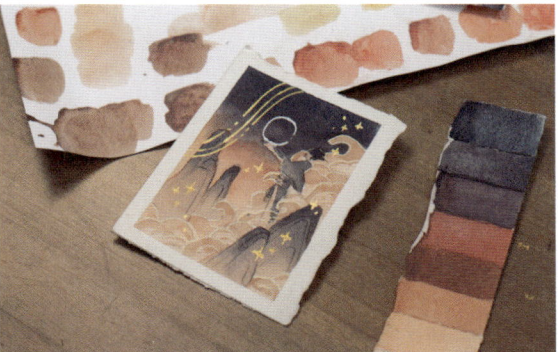

VARIOUS WATERCOLOUR EXPLORATIONS AND TRIALS, ALONG WITH A MINI-PAINTING REFERENCE

04 TRANSFER LINE-WORK DRAWING

Time to work on the real thing! I print out the digital line-work drawing on transparent tracing paper (so I can see through the page) and transfer it onto proper watercolour paper using a light graphite pencil like 2H. I then refine and make any last adjustments to the line work until I'm happy and ready to paint. I usually use a much darker pencil like a 2B to clean up the line work here.

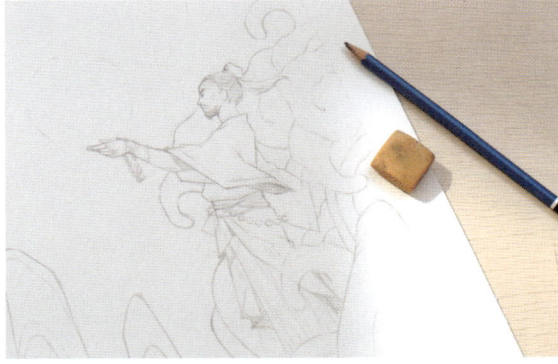

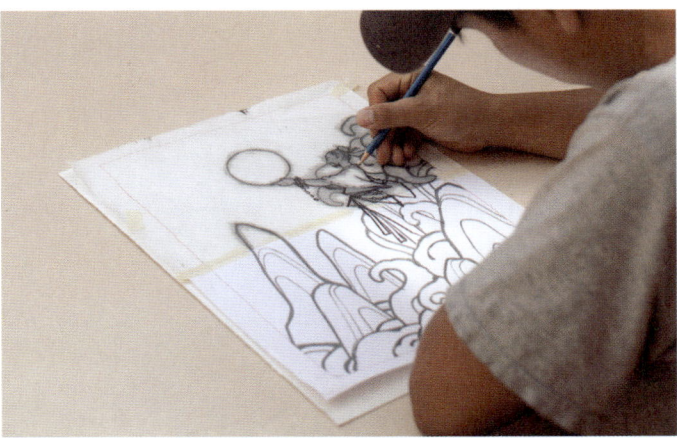

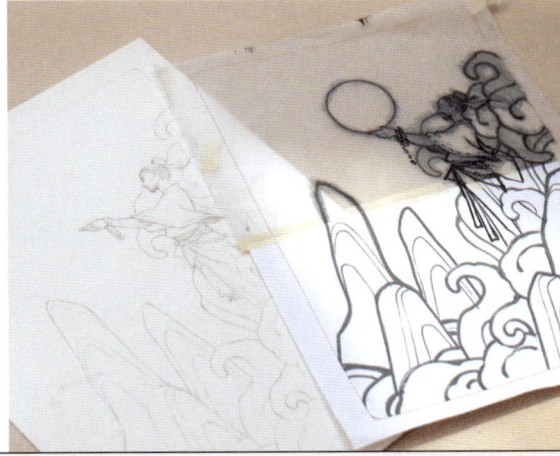

TRANSFERRING THE LINE-WORK DRAWING TO
WATERCOLOUR PAPER USING TRACING PAPER AND GRAPHITE

05 MASKING

I want to work on the background first, so to make it easier for myself, I carefully mask the whole area I don't want painted. Doing this allows me to focus solely on painting the background without having to worry about painting over the edges of the figure, clouds, mountains, and so on.

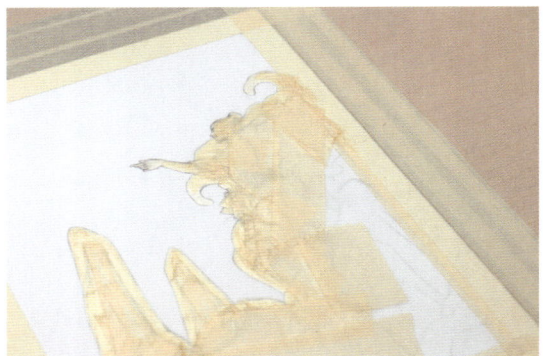
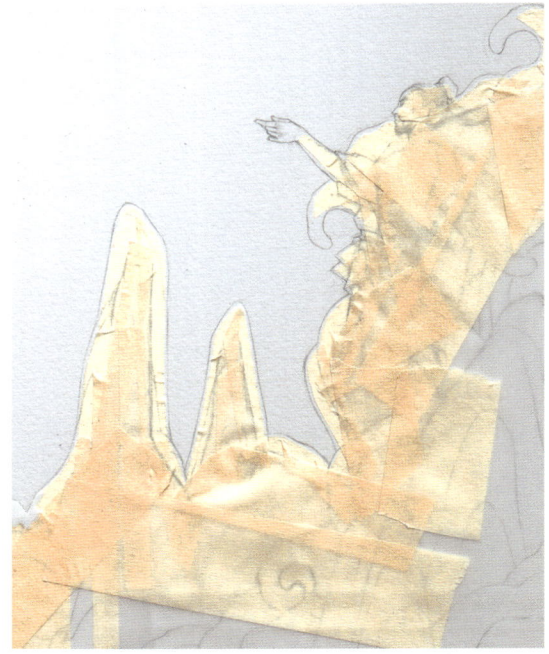

APPLYING MASKING TO THE AREAS OF THE PAINTING I WANT UNPAINTED

06 BACKGROUND LAYERS

With the area masked, I am able to paint a clean gradient skyscape in the background – warm pink to dusky indigo. I want the work to resemble and pay homage to Japanese ukiyo-e works of art, which commonly have smooth, linear, and transitional colour gradients. There is often a horizontal texture in ukiyo-e works created by brushstrokes on woodblock grain, so I try to leave a similar sort of horizontal brush texture in the background gradient (and later, throughout the entire piece). This helps tie my own style to the traditional elements, blending both into a harmonious composition.

FIRST BACKGROUND WATERCOLOUR LAYERS PAINTED TO ACHIEVE A CLEAN GRADIENT

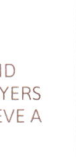
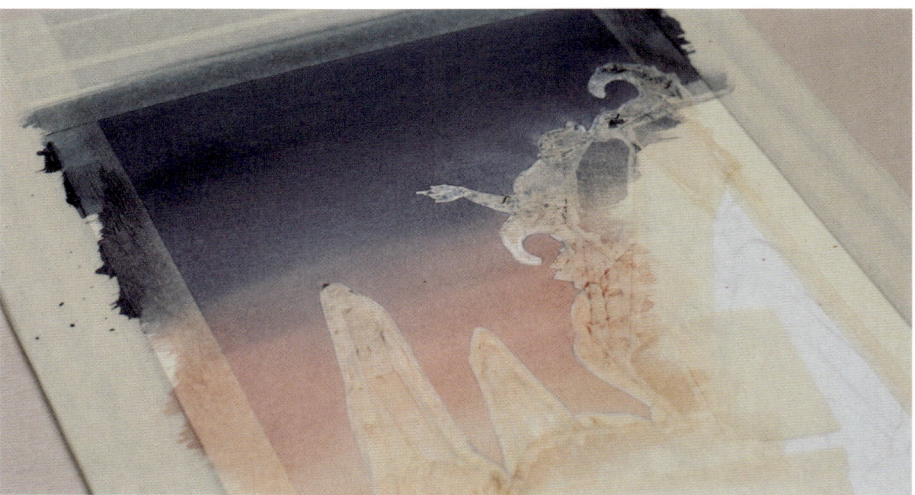

07 LIFTING (ADDING STARS)

The scene is set somewhere high above the mountains and clouds, so I want the background skyscape to also be dotted with some stars. To make them glow, I use a small brush with clean water and lift the paint (a technique of removing pigment from the page) to create these small impressions of stars. Later, I will add white ink to make the effect more pronounced.

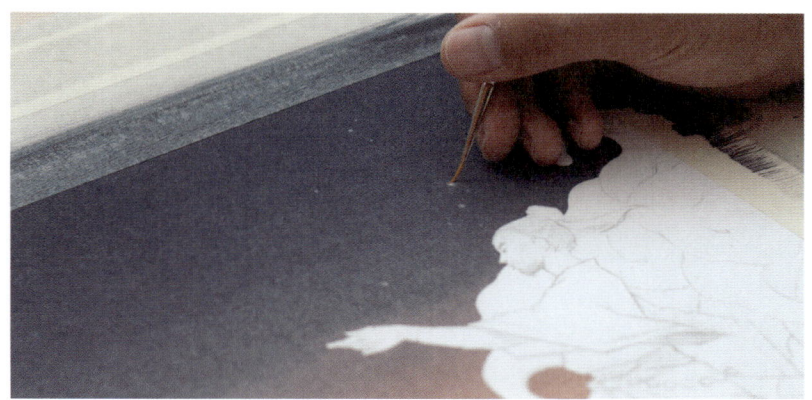

ADDING GLOWING STARS TO THE BACKGROUND USING A WATERCOLOUR LIFTING TECHNIQUE

08 MOUNTAINS

Revisiting the inspiration from ukiyo-e woodblock prints, I want to paint the mountains with a smooth, flat colour gradient. By using that same light-to-dark transition shown in the sky in the background, the scene is seemingly illuminated from below, subtly introducing dimensionality to the piece. It maintains the clean, flat colour layers while creating a sense of light that adds depth without overwhelming the simplicity.

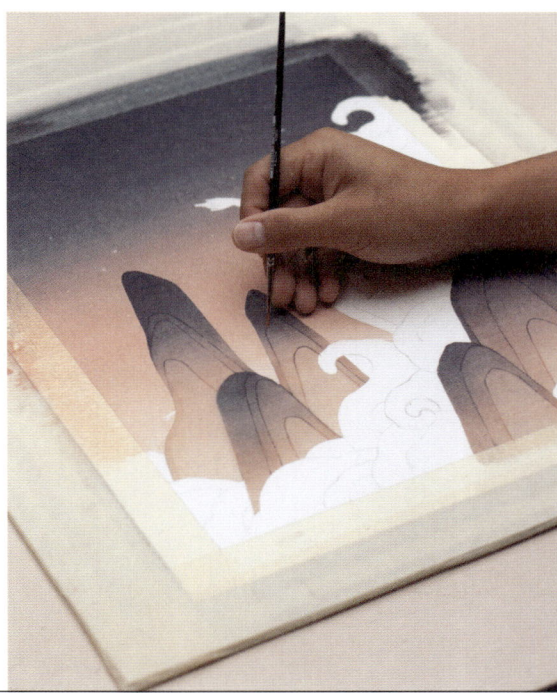

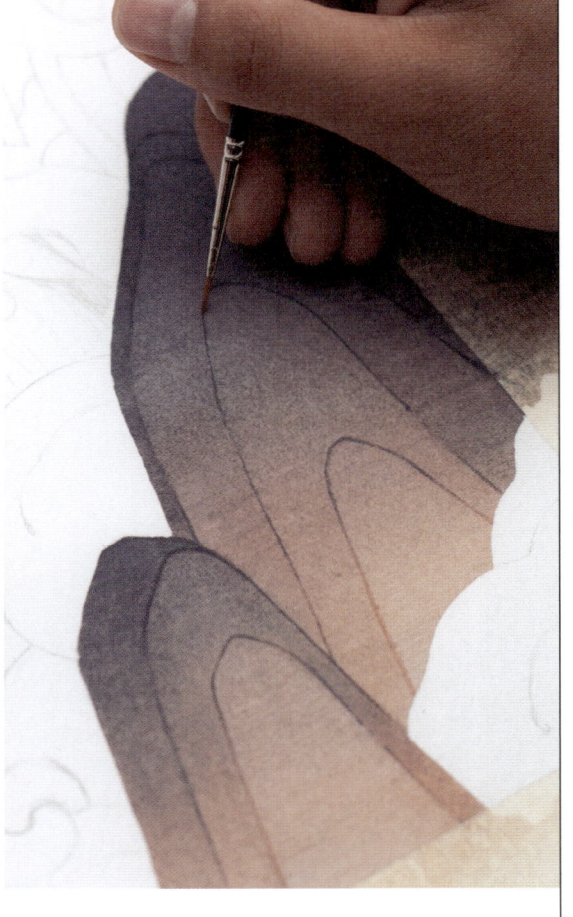

PAINTING IN THE SKY-HIGH MOUNTAINS USING A CLEAN GRADIENT, AND ADDING LINE WORK TO FOLLOW THE FORMS AND GIVE DIMENSIONALITY

09 CLOUDS

I want to paint the clouds in an illustrative, graphic style. It's a cloud form I've been experimenting with in my recent works, inspired by the decorative, stylized cloud patterns often seen in traditional Chinese art and textiles. Even though this style is quite different from the smooth, flat gradients I used for the mountains and sky, I try to create cohesiveness between the styles by using a similar light-to-dark gradient within the cloud forms as well.

I also want to re-emphasize the grain texture of the ukiyo-e works and make sure to leave horizontal brushstrokes throughout the clouds.

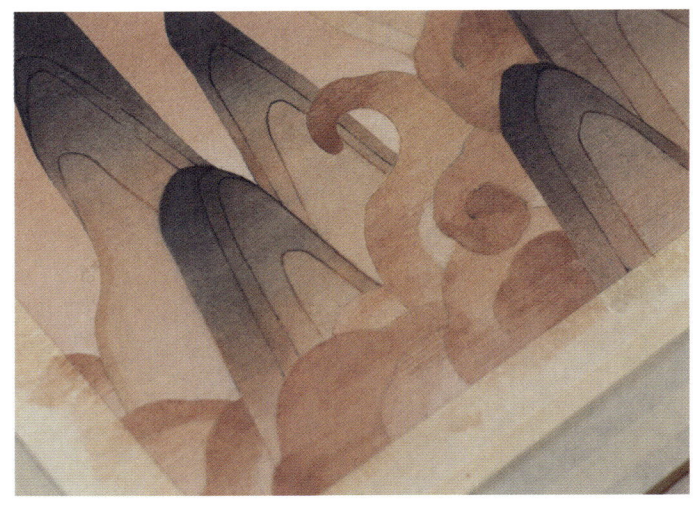

CREATING TEXTURED CHINESE DECORATIVE CLOUDS TO DEPICT THE CLOUD-LADDER THE MONK ASCENDS TO GET TO THE MOON

10 DAOIST MONK ZHOU SHENG

While painting the monk (Zhou Sheng) and his clothes, I want to avoid making things appear too realistic. Since the other parts of the painting are graphic, simple, and illustrative, too much realism would feel out of place. This is a common approach I use to unify contrasting styles in my work: I paint him in a simplified way, but with enough depth to keep him cohesive with the rest of the piece, while also considering the light coming from below.

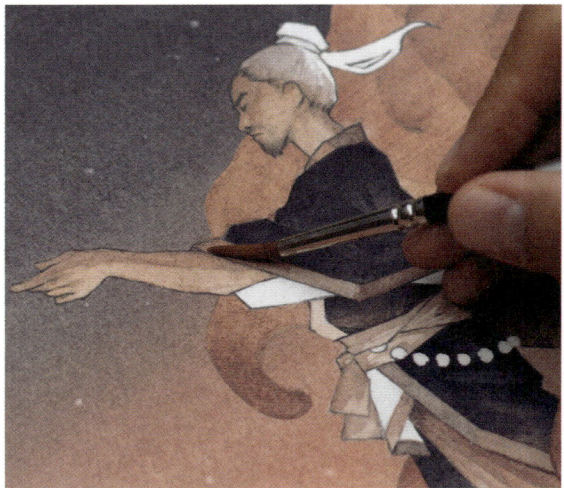

PAINTING AND FILLING IN THE DETAILS OF THE DAOIST MONK

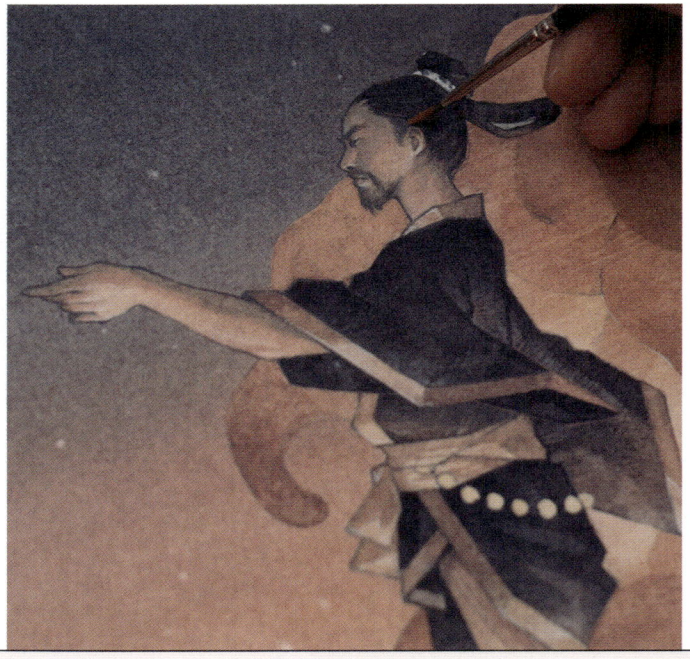

11 WATERCOLOUR LINE WORK & DETAILS

Once everything is painted in, I find there is still a lack of both cohesion and definition with all the different elements and their respective styles. To bring things together, I create thin outlines with watercolour on the clouds, monk, and mountain. Using that predominant blue and orange colour in the line work creates a sense of uniformity.

CLEANING UP THE PAINTING BY REINTRODUCING LINE WORK

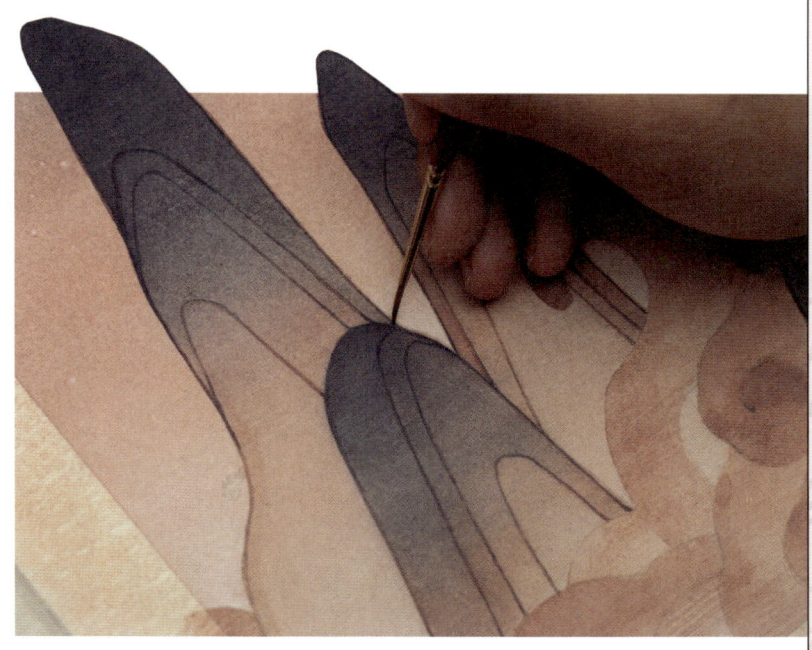

12 CLOUD LINES

To stylize the clouds even more, I use opaque gouache to create outlines of the shapes, forms, and curls. It makes the clouds appear more dreamlike and illustrative. I also specifically use a lighter colour as it gives the clouds a more dreamlike effect, as if they are illuminated and glowing.

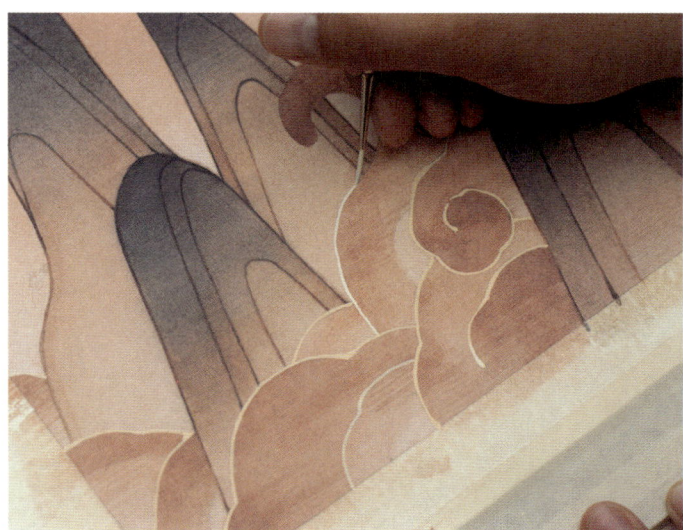

STYLIZING THE CLOUDS WITH GRAPHIC LINE WORK USING GOUACHE

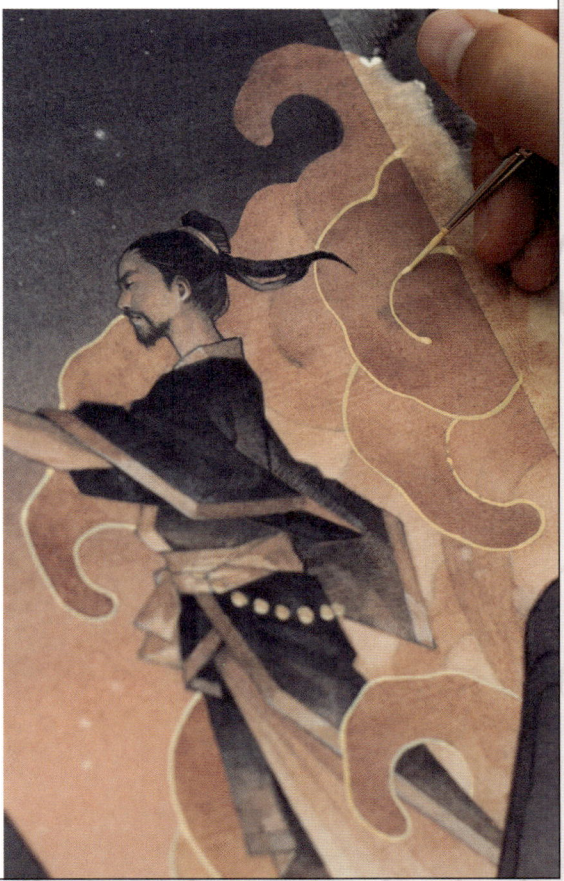

13 WHITE INK

Watercolour can't be used to paint opaque details, so getting white to show up in paintings can only be achieved in two ways; either leaving it unpainted (the paper shows through) or by using mixed media. In this case, I use opaque white ink to outline the moon, as well as painting little white specks and glints in the sky as stars.

PAINTING IN THE MOON USING
A THIN WHITE INK OUTLINE

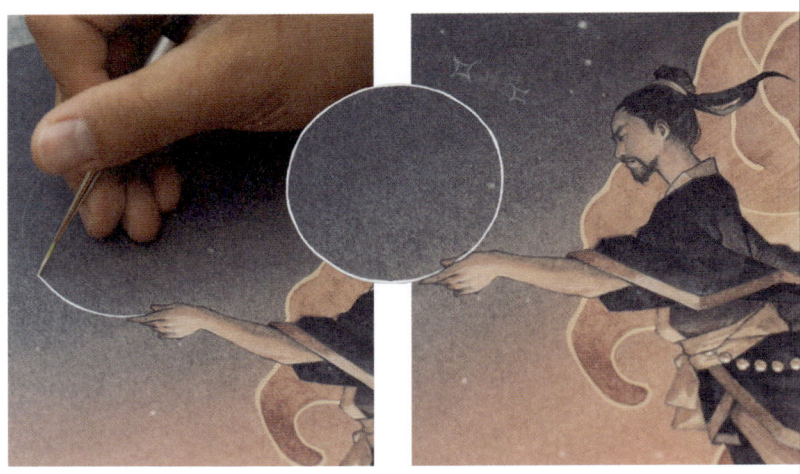

14 GILDING

I often add gold leaf to my paintings to provide extra dimensionality and depth. I find that it also makes the viewer look at the painting twice, as the effect shifts depending on the light source and angle. I try to incorporate the gold detail to my paintings in a very fine and subtle way. In this work, I want the gold to add a sense of flow to break the overwhelming negative space of the sky, while also adding little graphic gold stars throughout the composition.

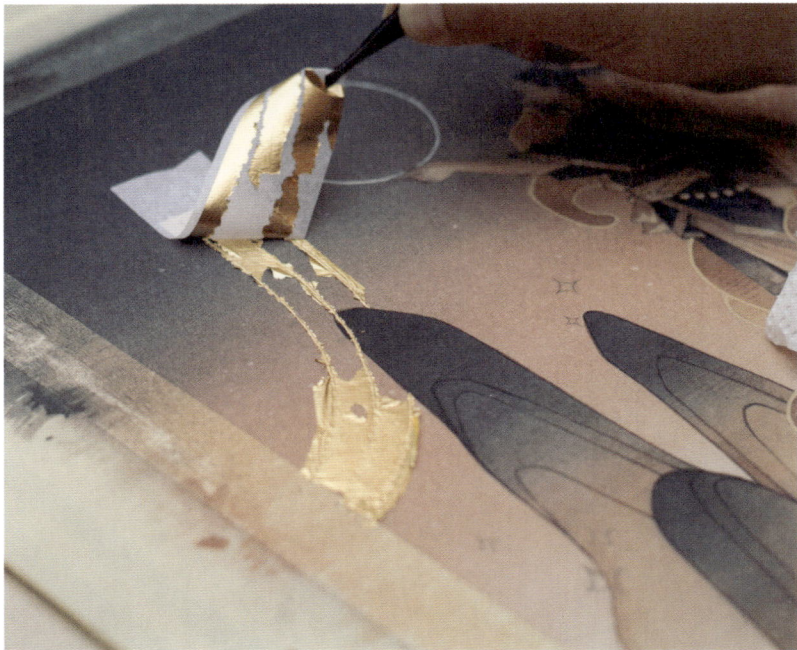

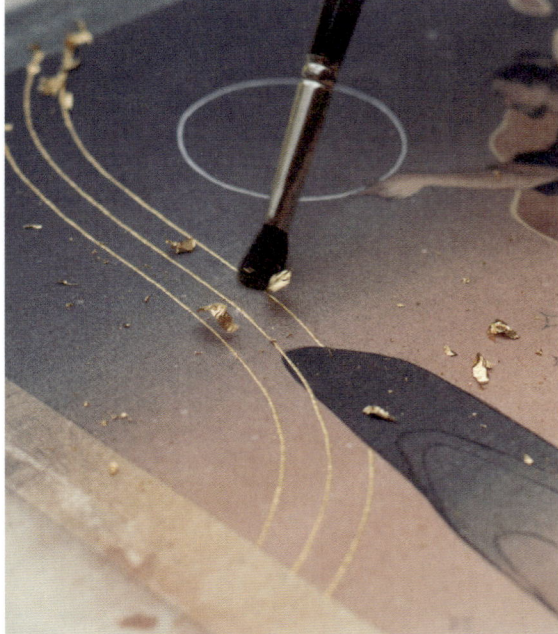

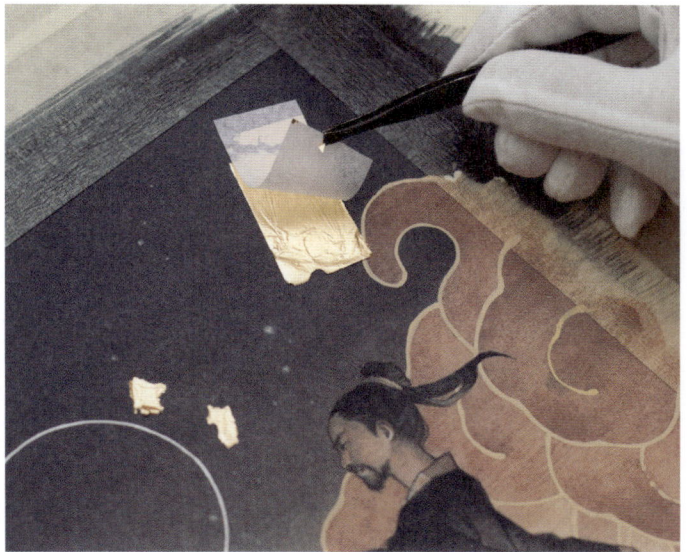

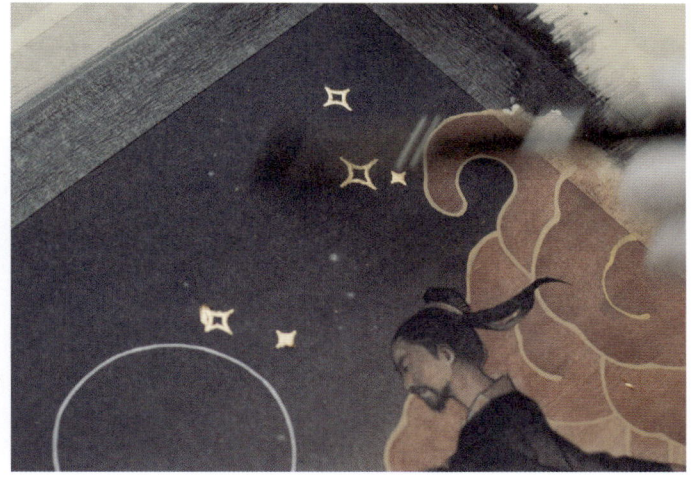

INTRODUCING DIMENSIONALITY TO THE
PAINTING USING METALLIC GOLD-LEAF DETAILS

15 FINISHING TOUCHES

To finish the painting, I add final details and textures. I build patterns into the monk's robe, sharpen some outlines and details, and also loosen up the painting by reintroducing some watercolour textures in the form of splatters and loose brushstrokes. Prior to this stage, the painting is very separated and almost 'perfect', as the elements are painted individually (sky, background, mountains, and so on). So, to unify the painting and help the elements connect, I use the watercolour textures throughout.

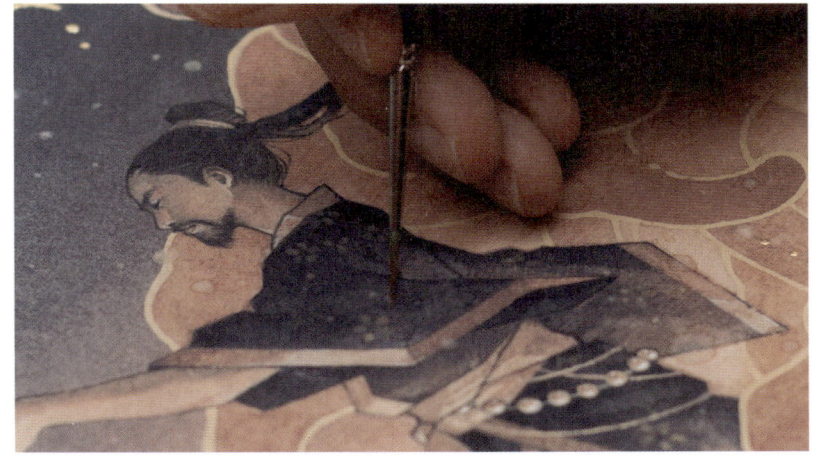

ADDING FINISHING DETAILS AND LOOSENING UP THE
PAINTING BY INTRODUCING WATERCOLOUR TEXTURES

CONCLUSION

I'm really proud of this work. It definitely was a challenge to reinterpret Hokusai's piece. I needed to maintain all the original elements of the composition while modernizing it in my own style with the utmost respect for its cultural background. I tried my best to pay respect and homage to the work's roots, considering inspiration and references like ukiyo-e and using specific techniques to achieve similar qualities – gradients, flat-painting layers, clean line work, and clean, minimal compositions. The best part was reimagining an original black-on-white piece of ink work to a colourized rendition. I felt that a dreamy, sunset skyscape was fitting.

Kelogsloops

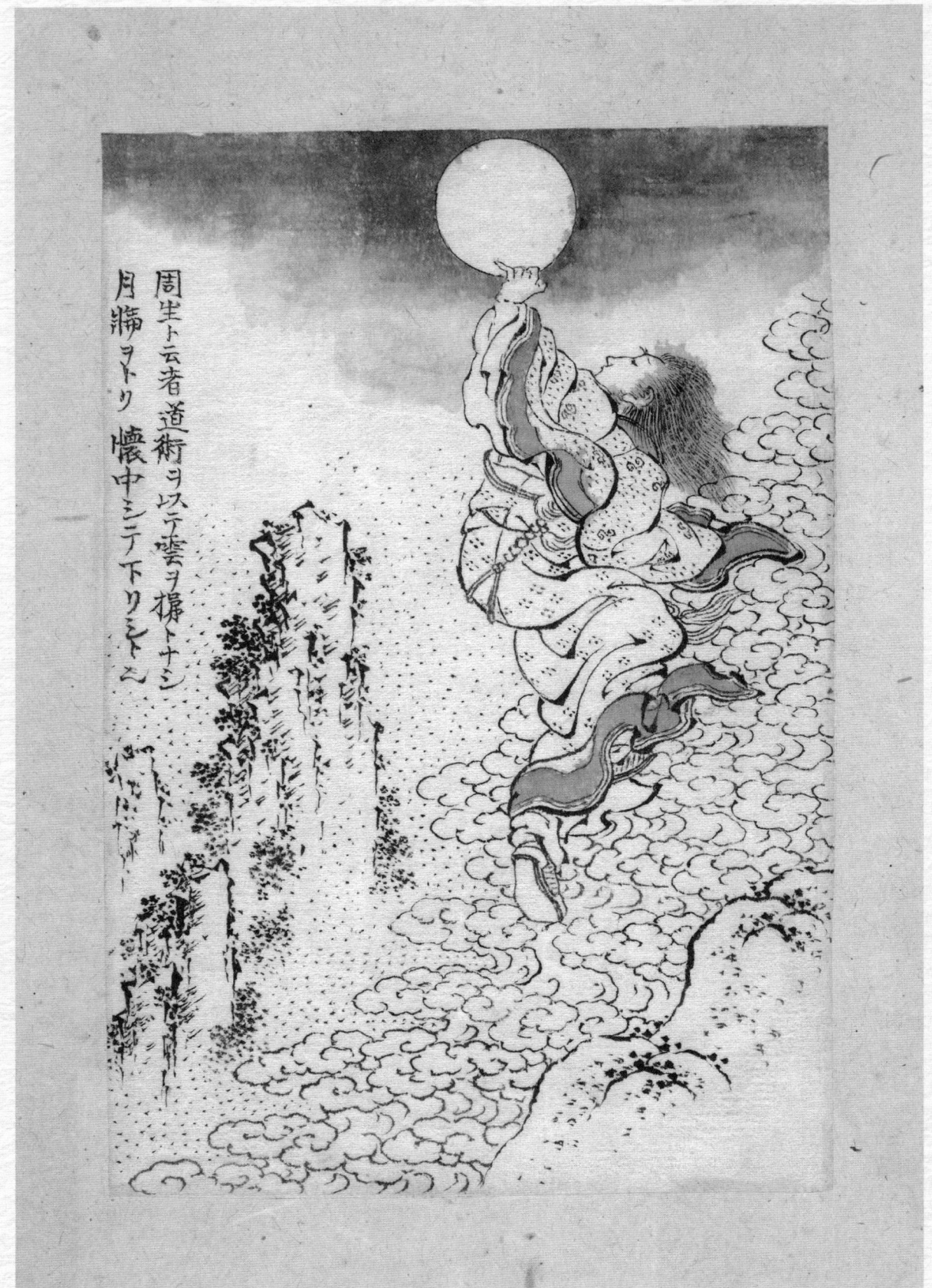

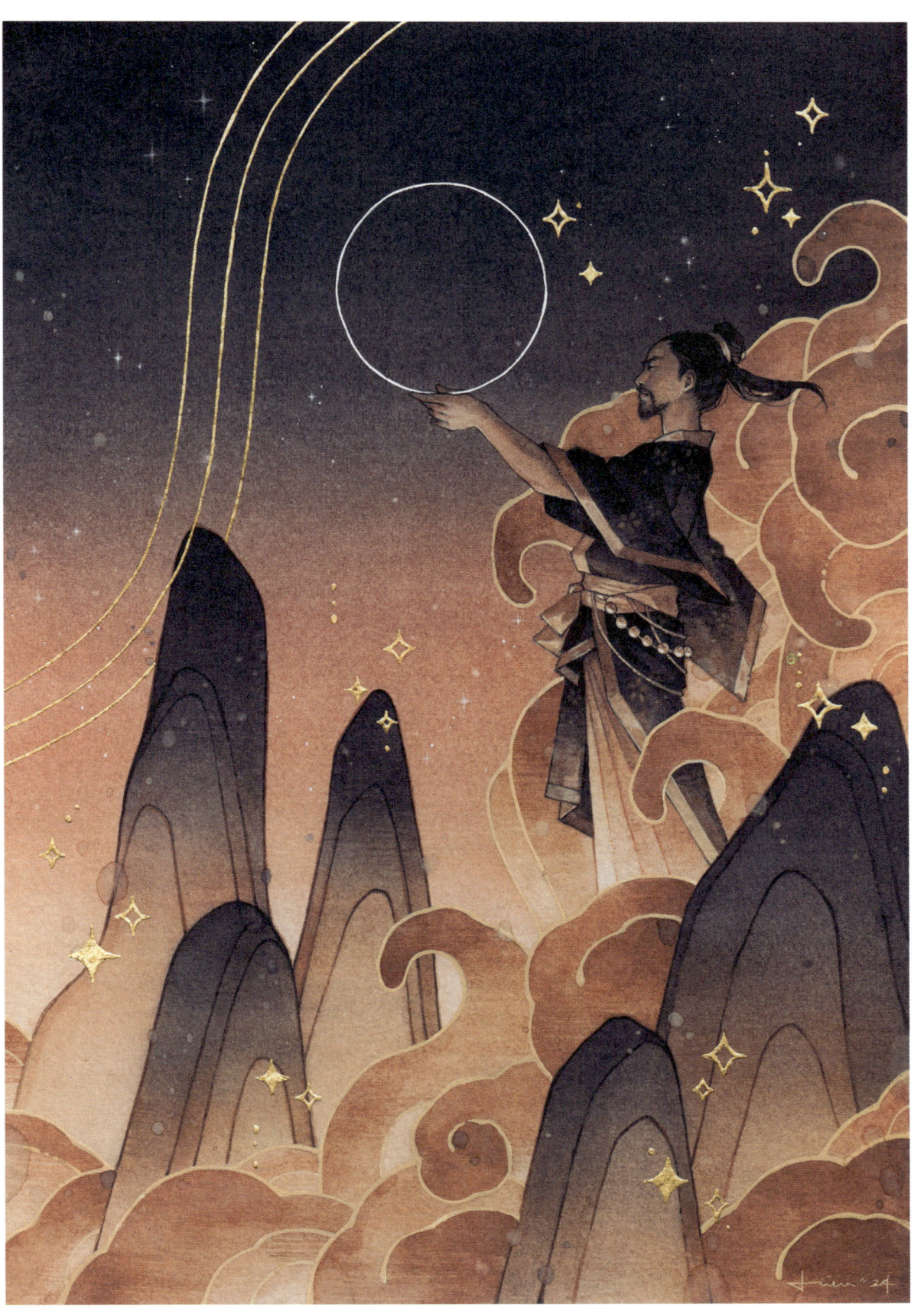

DAOIST MASTER ZHOU SHENG ASCENDS A CLOUD-LADDER TO THE MOON

KELOGSLOOPS

RIGHT: *Kappa*
A kappa (a Japanese yōkai) that sits atop a rock, fishing on a rainy day

OPPOSITE PAGE:
For the World
A piece about vulnerability and the capacity to open up

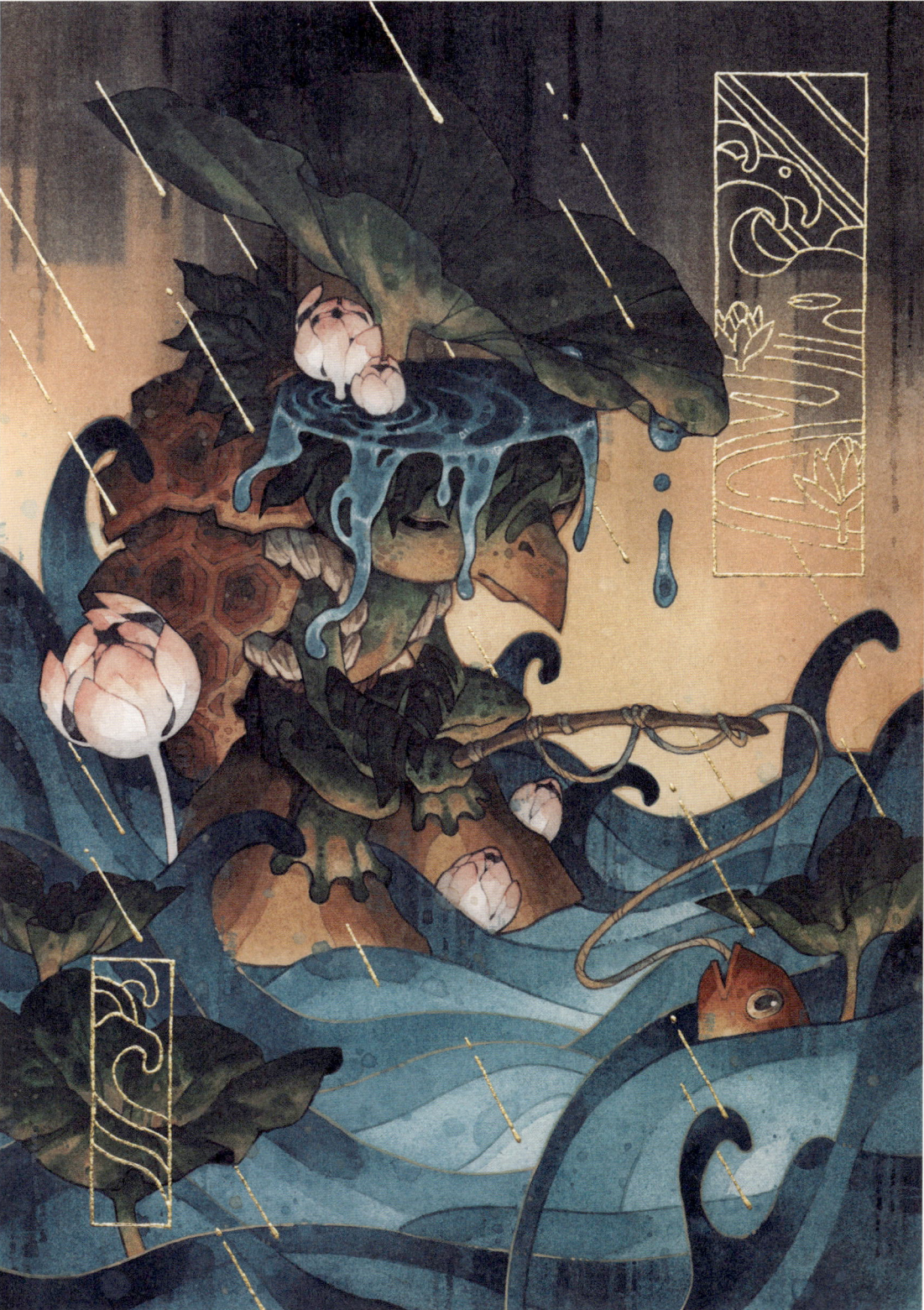

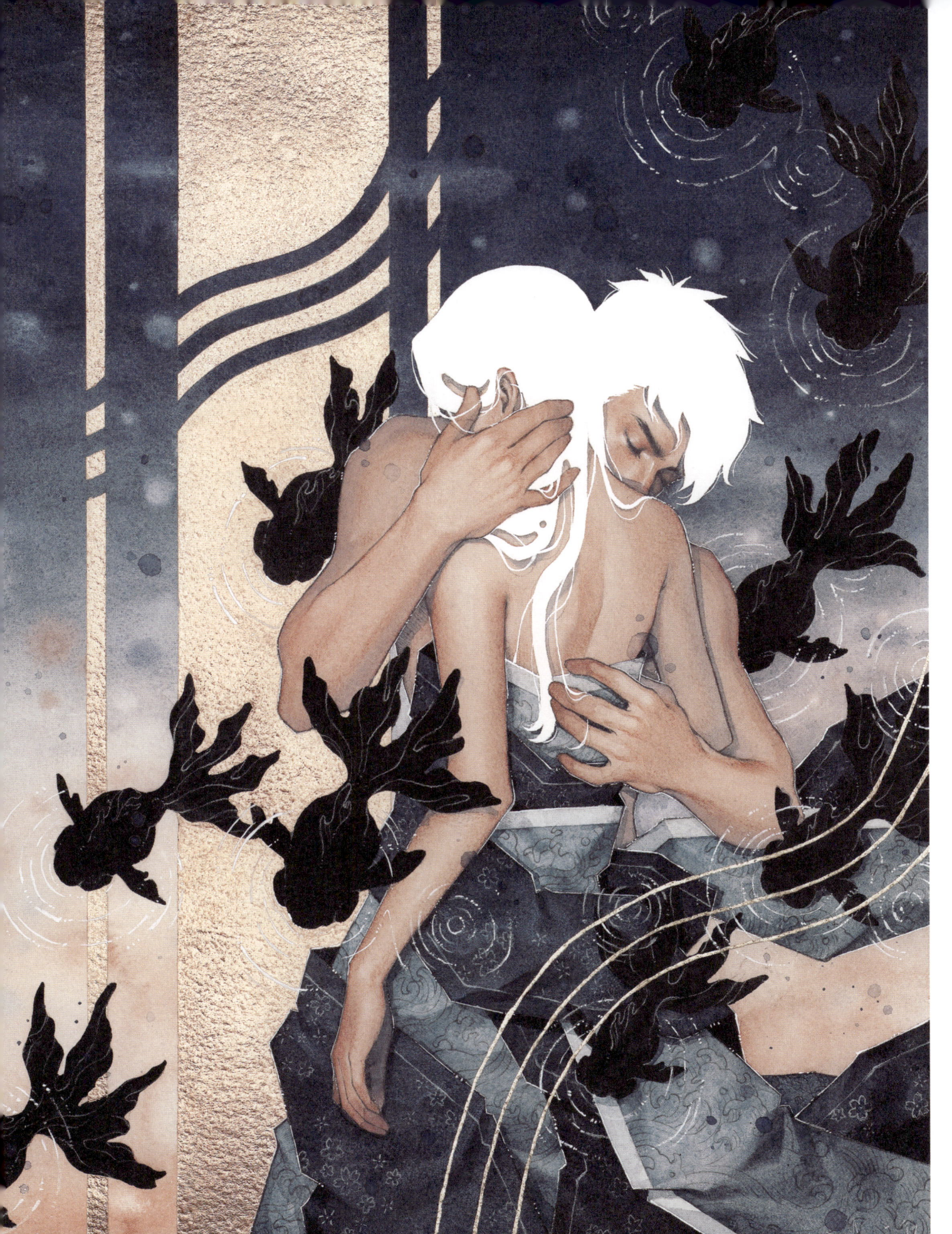

Kelogsloops

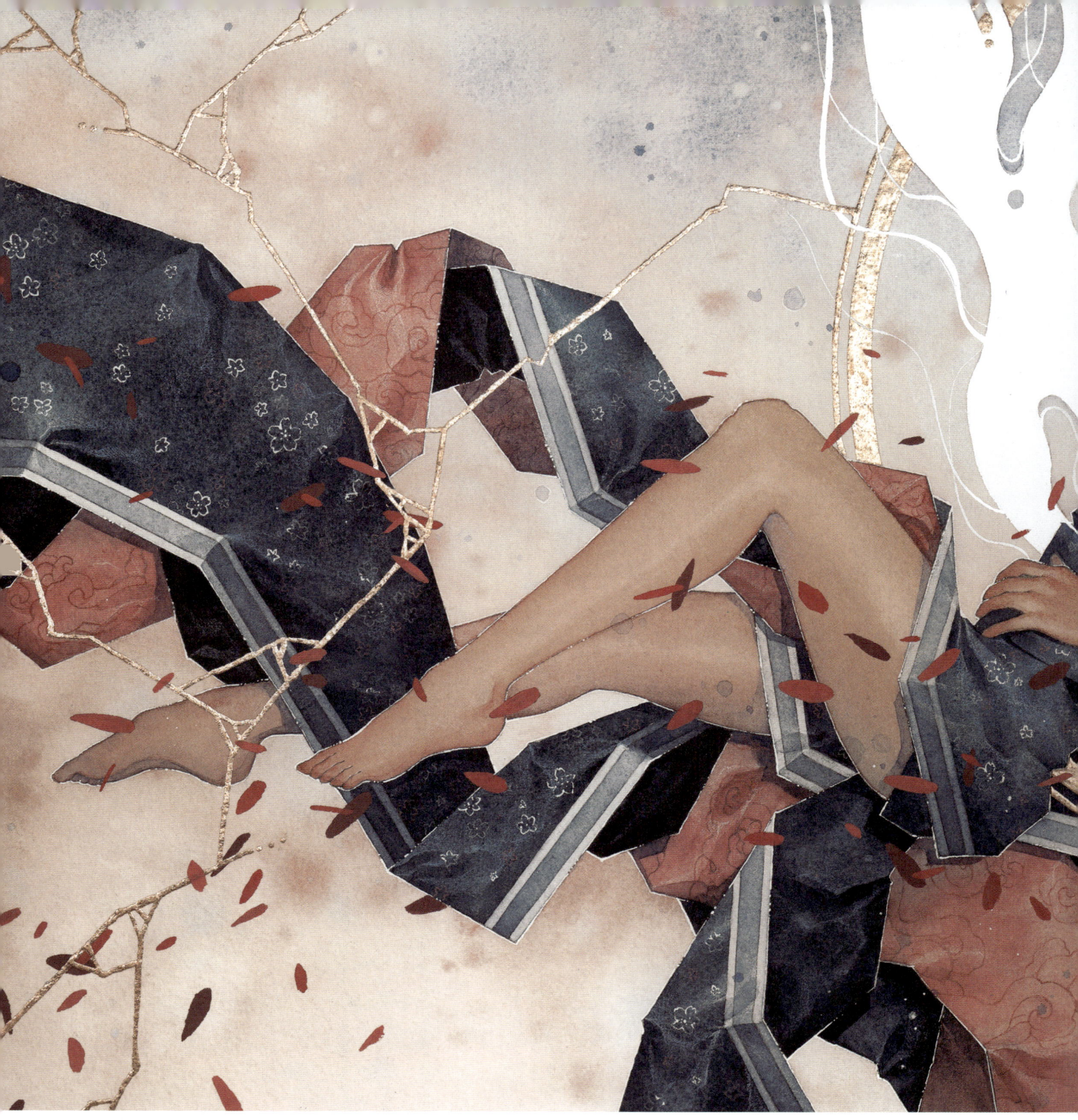

Inhale, Exhale
The hero piece from my collection
of works from 2018, themed *Breathe*

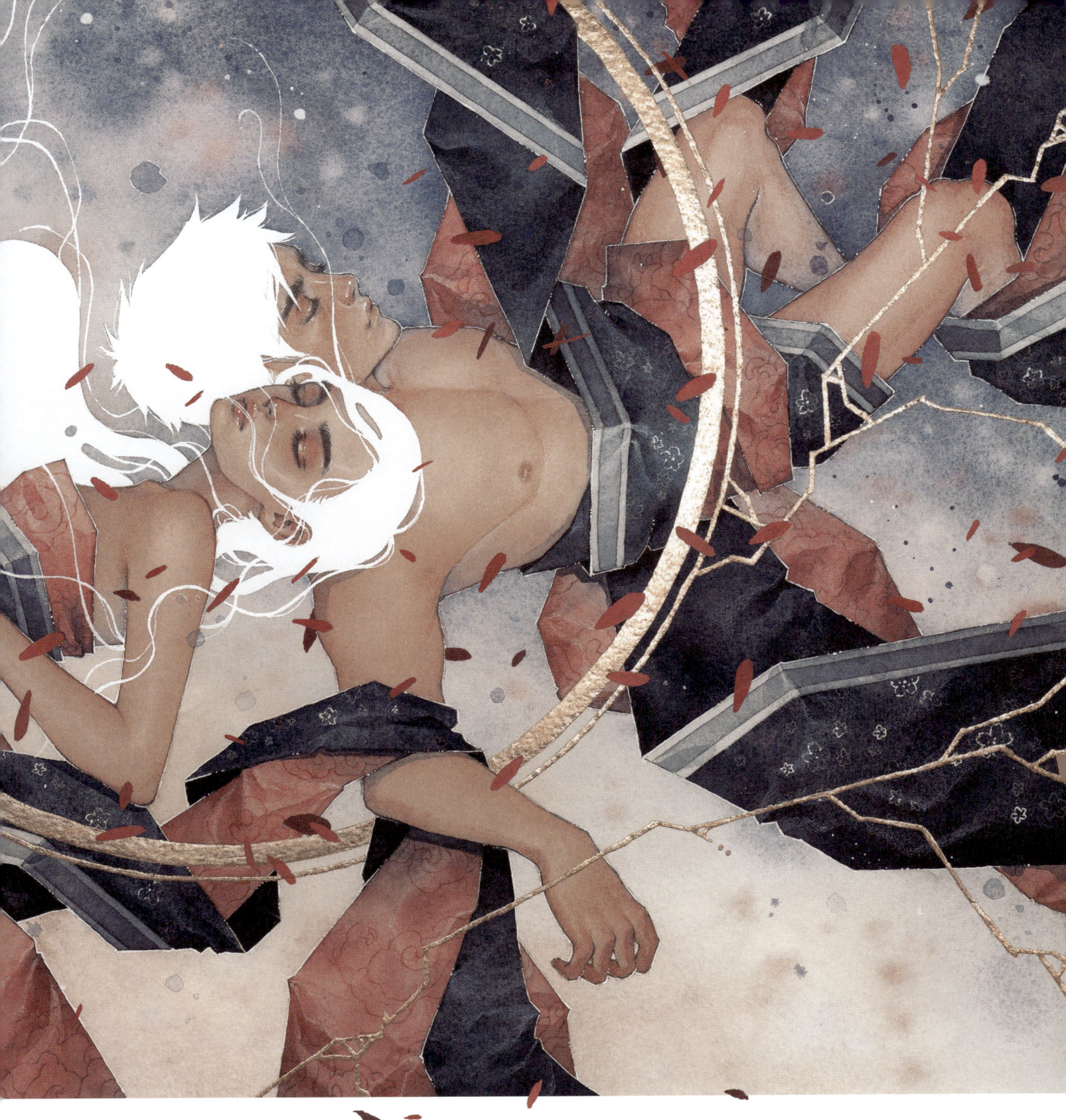

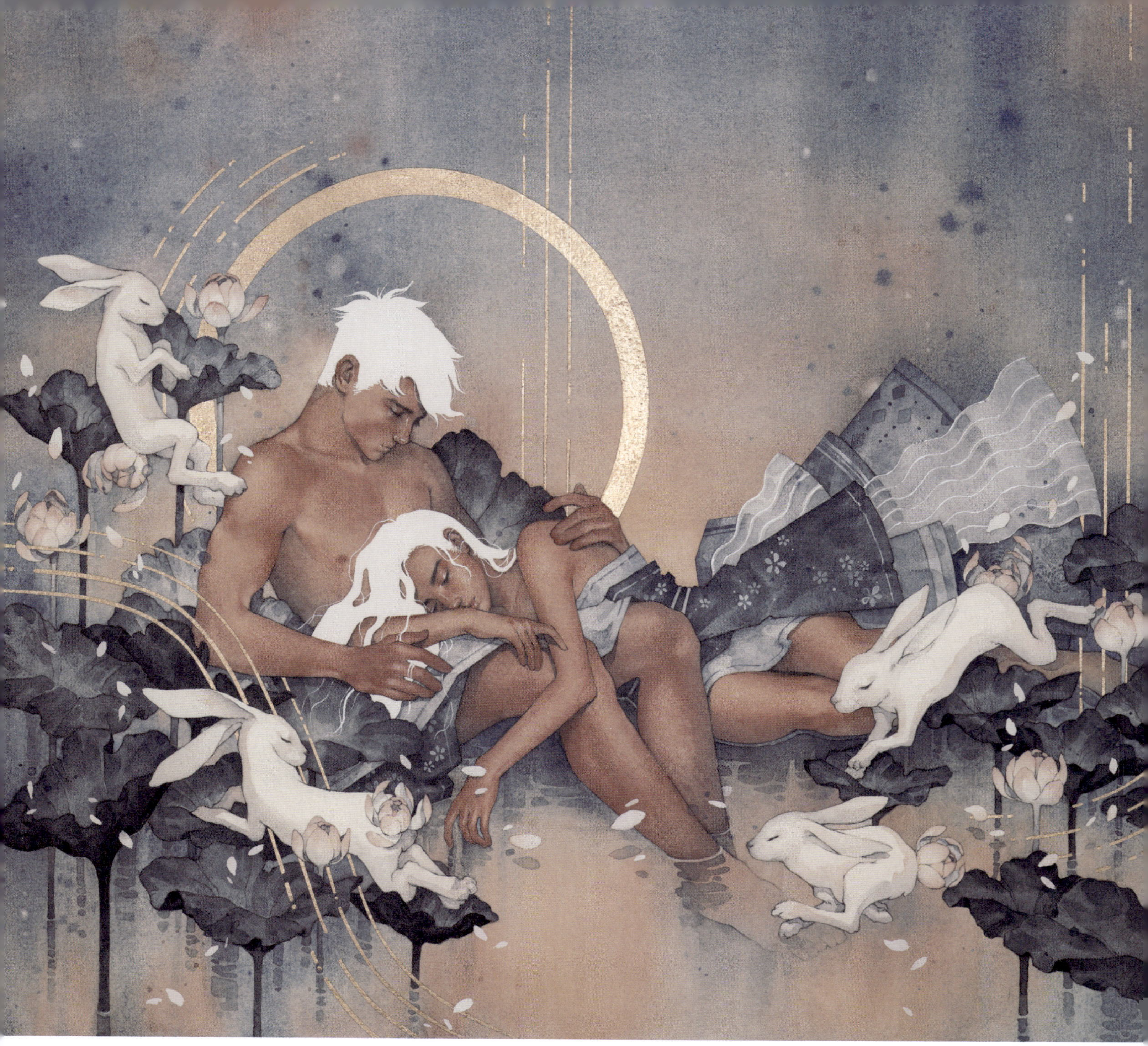

ABOVE: *Someday*
A hero painting from my
exhibition, *The Dream*, which was
heavily inspired by *Final Fantasy X*

RIGHT: *Hiding Place*
One of my personal favourite
pieces of all time, from my
Breathe collection

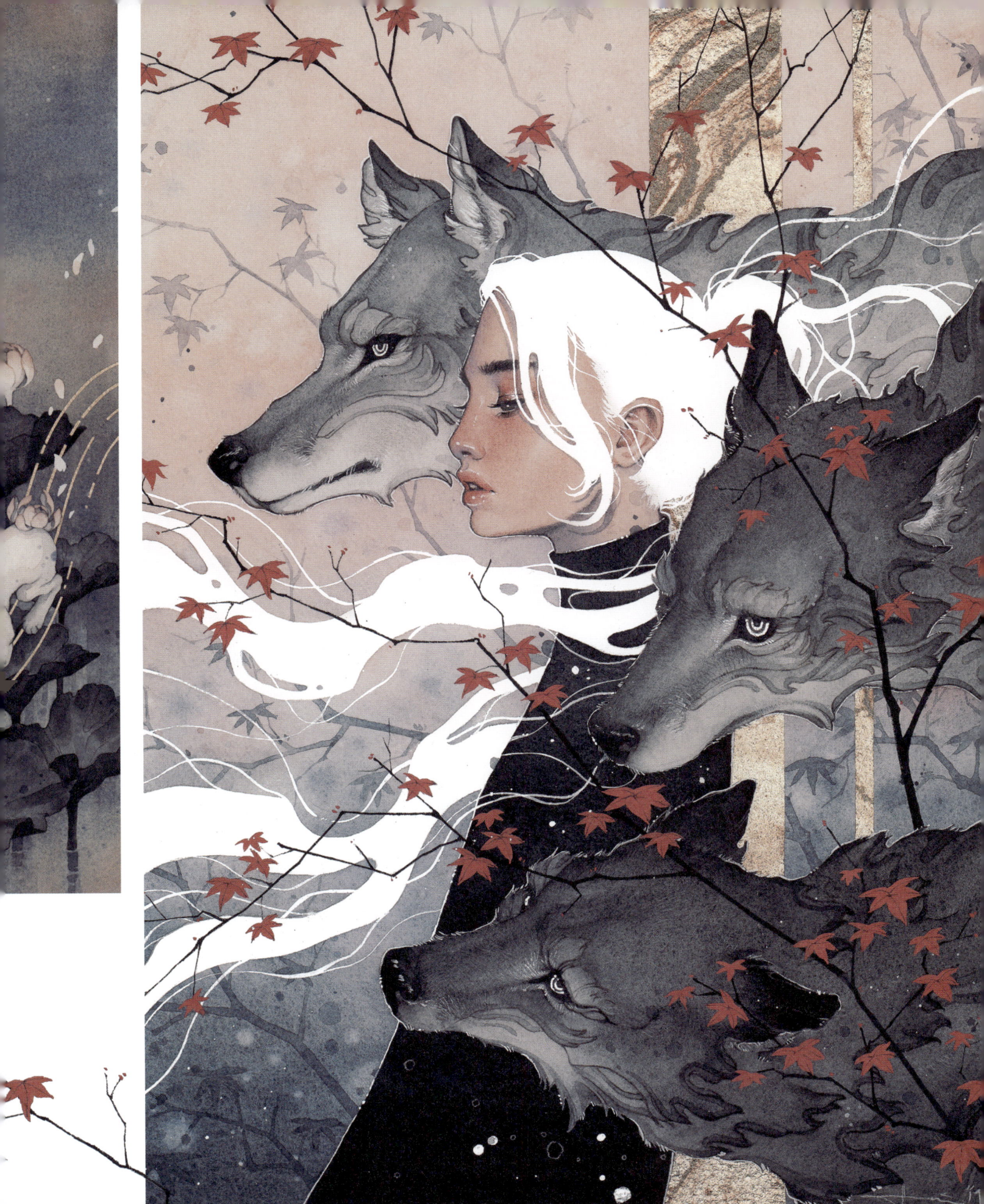

AVALOKITEŚVARA SEATE
ON THE HEAD OF A DRA

BY HAGUSHKA

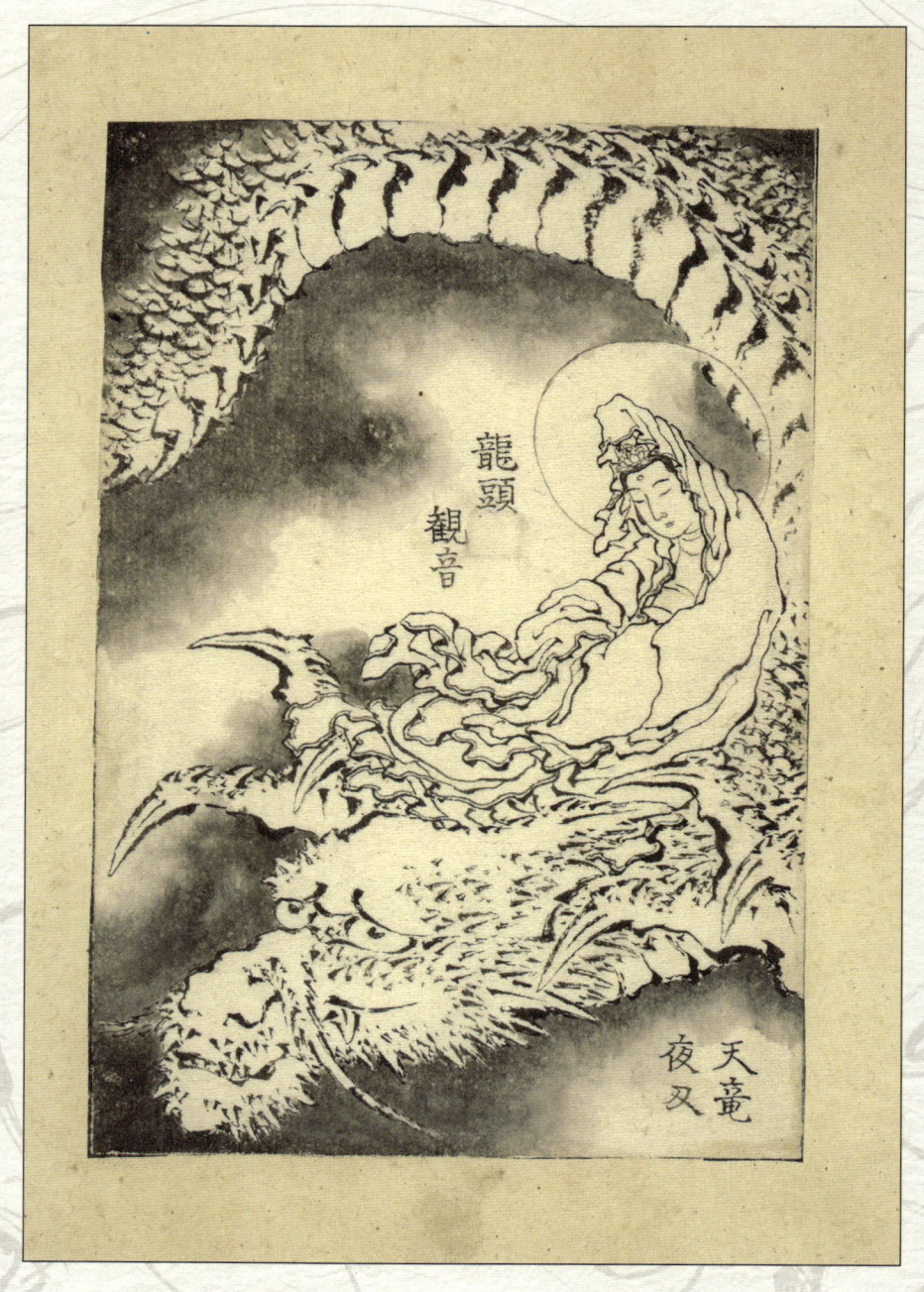

龍頭
観音

天竜
夜叉

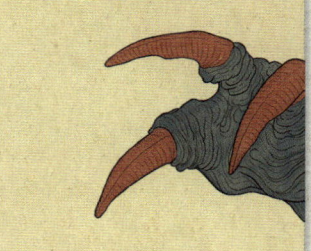

DISCOVERING HOKUSAI

I've enjoyed watching anime since childhood. Among the bold and colourful animation, unique character design, and complex stories, my favourite thing above all else is the character development. There is just something special about watching characters evolve alongside the narrative. Perhaps that's why I've always loved drawing and recreating characters from my favourite shows and video games. Over the years, my technique experienced its own sort of evolution into a more realistic and complicated style. But thanks to the discovery of artists such as Takato Yamamoto, Suehiro Maruo, and Haruko Ichikawa, I began to notice that I preferred simple lines and shapes; how I used to draw when I was younger.

During that time, I didn't know much about Katsushika Hokusai, but it is difficult *not* to know *The Great Wave off Kanagawa*. It wasn't until much later on that I understood that the people I sought inspiration from had sought that same motivation from Hokusai's art. He laid the foundations of this style for many artists: simplicity of backgrounds, emphasis on line art, and an absence of shadows. I am glad to have discovered more about this art master, who many call the 'Father of Manga', and I am equally thrilled that his art continues to inspire people today – including me.

01 INITIAL SKETCH

Before I start drawing, I look at the direction of lines and the location of Hokusai's characters, Bodhisattva Avalokiteśvara and the dragon. Together, they create a spiral shape that perfectly matches the composition of the drawing. It makes the eye perceive the characters to be flying or floating in the air.

I sketch out the general placement of figures on the canvas, following the direction of lines. You can see that my lines are sloppy and imprecise, but my main mission here is to get a feel for the composition.

SKETCHING THE
GENERAL PLACEMENT OF
FIGURES AND PICTURING
THE COMPOSITION

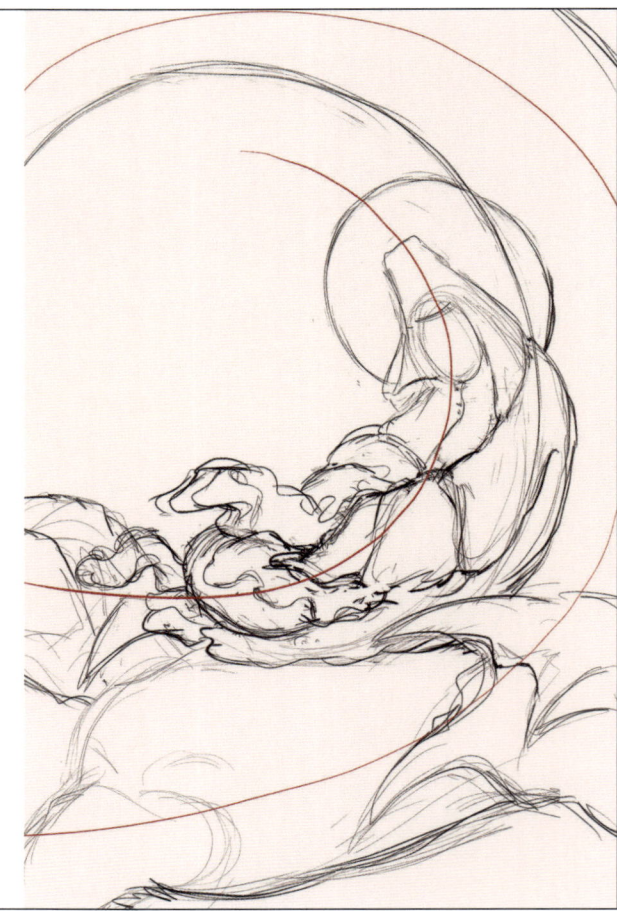

02 LINES CREATE TEXTURE

Hokusai skilfully creates motion through dynamic lines. This catches the eye and forces you to explore the drawing by looking at it from different angles. The pattern made by the windswept folds in the character's clothing is mesmerizing.

I use Hokusai's line art as a guide, but make sure to add changes to Avalokiteśvara's clothes. By adding curving lines, I create smoother shapes that flow down like tides from the character's head. Notice how the detailed folds on their clothing add texture to the drawing.

USING LINES TO CREATE TEXTURE

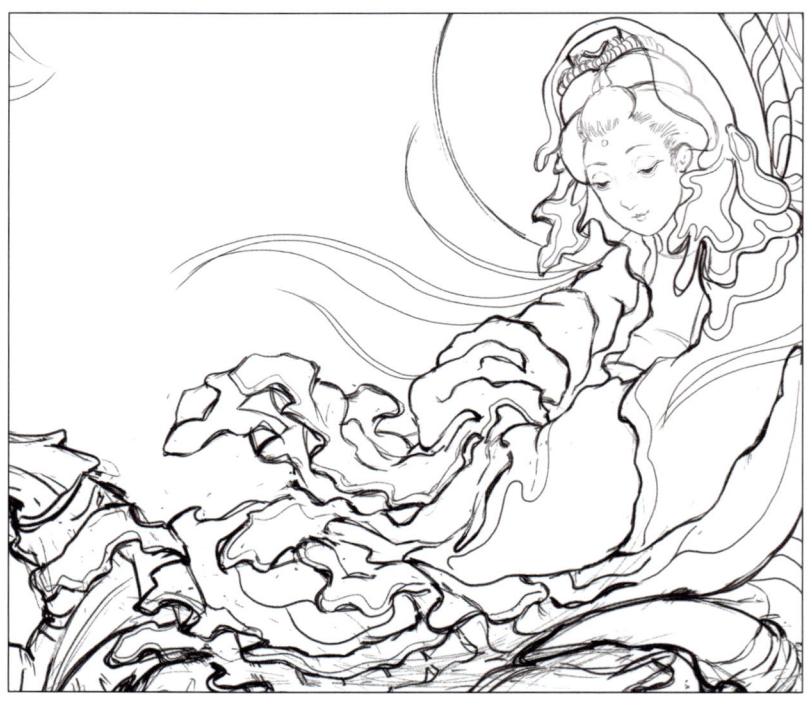

03   LINES CREATE MOTION

To show motion, Hokusai uses line strength; he draws the same pattern over and over on the dragon's back, which creates a repetitive cycle. For my recreation, I also draw in the direction of the spiral, but instead of simple lines, I try to create more of a complex pattern for the dragon's back. I add big brows, fur, and scales, playing with the texture lines. I need *more* detail on these characters! The dragon *must* be in motion.

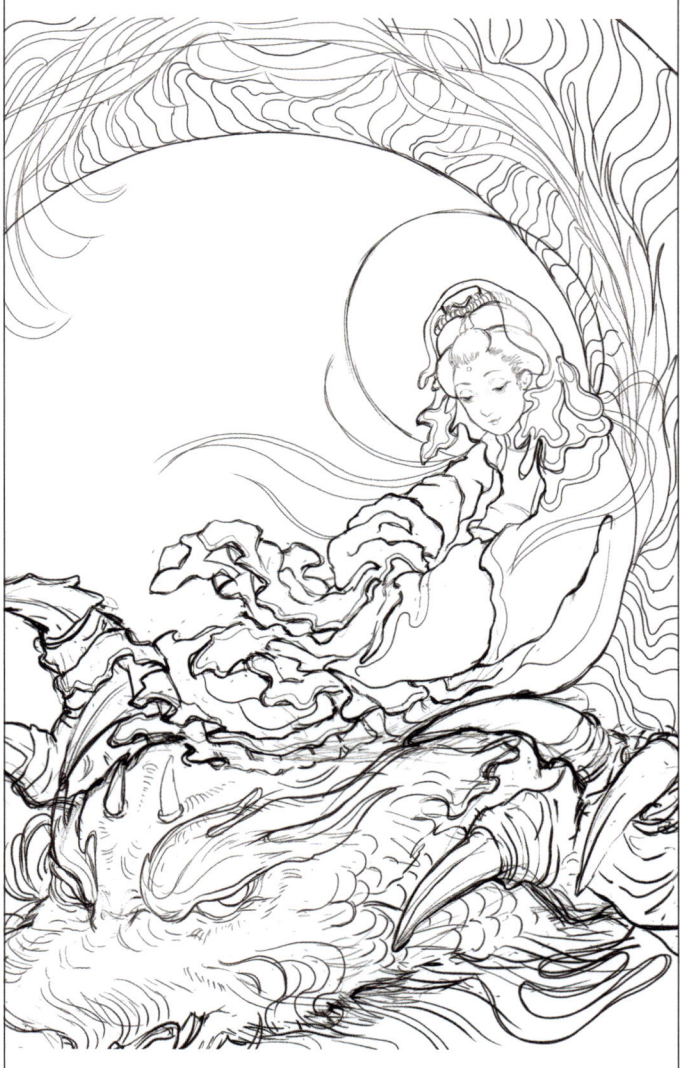

USING LINES TO CREATE A SENSE OF MOTION

04   BEGINNING THE LINE ART

When I am fully satisfied with the sketch, so begins one of the most difficult parts of drawing: the proper line art. Eyes are very important for me, so I start with them and then work my way outwards. When sketching loosely, the lines can look a little messy, but I think it's important to keep some that way as they add a certain charm to the drawing. Right now, my mission is to keep the playfulness of these lines and understand which ones should be thicker or thinner.

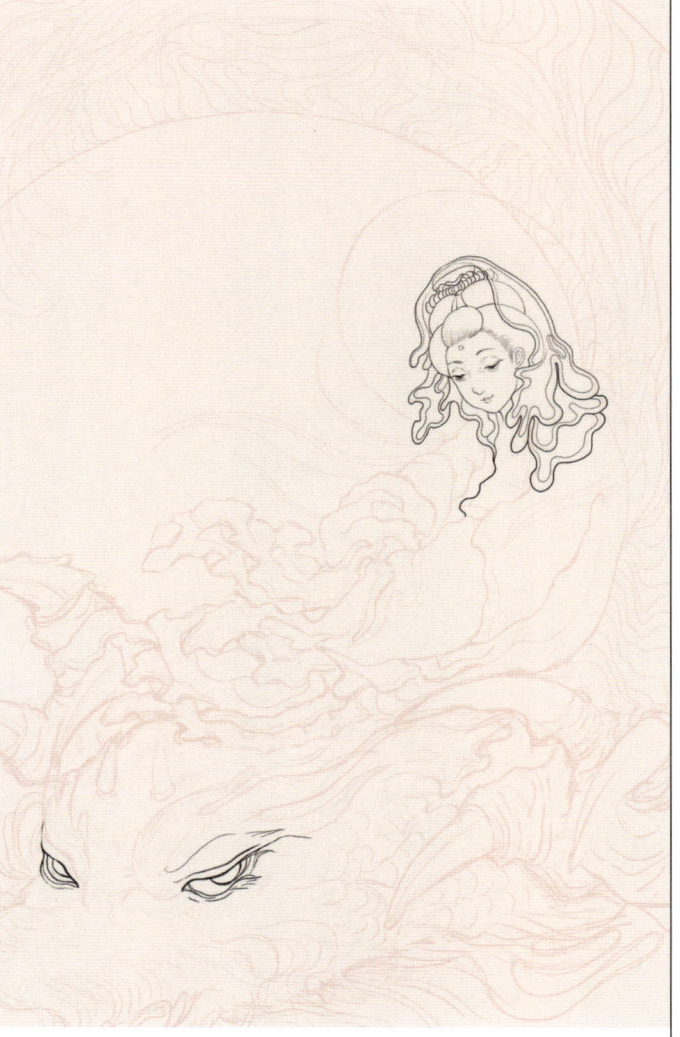

I USUALLY START WITH THE EYES AND WORK MY WAY OUTWARDS

05 RENDERING THE CLOTHING FOLDS

Time to focus on Avalokiteśvara. I start by drawing smooth lines on the folds of their clothing. I follow the sketch, but the line work isn't thick or thin – it's just stable. I do this to create the foundation of an outer contour. While working on the headpiece, I add a very thin inner contour for depth and texture.

WORKING ON THE
CHARACTER'S HEADPIECE

06 HEAD OF THE DRAGON

Earlier, I added unique and varying line patterns to this magnificent creature. I decide to add more fur to the dragon's face, which is made up of thin lines. I also add very big brows that create volume and add diversity to its shape. I want to give the dragon horns that mimic the shape of its claws and make its scale shape more complex. Notice how the dragon's face is now very rich in texture.

FOCUSING ON THE DRAGON'S
HEAD BY ADDING FUR, HORNS,
AND DIFFERENT SCALE SHAPES

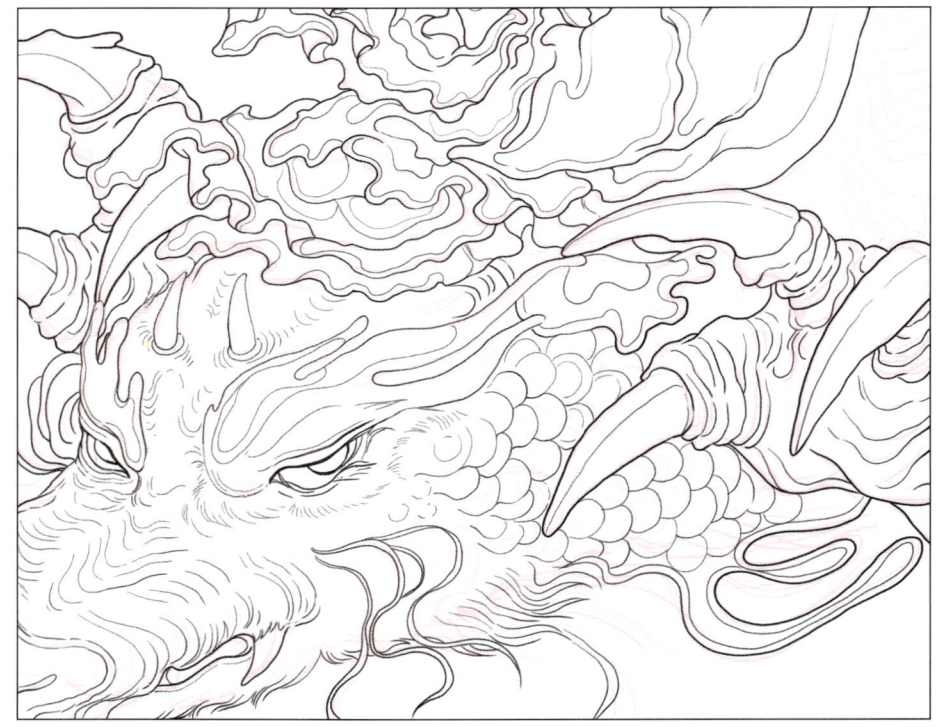

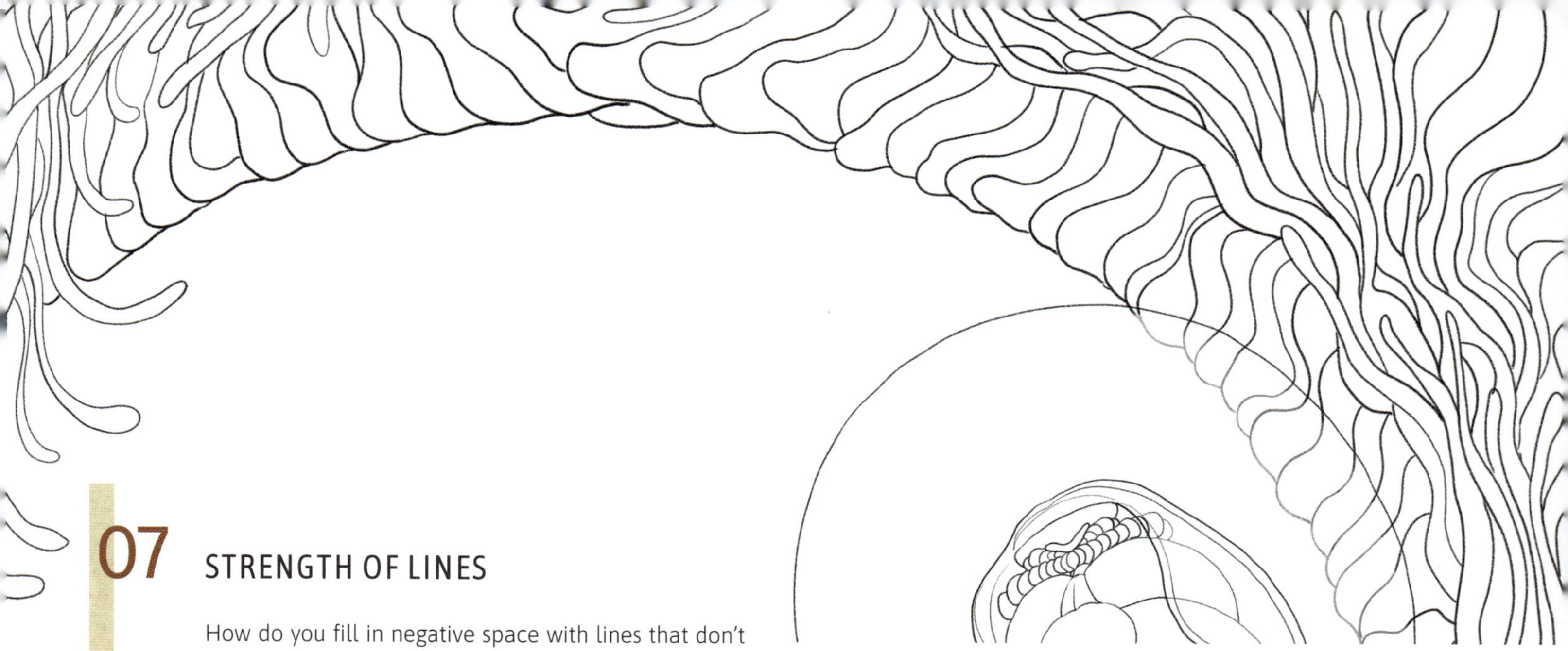

07 STRENGTH OF LINES

How do you fill in negative space with lines that don't make the eye feel tired or bored? First of all, you need to understand the direction of motion – in this case, the dragon's arc. I divide this space with many lines that combine to make a complex texture. I decide to draw the dragon's hair to resemble seaweed flowing in a stream of water. I spread it out unequally, starting with a few strands at the beginning, slowly increasing the amount of hair until it peaks at the tail end. I really want it to be visually stimulating. No room for boredom – I need dynamics and motion. The body lines start to appear near the centre of the arc; I slightly change its position, but not too much. I want to keep the shape as much as possible. I am pleased with how it's looking – by playing with shape, there is now an interesting body that is full of different textures.

DYNAMICS AND MOTION MAKE THE COMPOSITION APPEAR MORE PLEASING TO THE EYE

08 FINAL LINE-ART TOUCHES

When drawing contours, I try to highlight the most important part of the canvas. By doing this, I add depth and readability to the drawing. I also add variability of details, which makes it easy for the eye to find the most important parts. Avalokiteśvara is one of these important areas, and I definitely need to highlight that. Once again, I outline the outer contour.

Next, I focus on the claws – they must be distinguished from the dragon's body – and the brows, as they draw the viewer to the dragon's face.

APPLYING FINAL TOUCHES TO THE LINE ART

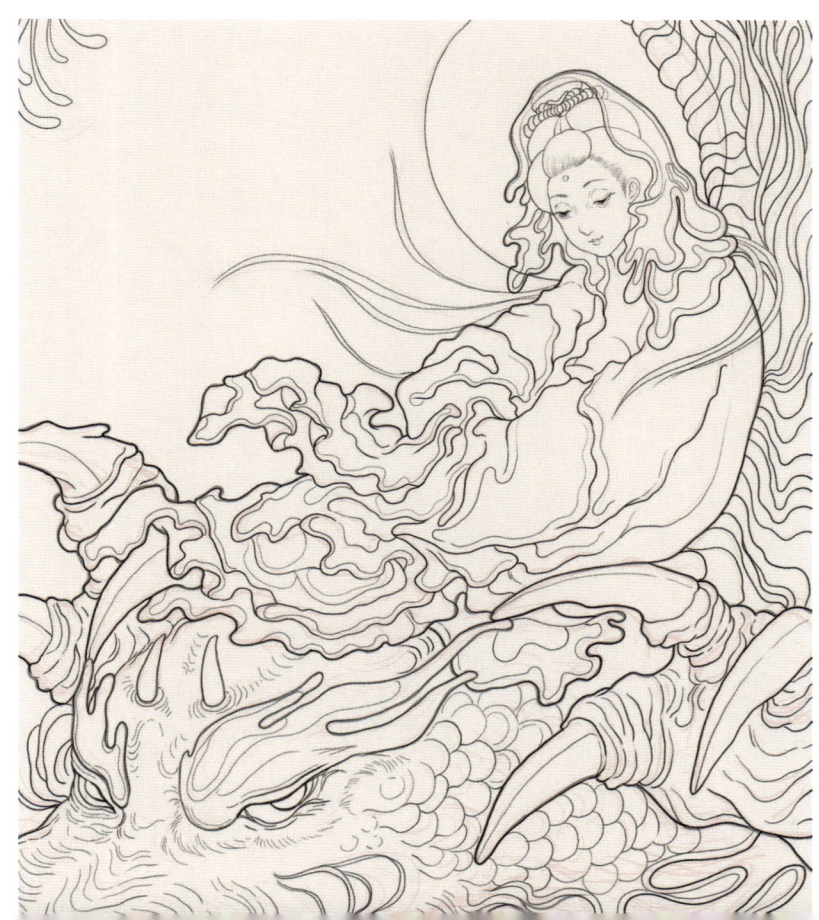

09 COLOUR SOLUTION

As I begin working with colour, I am not scared of spilling paint over different shapes. It is a normal part of the process for me, and I will deal with those details later. I like combining bright colours with duller ones, playing on contrasts in action. The first thing I decide is which colour gamma to use. I choose different shades of peach, pink, and lilac, just like you'd find on flower petals, which I think makes the image look unique.

For the dragon, I decide to use a colder gamma, contrasting it to the central character. To bring focus to its paws, I choose a dark colour, but make the claws a warmer colour to visually connect them to the character.

INTRODUCING COLOUR TO THE CHARACTER AND DRAGON

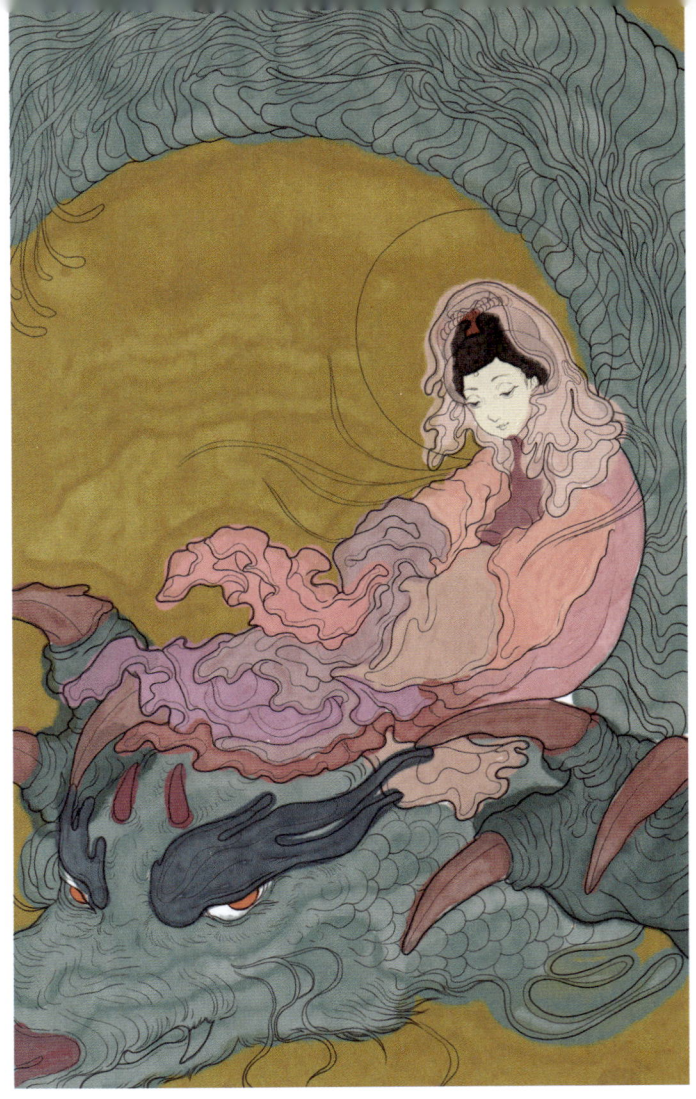

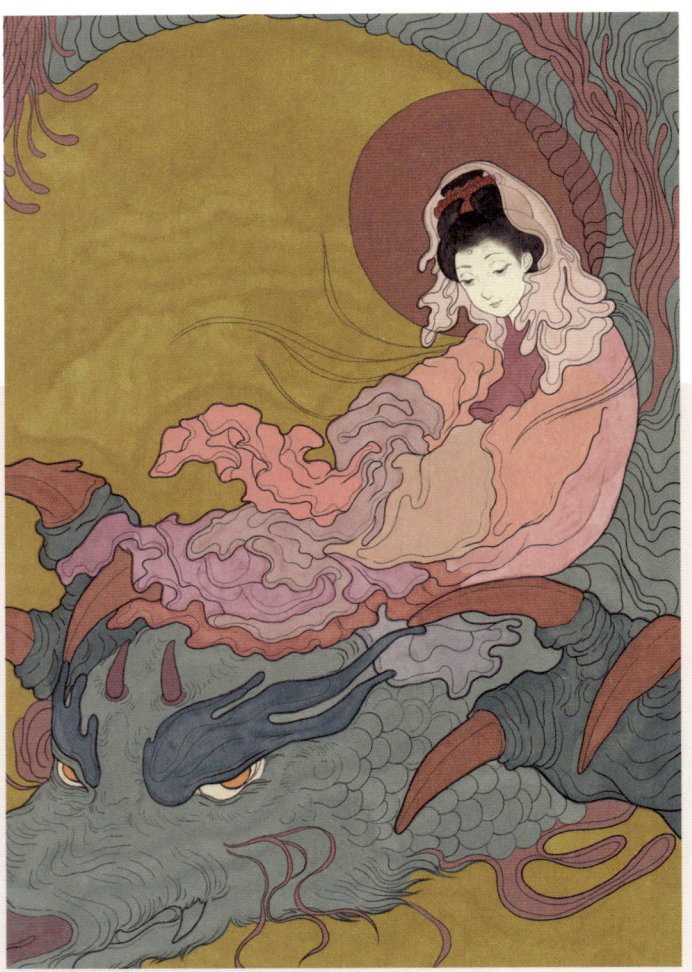

10 BASE COLOURS

I add a thick, warm line down the dragon's back, connecting it with the central figure. By using colour layers, I can create a feeling of depth without using shadows. Contours I created during the line-art phase also help me with that. It's a simple way of filling empty space, and one of the most impressive skills in Hokusai's arsenal. Now I have a canvas with general colours that I can add details to later.

HOKUSAI ALSO USES COLOUR LAYERS TO CREATE DEPTH WITHOUT APPLYING SHADOWS

11 SLIGHT CHANGES

To create a drawing that is bright and full of life, I add a gradient to the dragon's body. It highlights the character's motion and direction.

Looking at the illustration, I think there is currently too much blue around the dragon's head. To counter this, I add warmer colours. Next, I continue adding darker colours on Avalokiteśvara's clothes, dividing large shapes into smaller sizes, which amplifies the depth. Lastly, I make their halo light more transparent, as things look a bit crowded around their face.

ADDING GRADIENTS
TO THE DRAGON AND
IMPROVING THE HALO

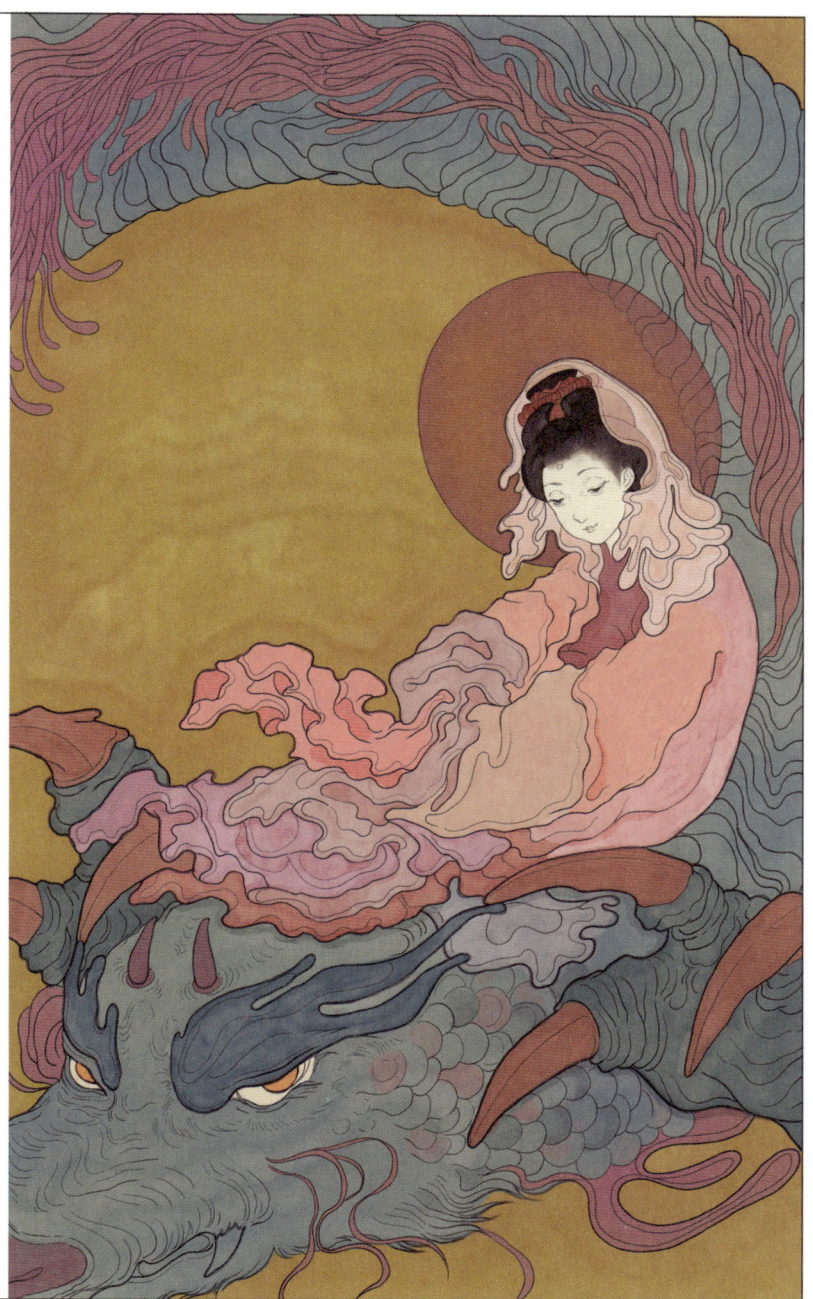

'I AM NOT SCARED OF SPILLING PAINT OVER DIFFERENT SHAPES. IT IS A NORMAL PART OF THE PROCESS FOR ME'

12 EXPRESSIVENESS

Unlike Hokusai's original work, I want to make Avalokiteśvara more feminine. I give them a different hairstyle; I want to show as much hair as possible to create a dark area that attracts the eye. I like to create hair using hatching, applying strokes according to the shape size. This makes it easier to read different planes on the drawing. A bright-red accent on the hairclip helps to break up the darker hair colour and draws in the eye. To create a calm atmosphere, I make sure the expression is soft and gentle. If you look closely, you will notice that their eyes are not fully closed. Lastly, I add shadows, highlight the lips using a red colour, and make the character's face appear less pale.

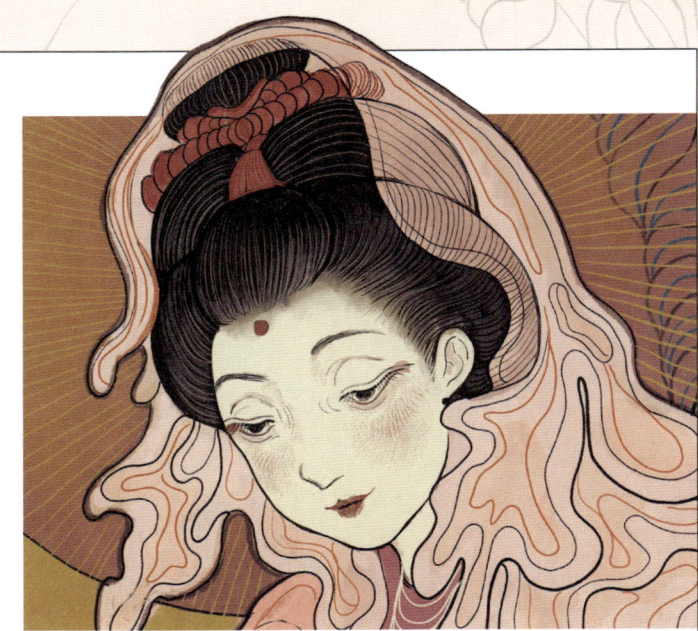

FOCUSING ON AVALOKITEŚVARA'S EXPRESSION AND BRINGING THE CENTRAL CHARACTER TO LIFE

13 HATCHING LINES

Now for my favourite part! I like it when my drawings have their own textures, so when they are seen from a distance, the viewer can understand the general shapes, but if they move closer, many more smaller details will reveal themselves. This is my aim for this stage: creating more texture. The first step for creating texture is drawing its base with lines. I start from Avalokiteśvara's clothes. Since there are many different planes that contain different folds, I choose one and then gradually fill in each one. I choose a darker colour than the main colour and fill the space with repetitive lines, leaving some empty spaces between them.

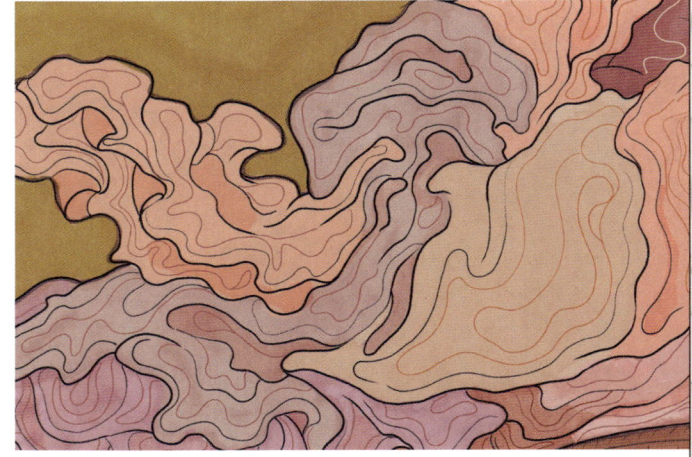

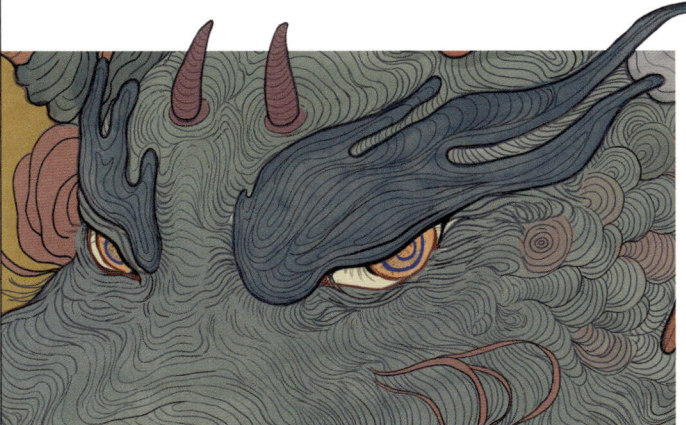

Next, I tackle the dragon's head. The lines here have a different structure; since the dragon has fur, the lines are situated closer to each other. The same concept applies to its scales. As for its body, I add multiple hatch lines, using darker colours for additional texture.

THIS IS ONE OF MY FAVOURITE
STAGES OF ILLUSTRATING

14 VOLUME

Now I move on to the second stage of creating texture. In this stage, I add depth to my hatch work. I choose a very dark colour (though not black), and on each section of clothing, I decide upon a point of interest that becomes the centre of motion. These areas are darker due to added lines, which improves the shape's readability. Notice how the dark lines that are closest to the edges emphasize the clothing's shape and volume. Thanks to these floating lines, the fabric now has texture, too.

ADDING DARKER LINES AROUND THE
CLOTHING EDGES CREATES A SENSE OF VOLUME

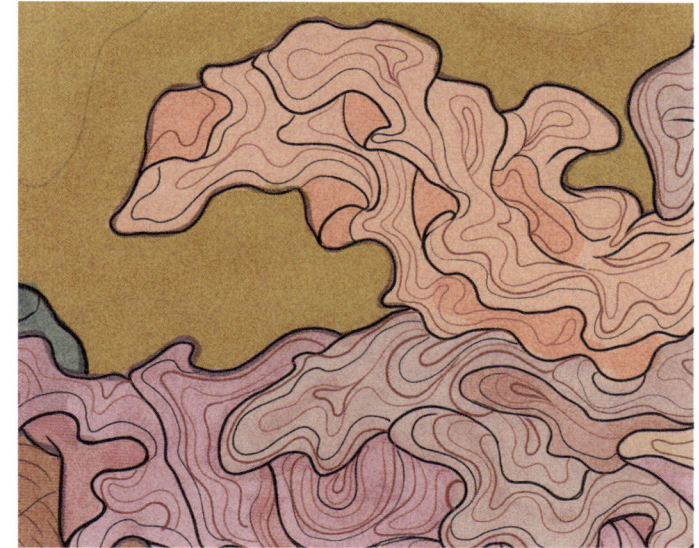

15 FINAL SHAPE

This is the best time to highlight the dragon's face. Using dark paint, I follow the existing lines, while simultaneously adding extra ones to distinguish its face from its neck. For a slight shine, I add small bright strokes to the face. To add more variability to the pattern on top of its head, I also include more coloured lines, redraw some on the horns, and focus on building more depth to the dragon's scales by darkening the lines. It's important not to overwork this section as it will make the pattern appear too repetitive. As for the dragon's body, I highlight the original contours and put emphasis on the original shapes.

FINAL TOUCHES ON THE DRAGON,
AND THEN THE PIECE IS FINISHED!

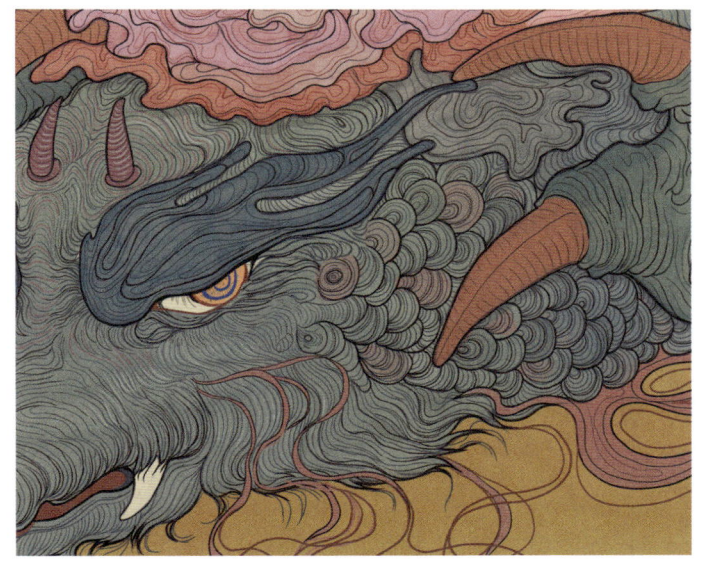

CONCLUSION

Right from the start, I loved the idea for this project. It was a great opportunity to learn more about Hokusai by studying his artwork. My favourite part was drawing Avalokiteśvara's clothes – not only did it turn out to be the most attractive part for me, but also the most educational. This is why I tried to recreate the same outline of folds, then later gave them their own meaning. It was so much fun!

I've never drawn dragons before, so that was another first. I wanted to give the creature many complex layers, and I feel like I was able to achieve that. This whole project reminded me of how wonderful it is to focus on lines and play with them to create different volumes and various textures – something I believe Hokusai may have considered himself.

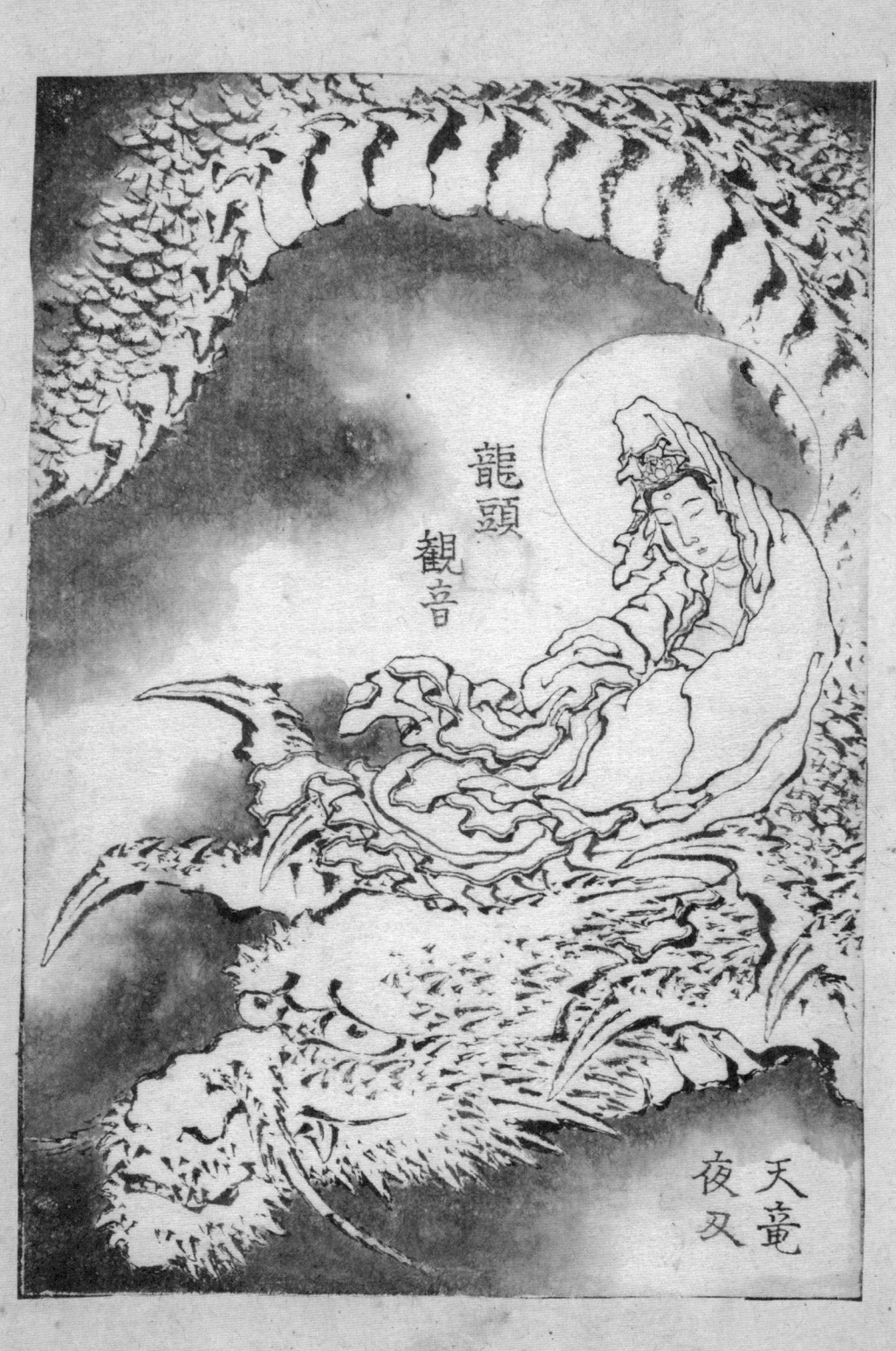

龍頭

観音

天竜
夜叉

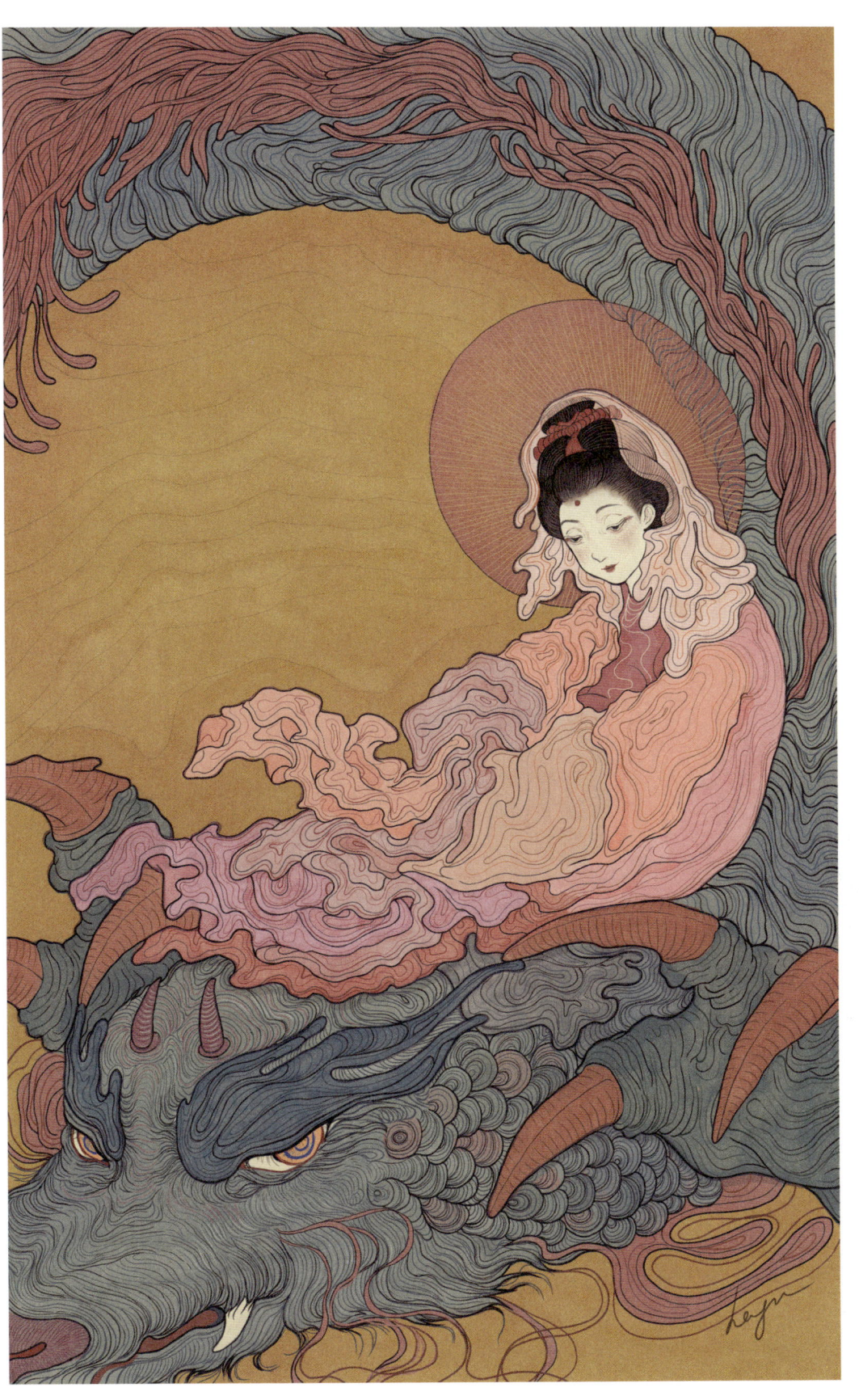

AVALOKITEŚVARA SEATED ON THE HEAD OF A DRAGON

HAGUSHKA

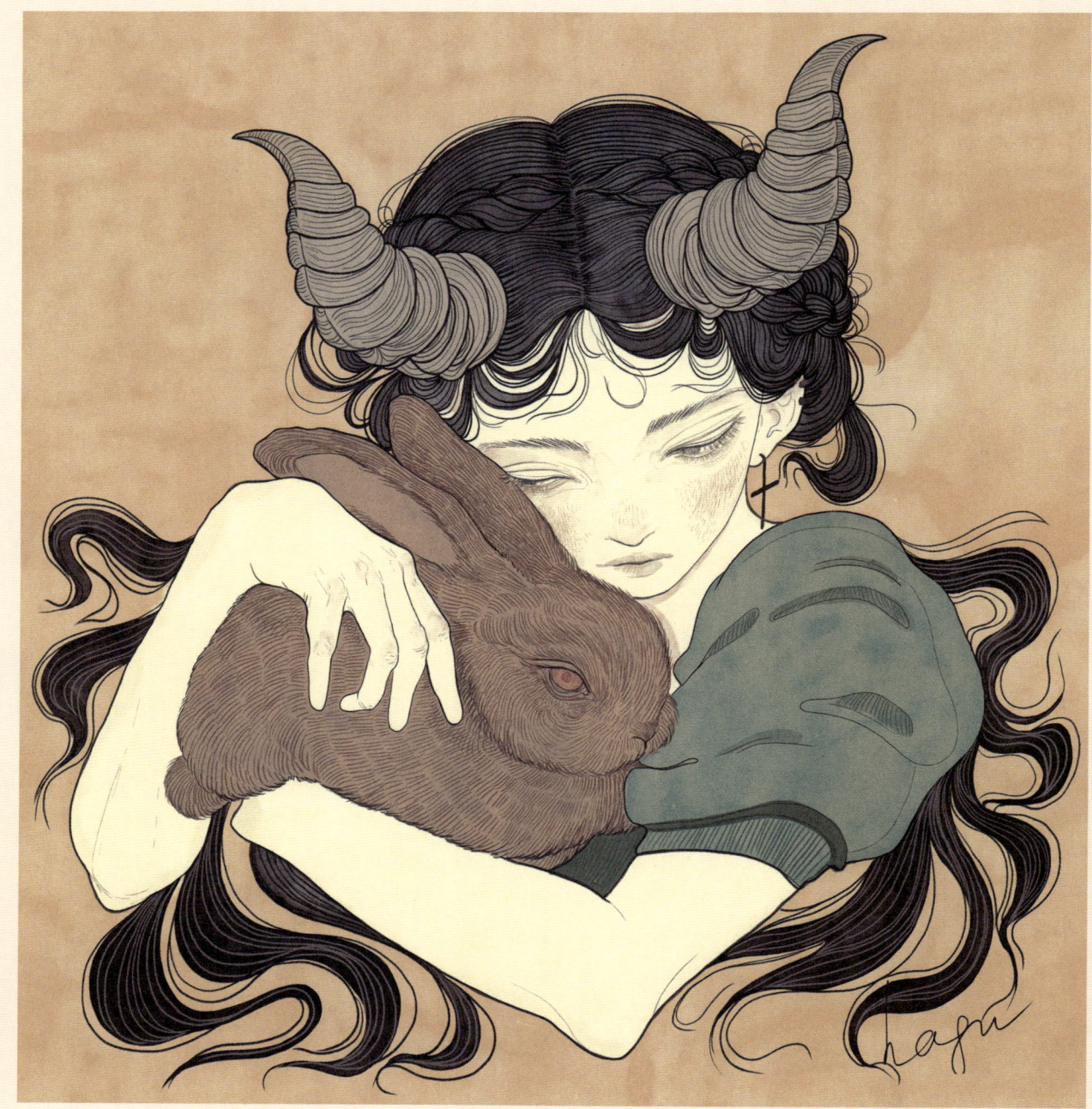

ABOVE: *Harmony*
Animals can't communicate through human language, but they can listen to us

RIGHT: *Fearlessness*
We can find courage to love those who can be unloved by society

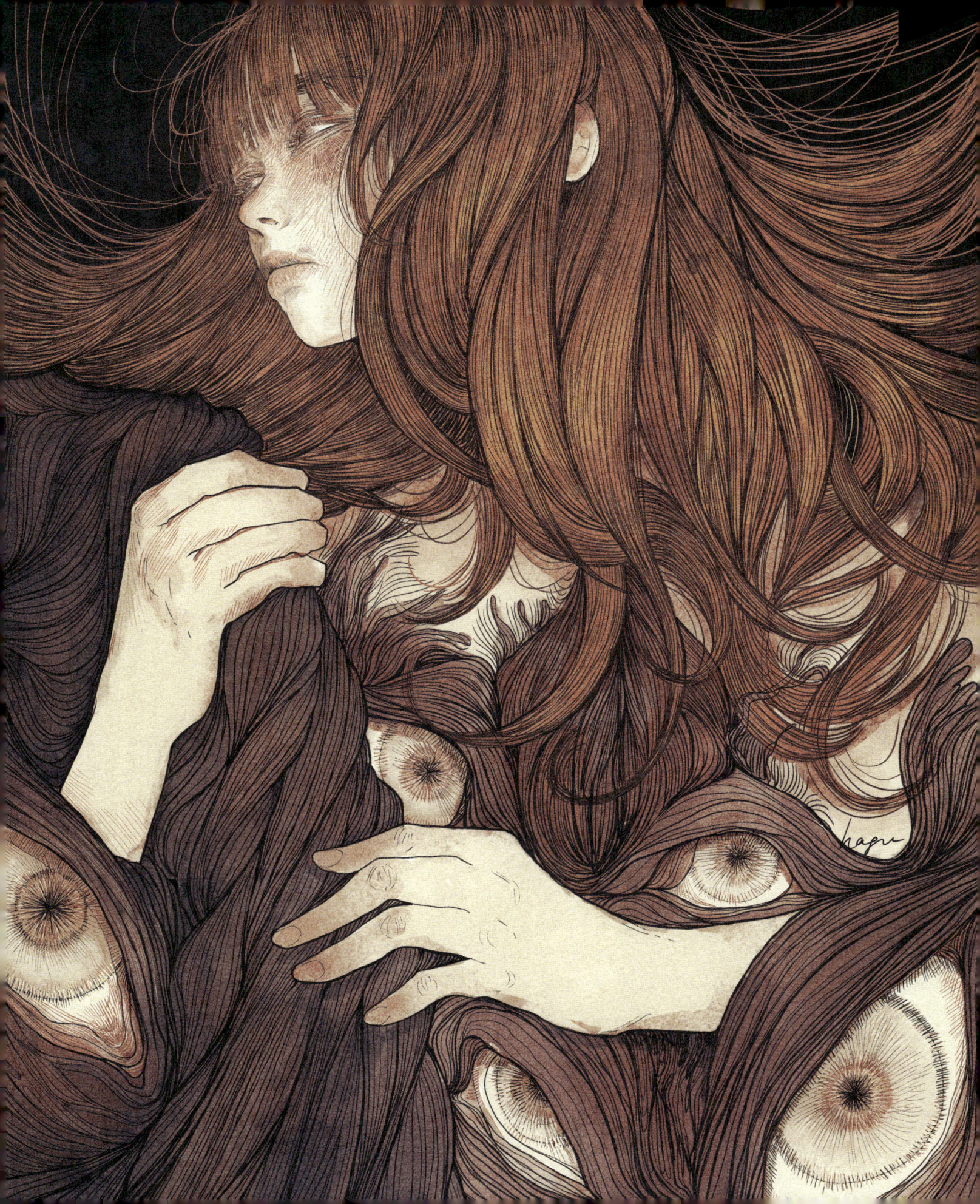

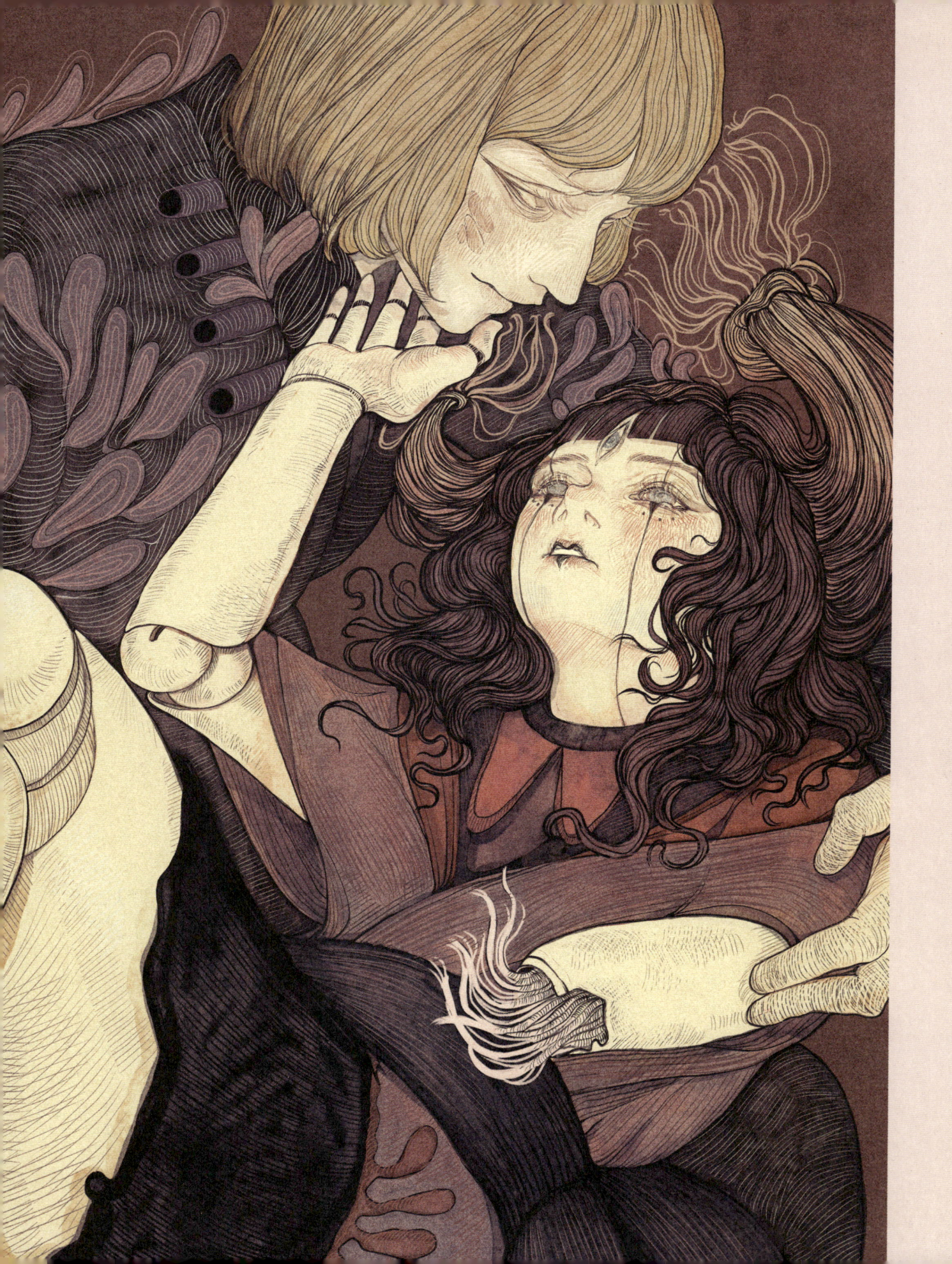

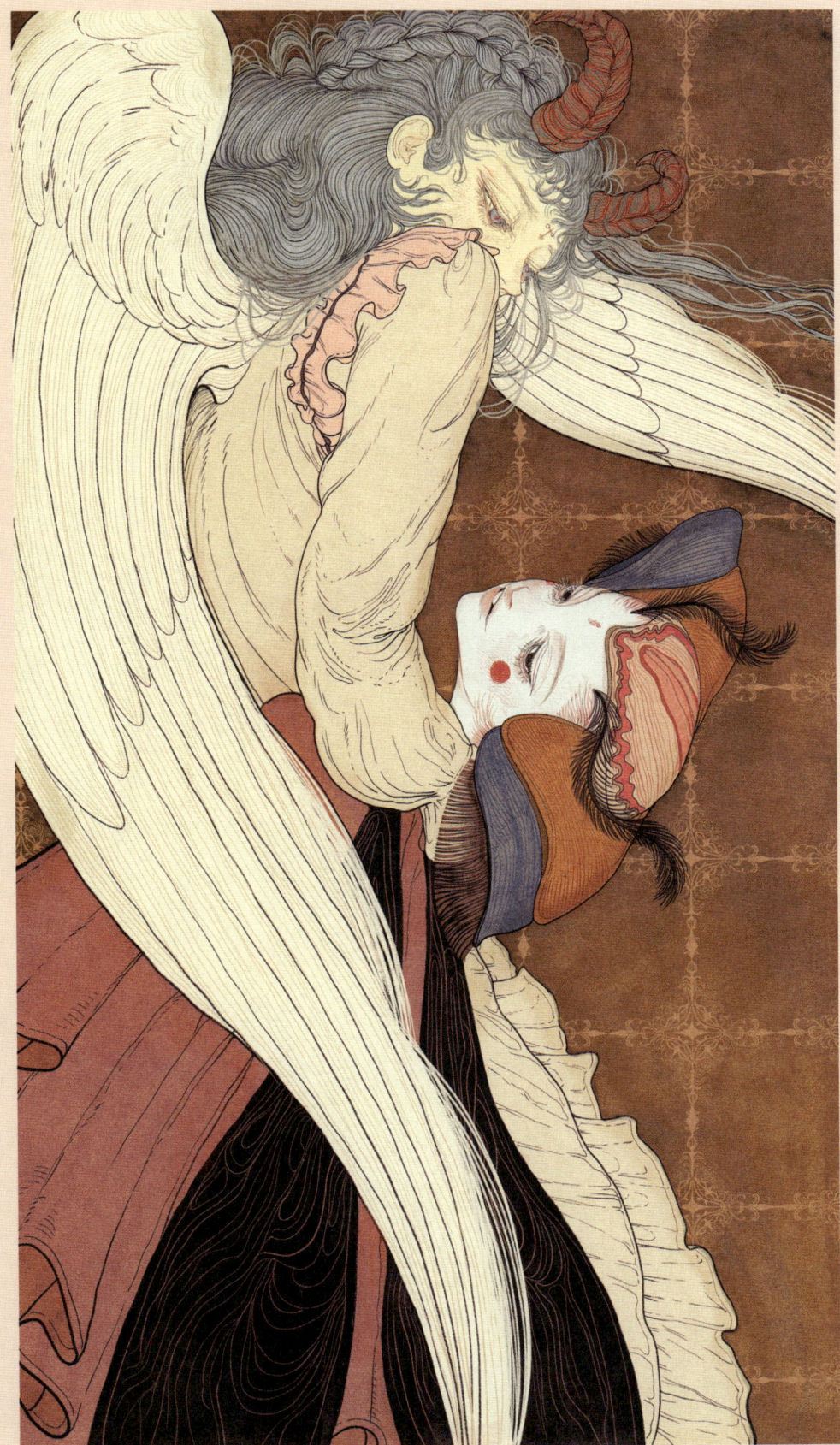

OPPOSITE PAGE: *Inevitability*
Time is not on our side

——————————————————

LEFT: *Gravitation of Souls*
There can be a connection
between you, but this connection
can be lost in a heartbeat

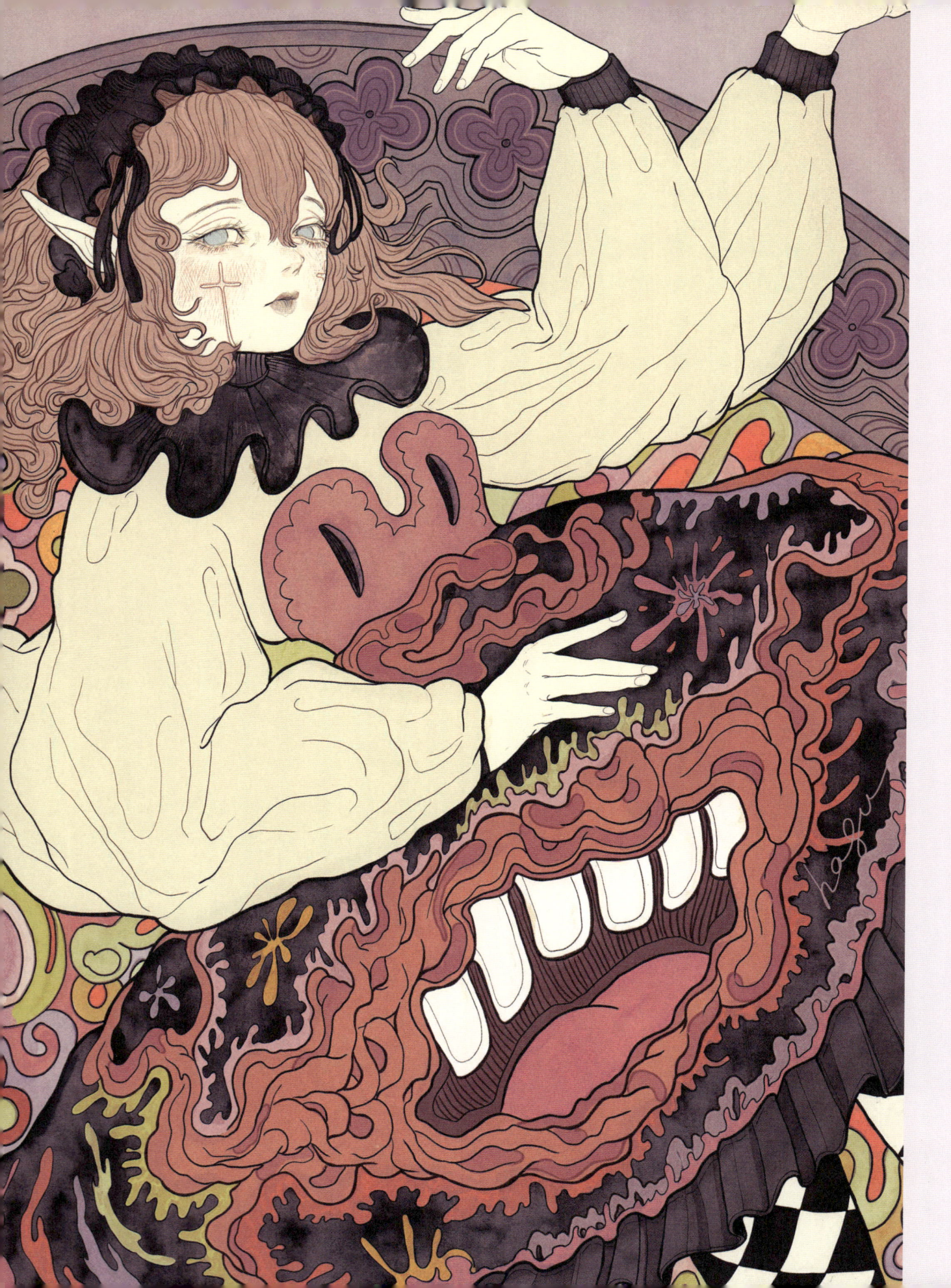

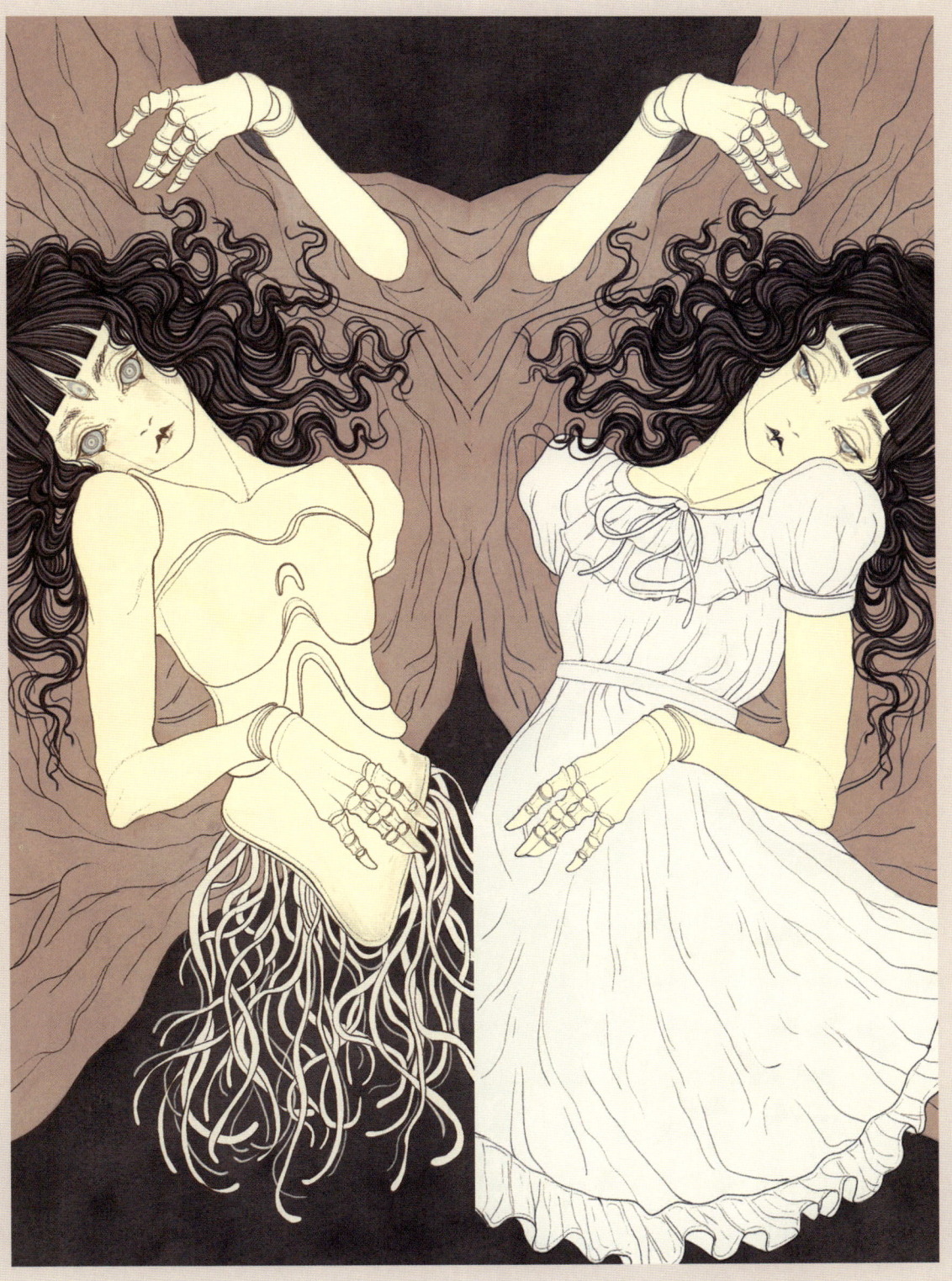

LEFT: *It's Eating Time!*
You never know which dress you'll choose this time

ABOVE: *Two Halves of One*
Appearances can be deceiving

Hagushka

TWO CATS BY HIBISCUS

BY TESSA NELISSEN

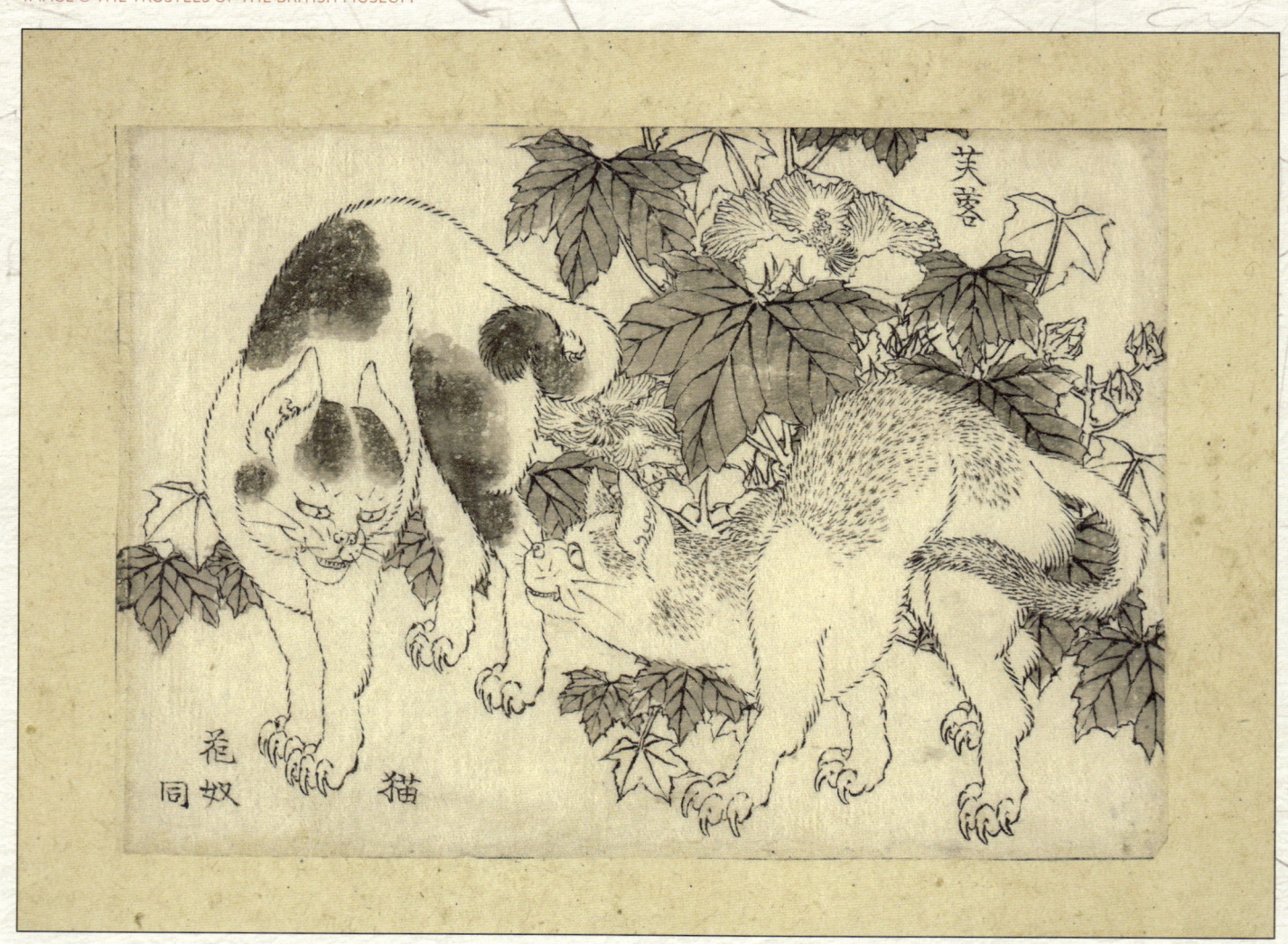

DISCOVERING HOKUSAI

I tend to draw what puts a smile on my face and lightens my heart. I've loved illustrating ever since I was able to pick up a pencil, and believe I am a classic example of someone who has been indirectly inspired by Hokusai through the likes of anime and, of course, manga. As a kid, I fell in love with all the classic shows like *Pokémon*, *Cardcaptor Sakura*, and *Dragon Ball Z*. Naturally, I had to try drawing all the characters from these shows myself, never realizing that they all sprouted from the same root: Katsushika Hokusai.

I properly discovered manga in my teens and became even more obsessed with Japanese culture and style. When I eventually joined the DeviantArt community and saw all the amazing artists on that platform, I realized that I wanted to improve my skills and started taking my art more seriously. However, I didn't pursue a career in art. Instead, I studied dentistry for six years, and when I graduated, I was the most unhappy I'd ever felt. But I never stopped drawing; there was always some part of

me that felt encouraged to keep learning and improving. Finally, after twenty-six years, I decided to listen to that part of myself and actively pursued a career in art. I felt so behind with my artwork, though. There were plenty of artists who had started their journeys earlier and were way better than me. But it didn't matter – being an artist made me happy.

In 2023, I posted an illustration to Instagram of two cats in a Japanese-inspired garden. Someone commented that my work reminded them of the ukiyo-e art style, and I had to look up the term as I didn't know what it was at the time: defined line art, vibrant colours, and scenes that showcased harmony in everyday life. I found it fascinating how my art style reminded others of Edo-era art without my own awareness of it. Simply, I believe it's because Hokusai's work has inspired so many modern-day shows, mangas, and artists. His style inspired my own without me realizing it. Now I actively look for inspiration from the artworks of the Edo period.

01 ANALYSING THE ORIGINAL

I picked this piece first and foremost because I love drawing cats. But before jumping into drawing, let's have a proper look at the original artwork by Hokusai. I ask myself: what do I see? Two cats by a hibiscus plant, yes. But what else? The cats have their claws out, backs high in the air, and you could argue that their faces don't look particularly happy. So, I wonder what the story could be here. Maybe they are fighting over something?

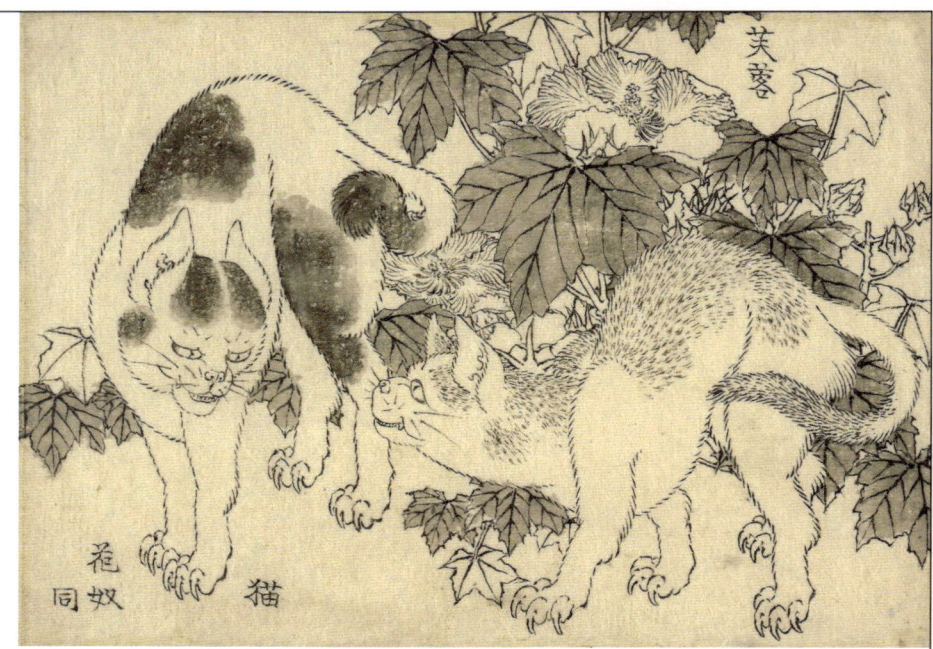

02 INITIAL SKETCH

I start by sketching the two cats and the hibiscus plant in the background, just like in Hokusai's original. To make the piece feel more dynamic, I slightly alter the cats' poses and change their facial expressions to be cheekier and more challenging, instead of straight-up angry. For more visual interest, I give the cats belts and knapsacks, decorated with patterns inspired by artworks of the Edo era. At this point, I'm quite happy with the sketch, but it feels like something is missing.

SKETCHING THE TWO
CATS IN MY OWN STYLE

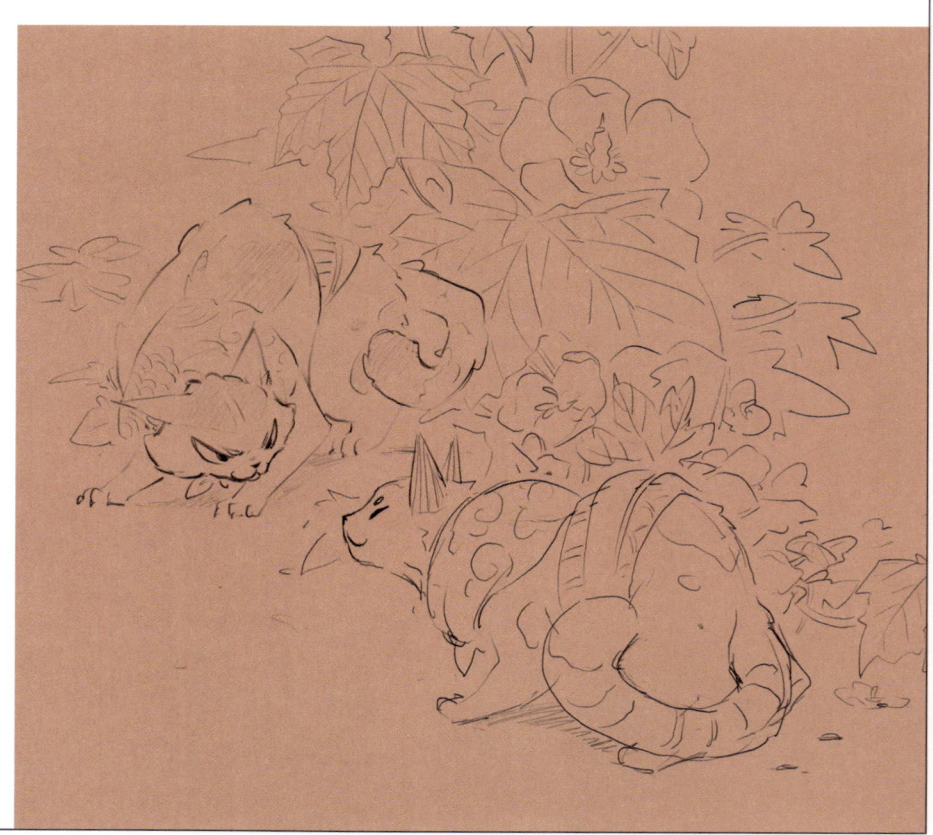

03 ADDING ANOTHER CHARACTER

I decide the piece could use another character. All good things come in threes, after all! I channel my inner Utagawa Kuniyoshi (my favourite artist from the Edo period, who drew plenty of cats in kimonos during his time) and add another cat wearing a kimono and holding a shamisen (a traditional Japanese three-stringed lute with a square body, played with a large plectrum).

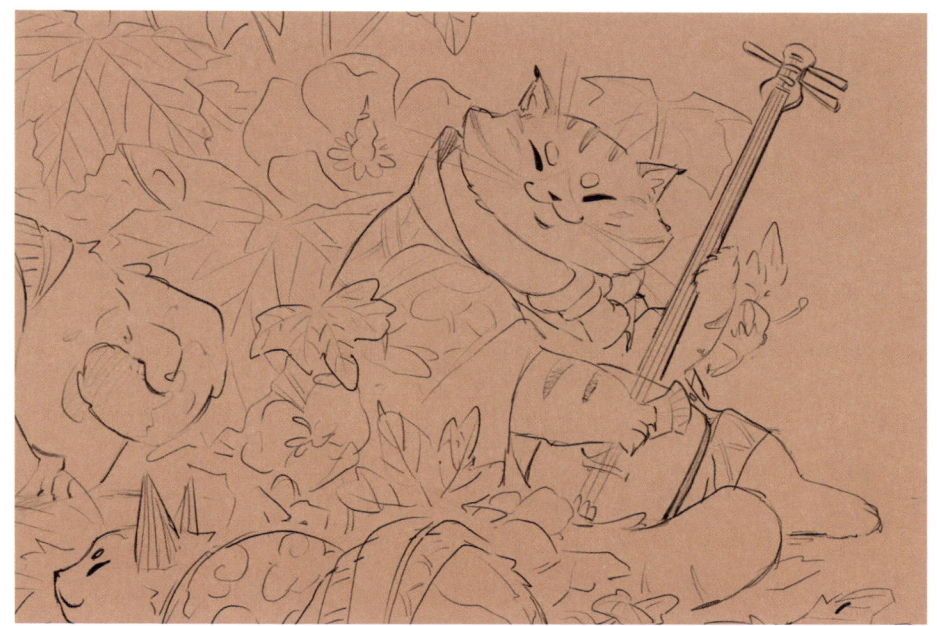

ADDING PERSONAL FLAIR BY DRAWING A THIRD CHARACTER

04 ADDITIONAL STORY ELEMENTS

I feel like the piece could use some more details that add to its storytelling ability, or can at least spark the imagination. My mind goes to some typical Japanese food and drink. Our chubby cat character on the right gets his own little table with noodles, sake, and fish. Now when you view the piece, you may think that he looks very pleased with himself whilst looking over at his two friends who have to share one fish.

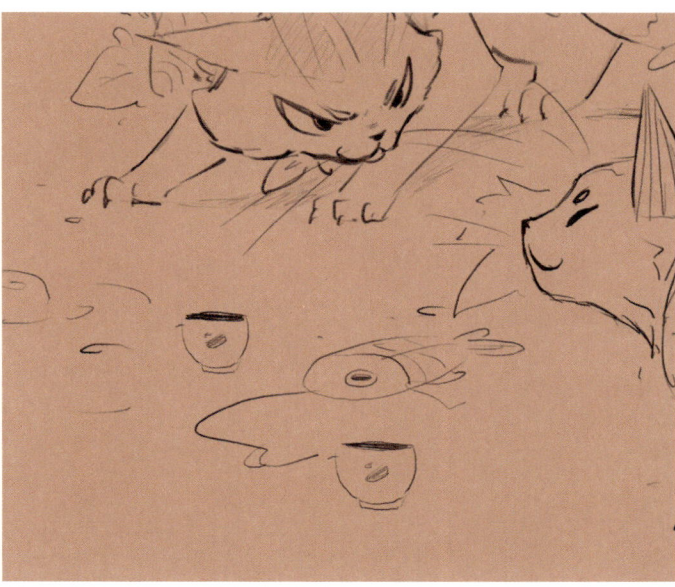

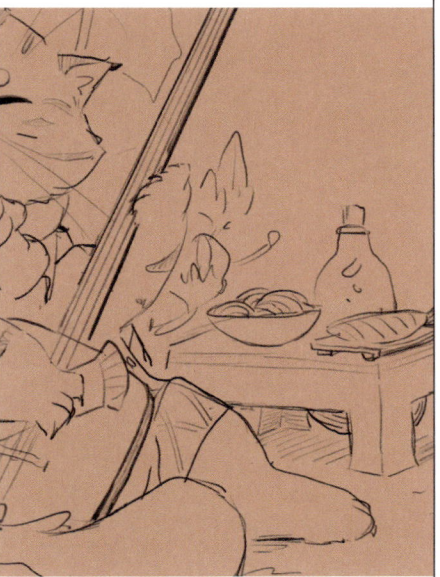

NOW THE TWO CATS ARE ARGUING OVER A FISH

Tessa Nelissen

05 COMPOSITION

Now that the sketch is done, you can clearly see how the different elements connect in triangular shapes: two points are closer to each other, and one point is further away. In my opinion, this is a great way of filling the canvas and making the composition feel organic.

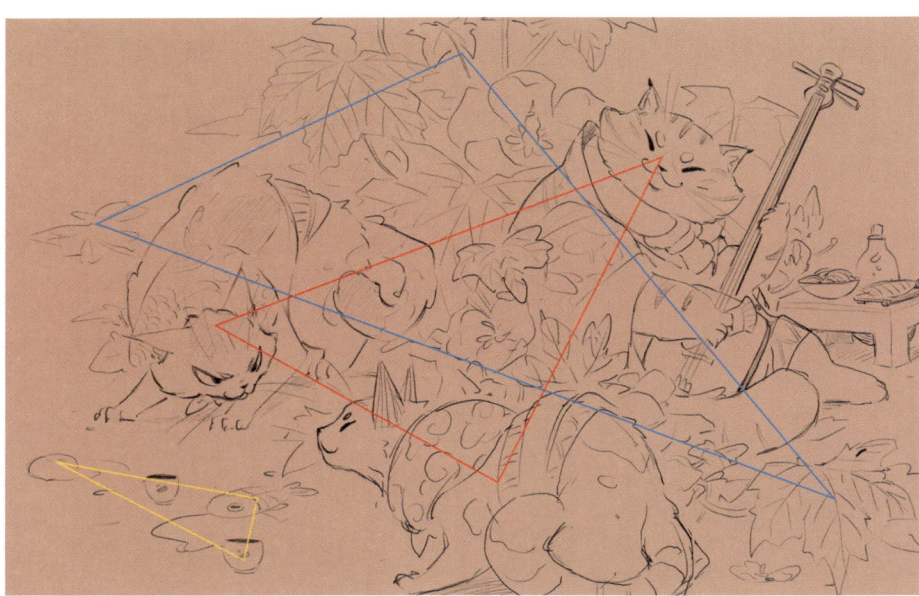

06 REFINING THE LINE ART

Now it's time to refine the line art and add line weight (the thickness of a line) to the characters and elements that make up the foreground. I tend to make the lines in shadowy areas a bit thicker, as well as areas in the drawing where two elements overlap each other. This step really makes the characters stand out. I rarely start a new layer for the final line art. I much prefer going directly over my initial sketch and erasing lines that are too messy with the same brush setting as the one I use for the line art. It gives it more of a traditional feel, in my opinion, and I like that.

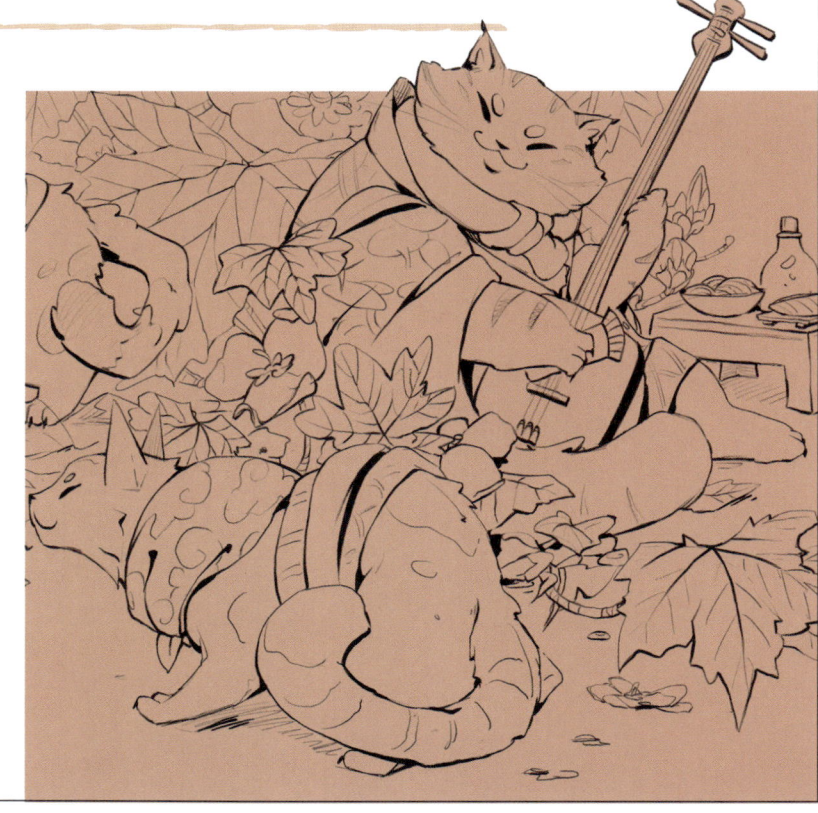

07 BASE COLOURS

Time to choose the colours for this piece. Hokusai's original was black and white, so here I am free to pick whatever palette I want. I go online to look for inspiration in coloured artworks from the Edo era; for example, this piece from Utagawa Kuniyoshi showing three cats in kimonos sharing a meal. I let this artwork inspire the colour palette for my own piece.

A SOFT GREEN WITH BLUE, GREY, AND ORANGE ACCENTS

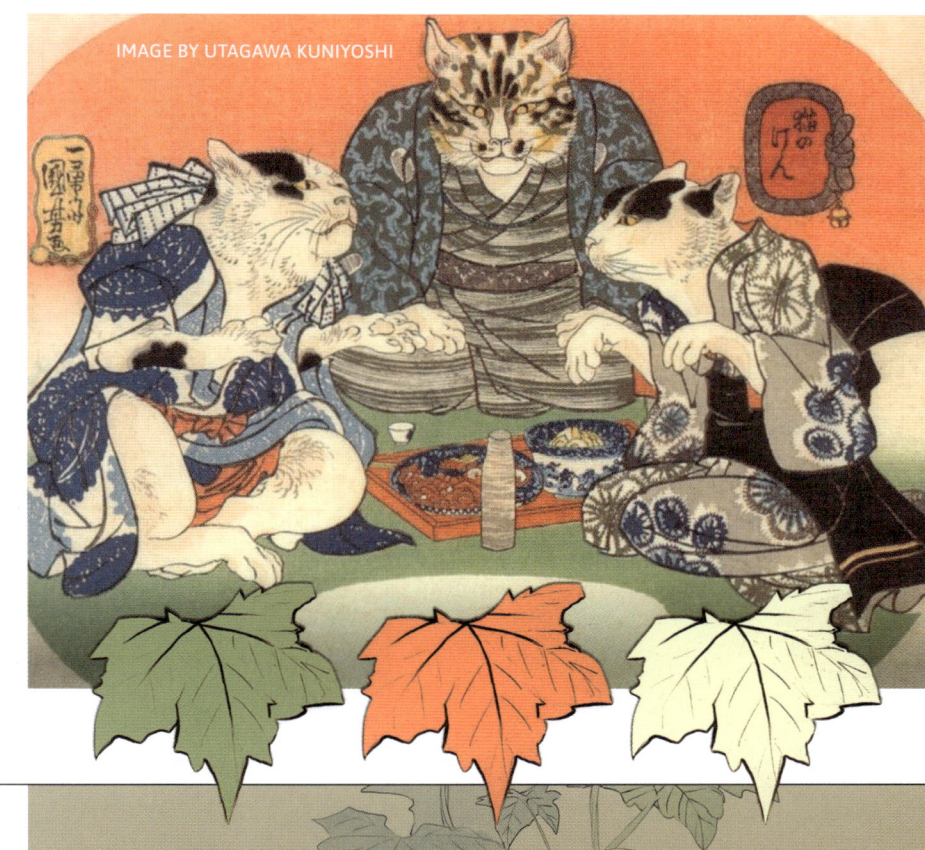

IMAGE BY UTAGAWA KUNIYOSHI

08 SUBTLE COLOUR VARIATIONS

To make the front part of the hibiscus plant stand out from the back, I make sure the colours are a bit more saturated. This way, I can make the background plants blend in with the colour of the sky (soft green, in this case). I do this by using the selection tool and reducing the opacity of those elements. By doing things this way, I ensure that the initial focus remains on the characters and not the background details. Those must be secondary.

COLOUR CAN REALLY GUIDE THE VIEWER'S ATTENTION

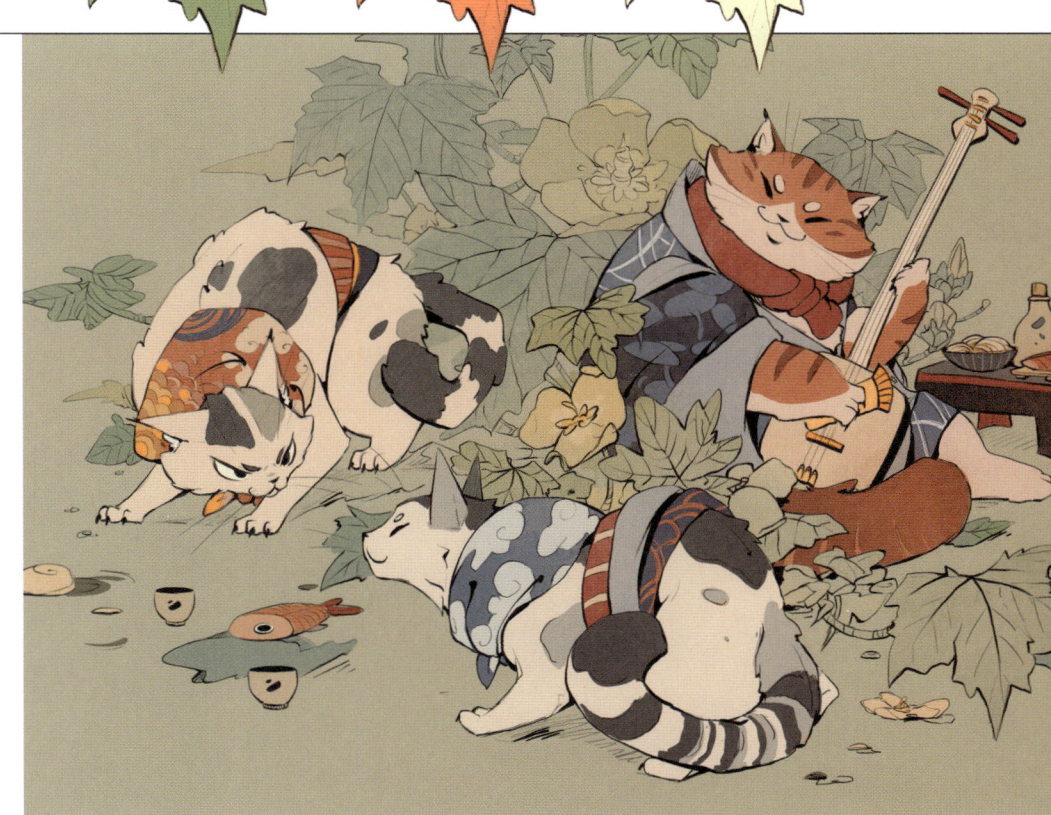

Tessa Nelissen

09 PATTERNS

For the patterns on the cats' outfits, I look again to the works of Hokusai and other Edo-era artists for inspiration. I find that these artists tend to use simplified shapes of natural elements like clouds, waves, leaves, and plants, so I translate that to the garments.

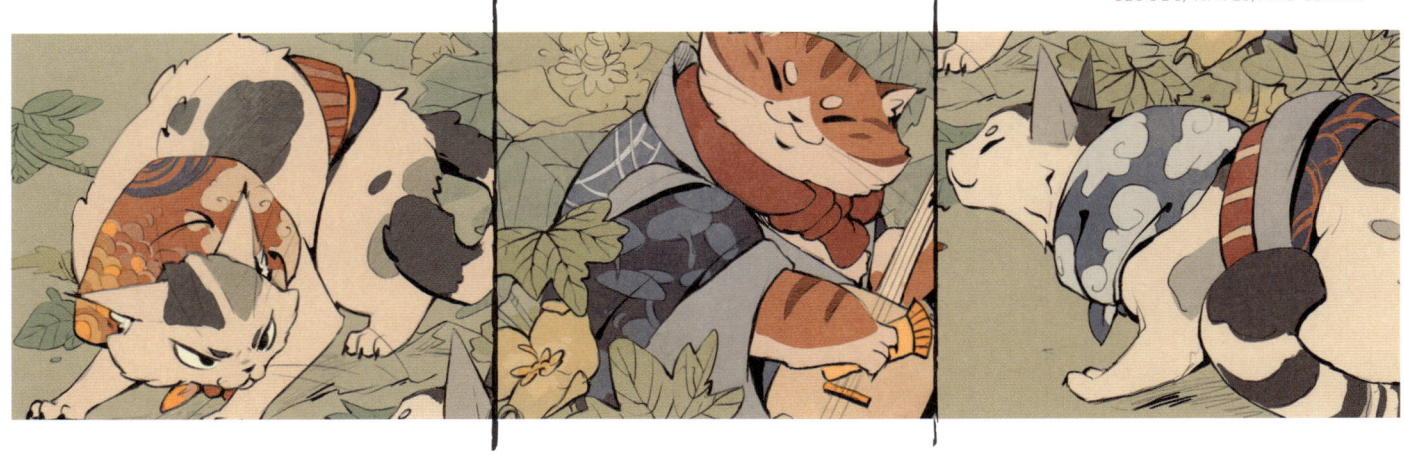

10 (HEART)WARMING

Looking at the piece so far, I feel that I'm missing more of that soft orangey-pink colour shown in the inspiration artwork. So, I make the ground this colour and it warms up the whole thing. And since we are on the topic of 'warming up' the piece, I'd like to take this moment to explain that the colours I chose for the third cat character actually reflect the coat colours and patterns that were on my own (late) cat, Chuntaro. I catch myself adding personal touches like this to my artworks whenever the opportunity arises. It warms my heart every time I look at them.

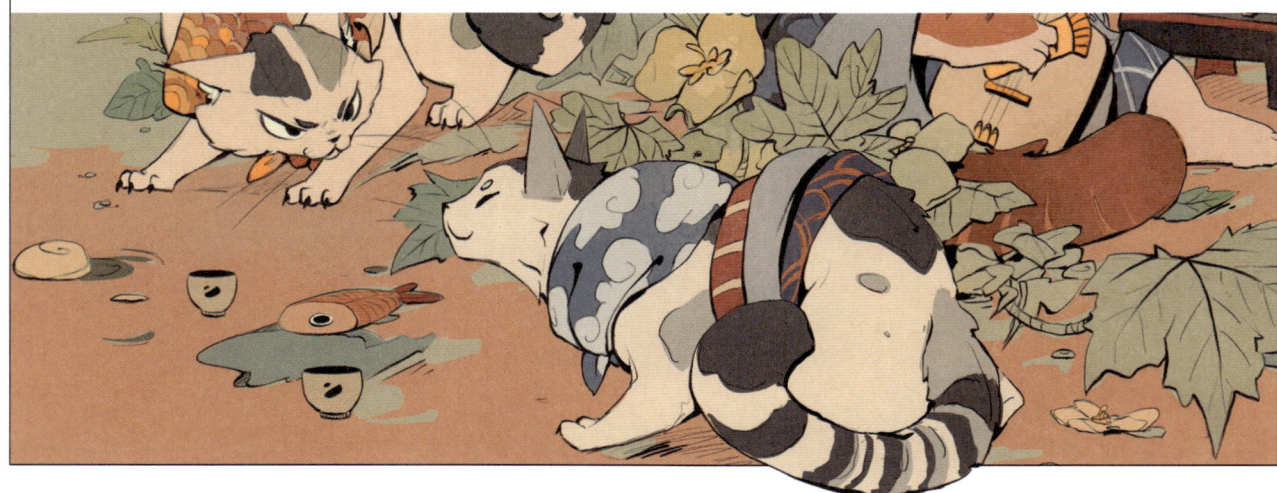

11 SHADOW & LIGHT

The next step is adding a light source and, with that, the shadows it creates. This makes all the elements in the artwork feel a bit more three-dimensional. But I don't want to make the contrast between light and shadows too strong because I want to keep the feel of an artwork from the Edo era and let the line art and colours be the stars.

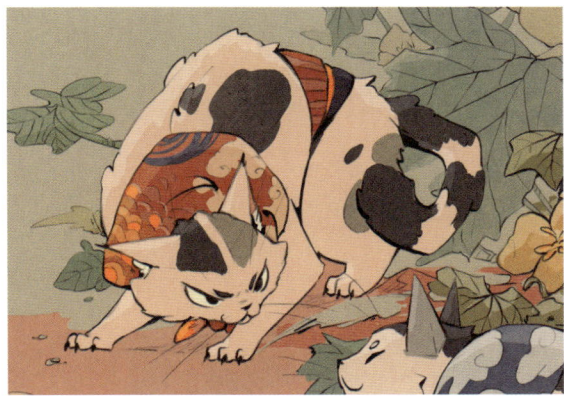 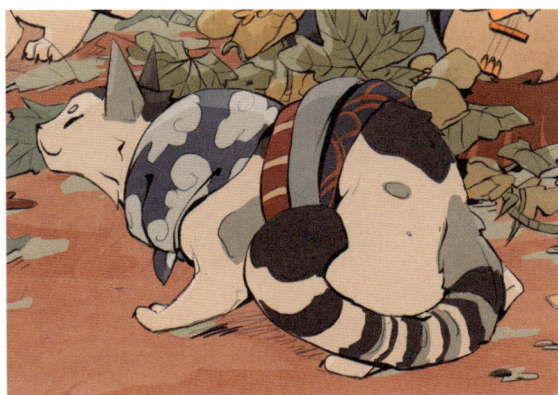

SUBTLE ADDING OF A LIGHT SOURCE AND SHADOWS TO MAKE THE PIECE MORE THREE-DIMENSIONAL

12 CONTRAST

I really like the effect of making some shadows under characters, objects, and in the deepest nooks and crannies completely black, especially when the artwork showcases line art. The use of pure black in this way creates such a stark contrast between the characters' silhouettes and their surroundings. It is very pleasing to my eyes, and I apply it to this piece as well.

THE VISUAL POWER OF PURE-BLACK INK

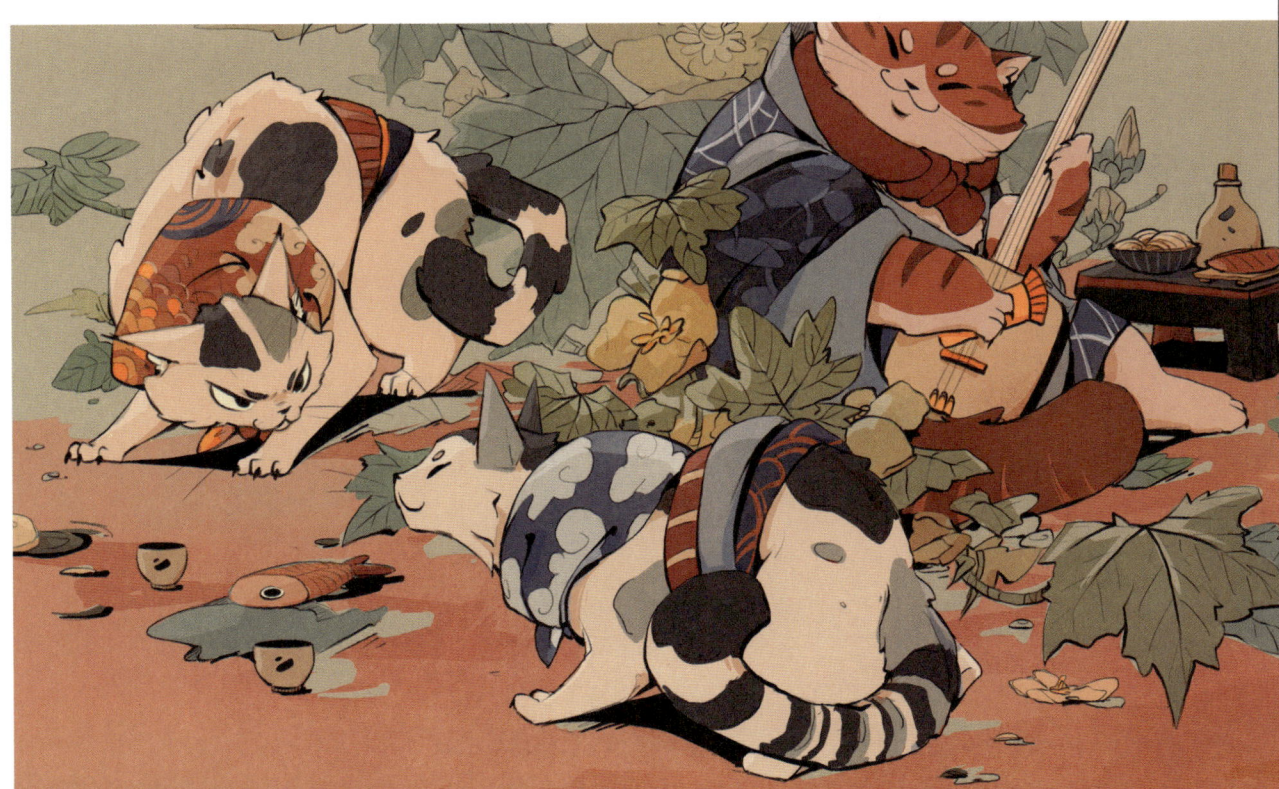

13 TEXTURE

I want to achieve more of a vintage/retro look like the traditional artworks from the Edo era, even though my own piece is made digitally. I do this by finding a nice, recycled-cardboard texture and, on a separate layer using the Overlay mode, putting it on top of the artwork. I play around with that layer's opacity until I get the desired look.

EVEN THOUGH AN ARTWORK IS DRAWN DIGITALLY, I STILL WANT TO ACHIEVE A TRADITIONAL FEEL

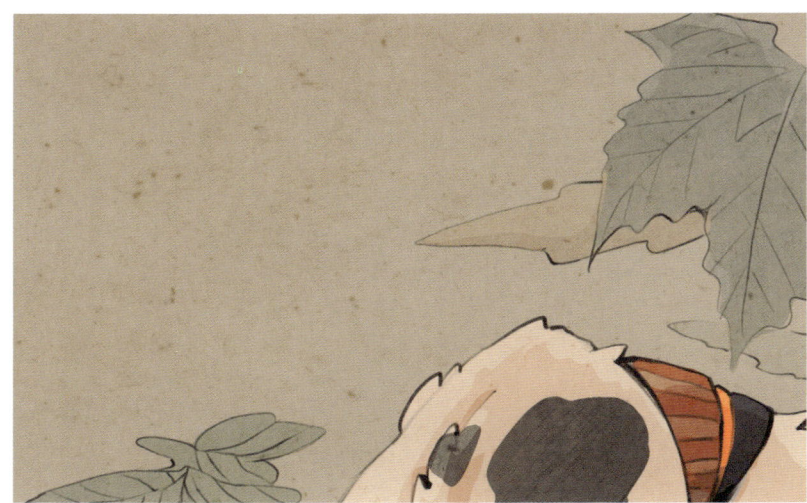

14 FINAL TOUCHES

For the first time (oh goodness, I should have done it sooner!) I flip/mirror the canvas to offer a fresh perspective and see if I screwed up any anatomical structures. Nothing that can't be fixed, especially with the help of the Liquify tool.

FLIPPING/MIRRORING THE CANVAS IS A GREAT WAY TO SPOT MISTAKES

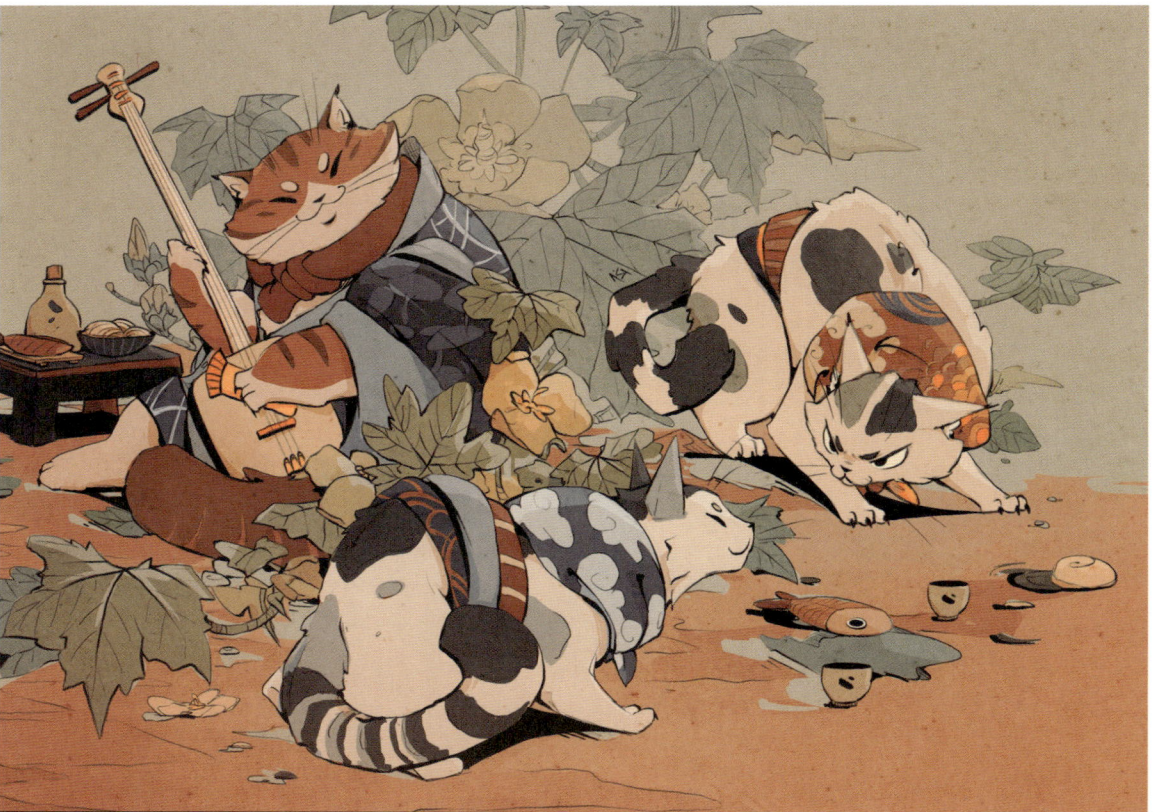

15 STEPPING BACK

I recommend always stepping away from your finished piece before reviewing it one last time. You tend to go blind to mistakes after staring at the same artwork for multiple hours in a row. The next day, you can look at it with fresh eyes and do whatever cleaning up the piece still requires. And after that, I declare this piece finished.

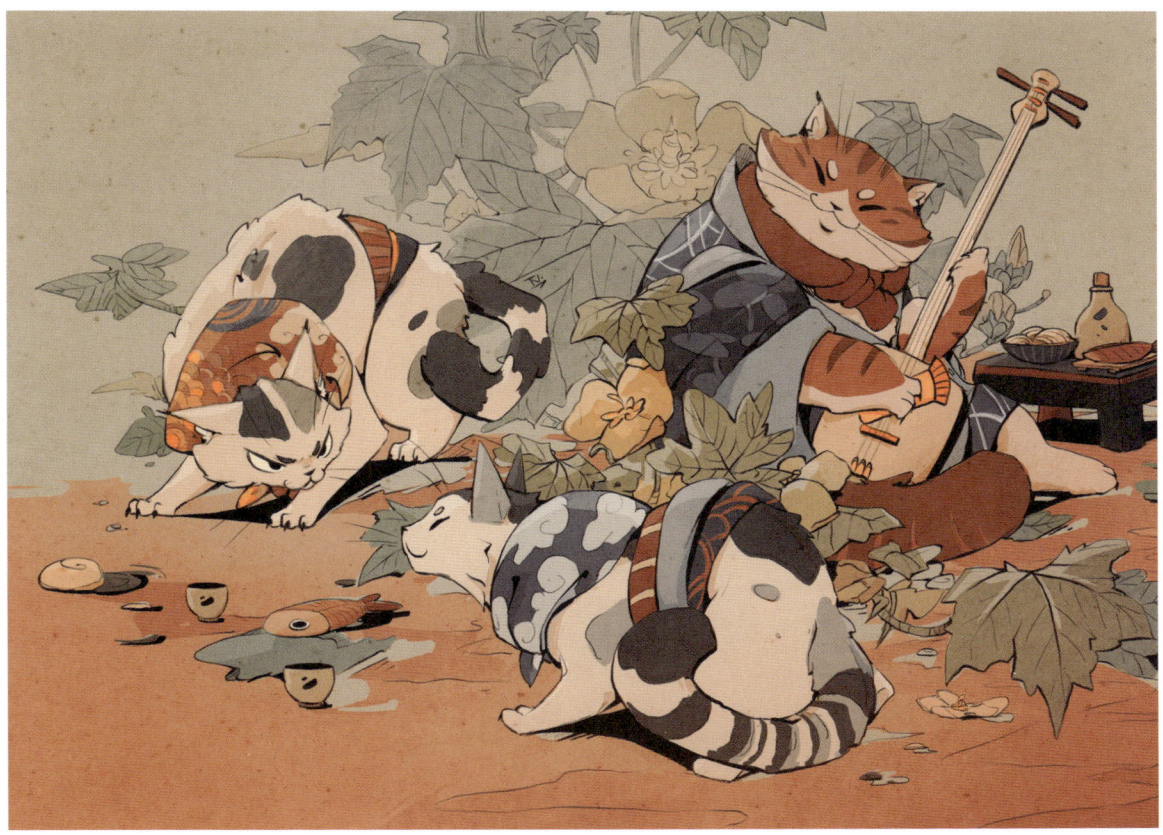

ALWAYS TAKE SOME TIME OFF FROM YOUR FINISHED PIECE BEFORE REVIEWING IT ONE MORE TIME

CONCLUSION

And that's a wrap! I feel like I was able to take Hokusai's original piece as the base and expand upon it by adding elements that I appreciate most from Edo-era art, like intricate kimono and pattern designs, as well as an appealing colour palette. Then adding my personal touches to the piece by translating the cats to my own style, putting in story elements like them fighting over fish, and of course, adding the third character who embodies my own (late) cat, Chuntaro.

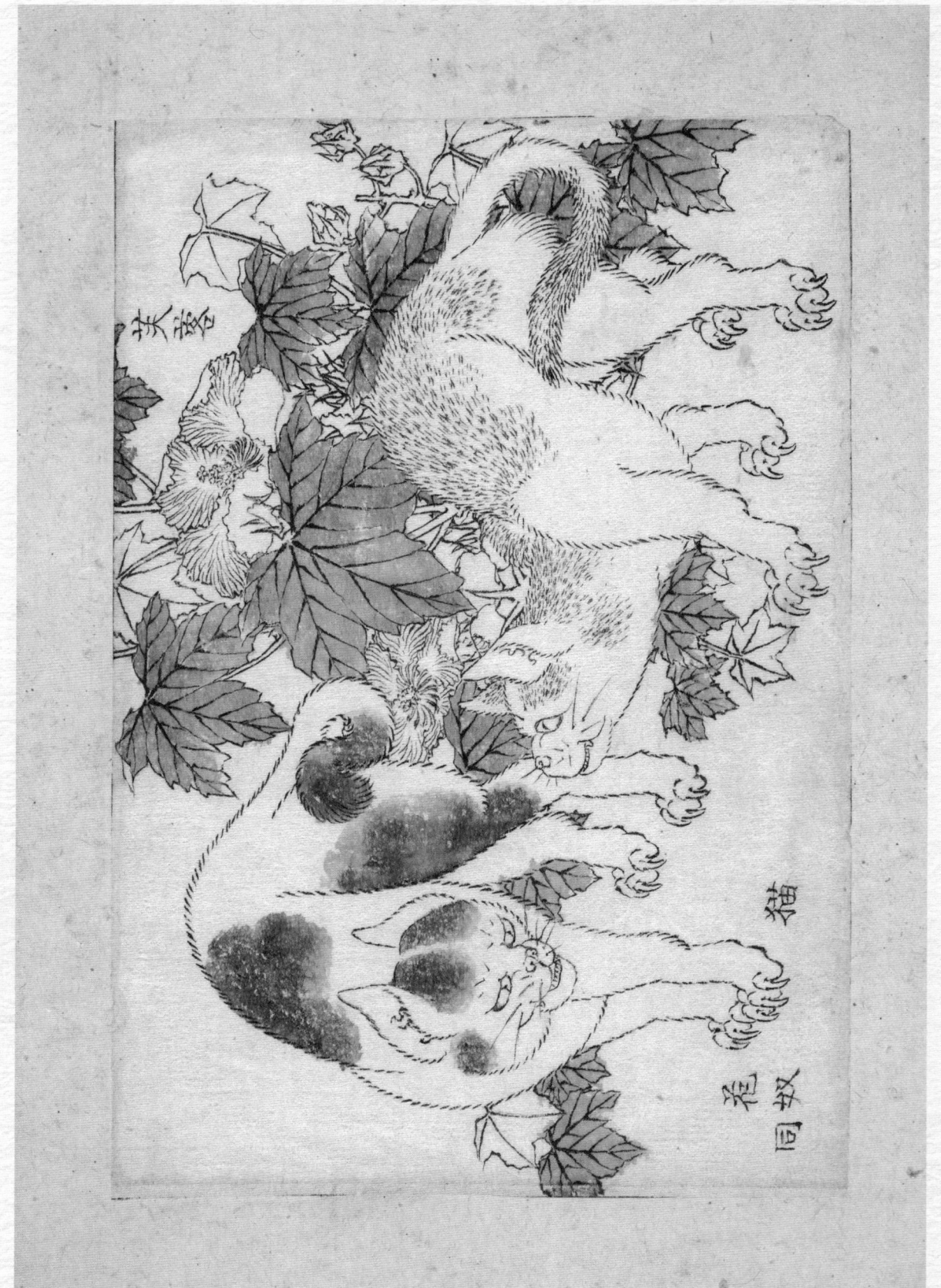

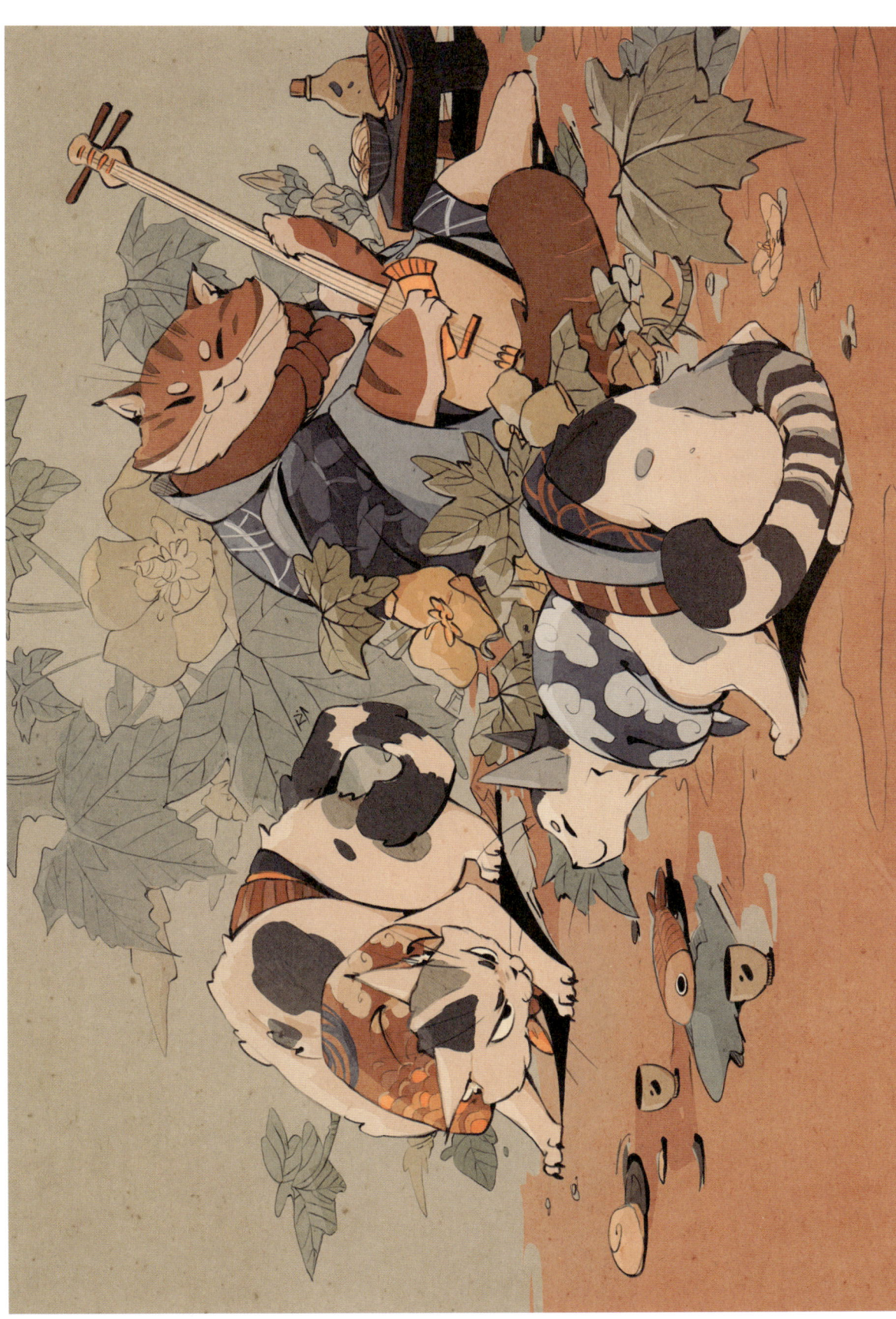

TWO CATS BY HIBISCUS

TESSA NELISSEN

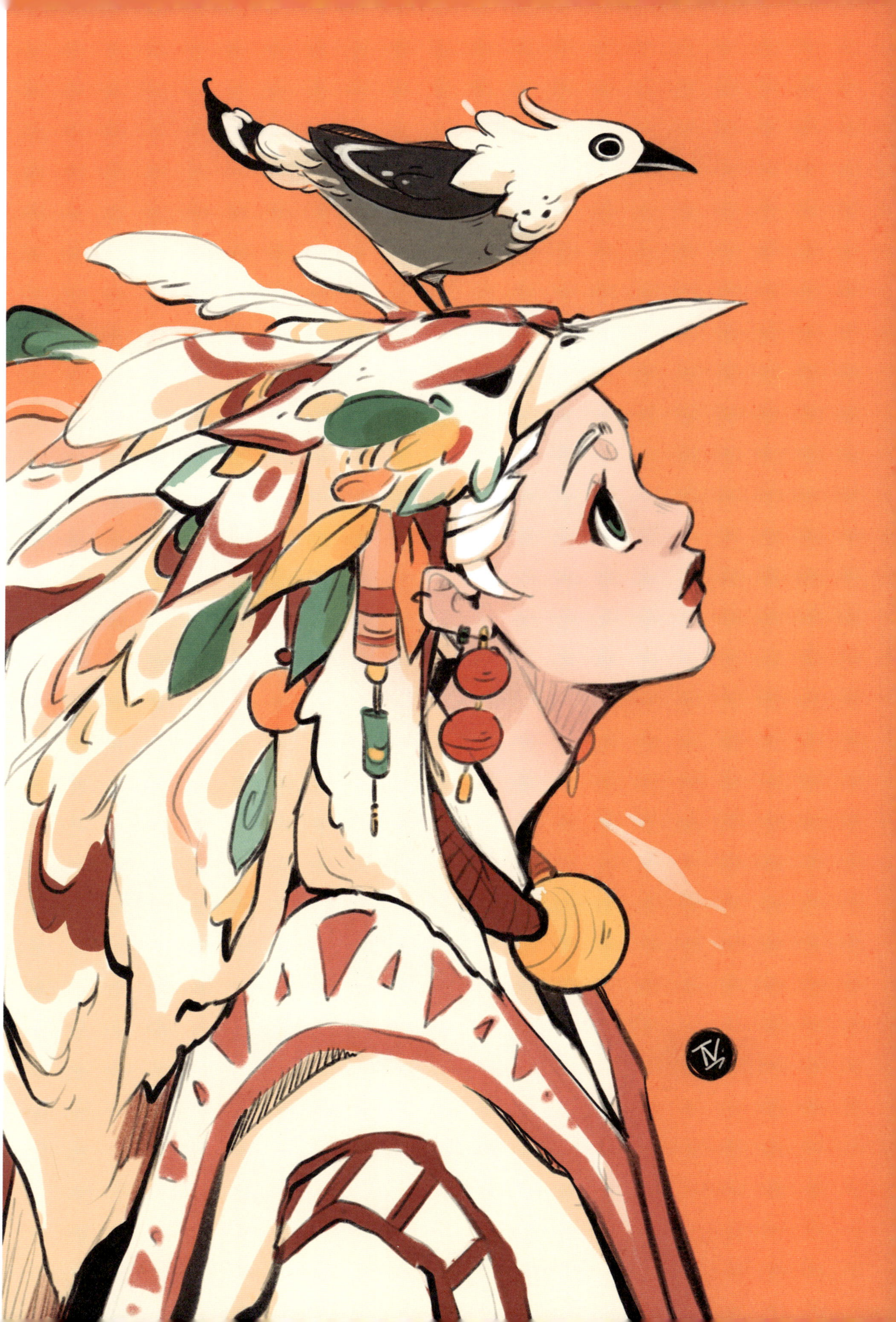

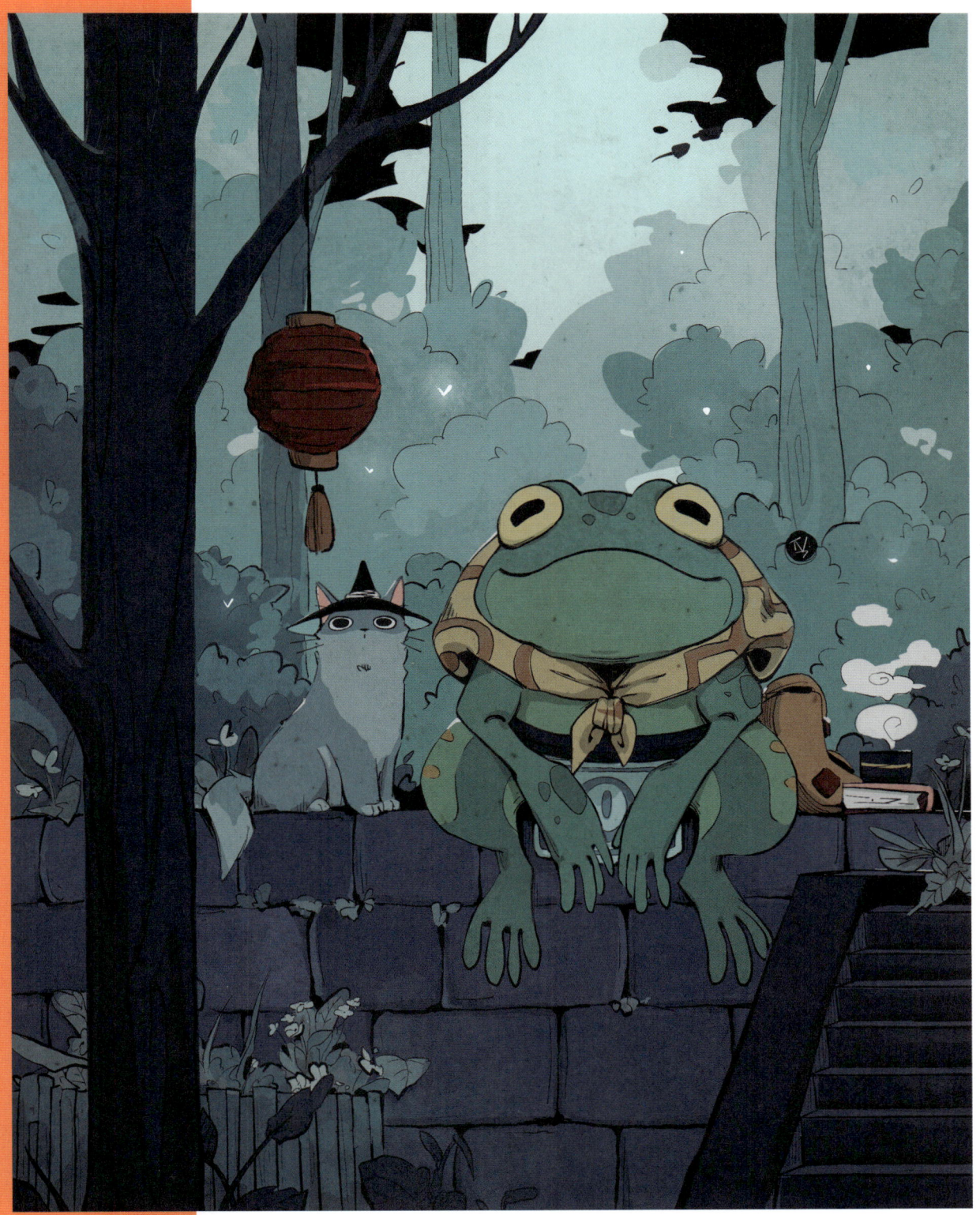

LEFT: *The Oracle*
The Oracle of feathers and beak speaks through the body of a young girl

ABOVE: *In The Woods*
An illustration of two travelling companions taking a break in the woods. I tried to achieve a Studio Ghibli kind of vibe

Tessa Nelissen

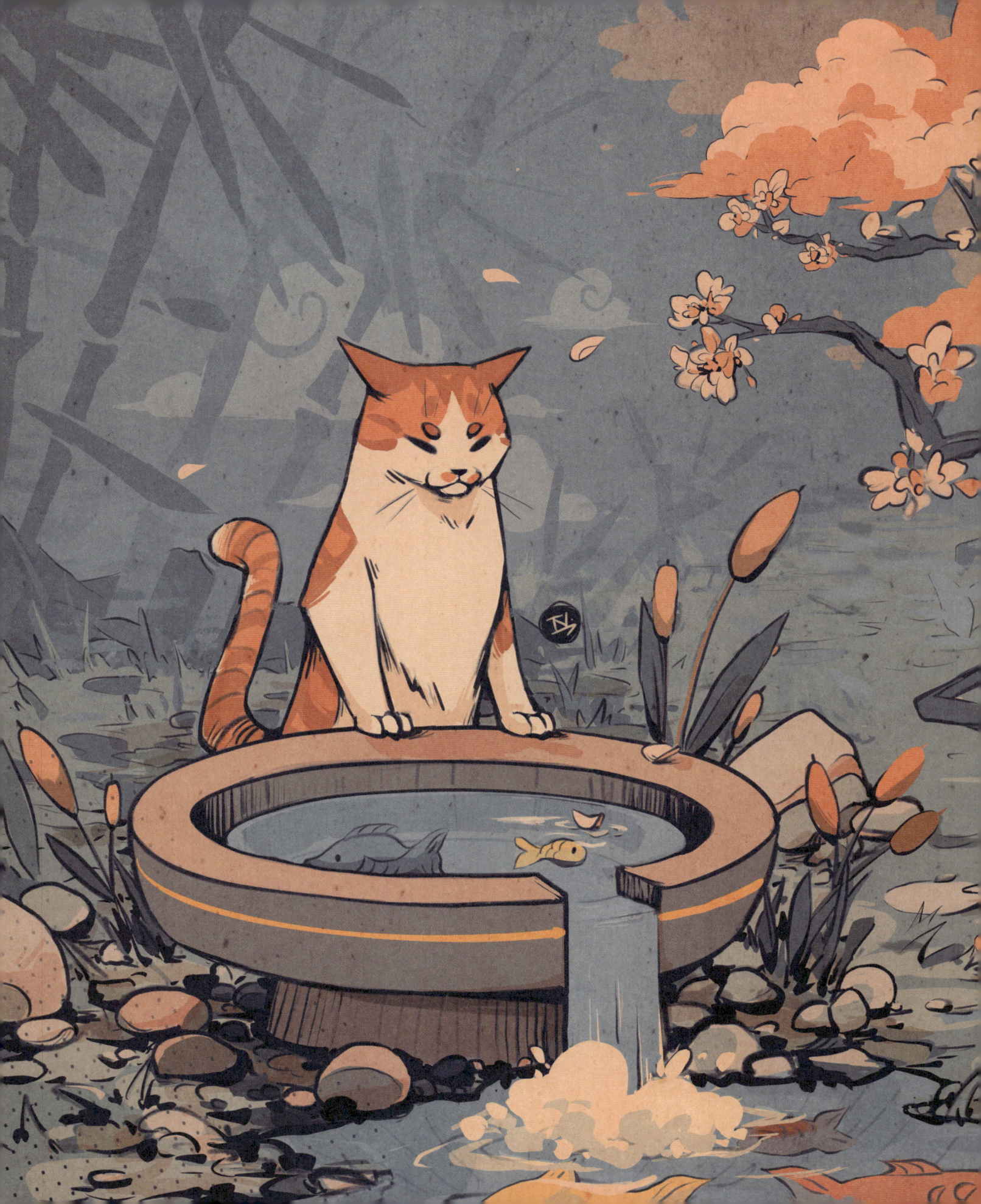

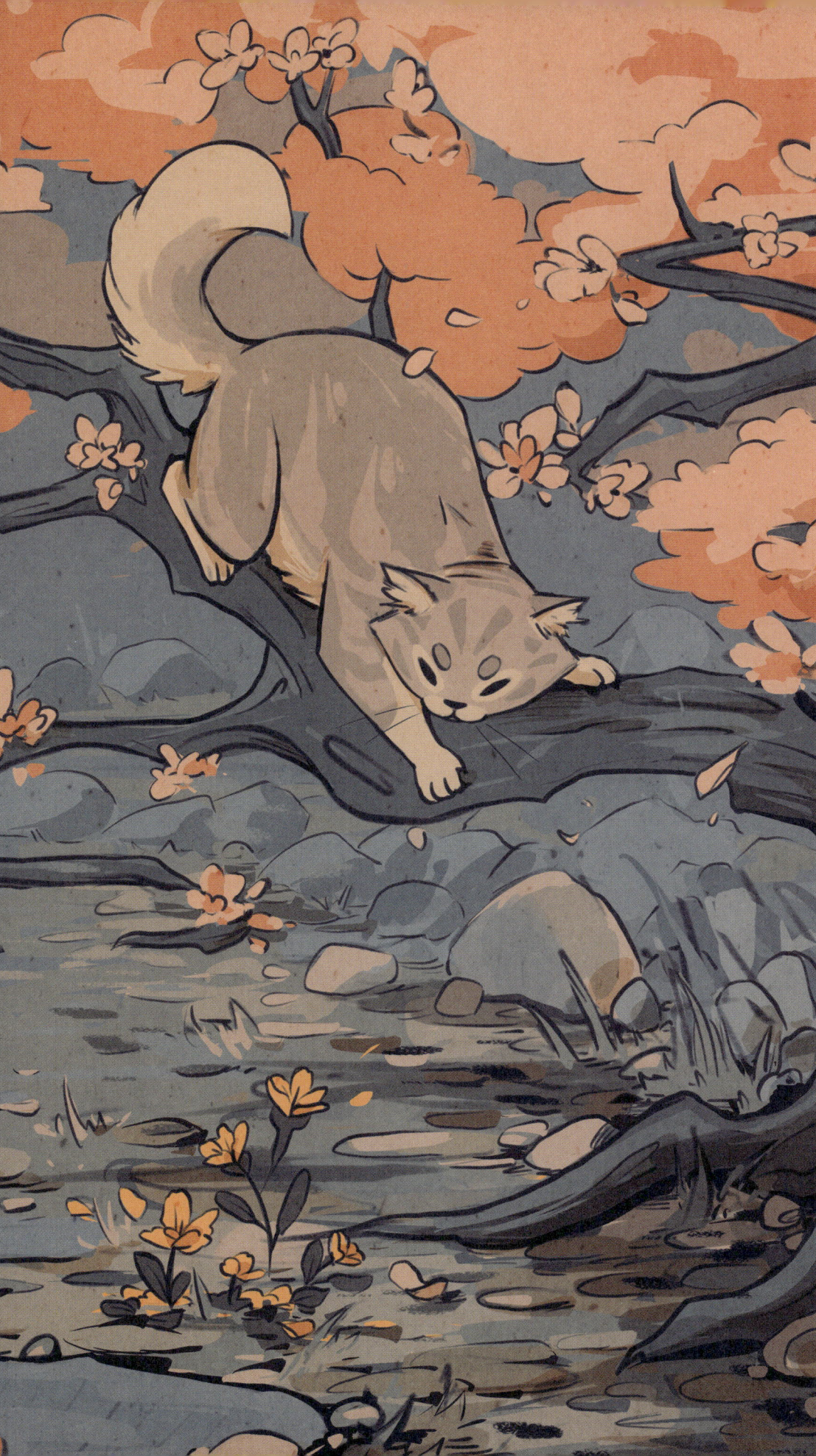

Japanese Garden
Cas and Finn hanging
out by the pond
under the cherry tree

Tessa Nelissen

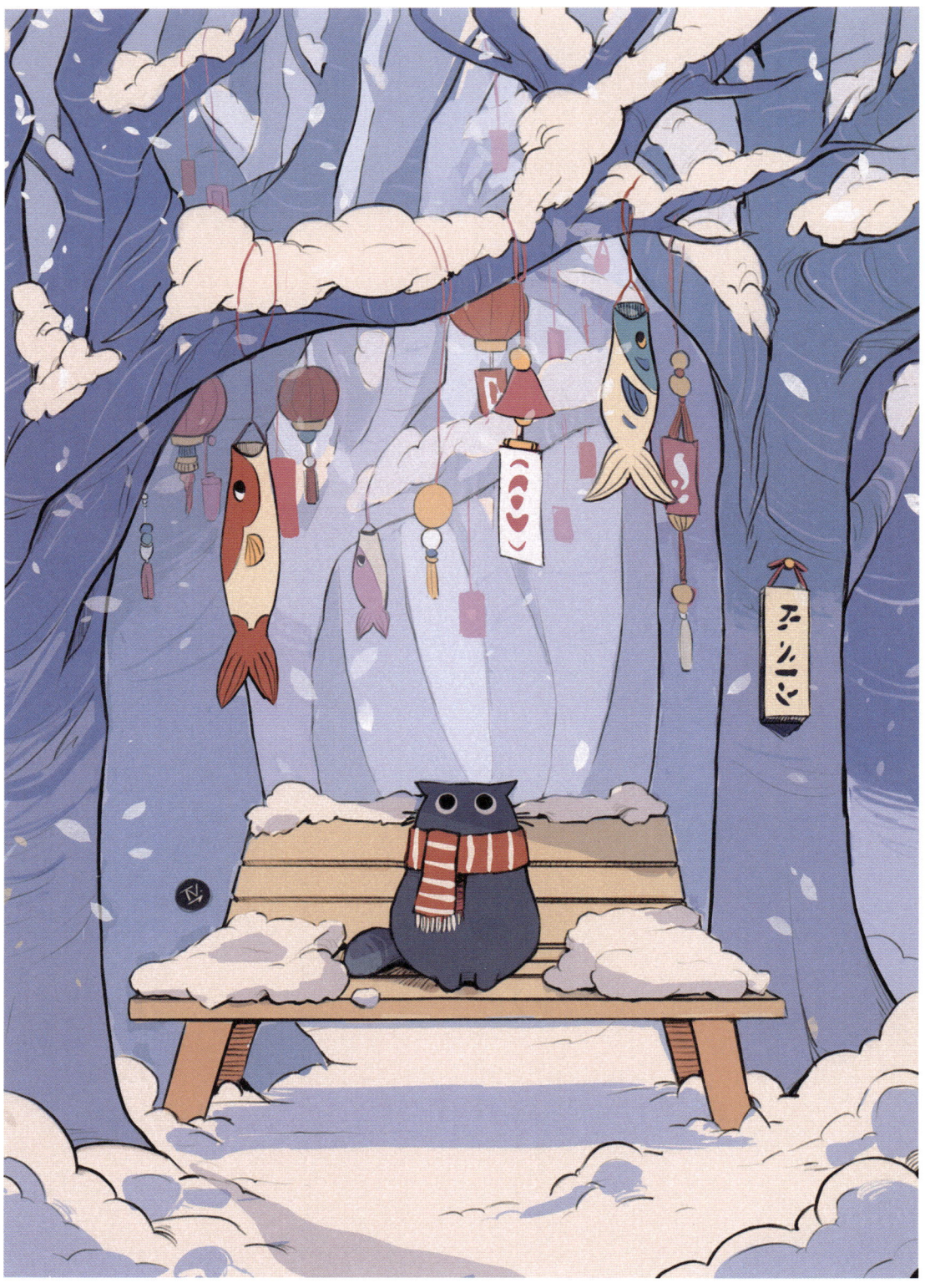

ABOVE : *Pooty In The Snow*
Is there anything more magical
than a winter wonderland?

RIGHT: *You Are Cute*
An angry kitty and his owner. The atmosphere and kimono design
are directly inspired by one of Utagawa Kuniyoshi's artworks

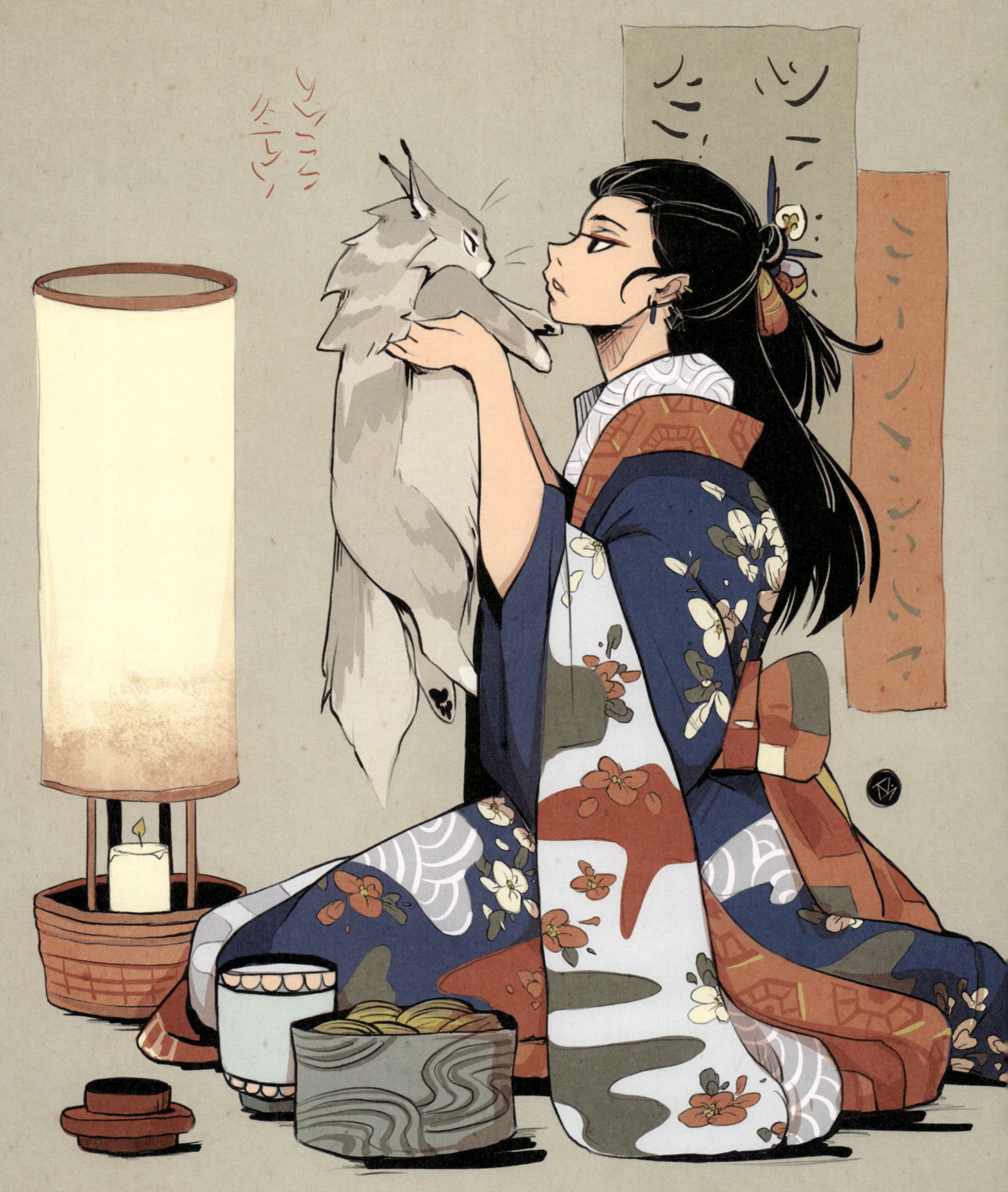

THE OLD TREE AT KŌNOMINE

BY JOHANNA FORSTER

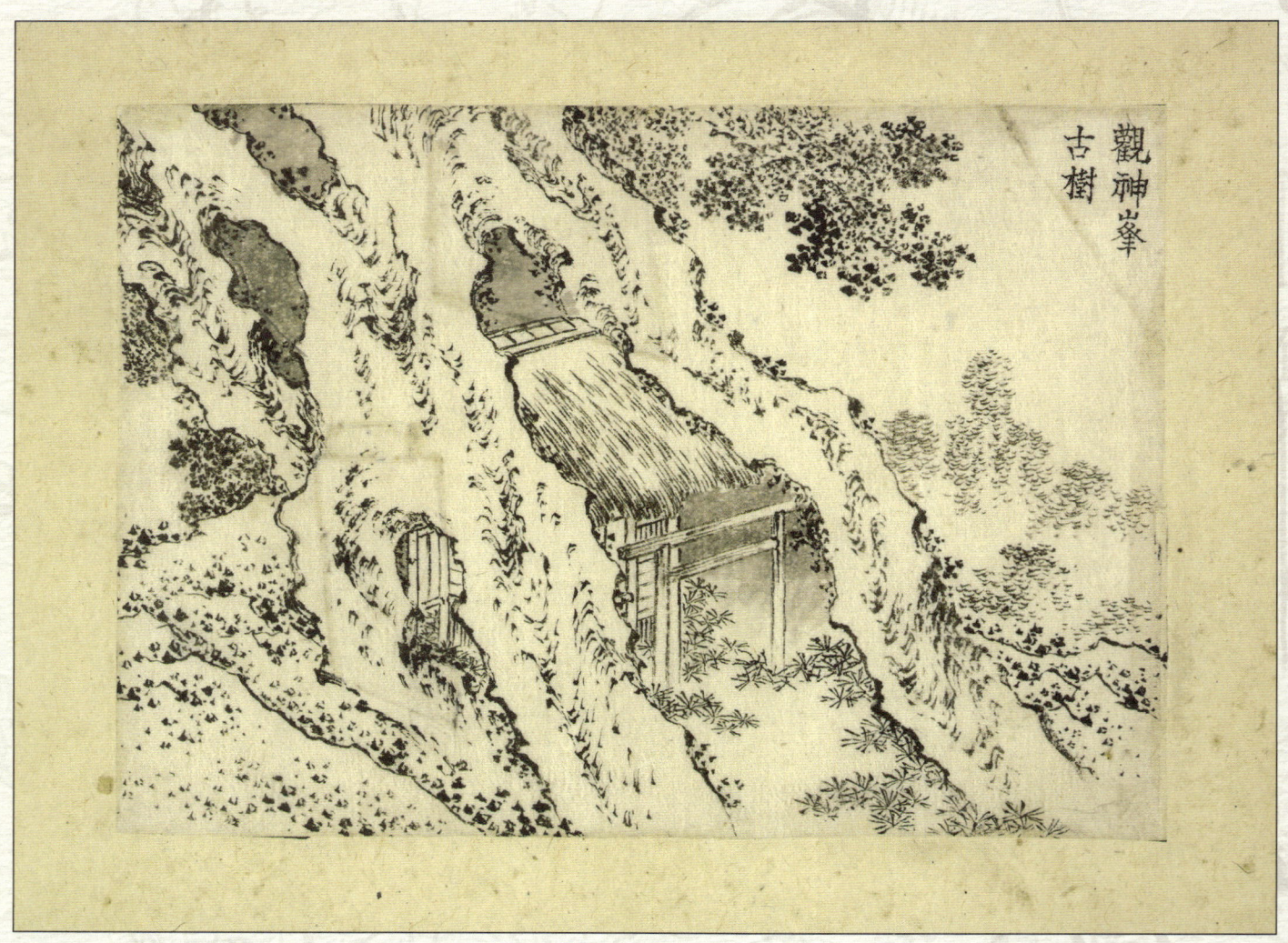

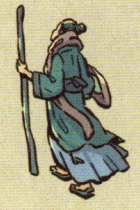

JOHANNA FORSTER

DISCOVERING HOKUSAI

For me, Katsushika Hokusai's paintings radiate a great sense of calm and harmony. His compositions are elegant and full of balance, and his contours are clear and dynamic. I particularly admire the sublimity of nature in his paintings: luminous landscapes, very small people between waves, seas of clouds, small houses hidden under the imposing roots of huge trees.

In my artistic work, I have had little direct contact with Hokusai's art. Of course, I was familiar with his best-known work, *The Great Wave,* and some of his depictions of Mount Fuji. However, Hokusai has had a considerable influence on manga and Japanese pop culture. Allegedly, he was one of the first artists to use the term 'manga' and his clean lines and dynamic compositions are clearly reminiscent of the style of modern manga. I grew up with Japanese video games and still remember my first sketchbook, which I filled with drawings of *Pokémon* and *Zelda* characters. Soon, I was inventing my own cute characters and dreaming of becoming a concept artist for games myself; I wanted to create these animated worlds full of wonder.

During my time at art school, I discovered the films of Studio Ghibli, which strongly influenced my current style. There are many parallels between Studio Ghibli and Hokusai's works in particular: the admiration for nature and for Japanese traditions, as well as the depiction of supernatural elements such as ghosts and other mythological creatures.

I actually achieved my goal of becoming a concept artist, and working as part of a team of game developers was a great experience. However, the urge to express my own imagination was a little stronger, so I am now a freelance illustrator and mainly work on my own projects. Like Hokusai and Studio Ghibli, my personal paintings focus on nature; I am fascinated by the relationship between us humans and the environment. Nature can be an endless source of inspiration, be it the colours of light shining through leaves, the textures of moss, or the exciting silhouettes of plants, animals, and landscapes. For me, nature is something overpowering that we still don't fully understand, and it makes our everyday human lives seem smaller in comparison.

Johanna Forster

01 CONSIDERING THE ORIGINAL

Hokusai's drawing *The old tree at Kōnomine* immediately stood out to me because it has such a mystical mood. It made me dream of being an explorer in 1800s Japan, finding a sacred place in an overgrown tree.

I think of the majestic roots of this tree as the main character of the scene; they flow from one corner of the canvas to the other, and their silhouettes reveal a hidden place, almost like a portal to another world. I definitely want to retain the shape of the tree in my interpretation. I try to keep my lines loose and dynamic.

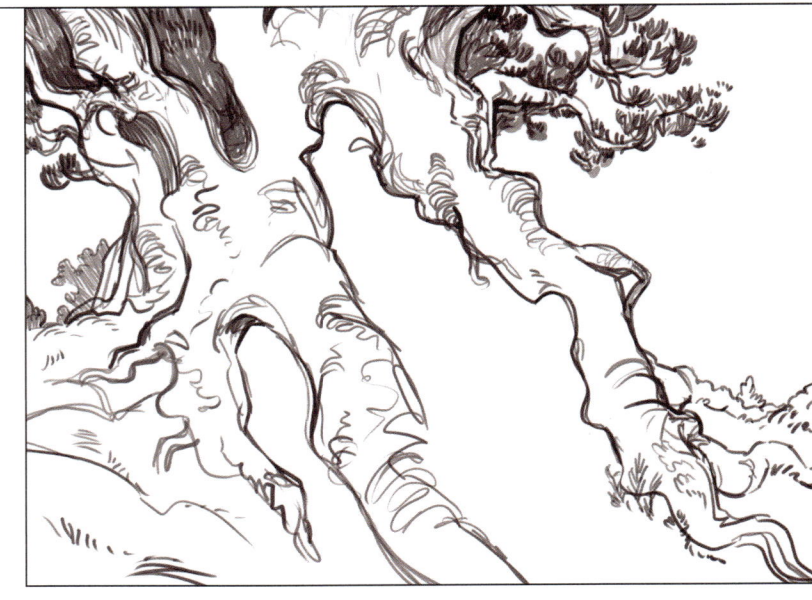

I WORK DIGITALLY IN PHOTOSHOP AND START WITH A SKETCH OF THE TREE

02 ADDING SCALE

I am not sure what kind of tree Hokusai depicted, but I imagine it to be a pine tree, which is iconic for Japan. The roots in the original drawing are huge, as if an entire building can fit inside it, and I want to reinforce this impression by placing smaller, normal-sized trees near it.

Hokusai's paintings are filled with depictions of Japanese landscapes. Steep mountains and lush vegetation are suggested in the background of his original piece, and I would like to retain these elements and their interesting silhouettes.

OBJECTS IN THE BACKGROUND CAN ADD TO THE SCALE OF A SCENE

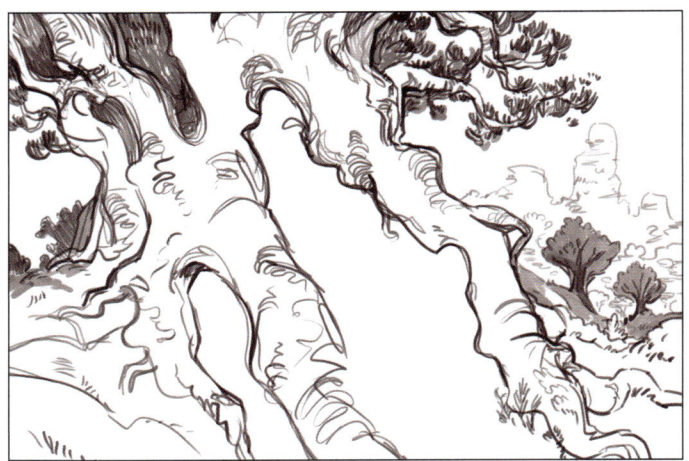

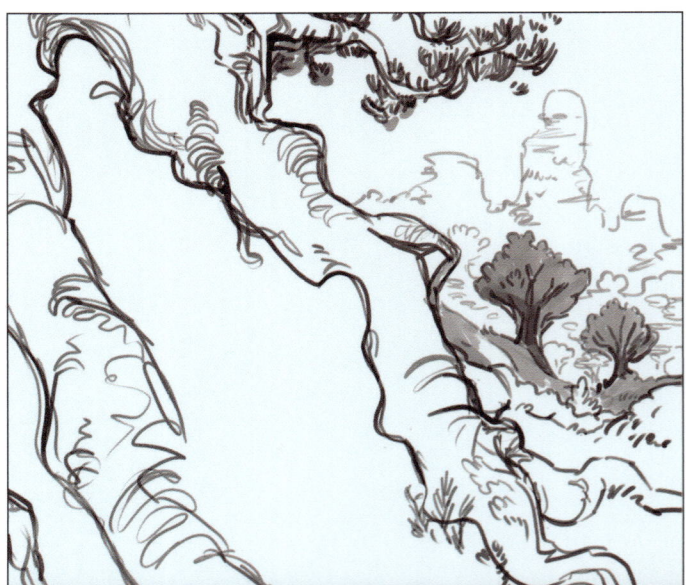

03 SIGNS OF CIVILIZATION

Now I turn my attention to the inside of the mystical tree. The gate in Hokusai's drawing is a Shinmei torii, a traditional Japanese entrance to a Shinto shrine, which marks a transition to a sacred place and the world of spirits. Kōnomine (the location described in the title) is a real temple in the middle-west area of Japan, where both Shinto and Buddhist gods have been honoured. It is part of a long pilgrimage and located on a steep mountain with many stairs. You can find pictures of the building and gate online – it's not in a huge tree, but it *is* surrounded by a beautiful forest.

For my drawing, I imagine nature spirits live here and that the inside of the tree offers even more space than it suggests from the outside. I decide to draw several little houses instead of one temple, and add signs of civilization in the form of lanterns.

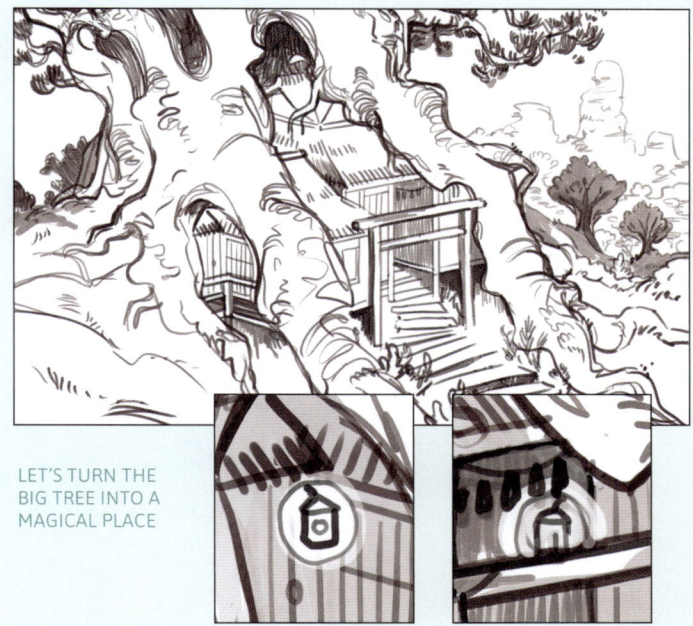

LET'S TURN THE BIG TREE INTO A MAGICAL PLACE

04 TOUCH-UPS

To give the scene even more of a sense of adventure (and a hint of romanticism), I place a wanderer in the foreground, climbing the steps. I also want the figure to add to the scene scale when compared to the tree.

My sketch is almost finished and I'm thinking about what is still missing without making things appear overloaded. To emphasize that the gate leads to a sacred place, I place paper ornaments on it, similar to the traditional shide garlands that symbolize the presence of spirits in Japan. I also draw additional vegetation to the crown of the tree because I think it looks a bit bare.

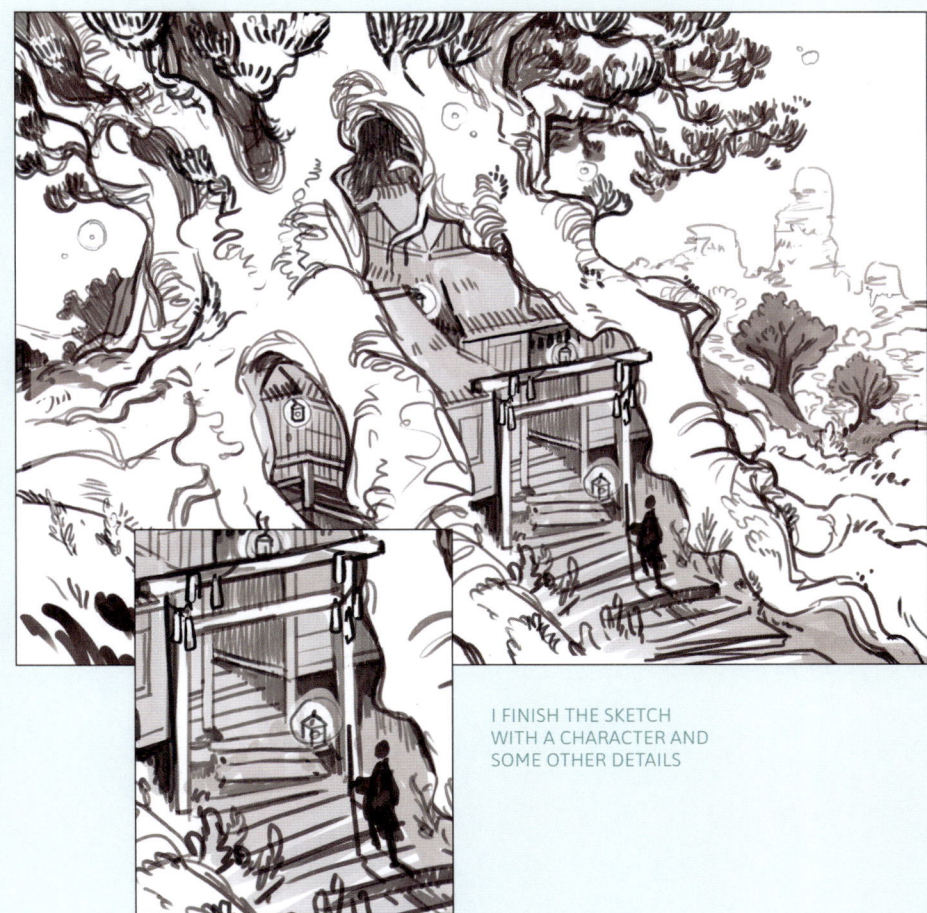

I FINISH THE SKETCH WITH A CHARACTER AND SOME OTHER DETAILS

Johanna Forster

05 MOSS & DETAILS

Before I finalize the line art, I draw a second, more detailed sketch over the first. This step always works well for me; it means I don't have to erase anything during the line-art phase. Since that takes a lot of momentum out of the lines, I draw over the previous layer with reduced opacity, emphasizing the lines that are important to me and filtering out the messy ones.

I think of a scene in the Studio Ghibli movie, *My Neighbor Totoro*, which shows the burrow of the great forest spirit with the same name. It is surrounded by roots that are overgrown with moss and other plants in countless shades of green. I want my tree to have a similar look. At this stage, I pay particular attention to details on the tree bark.

WITH A REFINED SKETCH, I CLEAN UP THE FIRST DRAWING

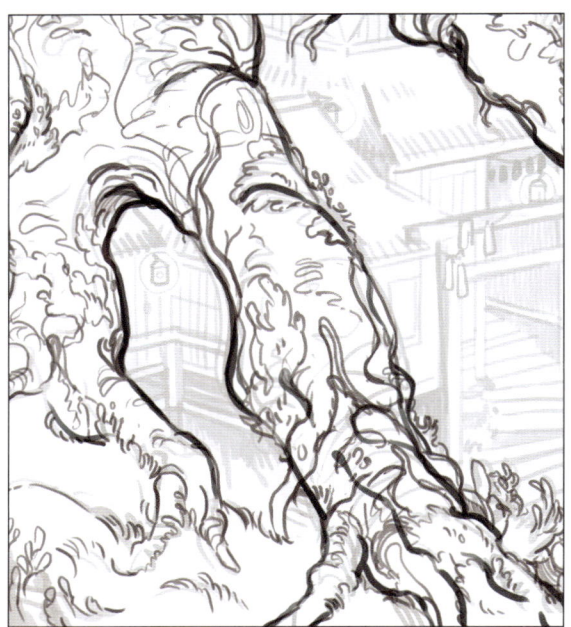

06 ADVENTURER

I decide that the steps to the mysterious place should also be overgrown with moss. I'm also thinking about what my adventurer should look like: should I draw modern clothes? Should I make them look like a fantastical creature? I eventually choose to give them traditional clothing that would fit into 18th-century Edo-era Japan, and try to keep the exact features of the face and the gender vague to leave room for the viewer's imagination.

CHARACTERS ADD A LOT TO THE WORLD-BUILDING OF A SCENE

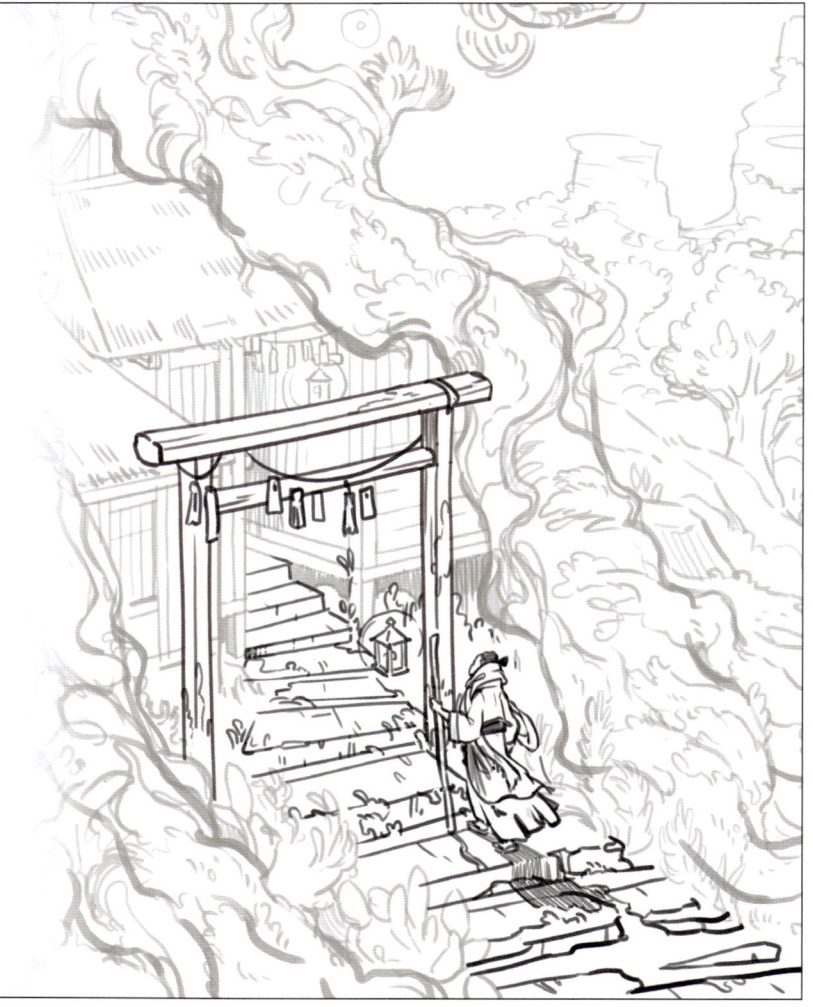

07 FINISHING THE SECOND SKETCH

For the details on the houses, I research traditional architecture of the Edo period. I use reference photos of the current temple in Kōnomine, and of historic houses with thatched roofs and half-timbering as models. To ensure credible world-building, it is important to use plenty of real references. A fantasy aspect is created by combining real elements with something unusual – in this case, the proportions.

In this scene, something interesting and mythical is also created by the dark areas in the tree, which I deliberately leave undetailed with dark hatch lines. Those are intended to fuel the question: what exactly is going on inside?

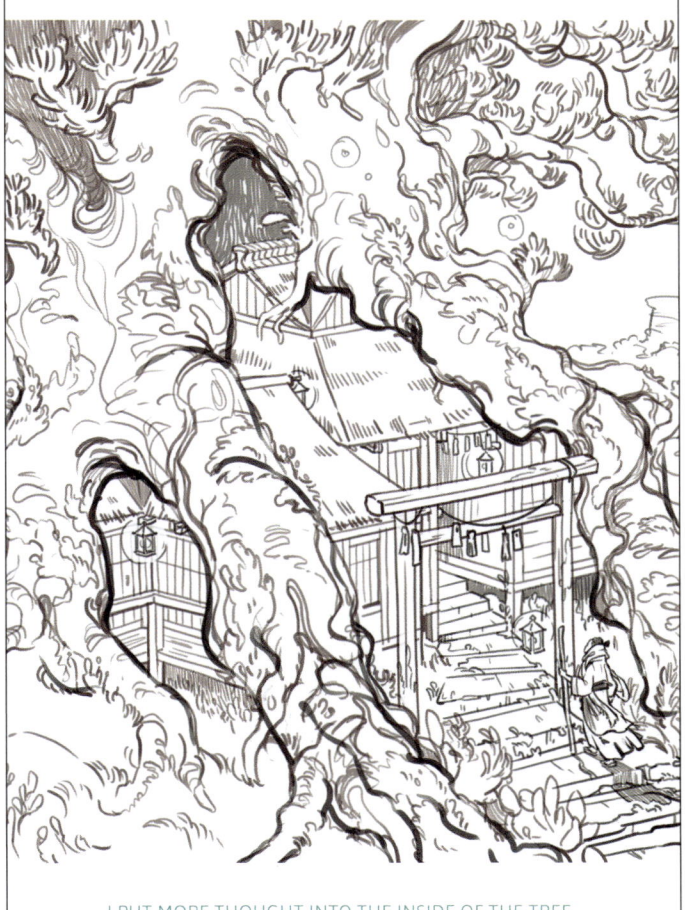

I PUT MORE THOUGHT INTO THE INSIDE OF THE TREE

08 PAPER

Hokusai worked with traditional black ink mixed with water on washi paper that smoothly absorbed the ink. Although working digitally is versatile, I love the traditional look of brushstrokes on textured paper, and I want to recreate that in Adobe Photoshop.

Before making a start with the outlines, I add a watercolour-paper texture in the background. I also add another texture using Overlay and reduce the transparency over my existing layer so the lines look more vivid. This method looks even more natural if you use lighter coloured lines instead of black ones. I start tracing my sketch with an ink-mimicking brush.

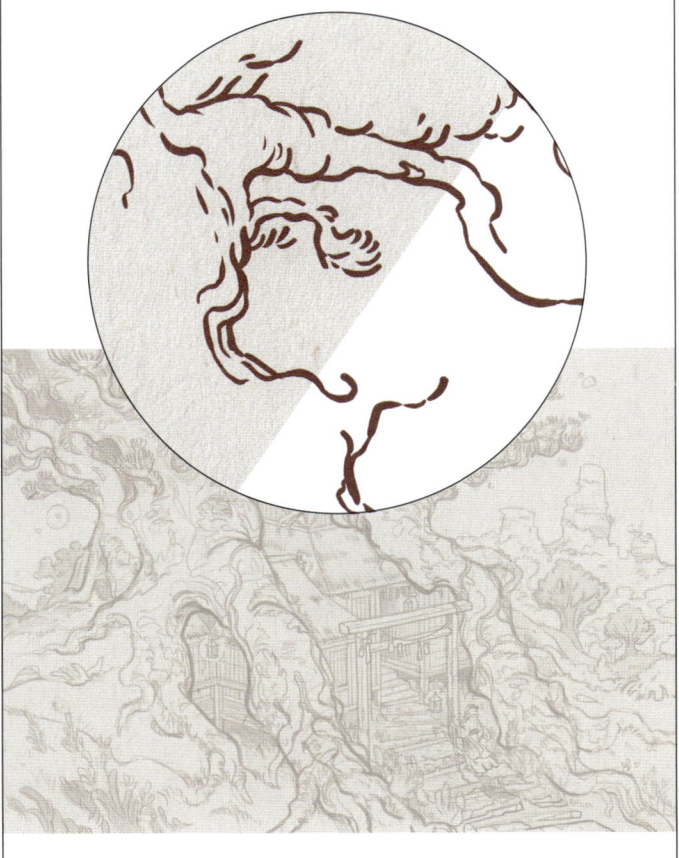

I ADD MORE TEXTURE TO MY CANVAS

Johanna Forster

09 INTENTIONAL LINES

Hokusai was a master of sumi-e art, an ink-painting technique that emphasizes simplicity. It is typical of this approach to capture the essence of a subject with minimal brushstrokes and execute them with confidence and spontaneity.

I can really relate to sumi-e being a meditative practice because inking is my favourite part of the process. It's important for me to draw outlines loosely, but with a lot of intention. I don't erase mistakes (only sometimes redoing a whole stroke) because the lines should appear organic through small imperfections.

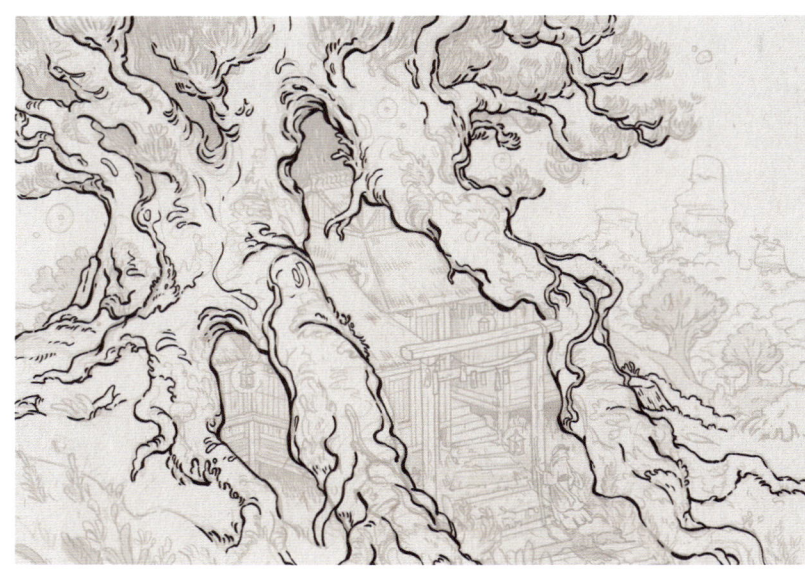

MY DIGITAL PAPER IS SLOWLY BEING FILLED WITH INK LINES

10 THICKER, THINNER & LIGHTER LINES

One technique I learned to use and love in my art is also essential in sumi-e and for Hokusai: the variation of line thickness. Right from the start, I think about where the light is coming from in the scene. On the shadowed side, usually along the underside of things, I apply more pressure and draw the outline thicker. Where there is a lot of light, I leave gaps to allow the shapes to breathe, creating negative space. Sometimes less is more and the eye can complete the picture in these places.

I draw elements that should move further into the background with less transparency, like the moss on the tree or the mountains in the background. In traditional ink drawing, artists used to dilute ink with water for a similar effect.

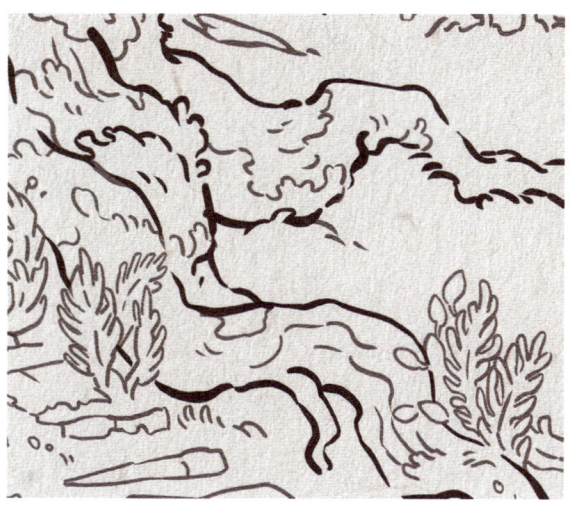
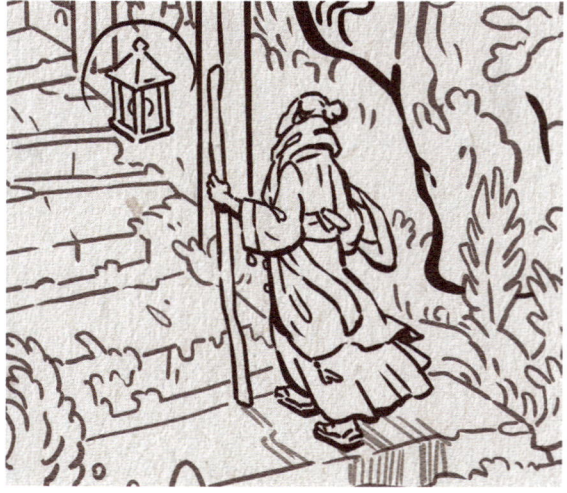

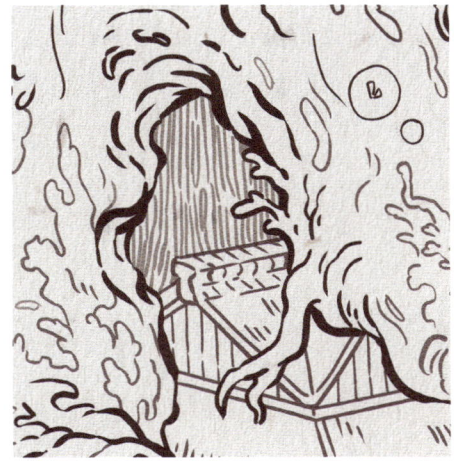

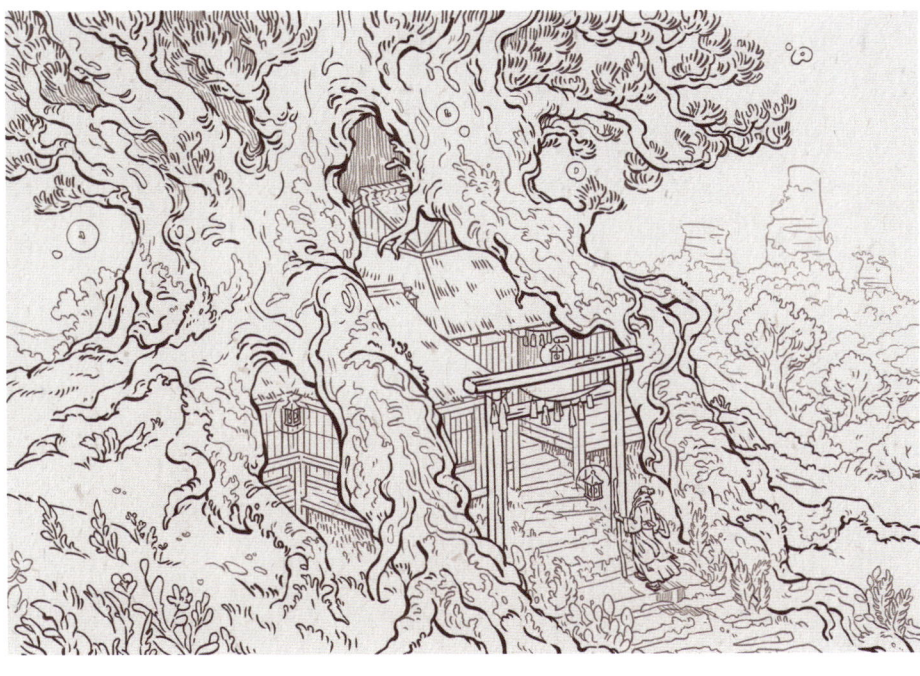

11 COLOURS

By referencing Hokusai's original work, I can only fall back on a line drawing, but I want to create a fully coloured illustration in my usual style. For the base colours, I get inspired by other completed Hokusai paintings showcasing trees and grass. He often paints mountains and water in a deep blue, which I don't usually use, but I can also find many works of his with lots of sage green, sky blue, and brown colours. I pick my favourites and put them down as a base for my interpretation.

I KEEP MY
FIRST COAT OF
COLOUR SIMPLE

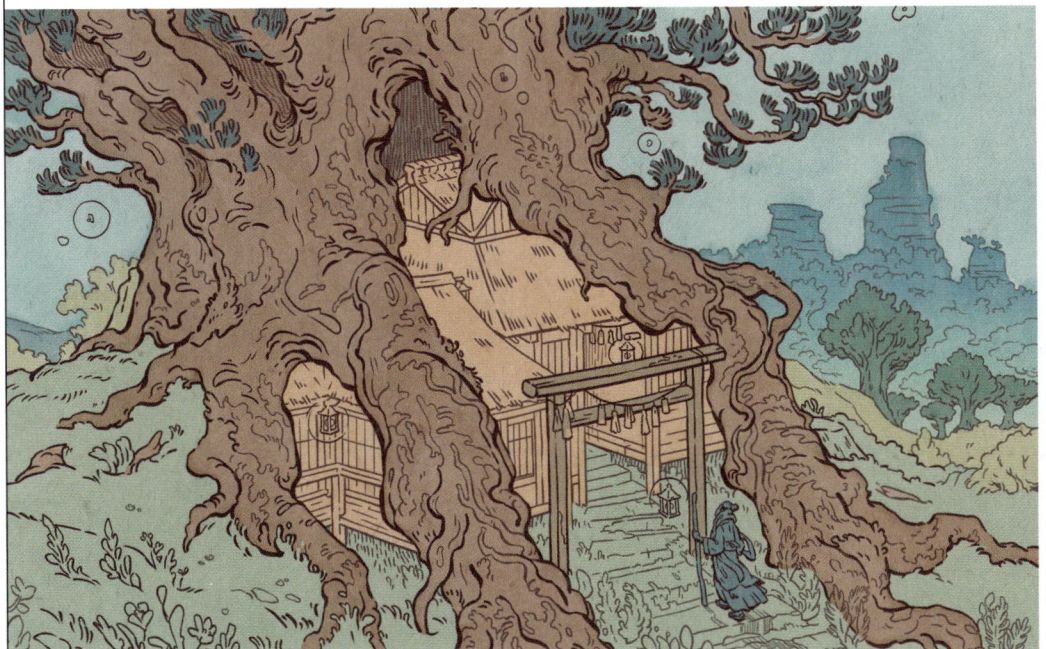

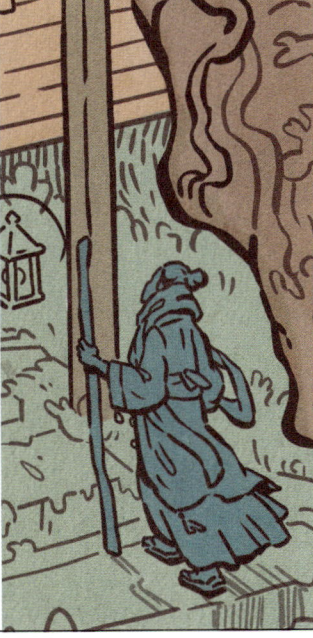

Johanna Forster

12 COLOUR DETAILS

I use a soft, watercolour-like brush and make sure to set my paper layer on top using the Multiply setting so its effect works on the colour as well. In the next step, I add more colour details on top of the previous step to create texture with splashes of colour and gradients for a traditional look. I keep looking at the image as a whole to assess how all the colours work together.

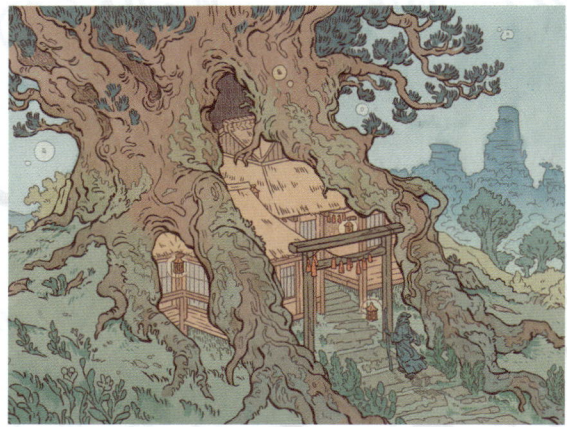

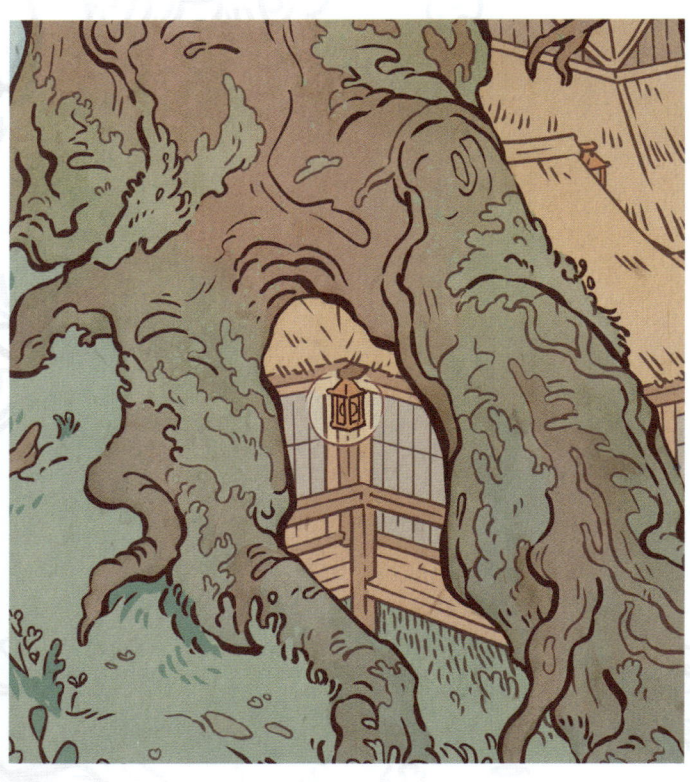

I BREATHE MORE LIFE INTO THE COLOURING WITH DETAILS AND TEXTURES

13 SHADOWS

I want to give my illustration a bit more depth, so I add shadows on top using a transparent layer. The inside of the tree becomes darker to emphasize the mystery within. Shadows are also a good way to create beautiful patches of light on the meadow, as well as the tree, emphasizing the texture of the bark. I usually paint purple shadows for reddish areas and blue shadows for greenish areas. This creates a softer, livelier look than black shadows.

A LAYER OF SHADOWS ADDS TO THE VOLUME OF MY PAINTINGS

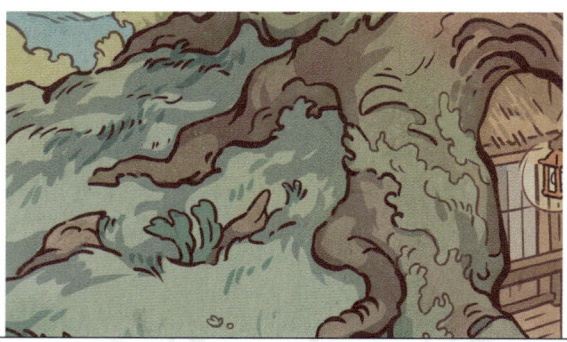

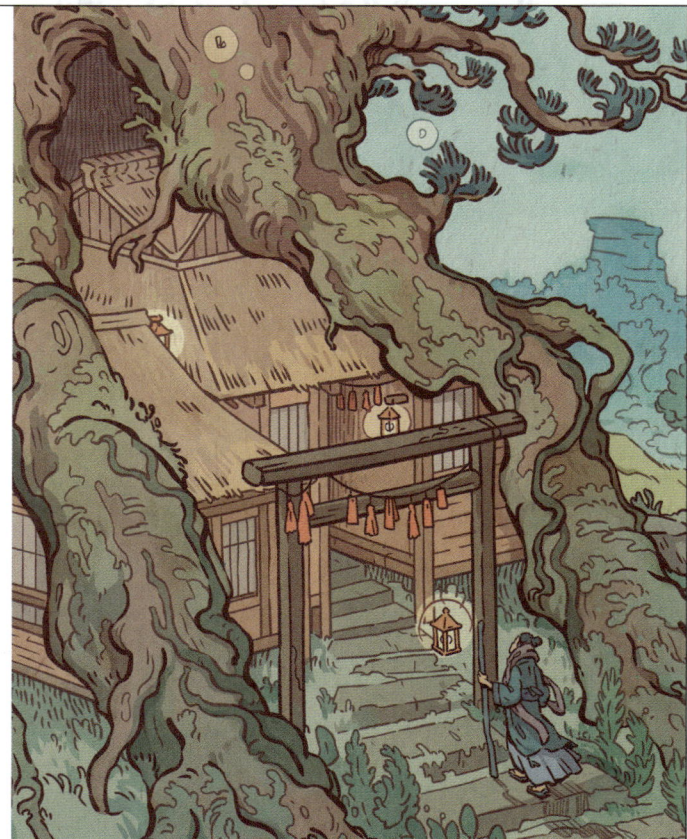

14 LIGHTS

Next, I give some more attention to the parts of the painting I want to highlight, like the lanterns and the fireflies. I imagine how they would light up the surroundings and create a little more three-dimensionality. I prefer to apply them in a slightly dotted pattern like you'd find in a cosy Impressionist painting. At this point, I consider making the buildings way darker and colouring the gate a lighter tone instead. Mysterious blue or violet lights would also look great, but I decide to go for a warm and welcoming feel.

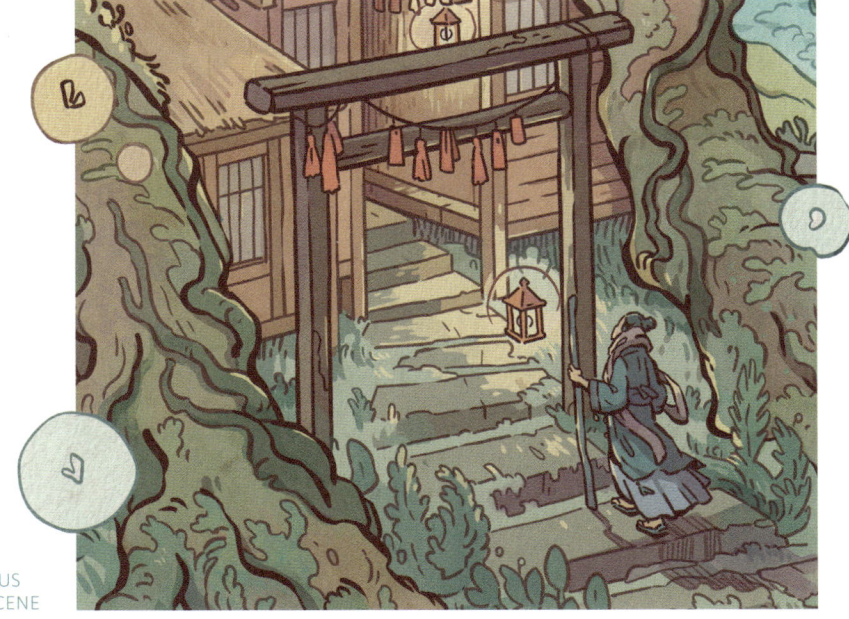

AFTER PAINTING SHADOWS, I FOCUS ON THE LIGHT SOURCES IN THE SCENE

15 FINAL TOUCHES

Almost done! I always make sure to colour the outlines to make them blend in a bit better. I edit the adventurer to be a little smaller to form an even stronger contrast with the tree. When I'm happy with the rest, I play around with the sliders in Photoshop and improve the overall contrast and saturation of the image. Finally, I add the smallest details, such as the flowers in the meadow and additional highlights on the tree bark.

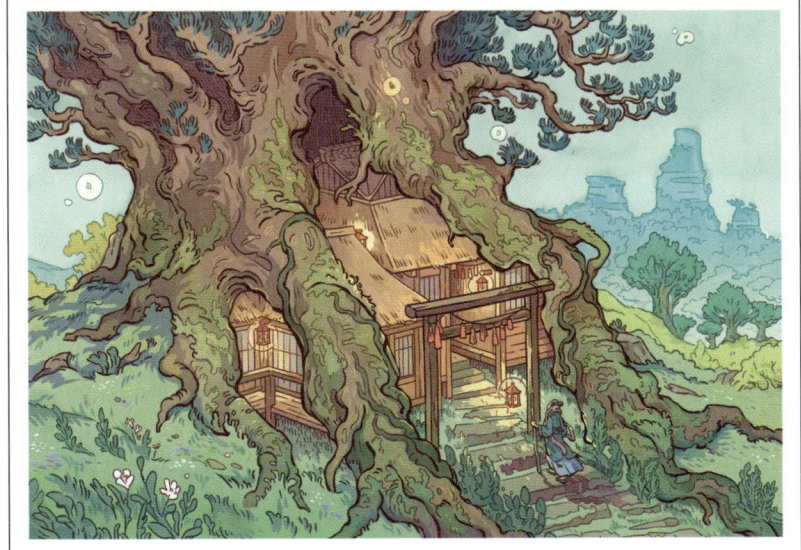

I TAKE A STEP BACK AND FINISH THE ILLUSTRATION WITH SOME FINAL DETAILS

CONCLUSION

It was a lot of fun getting to know Hokusai better. When I look at his works, I would love to step into them for a moment and breathe in the atmosphere of huge trees and mountains painted in elegant lines and beautiful compositions. Hokusai's art is a bow to nature's greatness. His drawings can inspire us all to strive for more balance within our environment and, as an artist, I hope to capture a similar magic by painting.

Johanna Forster

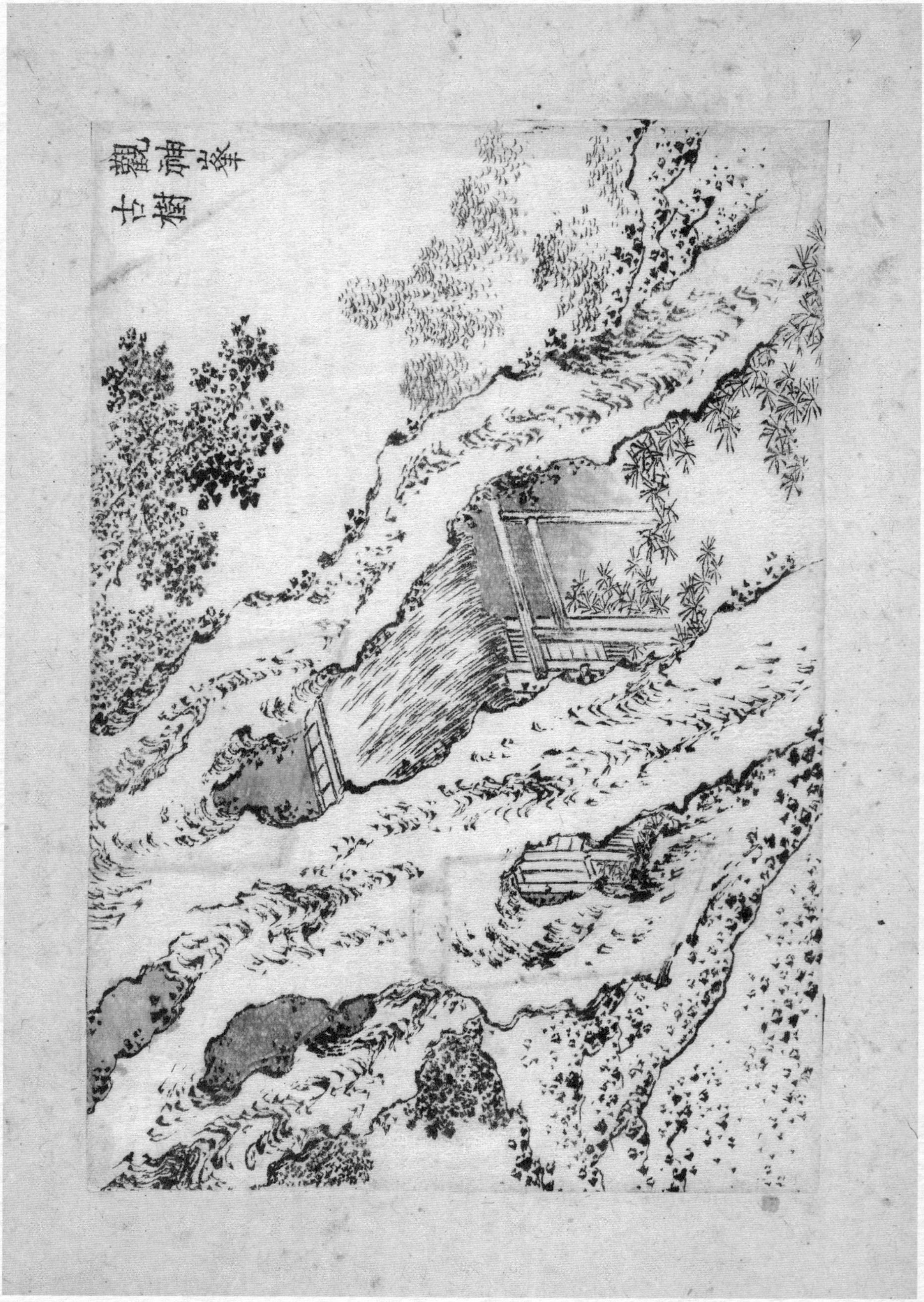
觀神峯
古樹

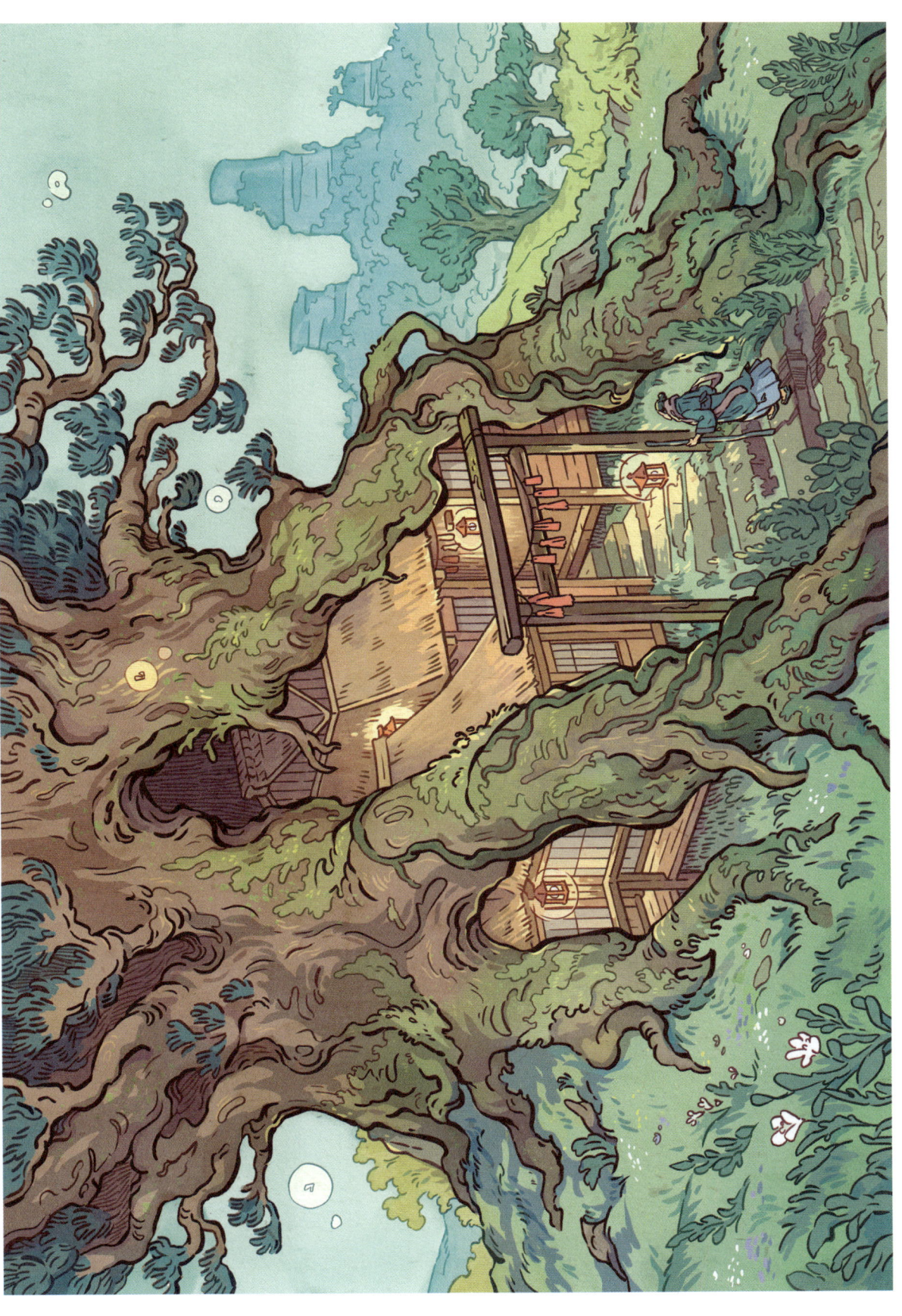

THE OLD TREE AT KŌNOMINE

JOHANNA FORSTER

GALLERY: JOHANNA FORSTER

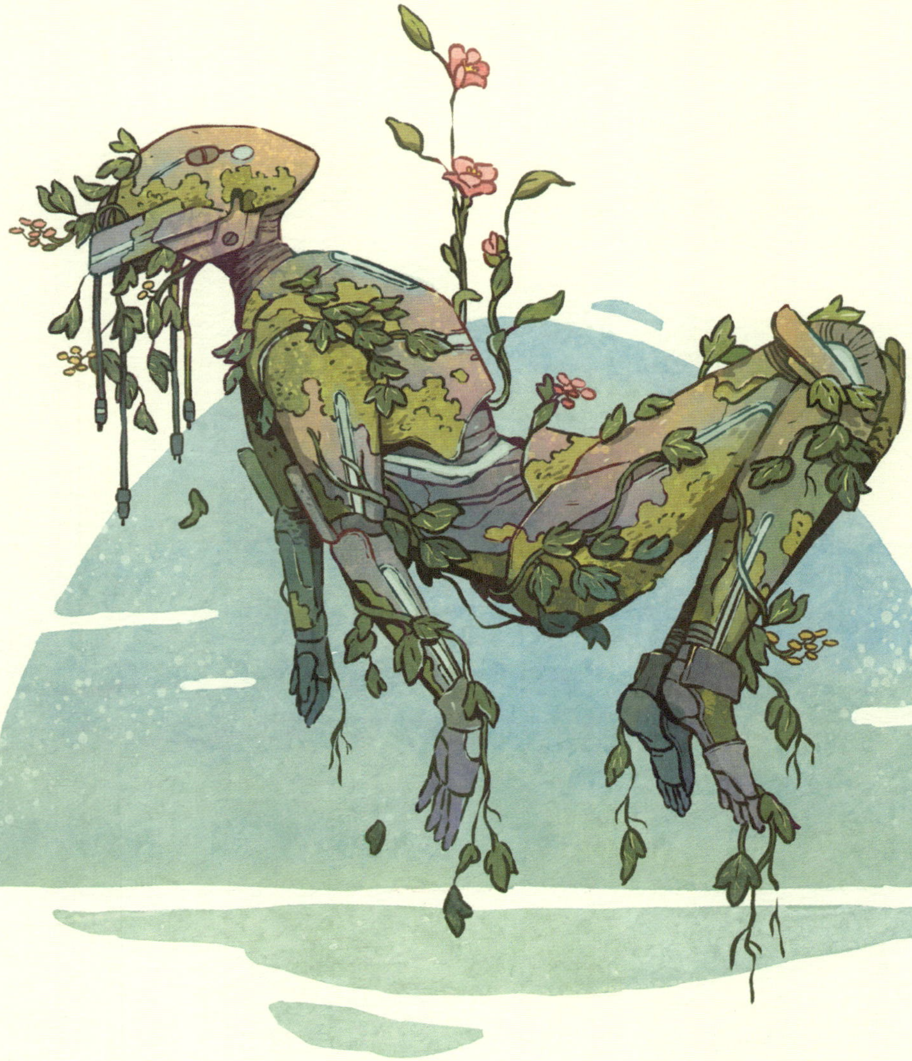

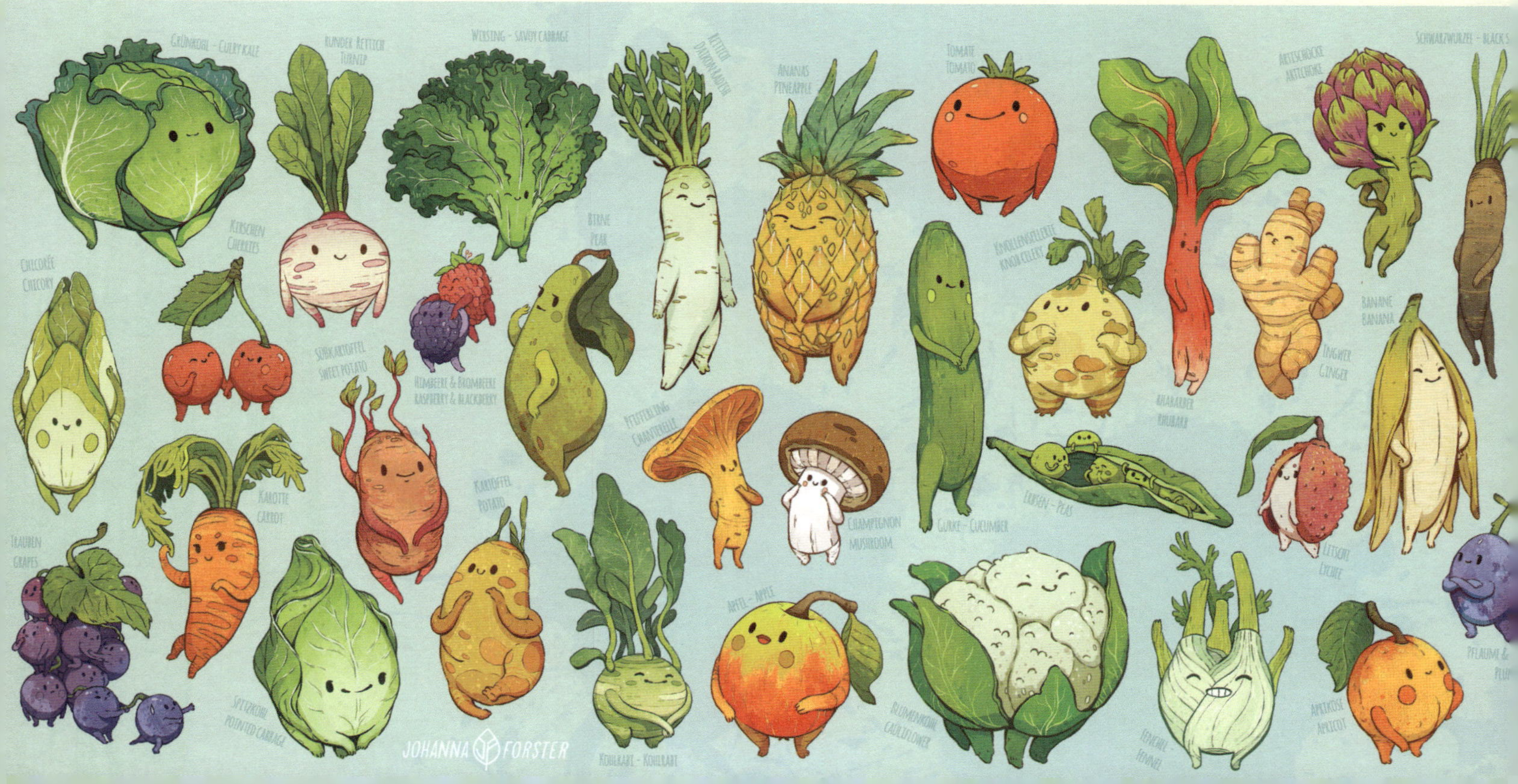

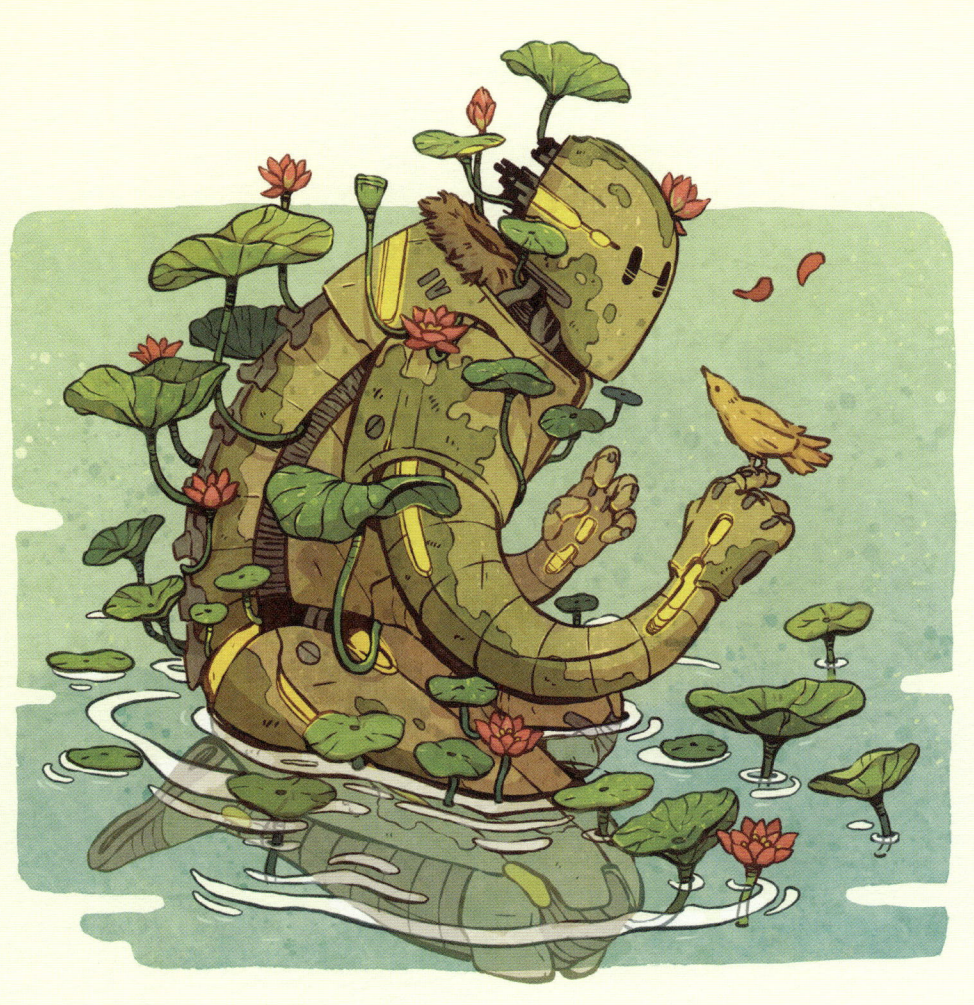

LEFT AND FAR LEFT: *Botanical Bots*
Two of my Botanical Bots: gentle overgrown machines and a tribute to Studio Ghibli's *Castle in the Sky*

BELOW: *Grunling Panorama Breit*
I imagine the Grunlings as friendly nature spirits who are good at hiding and have magical powers

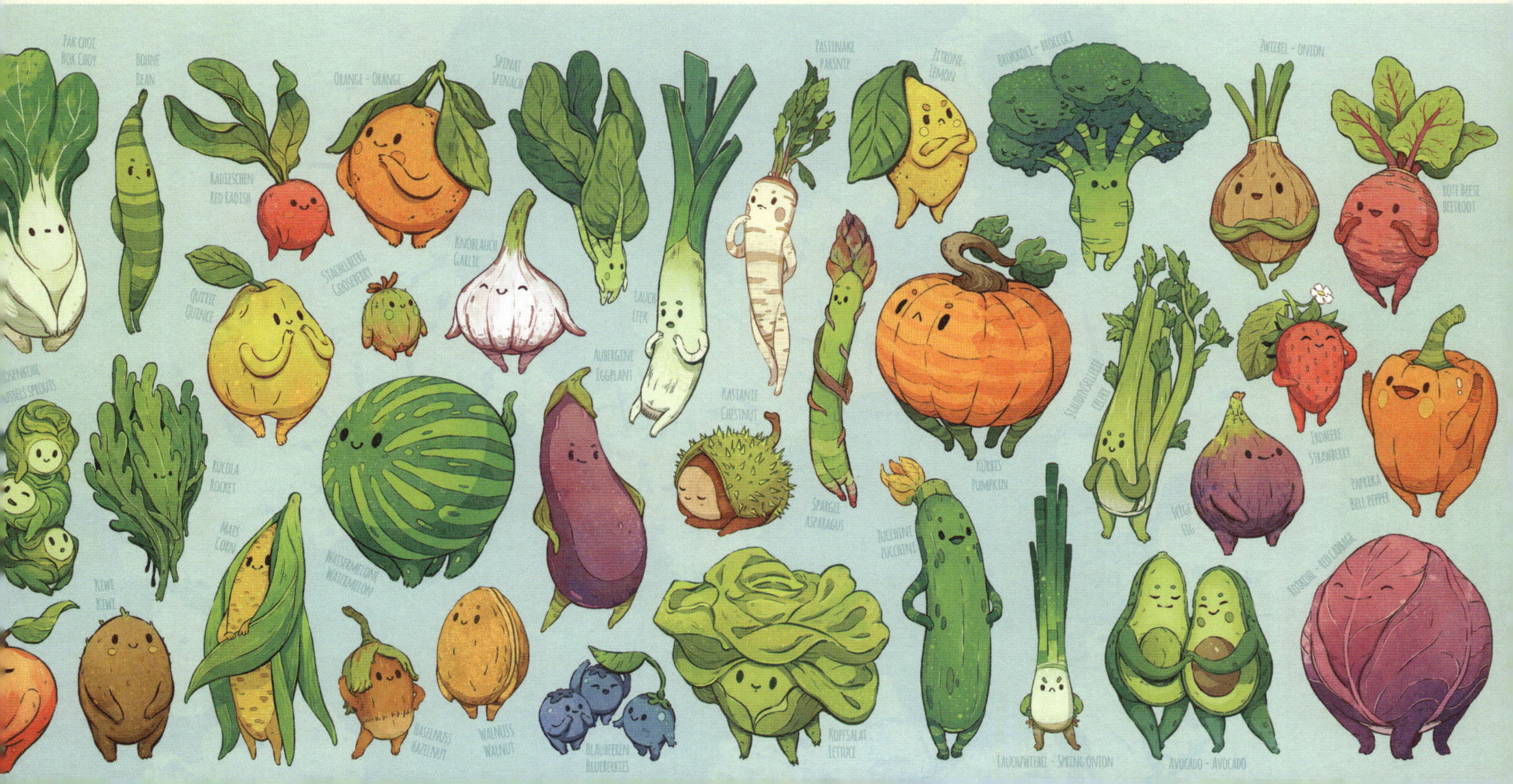

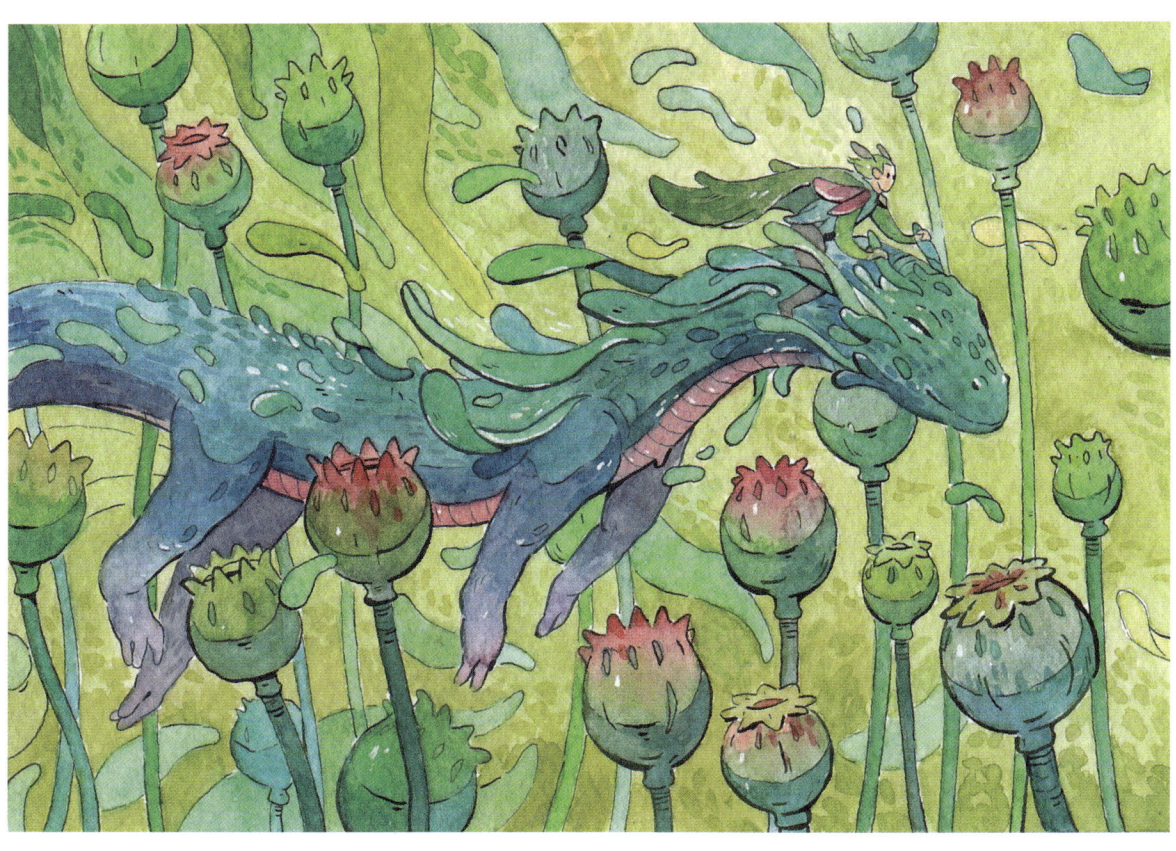

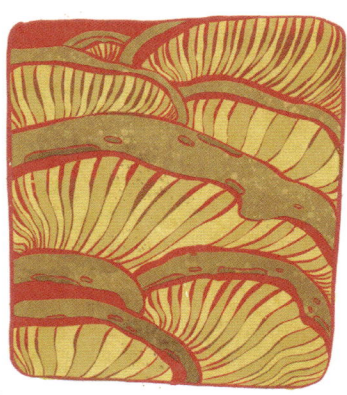

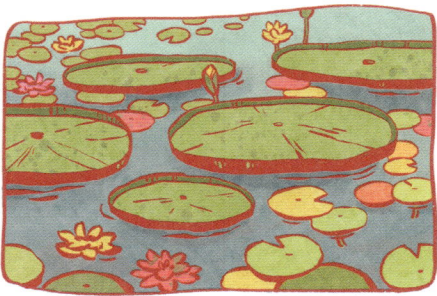

ABOVE: *Mohnreiter*
I think the dynamic composition of this watercolour poppyseed dragon has some similarities to Hokusai's art

LEFT: *Summer Moments*
A collection of warm summer memories

RIGHT: *Bananabird*
I practised more of a simplified human depiction here, inspired by the proportions of Studio Ghibli's Chihiro from *Spirited Away*

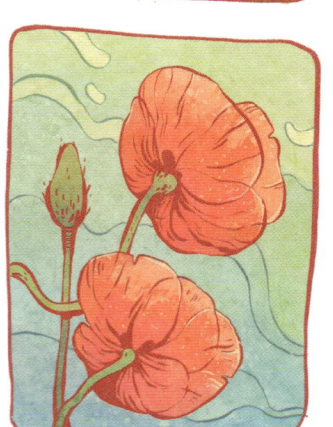

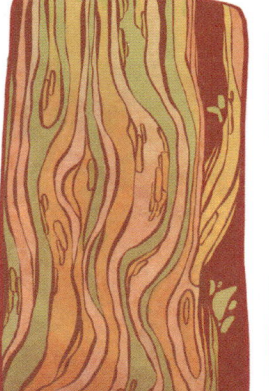

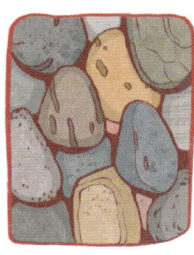

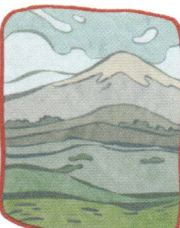

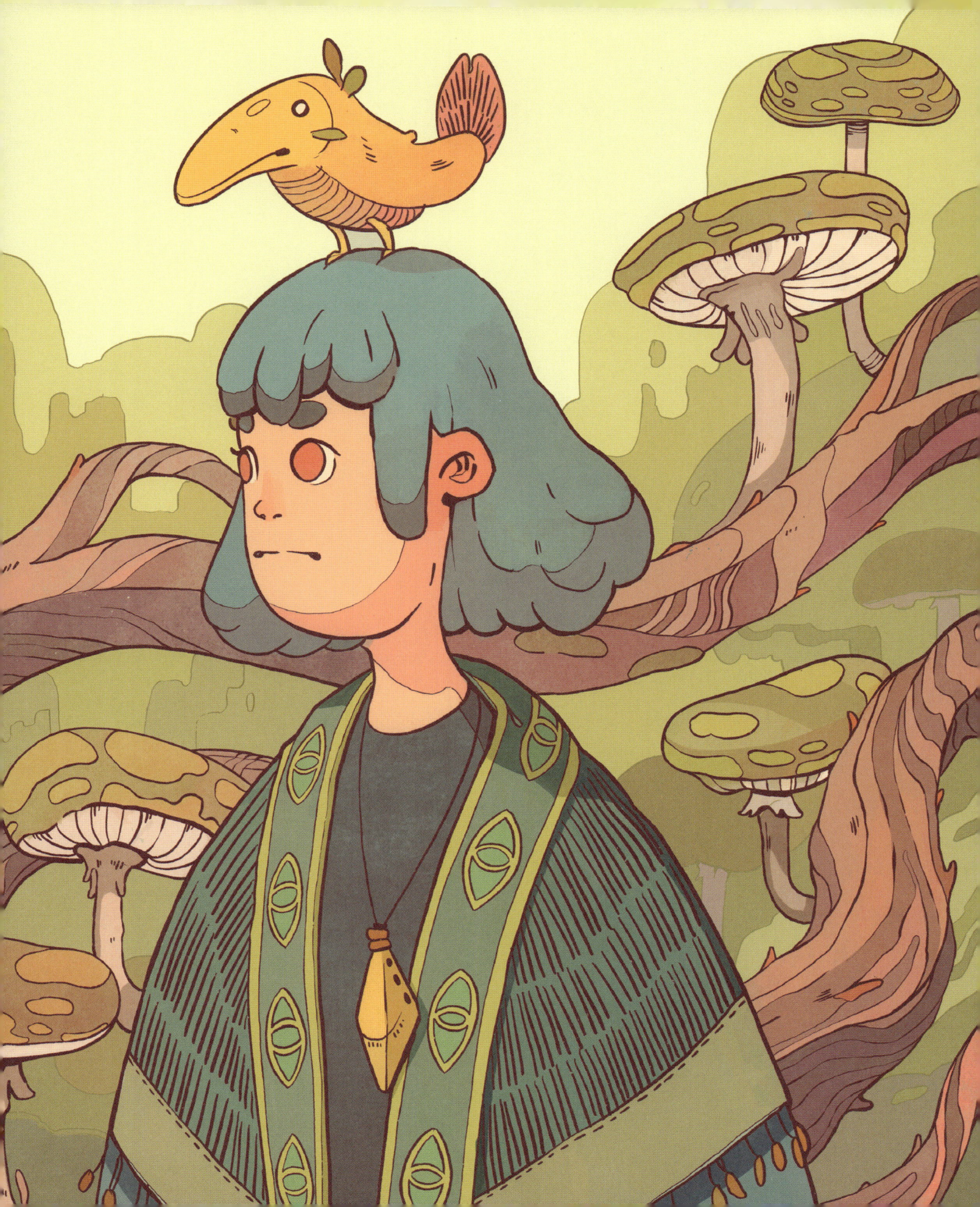

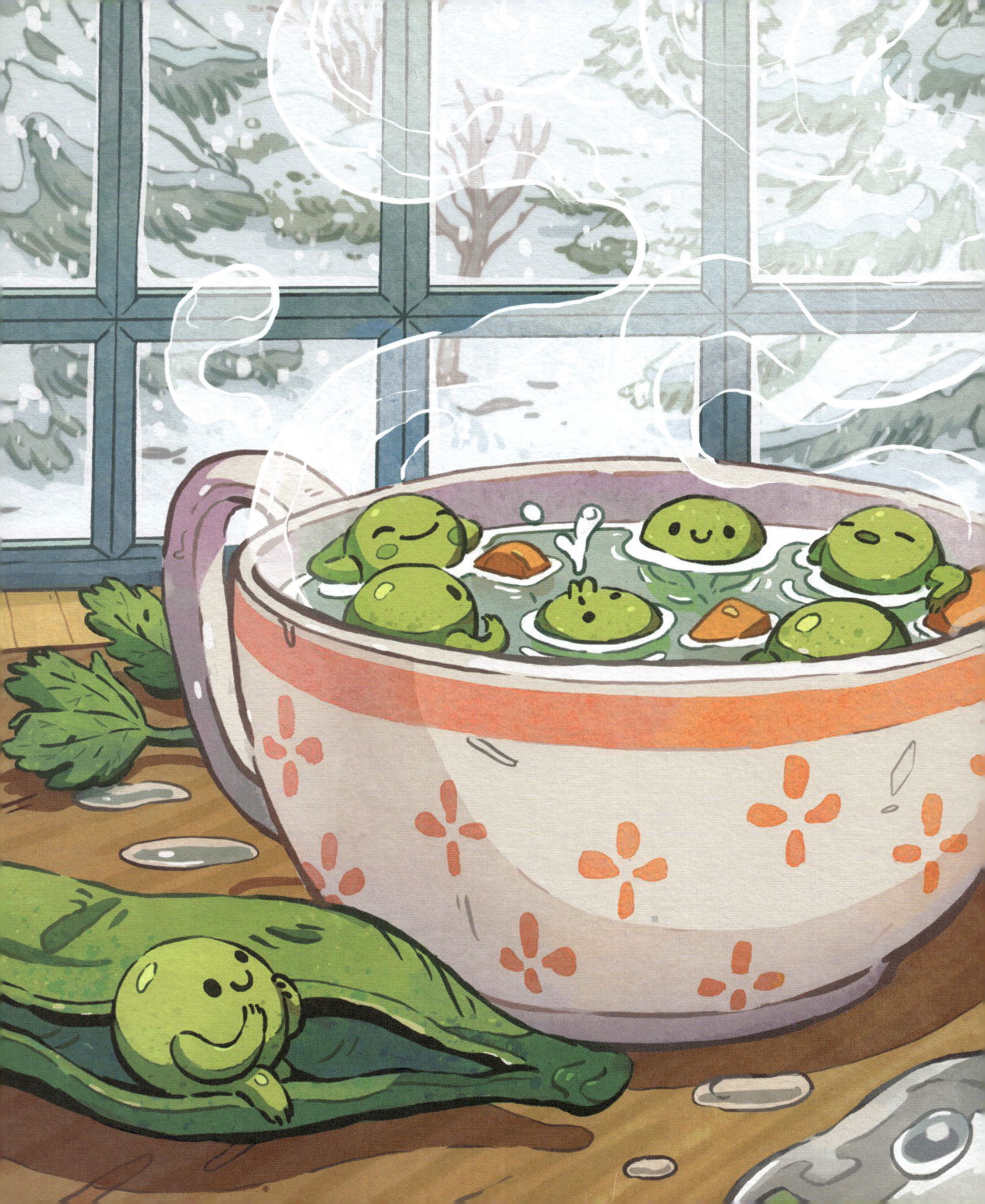

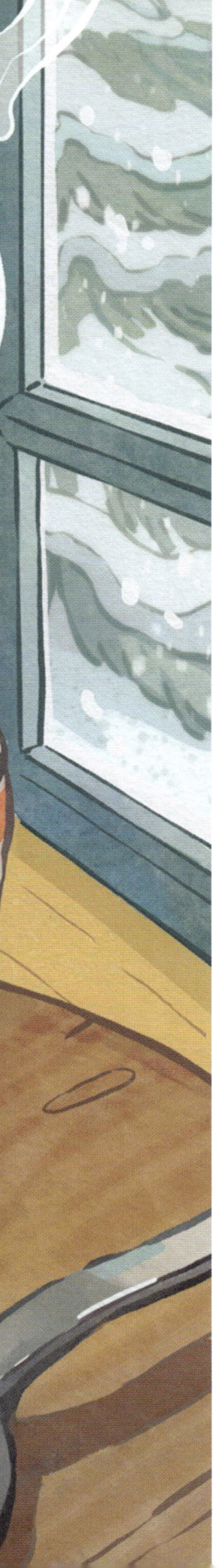

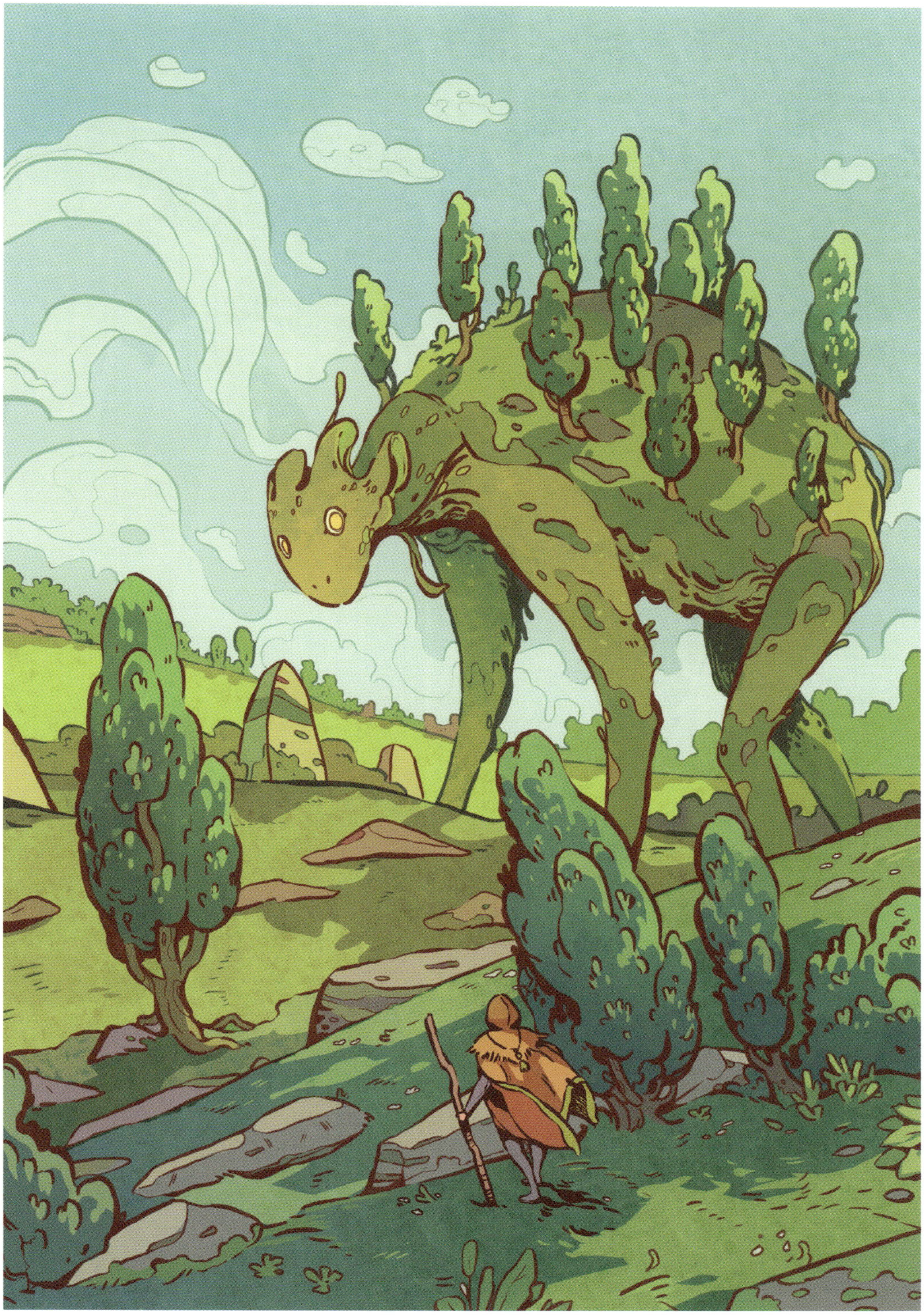

LEFT: *Grunling Peas Spa Time*
The pea Grunlings turn a bowl of soup into a relaxing onsen

ABOVE: *Forest Guardian*
One of my first illustrations in that style. I'm still proud of the composition and overall mood

Johanna Forster

PALM TREE AND MYNA BIRD

BY JANICE SUNG

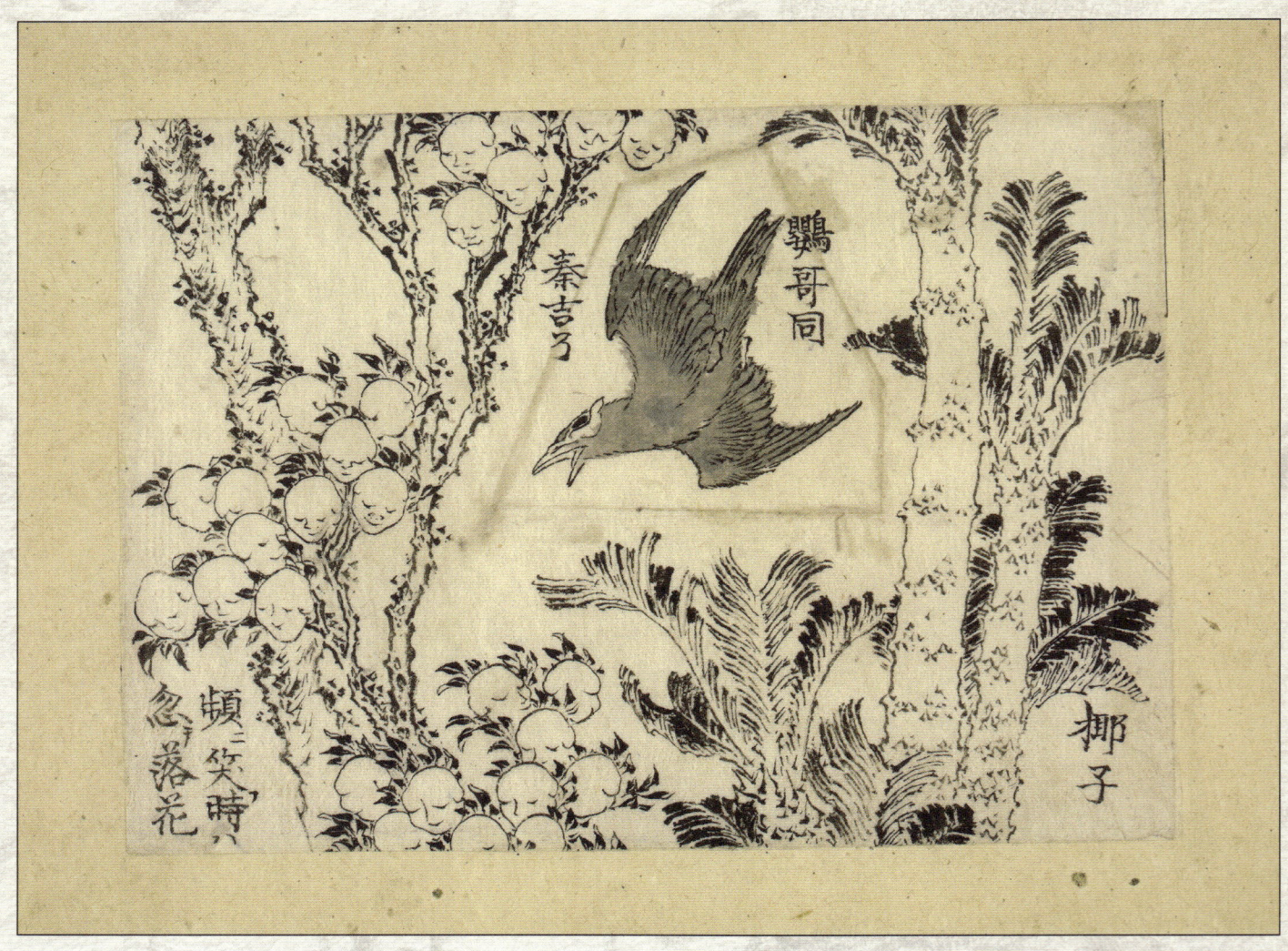

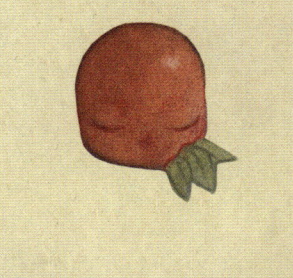

DISCOVERING HOKUSAI

My work often explores recurring themes of flora, fauna, and feminine subjects. My artistic style, though ever-evolving, is often a delicate exploration of emotions and ethereal beauty, blending the human form with elements of nature, such as flowers and animals. Over the years, I've drawn inspiration from a diverse range of artistic influences, including Neoclassical, Baroque, and traditional Chinese and Japanese art. By blending these influences, I strive to create pieces that are both captivating and timeless, working across multiple mediums that include watercolour, gouache, oil, acrylic, and digital tools.

Japan and its culture have always had a huge influence on me. Growing up, I watched a lot of anime and read manga, all of which helped spark my creativity and further deepened my admiration for Japanese artists. Their dedication and creativity continue to amaze me every day. Over the years, some of my greatest artistic influences have included Gustav Klimt, Audrey Kawasaki, Yoshitaka Amano, Ferdinand Keller, and many others. Among them, Hokusai has made a significant impact, not only on me but on the art world as a whole. What stands out most to me about his work is his bold and unconventional use of composition, which creates a sense of dynamism and depth that is truly unique. I'm also drawn to how he captures everyday life in such a beautiful way, especially with his recurring themes of nature that resonate deeply with me. When I come across one of his pieces, I find myself studying it for long stretches, analysing each brushstroke or carved line, and admiring the meticulous care and thought he poured into each detail.

01 INITIAL SKETCH

I start with a simple sketch, focusing on capturing the movement and flow of the bird and branches. Using Hokusai's original as a foundation, I want to stay true to the piece while introducing my own style. For me, this stage is all about finding balance between tradition and my personal interpretation.

ROUGHING OUT A CONCEPT USING HOKUSAI'S ORIGINAL AS A FOUNDATION

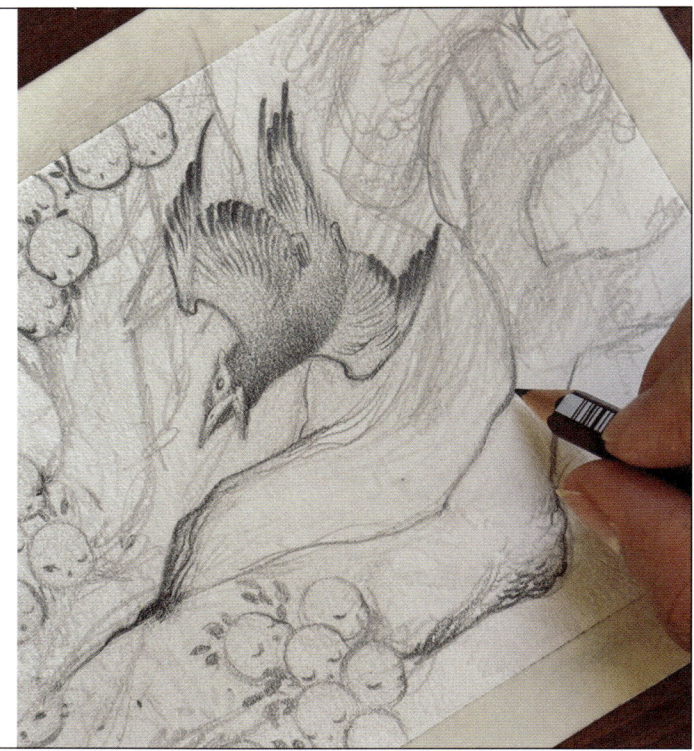

02 REFINING THE COMPOSITION

As I finish the preliminary sketch, I focus on refining the composition and adding details to the bird and branches. I love the fluidity and grace of the bird in the original piece, so I want the tree to follow that same flow. I envision a large tree with branches that twist and weave around each other, enhancing the sense of movement. While adding delicate details, I remain mindful of preserving the simplicity and elegance found in Hokusai's original.

REFINING THE COMPOSITION AND ADDING DETAILS

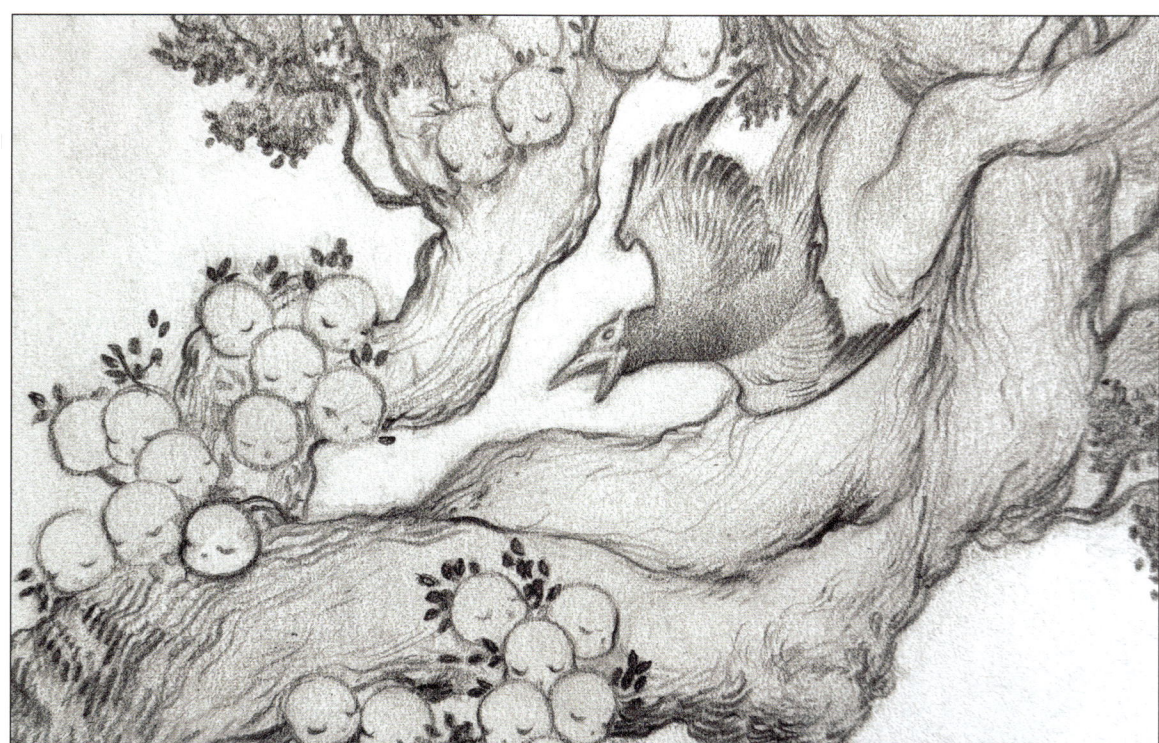

03 FRUIT CONCEPT

What initially drew me to Hokusai's piece were the sleeping fruits. I thought the concept was so fun and unique, and I was excited to put my own spin on it. I decide to take it a step further by giving the fruits more detailed and distinct expressions. Some have their eyes open, while others are peacefully closed, adding a layer of imagination that contrasts with the natural elements around them. It is important to me that the fruits aren't just part of the background, but characters with presence, enhancing the dreamy atmosphere I want to create.

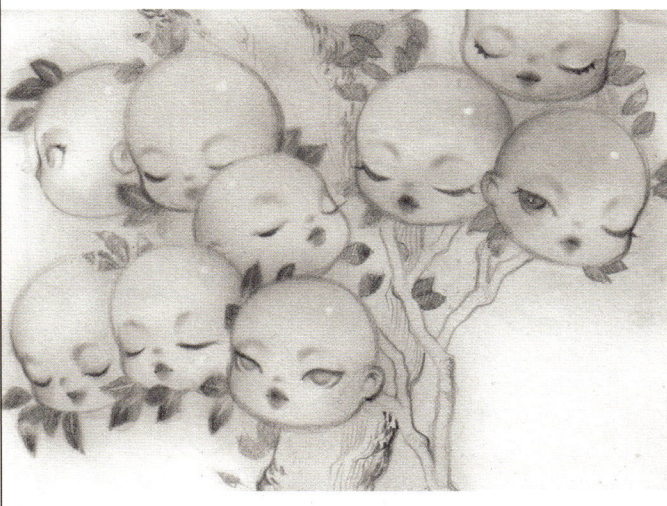

EXPLORING CONCEPTS AND STYLING THE FRUITS

'WHILE ADDING DELICATE DETAILS, I REMAIN MINDFUL OF PRESERVING THE SIMPLICITY AND ELEGANCE FOUND IN HOKUSAI'S ORIGINAL'

04 CHOOSING THE MEDIUM

I'm just about to start painting over the sketch; I decide to go with watercolour for this piece because it lets me build up the colours gradually and create the ethereal, dreamy feel I'm aiming for. I especially love how it adds a sense of softness and transparency. Hokusai often worked with woodblock prints and inks, which have a similar fluidity, so using watercolour feels like a natural way to pay homage to his style.

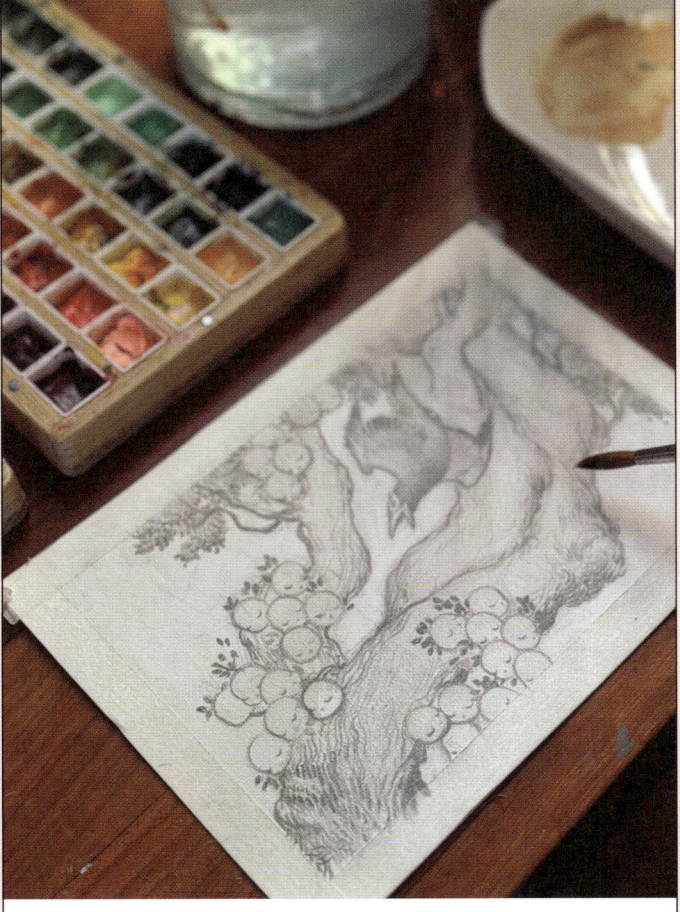

CHOOSING WATERCOLOUR AS THE MEDIUM

Janice Sung

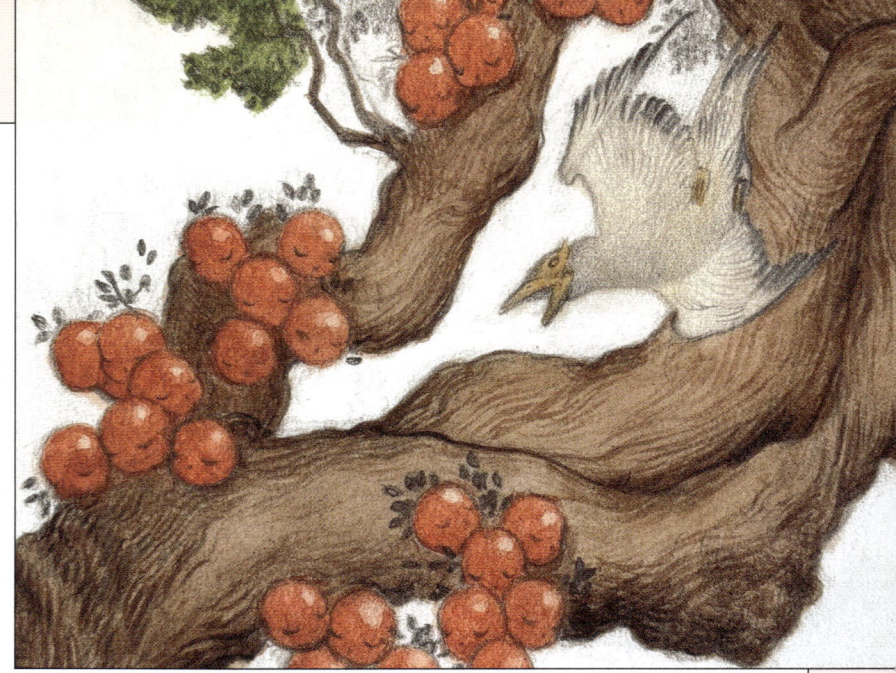

05 CHOOSING COLOURS

I start by painting the fruits and branches. I love Hokusai's colour choices in his paintings, particularly his use of bold complementary colours like blue and red or orange and green. I choose a vibrant red for the fruits and warm brown for the tree. These warmer tones will create a beautiful contrast with the blue sky I plan to add next. The contrast between the warm fruit and the cooler background creates visual balance, allowing each element to complement the other.

CHOOSING COMPLEMENTARY COLOURS TO CREATE A VISUAL CONTRAST

06 FINAL PREPARATION

At this point, the sketch is complete, and all the colours are applied. Now I'm ready to move forwards with the final piece, where I'll redraw this concept on a larger canvas. The sketch is essential in the planning phase, as it ensures that everything comes together exactly as I envision it for the final painting. It's important to get the composition and colours right at this stage so that when I scale up, everything feels balanced and cohesive. It gives me the confidence to bring this idea to life.

FINISHED SKETCH/CONCEPT. GETTING READY TO START THE OFFICIAL PAINTING

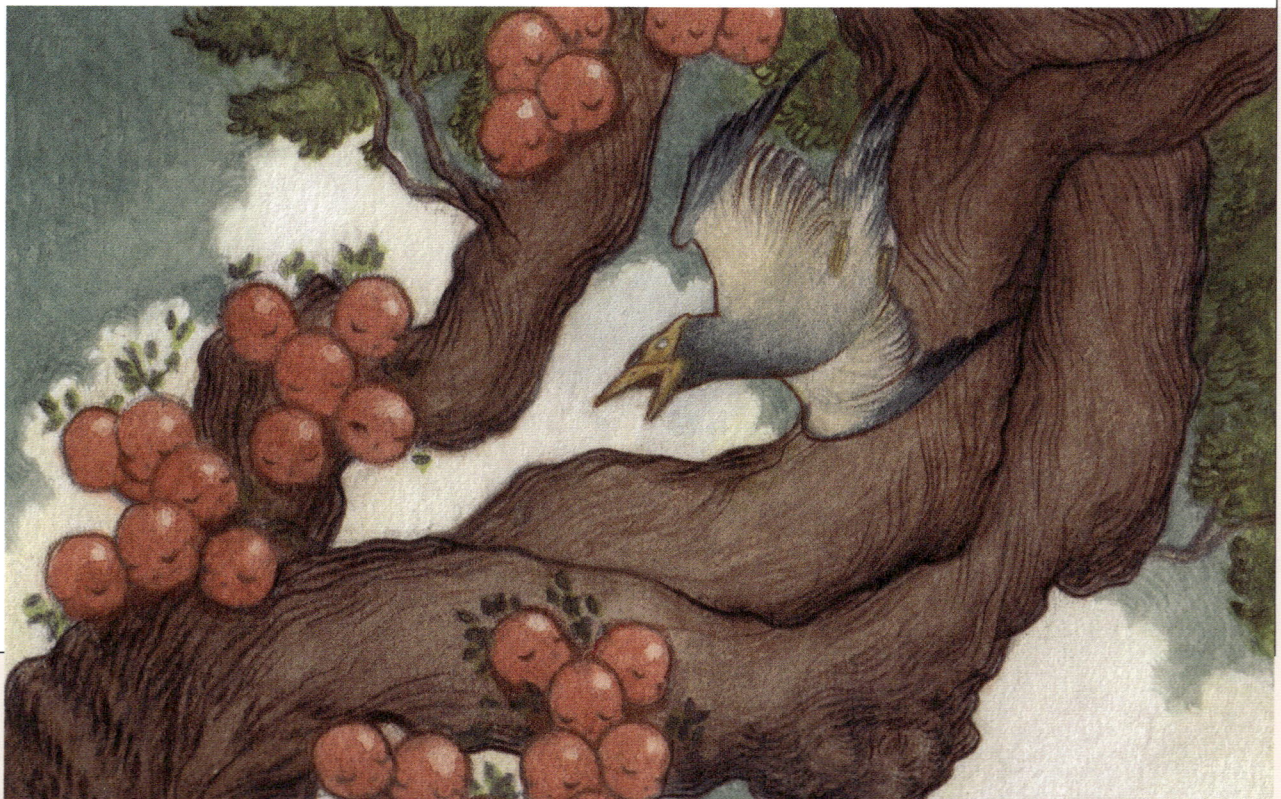

07 SCALING UP

I use the original sketch as a guide to map out the larger version of the piece, which is about four times the size. Scaling up allows me to refine each element, adding more intricate details such as the expressions on the fruit, and making adjustments to areas I was not completely satisfied with in the initial sketch. This process gives me the freedom to explore new ideas while staying true to the original concept. Working from the smaller sketch helps ensure the proportions and overall flow remain intact.

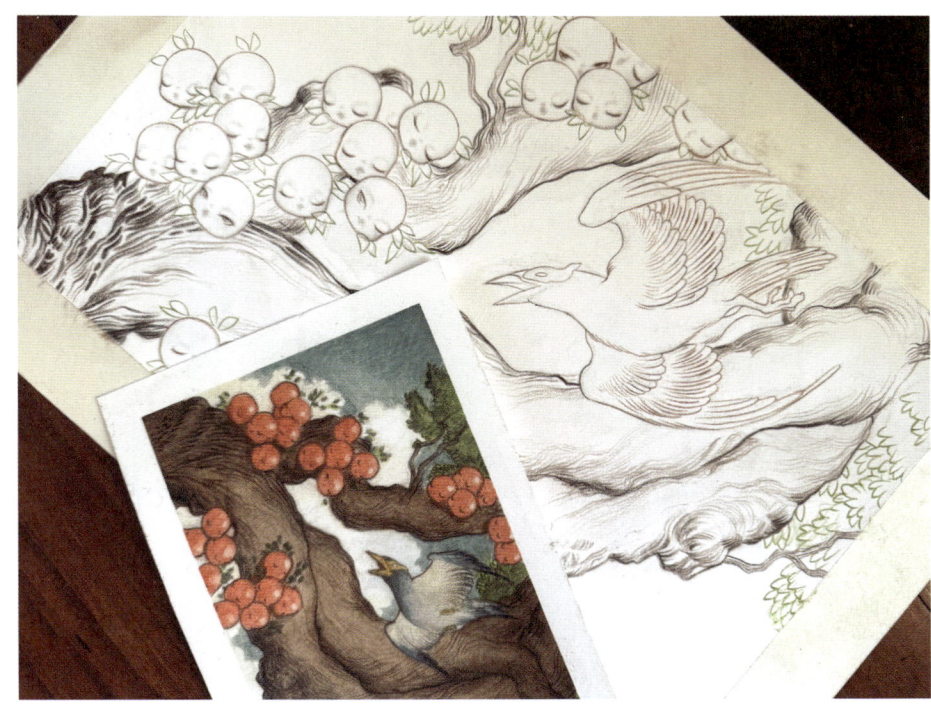

USING MY SKETCH AS REFERENCE, I SCALE UP THE PAINTING TO A LARGER CANVAS

08 REFINING THE LINE WORK

Keeping the line work clean and precise is absolutely essential, as I want to stay true to Hokusai's work. This phase is likely the most time-consuming and meticulous. I'm choosing to use coloured pencils for the line work to preserve that traditional feel, while giving the piece a soft, subtle texture. The pencils also allow me to layer watercolour over them without disrupting the lines.

REFINING THE LINE WORK, ENSURING THAT IT IS CLEAN AND PRECISE

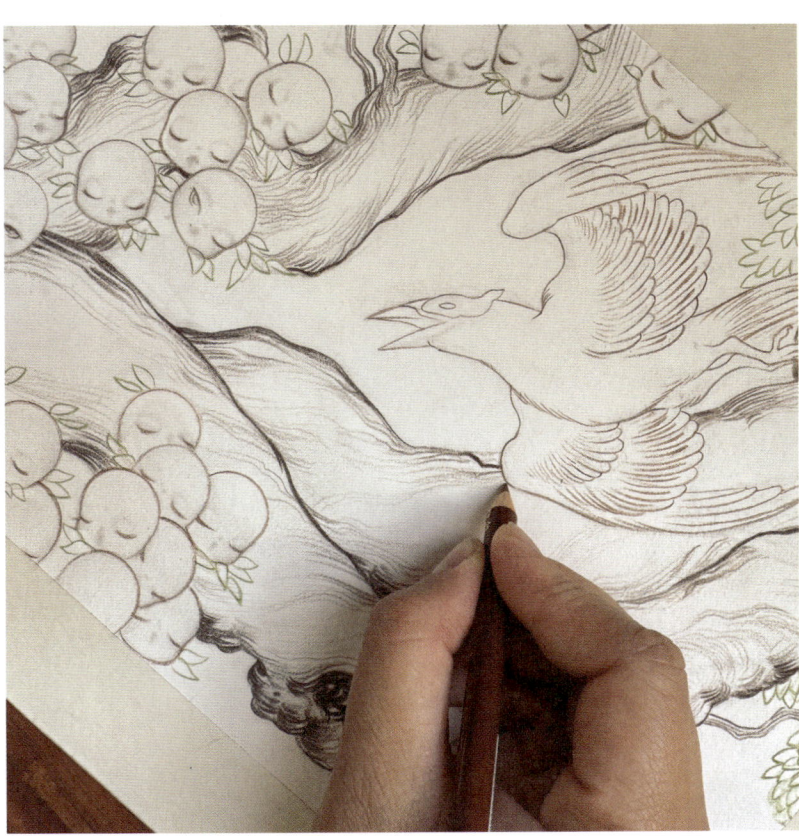

Janice Sung

09 DETAILING THE FRUITS & BRANCHES

The fruits in this piece are inspired by modern Japanese vinyl toys with anime-like faces, adding a subtle yet playful element. I want them to feel cute and light-hearted. The tree, on the other hand, is influenced by various Hokusai works and other manga artists. I aim to strike a balance between being detailed and minimal. Ultimately, I want to create a harmonious blend of traditional and modern influences.

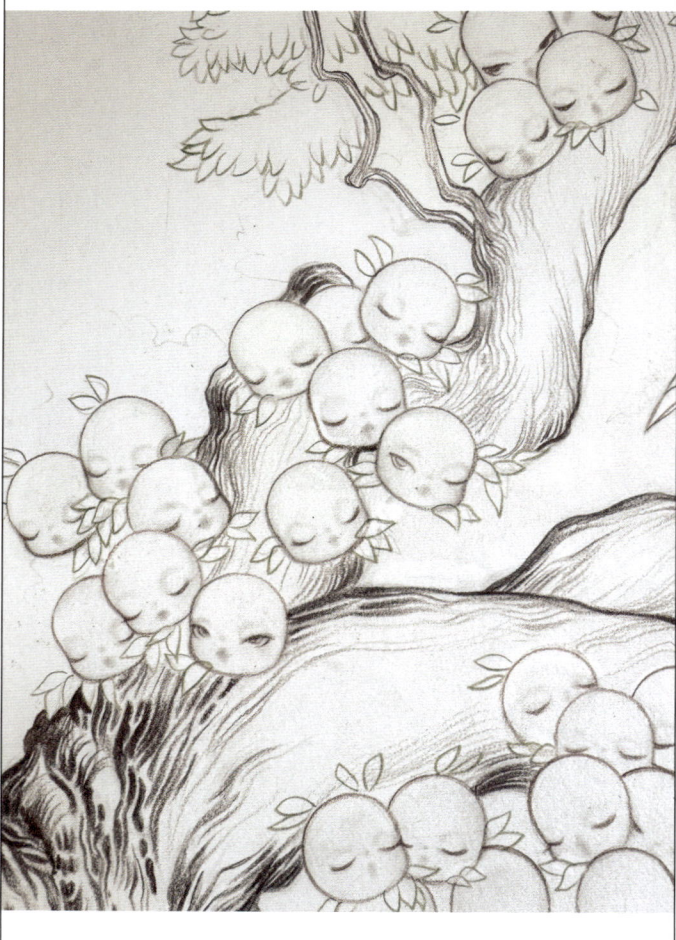

DETAILING THE FRUITS AND BRANCHES WITH JAPANESE INFLUENCES

10 SETTING THE TONE

I paint the fruits first. For me, starting with the fruits helps set the tone for the overall colour palette and mood of the piece. The bright red serves as the focal point, so I want to ensure they are established right from the start. By focusing on them early in the process, I can build the rest of the composition around them.

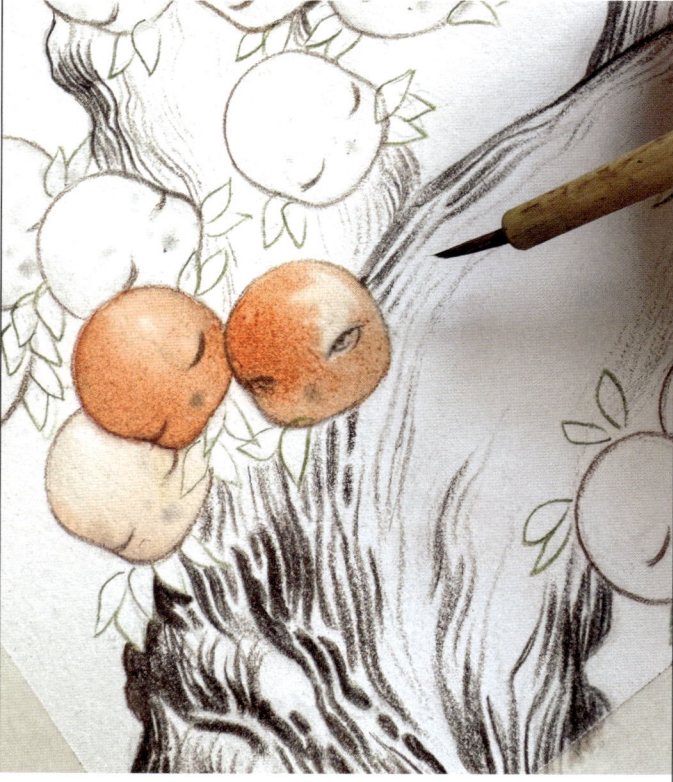

SETTING THE TONE BY PAINTING THE FRUITS FIRST

11 LAYERING PAINT

Next, I move on to painting the branches. When working with watercolour, I prefer to begin with very diluted pigments, gradually building up layers to create depth. This approach not only adds dimension but also subtle transparency, something I've always admired in Hokusai's work.

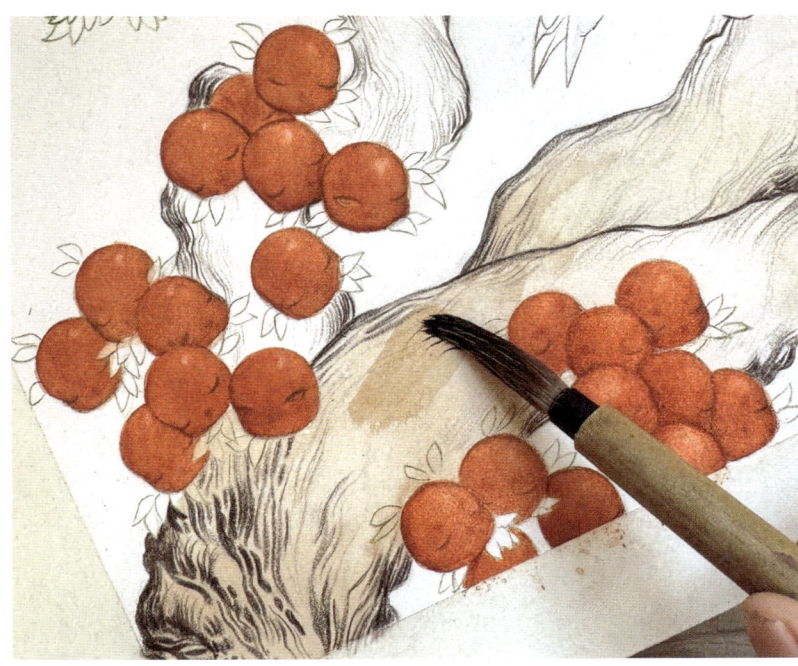

LAYERING PAINT TO ACHIEVE DEPTH AND SUBTLE TRANSPARENCY

12 SUBTLE DETAILS & TEXTURE

I use very small, deliberate strokes when building up the texture of the tree. Though they may seem subtle, these strokes are what really bring the tree to life. Each layer adds more form, depth, and dimension.

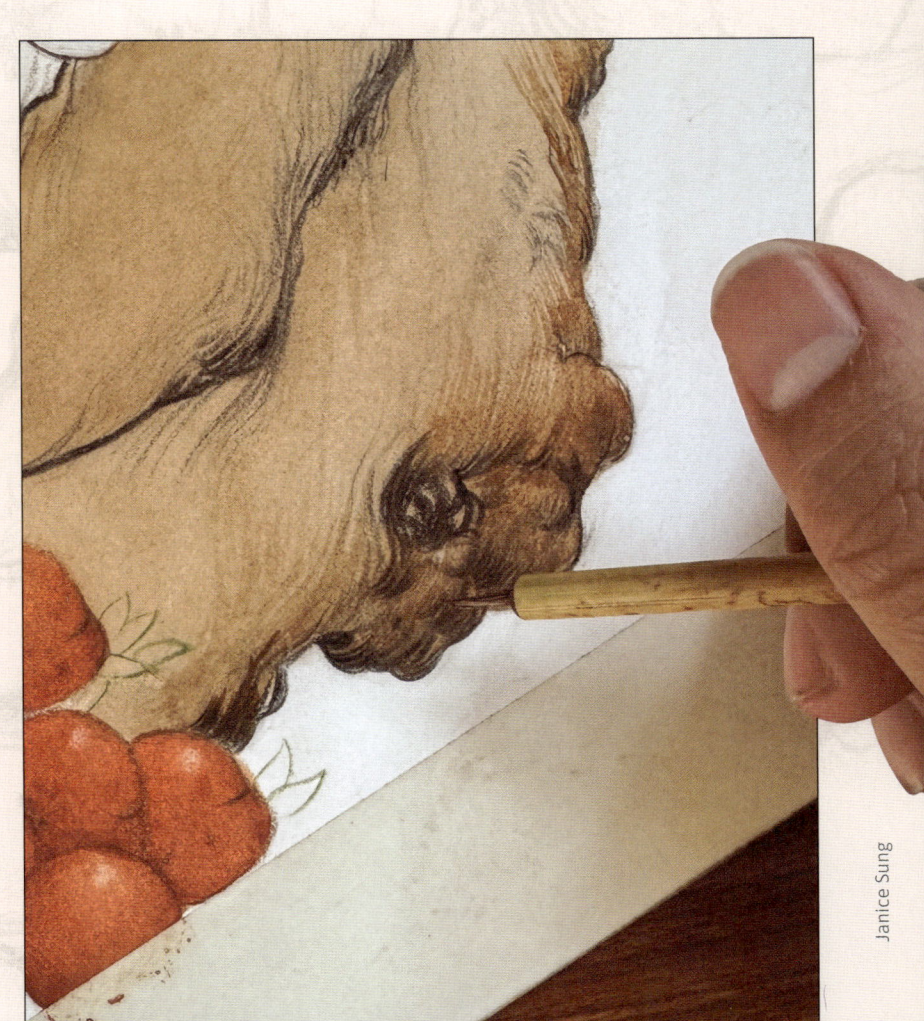

BUILDING TEXTURE WITH SMALL DELIBERATE STROKES

Janice Sung

13 ENHANCING DETAILS

Although most of the line work is done with coloured pencils, I want the texture and details within the tree to feel more delicate and refined. To achieve this, I use a thin brush with a more concentrated pigment. This technique allows me to create even finer lines and add greater detail, especially in areas where the coloured pencil wasn't quite as precise. This combination of coloured pencil and brushwork gives me the flexibility to emphasize different elements while maintaining the softness I want throughout the piece.

ENHANCING THE LINE
WORK WITH BRUSHES

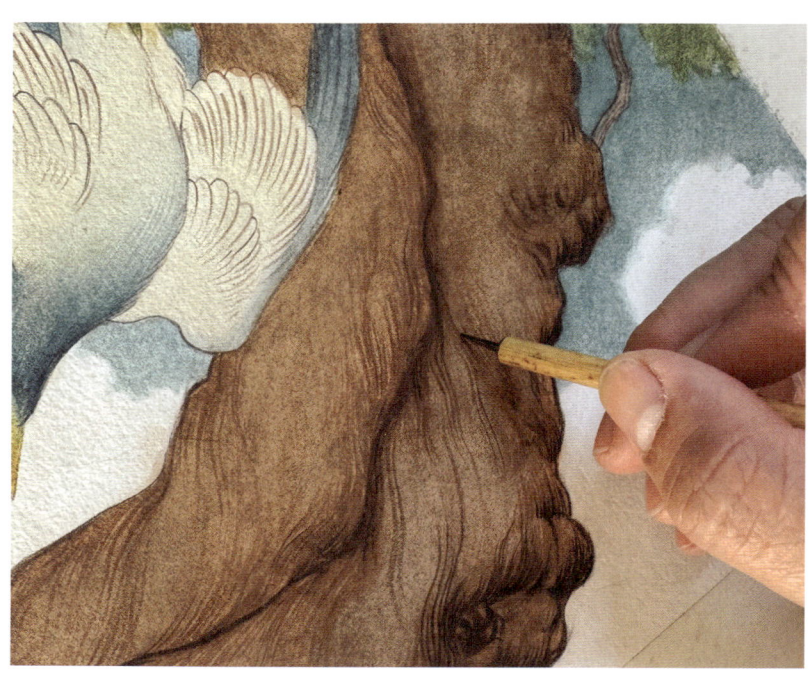

14 REFINING THE LINE WORK

For the final step, I go over all the line work with coloured pencils again to further define and sharpen the details. This process is especially important because the line work is often the focal point in Hokusai's work. This not only adds clarity, but also helps to clean up the entire piece, giving it a more polished and cohesive look.

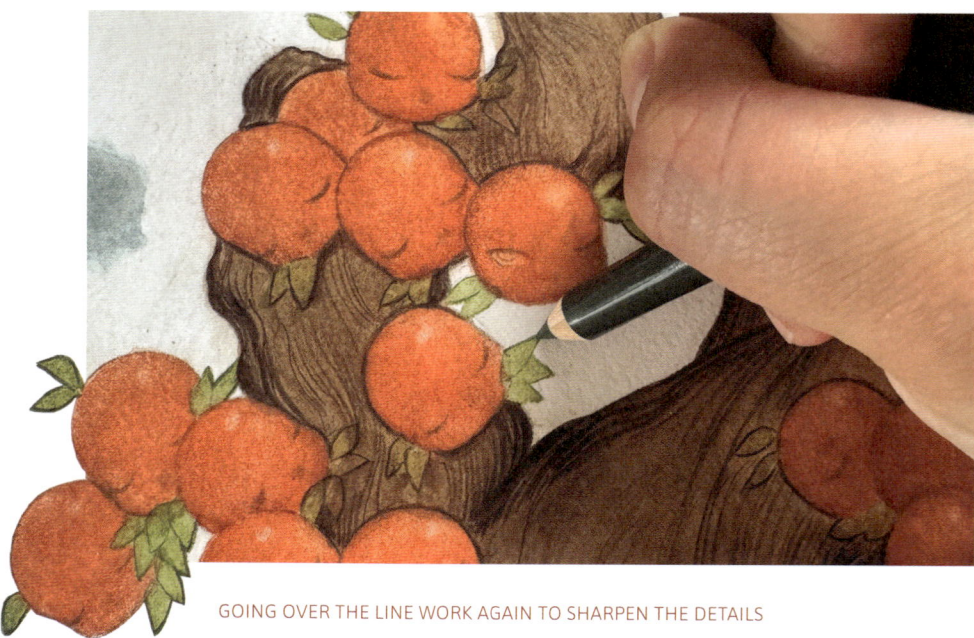

GOING OVER THE LINE WORK AGAIN TO SHARPEN THE DETAILS

15 FINAL TOUCHES

With the painting finished, I scan it into Photoshop to add a few final touches. I want to give the piece the feel of a vintage print, so I'm adding a subtle glow and vignette around the edges to provide a sense of nostalgia. These small adjustments really help tie everything together and give the artwork a soft, aged appearance.

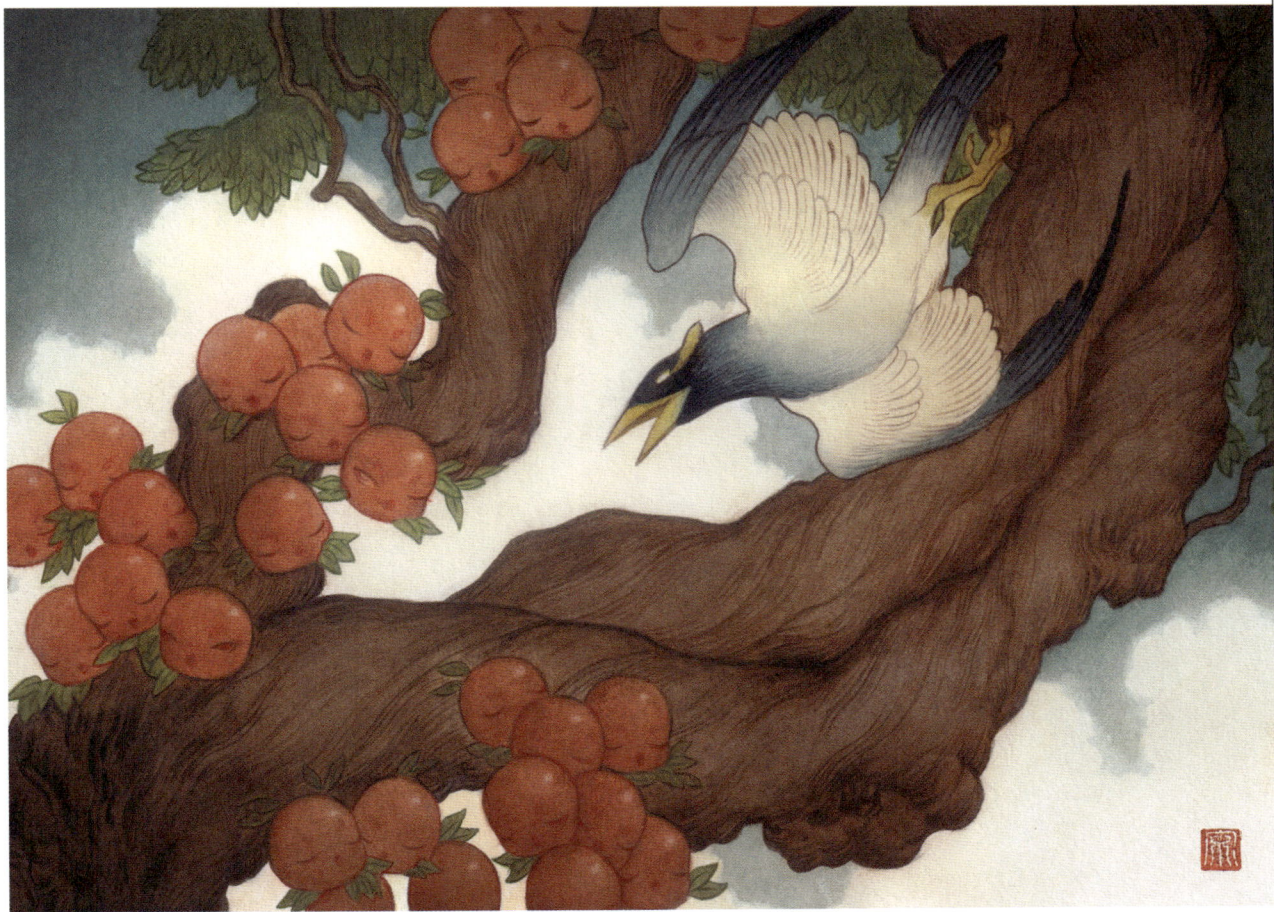

ADDING FINAL TOUCHES TO GIVE A NOSTALGIC, VINTAGE FEEL

CONCLUSION

Creating this piece was an incredibly rewarding experience, as it allowed me to merge my personal artistic style with a heartfelt tribute to Hokusai. The process of interpreting his iconic style while weaving in my own creative vision was both challenging and deeply inspiring. Each step – from the initial sketch to the final brushstroke – felt like a journey that bridged his world and mine, offering me the chance to explore new artistic possibilities. I hope this comes through in the final piece, as it serves as a deeper expression of my love for art and storytelling, and of course, my admiration for Hokusai's enduring legacy.

Janice Sung

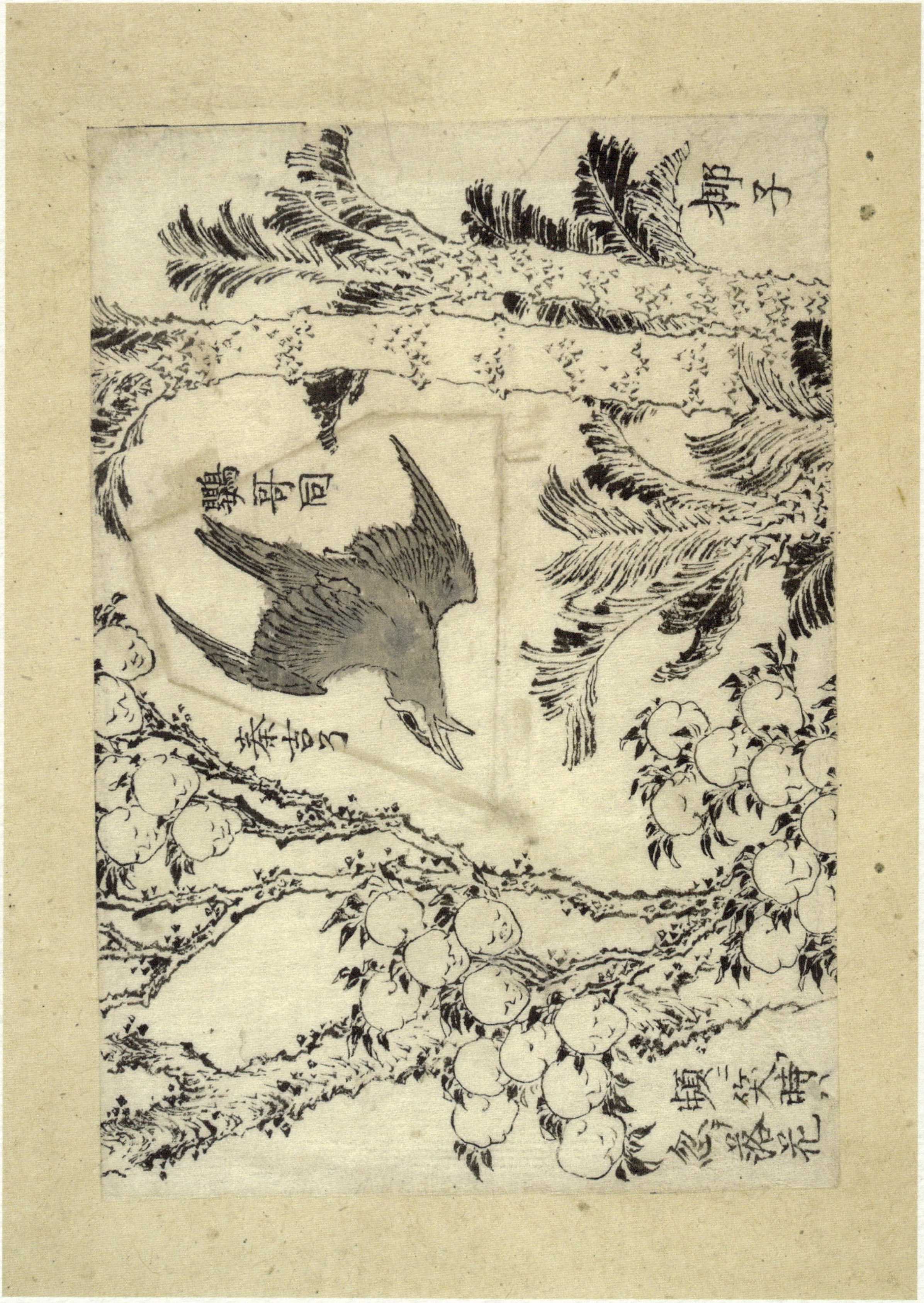

PALM TREE AND MYNA BIRD

JANICE SUNG

Janice Sung

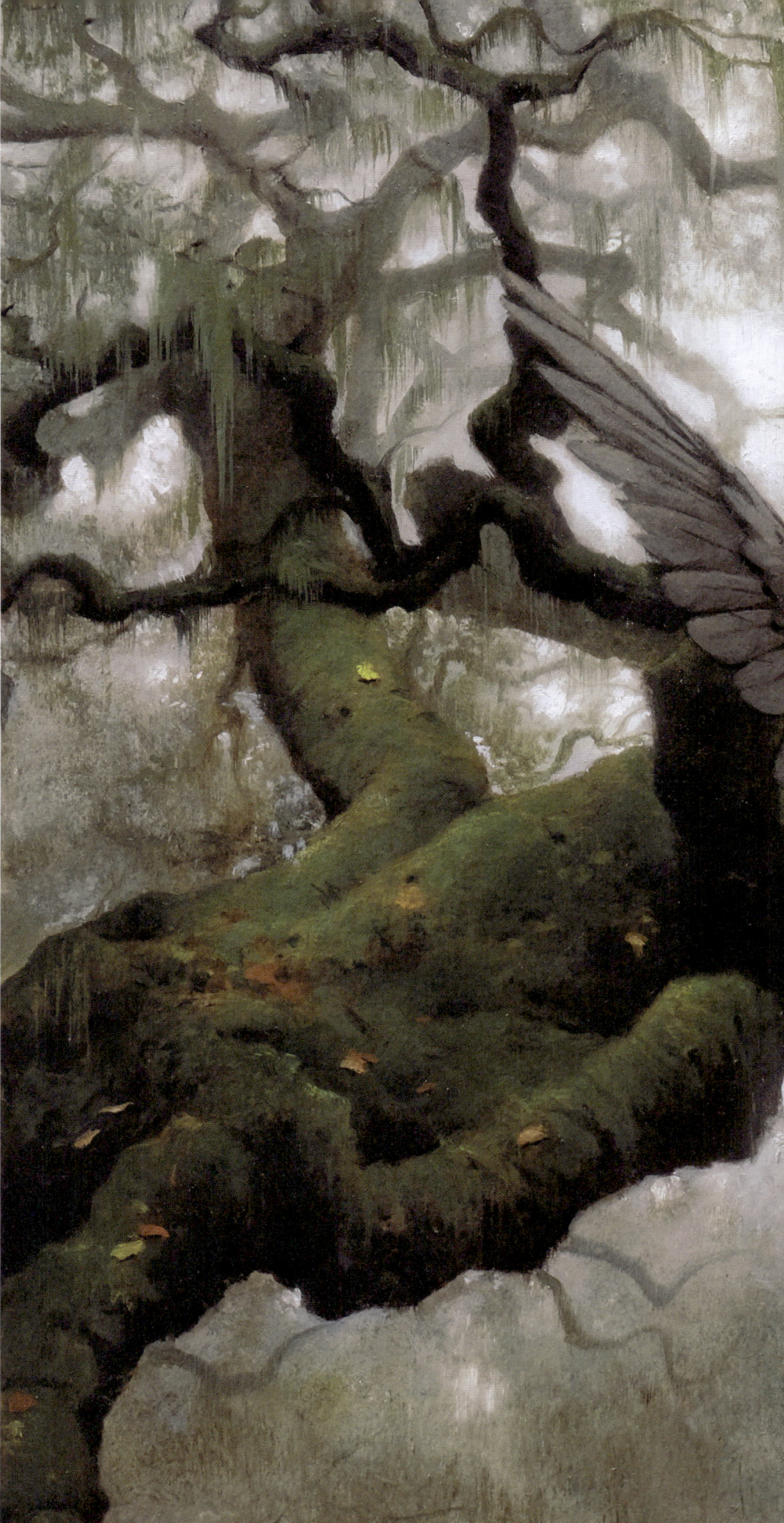

GALLERY: JANICE SUNG

Raventhorn Forest
Oil on paper

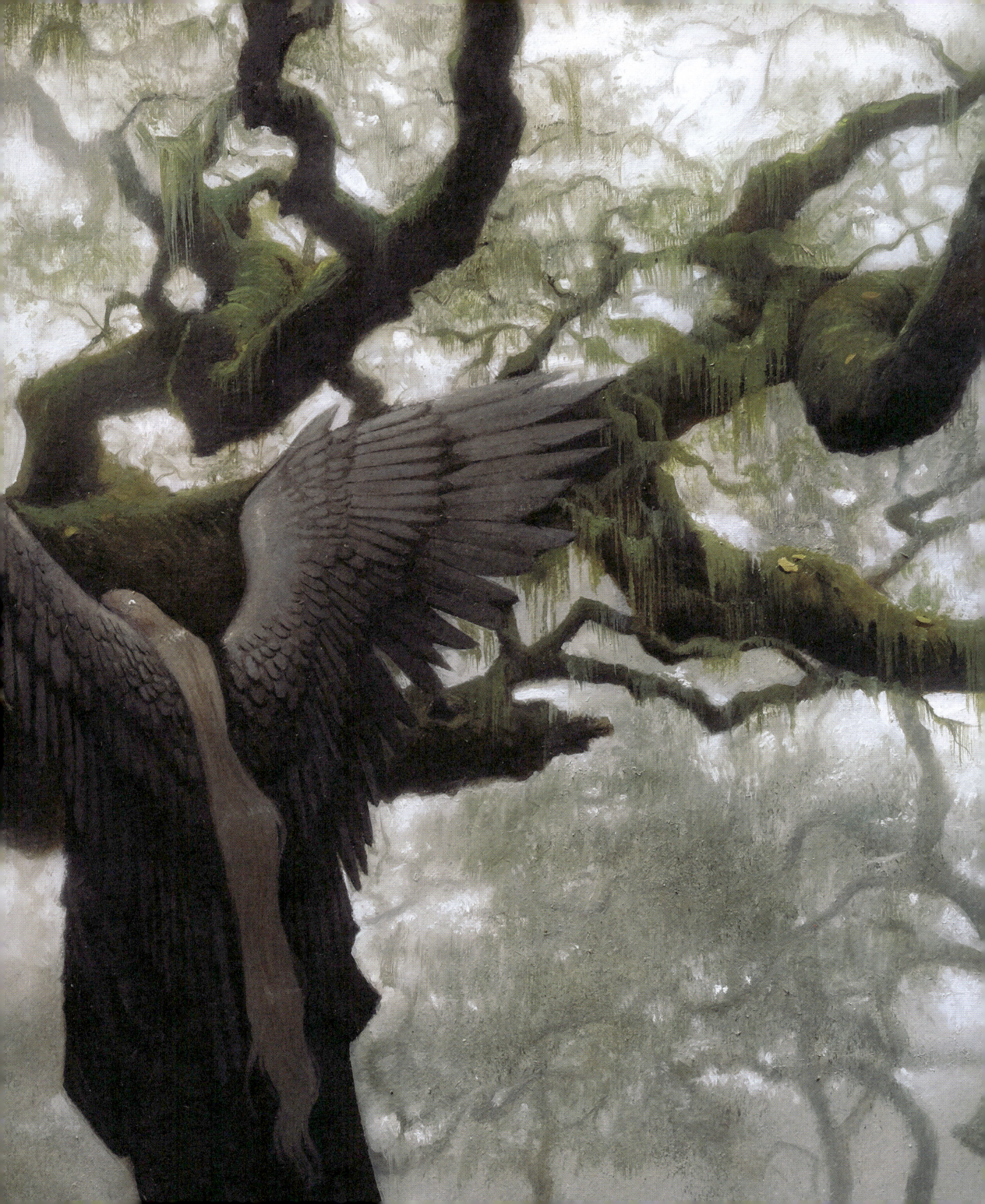

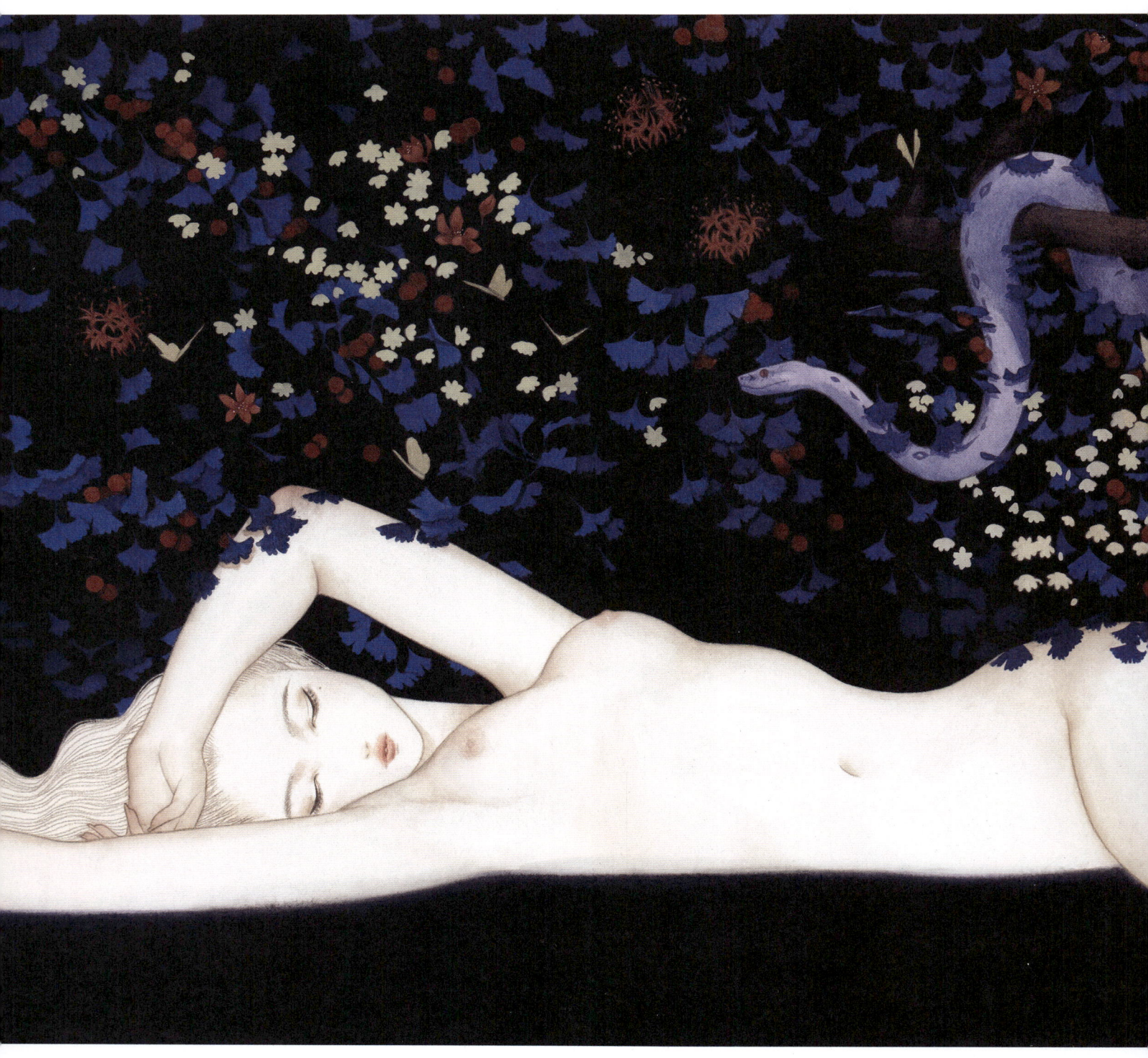

ABOVE: *Pandora*
Watercolour and
gouache on paper

RIGHT: *Morning Glory*
Oil on paper

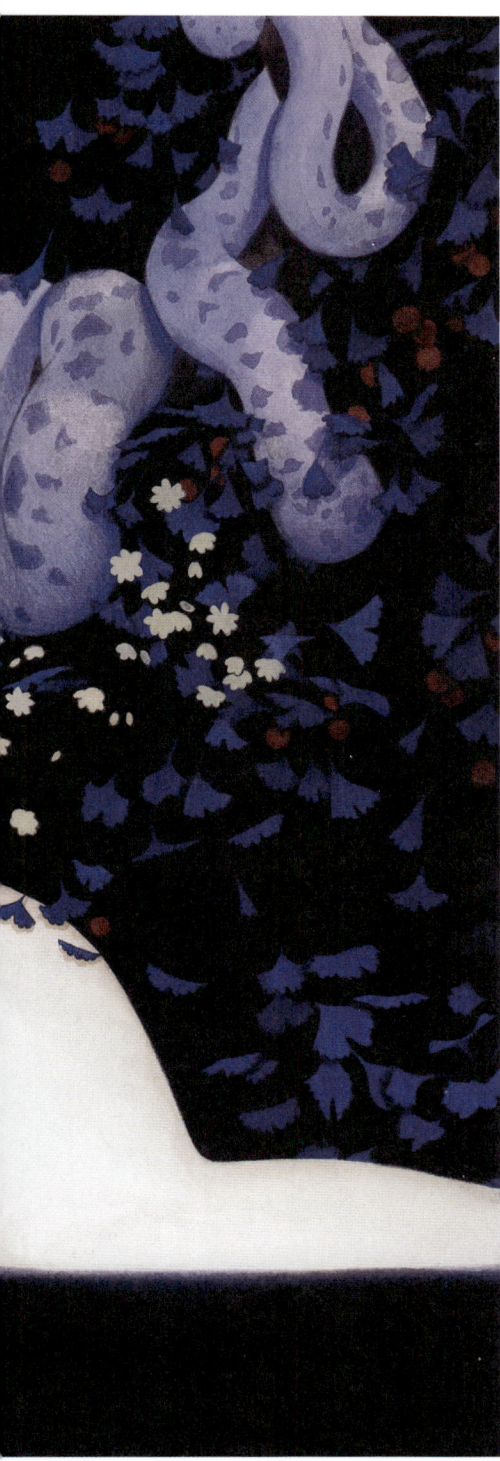

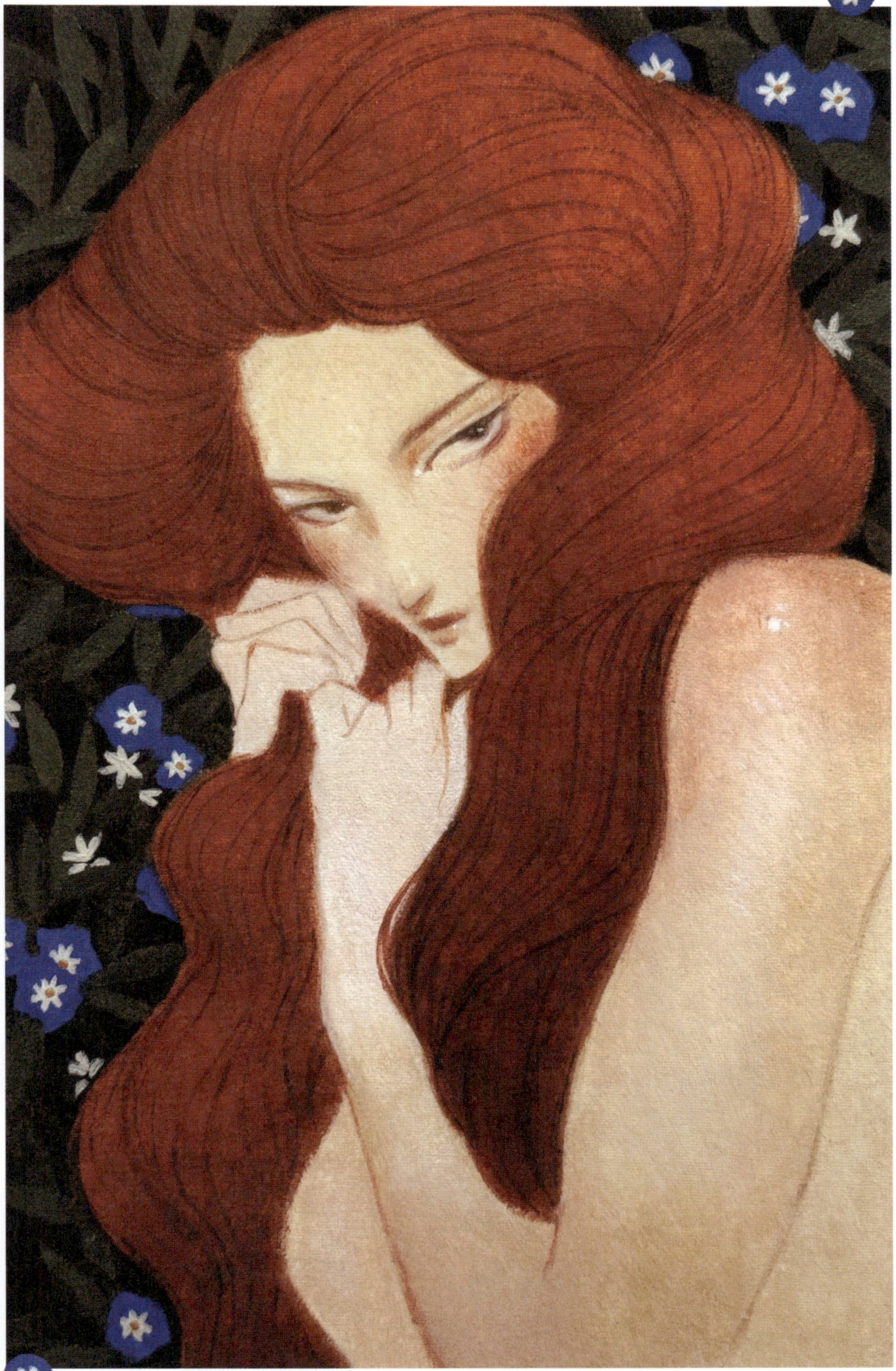

NEXT PAGE: *Cascade of Solace*
Watercolour on paper

Janice Sung

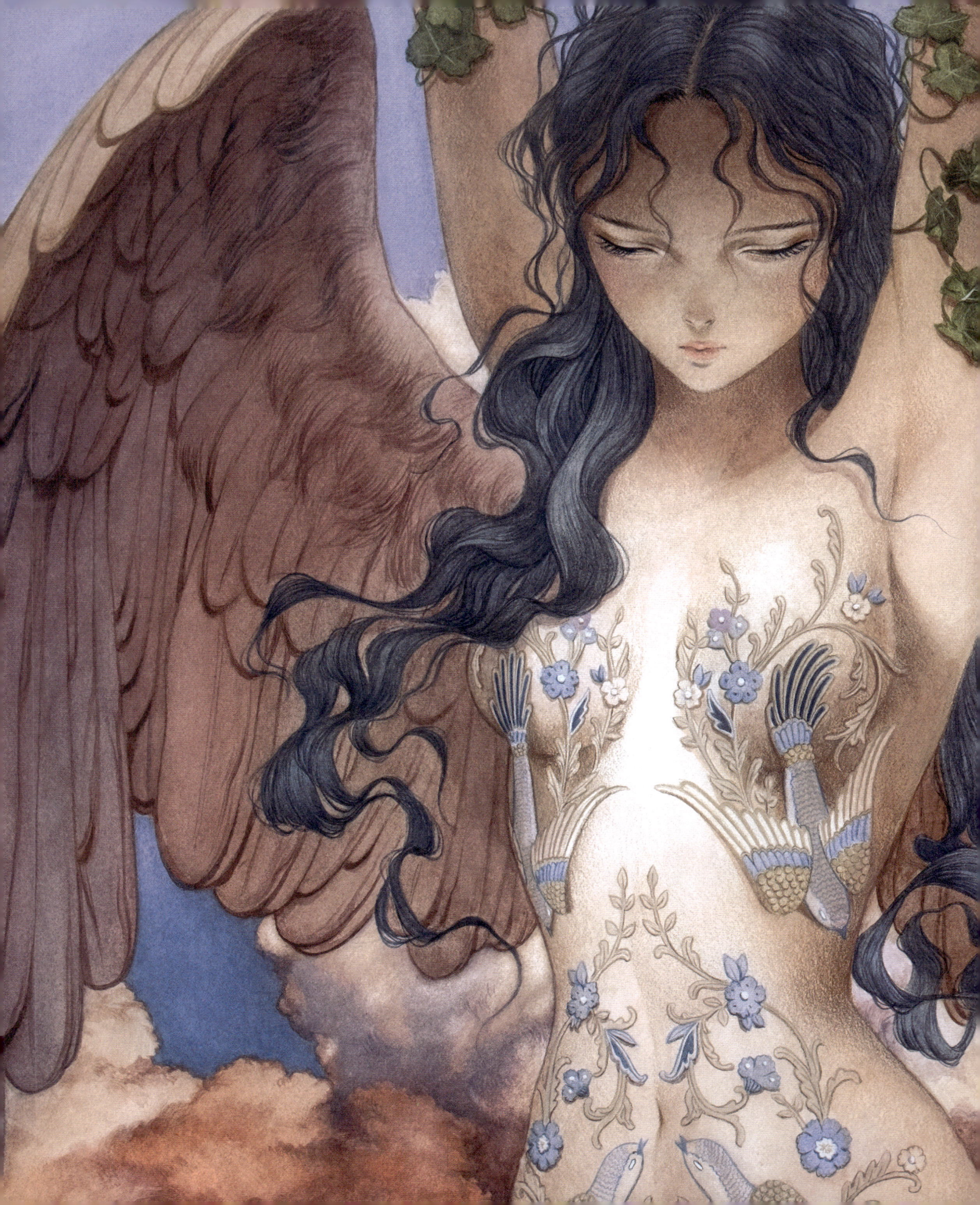

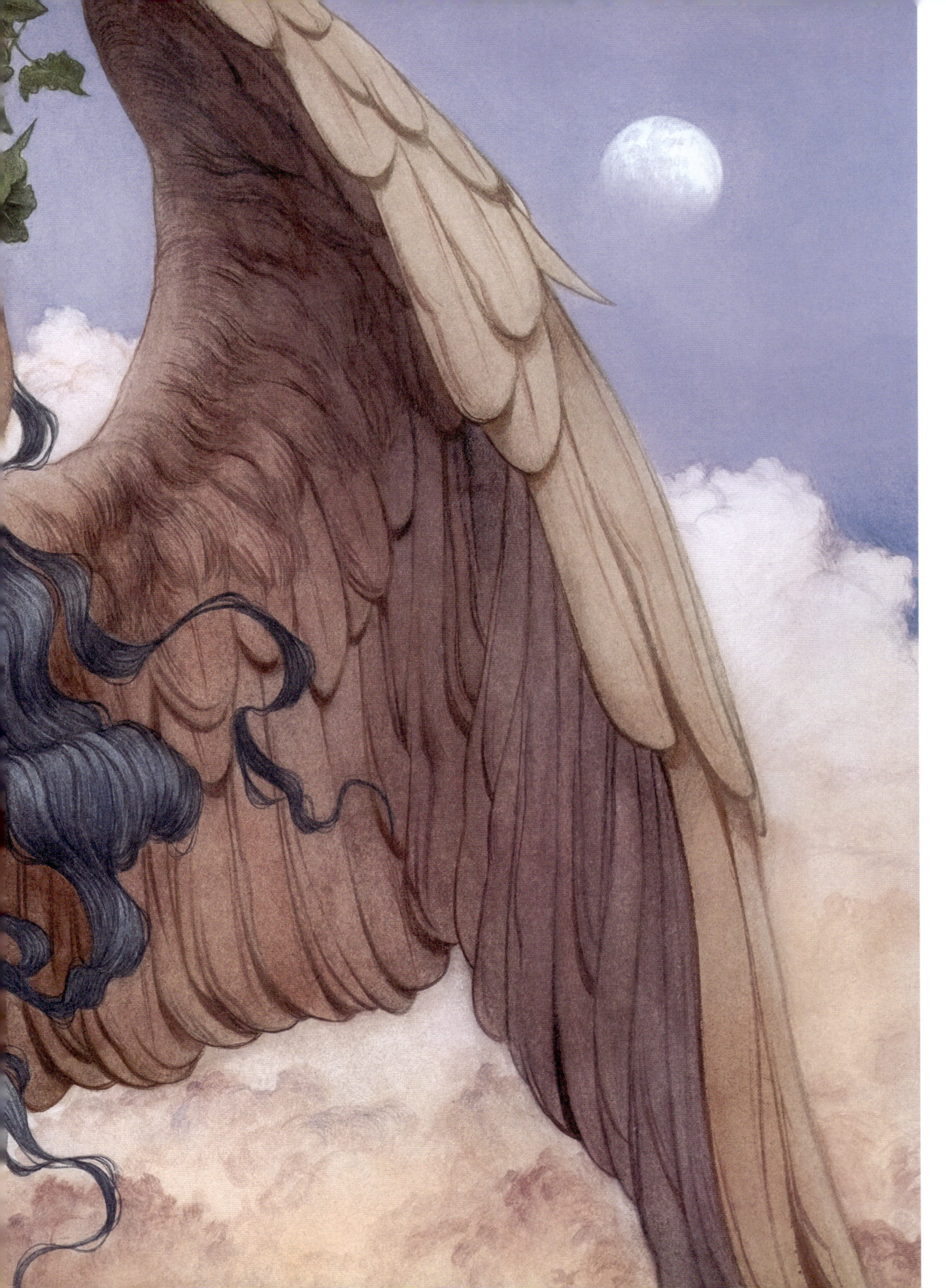

Janice Sung

DEVADATTA SURROUNDED BY EVIL SPIRITS

BY MONA FINDEN

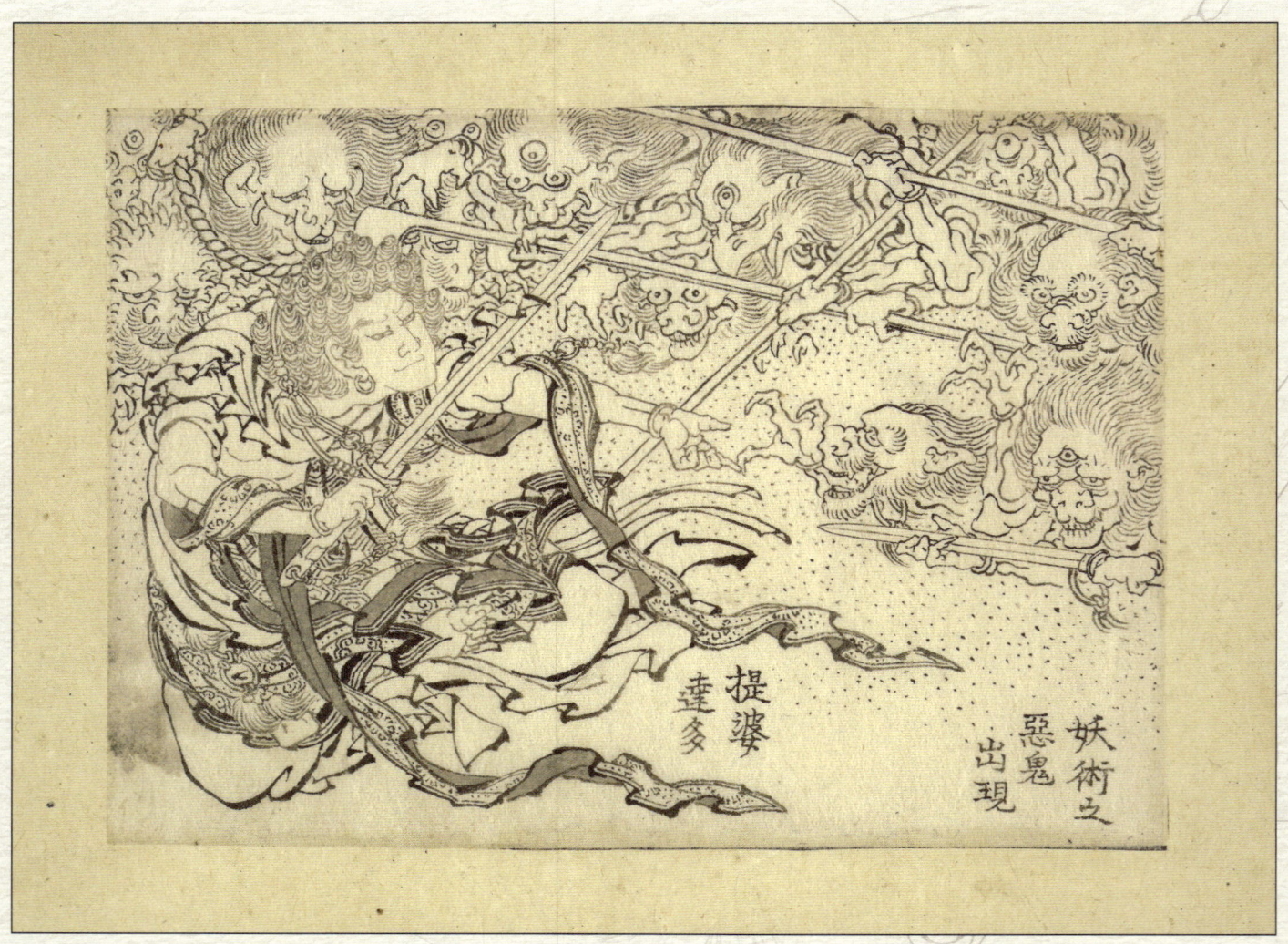

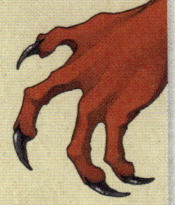

DISCOVERING HOKUSAI

In my work, I like to explore fantasy themes and myths through an emotional lens. A lot of focus goes into my line art, and I often use patterns, animals, and floral shapes to add symbolism or motion to a piece. More often than not, my artwork ends up embracing some level of melancholy or nostalgia.

For a while now, Hokusai has had a direct impact on my style and what I draw in general, especially since I started drawing heavy inspiration from ukiyo-e art, particularly woodblock prints. I really like how his work is both graphical and impressionistic, but specifically, it's the detailed line work that really resonates with me. I feel the same about modern artists who I'm also influenced by: James Jean, Akihiko Yoshida, and Yoshitaka Amano, to name a few. All of them make art with beautiful line work, and I can't articulate the exact reason why, but it always feels familiar and brings me joy.

Mona Finden

01 THUMBNAILS

My thumbnails are usually pretty rough – just a loose idea to warm up the brain. For this illustration, I want to keep things relatively close to the original, but with more of a focus on Devadatta and his wickedness.

The first thumbnail deviates most from the original composition, but puts Devadatta in the centre. The second is the closest to the original; his body language is more active and reaching. In the third thumbnail, he is falling back while reaching out to the spirits.

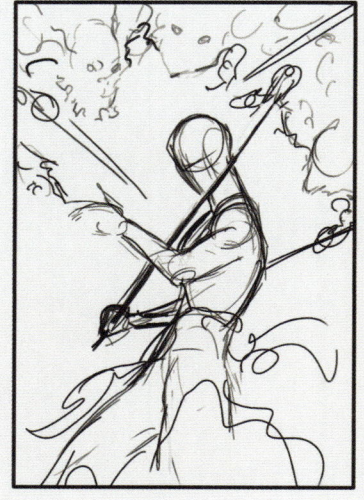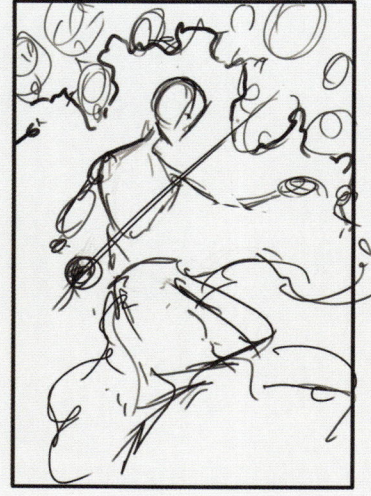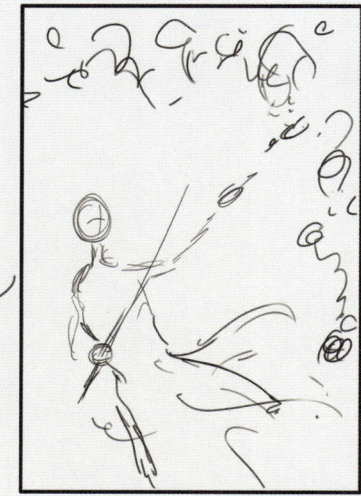

THREE ROUGH
THUMBNAILS
TO START

02 EARLY ROUGH SKETCH

I decide to go with the first thumbnail as I want to keep the focus on Devadatta. Since this scene is about the main character calling forth evil spirits to kill Buddha (who – fun fact – is also his cousin), I want to add a sense of inner turmoil, simultaneously showing his hesitation and determination.

At first, I'm a little uncertain about how much I want to push the piece in either direction. Is he smiling? Does he look scared? I try to work out the feel of the character before I put any focus on anatomy and pose. The composition is still not there yet. Right now, it's just about the character.

DEVELOPING THE
EMOTIONAL ASPECT
OF THE CHARACTER

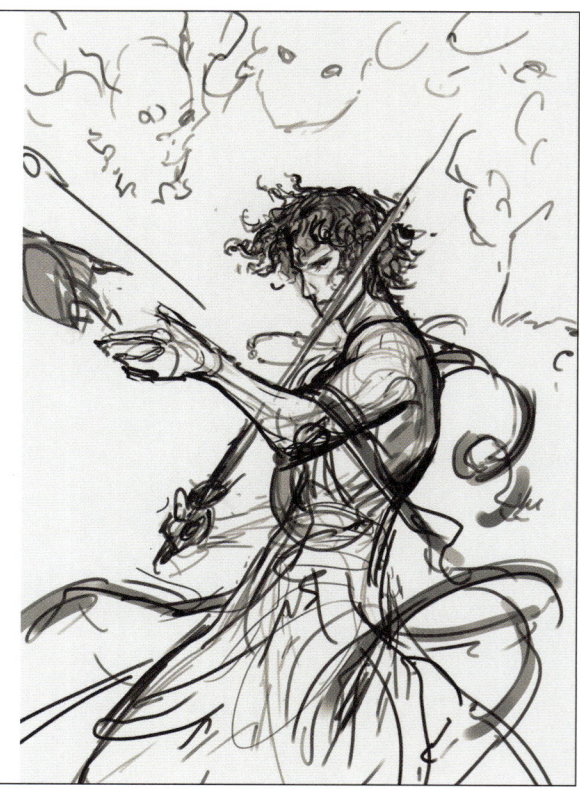

03 ROUGH SKETCH

I move back and forth quite a bit between the character and his surroundings until I have a solid composition. I choose to keep his face as the focal point, and even though it's partially overlapped by his sword, it's also framed by two other swords. These are elements from Hokusai's depiction and one particular detail I really liked.

I do everything I can to make sure that direct and indirect elements lead to the focal point. These include weapons, the spirits' gazes, and the flowing fabric, though I make sure it's not too obvious by breaking the lines with other details. I also fill in areas to get a better understanding of how the piece will eventually look and if the silhouettes look good together. This part of the process is very much trial and error, so I keep moulding it until it looks decent enough to move forwards. I don't include every little detail, but enough of them to get an idea about each section in the illustration.

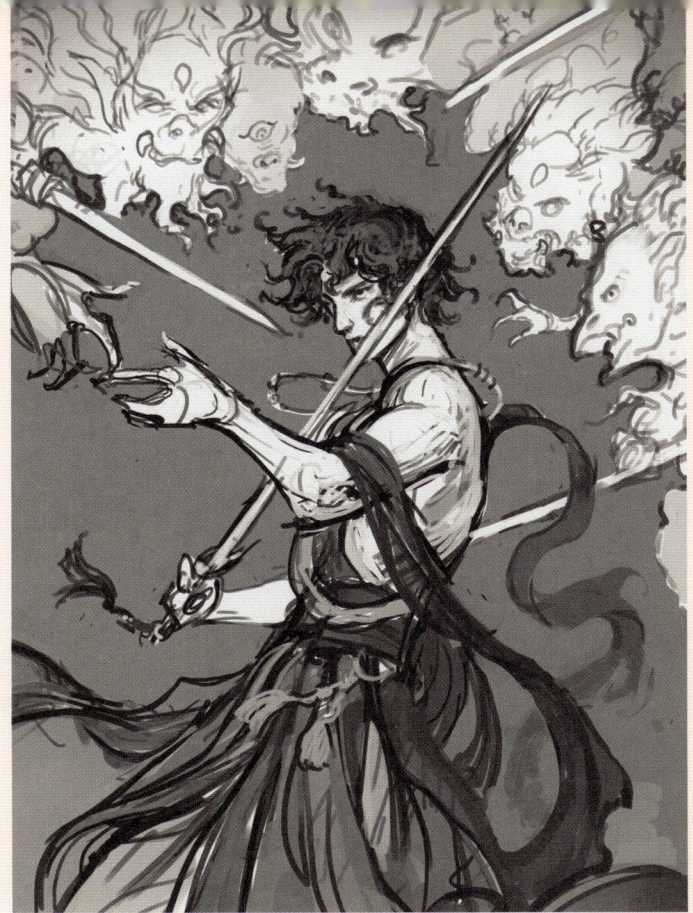

SKETCHING OUT THE COMPOSITION, FOCUSING ON ANATOMY AND POSE

04 REFINING THE SKETCH

Once I have a solid composition and I'm happy with the feel of the rough sketch, I lower the opacity and create a new layer so that I can begin working on the refined sketch. I will have to nail down each detail before I get started on the line work. Sometimes I freehand things, but it's easy to get stuck in a corner that way.

I start by roughly lining the face and hair, making sure I retain the same look and motion. Once details such as the hands and clothes are refined, I add in patterns. I try to keep the character design relatively close to Hokusai's version since I've already changed the original composition quite drastically.

REFINING THE DETAILS ON DEVADATTA

Mona Finden

05 INDIVIDUALIZING THE SPIRITS

Now, I try to uncover the spirits' personalities by adding in some details. Hokusai's way of drawing spirits and demons is very different from what I normally do, so I want to find a happy middle ground. I also aim to individualize each spirit without drawing in too much focus; I still need them to work as a whole. Starting with the larger spirits, I work from left to right before adding in the smaller spirits. I treat them almost like a pattern and fill in gaps with their hair. At the end of this step, I am pleased to see that I've managed to retain some of the spirits' original depiction.

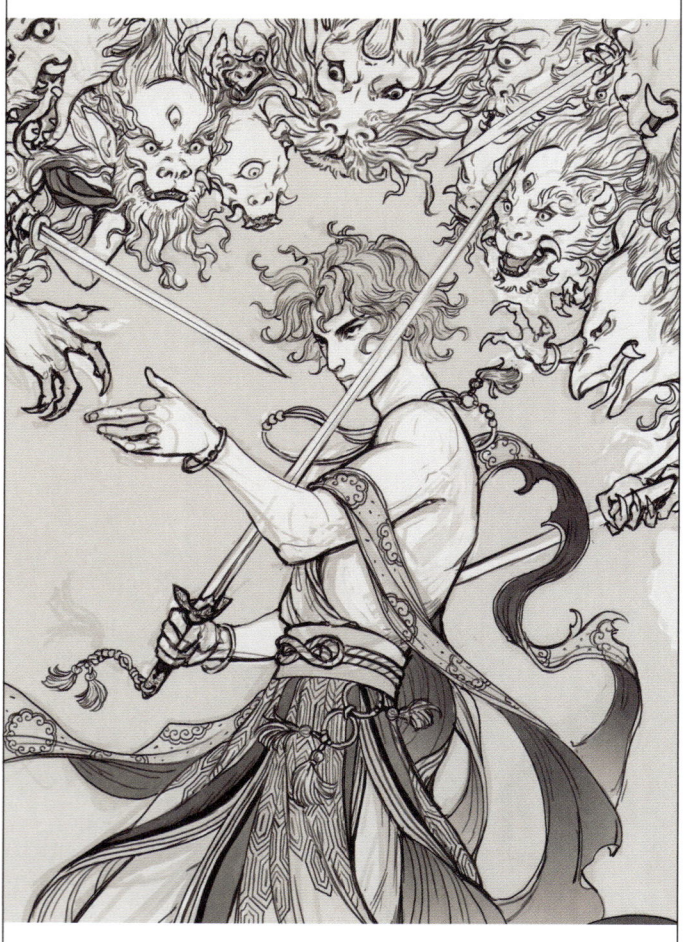

REFINING THE SPIRITS TO ACT AS A WHOLE CHARACTER

06 STARTING THE LINE ART

Now that all the details are set, I begin the line art. I start the same way I did with the refined sketch, but I keep the lines as clean as possible. It's easy for the line art to end up looking stiff, so it's important that the refined sketch is correct and that I have a good base to work from. I keep most of the lines the same, but I update a few details along the way.

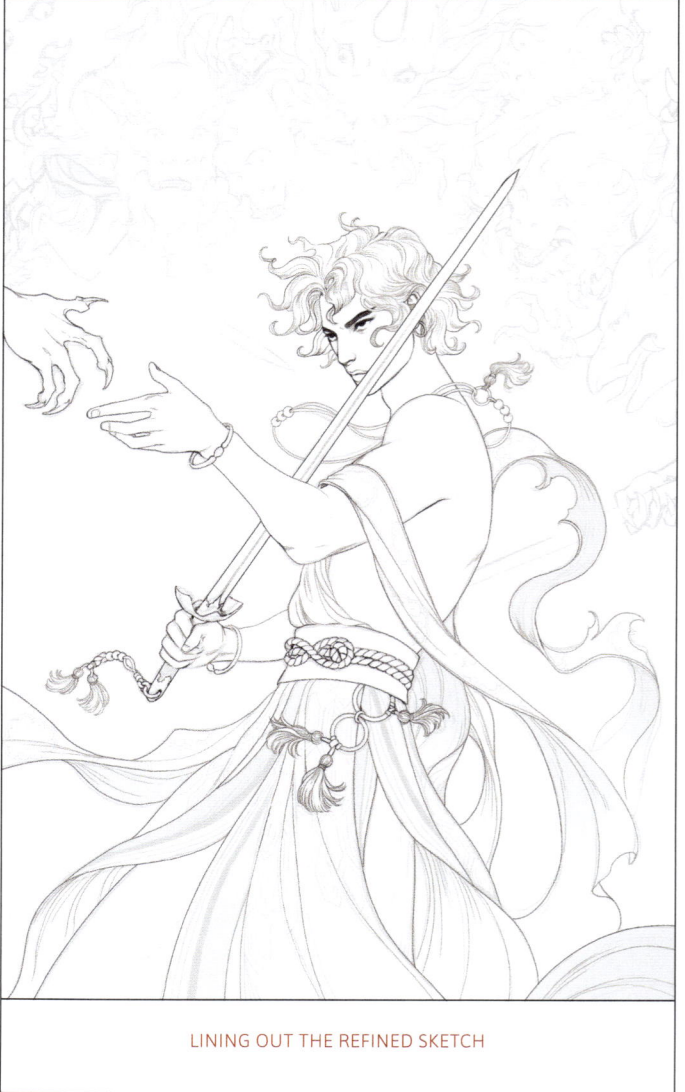

LINING OUT THE REFINED SKETCH

07 ADDING PATTERNS

I draw all patterns on a separate layer so that I can change them later, if needed. I also add in some extra patterns to the sword's armguard, as well as the bracelets. Once everything is lined, I lower the brightness in the background and add base colours to Devadatta. This way I can make sure the silhouette works. Keeping the base colour grey means I won't feel locked into any particular colour palette.

ADDING PATTERNS AND FILLING IN DEVADATTA'S BASE COLOURS

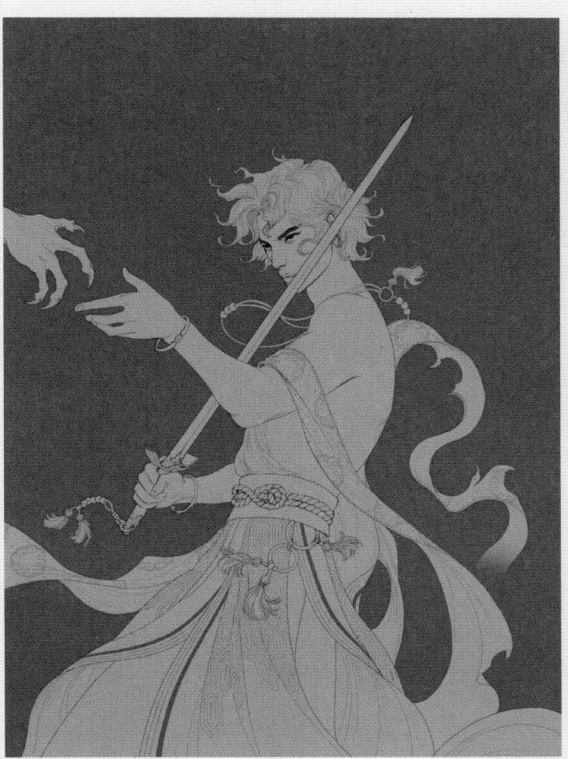
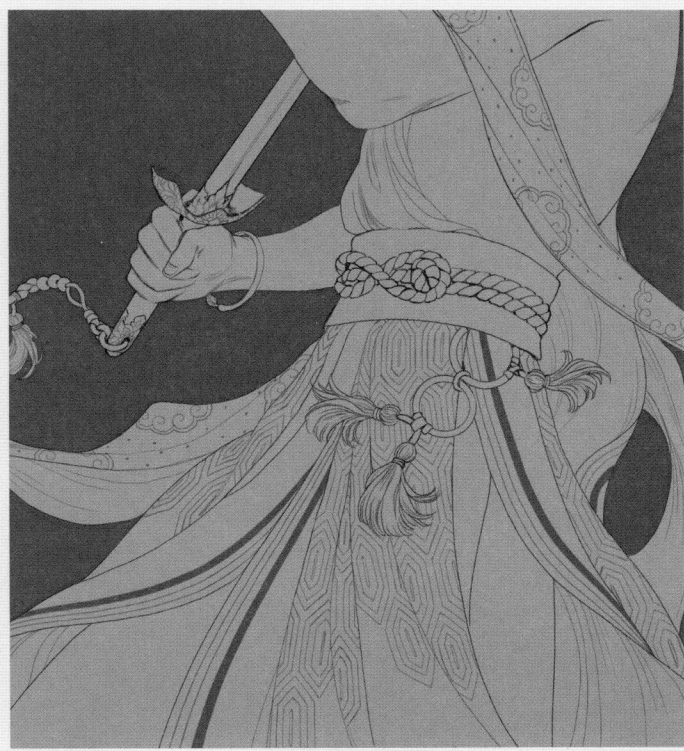

08 EVIL SPIRIT LINE ART

For this next step, I move on to the evil spirits, lining them in the same way I lined Devadatta. First, I flip the image to make sure everything looks alright and notice that some of the evil spirits look wrong. I fix them before finishing the line art.

Hokusai's spirits look like variations of monkeys, dragons, and birds, so I try to stay true to his vision. Now the line art is complete!

DRAWING LINE ART FOR THE EVIL SPIRITS

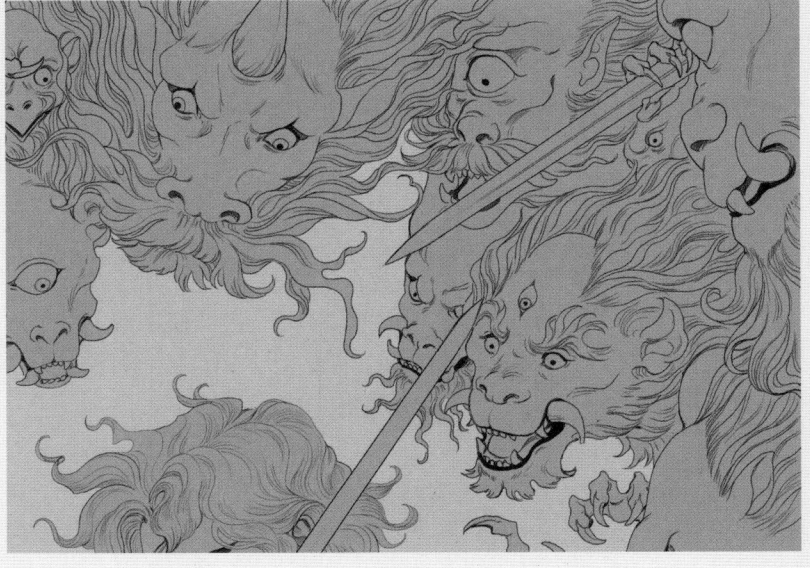

Mona Finden

09 COLOUR BASE

Hokusai's illustration did not have any colour, so from now on, I rely on my own vision and taste. Unlike the sketch and line art, I start with the background and work my way to the foreground. This is so that I can build the atmosphere around the character, making him appear more immersed into the scene.

Hokusai used dots in his original illustration, which I translate as darkness and shadows. In the rough-sketch stage, I already decided on a black background, but I decide to add a little light to make the darkness look more like a void. This makes the whole scene feel more intimate and crowded. I also decide to paint the spirits red as I want them to have a warm, threatening aura.

FILLING IN THE BACKGROUND BASE COLOURS

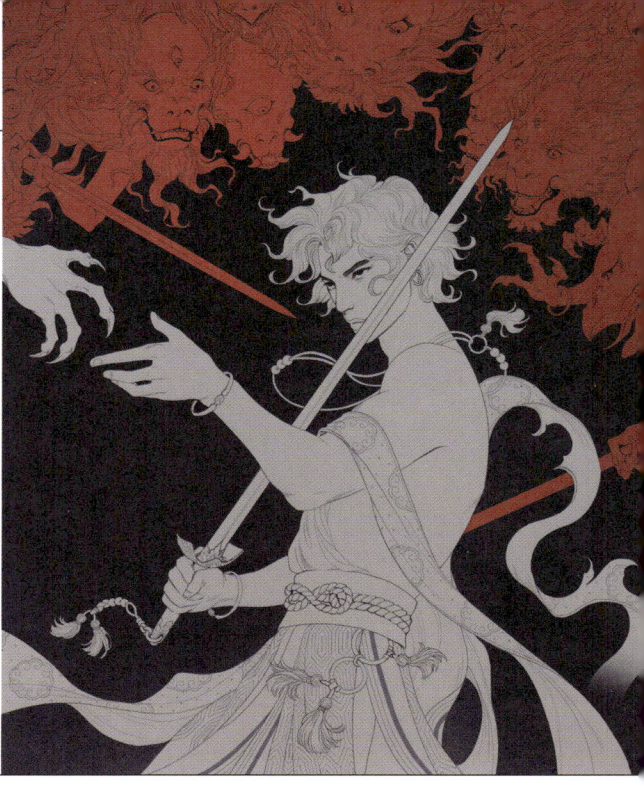

10 COLOURING IN THE SPIRITS

I fade the colours into lighter and darker sections before dividing each new colour (hair, claws, teeth, horns, and weapons) into separate clipping masks. I play around with the colours on each element until I find a sweet spot. Then the rendering begins! I start with the skin, colouring it as best as I can before continuing on to the other details. Right now, it looks more like one big blob instead of individual spirits, but I will divide them more clearly later on.

EARLY STAGE OF COLOURING THE SPIRITS

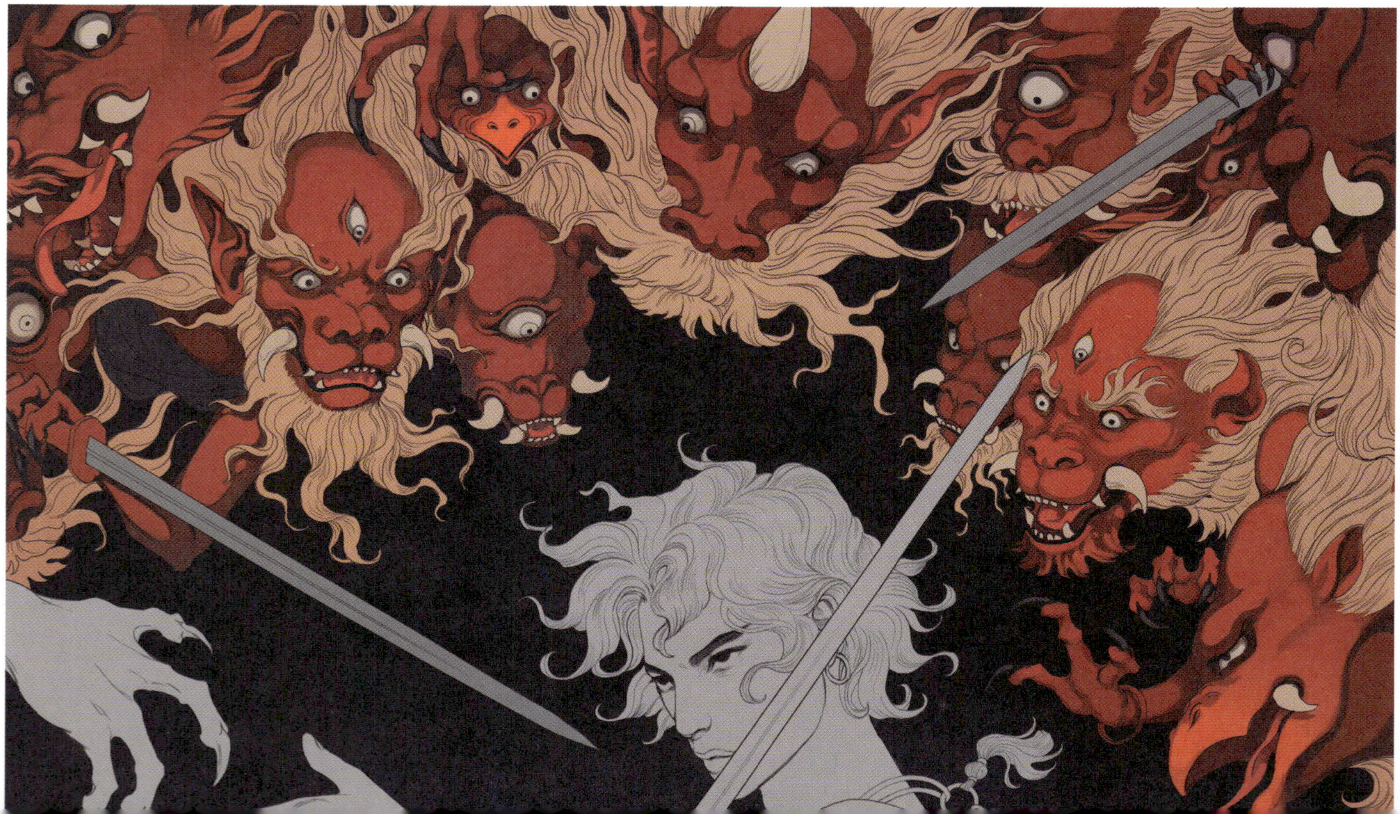

11 RENDERING THE SPIRITS

Rendering the hair needs just as much attention as the skin. By adding more pink hues and purple shadows to the skin and hair, they instantly have more depth. As I continue to render back and forth between layers, I add in more shadows to certain areas, making sure to colour-correct as I go so the spirits blend seamlessly with the environment while remaining distinct and separate from one another.

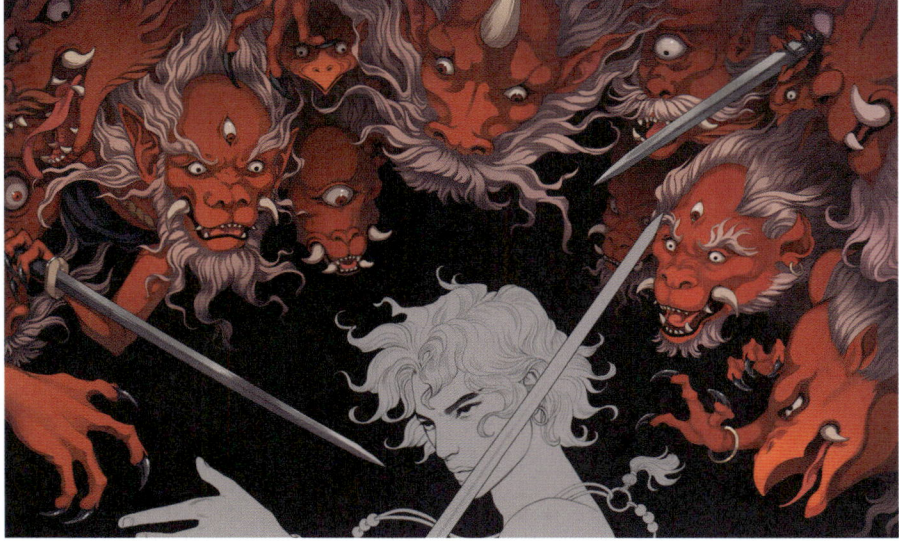

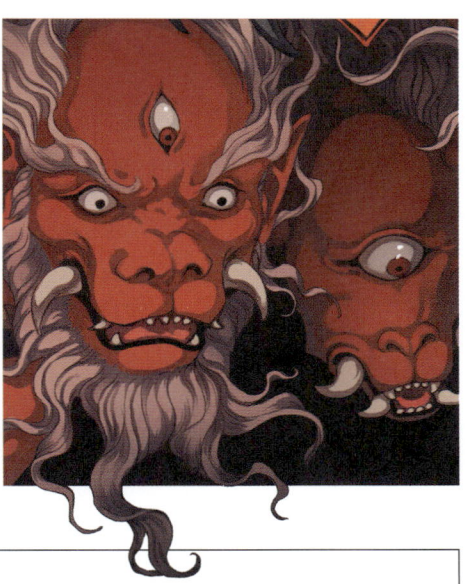

FINAL STAGES OF
COLOURING THE SPIRITS

12 FINDING DEVADATTA'S PALETTE

Before I start colouring Devadatta, I have to find the right combination for his attire. I initially want it to be black and gold, but I don't want it to blend too much with the background, so I decide to make a few tests with muted colours and pops of vibrancy here and there.

FINDING THE RIGHT
COLOUR COMBINATION
FOR DEVADATTA

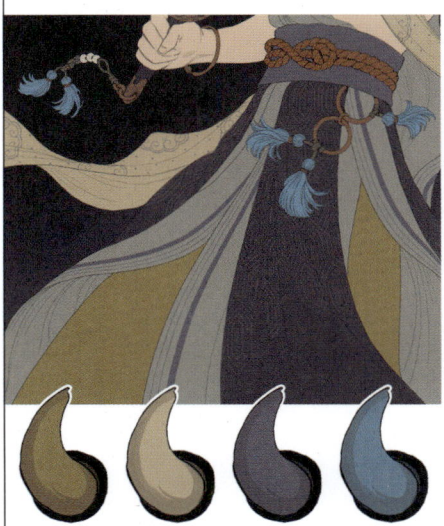

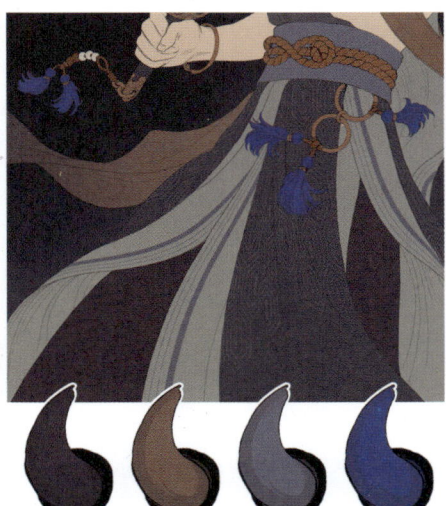

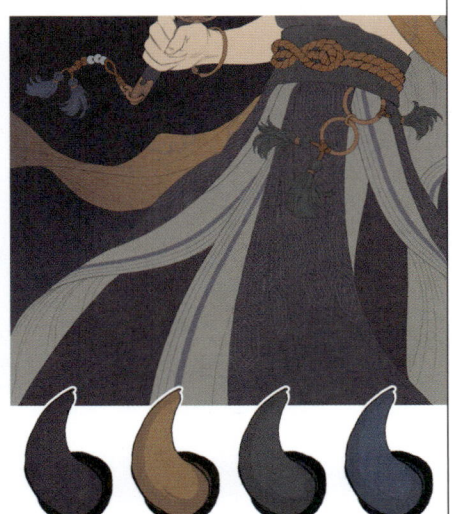

13 FIXING EXPRESSIONS

Once I begin rendering the character's skin, I find that I have lost the facial expression I initially wanted him to have. He looks too angry, and although it is fitting for his character, it's not what I'm aiming for. My vision is for him to have an intense yet calm look in his eyes, as if entranced by the spirits. From here, I just have to make sure the anatomy is correct.

RENDERING THE SKIN AND HAIR

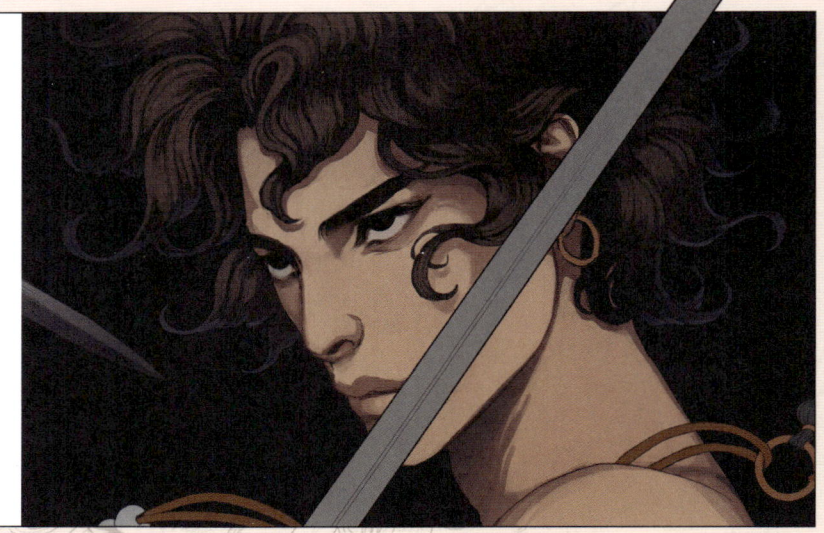

14 FINAL COLOUR CHANGES

As I continue to render Devadatta, I keep changing the colours of his attire. It looks too grey overall, and I need him to stand out since the spirits are so intense. I increase the contrast, fill in the patterns and small details, and just try to find ways of bettering the overall colour scheme.

RENDERING THE REST OF DEVADATTA

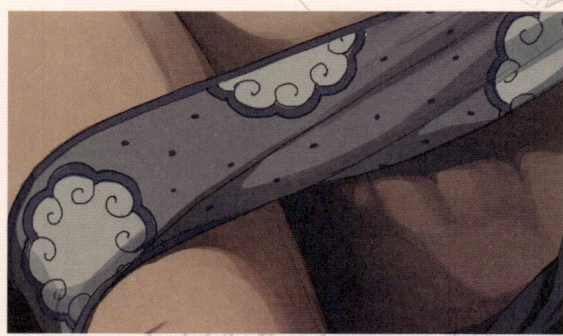

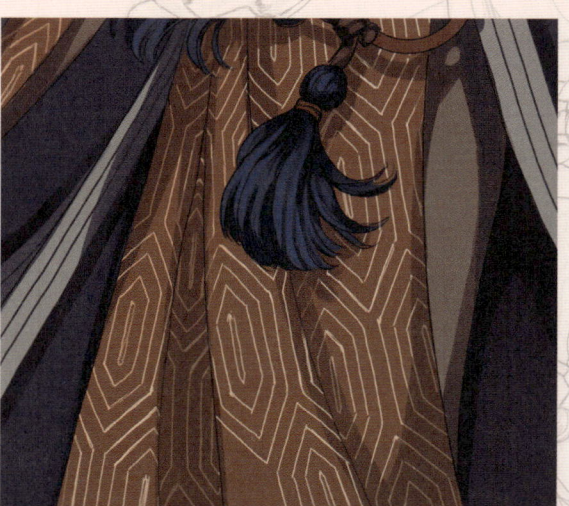

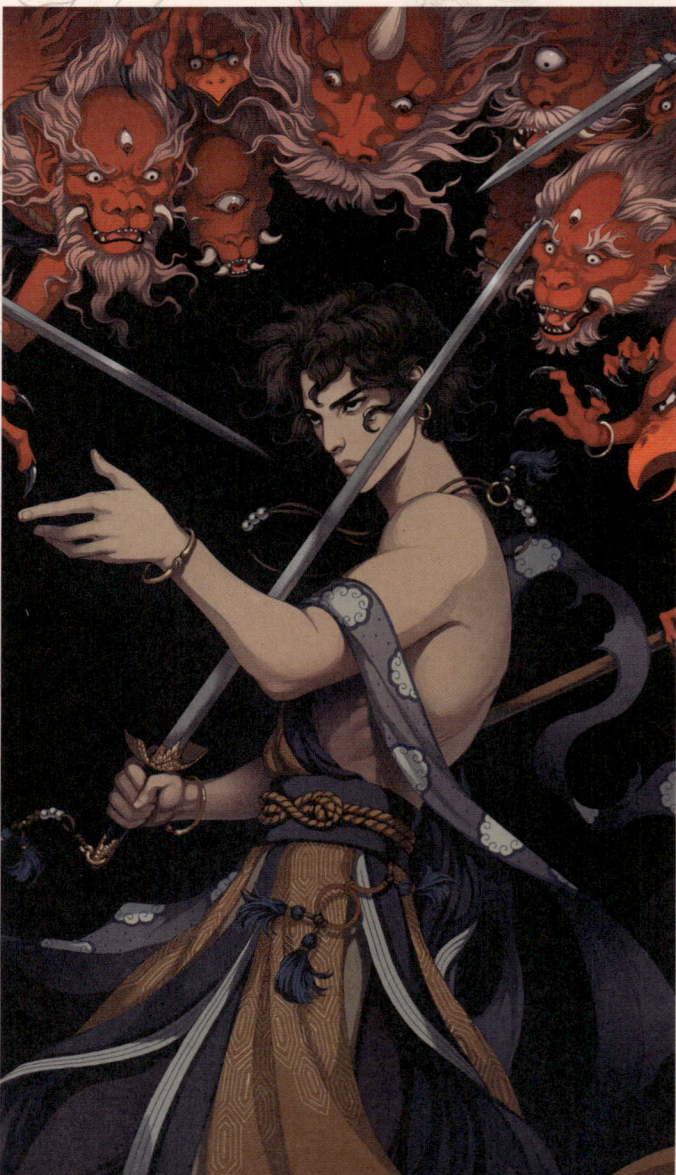

FINAL TOUCHES

I eventually land on a colour scheme that makes him stand out. It's close to my original idea with darker colours paired with gold, as well as a few lighter colours in between. I make some final colour edits and clean up some details. Then I'm done!

MAKING FINAL TOUCHES ON THE OVERALL ILLUSTRATION

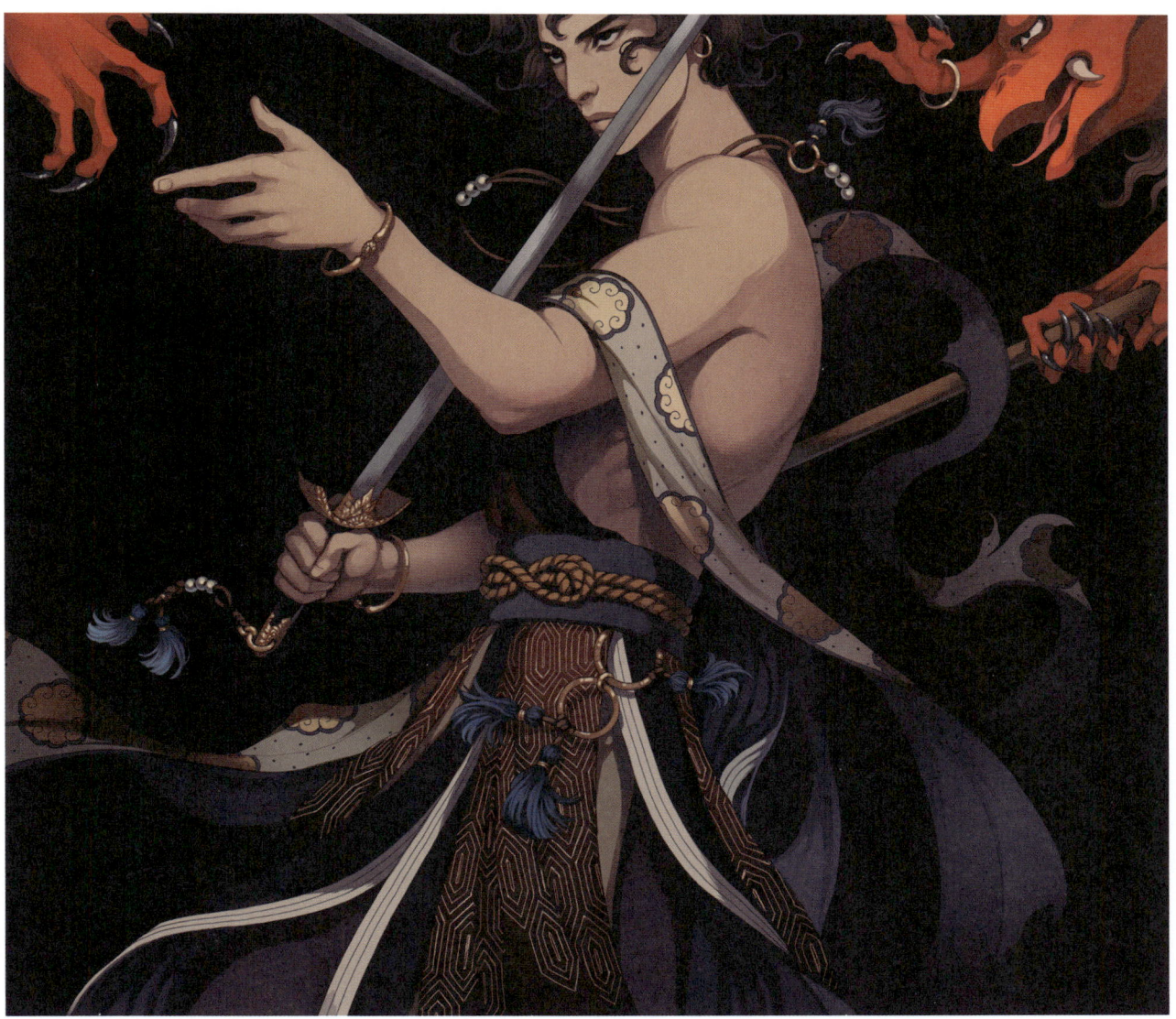

CONCLUSION

I'm quite happy with the end result, particularly the composition, Devadatta's expression, and the collective intensity of the evil spirits. I hope the piece will evoke some sort of emotion in the viewer. I consider myself to be a very intuitive artist, so putting my process into words has been the biggest challenge, but something I'm very glad I got to experience.

Mona Finden

妖術之
惡鬼出現

提婆
達多

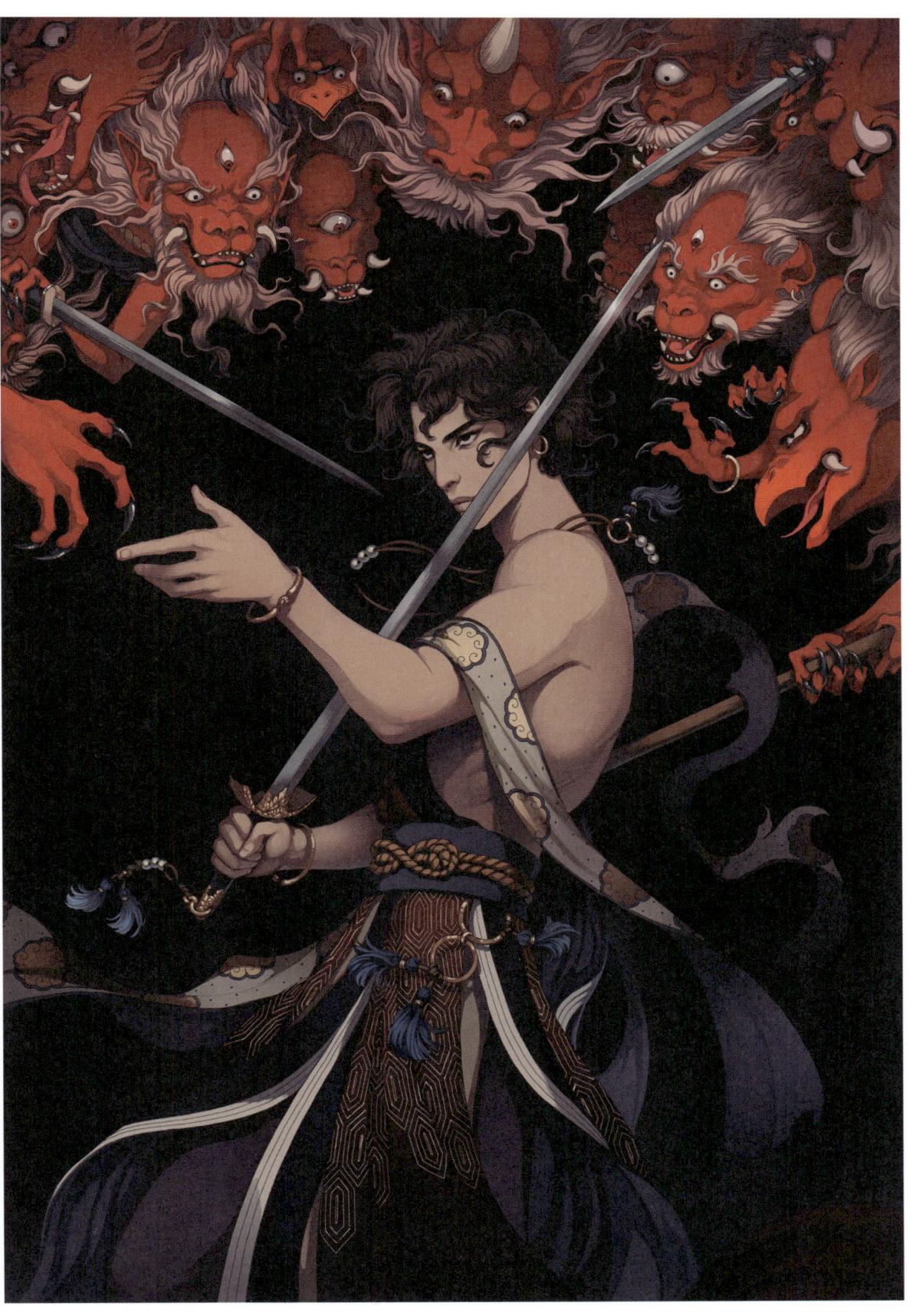

DEVADATTA SURROUNDED BY EVIL SPIRITS

MONA FINDEN

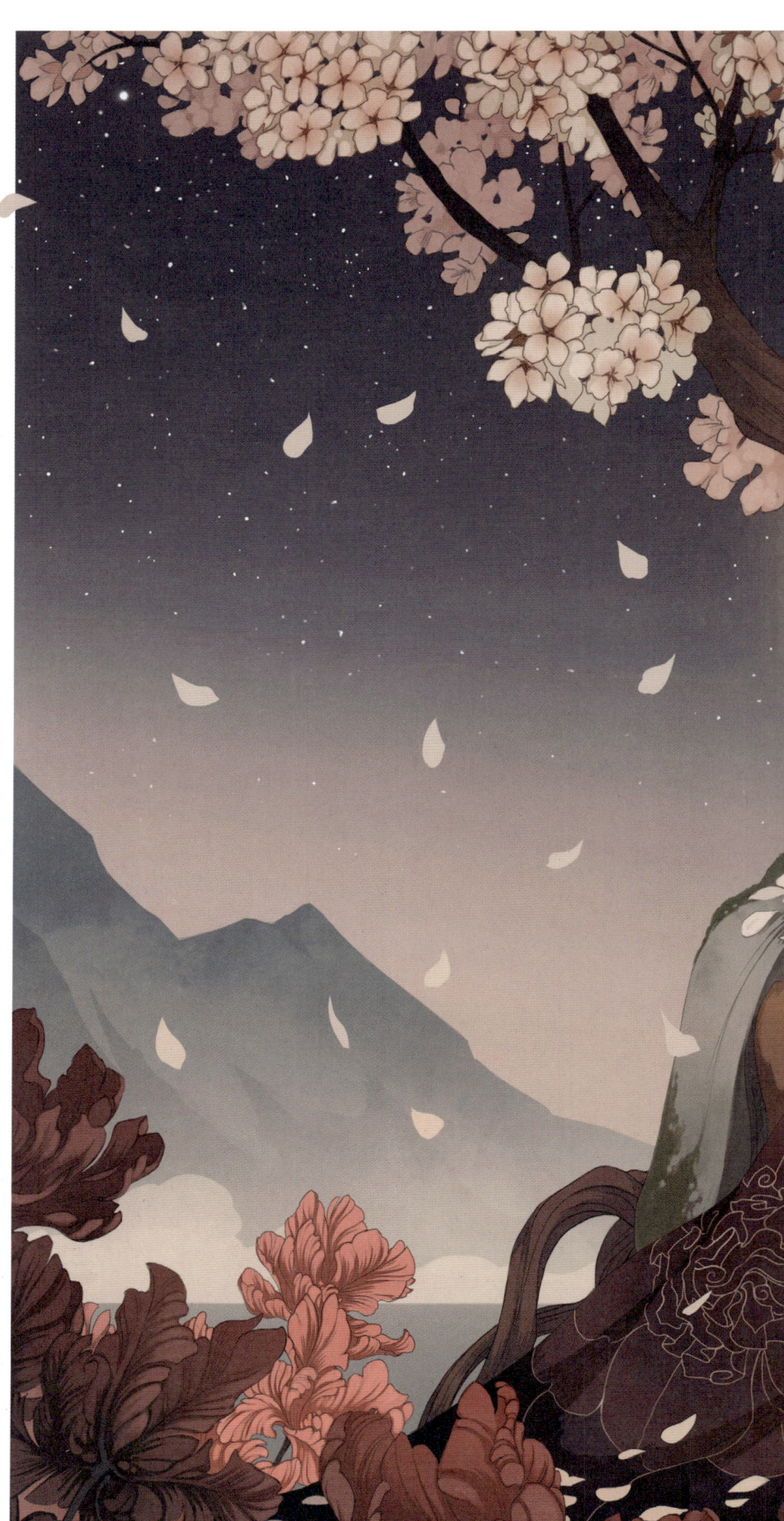

GALLERY: MONA FINDEN

A Forgotten Love Story
A defeated warrior holding
on to his long-lost love

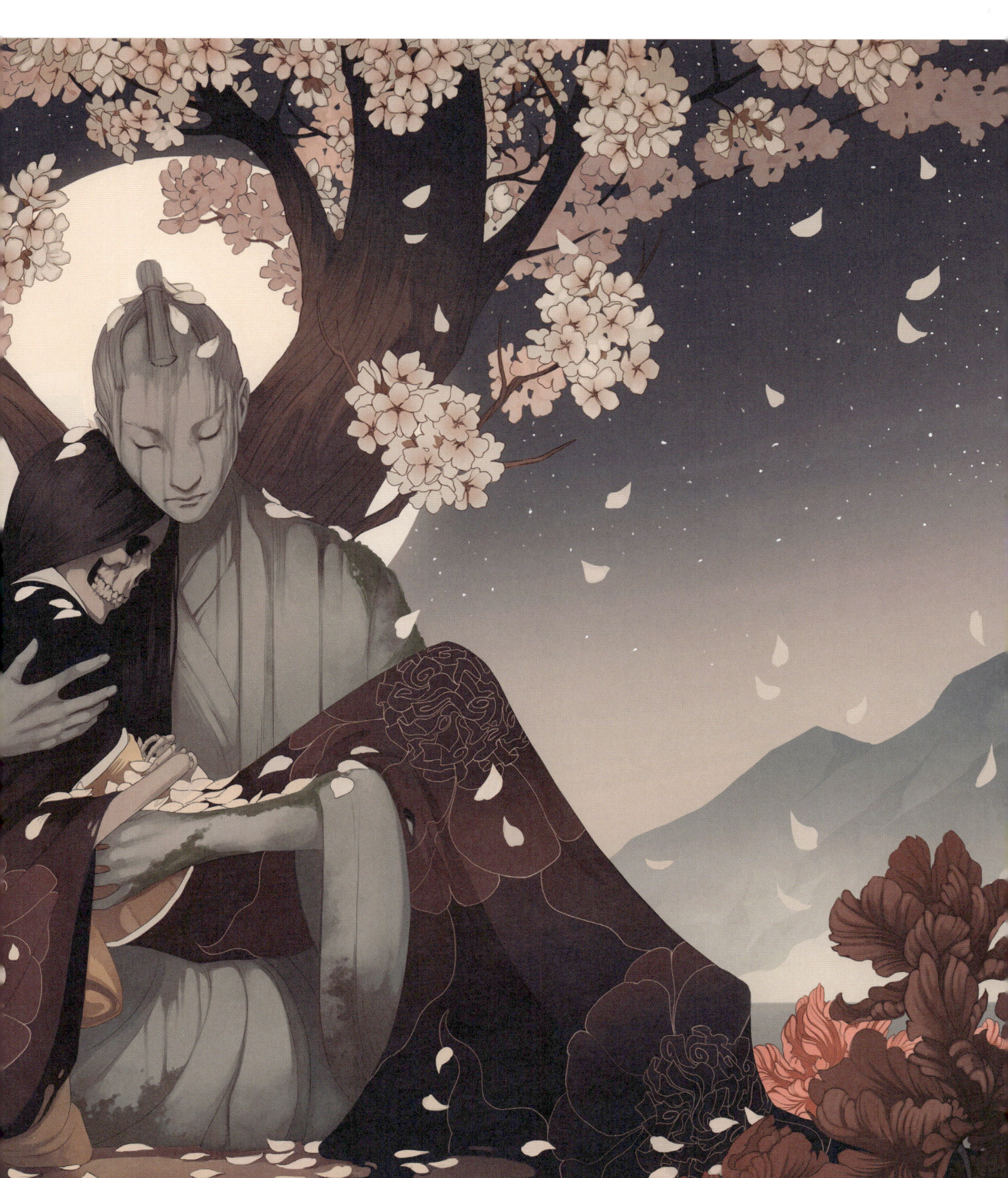

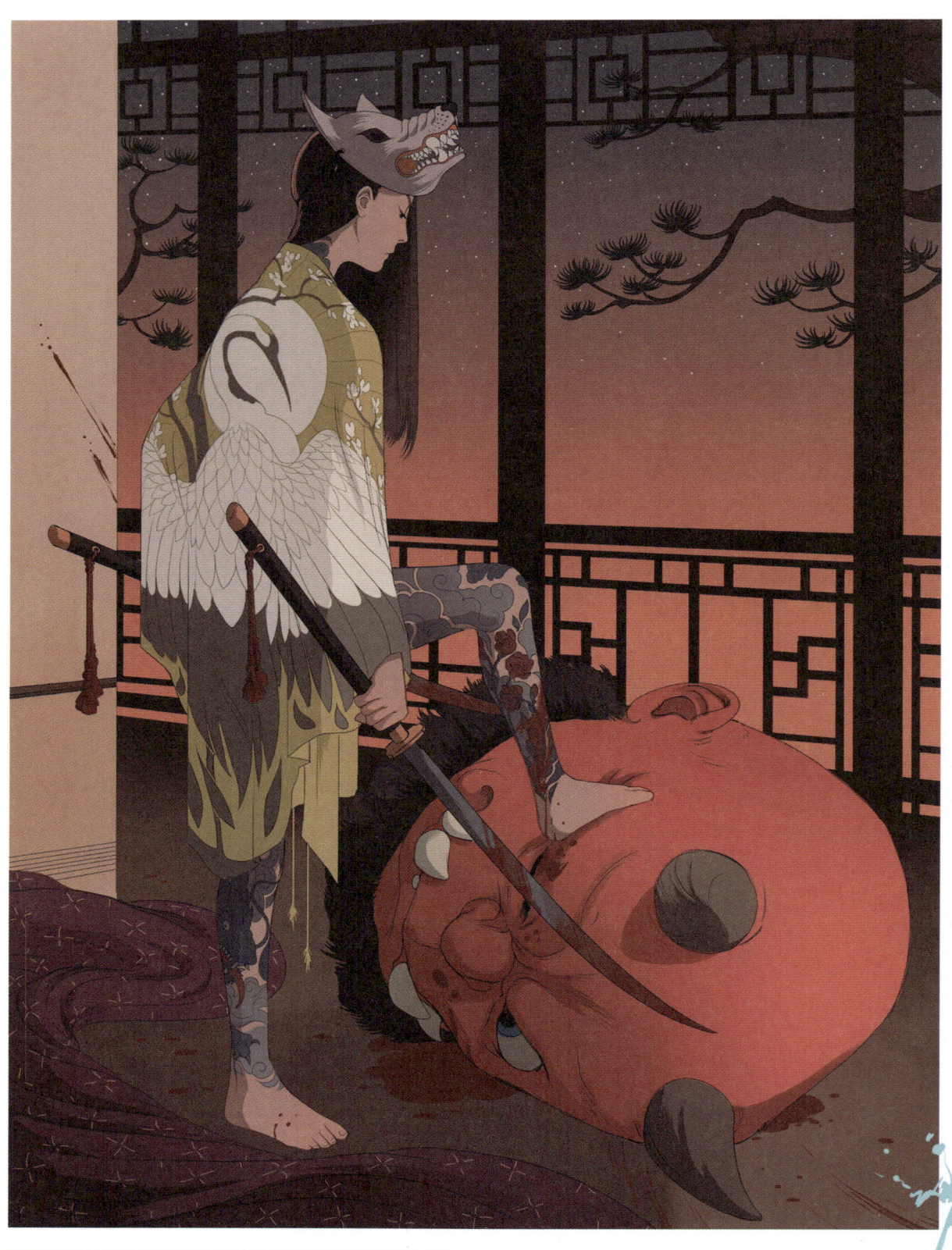

ABOVE: *Defeated*
The battle was over and her enemy – what was left of him – squirmed at her feet

RIGHT: *Broken Synth*
A synth broken from battle, but not yet defeated

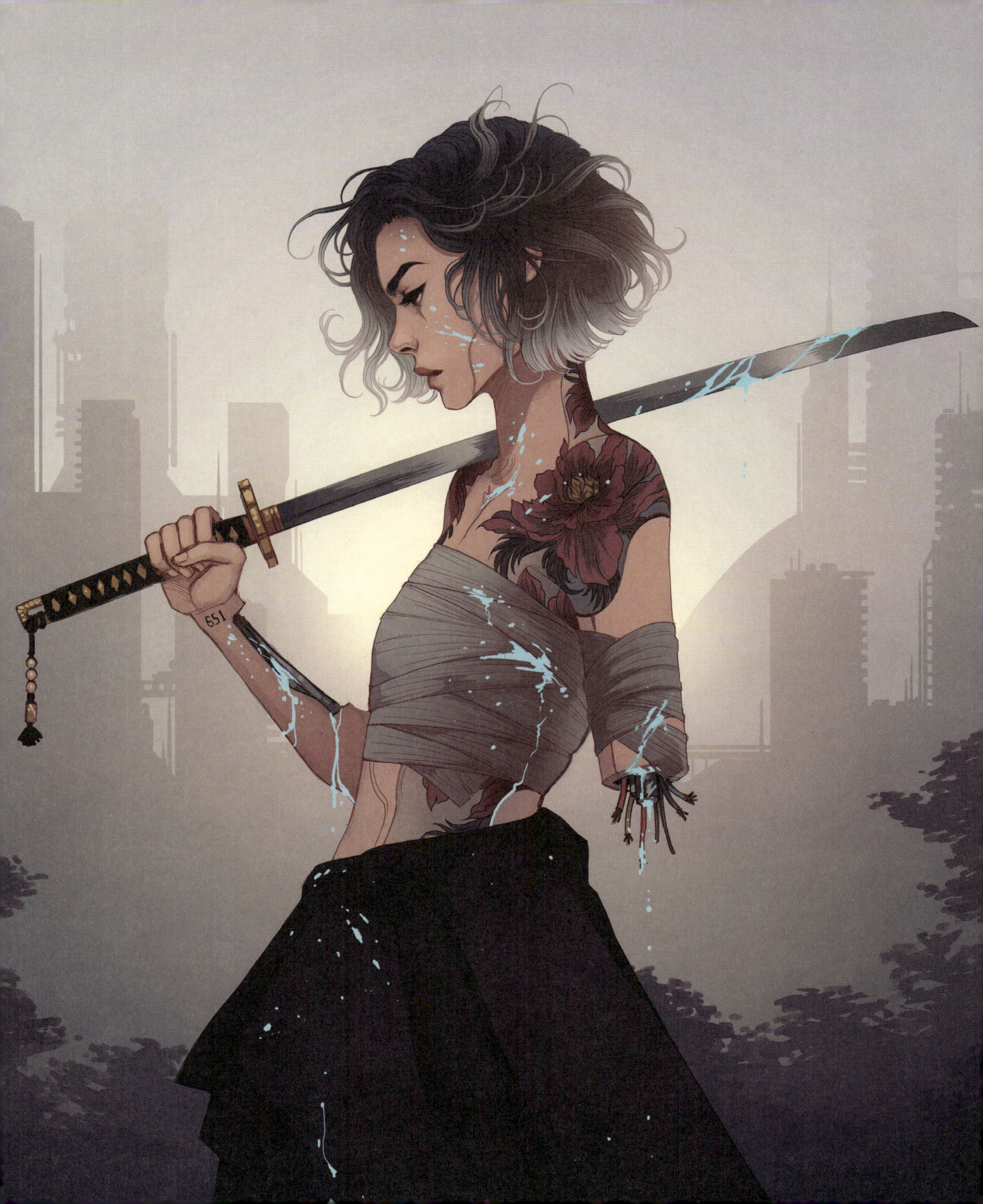

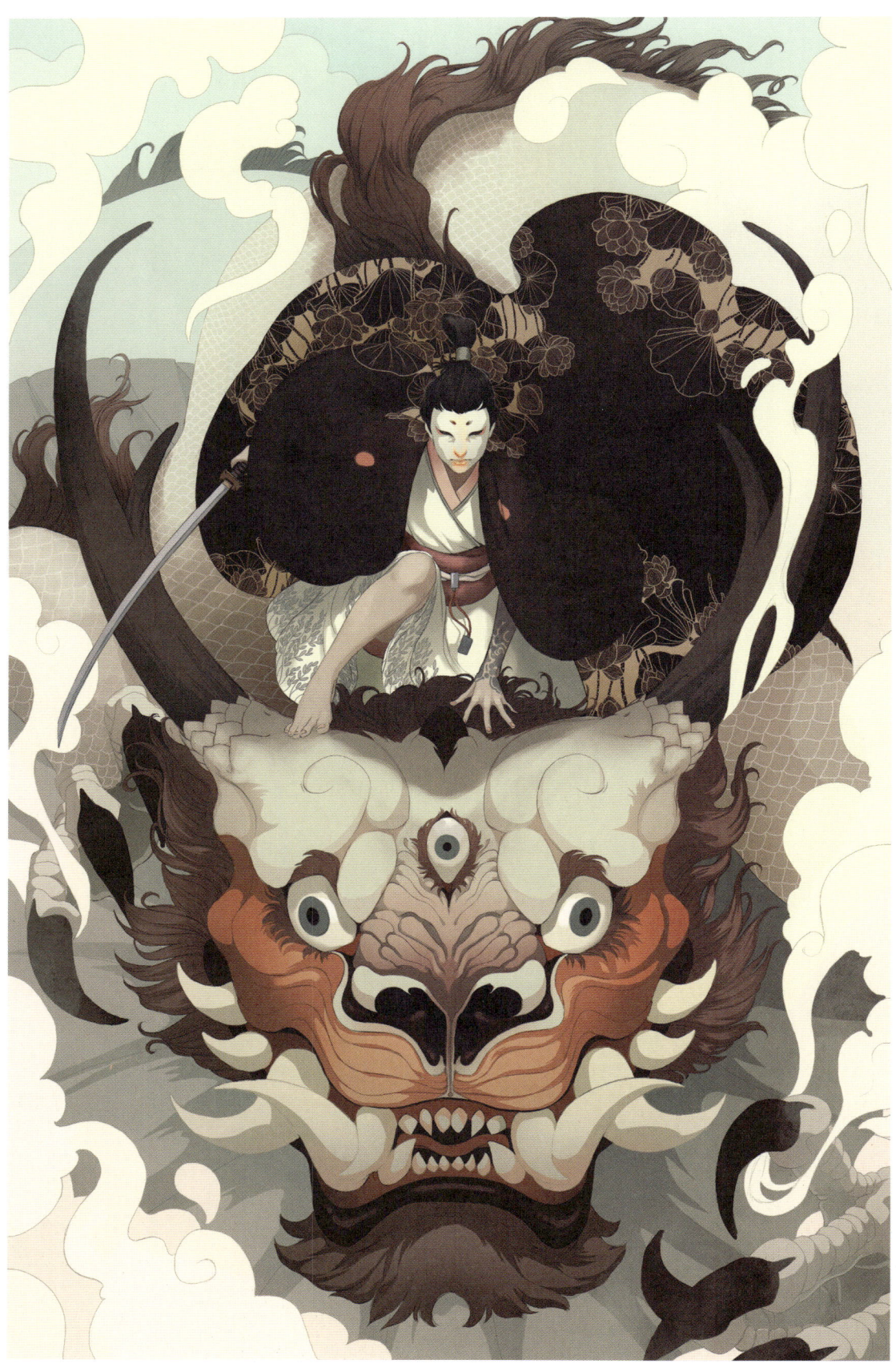

LEFT: *Windrider*
A dragon rider and her dragon of wind

RIGHT: *Knight*
A warrior finding inner courage as she lifts her blade

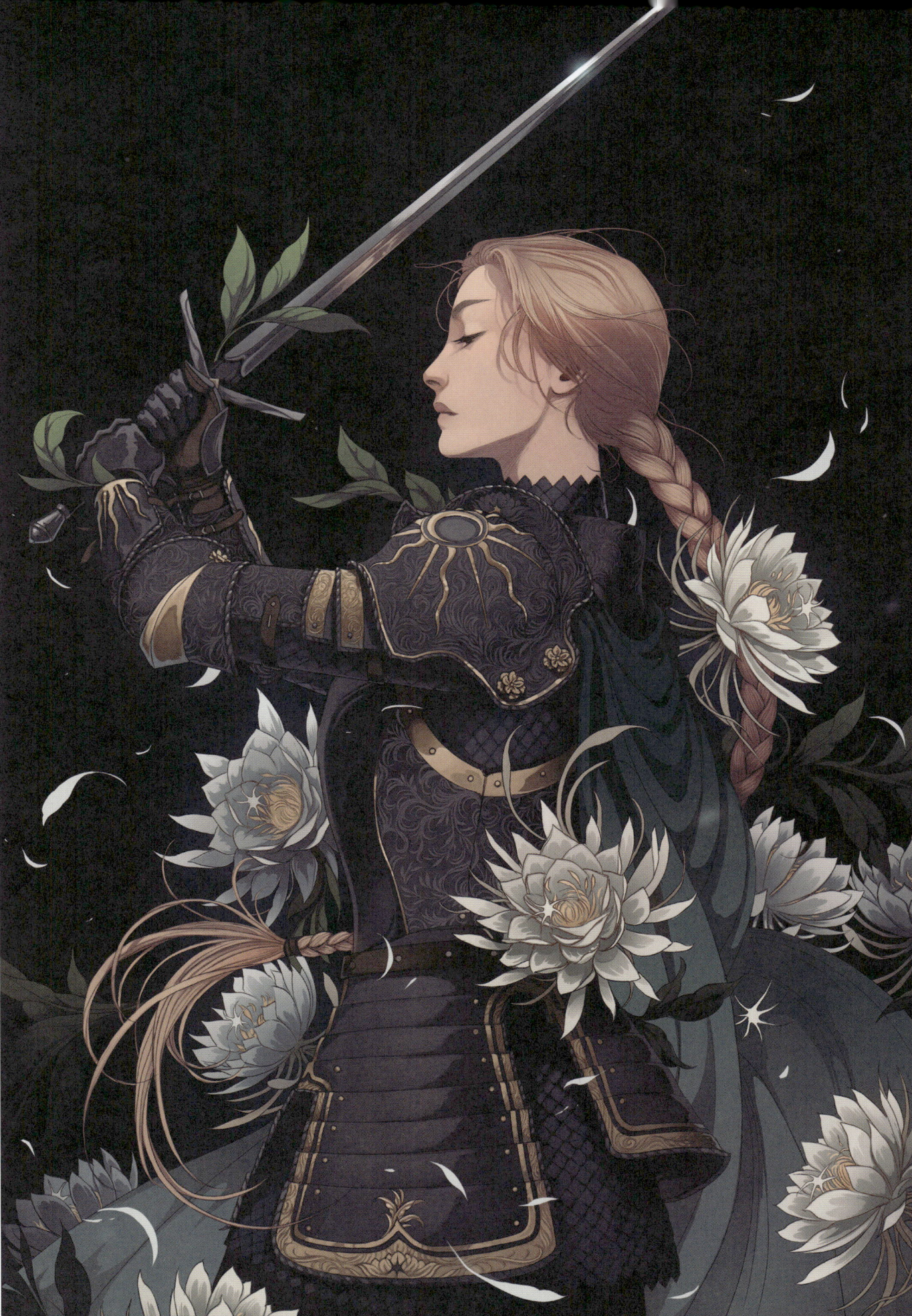

A BOLT OF LIGHTNING STRIKES VIRŪDHAKA DEAD

BY LUOMAN

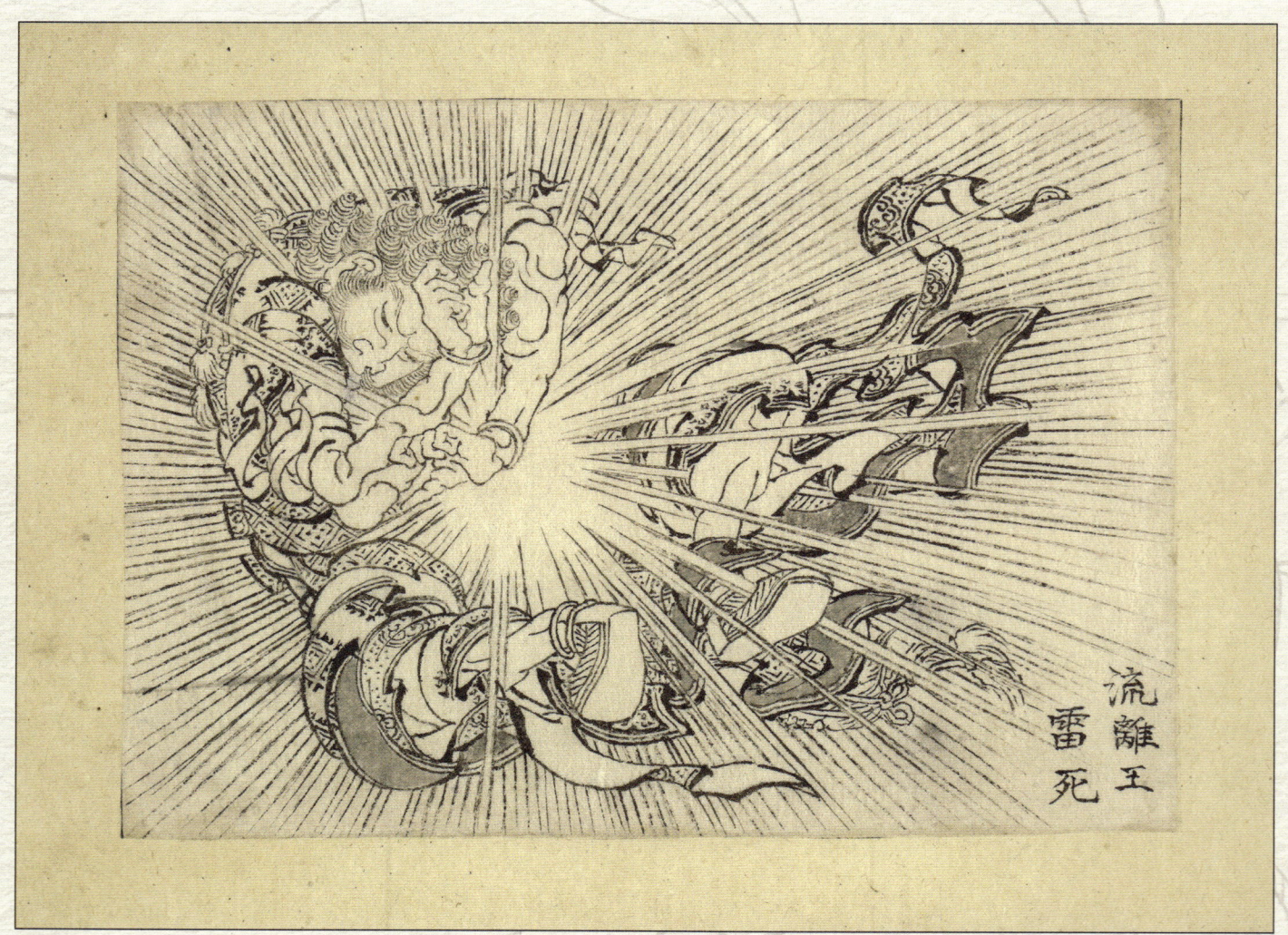

DISCOVERING HOKUSAI

Hokusai's art always astonishes me, offering a distinct and unconventional take on Eastern aesthetics. A *bolt of lightning strikes Virūdhaka dead* is a particularly noteworthy piece. It embodies both poetic grace and a striking sense of power, evoking a feeling of excitement and awe. The dynamic energy in this work ignites a sense of passion, and I hope to capture some of the brilliance and inspiration it holds in my own artistic journey.

01 SKETCHING THE OUTLINE

Since the central focus is the character Virūdhaka, I start by establishing his form posture early on in the sketch. Even though it's still in the rough stage, I make sure to define the essential proportions and anatomy of the figure. I sketch a lightning bolt striking down from the upper part of the composition, which will later be a major part of the scene. Though simple at this stage, it's important to map out the overall flow and visual direction, ensuring the lightning leads directly to the main character's body. By the end of the sketching process, I have a rough but clear sense of Virūdhaka's form, movement, and the dramatic action surrounding him. This foundation allows me to move forward into refining the details in the next step.

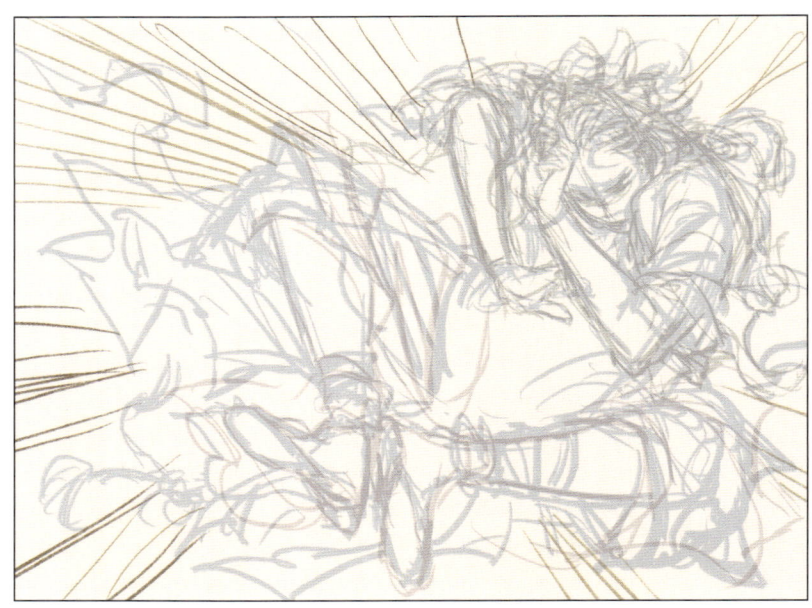

I MAKE SURE TO ESTABLISH THE CHARACTER'S FORM EARLY ON

02 BASIC SHAPES

I first begin with basic shapes – circles and ovals to represent the head, torso, and limbs – allowing me to quickly block out the character's position. Virūdhaka's pose is dynamic, showing the exact moment he's struck by lightning, so I emphasize an arched back and limbs extended outward to convey the force of the impact. The expression on his face is also key, so I roughly indicate the position of the eyes and mouth to capture the agony and shock of the moment.

ADDING IN SHAPES TO
CONVEY FORCE OF IMPACT

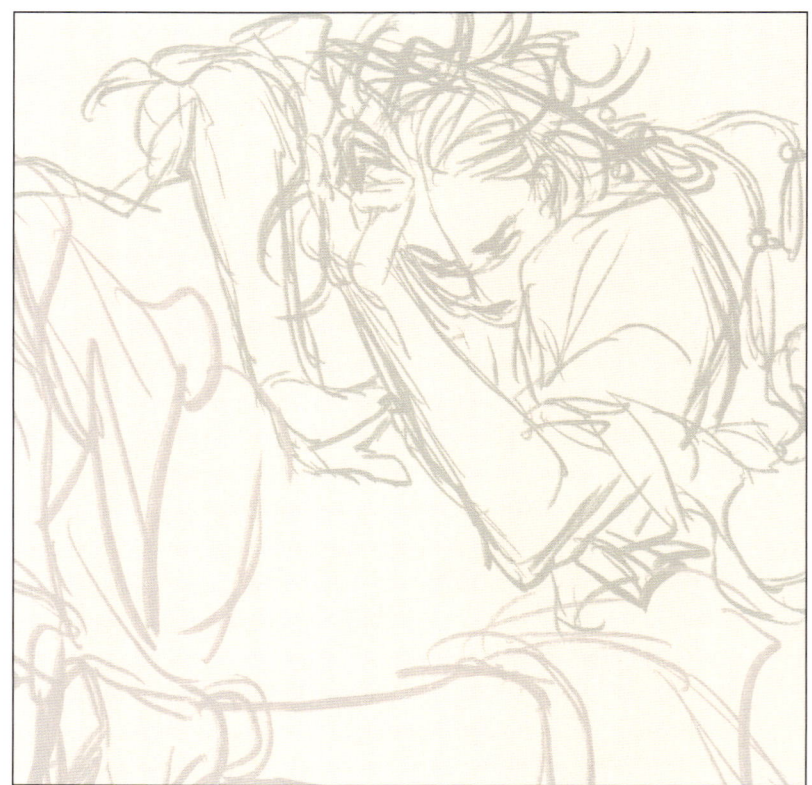

03 SPEED LINES

Around the figure, I add in some speed lines, which are crucial to directing the viewer's gaze towards the central action. These lines radiate from various points around Virūdhaka, pulling attention to his body as it reacts to the lightning strike. The speed lines not only add energy to the composition but also reinforce the idea that the force hitting him is sudden and powerful.

GUIDING THE VIEWER'S GAZE TOWARDS THE CENTRAL ACTION

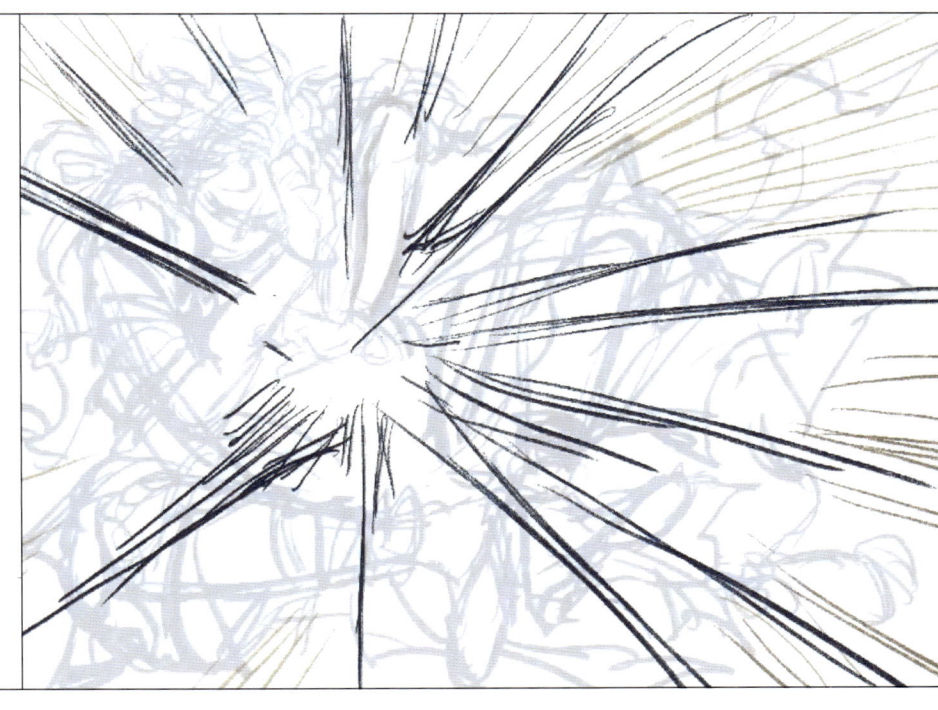

'THE SPEED LINES NOT ONLY ADD ENERGY TO THE COMPOSITION BUT ALSO REINFORCE THE IDEA THAT THE FORCE HITTING HIM IS SUDDEN AND POWERFUL'

SHARPENING THE SHAPES

04 INKING THE LINES

Once the sketch is complete, I move on to inking the lines. Since my colouring style involves flat shading, it's essential at this stage to create clean, precise line work that clearly defines the content of the illustration. The inking process ensures that the shapes and forms are sharp and ready for the colouring phase, so attention to detail is key here.

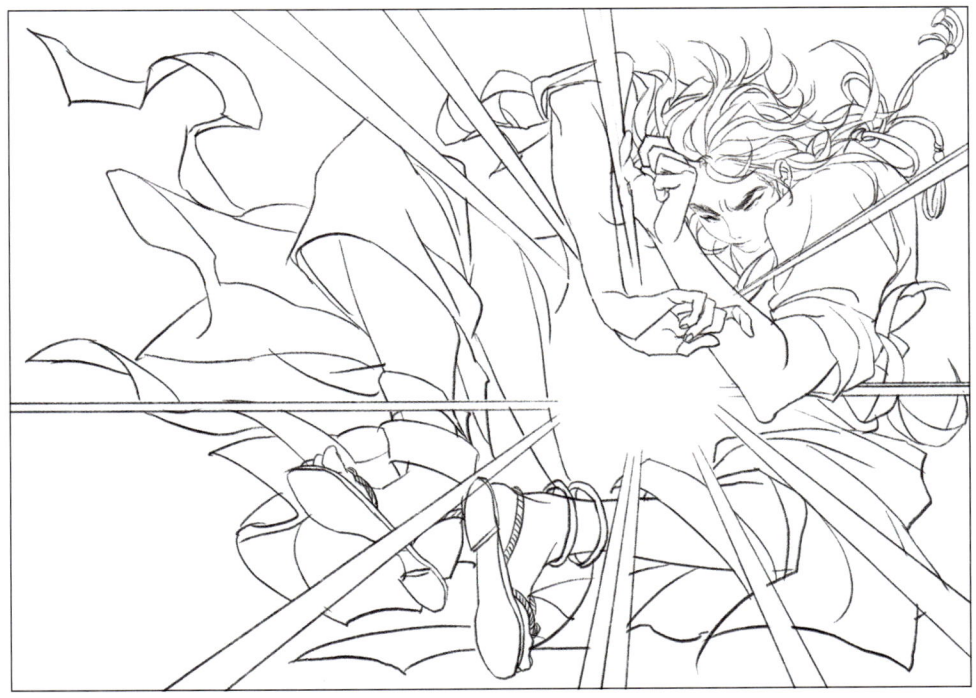

05 LAYER MANAGEMENT

To keep the illustration organized and visually clear, I also establish layer management. For this particular piece, I divide the image into three main layers:

I DIVIDE THE IMAGE INTO THREE LAYERS TO CONTROL SCENE DEPTH

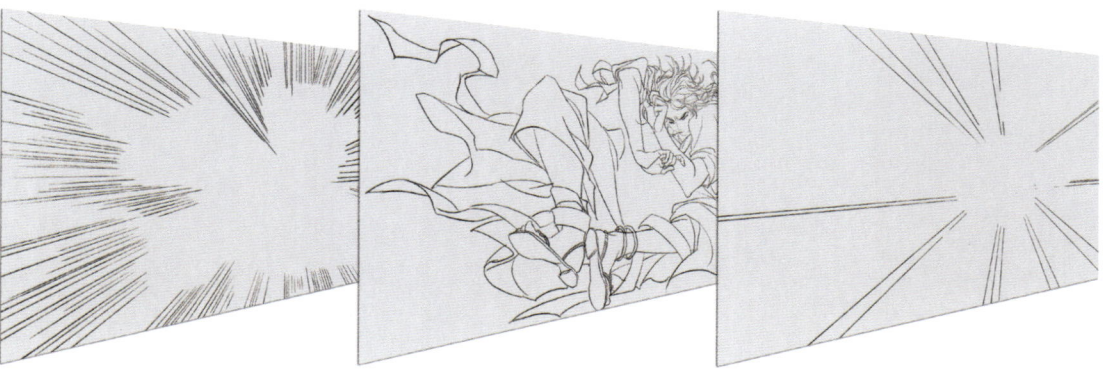

Background: the speed lines, which amplify the sense of action and lead the viewer's eye towards the central figure

Middle ground: the character, Virūdhaka, who is the main focal point of the composition

Foreground: the lightning bolt, which takes priority as it interacts directly with the character

Careful layering helps me control the depth of the scene and ensures that each element stands out in the final composition.

06 REFINING THE INKING

When refining the details, it's crucial to have a clear sense of direction and flow in mind. For example, I make sure that the direction of Virūdhaka's hair and the folds in his clothing align with the movement created by the lightning strike and speed lines. These elements aren't just random – everything is designed to converge towards the visual centre of the illustration, emphasizing the force of the impact and keeping the viewer's attention on the character. Additionally, as I refine the inking, I pay special attention to maintaining consistent line weight. Thicker lines are used to emphasize the outline of the character and major elements, while finer lines bring out the smaller details such as the intricate folds of fabric or strands of hair. This variance in line weight adds depth and dimension to the illustration, making it more visually dynamic.

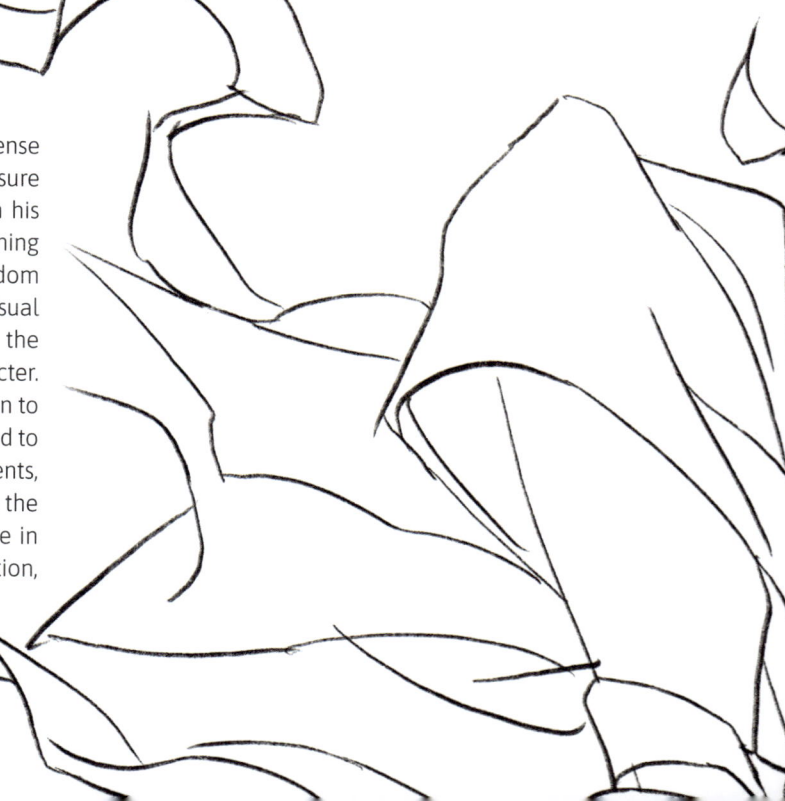

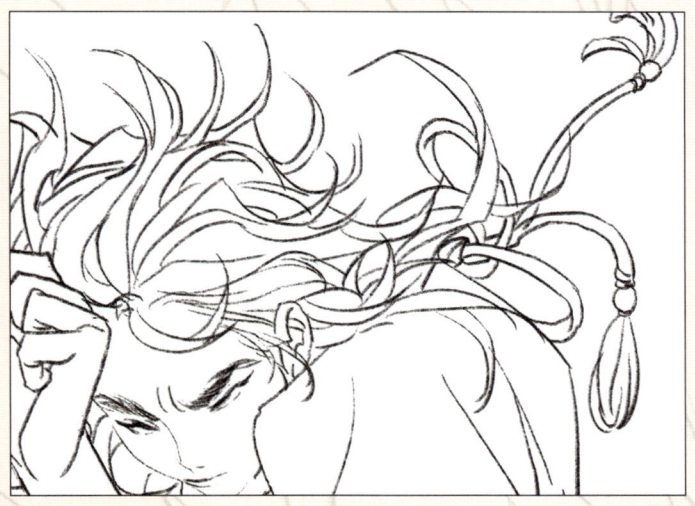

By the end of this step, the drawing is clear, structured, and ready for the colouring process. The visual hierarchy is established, and the flow of movement is captured in the inked lines, ensuring a strong foundation for the next phase.

I TRY TO MAINTAIN A
CONSISTENT LINE WEIGHT

07 ADDING PATTERNS

At this point, I felt the illustration lacked some details, so I added intricate patterns to the clothing, choosing some traditional designs.

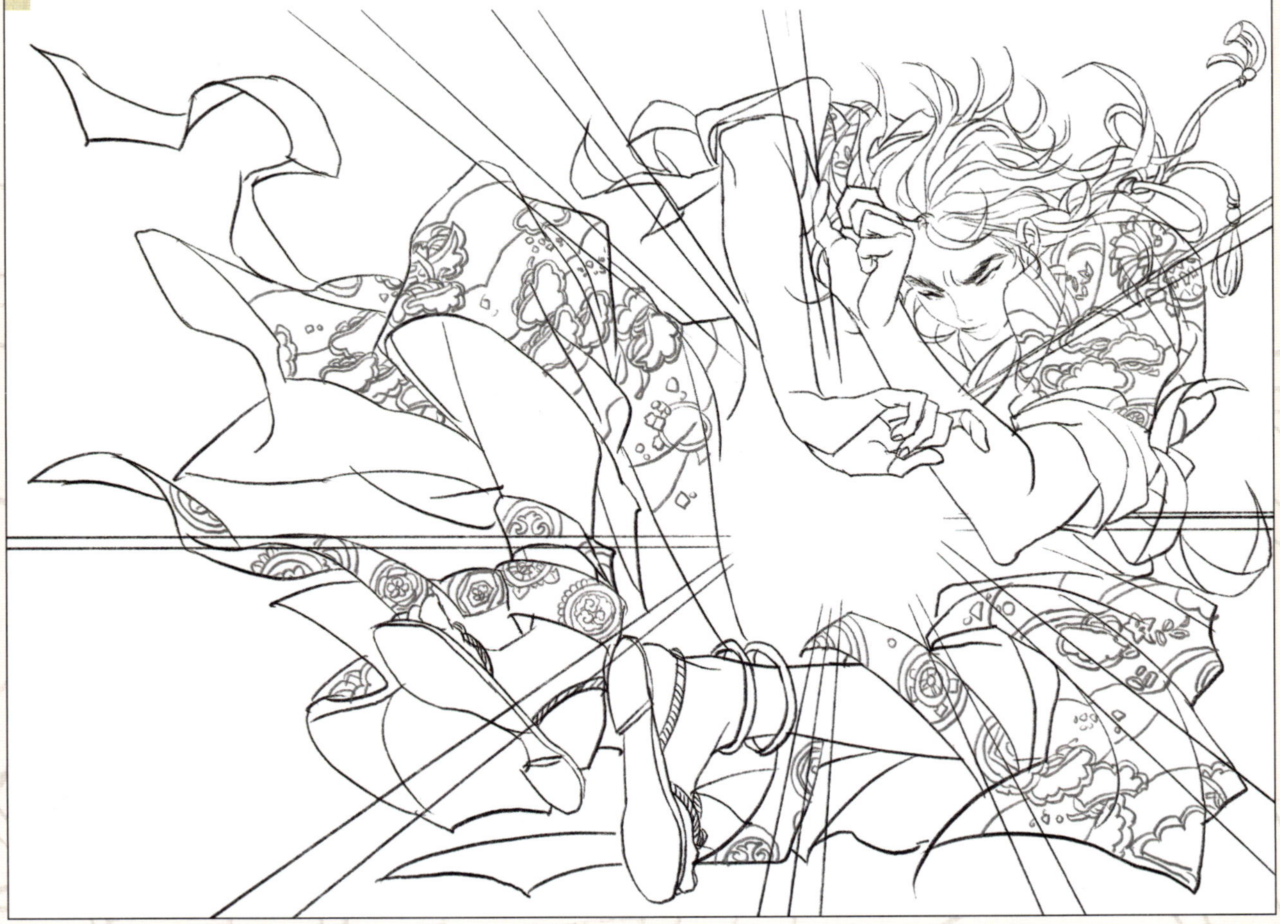

Luoman

08 COLOUR BLOCKING

Now, it's time to move on to the colouring phase. I begin by roughly blocking in the main colour areas. At this stage, it's important to keep things simple, focusing only on the base colours of each element without worrying about too many details. This helps avoid creating unnecessary complexity, which could disrupt the overall composition. For this illustration, I opt for a warm palette, using yellow as the dominant colour to set the tone.

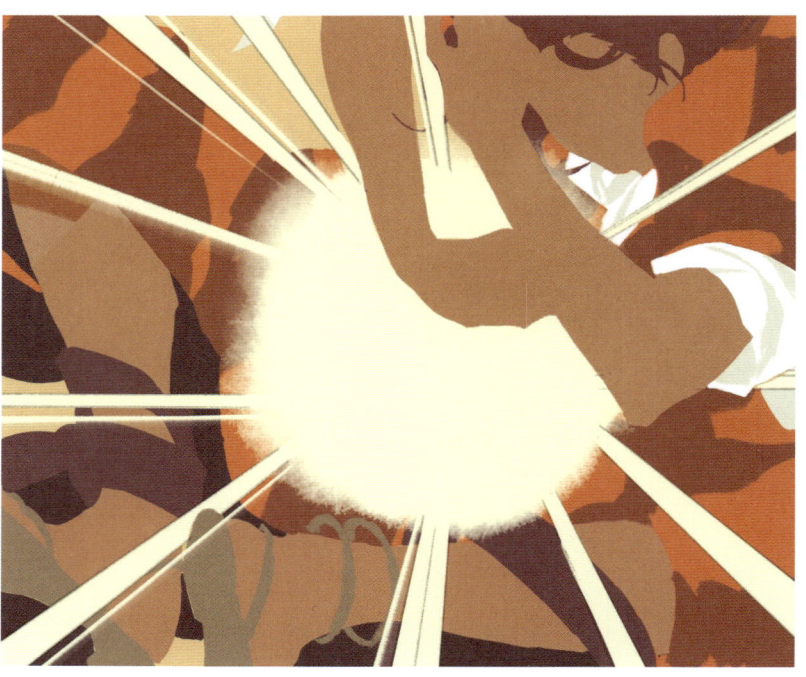

I DON'T WORRY ABOUT DETAIL AS I BLOCK IN COLOUR

09 SHADOW DEFINITION

Once the base colours are established, I start adding shadows to define the forms of different objects. Since the line work was already made precise during the inking stage, the shadows only need to be applied at key points of transition and form, like where surfaces curve or overlap. This is where the accuracy of the line work becomes essential – it guides the placement of shadows, allowing for smooth and efficient rendering of the volume and depth of each object.

SHADOWS HELP TO DEFINE FORMS

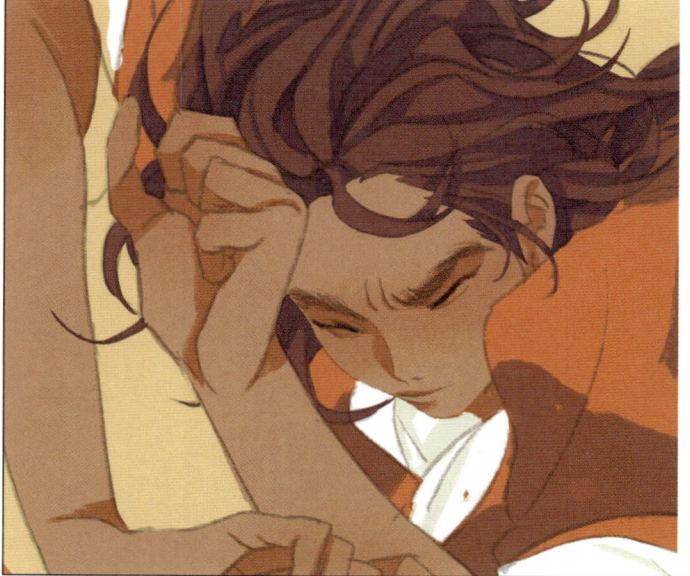

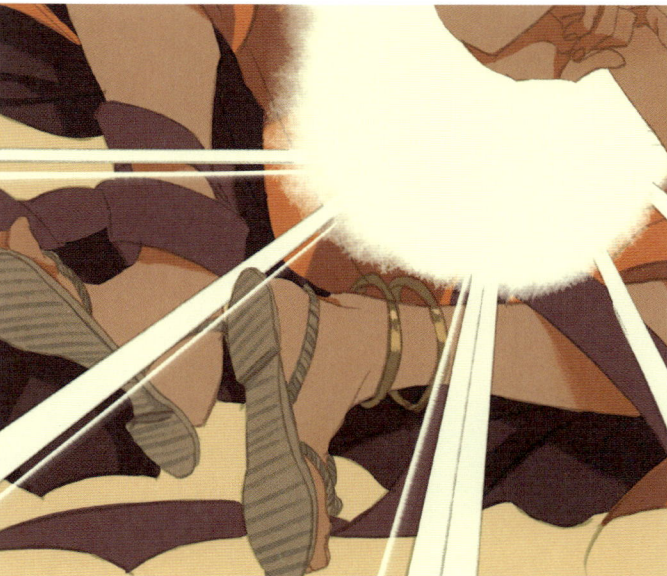

10 COLOURING INTRICATE PATTERNS

Finally, after completing the overall light-and-shadow relationship, I move on to colouring the intricate patterns on the clothing. To prevent the image from becoming cluttered or messy due to an overabundance of colours, I choose instead to fill the complex patterns using analogous colours (those that are similar in hue). This approach helps maintain harmony in the image, allowing the intricate details to stay visually cohesive within a unified colour palette, rather than overwhelming the composition.

By carefully managing colour choices for the patterns, I ensure that the richness of the design remains without compromising the overall cleanliness of the illustration.

I USE ANALOGOUS COLOURS TO MAINTAIN HARMONY IN THE IMAGE

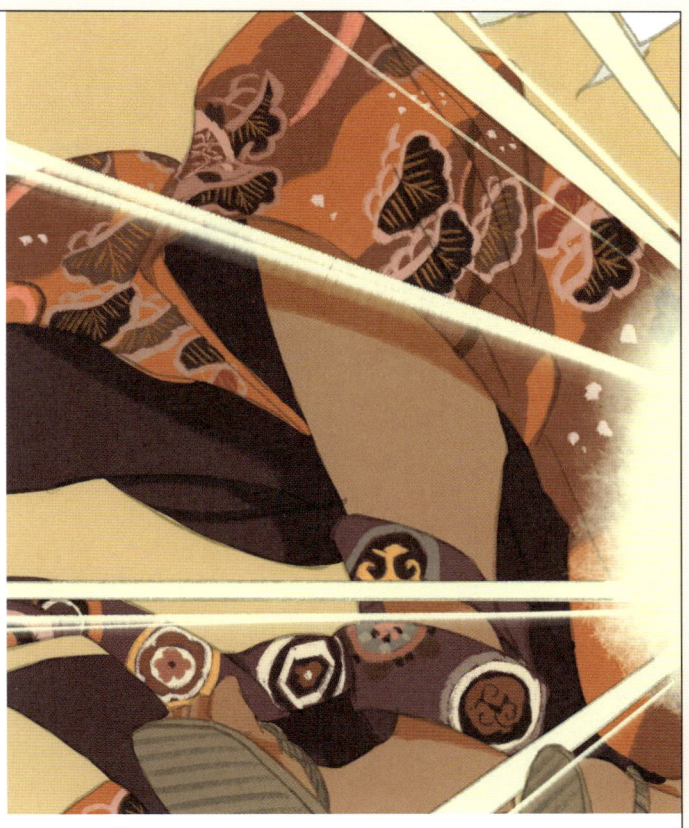

11 MODIFYING THE SPEED LINES

Next, I move on to the speed lines. To ensure they blend more harmoniously into the illustration, I modify the colour of the line work. This subtle adjustment helps the speed lines feel more integrated with the overall composition, rather than standing out too sharply or competing with the main elements of the piece.

I DON'T WANT THE SPEED LINES TO COMPETE WITH THE MAIN ELEMENTS

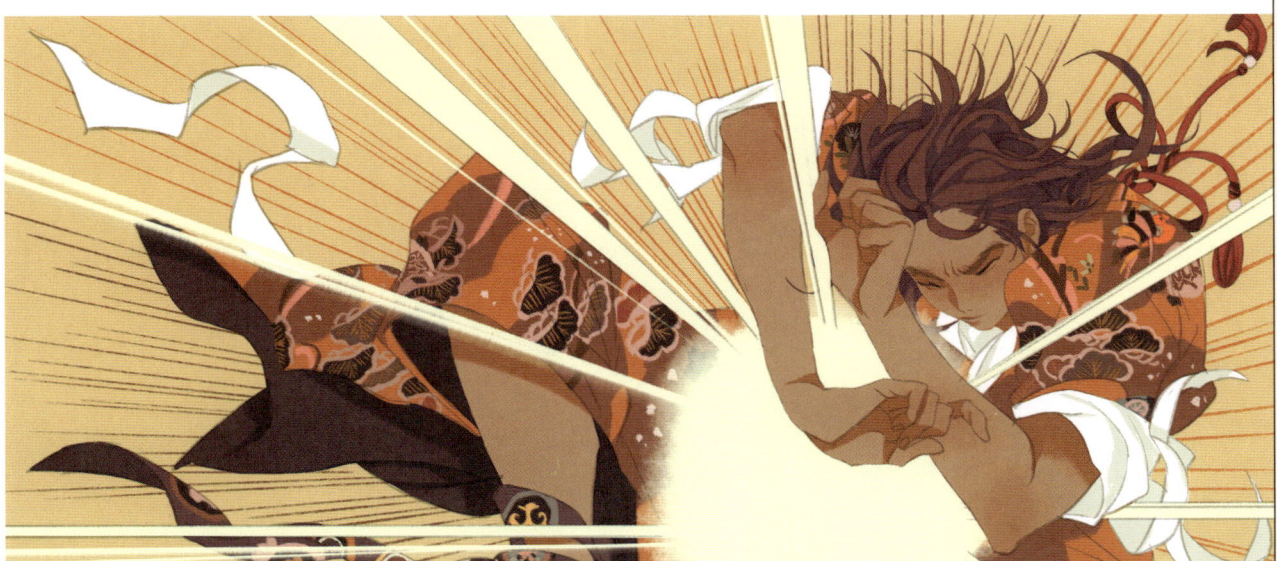

12 ADJUSTING THE BASE COLOUR

After that, I begin layering in some textures to bring more depth and richness to the artwork. To do this, I first choose materials with a watercolour texture and a paper grain. By adjusting the layer properties – such as using blend modes like Multiply or Overlay – I seamlessly merge these textures with the base illustration, enhancing the hand-drawn feel of the piece. This layering of textures adds a level of detail that makes the image feel more tactile and visually interesting.

The goal here is to give the artwork a handcrafted, organic quality while maintaining control over how the textures interact with the colours and line work. With this method, the image gains a more authentic, painterly look, while still preserving the clarity of the character and action at its core.

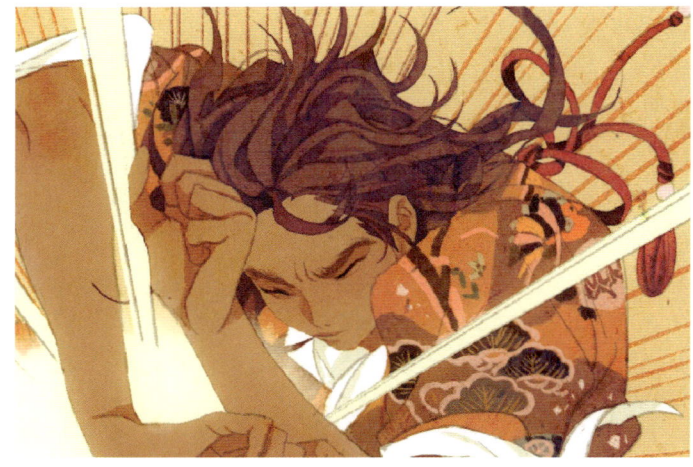

BRINGING IN SOME TEXTURE

13 GRADIENT MAPPING

At this stage, I create two new layers and apply a gradient-mapping effect to them. Then, by adjusting the layer properties, I blend them to achieve the desired result. The purpose of this step is to retain the original light-and-shadow relationships while adding more vibrant colours to enrich the overall composition.

BLENDING LAYERS WITH A GRADIENT-MAPPING EFFECT

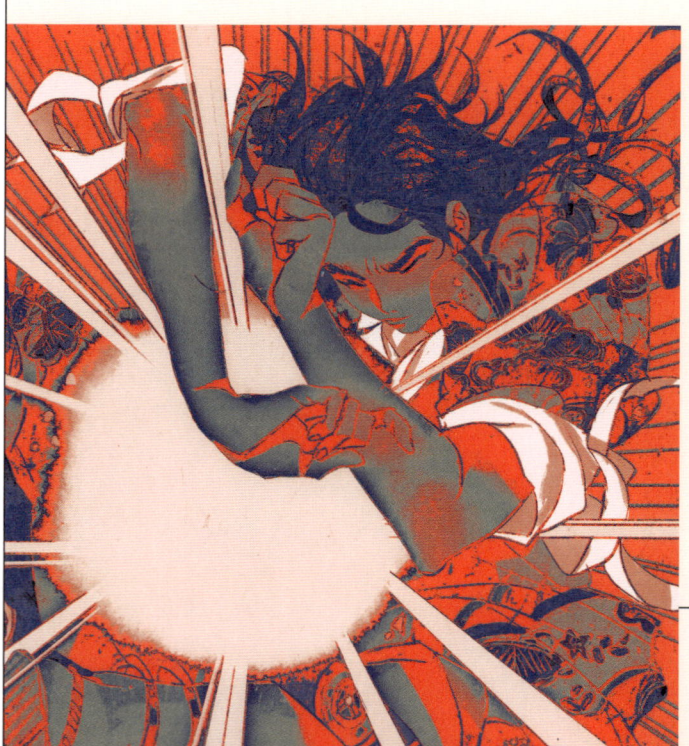 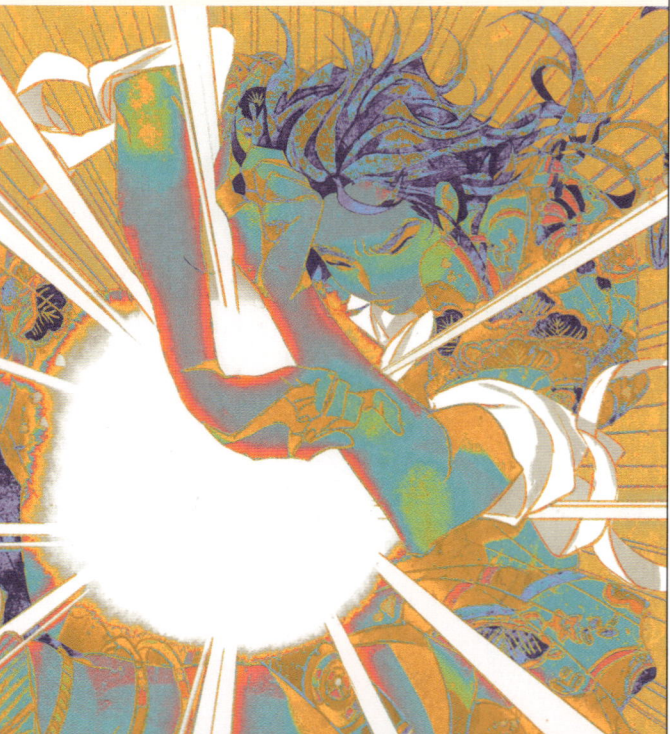

14 TWEAKING THE CURVES

To wrap up the illustration, I make one final adjustment to unify the layers. By tweaking the curves of all the layers, I refine the overall colour contrast, ensuring that the tones across the image are harmonious and balanced. This step helps emphasize key areas, subtly enhancing the contrast without overwhelming the finer details.

In this process, I also bring out some of the texture effects that were added earlier, making sure they integrate smoothly into the composition. This gives the illustration a more cohesive and polished feel, allowing the textures to subtly enhance the overall hand-drawn aesthetic.

With the colour contrast adjusted and textures in place, the illustration reaches its final form. The dynamic elements, detailed patterns, and rich textures come together, creating a visually engaging and well-balanced artwork.

And, with that, the piece is complete!

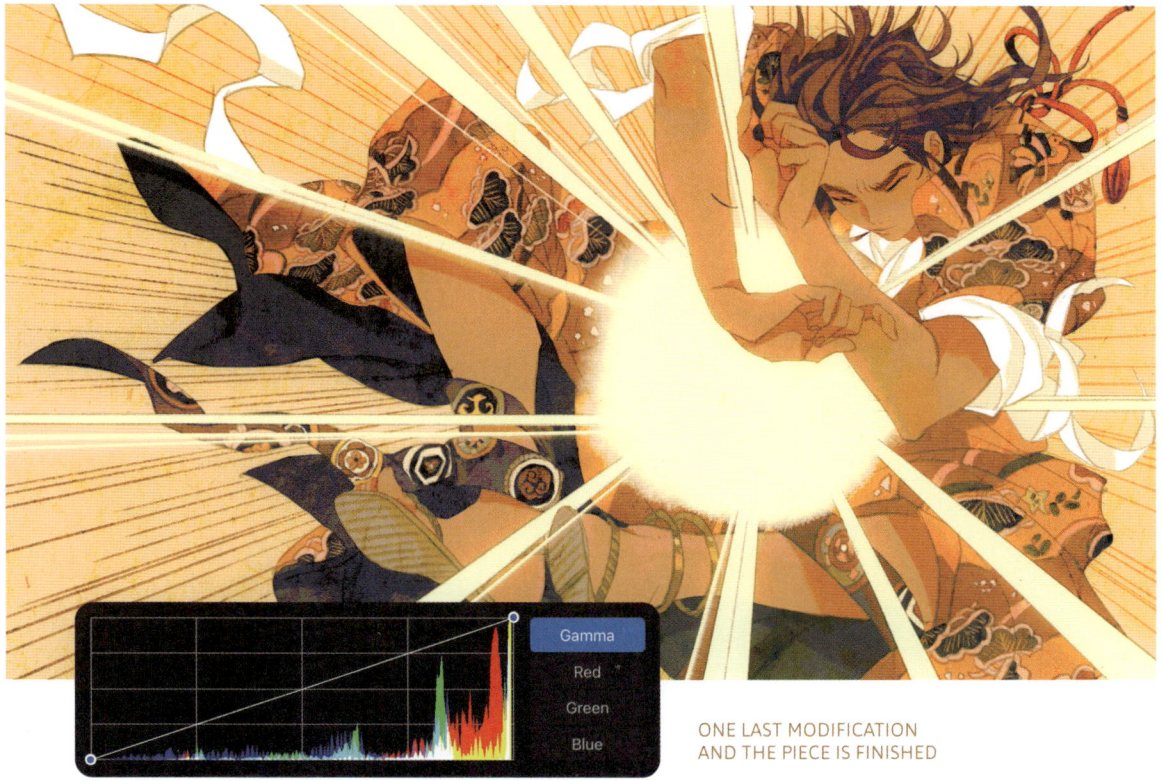

ONE LAST MODIFICATION
AND THE PIECE IS FINISHED

CONCLUSION

By completing this piece, I gained a deeper understanding of Hokusai's pursuit of formal aesthetics, which holds significant artistic value. I hope that through my own interpretation, I can offer a fresh perspective on his work, honouring his legacy while adding my unique voice to the conversation. This journey has allowed me to connect with the essence of his art, and I aspire to continue exploring and reimagining such timeless creations.

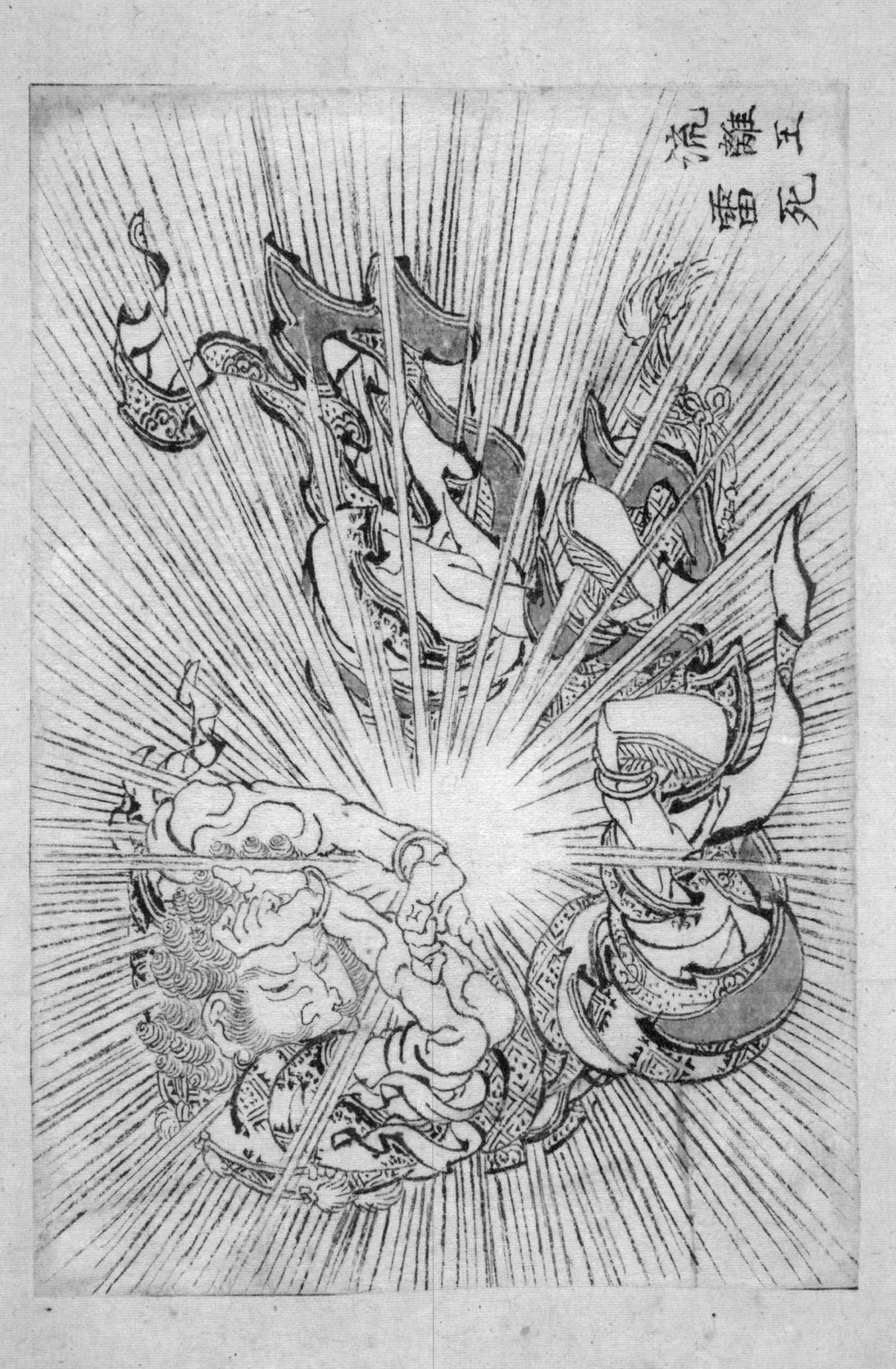

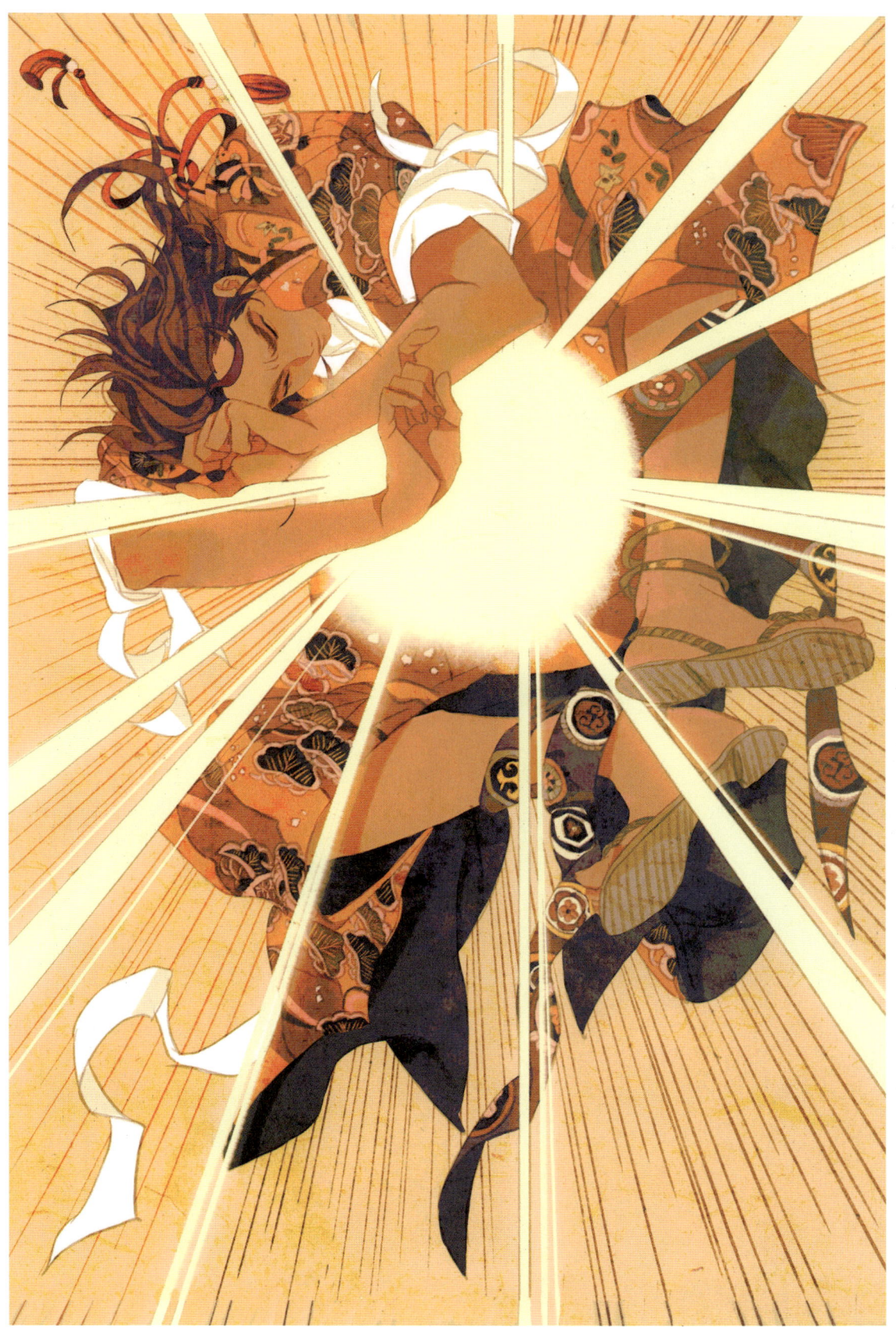

A BOLT OF LIGHTNING
STRIKES VIRŪDHAKA DEAD

LUOMAN

BELOW: *Eros*
As the goddess of love, Aphrodite cannot control her powers. Constantly thwarted by fate, she cannot find her true love and, as a result, humanity also cannot attain the fulfilment of perfect love and happiness

RIGHT: *Them*
I've drawn this couple for the past few years, always feeling that their days together are so sweet

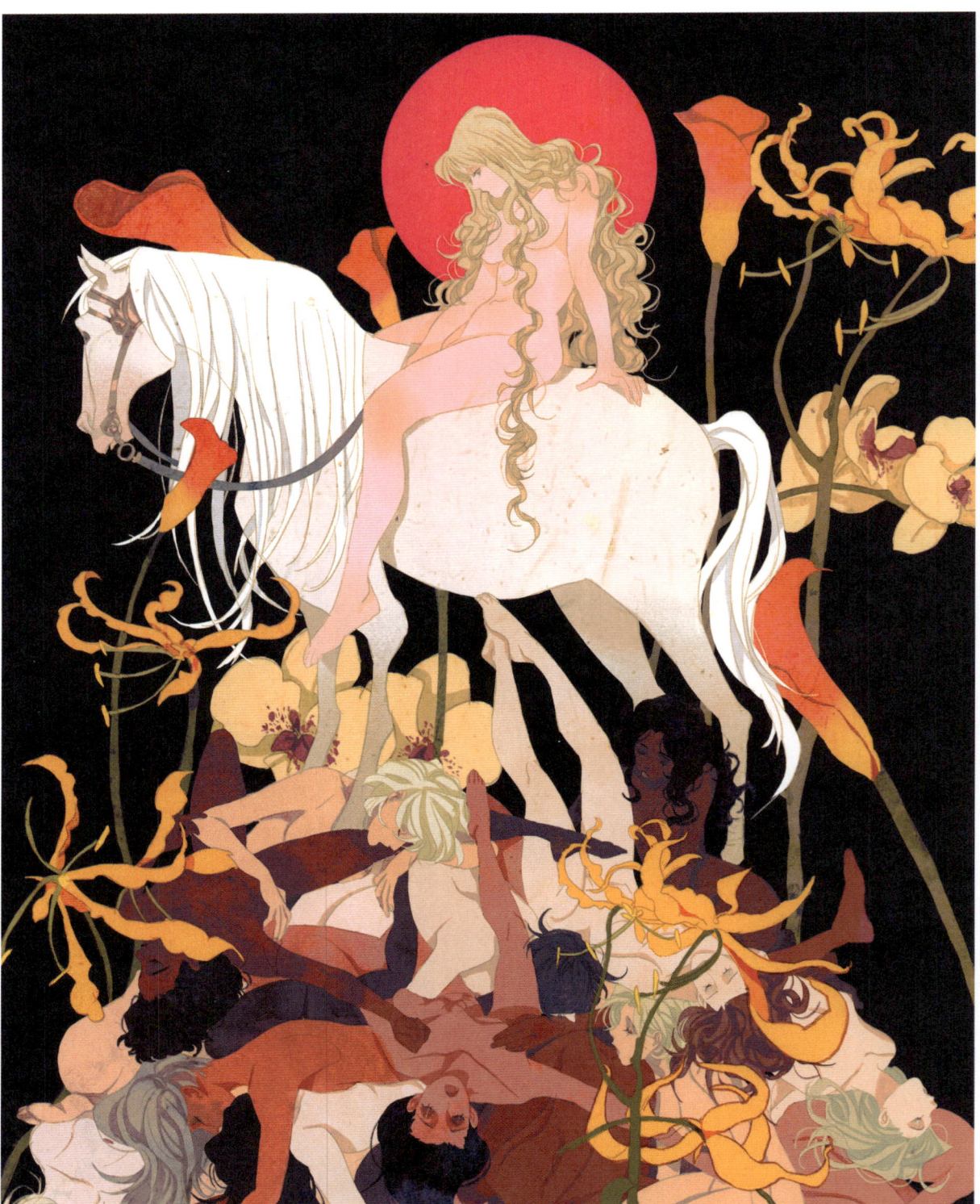

GALLERY: LUOMAN

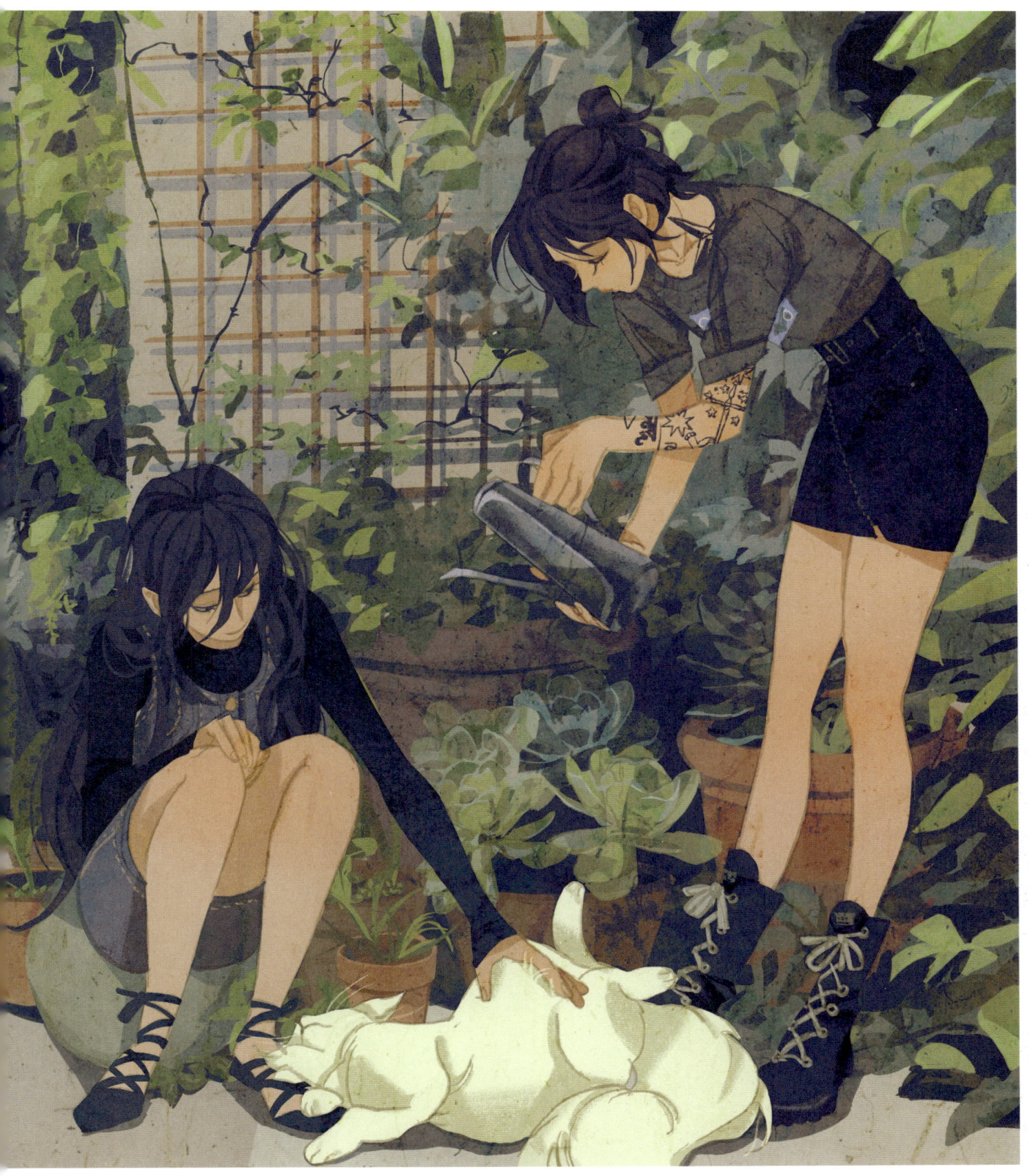

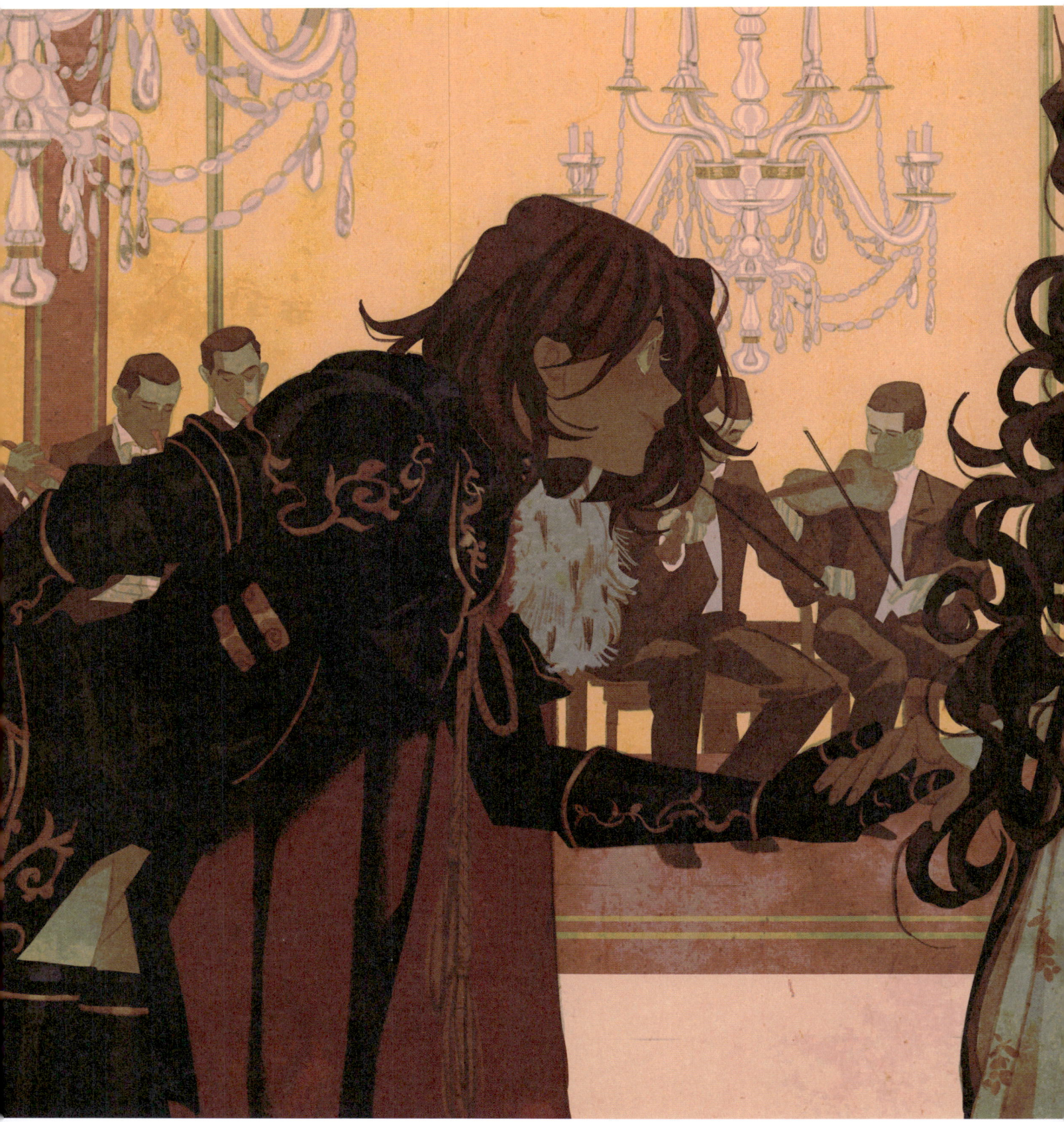

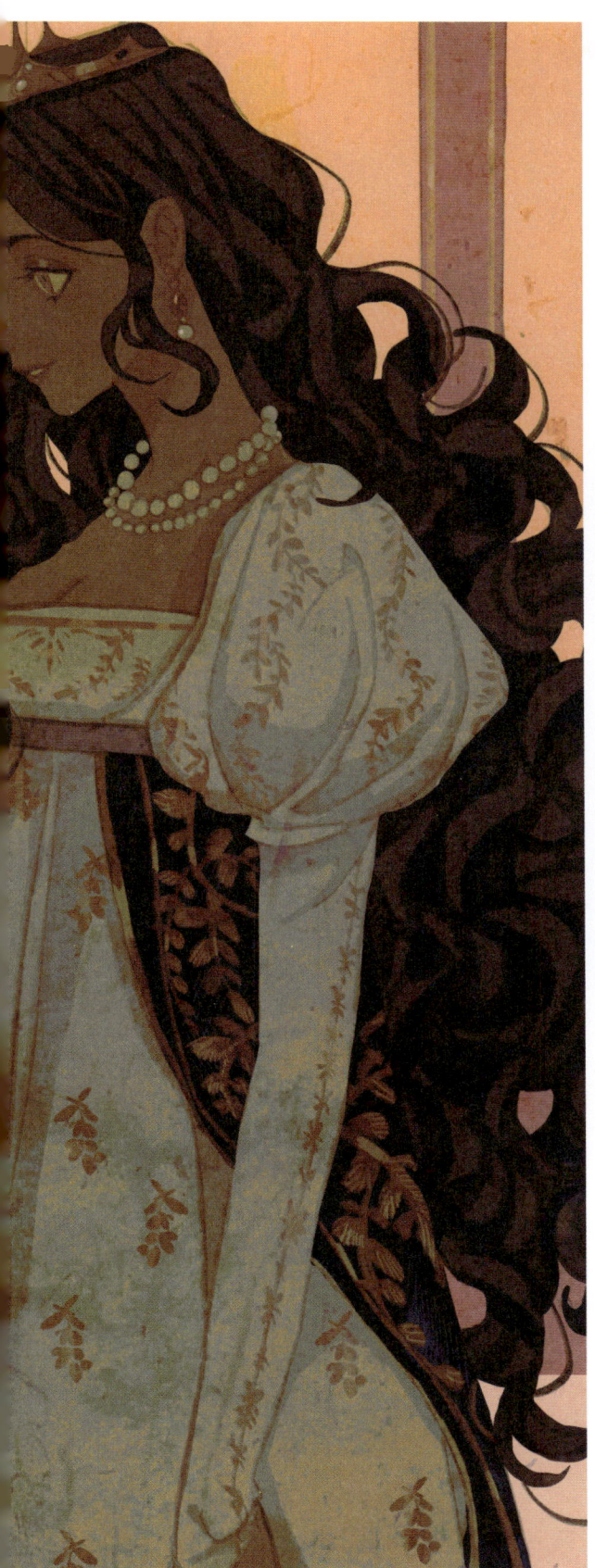

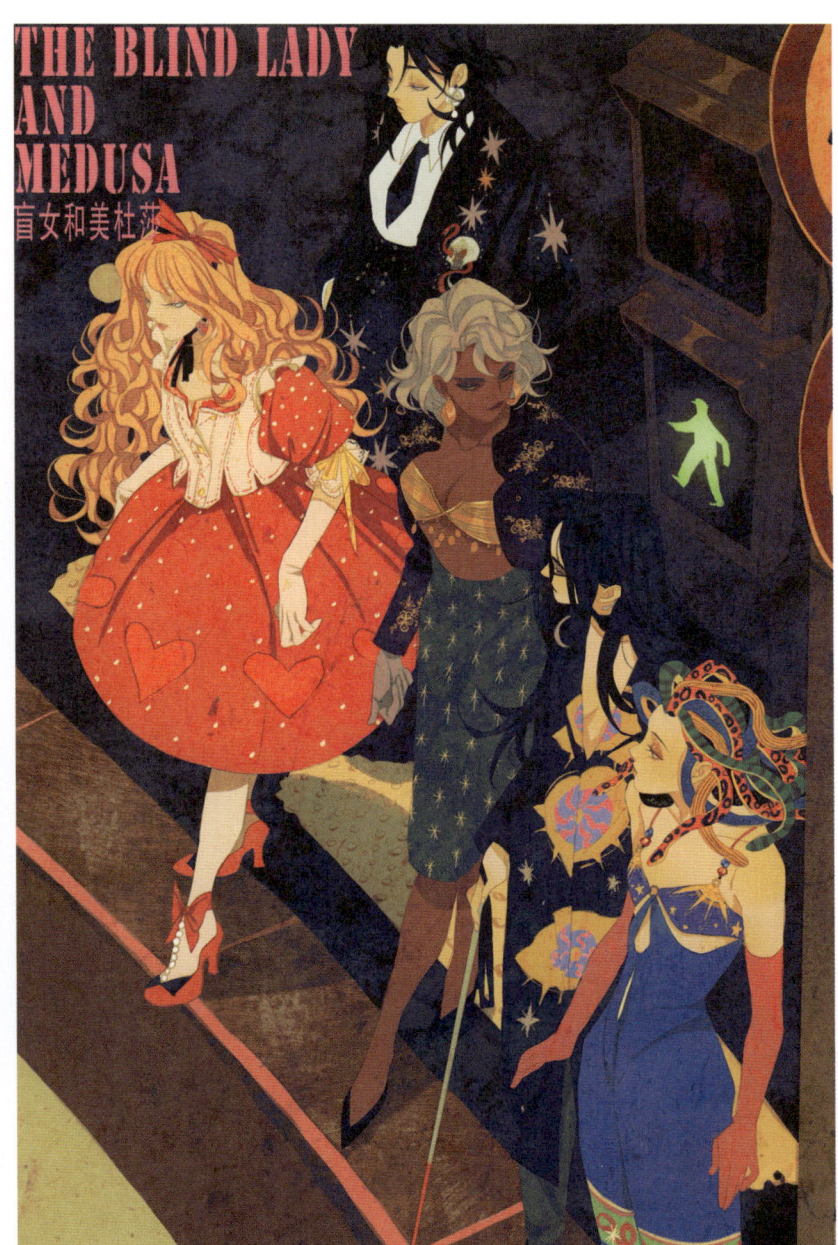

THE BLIND LADY
AND
MEDUSA
盲女和美杜莎

Left: *The Princess and the Knight*
The knight is inviting his queen to dance

ABOVE: *A Corner of the Street*
Two girls are walking on the streets of Paris

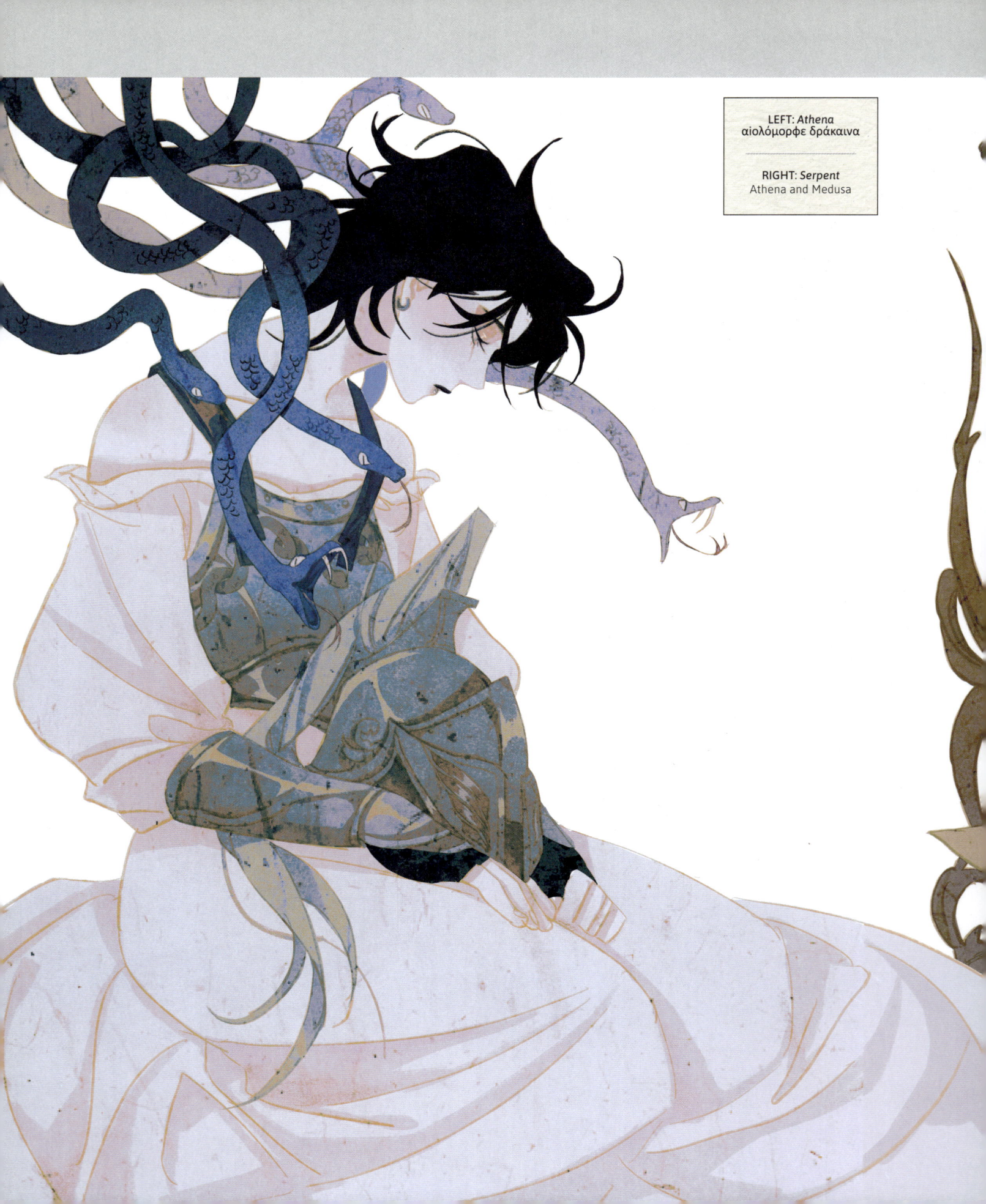

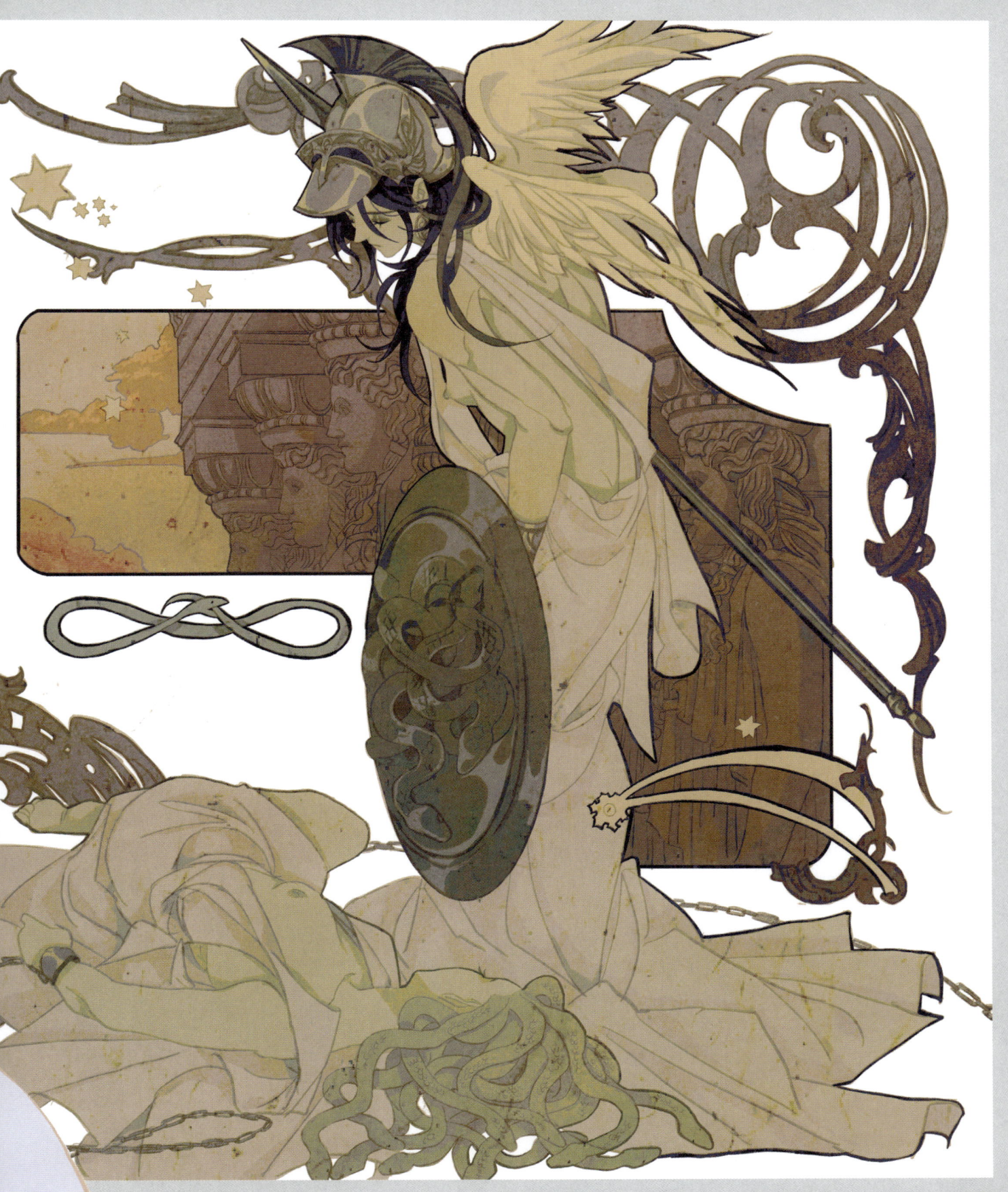

Luoman

PEPPER, PERILLA, SAFFRON AND CLOVE

BY MENGXUAN LI

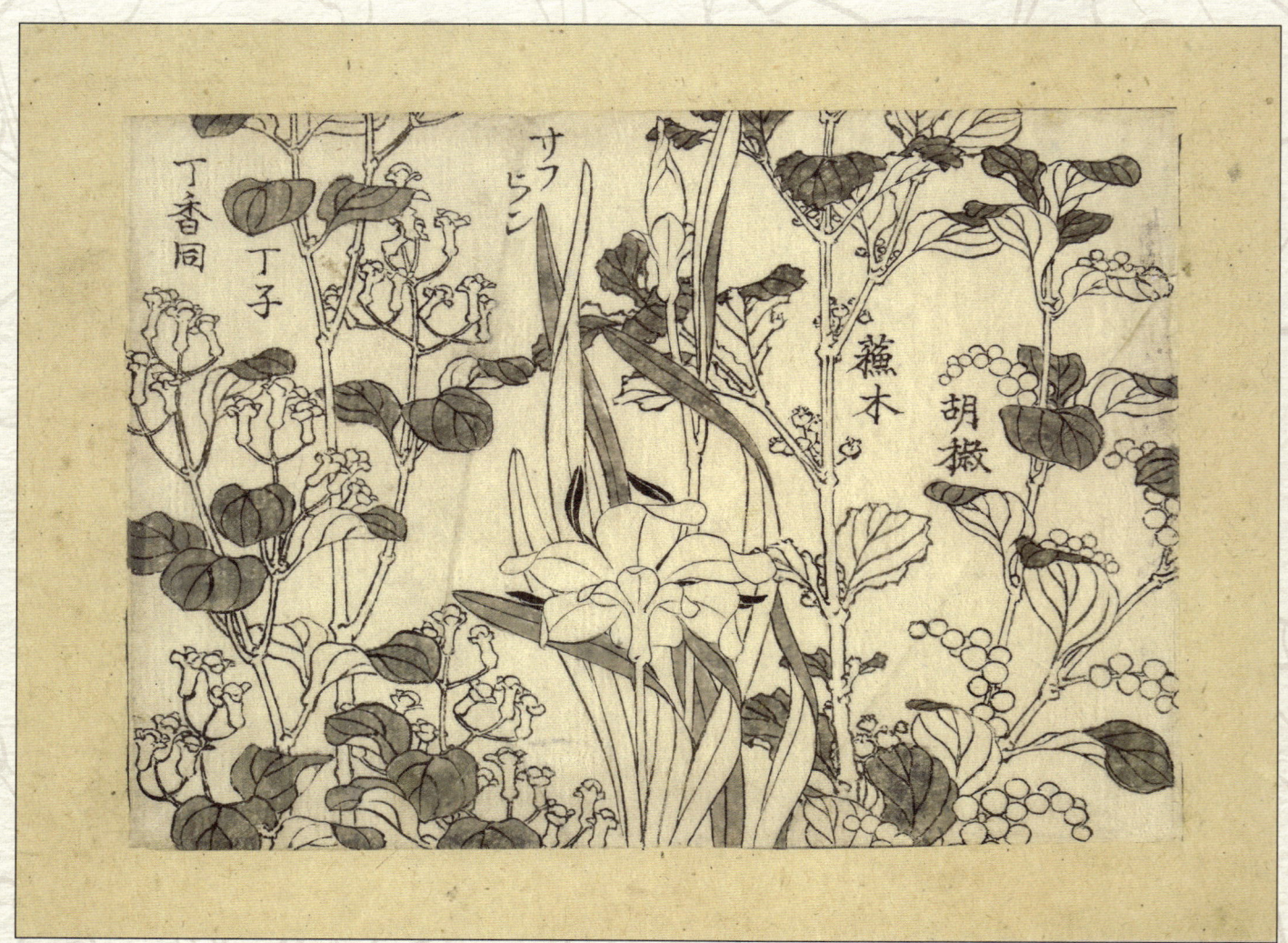

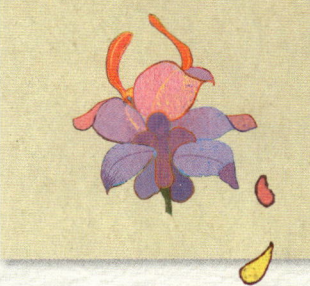

MENGXUAN LI

DISCOVERING HOKUSAI

I have been drawing since I was very young. After spending my childhood in China, I moved to Japan to specialize in traditional art and oil painting. During my art studies, I was influenced by many Japanese styles of art, including ukiyo-e and nihonga paintings, as well as Japanese manga and anime. I have also been inspired by the Impressionist and Nabis artists, and a variety of children's picture books. While studying, I often observed Hokusai's works, taking time to learn how he painted natural scenery and where he found motivation for his art. I discovered that Hokusai's observation of life was very detailed, and that he summarized natural things in his own shape language. In the same vein, I also like to observe things around me and draw inspiration from them, eventually turning them into my own creations.

01 INITIAL SKETCH

I usually draw a very rough sketch when I begin the painting process. I think the plant forms in Hokusai's original image are very distinct, and the line work also has a lot of things that I can learn from. So, I study it and create a rough line drawing.

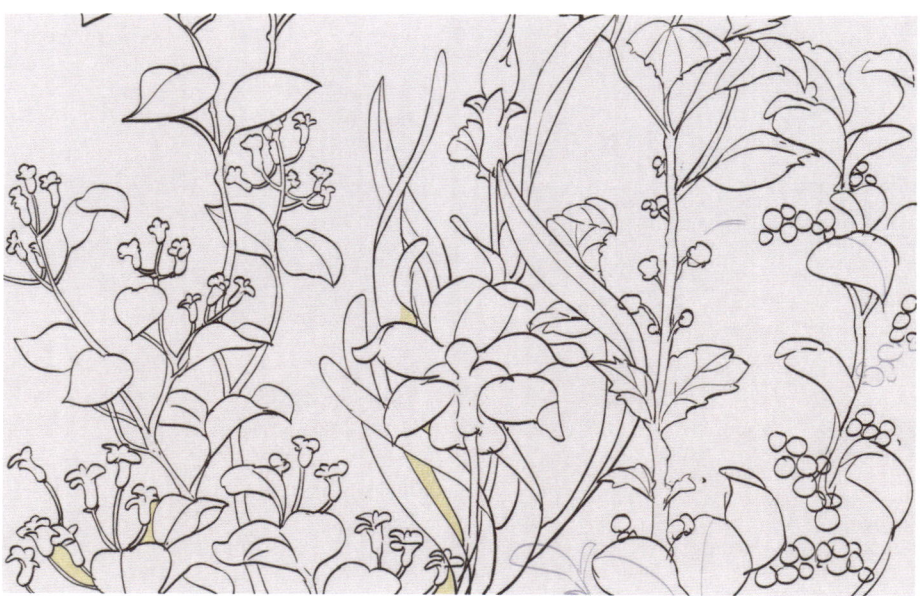

ROUGH LINE DRAWING

02 CHARACTER SKETCH

After I have the sketch of the plants down, I plan to add characters to the image to enrich the story of the painting. The symbolism of the lilac flower is innocence, so I draw two girls in the background.

ADDING CHARACTERS TO MY SKETCH

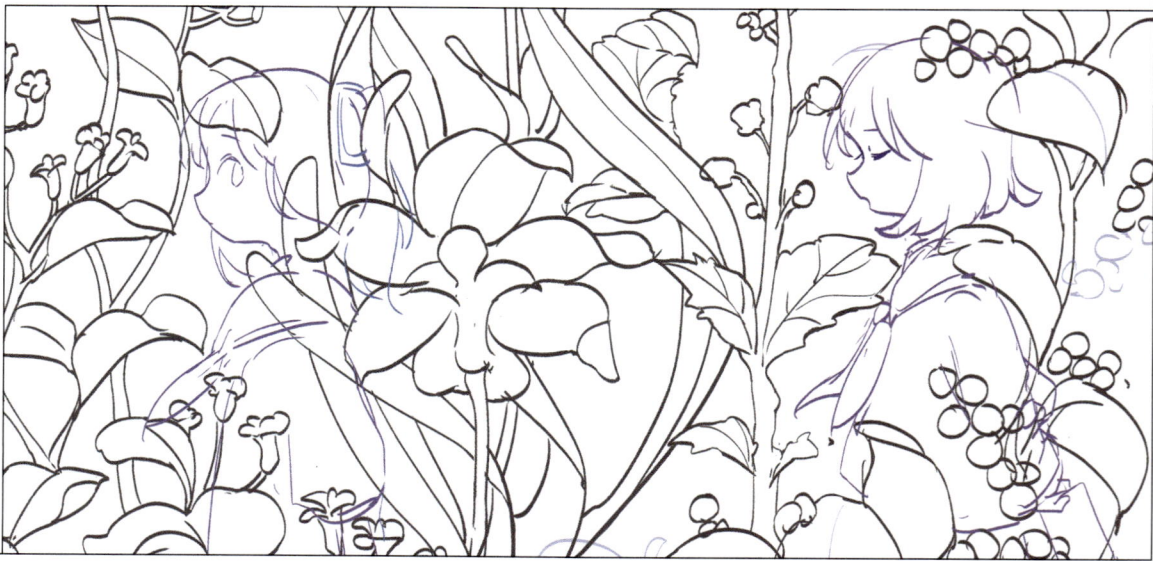

03 SIMPLE OVERALL COLOUR

Once the rough line drawing is determined, I simply add some local colours. Immediately, I think that the background could be yellow to resemble a Japanese ukiyo-e screen. If I'm sticking to the ukiyo-e style, that means the plants in the foreground should be flat colours. I don't use too many colours here; I just want to roughly distinguish the background and foreground to see the overall effect.

TESTING OUT SIMPLE OVERALL COLOUR TO EMULATE THE UKIYO-E STYLE

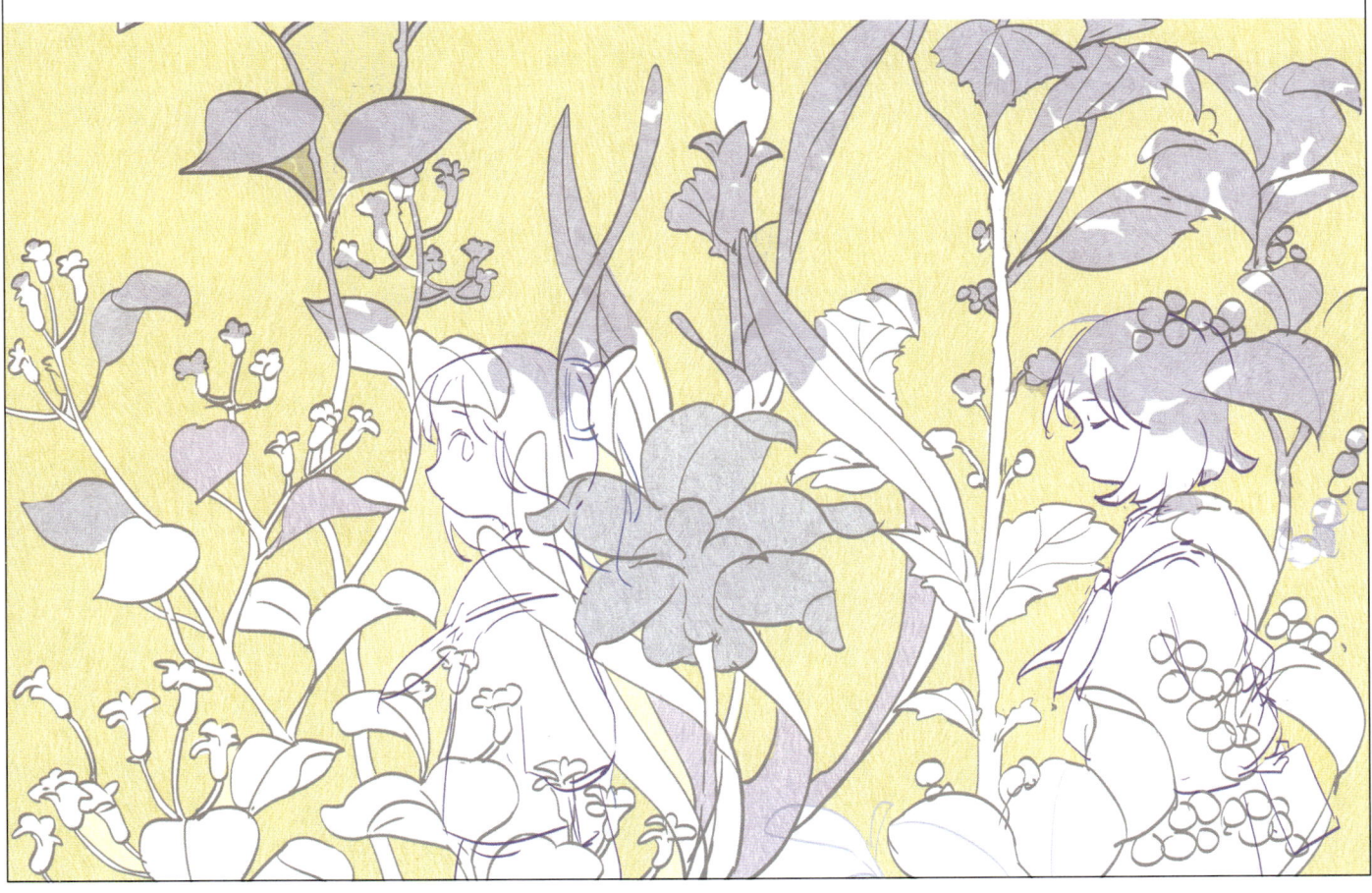

04 SIMPLE LOCAL COLOUR

Here, I start adding more colours to the image, drawing in the local colours of the plants and different flowers. Since the original Hokusai drawing names each flower in the title, I look for many real-life references to capture their likeness as best as possible in my own style. I also add a local colour for each character. By zooming out of the canvas, I can see the general colour relationship.

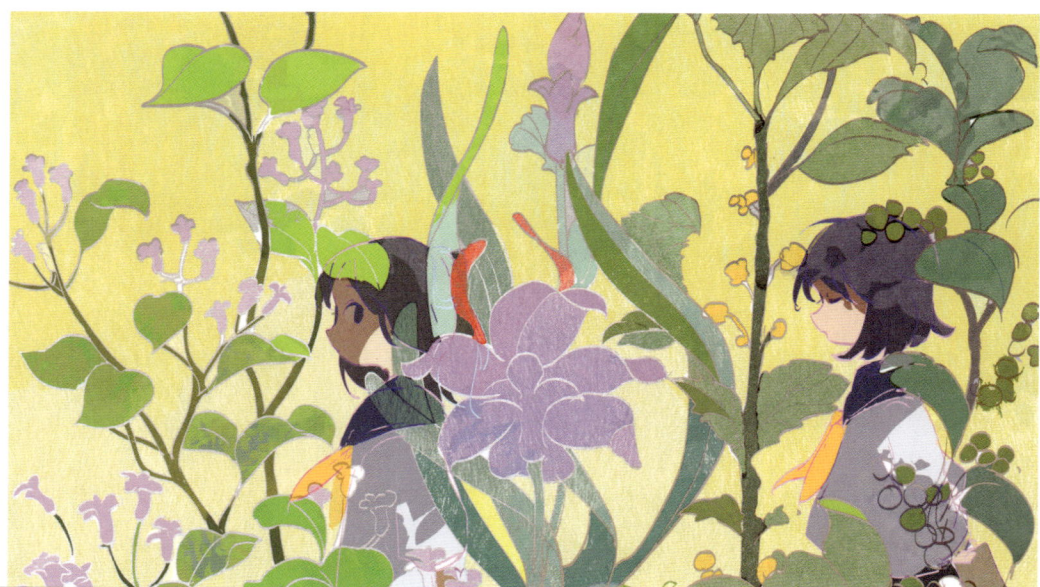

ADDING IN
SIMPLE LOCAL
COLOUR

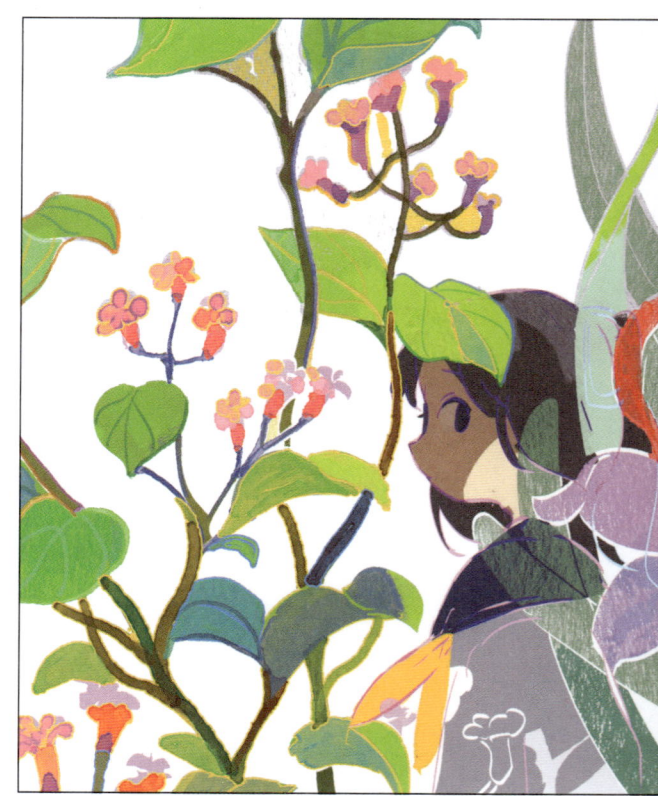

05 START REFINING

After laying out the basic colours, I continue to adjust the colour relationship. I try many colours to see which ones are most suitable and comfortable. While adjusting them, I also pay attention to the black-and-white relationship of the image and try to deepen the background to make the plants and characters in the foreground stand out more.

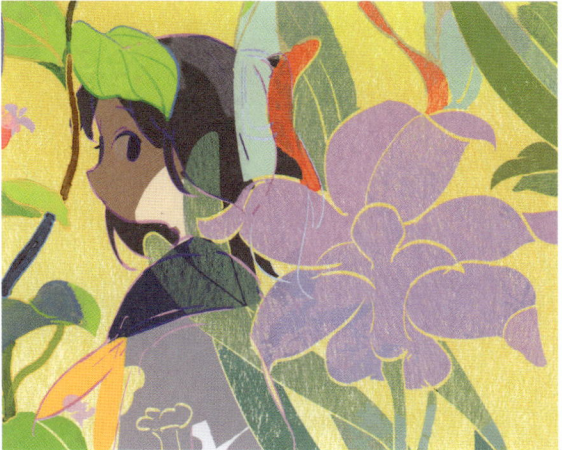

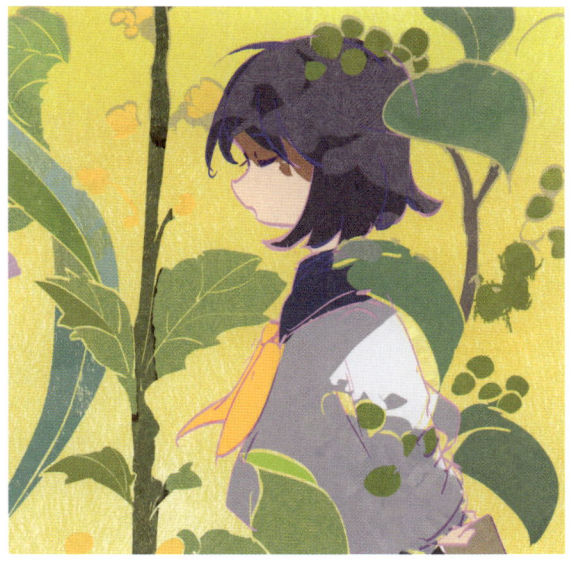

NOW TO REFINE

In some of Hokusai's paintings, you can see that he also simplified his backgrounds and often made them into plain colour blocks to emphasize his subjects and communicate his narrative.

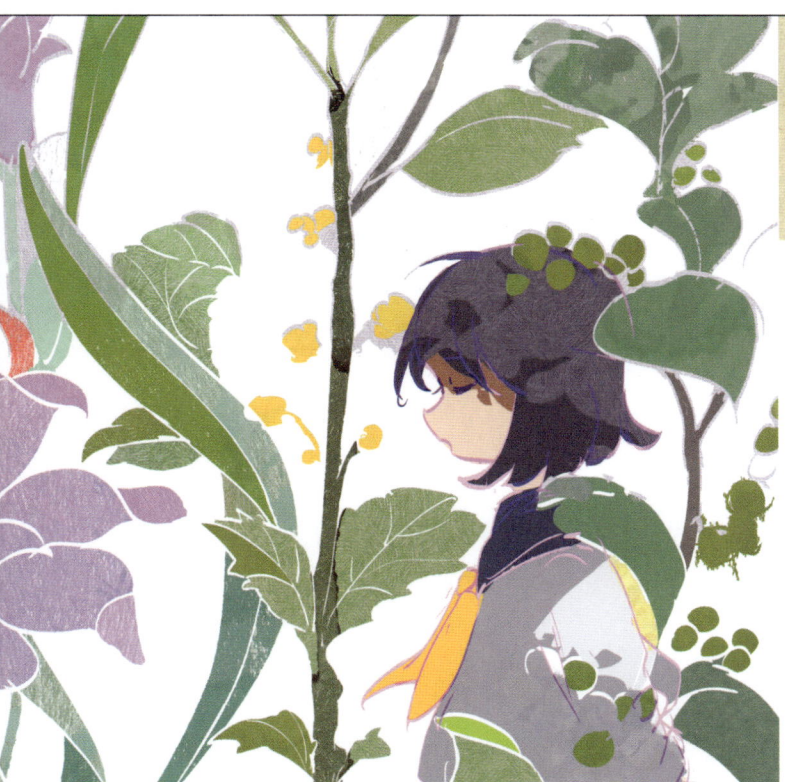

06 MAKING ADJUSTMENTS

In this step, I try a lighter, less-saturated background and it feels surprisingly good. The plants and people in the front are now better highlighted, so I make the switch. I also want to reproduce the printmaking and hand-painted texture often seen in Hokusai's art, so I add some pencil textures.

ADJUSTING THE
BACKGROUND COLOUR
AND ADDING SOME
PENCIL TEXTURES

07 MORE REFINING

Once the rough draft is finished, it's time to start refining it. I add more details and colour variations to the image and start to characterize the leaves. I also add different colours to their outlines.

ADD DETAILS AND
COLOUR VARIATIONS
TO THE IMAGE

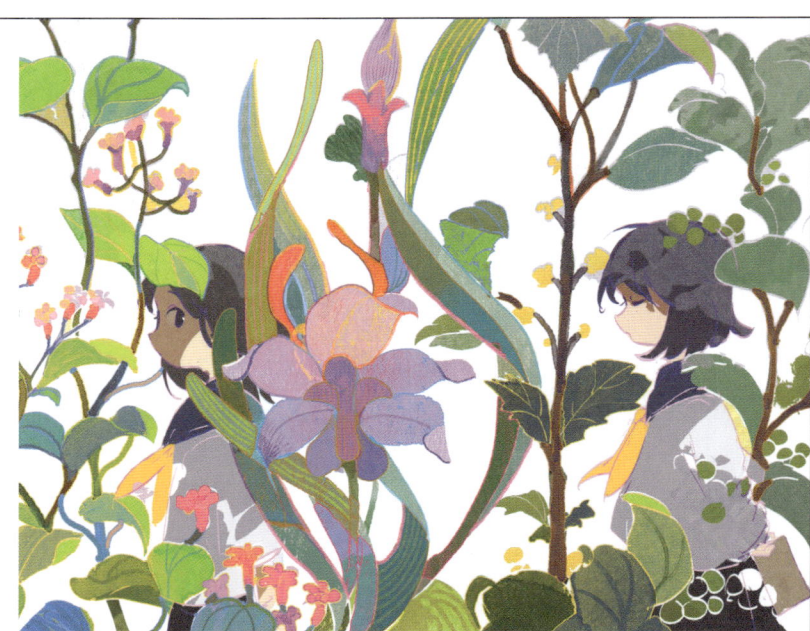

08 ADDING TO THE PEPPER PLANTS

Time to focus on adding to the plants on the right. After looking up reference pictures, I now know that pepper fruits (far right) are also green and brown, so I include these two colours to make it appear less monotonous. Slowly, I refine the leaves and flowers, adding details and more brushstrokes.

STICKING CLOSE TO MY REFERENCE ISSUES

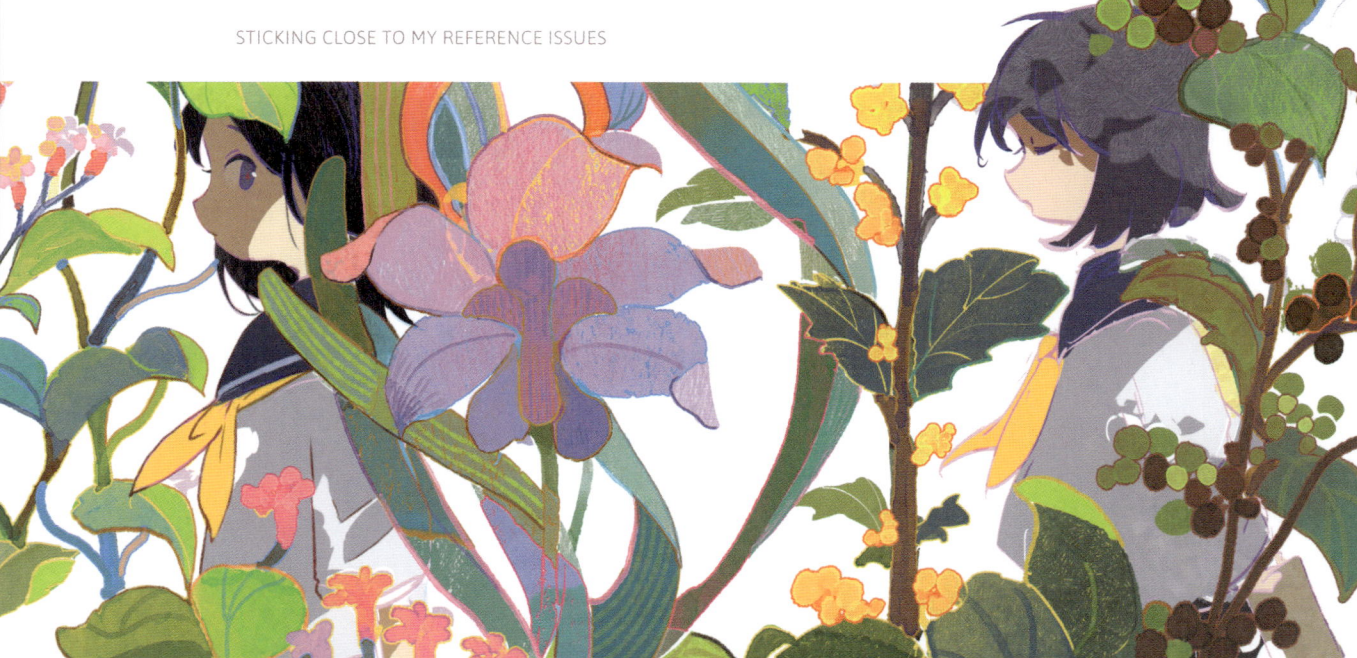

09 COLOUR SOLUTION

At this stage, I play around with different forms and arrangements. I like how the characters are broken up into two different sections, highlighting the various plants and presenting a kind of story with colour. Though I don't decide to keep the layout this way, I had a fun time experimenting.

TRYING OUT
DIFFERENT LAYOUTS

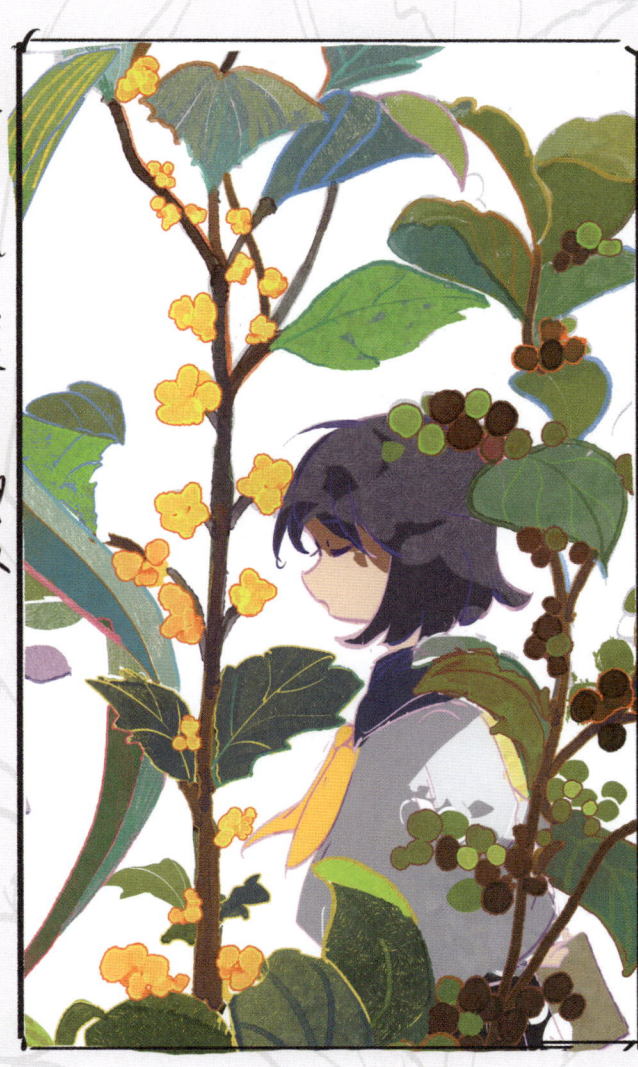

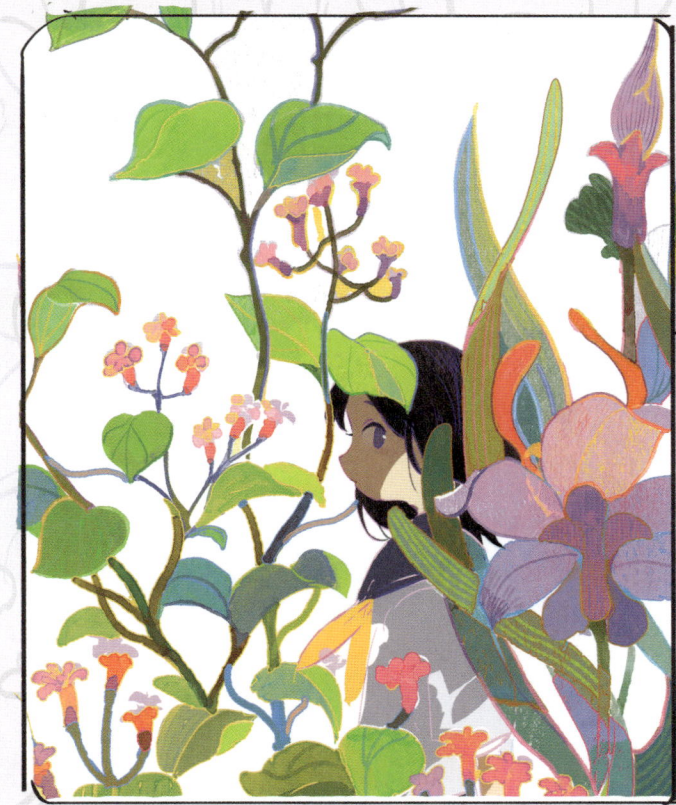

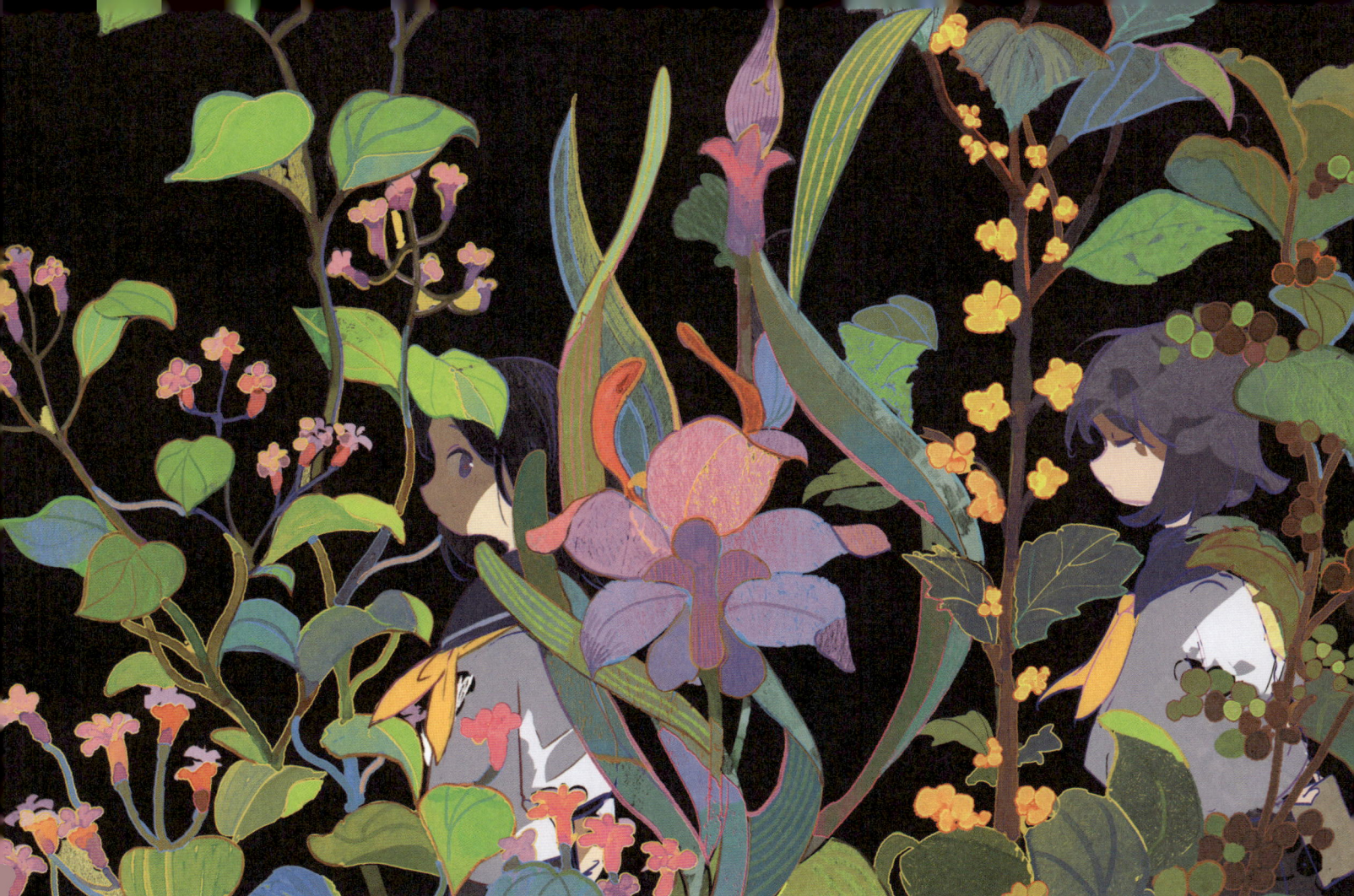

10 DECIDING ON A BACKGROUND

I often try different things to see which solution is best, and I don't decide on it all at once. I've adjusted the background again here, changing it to black. I feel that this choice makes the colours on the plants appear richer, and the effect is pleasing. I'm locking the background in.

11 ADDING DETAILS TO THE CHARACTERS

Now it's time to refine the characters. I organize the characters' shapes and colours, cleaning up their line work to make them look more integrated yet prominent. At the same time, I adjust their structures and proportions.

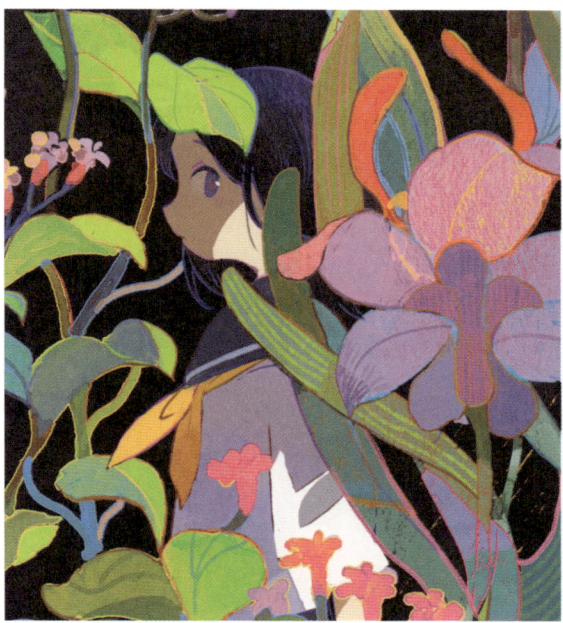 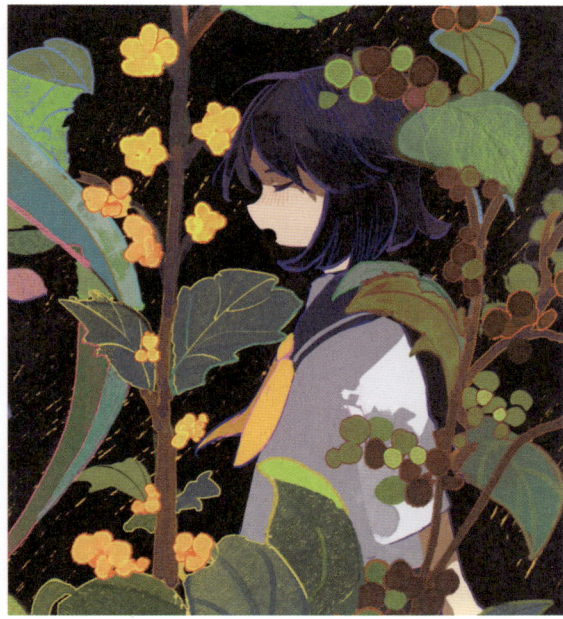

REFINING DETAILS ON THE CHARACTERS

12 TEXTURE

On second thought, I make the background a little lighter so it looks more comfortable. I also add texture and slightly adjust the outline and internal lines of the plants. I incorporate some small dots in the background to float around like pollen.

I ADD LITTLE DOTS TO THE BACKGROUND TO RESEMBLE POLLEN

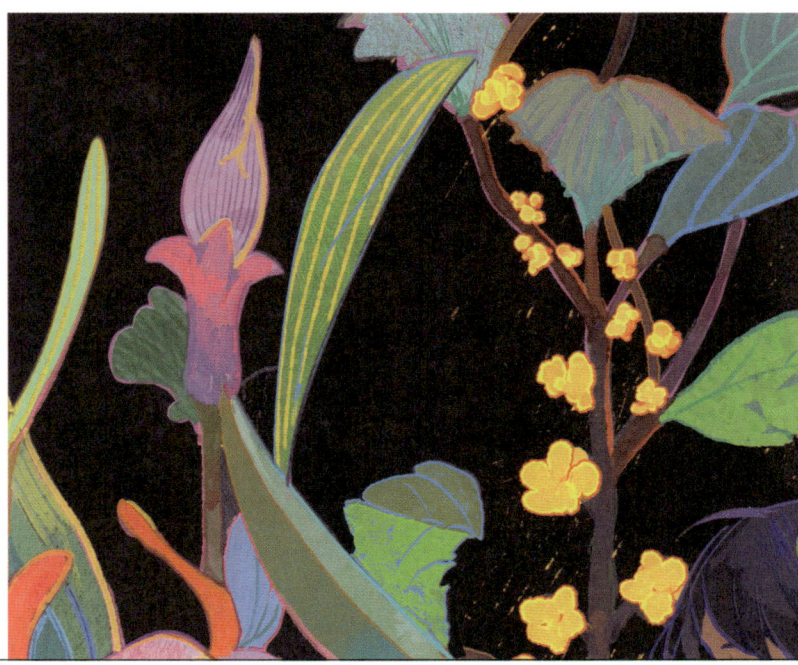

DEFINING THE PLANTS

Continuing to sort out the plant shapes and subtle colour changes within them, I add some coloured lines to the flowers and adjust the colour of their branches and stems. During the painting process, I constantly tweak the colours in various places to see which ones are the best fit for the painting.

ADJUSTING THE SHAPES AND
SUBTLE COLOUR CHANGES

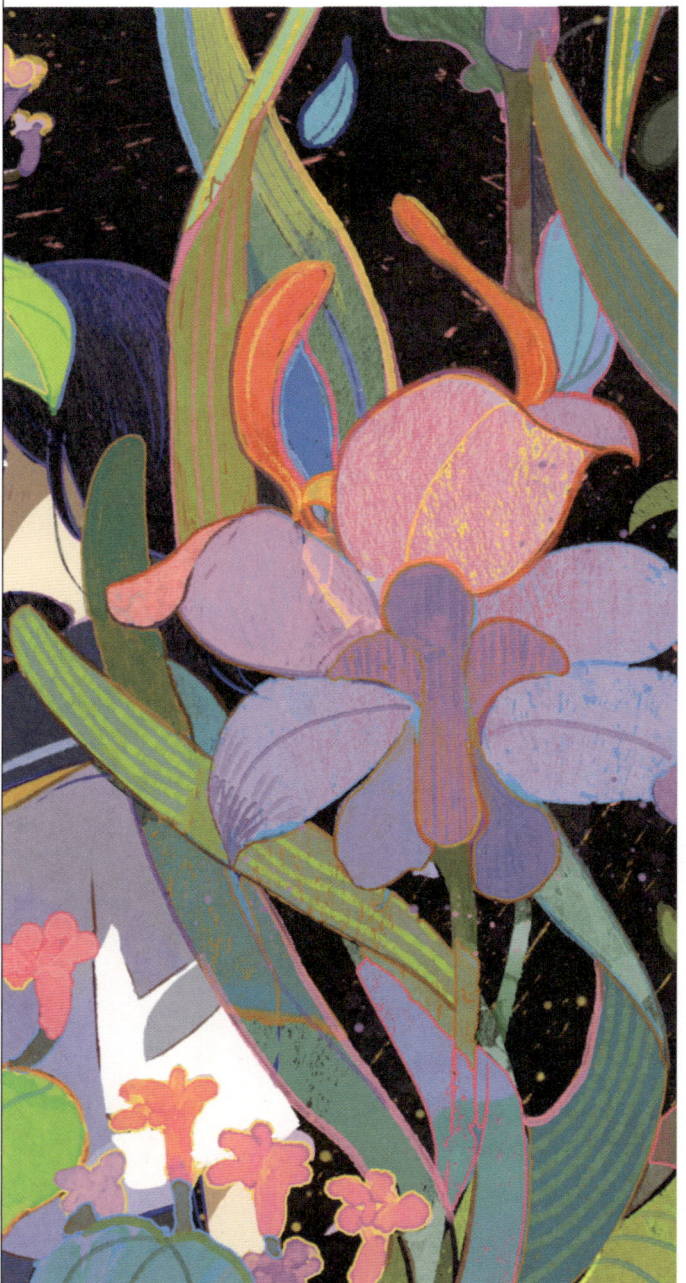

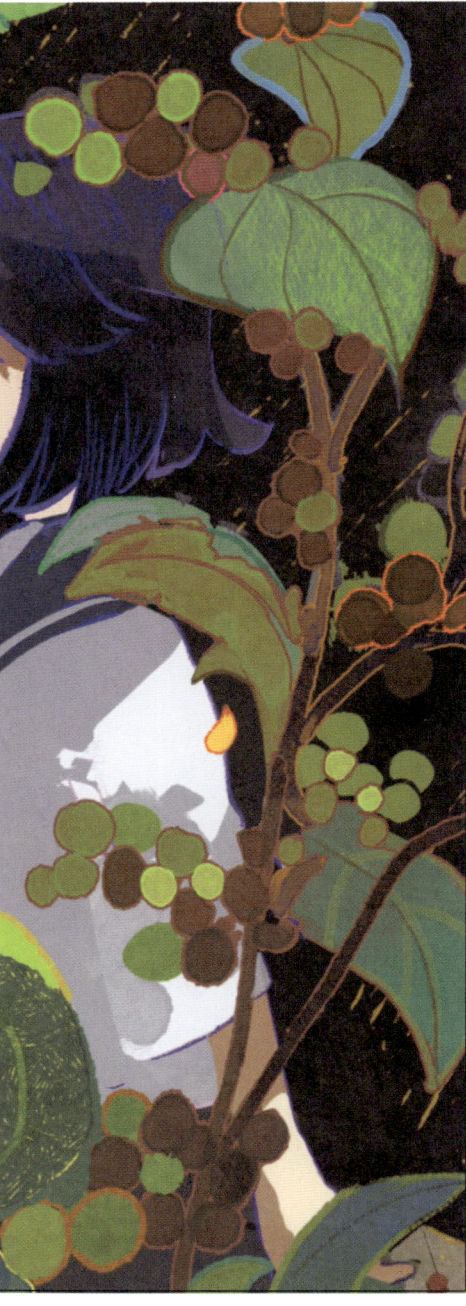

FINAL TOUCHES

Next, I add some more detail to the background, such as tiny falling petals, to give the shapes a contrast between large, medium, and small. I also draw more dots around the flower to appear like pollen blown by the wind. Finally, I use filters in Adobe Photoshop to adjust the overall colour and contrast of the painting. And with a little sharpening effect, the image is complete.

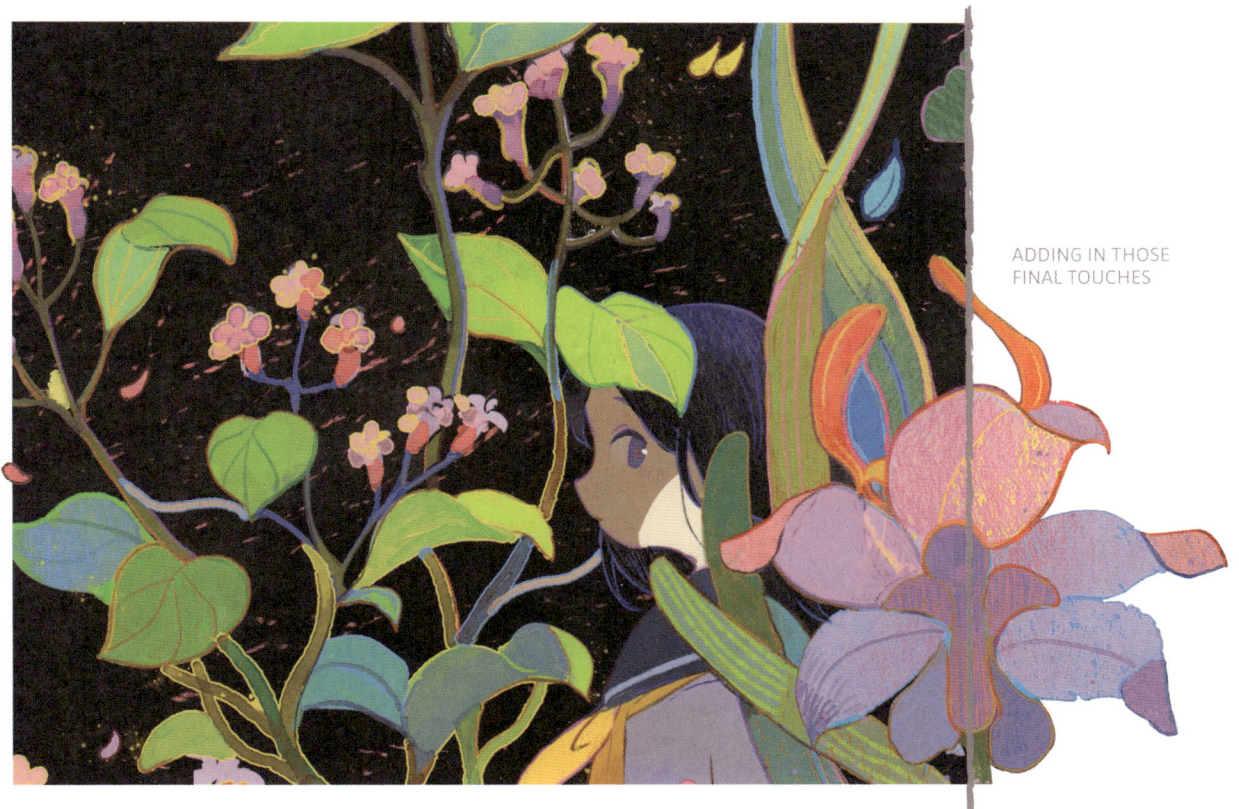

ADDING IN THOSE
FINAL TOUCHES

CONCLUSION

Through this study of Hokusai, I realized the wonderful and varied scope of his compositions, particularly his depictions of plants. His line work is very interesting and, though simple, beautifully considered and designed. Among his artwork, I also love his illustrations that showcase fantasy animals, as well as his vivid and exquisite depictions of historical figures. It is clear why Hokusai had a profound influence on modern comics. There is endless invaluable inspiration to be found in his ukiyo-e style and composition methods.

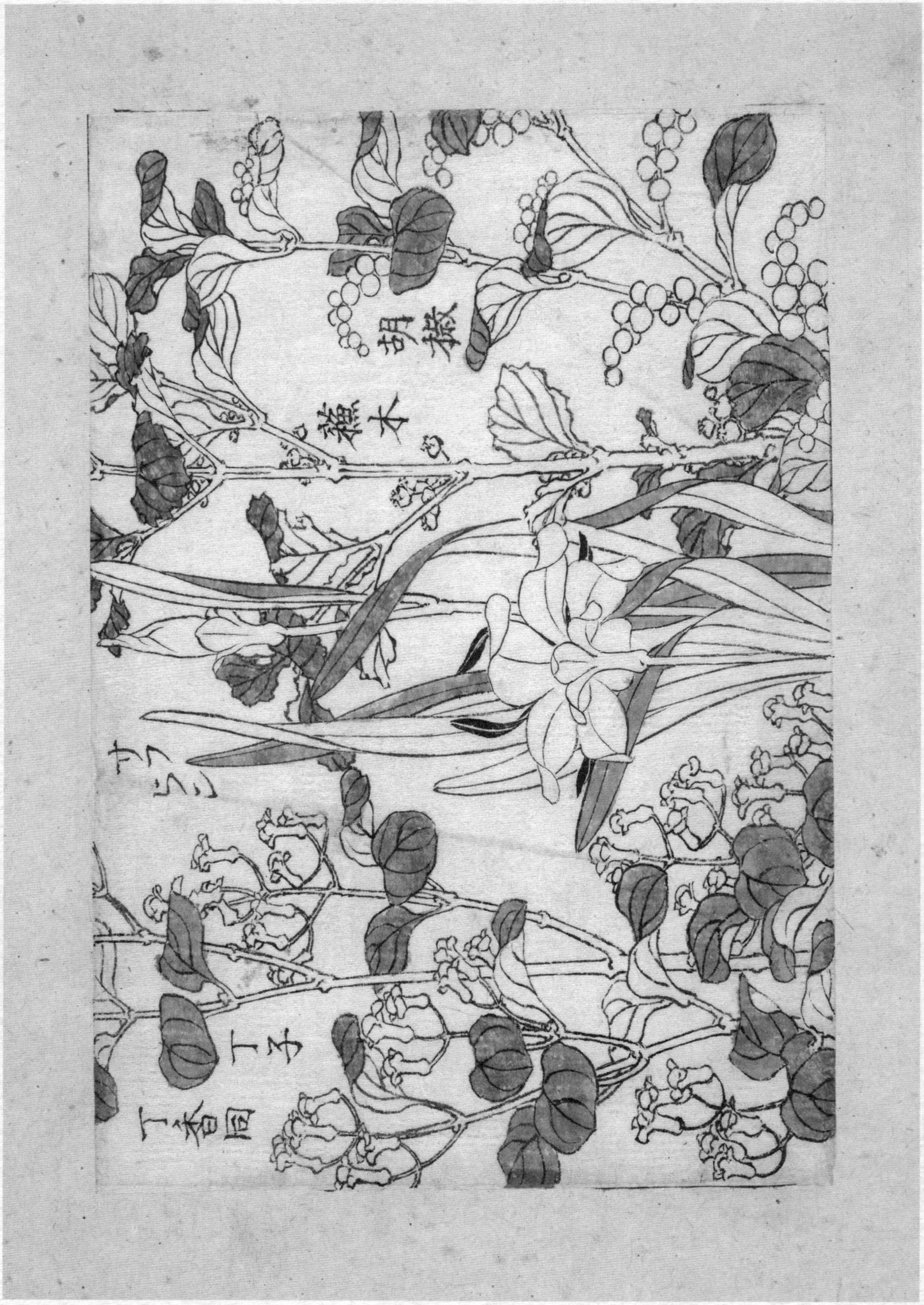
胡椒
丁子

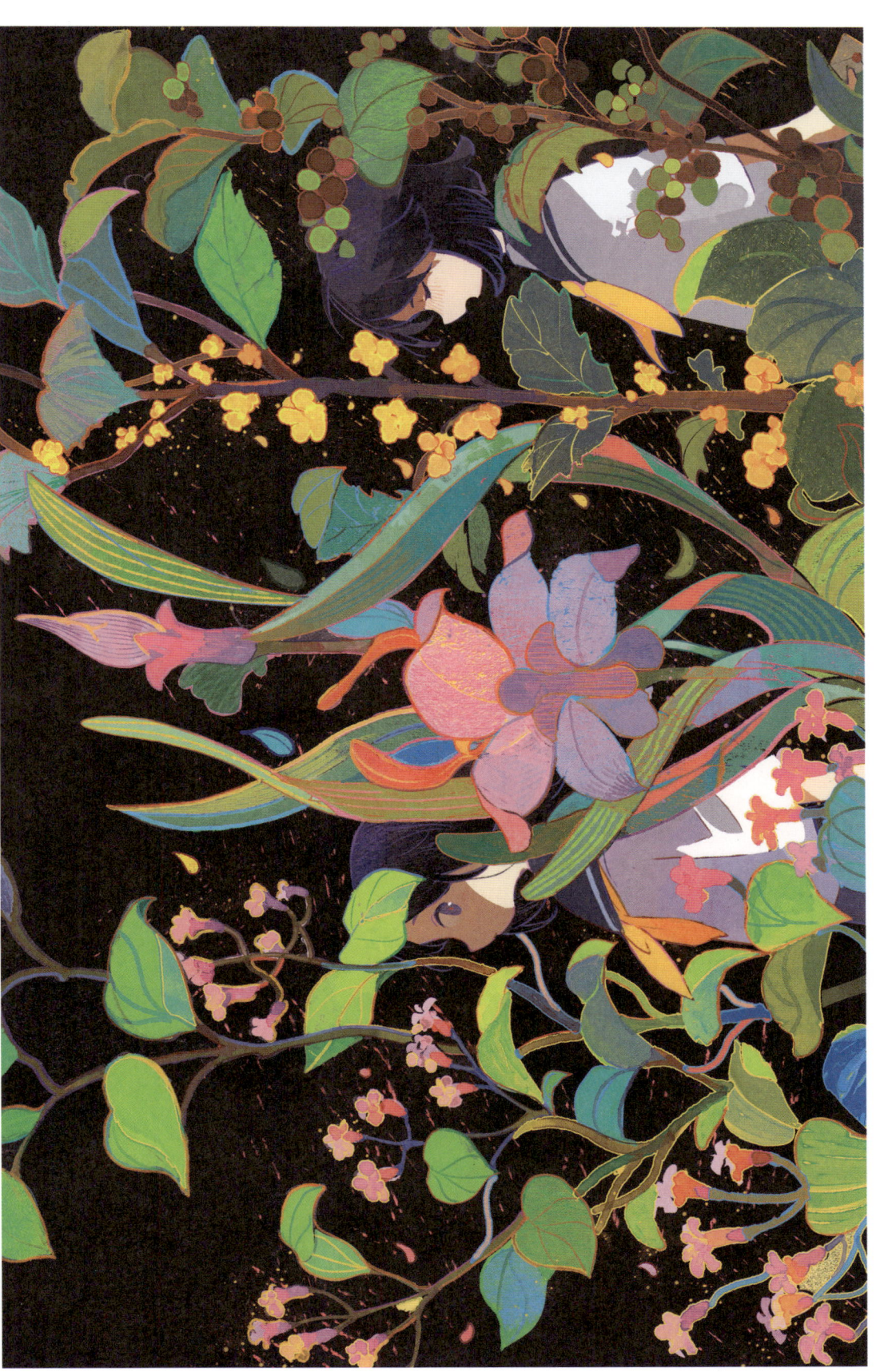

PEPPER, PERILLA, SAFFRON AND CLOVE

MENGXUAN LI

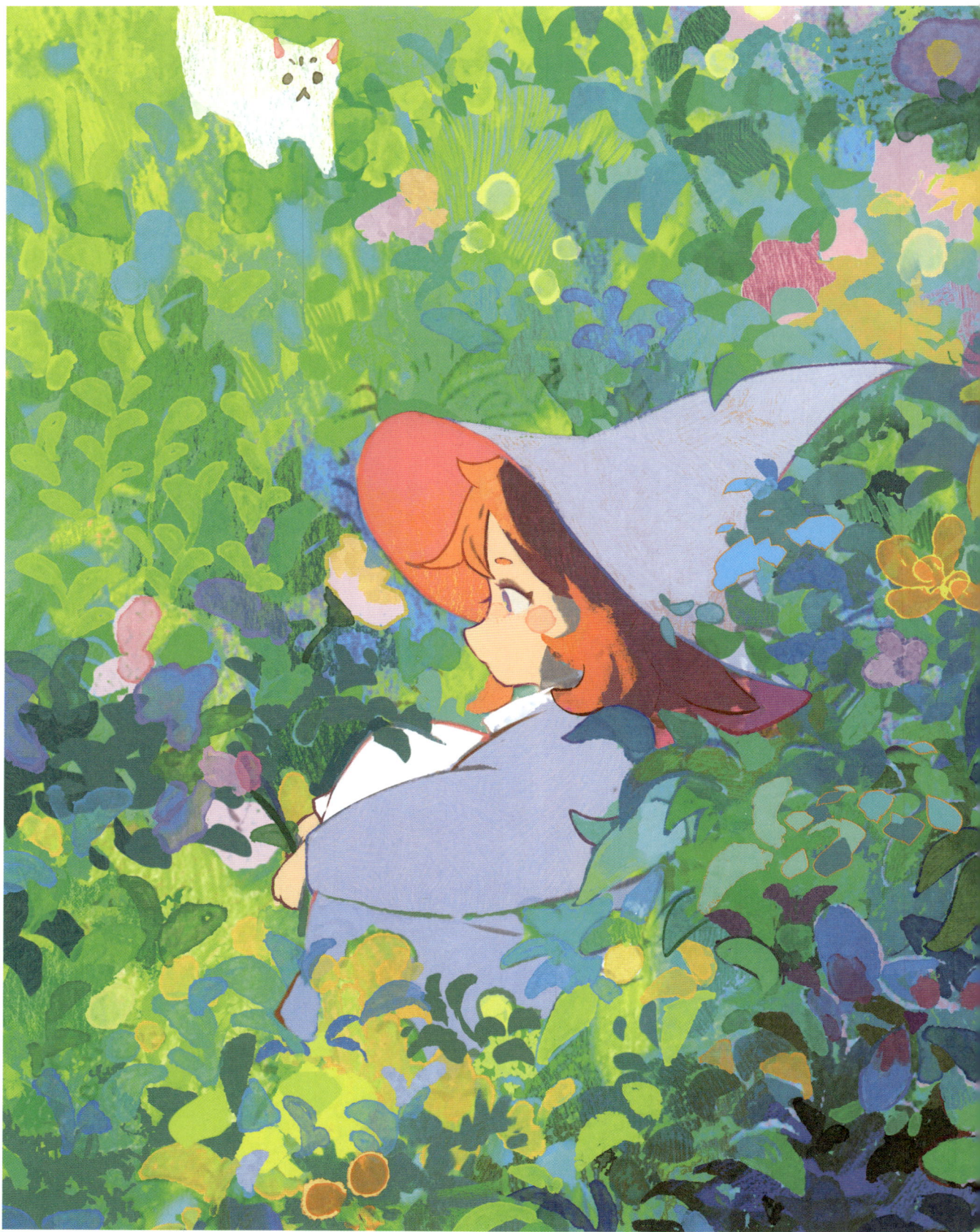

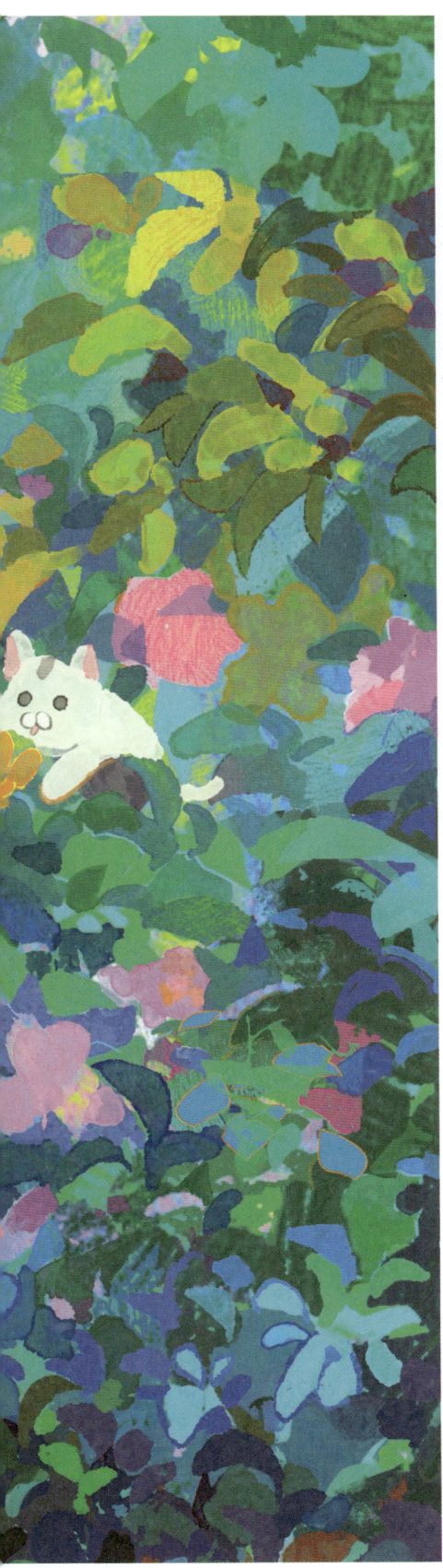

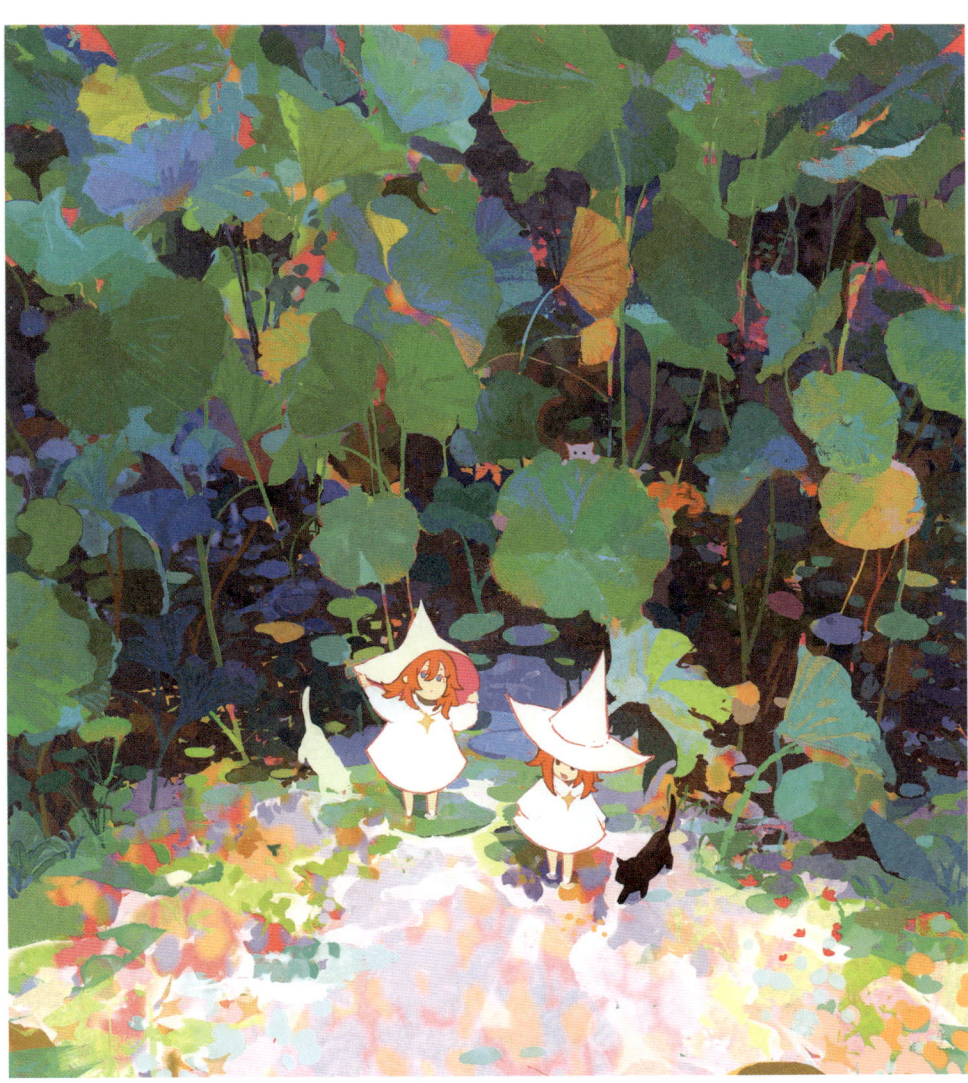

LEFT: *Secret Garden*
I just really wanted to draw some green foliage

ABOVE: *Lost in Lotus Leaves*
In this painting, I imagined the lotus leaves suddenly becoming huge, and the little witches getting lost in them

Mengxuan Li

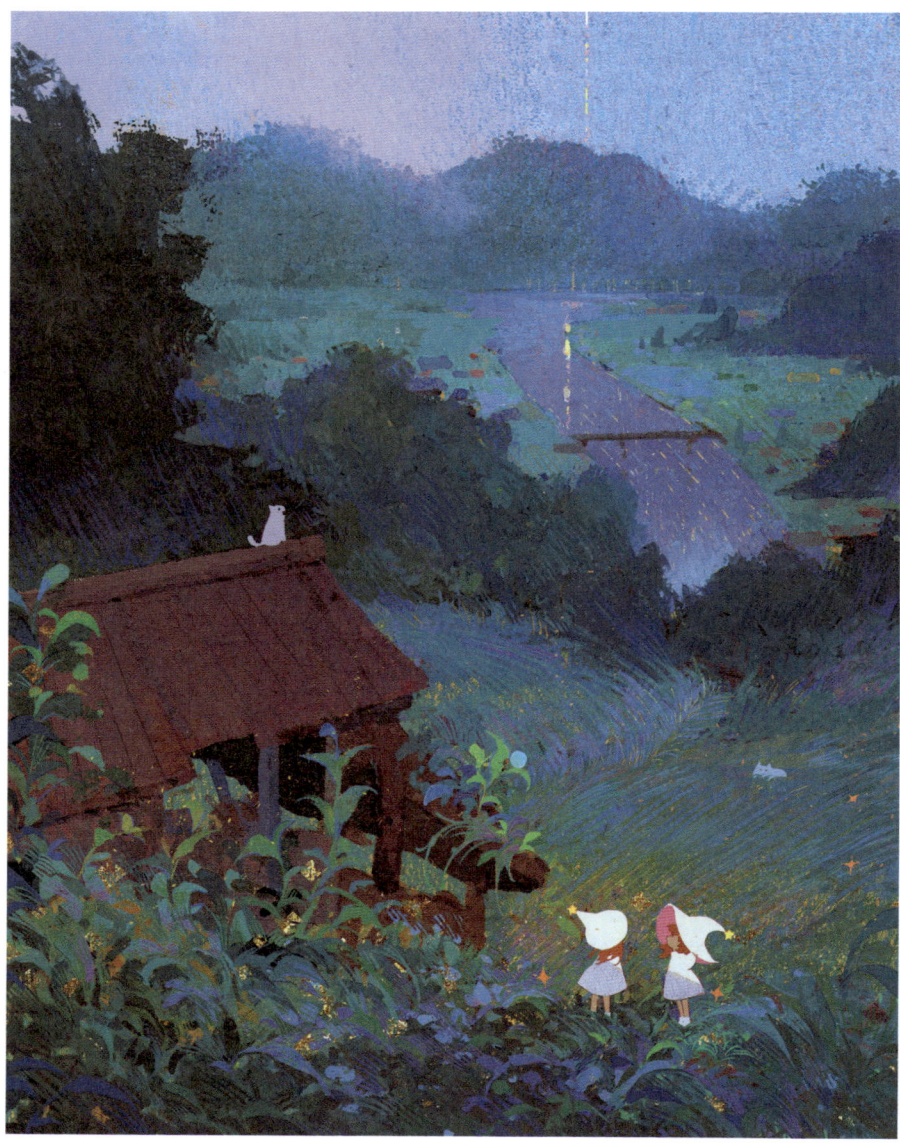

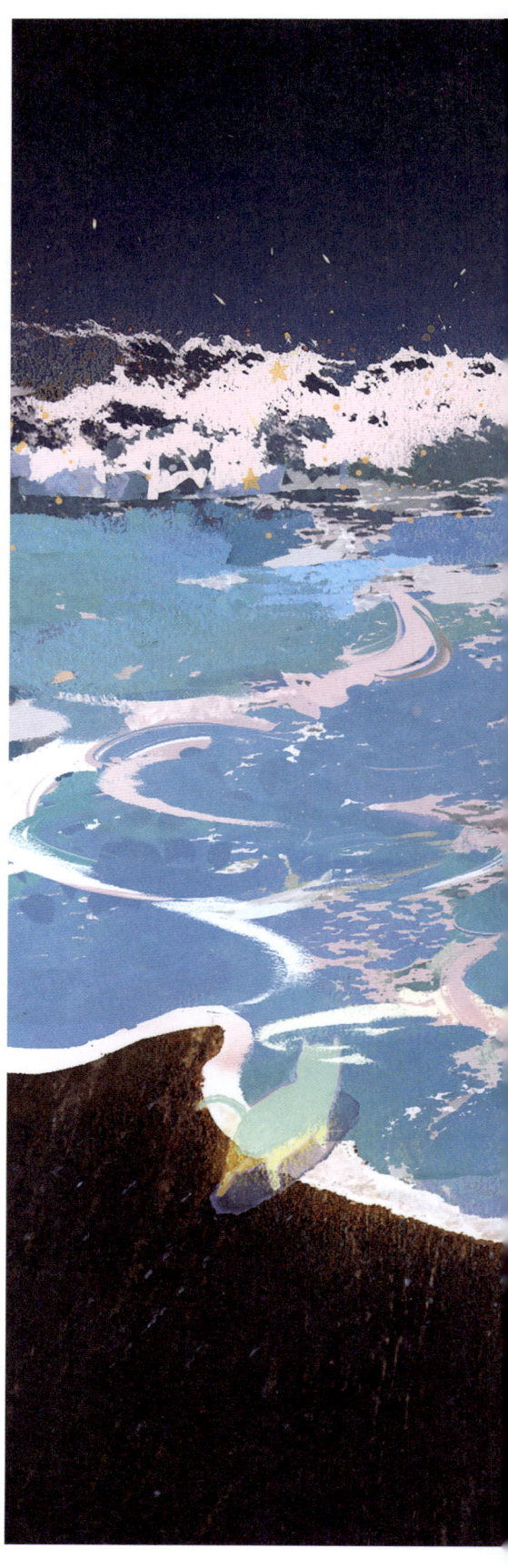

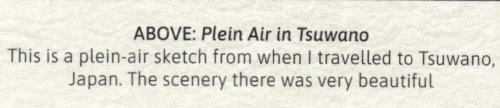

ABOVE: *Plein Air in Tsuwano*
This is a plein-air sketch from when I travelled to Tsuwano, Japan. The scenery there was very beautiful

RIGHT: *New Dress*
I associated the witch's dress with the sea, turning into waves

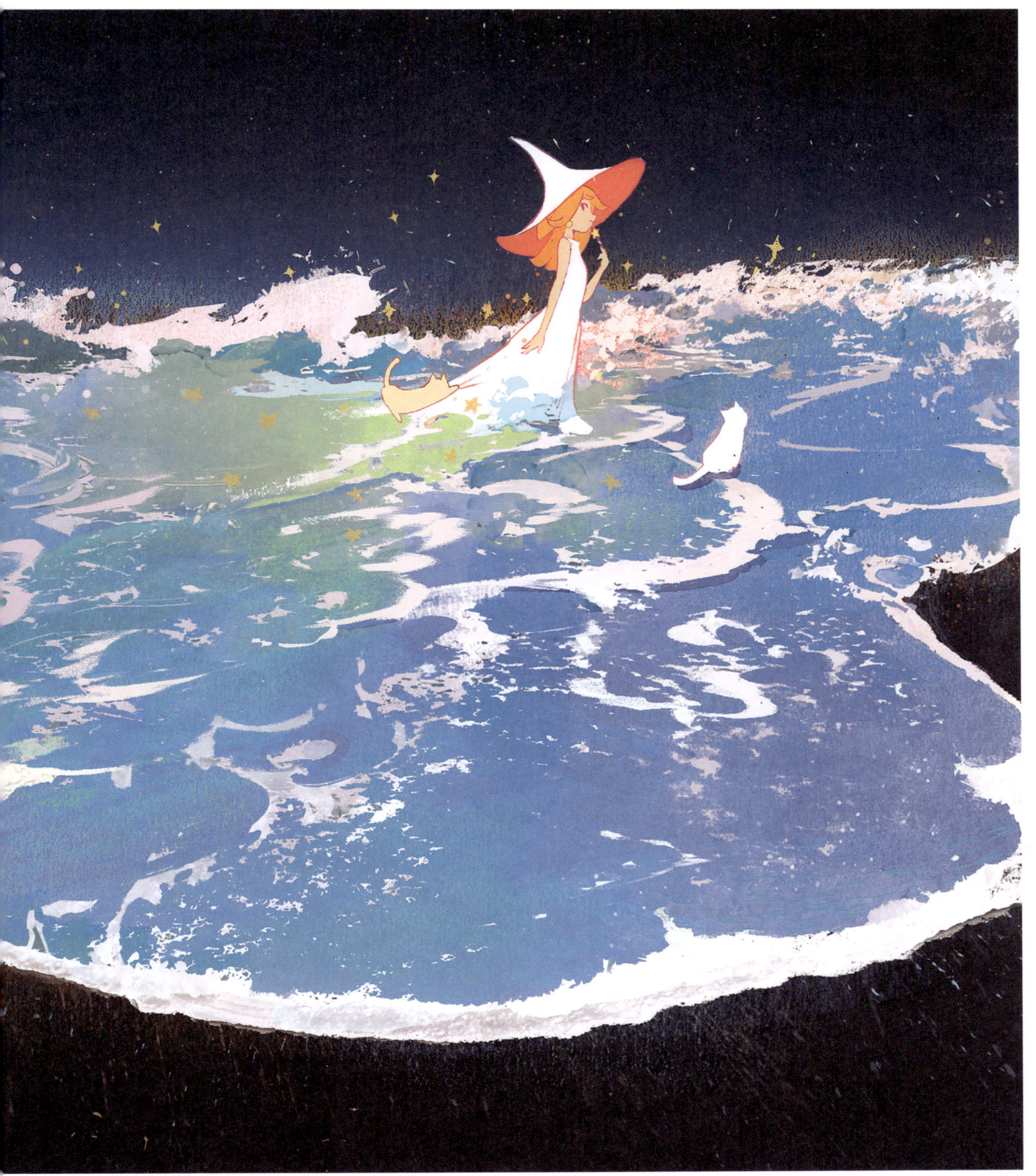

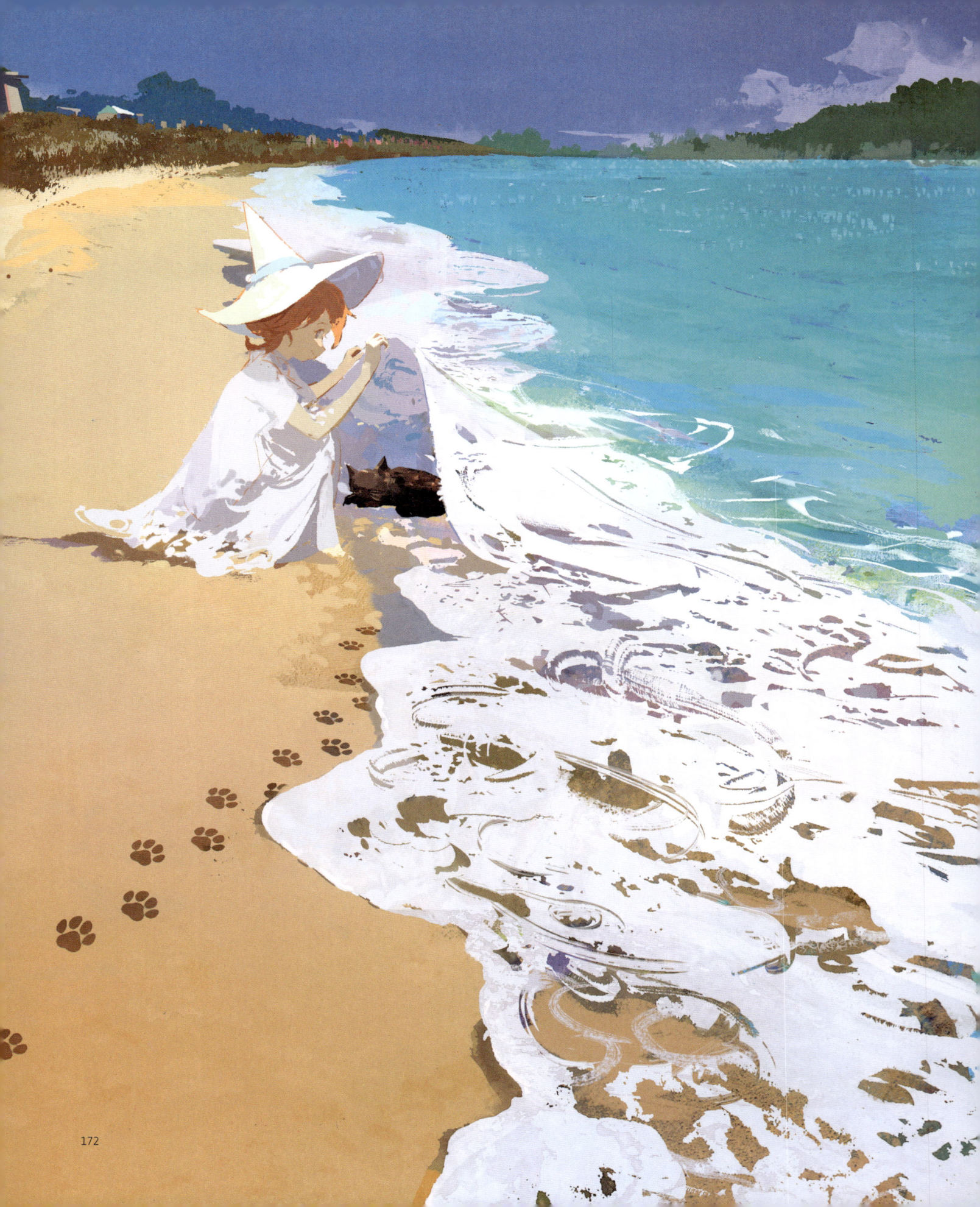

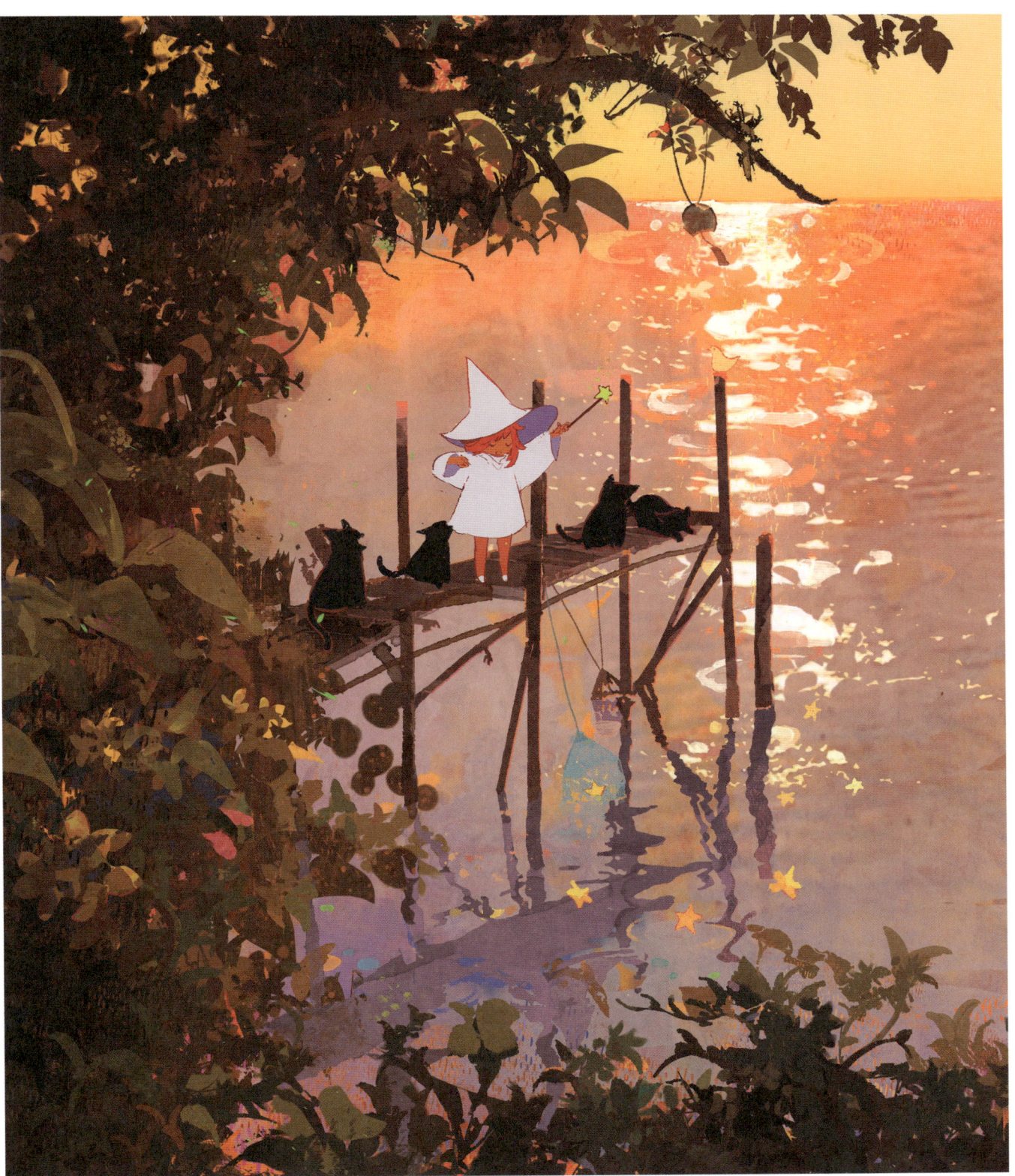

LEFT: *Looking for the Cat*
This image is a tribute to Guy Billout. The little witch found the sleeping cat under the ocean waves

ABOVE: *Chorus Practice at Sunset*
The witch and her cats practise singing together at sunset. This is a small bridge I found while walking near my home

Mengxuan Li

ESCAPING A SANDSTORM

BY JAMIE CHEN

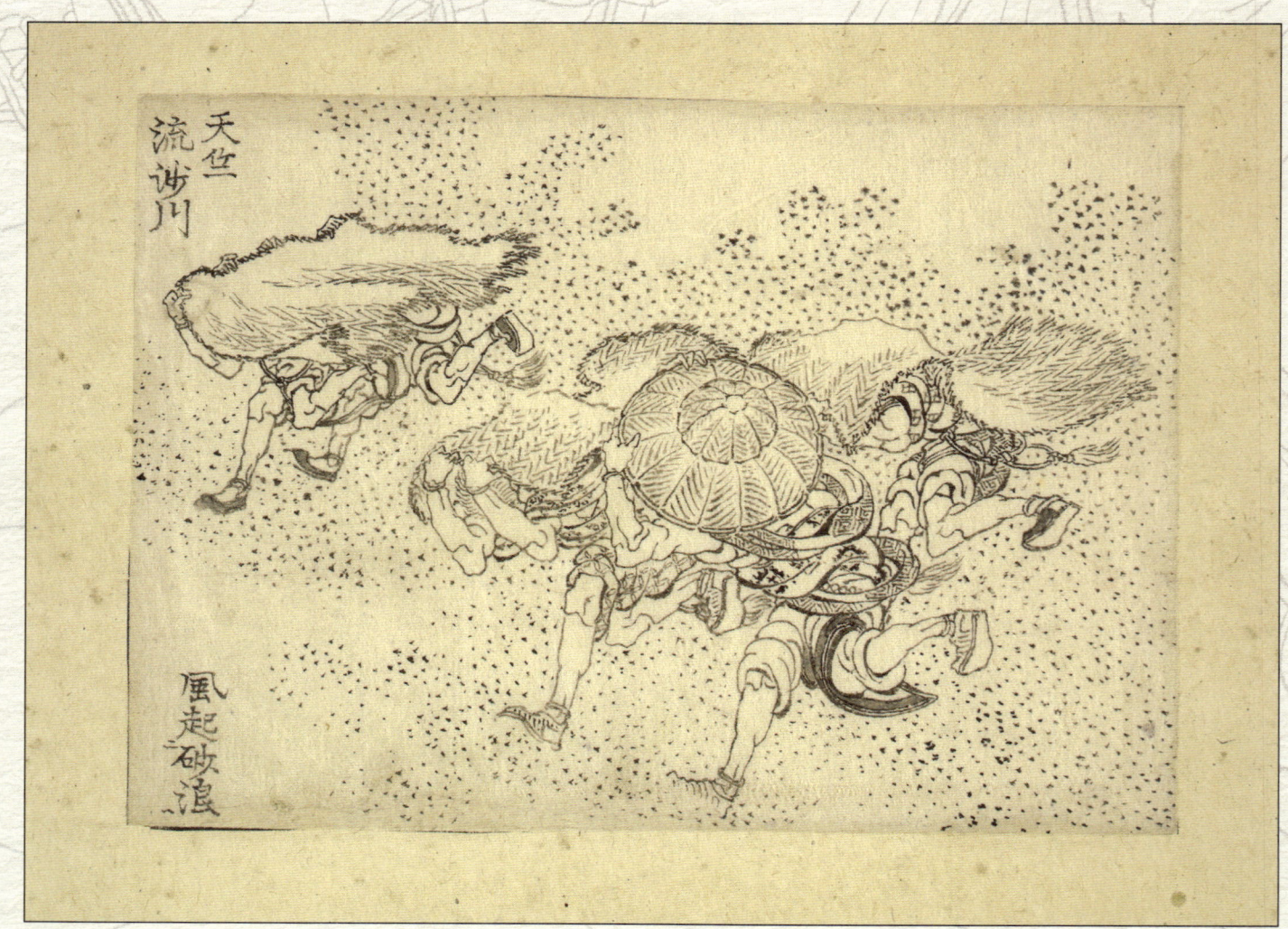

JAMIE CHEN

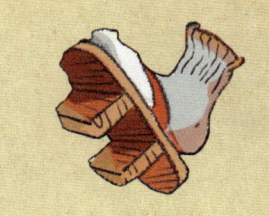

DISCOVERING HOKUSAI

I began learning how to draw traditionally with gouache and coloured pencils from a young age. At the same time, reading manga and watching anime played a big role in my artistic sensibility and influenced my decision to pursue a career in design and art. In 2017, I earned a degree in graphic design at Rhode Island School of Design, and have continued to work as a designer since. In 2018, I started illustrating digitally, combining my background in design and my love for Japanese art, which continues to shape my work.

Although I was familiar with Hokusai's paintings, especially *The Great Wave*, his work always felt distant from the art style I grew up with. I admired works by CLAMP (*xxxHolic, Tsubasa*), Rumiko Takahashi (*Ranma 1/2, Inuyasha*), Tite Kubo (*Bleach*), and films by Studio Ghibli (*My Neighbor Totoro, Nausicaä of the Valley of the Wind, Princess Mononoke*) for their storytelling, clear graphic lines and patterns, and emotional depth. Little did I realize, all the artists I loved are, in fact, successors of Hokusai's work. His impact is inescapable.

Comparing my work to these artists, and tracing back to the contributions of Hokusai's paintings, reveals a direct line from his work to mine through elements such as formatting, line work, and graphic colours. While I still look to modern artists who have also found inspiration from manga and anime, understanding the history of the art form has expanded my perspective. It has deepened my appreciation for Hokusai and made me see how influential he is and will continue to be in modern aesthetics.

01 SEEKING INSPIRATION

In general, Hokusai's work is very masculine, depicting battles, large animals, and natural disasters. For *Escaping a sandstorm*, I'm noticing a similar theme where most of the people are male and the scene is chaotic. Although I'm inspired by his style, I believe the most compelling stories come from our own experiences. Therefore, I start by transforming all the people to young women and play up the colour and pattern of the clothes. Instead of running from a sandstorm, I envision they are playfully chasing each other. Since nature plays a significant role in my work, I replace the straw hat and mats with large flowers.

With a general approach in mind, I start looking for references. Even the best artists don't draw solely from memory. For this particular piece, I look at traditional kimonos, traditional Japanese pattern-making (this is not limited to clothing, but also in architecture, crafts, and modern mark-making), different types of flowers, and drawings by other artists that depict groups of women. I want to see how other artists have approached the same subject, but also to make sure I don't accidentally draw something that's already been done.

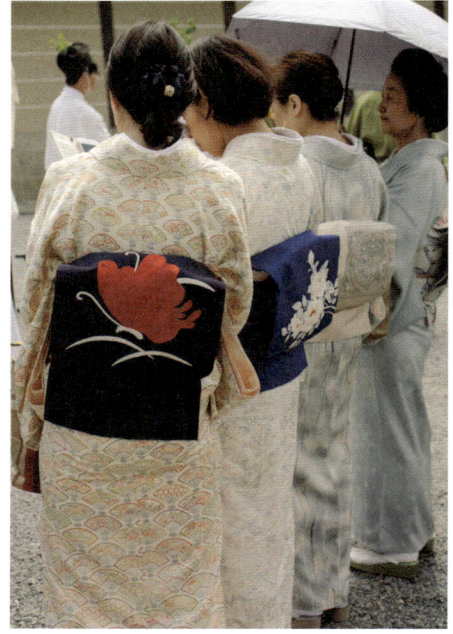
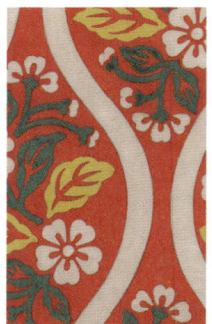
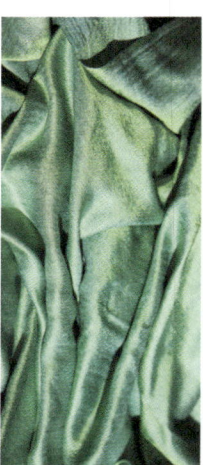

EXAMPLES OF REFERENCES GATHERED BEFORE SKETCHING

CLOCKWISE FROM TOP LEFT IMAGE:
PHOTO BY DARIA AVERINA – UNSPLASH.COM
PHOTO BY LIBRARY OF CONGRESS – UNSPLASH.COM
PHOTO BY ALEXANDER GREY – UNSPLASH.COM

02 CREATING THE LAYOUT

At this stage, I want to ensure my final piece is easily recognizable as a recreation of Hokusai's work, including common elements to draw the two pieces together while still maintaining my style. Since I'm changing many basic elements, the general layout should be preserved. The challenge is translating the new elements into the same position as the original. For example, I need to design the flowers to echo the shape of the straw hat and mats. This involves adjusting the perspective of the flowers and selecting the right type of flower. I overlay the original work onto my sketch to help me with this.

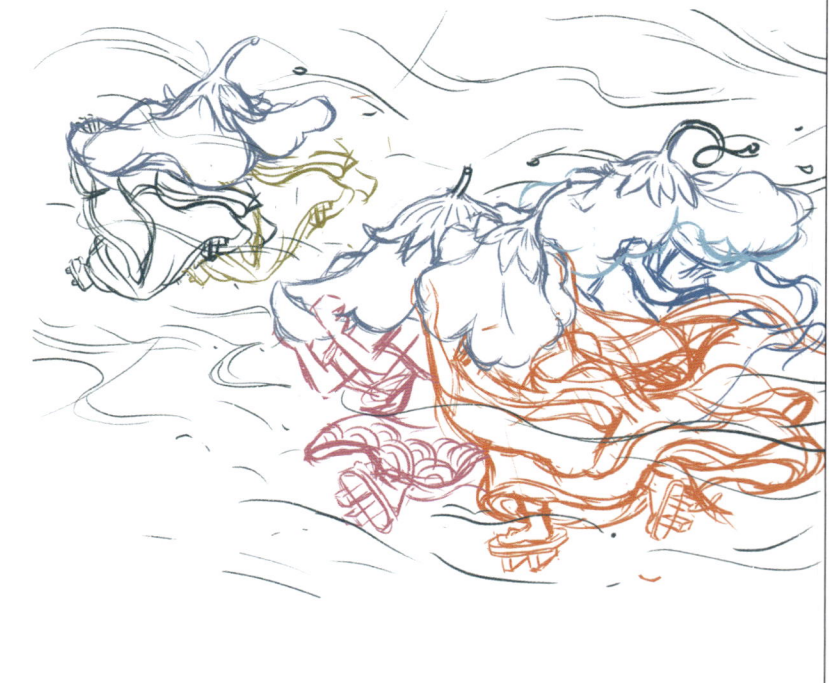

I USE DIFFERENT COLOURS TO DISTINGUISH BETWEEN THE SEPARATE LAYERS

03 SKETCHING THE BACKGROUND

I also need to recreate the background in my style. While the dots in Hokusai's piece make sense, they don't have enough movement. Although my final piece will not take place in a sandstorm, I draw lines inspired by the motion and the wind of Hokusai's storm to maintain the spirit of the original work. This makes the piece more dynamic but also distinguishes the work as my own. I know many artists struggle to find the type of mark-making that captures their artistic expression and are eager to find their 'style'. It can be frustrating, but this comes with practice and time. As you draw more, you'll find certain patterns and objects that you draw more frequently, or excel at, and the culmination of those experiences will become a part of your style.

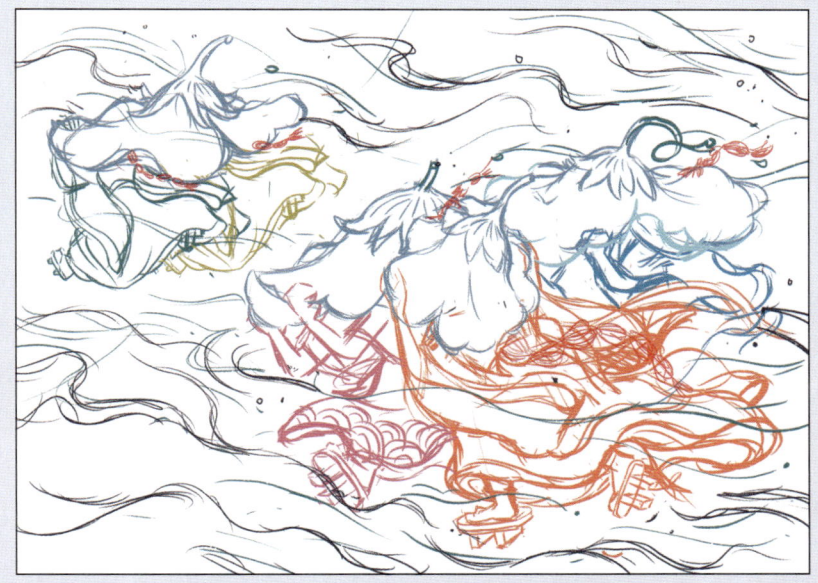

ADDING MORE DETAILS TO THE BACKGROUND

04 REFINING THE SKETCH

Now that I have the layout ready, I add details to my sketch. This includes defining the hands, feet, and folds of clothing as well as adding texture to the flowers. Many artists don't need to have all the details fleshed out in the sketch, but because my style, as well as Hokusai's style, features strong and intricate line work, I want to know what I'm drawing so that my final line work looks intentional and smooth. If I'm unsure of what I'm drawing, the lines will look choppy and less refined.

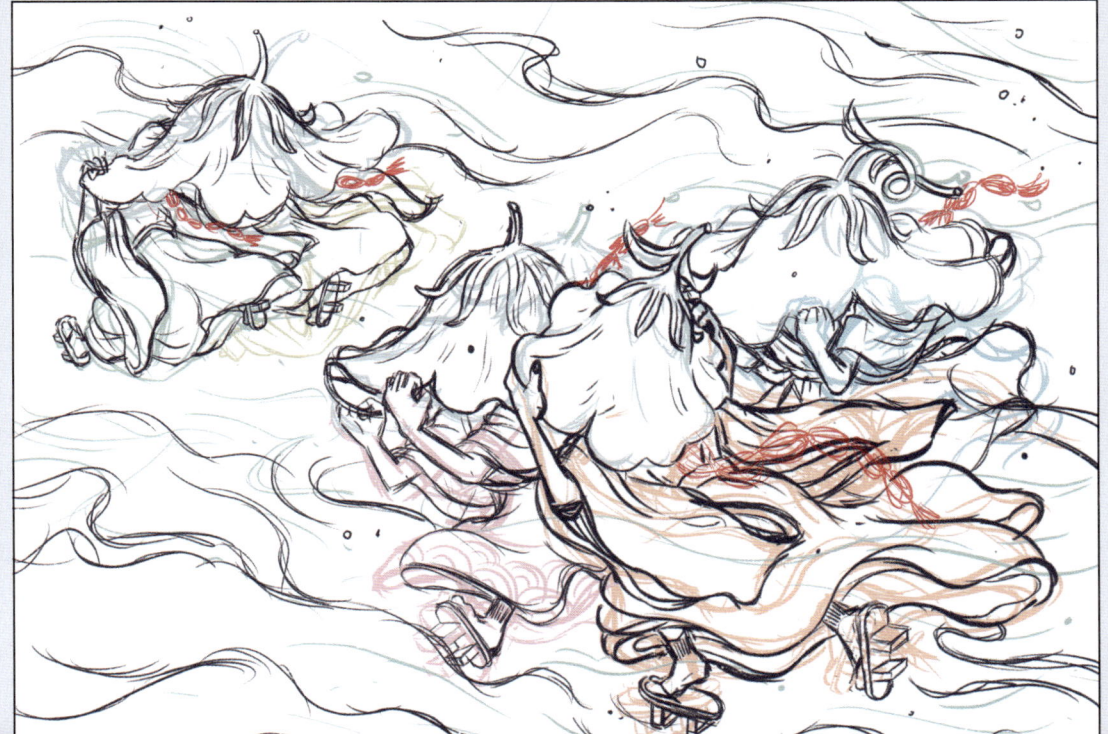

FLESHING OUT THE DETAILS SO IT'S READY FOR OUTLINING

177

Jamie Chen

05 OUTLINING

Once I'm comfortable with the level of detail in my sketch, I outline my drawing. Hokusai painted with a brush and ink that naturally created irregularities and depth to his drawings. This is hard to replicate with digital tools, so I like using brushes that have more texture. Here, I use a Procreate pencil that creates a texture similar to a sketching pencil. Using textured brushes creates humanistic qualities that can easily define your work.

Hokusai's line work is clean and decisive, yet delicate. I also like to outline my work this way. This type of line work is just thin enough to add details, but thick enough that people can easily decipher the image. This is common with many modern anime and manga artists; you want people to easily read what's happening, but also have enough detail to create a beautiful image.

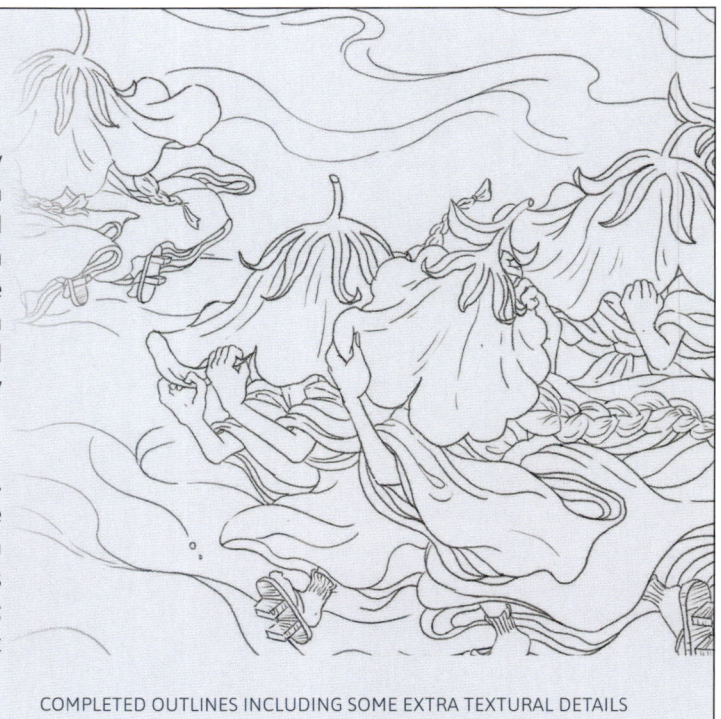

COMPLETED OUTLINES INCLUDING SOME EXTRA TEXTURAL DETAILS

06 ADDING SHADING & VALUE

An important step when illustrating or painting is adding value. Value is the lightness and darkness of a colour and it defines the different parts of a painting. Different colours inherently have different values. You usually want more value where you want people to focus, like the foreground or main characters, and less value on areas like the background. Shading is a way to define those values.

While I'm confident with my line work, I'm not so confident with shading. This is why I'm attracted to Hokusai's work and all the artists that succeed him. Hokusai relies on the inherent value of each colour, playing with gradation and saturation to define the shapes in his paintings, rather than shadows and light. So, although I still add shadows to my work, I don't worry about whether my execution is perfect; I will rely on my colour choices in the next step to properly define the different elements in my drawing. This will give my piece a graphic and abstract style, similar to Hokusai.

I TYPICALLY APPLY TWO TO THREE DIFFERENT LAYERS OF SHADING FROM LIGHTEST TO DARKEST

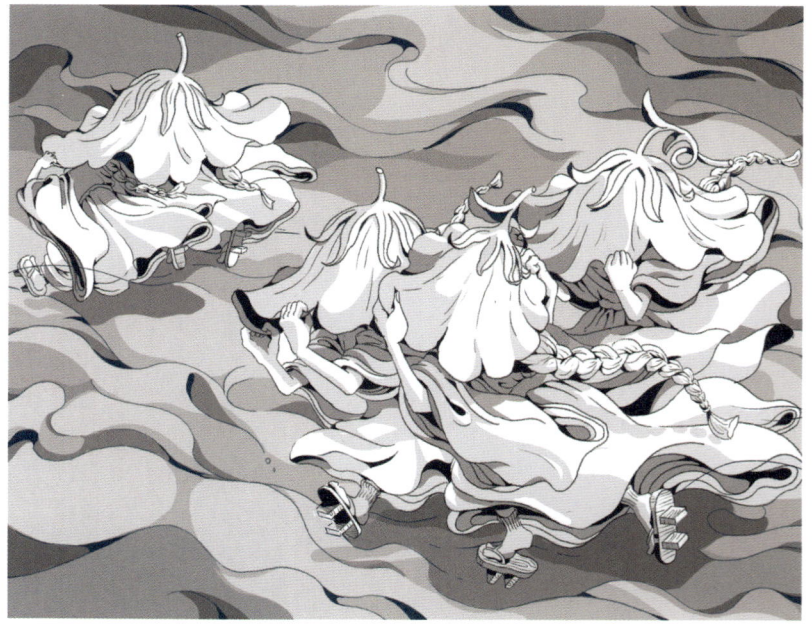

07 CREATING A COLOUR PALETTE

Before I add colour, I first create a colour palette. Colours can be overwhelming; there are so many ways to combine them. I typically limit my colour palette to three to seven colours. When I first started illustrating, I only used two to three. This seems counterintuitive at first, but a painting can look busy if there are too many colours. There's a tendency to think you need a lot of colours, but you really only need a handful to create a striking image. If you take a closer look at his work, Hokusai creates the illusion of a colourful painting, but he's only using a select number of colours.

Before jumping into the specifics, this is generally how I create a colour palette. A technique I rely on, which is also prevalent in Hokusai's work, is to either use analogous colours (blue, green, and yellow) or complementary colours such as blue and orange. You can choose a colour with high value, like a dark blue, and pair it with a colour that has less value, like a light yellow. For this specific piece, the main colour families I use are blue and orange. But unlike Hokusai's work, I like to add neighbouring colours to create more intrigue and depth (reddish orange or bluish green). I do this cautiously and intentionally. I control the amount so that holistically the piece still has a complementary colour palette. But even with an expanded palette, I'm only using eight swatches of colour.

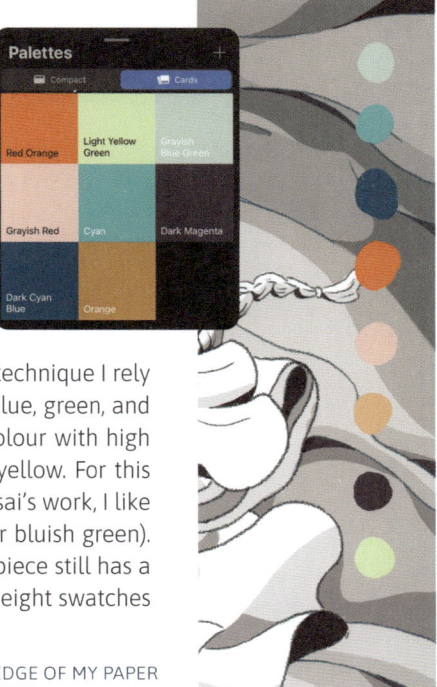

I LIKE TO SAMPLE THE COLOURS AT THE EDGE OF MY PAPER
SO IT'S EASIER TO EYEDROP THEM AS I DRAW

08 EXPERIMENTING WITH COLOUR

Deciding your colour palette also takes experimentation. This can mean trying a completely new palette or playing with the colour ratio of the same palette. Changing the ratio can drastically alter the look and feel of a piece. As you see here, I'm trying many versions, including analogous palettes, different ratios of the same palette, and other unexpected colour combinations. This can take a lot of trial and error. But what ultimately guides my colour choices is how I want the people – my focal point – to show up, which I'll describe in my next step.

TRYING OUT DIFFERENT COLOURS
CAN TAKE TRIAL AND ERROR. THIS IS
A SMALL SAMPLE OF MY ATTEMPTS

Jamie Chen

09 FINALIZING THE COLOUR

As I want to convey playfulness and joy, I use warm and bright colours for the characters' clothing. This choice is crucial for capturing the same energy. To create contrast and have my characters stand out, I use a dark colour for the background. Although this isn't my first choice – since I initially wanted to keep the background light, like Hokusai's drawing – I've decided to diverge from Hokusai's original sandstorm depiction while still maintaining a sense of motion and lightness in the background. Given that my style often features bold colours and high contrast, this colour combination, while different from my original idea, ultimately makes sense.

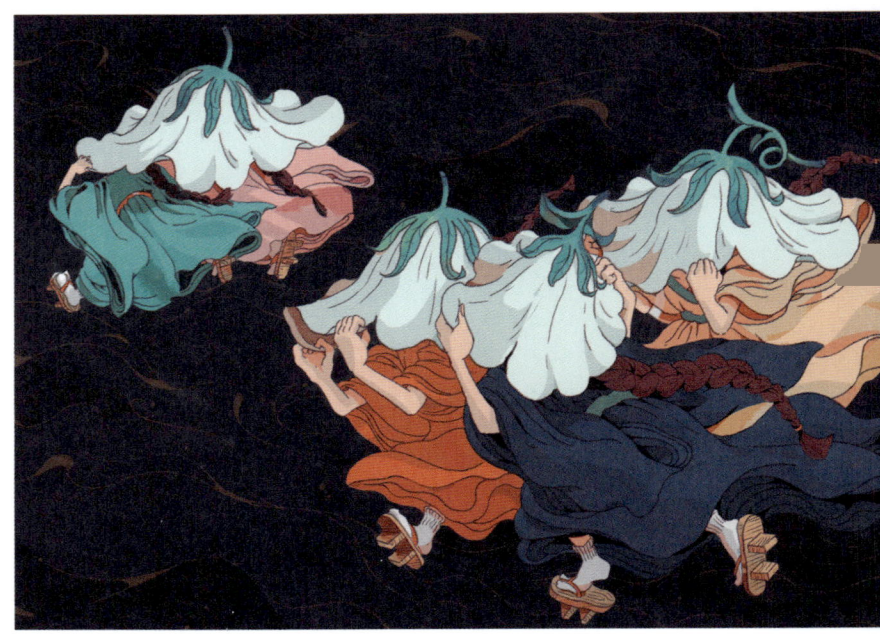

THIS FINAL COLOUR PALETTE IS OUTSIDE MY EXPECTATION BUT ACCOMPLISHES EVERYTHING I WANT IT TO

10 REVISITING YOUR REFERENCES

This is where I revisit the mood board I put together before starting. I do this at different stages of my work, especially if it's based on another artist. But in general, it's good to do this at least midway through your work. For this piece, I want to make sure it still feels reminiscent of Hokusai's original drawing, despite all the changes I've made. While it mostly does, the characters don't feel as integrated with the background as the original; they seem as if someone cut them out and pasted them on the paper. To address this, I add extra cloth to the characters that mimics the flowing lines of the background. I will also add a pattern or texture in the next few steps to better integrate the foreground.

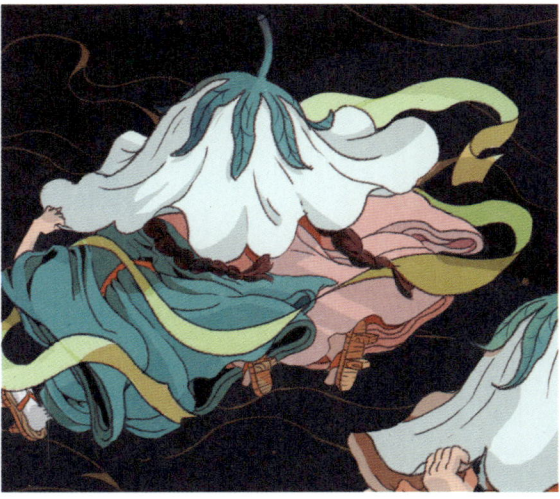

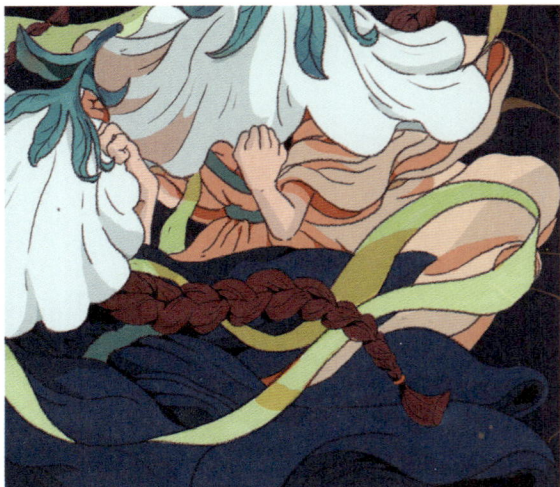

A DRAWING WILL EVOLVE AS YOU WORK ON IT. EMBRACE THOSE CHANGES EVEN IF THEY'RE DIFFERENT FROM WHAT YOU FIRST IMAGINED

11 ADDING PATTERNS

Sometimes I add details using line work, but since I'm incorporating patterns to the clothes in this piece, the details will integrate better through colour alone. At this point, I also go back to my references of traditional kimono patterns. I copy existing patterns but adapt what I find into my own style. I want graphic, abstract patterns to contrast with the flowy, humanistic lines I already have, rather than common kimono patterns like birds or leaves. For example, instead of drawing three-dimensional flowers, I draw clustered, flat circles that look like clovers.

The colour of the patterns is also important. Hokusai's original piece doesn't have colour, so it only has to contend with the balance of textures, but we have to be considerate of the contrast and value when pairing colours together. For example, if you have one pattern that is low contrast next to another that is very striking, your eye will be drawn to the bolder pattern. This will work if that's your intention, but you could accidentally create a focal point where you don't want one. It's important to be careful when pairing pattern colours. In this case, I want the patterns to all have relatively equal contrast with each other.

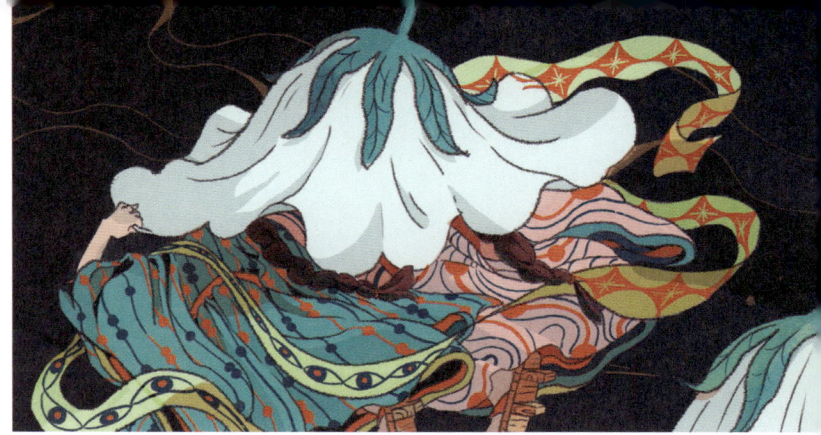
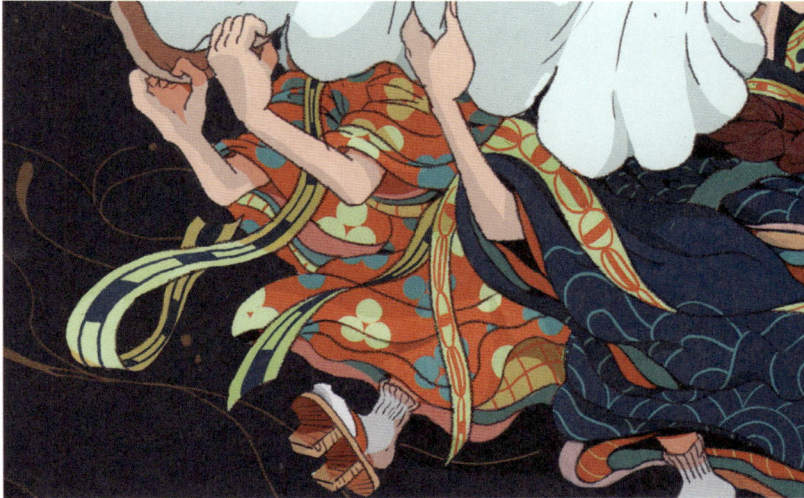

THE PATTERNS HIGHLIGHT THE FOCAL POINT
AND FURTHER ENHANCE THE DRAWING

12 ADDING TEXTURE

Now that the base colours and pattern details are done, I can add texture and richer colouration. I like to create clipping masks over layers and use brushes with watercolour effects to enhance the base layer. I don't use the same exact colour, opting instead for a neighbouring pigment to create more depth. For example, I add a clipping-mask layer over the blue dress and lightly go over this layer with a green watercolour brush. This helps add texture to my drawing and makes it feel more hand-drawn. I find using a neighbouring colour also mimics the way real watercolours pick up other pigments on the palette. Unlike what I'm doing here, Hokusai's drawings typically have smooth, solid colours that are quite abstract. But because he drew traditionally, he didn't have to imitate textures and imperfections that make a piece beautiful. As a digital artist, I find this step makes my drawings better.

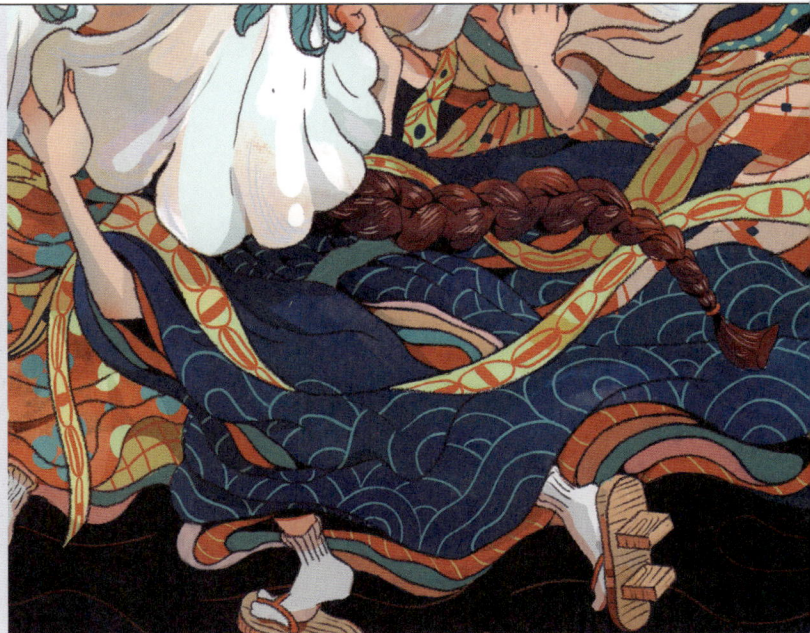

ALTHOUGH IT'S A SMALL DETAIL, ADDING
TEXTURE CAN REALLY MAKE A DIFFERENCE

Jamie Chen

13 CREATING COHESION & FINAL DETAILS

At this point, I step back and see if my piece looks cohesive. Earlier, my foreground didn't integrate well with my background and I took steps to fix that, but I want to integrate the two even more. Inspired by the sandstorm, I use dots to create an abstract sand pattern and have them overlap between the two layers. I also use the orange tones to bring some warmth into the cooler blue background. Since I lost some details in the background because of the dark colour, I go over the outline in a lighter colour to bring those details back.

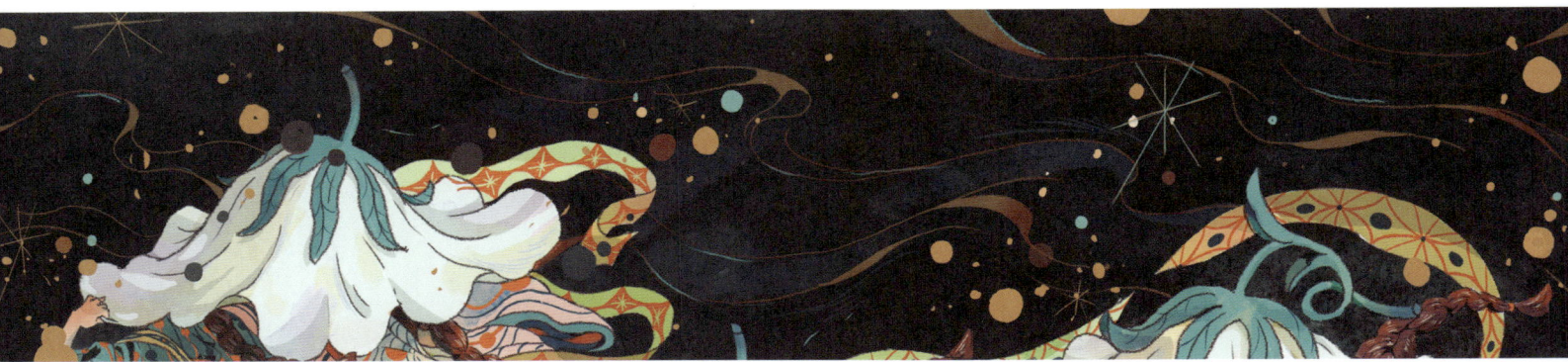

ADDING DIFFERENT SHADES OF ORANGE DOTS TO THE PIECE BRINGS TOGETHER THE FOREGROUND AND BACKGROUND

14 USING GRADIENT MAPS

For my last step, I use gradient maps to do a few things. First, I like to check to see whether my drawing has the correct values by using gradient maps to make the piece black and white. As I mentioned earlier, having more value on your focal point and less value on the background helps your drawing read better. If you can make out the drawing without colour, that means the values are in the right place. Here, you can tell my values are in the right place because the characters in my drawing are very recognizable. This technique can also be done on Hokusai's drawings; notice how the values are distributed.

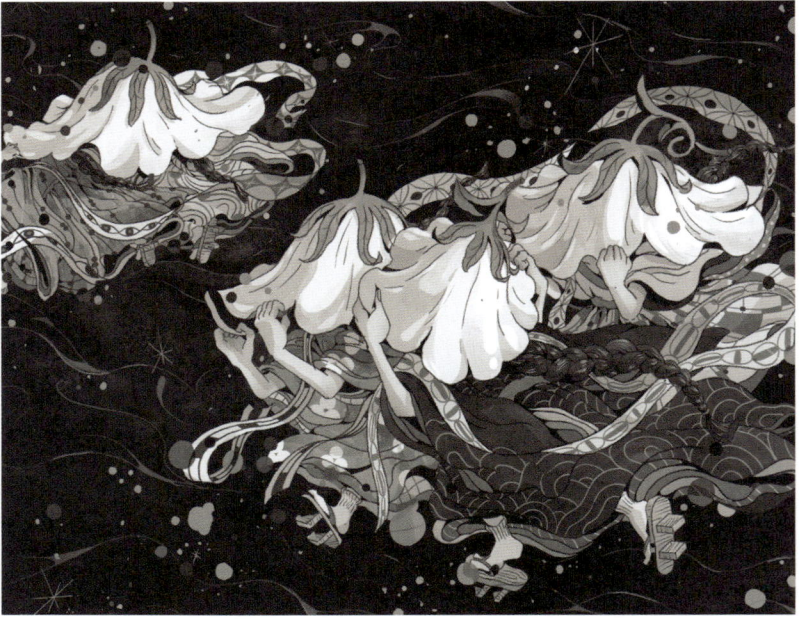

GRADIENT MAPS ARE ALSO GREAT FOR TRYING DIFFERENT COLOUR PAIRINGS

Using gradient maps is also a great way to explore different colour palettes. You can do this in earlier stages, but regardless, this technique can create unexpected results that are worth including in your work.

15 FINALIZING THE DRAWING

The final thing I do is compare my drawing to the original and make any last-minute edits. Playing with hue, saturation, brightness, and colour-balance filters help with making minor adjustments without too much effort. For example, I notice my drawing is slightly less saturated than I'd like (the whole piece feels a little dull) so I increase the saturation just a bit to improve the colours. Lighting and different illustrating software can change how you interpret colour, and sometimes you don't notice until you finish. You can use these settings to quickly make any necessary changes.

ALWAYS REMEMBER TO SIGN YOUR DRAWING WHEN YOU'RE FINISHED!

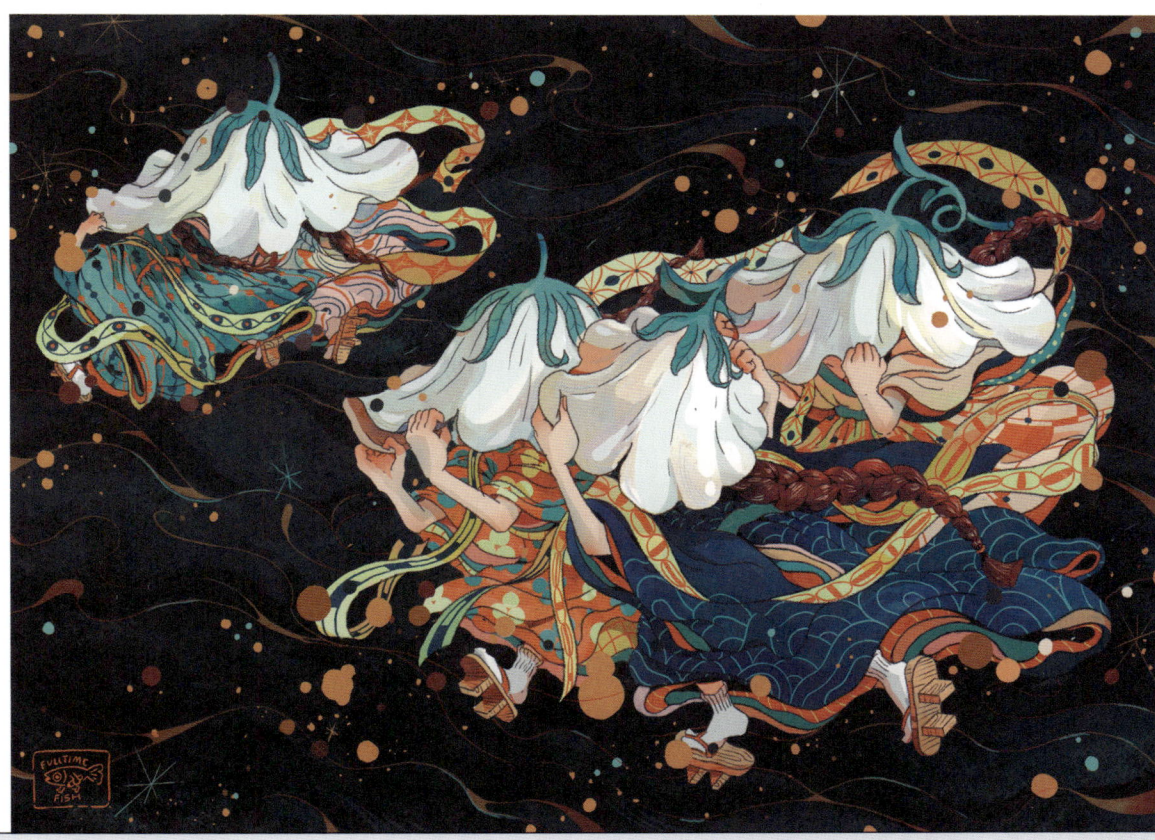

CONCLUSION

Working on Hokusai's uncompleted drawing has been an eye-opening and reflective experience. Despite having studied and admired many modern artists, it's obvious many contemporary techniques and styles owe their development to Hokusai's influence. The final piece definitely has my own unique style, but you can see how many techniques I use directly stem from Hokusai's artistic innovations. It's evident his work remains influential on artists like me and will continue to leave a lasting impact.

Jamie Chen

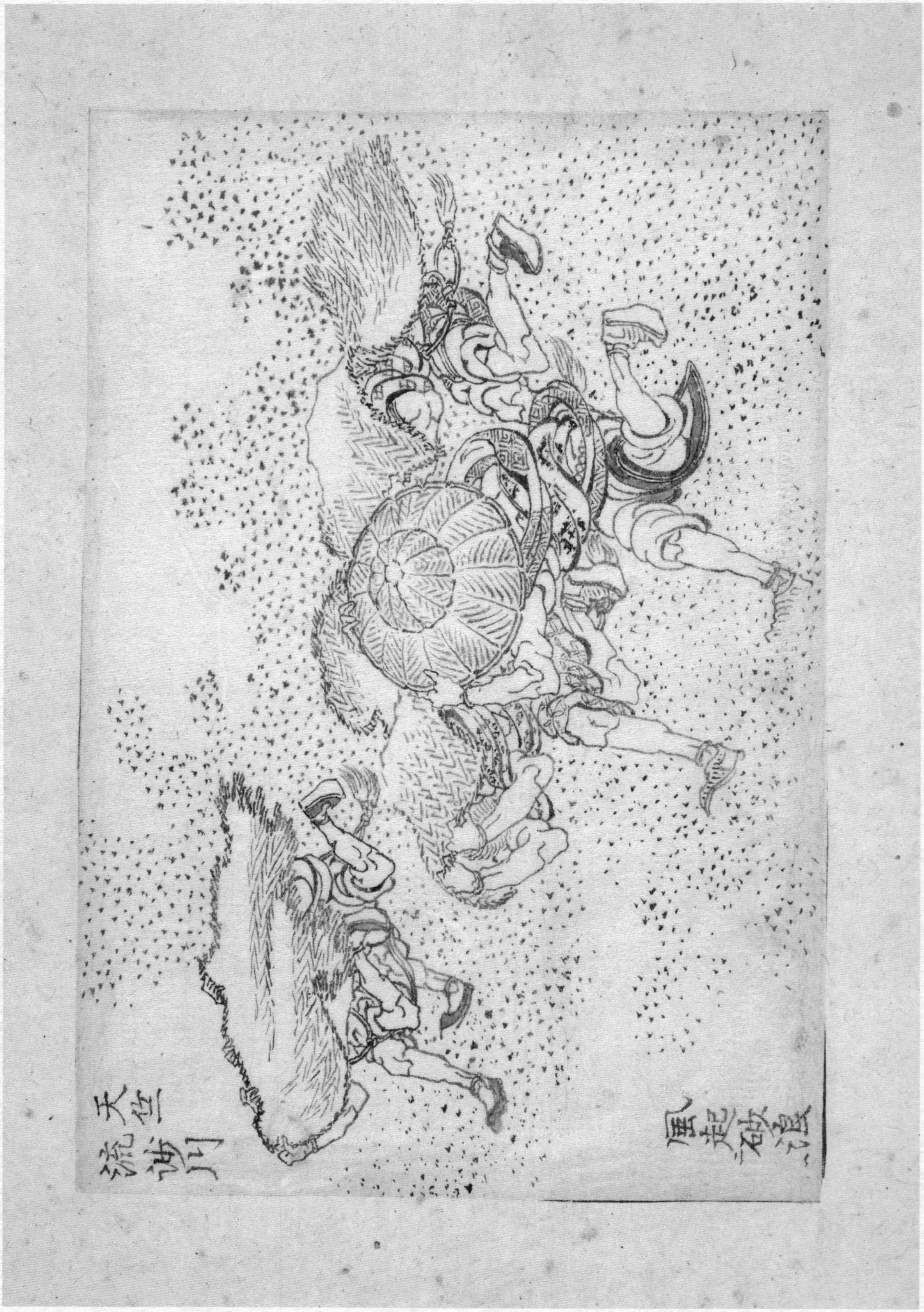

ESCAPING A SANDSTORM

JAMIE CHEN

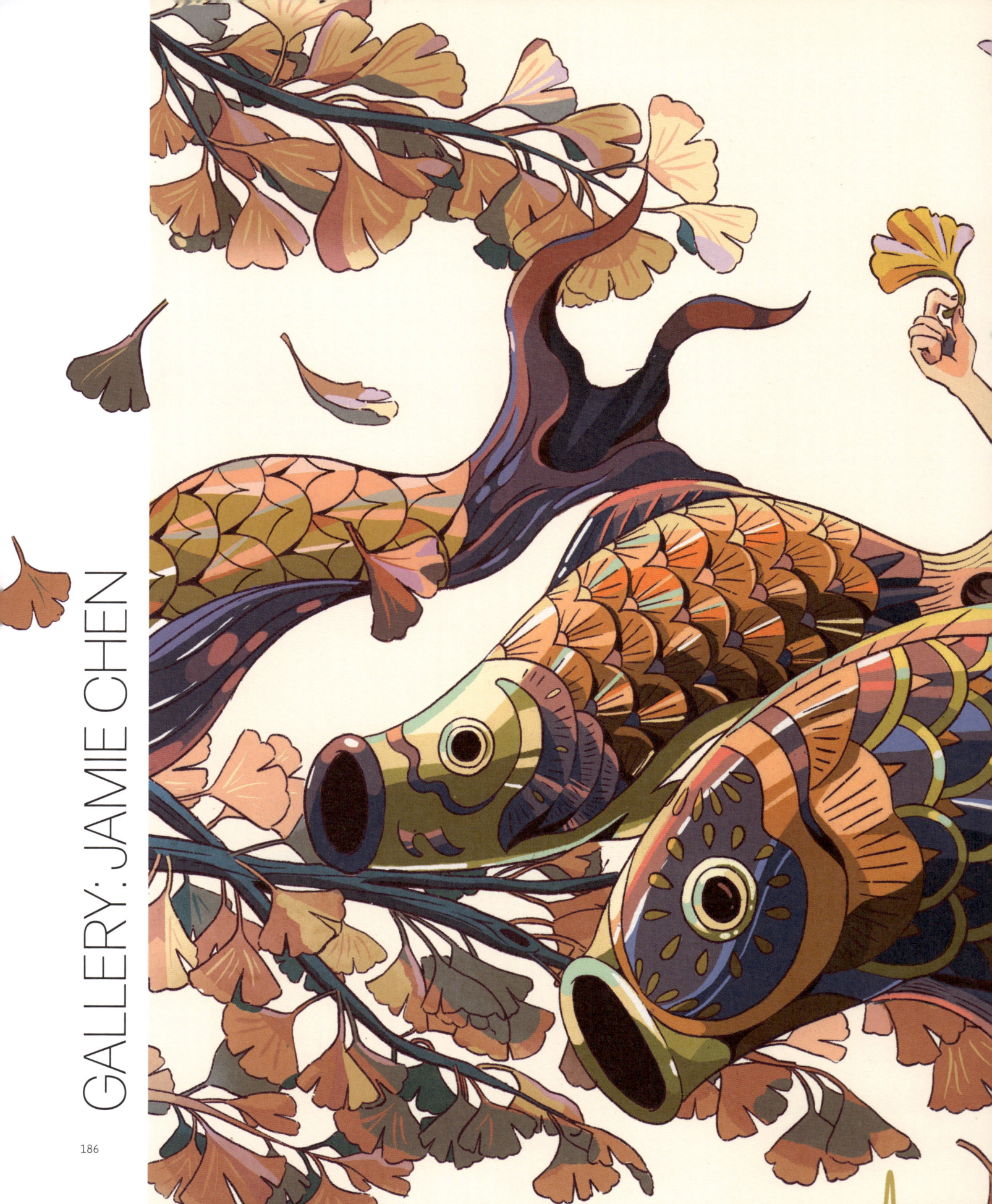

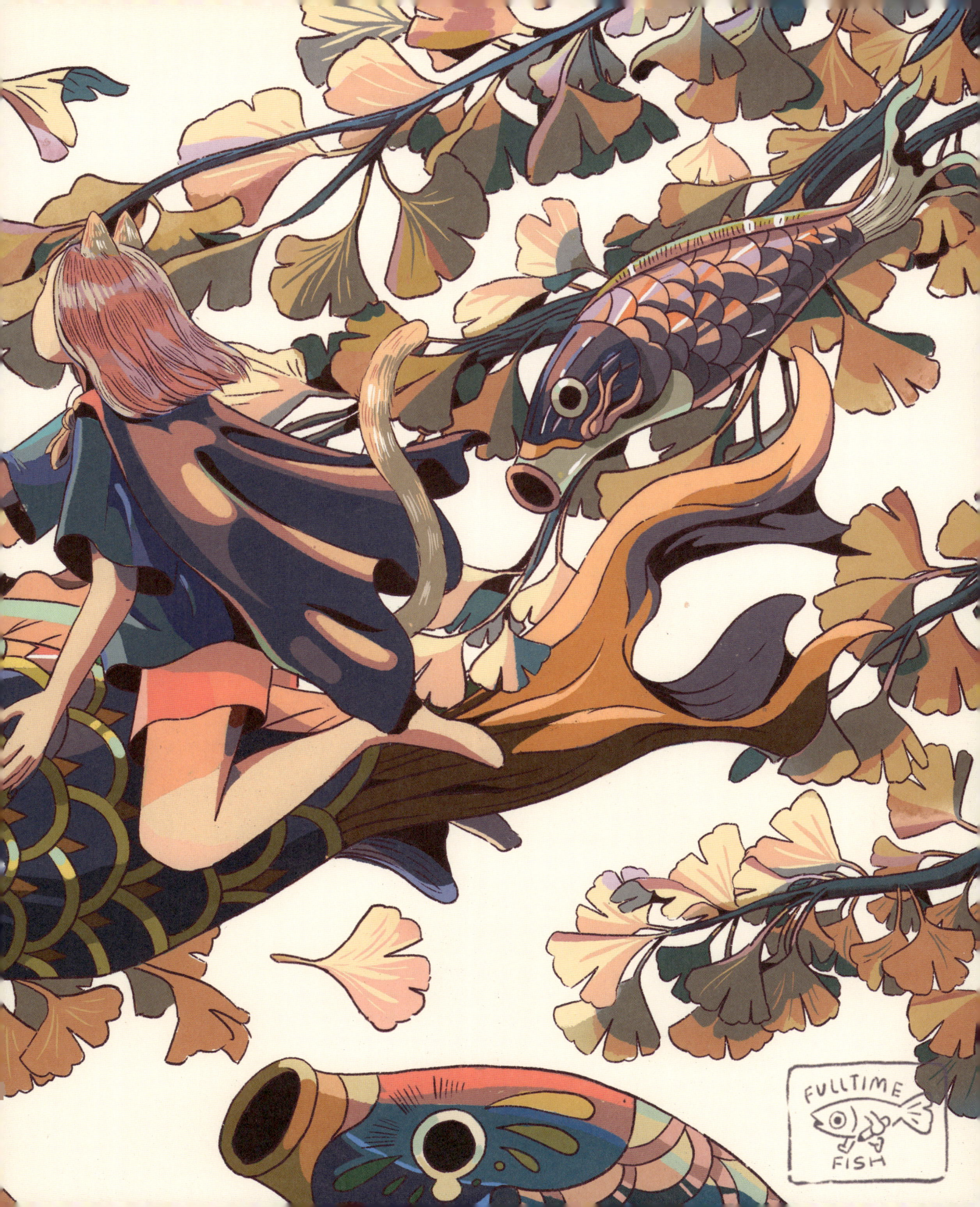

PREVIOUS SPREAD: *Koi*
A feline girl riding koi fish among gingko trees

RIGHT: *Headspace*
Girl with a restless mind

BELOW: *Flower Diptych*
Three flowers in unique vases

OPPOSITE PAGE: *Scissors*
Golden scissors cutting blue flowers after rainfall

NEXT SPREAD: *Sunfish*
Flying sunfish emerging from a field of sunflowers on a sunny morning

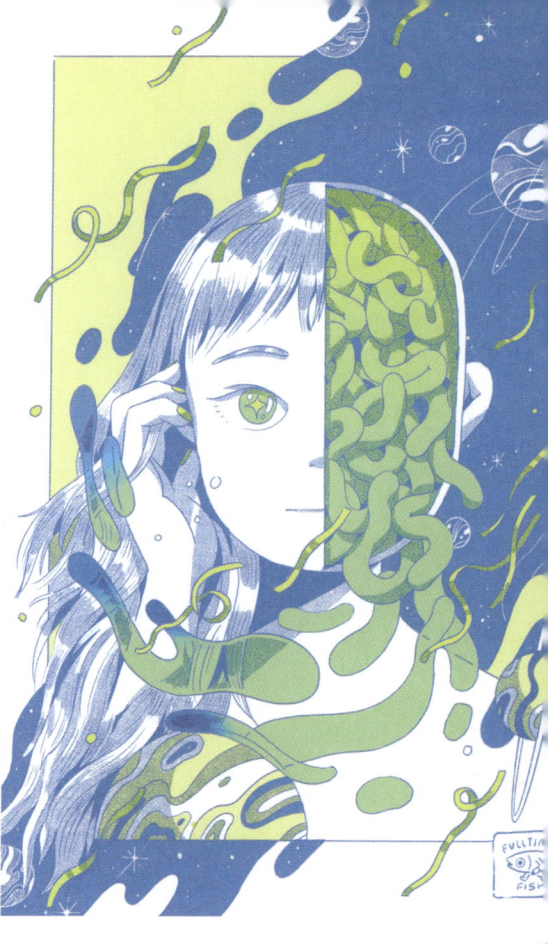

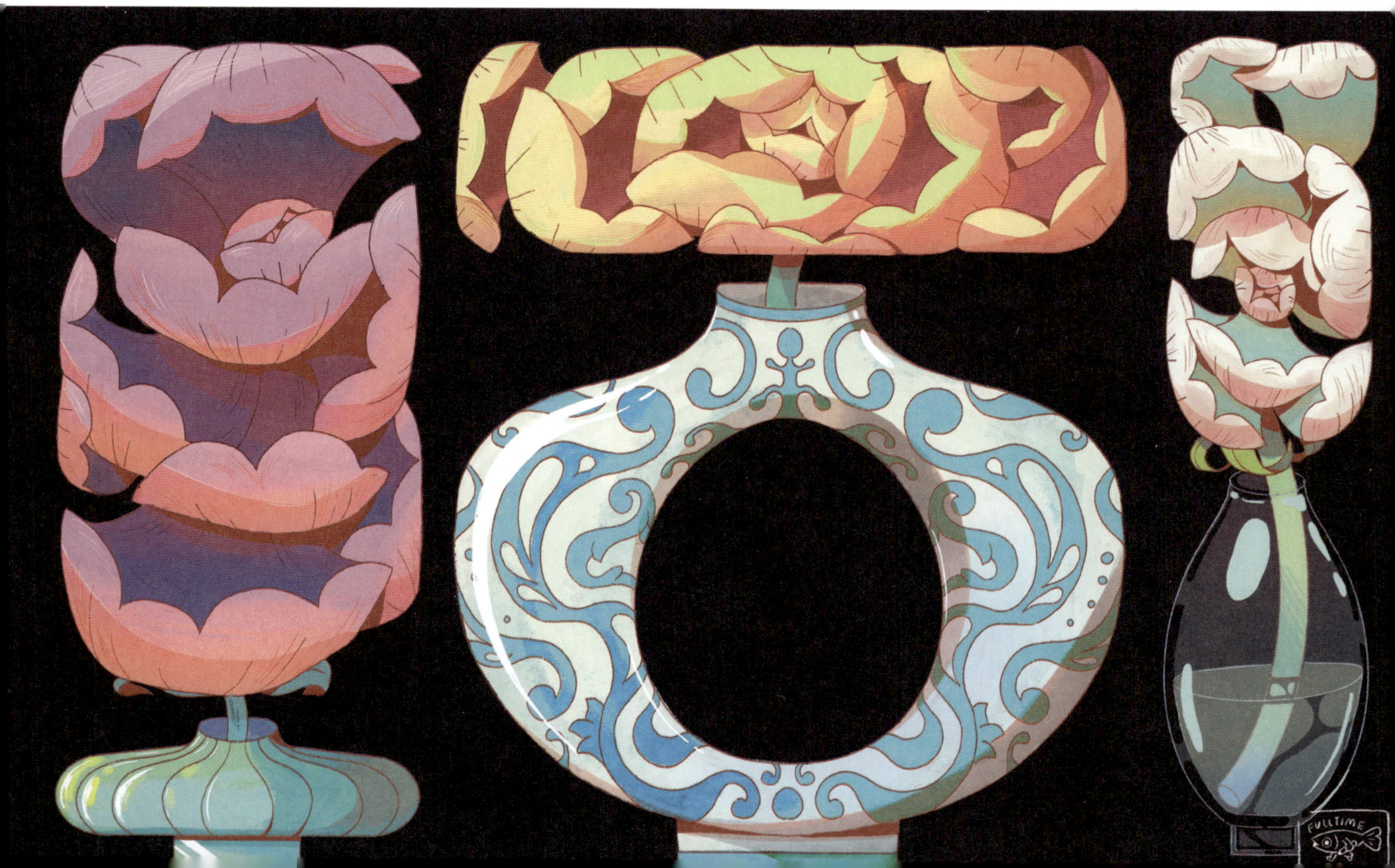

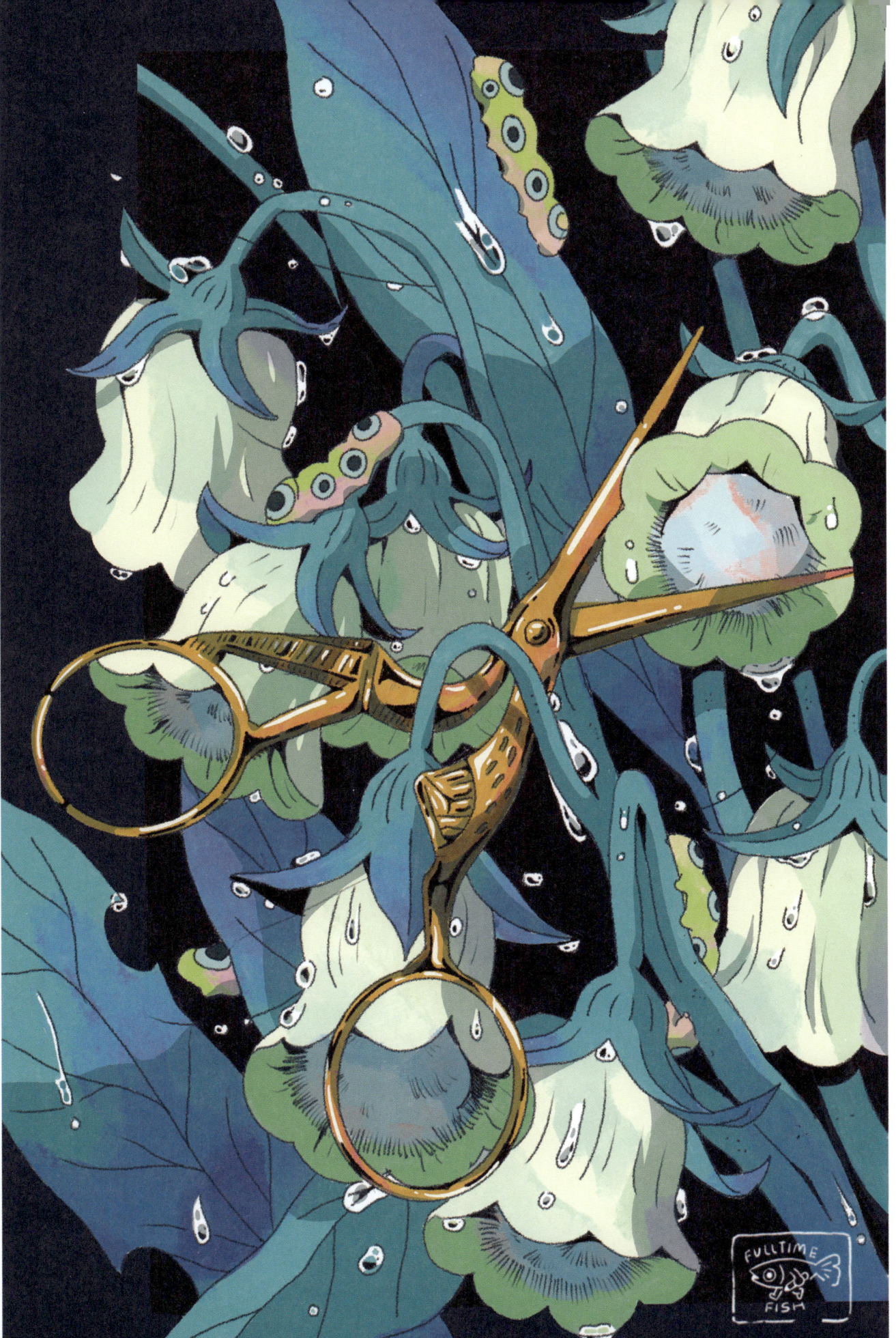

Jamie Chen

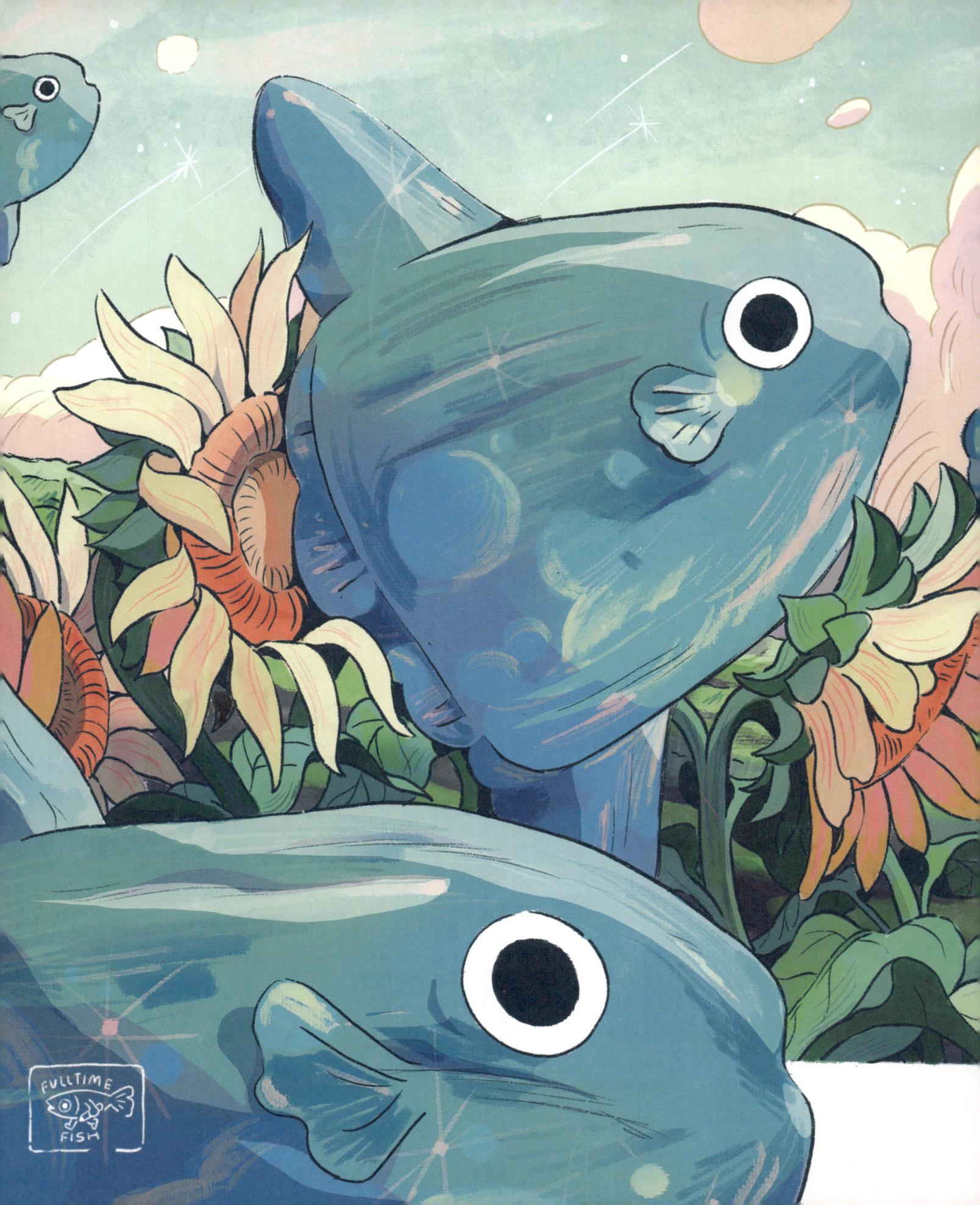

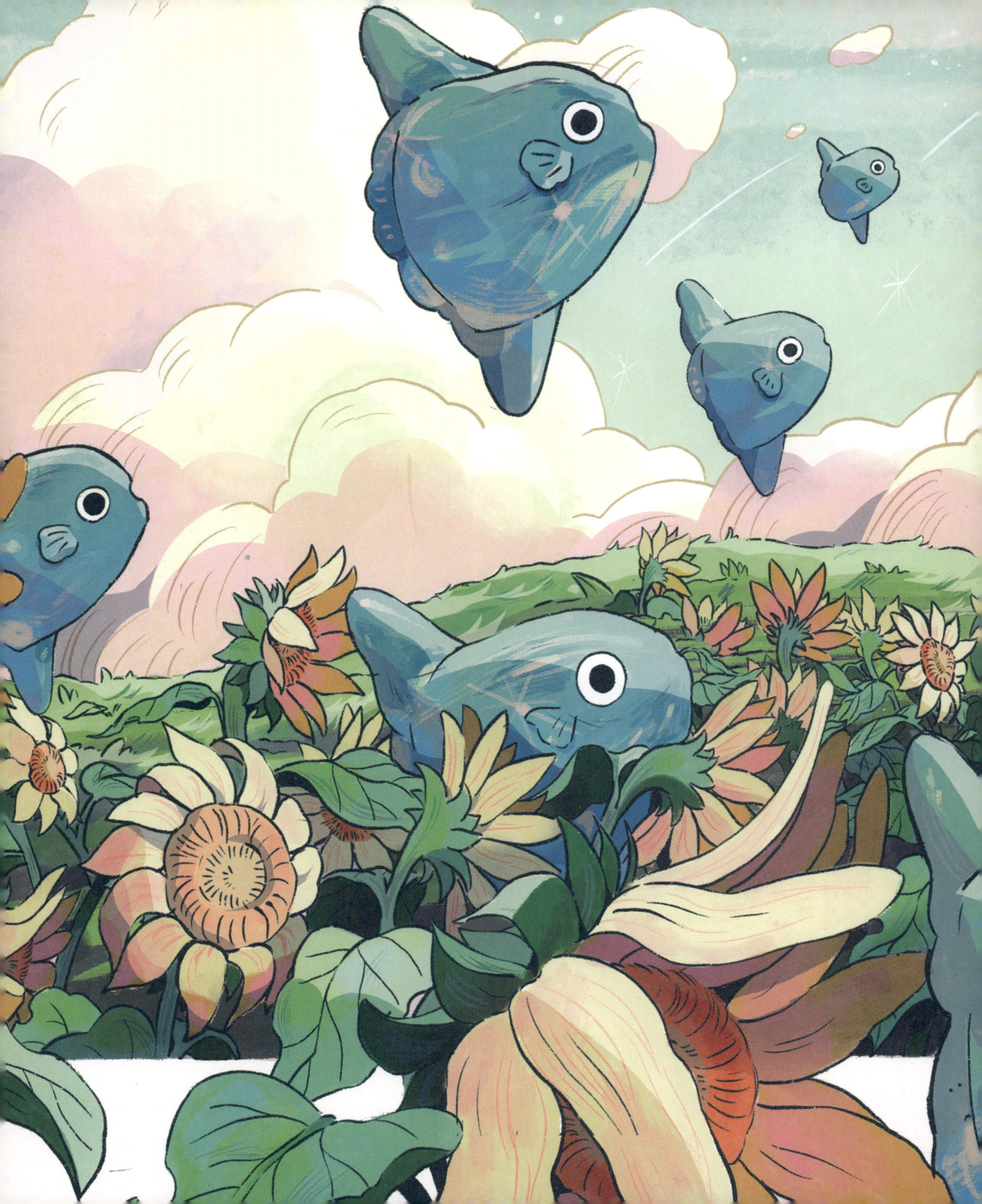

TIGER AND LEOPARD
BY JULIA SCHLEICHER

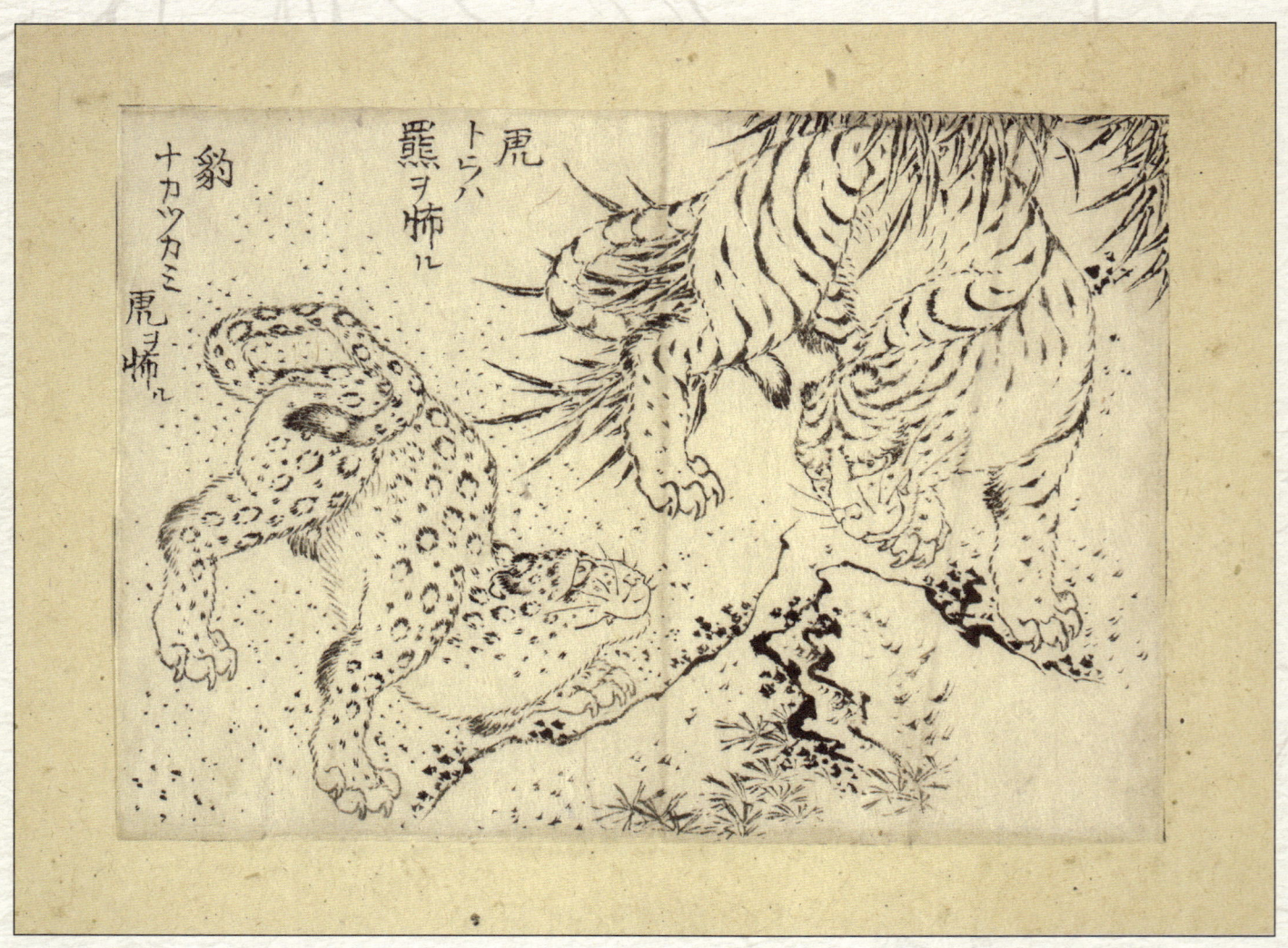

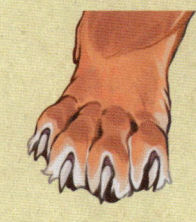

DISCOVERING HOKUSAI

When I first discovered Hokusai's work, it was in an unusual spot: a game where players could catch insects and fish, as well as collect fossils and artwork. Some of you might know what I'm talking about (that's right – it's *Animal Crossing!*). I remember coming across *The Great Wave* and it piquing my interest. Even though the screen quality was not the best, and Hokusai's image wasn't shown in its true glory, I redrew it on multiple occasions.

In art school, I came across more of Hokusai's work and even had the opportunity to mimic the same technique of printing with multiple woodblocks. It really allowed me to uncover and appreciate his work and artistic approach in a new light. But what I love most about his works is how calming they appear. He uses his masterful techniques to create such soft colour gradients that are unnoticeable at first glance, and works with shapes and a few select lines to bring life to a scene. His work is also a great reminder to not add details everywhere – having a few strong lines can be just as appealing as a fully rendered artwork.

Julia Schleicher

01 FIGURING OUT WHAT'S IMPORTANT

Drawing from an existing sketch is quite a different approach for me. I don't know everything the artist considered when creating the piece. What were his references and thoughts about the subjects? The first step to uncovering his musings includes identifying the dynamic shapes and form – everything that catches my eye that I find to be important.

THE FIRST SKETCH FEELS A BIT STIFF, BUT IT GIVES ME A DEEPER UNDERSTANDING OF WHAT I WANT TO CHANGE IN THE NEXT STEP

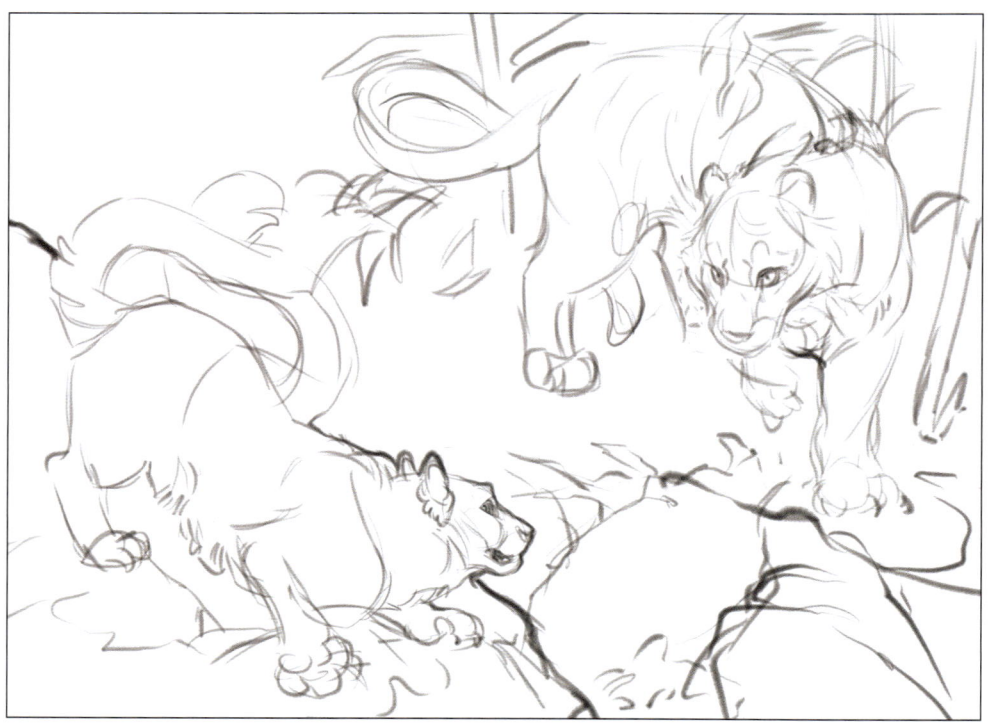

02 PLANNING

My first sketch tends to be messy. It's a playground where I can test things out and find the right lines for the second round. But this is also where I must plan the most, since it will set the foundations for the whole drawing. I try to spend a bit more time here.

THE VERY FIRST SKETCH IS LOOSE AND FULL OF IDEAS

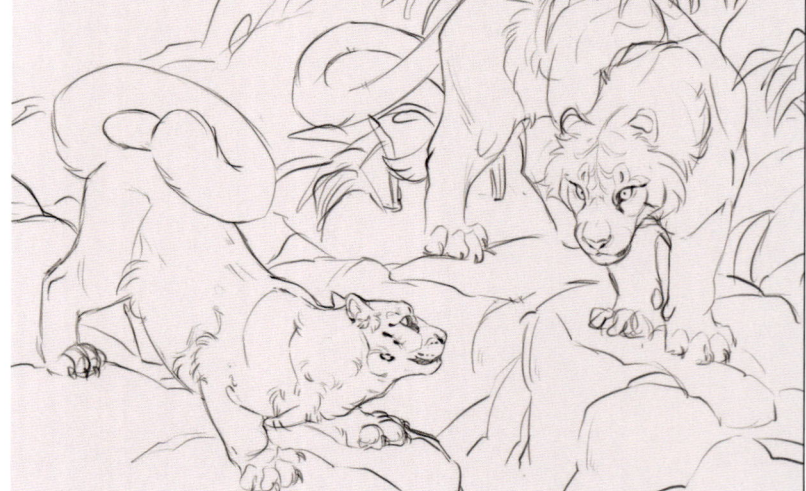

03 UPDATING THE SKETCH

The next step is, of course, a new sketch. I take what I like from the old one and focus on adding more action lines and a flowing sense of movement. I want the connection between the animals to be more playful. Overlapping the tails helps to make the connection even stronger than just having them sit next to each other with a large gap in between.

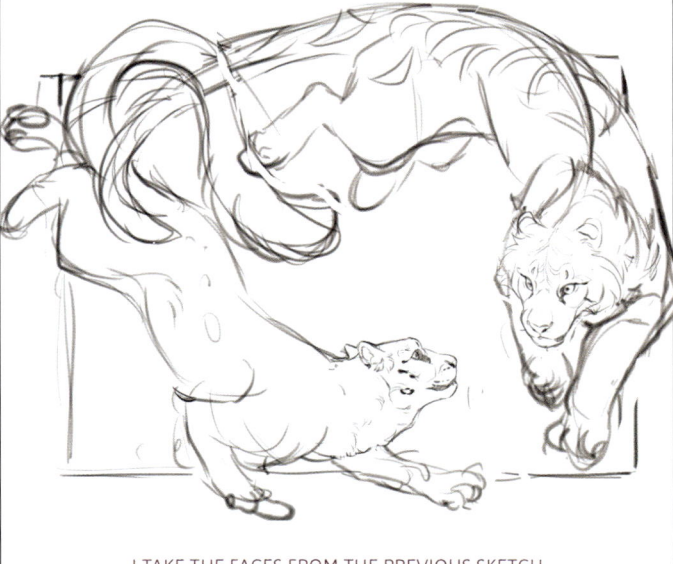

I TAKE THE FACES FROM THE PREVIOUS SKETCH AND CONSTRUCT THE BODIES FROM IT

04 FINDING THE STORY

Messy sketches also help to spark creative ideas, and I usually end up finding the story by accident. Maybe the tiger markings could be leaves? And wouldn't it be a nice contrast to the snow leopard's markings? Since it's a *snow* leopard, its fur pattern can resemble a flurry of snow, too. Finally, the story reveals itself: a winter and autumn spirit meet at the transition between seasons. Stories can be really easy to discover if you just look for them.

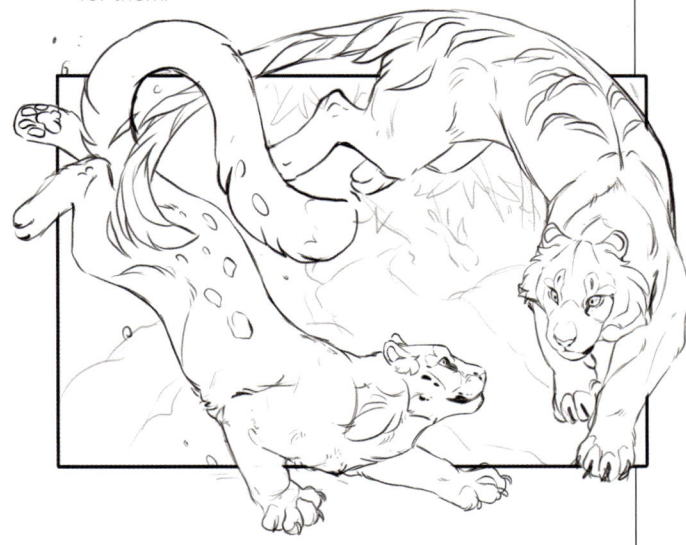

THIS IS THE FINAL STEP BEFORE I MOVE ON TO LINE ART. I HAVE ALL THE CRUCIAL INFORMATION I NEED TO MOVE FORWARD

05 FOCAL POINTS

In this cleaner sketch, I solidify the lines. At this stage, I pay a lot of attention to the focal points of the image: the faces and areas with strong contrasts. These are the areas we tend to look at first. It is where my eyes moved to in Hokusai's original drawing, and I want to establish this in my painting as well.

THE FOCAL POINTS OF THE IMAGE SHOULD INCLUDE ALL THE IMPORTANT STORY POINTS

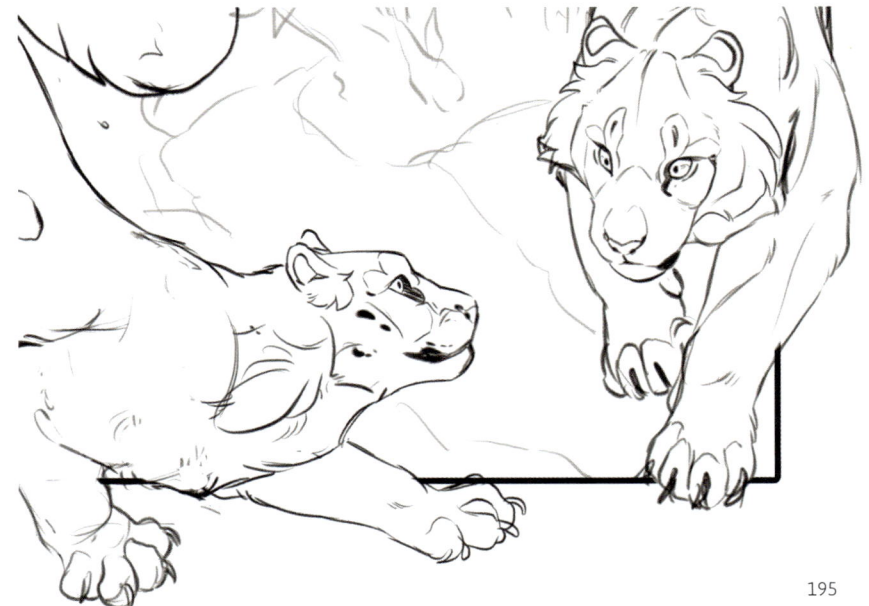

195

Julia Schleicher

06 LINE ART

The line art is the final stage before colouring begins. I now have a strong base to work from, as well as an idea of how I want the final painting to look. I start from the focal point and work my way through the drawing. Since I don't have to worry about proportions and composition, I can zoom closer and add details like fur spikes here and there, as well as important markings. I don't draw the spots of the snow leopard, since it will be easier to paint them instead.

LINE ART CLEANS UP THE SKETCH. I MAKE SURE THE SUBJECTS STILL FEEL AS ALIVE AS MY ORIGINAL SKETCH

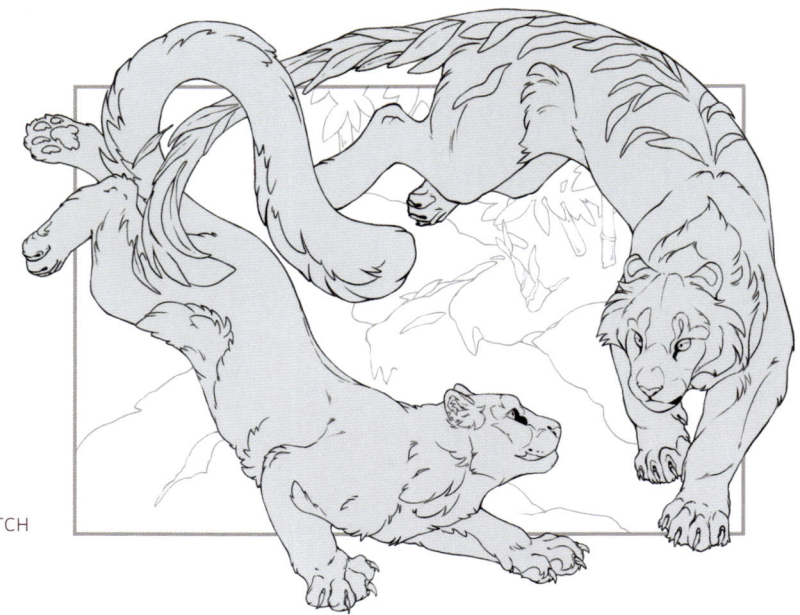

07 CREATING THE COLOUR SCHEME

Since the story is autumn and winter meeting, I already have an idea of how I want the colours to look. They should be inspired by nature, just like many of my favourite works by Hokusai. I don't include extremely saturated colour pops, but instead opt for a more harmonious and soothing colour scheme. I start with soft colours, separating the tiger with oranges from the leopard in greyish blues. The watercolour brush helps to bring all different kinds of mixes between the colours, creating a palette I can pick from later on.

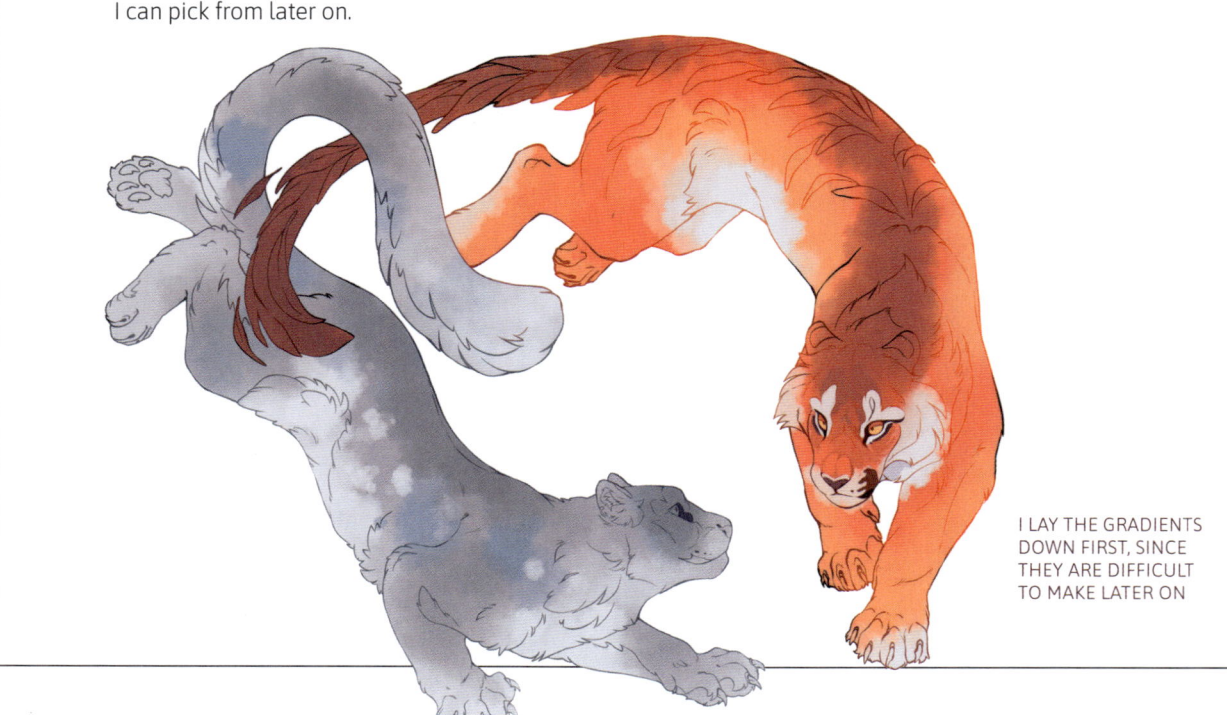

I LAY THE GRADIENTS DOWN FIRST, SINCE THEY ARE DIFFICULT TO MAKE LATER ON

08 FOCUSING ON WHAT'S IMPORTANT

Looking at the base colours, I decide I don't want any extreme light or shadows. Considering the patterns and scene as a whole, it would be an overkill of details and would most likely confuse the viewer instead of making things appear more interesting. Hokusai's coloured works tend to have a lot of flat colours due to the technique of woodblock printing, so I concentrate on shapes, patterns, and mostly flat colours.

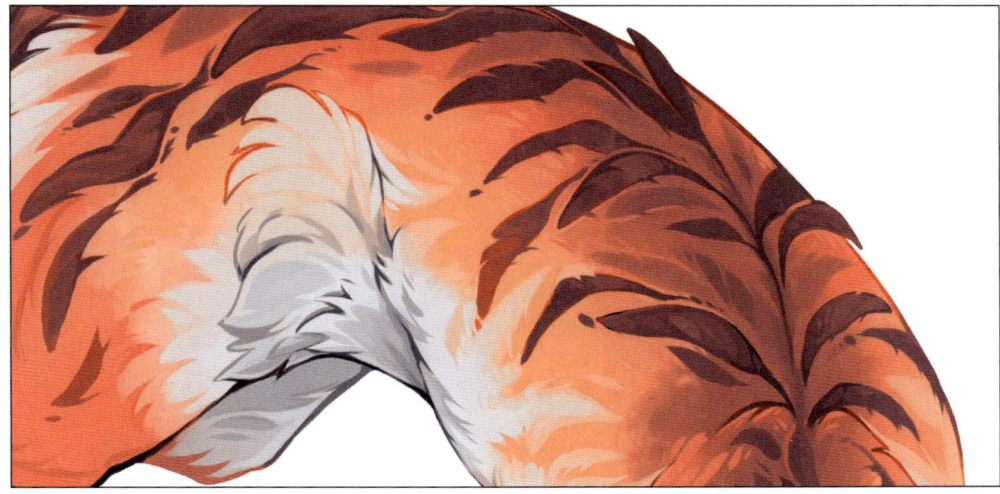

PATTERNS INSPIRED BY THE LEAVES OF THE BACKGROUND

09 THE 'UGLY' PHASE

Just like I did in the line-art stage, I start rendering the faces first. I painted with watercolour much of the time before moving over to digital mediums. With watercolour, there is normally always an ugly phase where colours have been laid down but there are no details yet. In the past, when I gave up on a piece because it didn't look quite right, it was always at this stage. It is helpful to finish the small parts, have a reference for the rest, and to not work on everything at the same time. This method helped me realize that sometimes you just have to push through that ugly phase, regardless of what medium you're using.

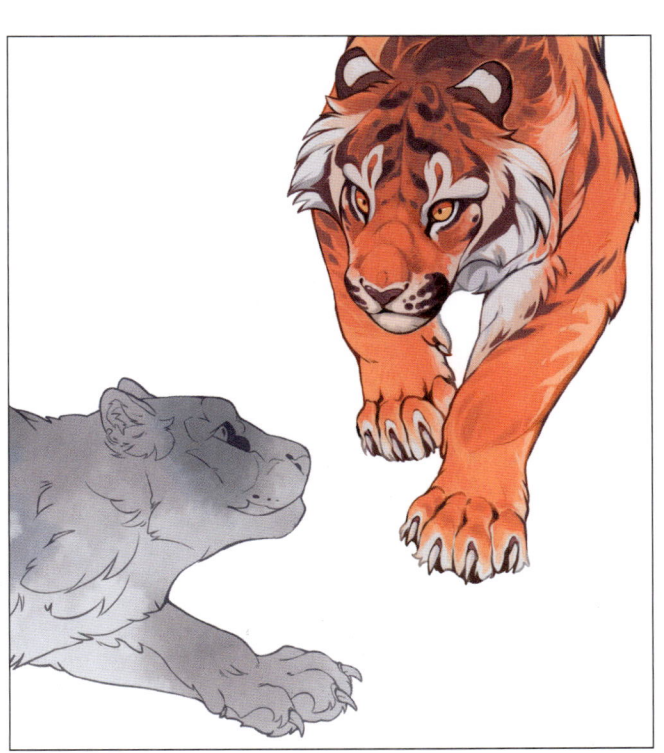

I WORK ON ONE AREA AND SUBJECT AT A TIME

Julia Schleicher

10 RENDERING

Rendering takes a lot of time, around two-thirds of the whole piece. It's really easy to get lost in the details. I have to add something here, make more contrast over there, and so on. It's important to remind myself that the piece as a whole should work, and that it shouldn't be overloaded with details so that the eye doesn't know where to look and rest. Ask yourself where the focal point is and if you need to add or subtract any elements. Also discern which lines are important and where you can apply more contrast.

While rendering, I work with colours from the base. It keeps me within a limited colour palette without the urge to use all the options provided in digital art. When I use the colour wheel, it's mostly to change the saturation or value, just like I did with the noses and eyes.

NOW THEY ARE STARTING TO LOOK LIKE SOMETHING. THE EYES OF THE SNOW LEOPARD ARE A STRIKING BLUE IN CONTRAST TO THE TIGER'S GOLDEN EYES

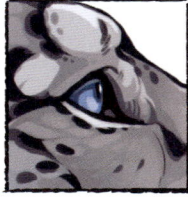
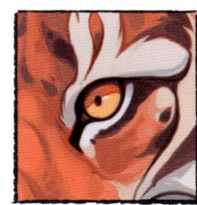

11 PAINTERLY TECHNIQUE

With the base colour added, I begin to render on top of the line art. It is a more painterly approach. I like having the brushstrokes visible and don't feel as limited. I just draw over lines if I don't like how they look.

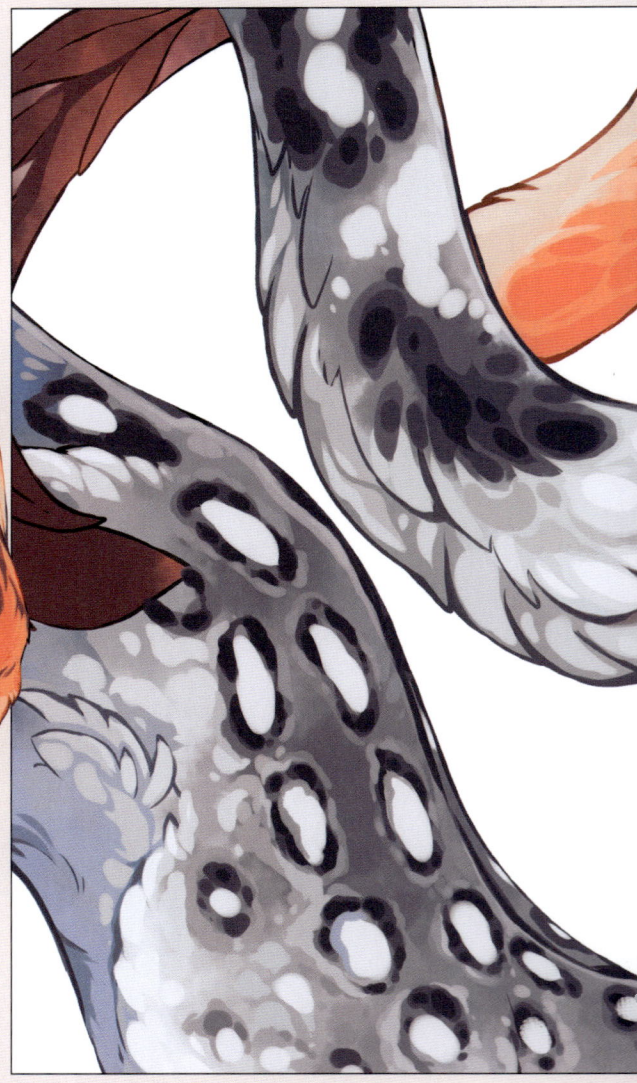

HAVING A FEW BRUSHSTROKES MAKES THE PAINTING FEEL ALIVE. THERE IS STILL THE ILLUSION OF DETAIL WHEN IT'S VIEWED FROM FURTHER AWAY

FILLING IN THE BACKGROUND

When the main subjects are mostly finished, I begin on the background. Since the tiger and leopard have many details and patterns, it's a logical choice to let the background be a resting point. A few lines help me to lay out all the important information. Next, I start with a soft colour gradient, which includes colours that are similar to the existing palette. With a few strokes, I add more details. I don't want the background to be too different from the foreground. It should still feel like one drawing.

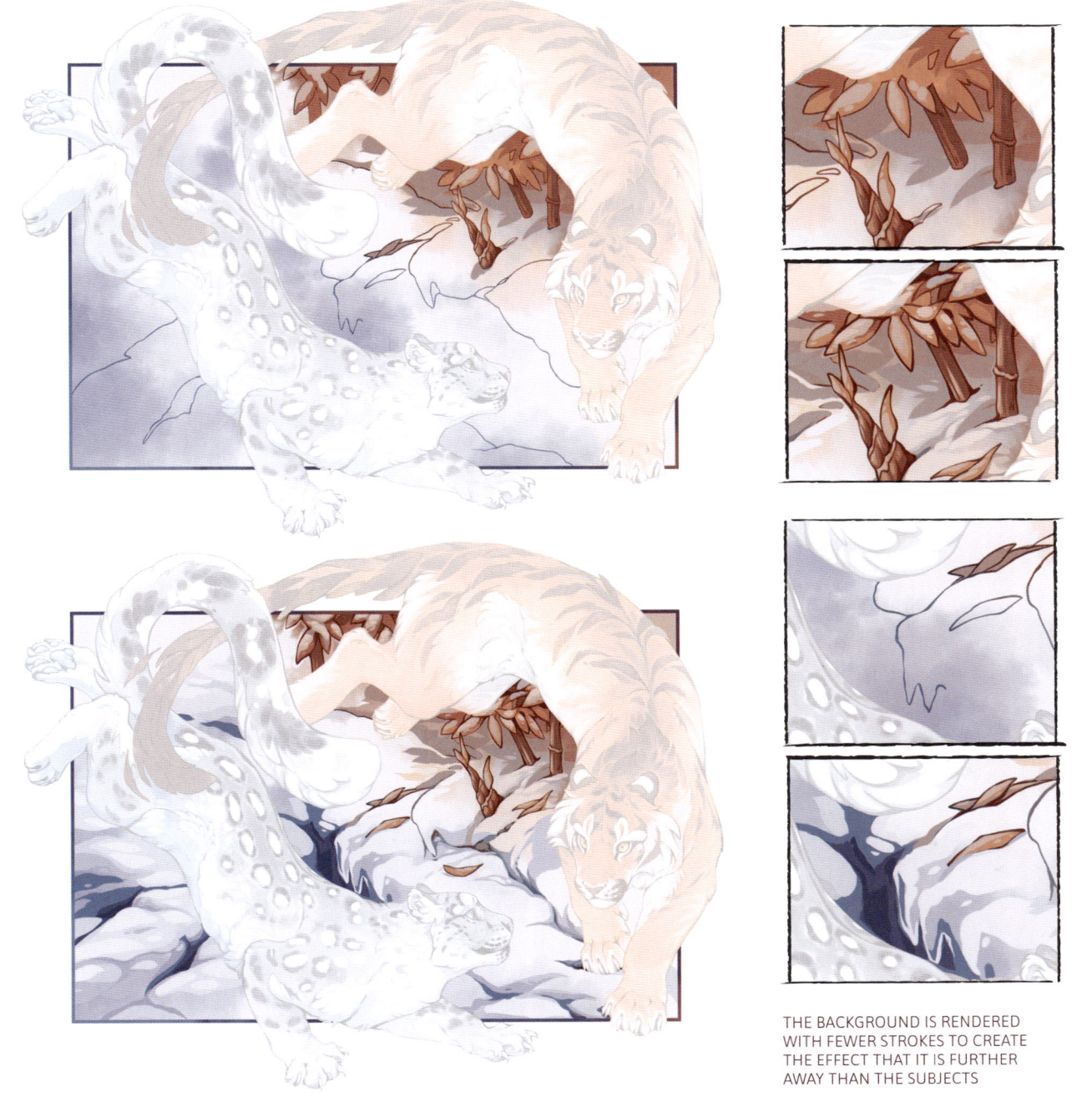

THE BACKGROUND IS RENDERED
WITH FEWER STROKES TO CREATE
THE EFFECT THAT IT IS FURTHER
AWAY THAN THE SUBJECTS

Julia Schleicher

13 CONNECTING THE BACKGROUND & FOREGROUND

Once the background is finished, I return to the main subjects and fix outlines that are not visible in the background, or ones that make things appear too busy. It's important for the entire image to function together.

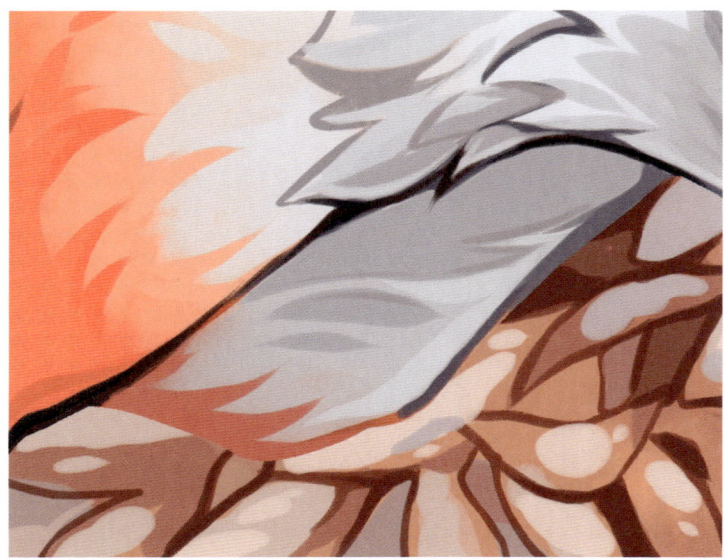

REVISITING THE OUTLINES MAKES A BIG DIFFERENCE TO THE PAINTING'S READABILITY

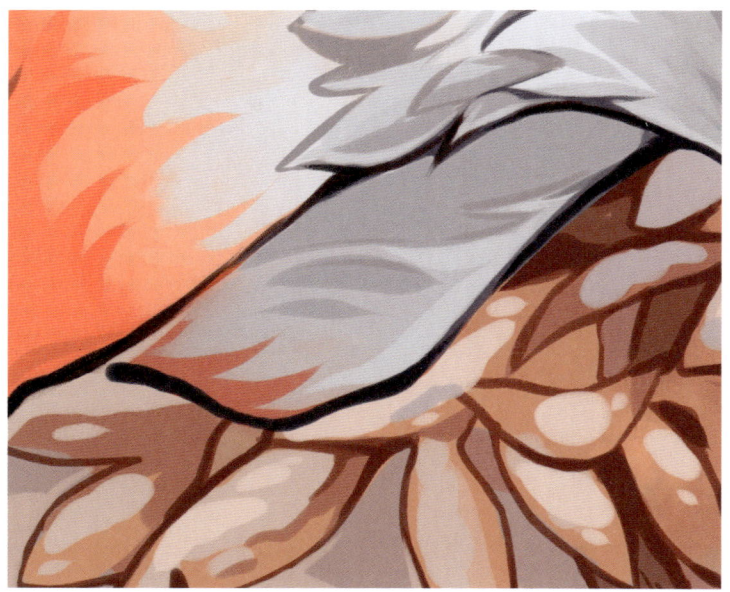

'THEY SHOULD BE INSPIRED BY NATURE, JUST LIKE MANY OF MY FAVOURITE WORKS BY HOKUSAI'

14 FINISHING TOUCHES

Lastly, I add the final touches. I look at the painting as a whole and see if it's still readable at a smaller size. Some lines need more contrast, while others are distracting. I like to outline shapes that are further away from the background with white or lighter lines to separate them from the background, almost like a cut-out piece. After I go through that process, I look it over one last time to see if I missed something. Then… it is finished.

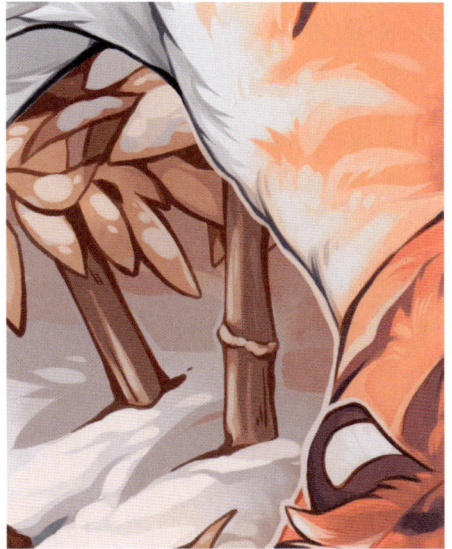

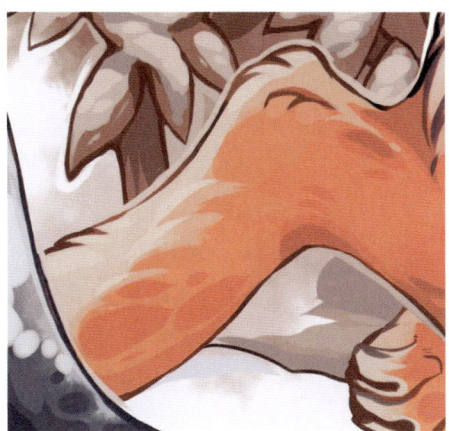

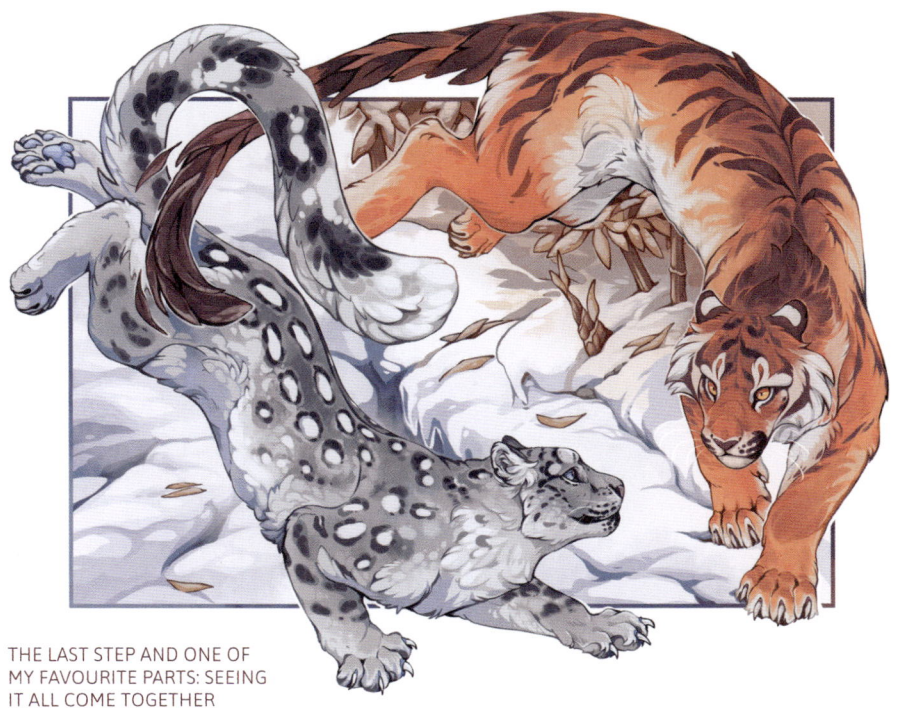

THE LAST STEP AND ONE OF MY FAVOURITE PARTS: SEEING IT ALL COME TOGETHER

CONCLUSION

Working from an existing sketch is not something I do very often. But I learned to love the process of discovering and interpreting Hokusai's work while mixing a few of my own ideas into the piece. I hope I did his work justice and implemented all the little things I felt were important, such as the dynamic between the two animals, as well as the movement. It was a joy to work on this project.

Julia Schleicher

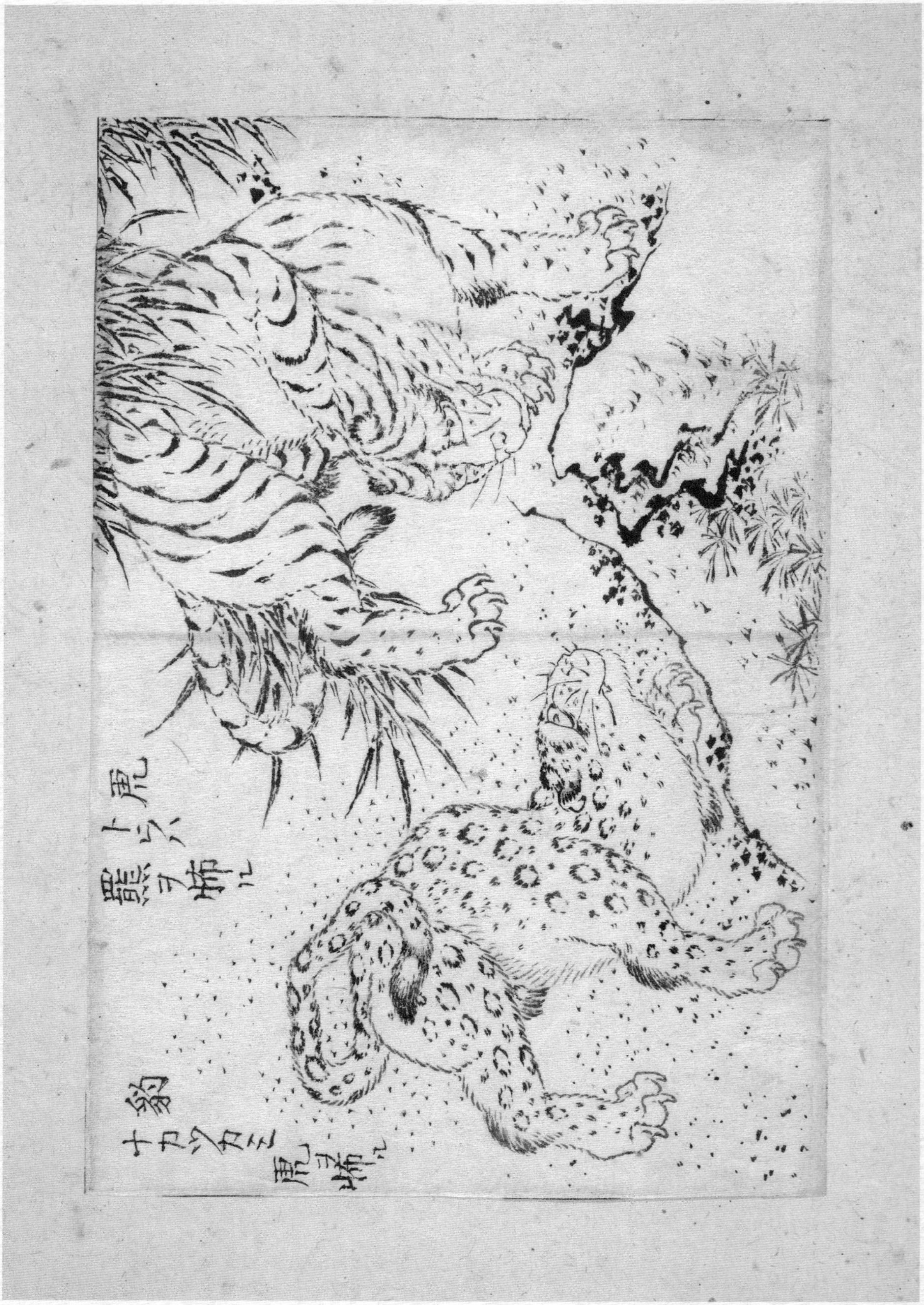

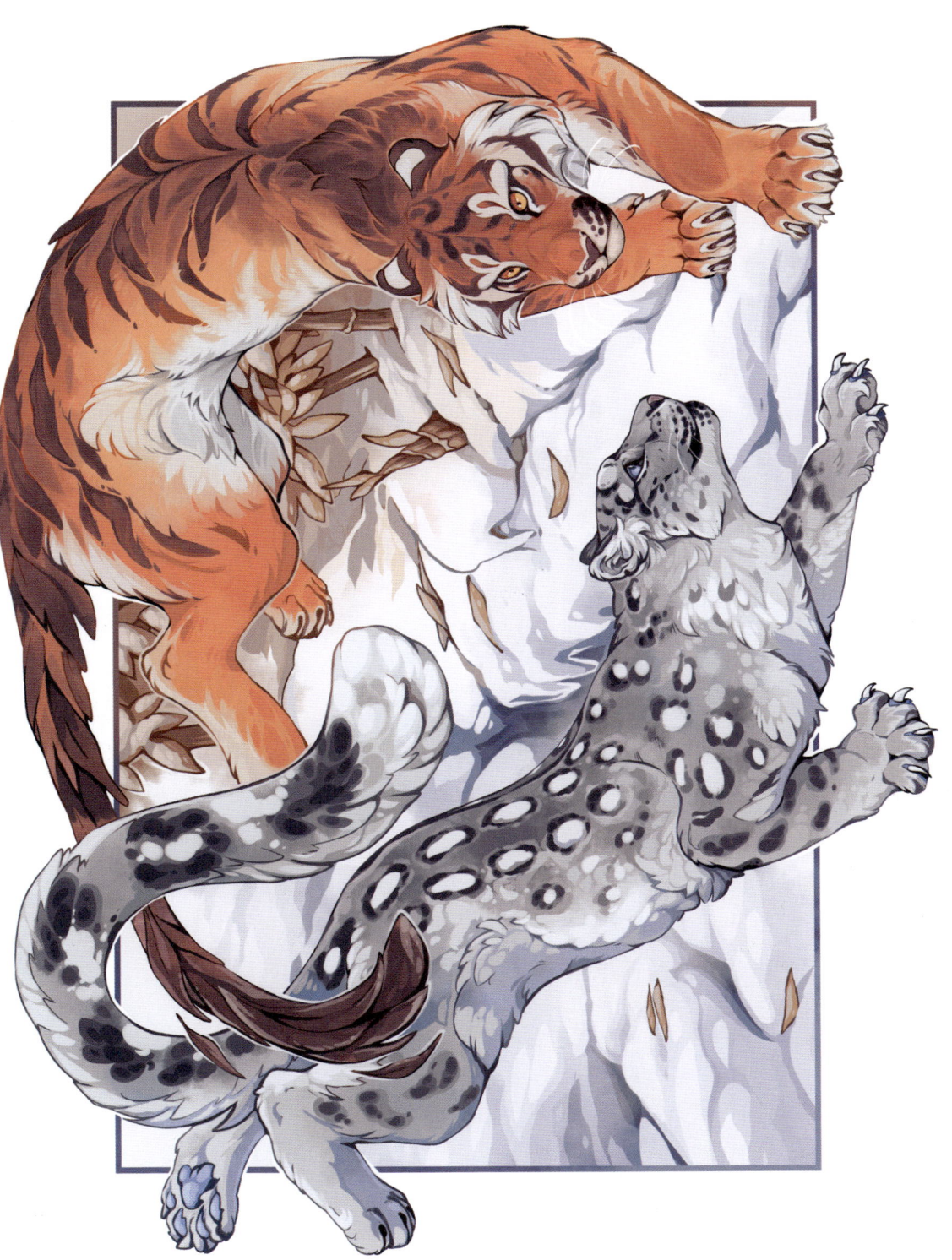

TIGER AND LEOPARD

JULIA SCHLEICHER

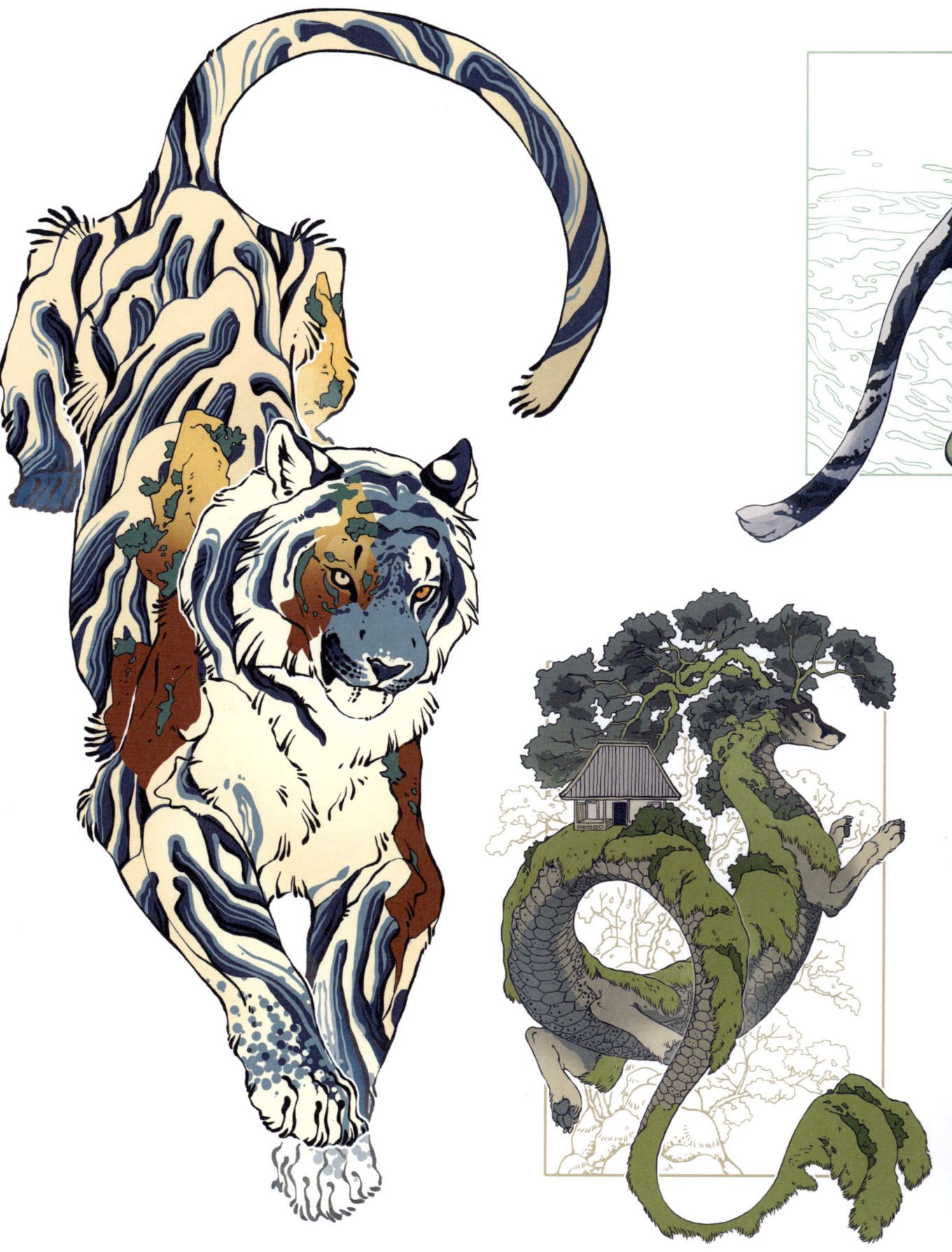

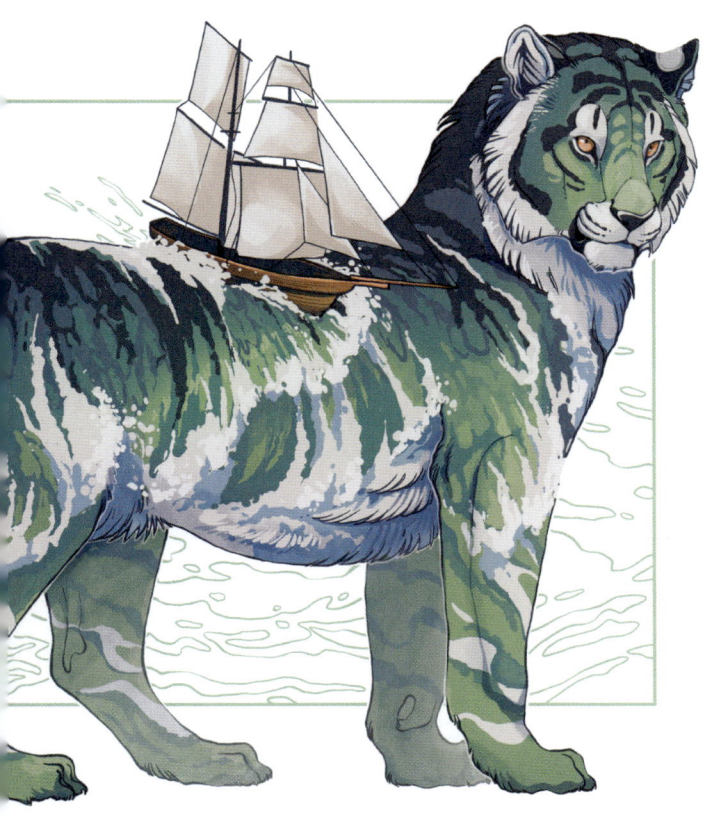
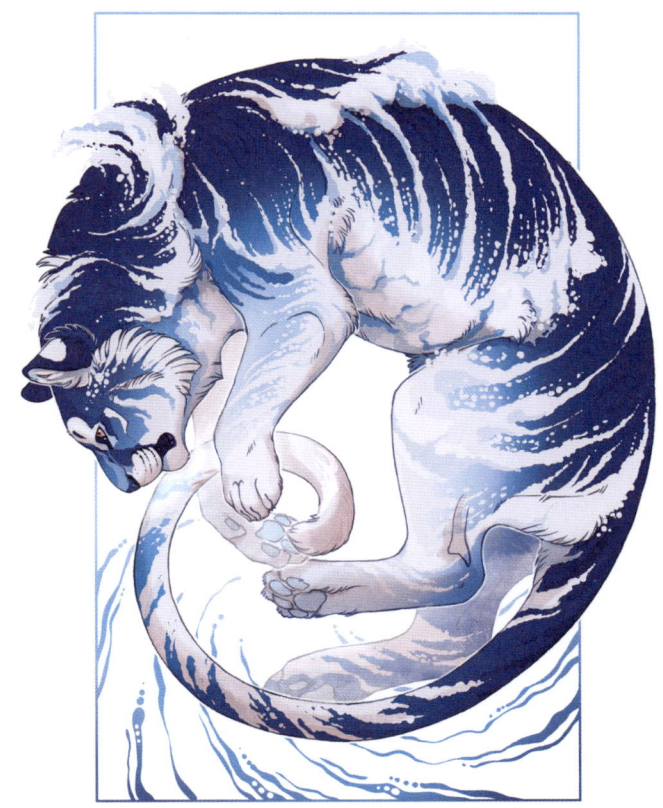

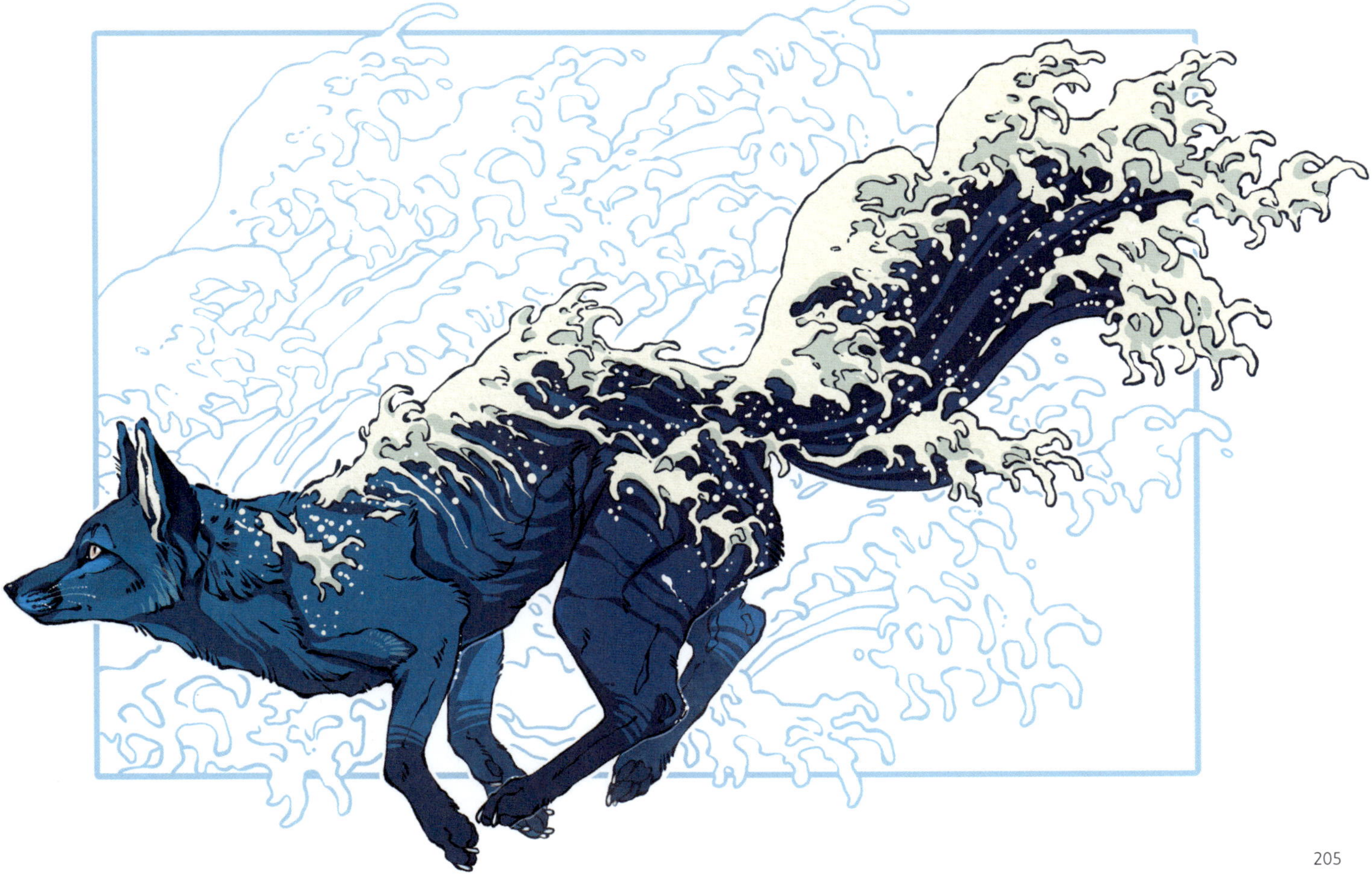

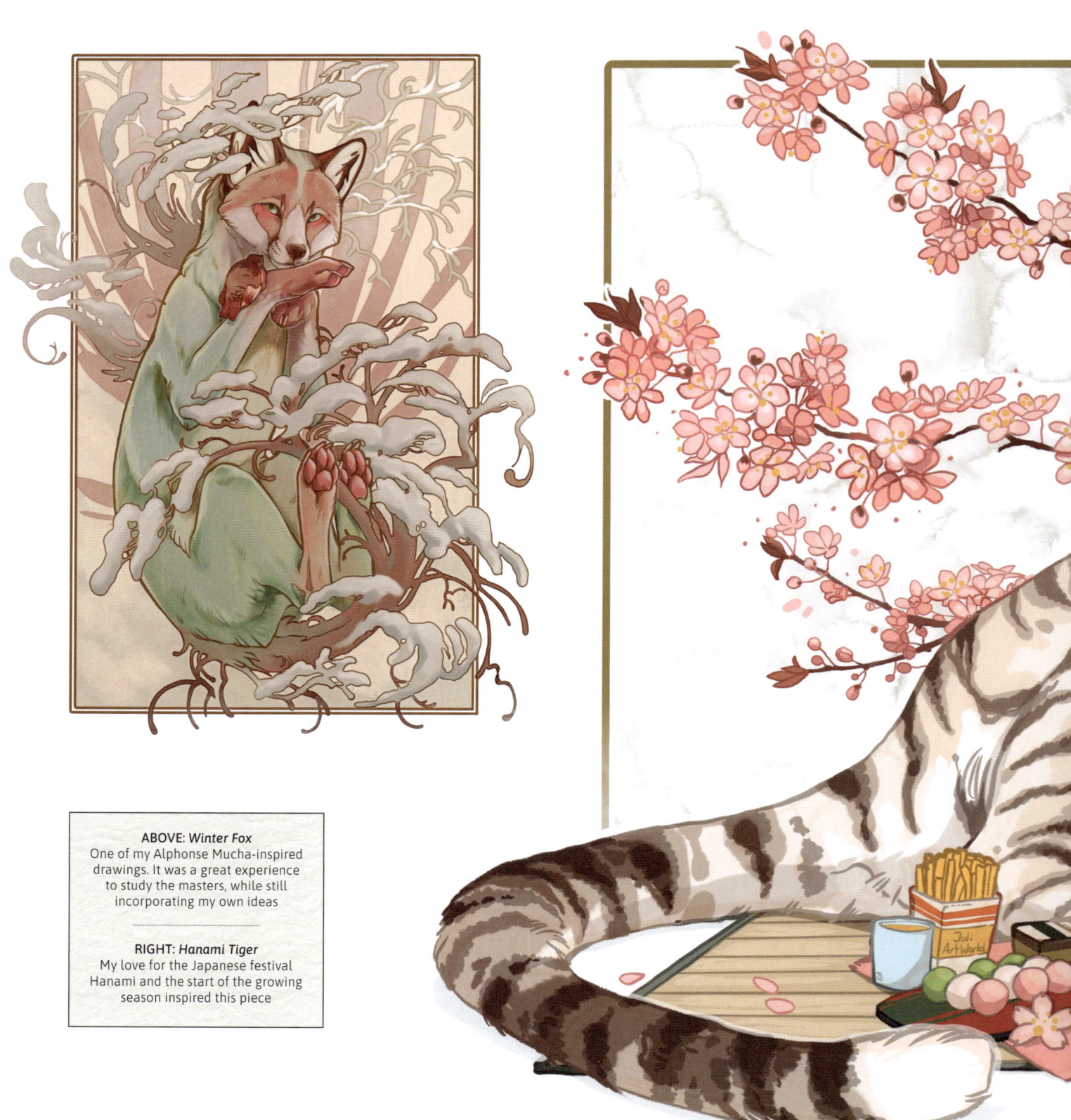

ABOVE: *Winter Fox*
One of my Alphonse Mucha-inspired drawings. It was a great experience to study the masters, while still incorporating my own ideas

RIGHT: *Hanami Tiger*
My love for the Japanese festival Hanami and the start of the growing season inspired this piece

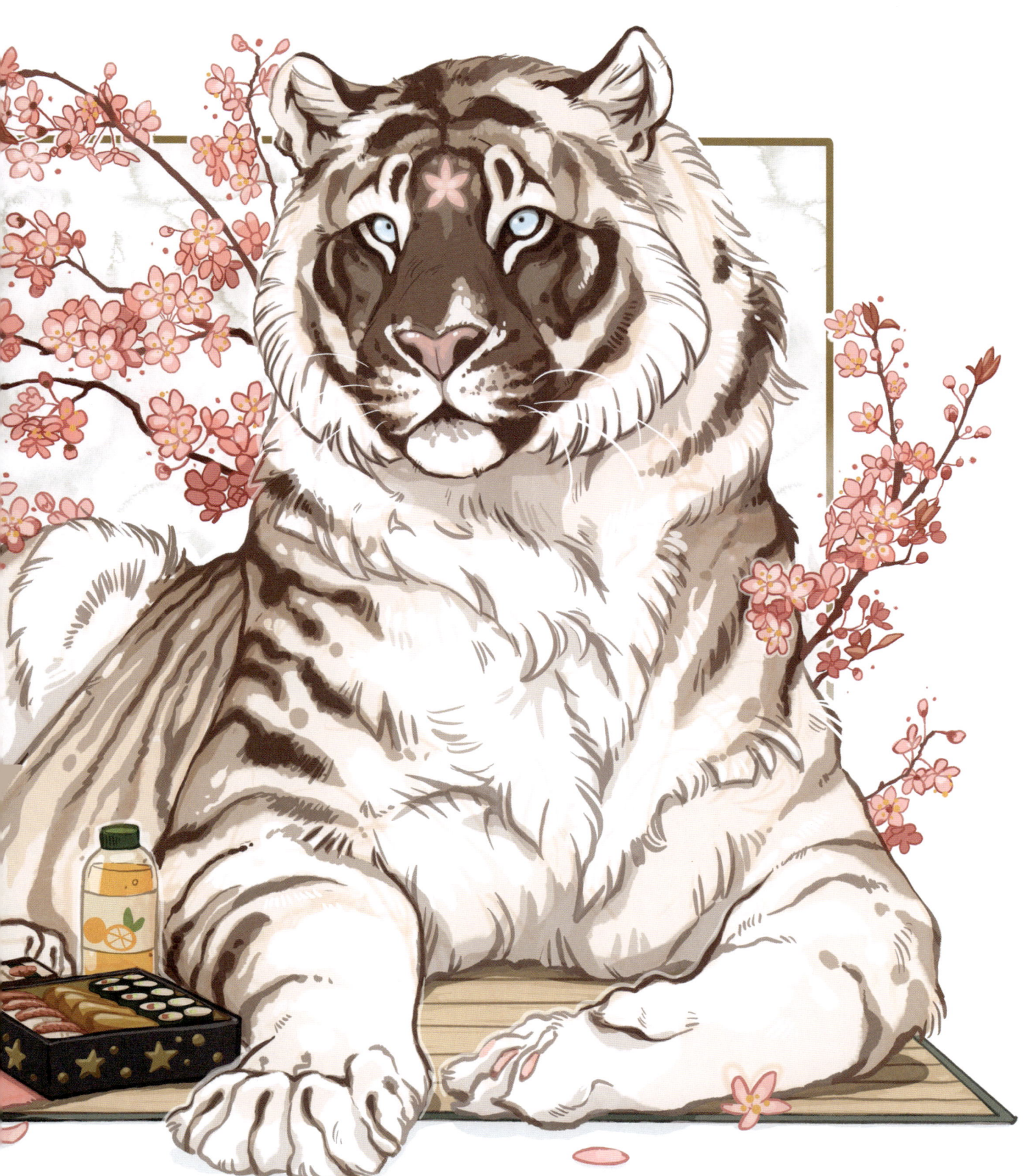

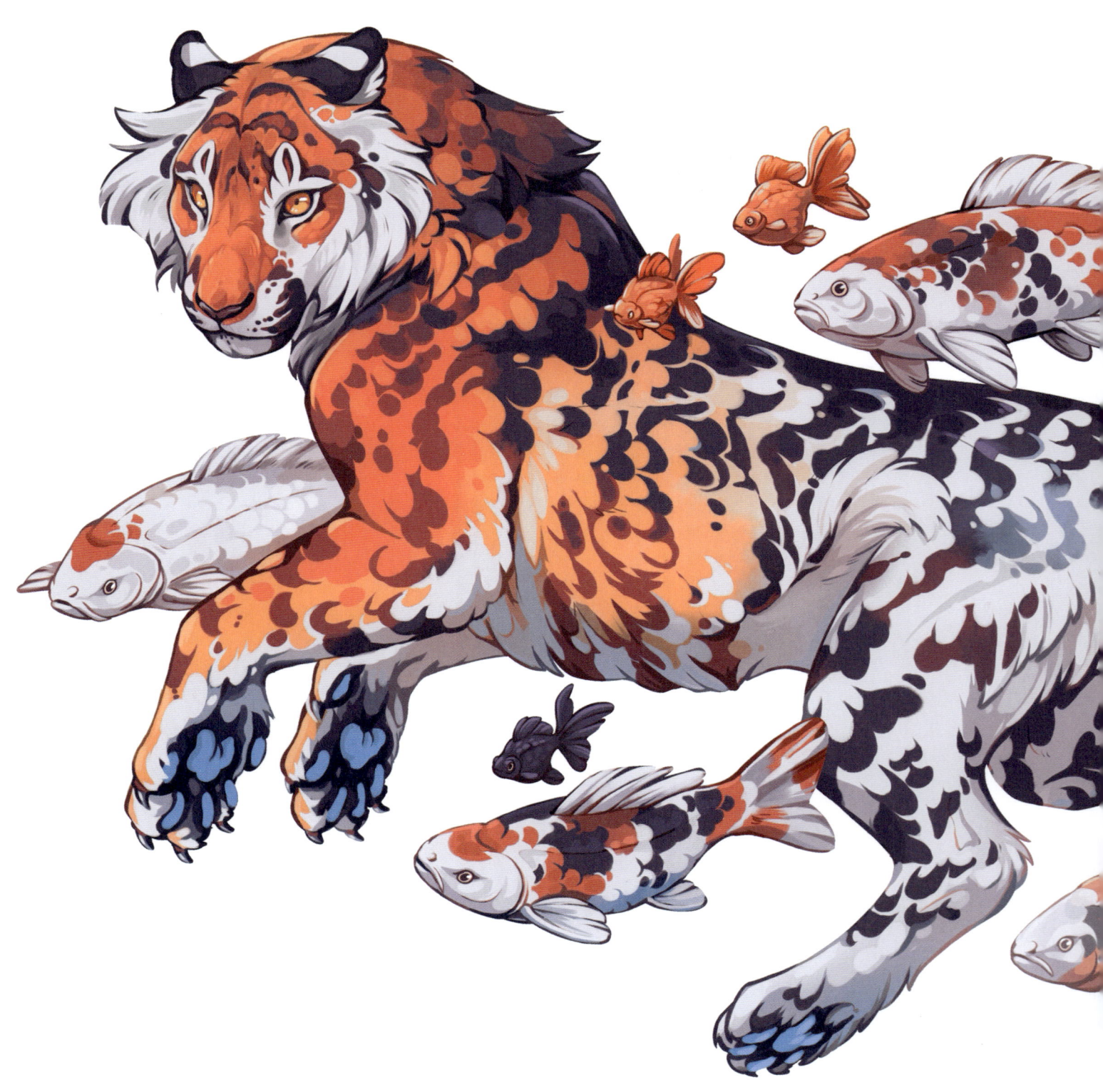

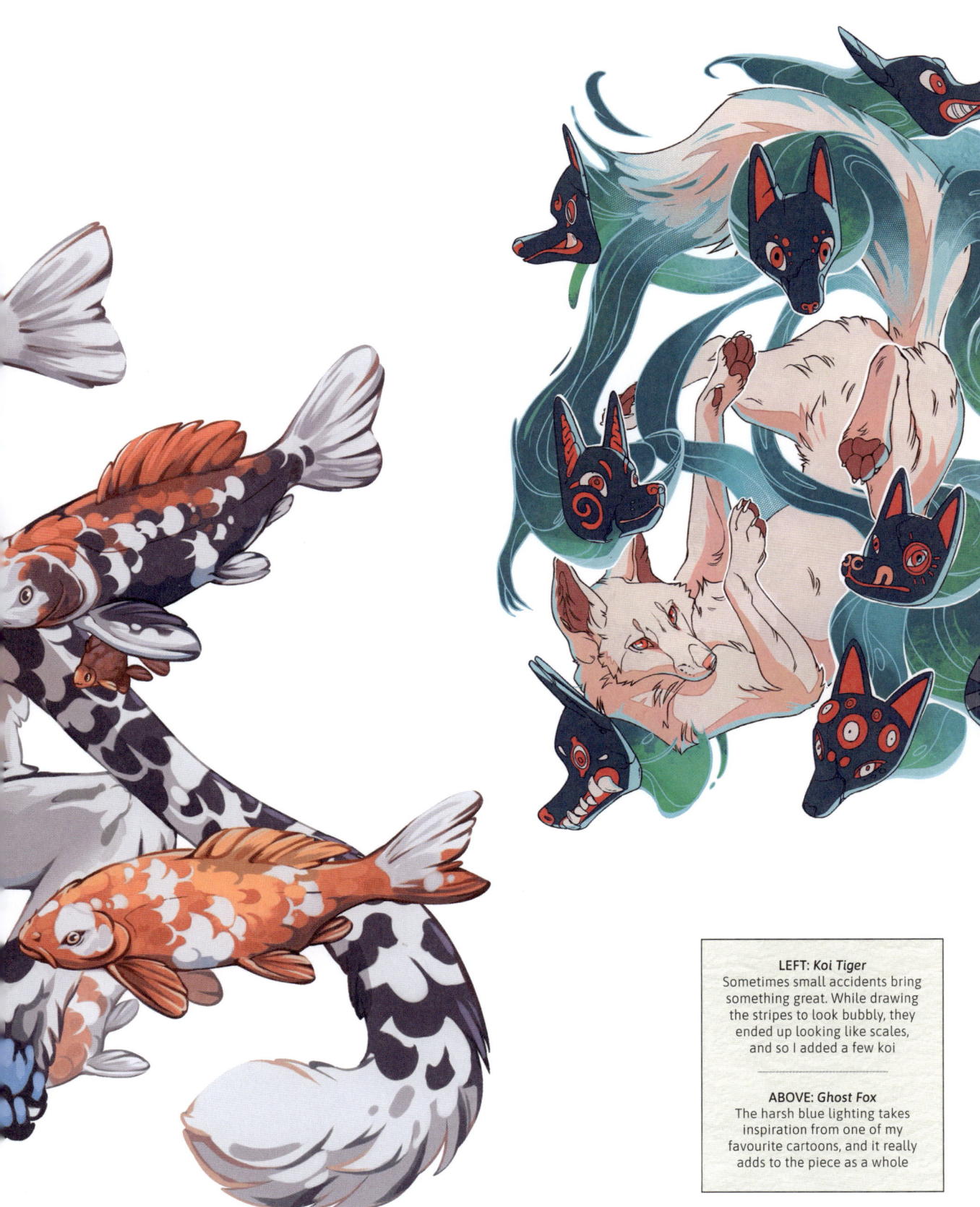

LEFT: *Koi Tiger*
Sometimes small accidents bring something great. While drawing the stripes to look bubbly, they ended up looking like scales, and so I added a few koi

ABOVE: *Ghost Fox*
The harsh blue lighting takes inspiration from one of my favourite cartoons, and it really adds to the piece as a whole

Julia Schleicher

ON MT JIULI, ZIFANG DE[FEATS THE] ENEMY BY PLAYING A ME[LODY]

BY ANGELA HAO

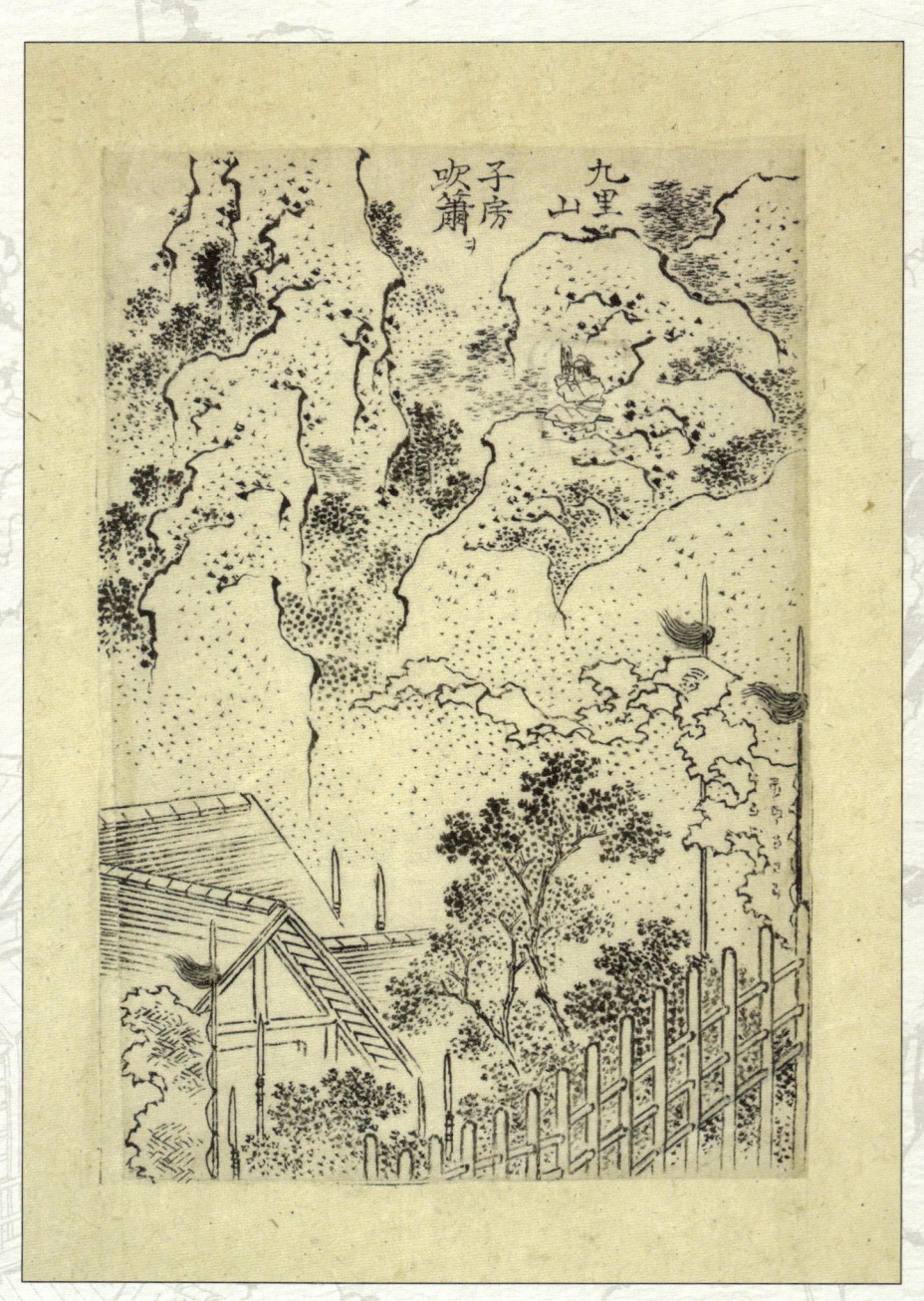

ORALISES THE
ANCHOLY TUNE

ANGELA HAO

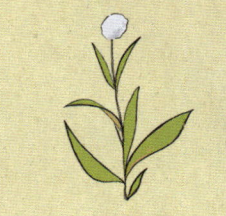

DISCOVERING HOKUSAI

My work is heavily influenced by Japanese animation, which itself draws inspiration from Japanese manga and art masters such as Hokusai, whose legacy extends far beyond traditional woodblock prints. Growing up, I was immersed in the world of Japanese manga, devouring stories by legends like Fujiko F. Fujio, Gosho Aoyama, Rumiko Takahashi, Akira Toriyama, Ai Yazawa, and so many more great manga artists. These works were my constant companions, sparking my imagination and fuelling my creativity. I spent countless hours drawing characters, backgrounds, and even transforming textbook figures into stylized manga versions, which was always a fun escape for me.

As I grew older, my fascination expanded to include Japanese animation, with Studio Ghibli films like *My Neighbor Totoro*, *Spirited Away*, and *Nausicaä of the Valley of the Wind* holding a special place in my heart. The vibrant colours, intricate details, and deep emotional resonance of these films profoundly influenced my approach to art.

Hokusai's influence is a cornerstone of my work. His mastery of line work and composition in iconic ukiyo-e prints have profoundly impacted Japanese visual arts, including manga and animation. Hokusai's approach to simplified yet expressive lines has indirectly shaped the development of Japanese manga and has clearly inspired the visual style of Studio Ghibli. This lineage of artistic clarity and depth informs my own work, as I strive to capture the essence of serene landscapes and intricate architecture with a simplicity and elegance that resonates deeply with viewers.

In my artwork, I love blending the vibrant colours of Japanese animation with the simplified, organic lines inspired by Hokusai and manga. This creative journey is something I truly enjoy, exploring how these influences come together in my pieces. Each illustration is a reflection of my passion for art, capturing the beauty of traditional subjects while letting my own style shine through. It's a continuous adventure, and I'm excited to see where it leads.

Angela Hao

01 INITIAL SKETCH

In Hokusai's original work, Zifang plays a bamboo flute on a rocky outcrop of Mt. Jiuli, slightly off-centre. Surrounded by rugged peaks and swirling mists, the composition uses delicate lines to highlight the serene connection between humanity and nature. In my interpretation, I envision returning to this storied location hundreds of years later, where time has left its gentle mark. The landscape remains largely untouched, preserving the essence of its natural beauty. The village, however, has grown and expanded, yet it has done so with a respectful nod to the past, integrating itself harmoniously into the surrounding environment. The natural setting endures, nearly unchanged, untouched by the heavy hand of industrialization, allowing the serene and unspoiled character of the landscape to continue shining through, as if time itself has stood still.

In my initial sketch, I embrace the same overall composition by placing the house prominently in the foreground on the bottom left, nestled among a cluster of trees. Behind the house, the mountain rises majestically, with its rugged, rocky peaks surrounded by bushes and trees, echoing the natural beauty and balance found in the original work.

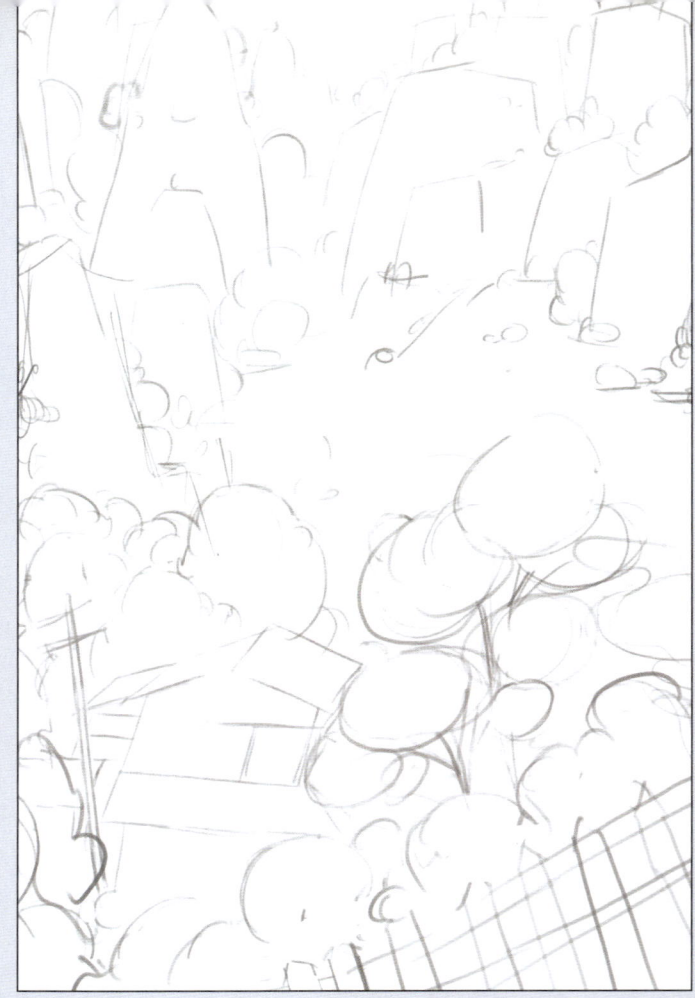

IN THE INITIAL SKETCH, I USE LIGHT, LOOSE LINES TO OUTLINE THE OVERALL COMPOSITION

02 REFINING THE INITIAL SKETCH

In the initial composition, elements feel crowded and too tightly packed. To enhance depth and create a more expansive feeling, I adjust the perspective by stepping back and viewing the scene from a higher vantage point. This approach makes the house appear smaller and pushes the mountains farther into the distance. Adding a snow-capped peak to the background further emphasizes depth. To bring more life to the drawing, I introduce plants and flowers in the foreground. Additionally, I include smoke, as depicted in Hokusai's original work, to echo its significance and infuse my piece with a similar atmospheric quality.

I ADJUST PERSPECTIVE, PUSH MOUNTAINS BACK, AND ADD A SNOW-CAPPED PEAK, PLANTS, FLOWERS, AND SMOKE FOR DEPTH

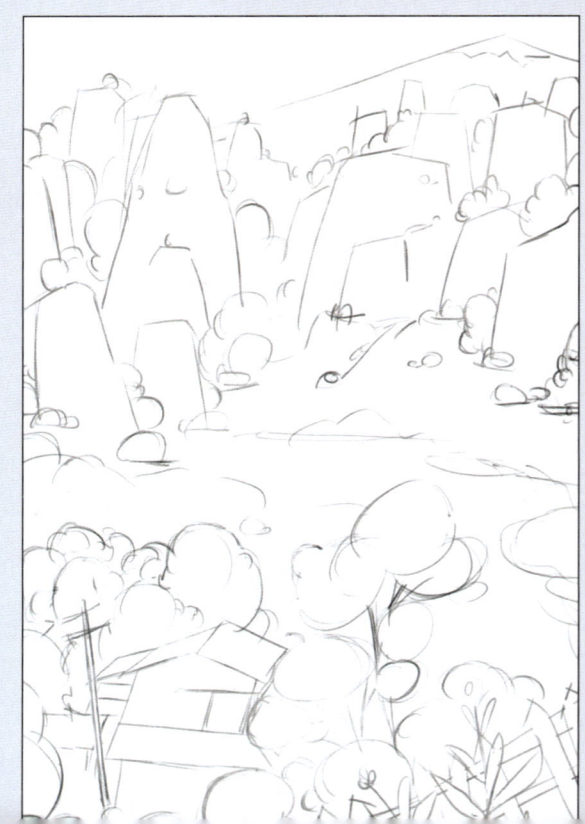

03 PLANNING

After reviewing the initial sketch, I notice that the mountains dominating the upper part of the drawing create an overwhelming sense of weight. This imbalance draws too much attention to the top area and skews the composition. To address this, I reposition the mountains lower on the page, which allows me to expand the sky and bring more balance to the scene. Adding expansive, fluffy clouds in the sky not only counters the visual weight of the mountains but also introduces a sense of depth and serenity.

To further enrich the scene, I introduce additional houses to the village, infusing it with a lively and vibrant atmosphere. This adjustment highlights the harmonious relationship between humanity and nature, echoing the essence of the original work. Since the architecture in the original piece reflects the Edo period of Japan, I adapt the building style to align with the traditional house designs of that era, enhancing the historical authenticity and visual coherence of the artwork.

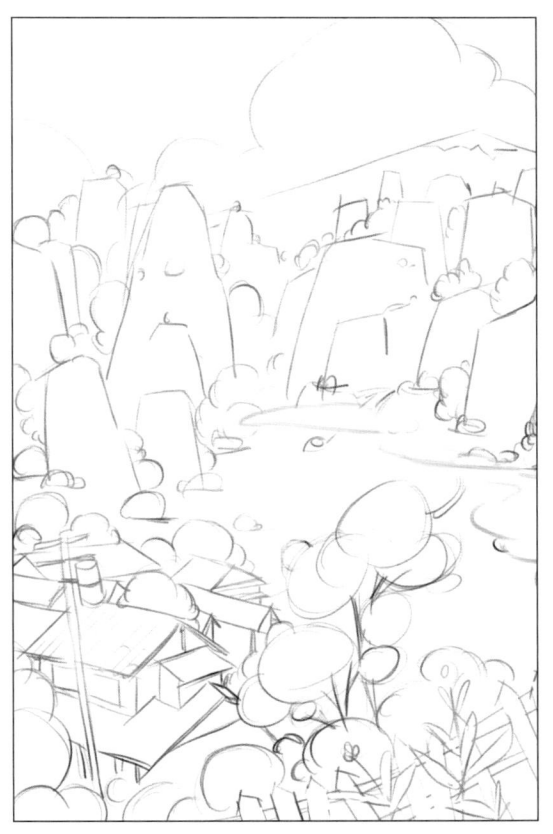

I ADJUST THE MOUNTAINS AND EXPAND THE SKY FOR BALANCE, AND ADD CLOUDS AND HOUSES FOR VIBRANCY

04 DEFINING THE FINAL SKETCH

In this final sketching stage, I start refining the drawing by adding a greater level of detail. The trees and bushes are now more clearly defined, with intricate detailing to enhance their natural shapes. The rocky mountains are outlined with cleaner, more precise lines, giving them a more structured appearance. The houses are further adjusted to reflect the architectural style of the Edo period, incorporating specific details to capture the historical accuracy of the era.

A crucial element in this step is the application of linear perspective. Linear perspective is a drawing technique that creates the illusion of depth and distance on a flat surface by converging lines towards a single point on the horizon. In this drawing, it's especially important for the trees. The closer they are to the viewer, the larger they appear, while those farther away gradually decrease in size. This technique not only ensures that the scene appears more realistic but also guides the viewer's eye through the composition, enhancing the overall sense of depth and dimension.

I REFINE DETAILS, APPLY LINEAR PERSPECTIVE FOR DEPTH, AND ENHANCE THE EDO-PERIOD ARCHITECTURE

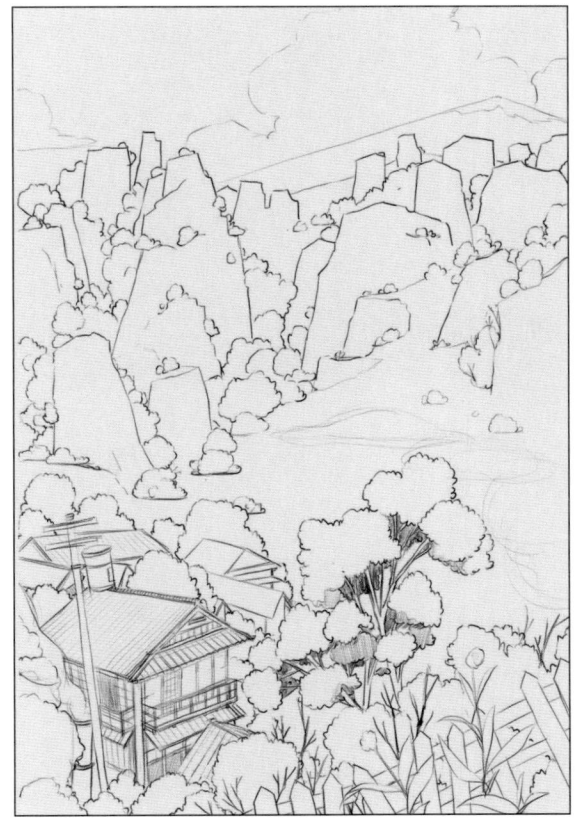

Angela Hao

'I FAVOUR LINES THAT ARE SLIGHTLY WIGGLY, BENT, OR EVEN OCCASIONALLY DISCONNECTED, WHICH ADDS A NATURAL, HAND-DRAWN FEEL TO THE ARTWORK '

I TRACE THE SKETCH WITH A TEXTURED INK PEN, EMBRACING IMPERFECT ORGANIC LINES FOR A NATURAL LOOK

05 INITIAL LINE WORK

I base my illustrations on ink lines, but rather than aiming for perfectly neat and clean strokes, I embrace a more organic approach. I favour lines that are slightly wiggly, bent, or even occasionally disconnected, which adds a natural, hand-drawn feel to the artwork. This method infuses the piece with a sense of authenticity and movement, making the scene feel more alive and less rigid.

In this step, I use a textured ink pen to carefully trace over the final sketch from the previous stage. The texture of the pen adds subtle variations that enhance the organic quality of the lines. At this point, the lines remain simple, without variations in thickness or colour, focusing on maintaining the overall fluidity and consistency. This foundational layer of ink sets the stage for the detailed work to come, ensuring the composition retains its natural and expressive character as I continue to build upon it.

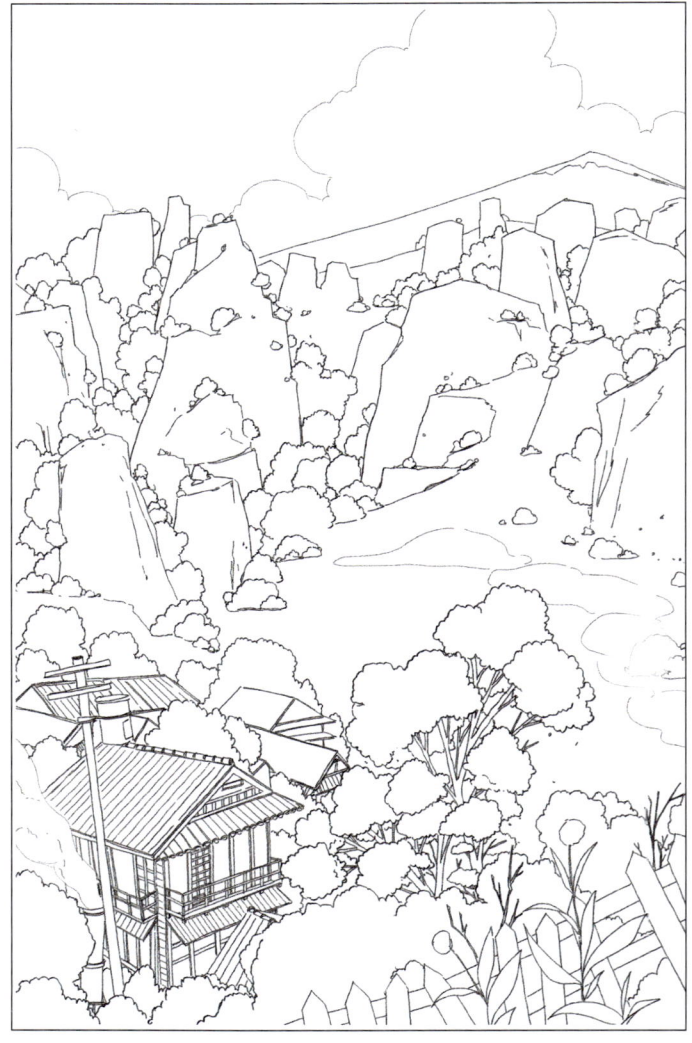

06 DEVELOPING DYNAMIC LINE WORK

In this refining stage, the lines play a crucial role in conveying perspective. On a separate layer, I selectively thicken the outlines of objects that are closer to the viewer. The closer an object is, the thicker its outline becomes, enhancing the illusion of depth within the composition. For example, the outlines of the flowers and leaves in the foreground are drawn with a heavier line weight compared to the tall trees next to the building. Similarly, the outline of the telephone pole is bolder than that of the architecture, which in turn is thicker than the lines used for the distant trees in the background. This technique not only adds depth but also guides the viewer's eye, emphasizing the spatial relationships between elements in the scene.

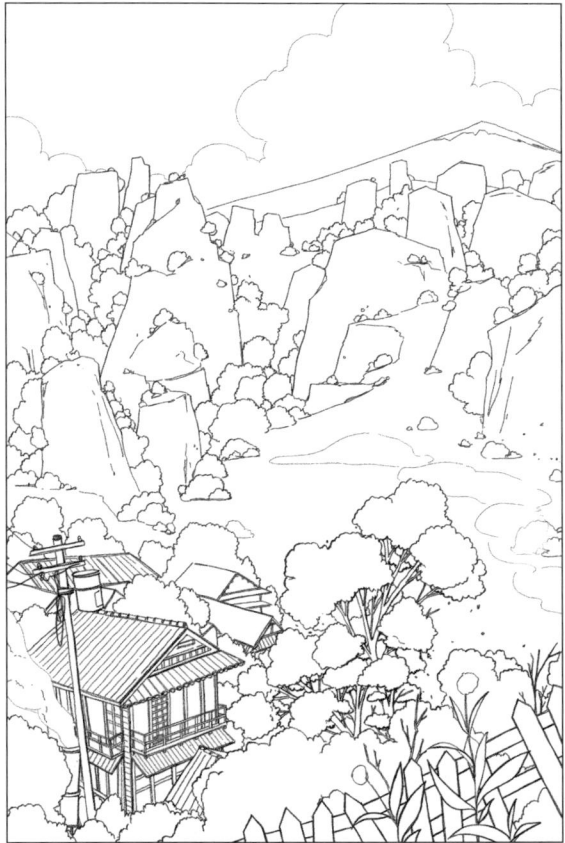

I THICKEN OUTLINES OF CLOSER OBJECTS TO ENHANCE DEPTH AND EMPHASIZE SPATIAL RELATIONSHIPS

Next, I refine the line work by introducing the darkest points of the illustration on a separate layer. This step heightens the overall composition, enhancing the sense of depth and adding a dynamic contrast that brings the final piece to life. By strategically placing these dark accents, I create a stronger visual impact, drawing attention to key areas and giving the artwork a more dramatic and polished finish.

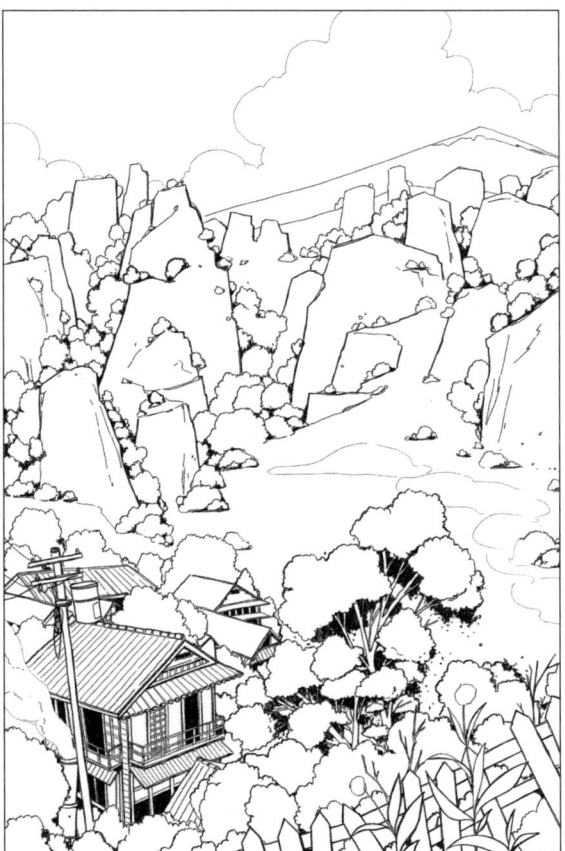

NEXT, I ADD THE DARKEST POINTS ON A SEPARATE LAYER TO ENHANCE DEPTH AND DYNAMIC CONTRAST

Angela Hao

07 COLOUR COMBINATION THUMBNAILS

Before I begin colouring my drawing, I always experiment with different colour combinations using quick thumbnail sketches. This step is crucial as it allows me to explore various moods and atmospheres that different palettes can evoke, ensuring that the final piece aligns with the intended emotional tone.

For this illustration, I test two different colour combinations – one with cooler tones and the other with warmer hues. The first combination with its cooler palette conveys a calm and tranquil atmosphere, while the warmer tones create a soft and inviting feel. Although I appreciate both approaches, I aim for a palette that captures a serene, peaceful mood while also evoking a sense of life and harmony. To achieve this, I decide to blend the best elements of both combinations. I use the darker sky colour from the cooler palette, paired with lighter, paler tones for the rocks. For the landscape, I incorporate warm greens for the grassland and a bluish green for the trees, striking a balance between tranquillity and vibrancy.

EXPERIMENTING WITH COLOUR THUMBNAILS TO EXPLORE MOODS AND ENSURE THE DESIRED EMOTIONAL TONE

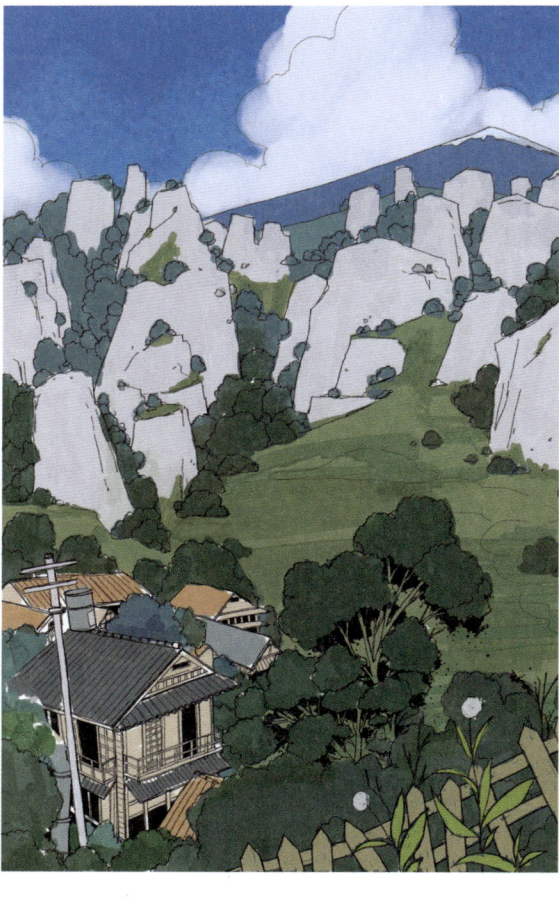
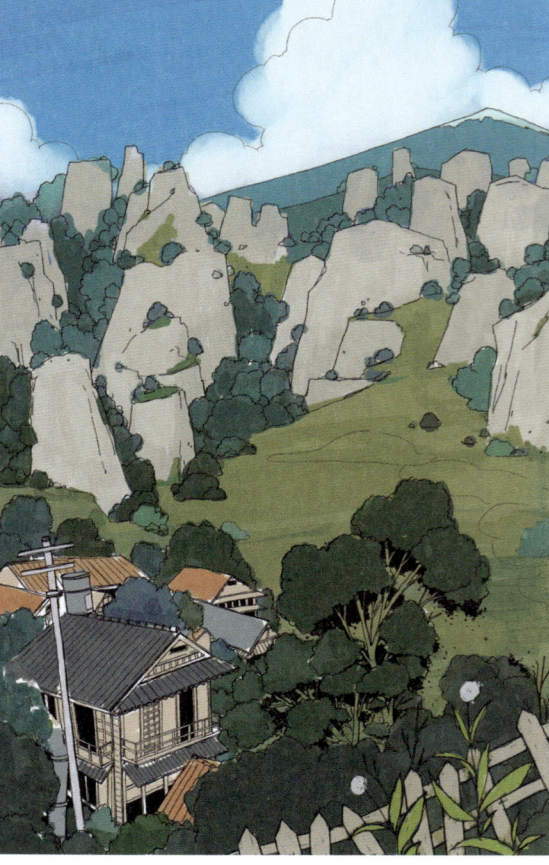

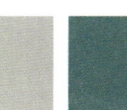
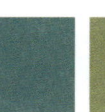

08 COLOURING THE BACKGROUND SKY

As I begin the colouring stage, I like to start by carefully planning out my layers. Each type of element gets its own layer for better organization and control. This organization makes it easier to modify specific areas without disturbing the rest of the composition. Typically, I work from background to foreground, gradually building up the scene in layers.

In this step, I focus on painting the background sky. I apply a soft gradient of blue using an airbrush tool, creating a smooth transition that captures the natural depth and atmosphere of the sky.

Next, on a separate layer, I use a soft-edged brush with a light-blue colour to gently paint the clouds. I vary my strokes to build a sense of softness and volume, blending edges for a more natural, fluffy appearance.

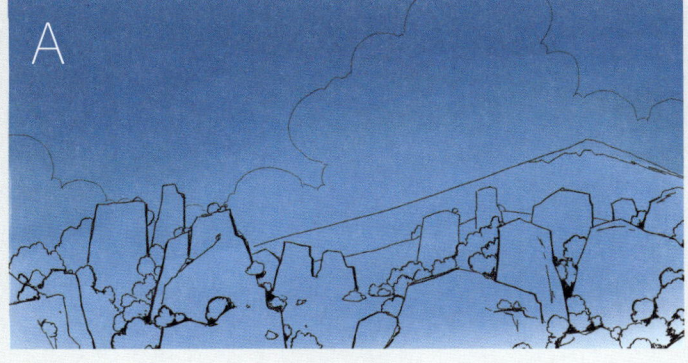

PAINTING A GRADIENT BLUE SKY WITH AN AIRBRUSH, ACHIEVING SMOOTH DEPTH AND ATMOSPHERE

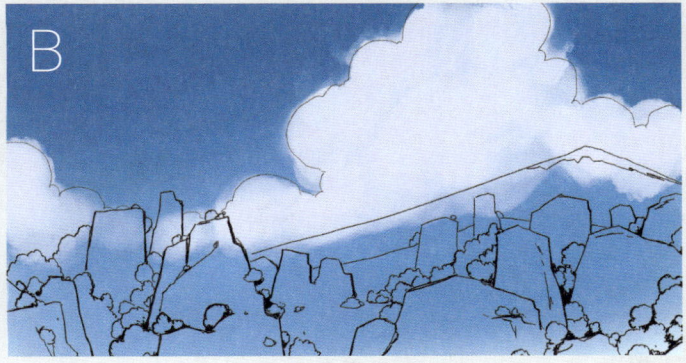

ON A NEW LAYER, I USE A SOFT BRUSH WITH A LIGHT-BLUE COLOUR TO PAINT AND BLEND FLUFFY CLOUDS

Then, on a clipping-mask layer above the cloud layer, I add shading to enhance depth and dimension. I use a soft, low-opacity brush with a slightly darker shade of the cloud colour to apply shadows along the cloud's base and any areas where light would be obstructed. I then blend the shading gently to maintain a smooth, natural look.

Finally, I remove the cloud outlines from the line-work layer to create a more organic, fluffy appearance. Without the outlines, the clouds will blend seamlessly with the sky, enhancing their natural, airy look.

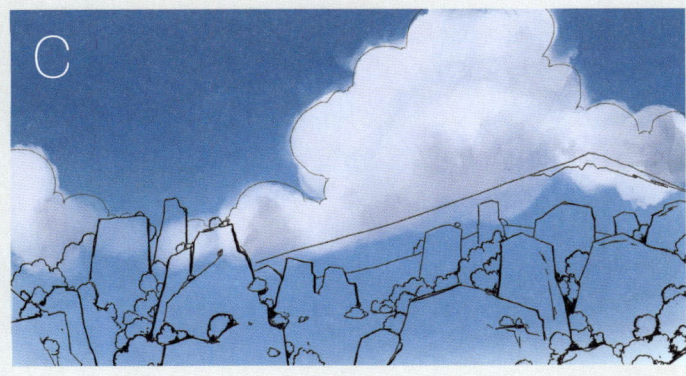

ON A CLIPPING-MASK LAYER, I ADD SOFT, DARK SHADING TO ENHANCE CLOUD DEPTH AND BLEND NATURALLY

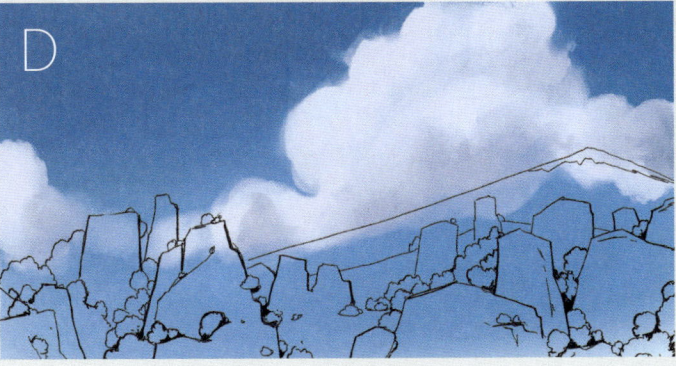

I REMOVE THE CLOUD OUTLINES FROM THE LINE-WORK LAYER

Angela Hao

09 COLOURING THE MID-GROUND ELEMENTS

In this step, I focus on painting the mid-ground elements, including distant mountains, rocks, grasslands, and trees. Each element is placed on its own separate layer to maintain control and flexibility. I apply colours following the principles of atmospheric perspective, where objects appear lighter and less saturated as they recede into the distance. This means the distant mountains will have softer, cooler tones, while the trees and grassland in the foreground will display richer, more vibrant colours. Atmospheric perspective is a technique that simulates how the atmosphere affects the appearance of objects based on their distance from the viewer. The further away an object is, the more the atmosphere scatters light, causing distant elements to look lighter, hazier, and often bluer compared to closer objects. This effect helps to create a sense of depth and realism in the scene.

To enhance the natural texture of these mid-ground elements, I use a hard-edged brush with Colour Jitter enabled. This setting adds subtle variations in hue and saturation with each stroke, giving the trees, rocks, and grasslands a more organic, textured appearance. The result is a dynamic mid-ground that complements the overall composition.

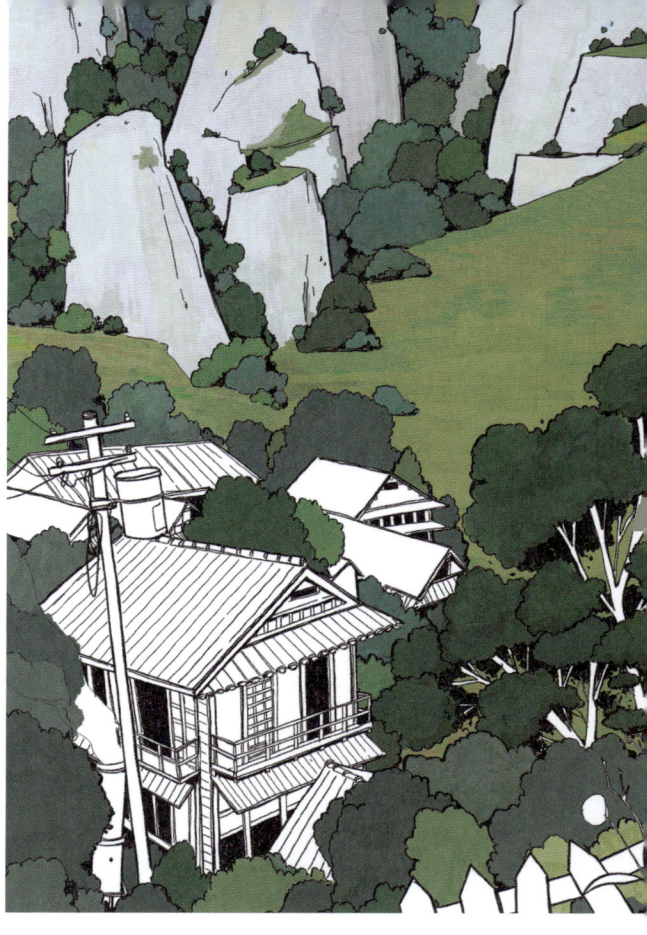

I PAINT MID-GROUND ELEMENTS ON SEPARATE LAYERS, APPLYING ATMOSPHERIC PERSPECTIVE AND USING COLOUR JITTER FOR TEXTURE

10 FURTHER DEVELOPMENT OF BASE COLOUR

On separate layers, I paint the base colours for the houses, tree branches, fences, and foreground plants using a Colour Jitter brush to add natural texture and variation. I opt for lighter colours for the tree trunks and foreground fences, ensuring they stand out against the background rather than blending in. In this step, I pay special attention to selecting the roof colours, aiming to echo the traditional aesthetics of Edo-period Japanese architecture. I also focus on creating visual layers among the buildings, ensuring that each structure has a distinct appearance, adding depth and interest to the scene. This careful colour selection prevents the buildings from looking uniform and enhances the overall composition's visual appeal.

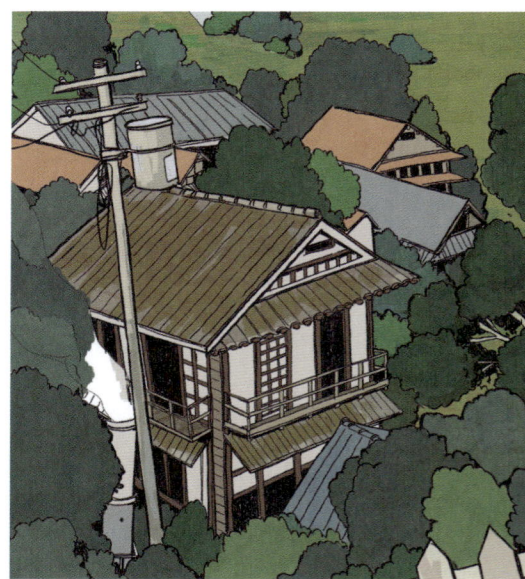

PAINTING TEXTURED BASE COLOURS ON SEPARATE LAYERS, EMPHASIZING DISTINCT ROOF TONES FOR VISUAL DEPTH

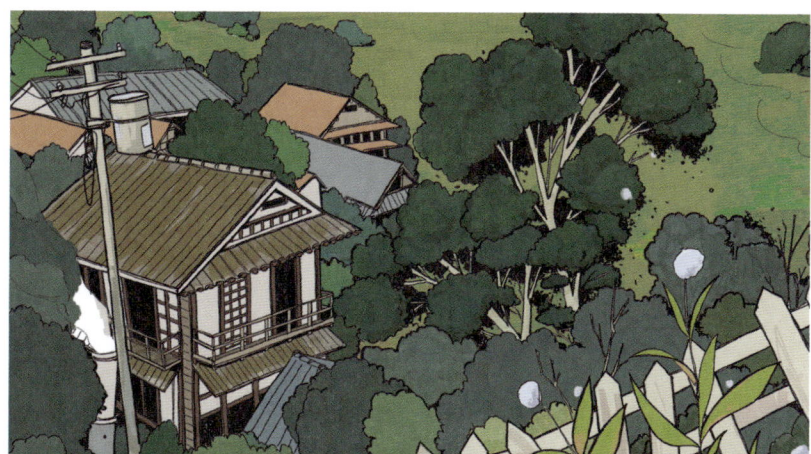

11 INCORPORATING HOKUSAI-INSPIRED DYNAMIC SMOKE

In Hokusai's original work, the smoke is more than just a visual element; it serves as a vital part of the composition, creating a sense of movement and flow that guides the viewer's eye through the scene. The swirling tendrils of smoke add an ethereal quality, connecting different parts of the artwork and enhancing its overall harmony. To honour this aspect, I've incorporated smoke into my painting as well, but with a personalized touch. I introduce smoke billowing from a chimney, infusing the scene with a sense of life and warmth. On the left side of the composition, the smoke curls from the right, creating an illusion of movement that mirrors the dynamic energy of Hokusai's original piece. To further echo his work, I intertwine ancient musical notes within the smoke, creating a subtle tribute that blends his timeless influence with my own creative expression.

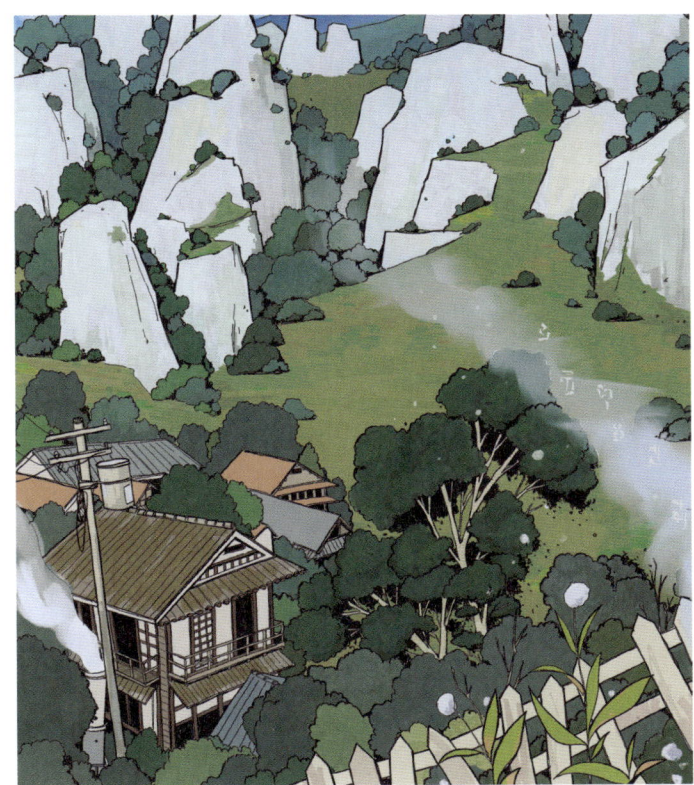

I ADD DYNAMIC SMOKE WITH MUSICAL NOTES, ECHOING HOKUSAI'S ORIGINAL ETHEREAL AND FLOWING ELEMENTS

12 ADJUSTING THE BASE COLOUR

Before diving into shading and lighting, I prefer to fine-tune the base colours to achieve a more cohesive and aesthetically pleasing composition. At this stage, the fence in the foreground appears too light, which might inadvertently draw the viewer's attention away from the focal points of the piece. To rectify this, I darken the fence while ensuring it remains distinguishable from the lush green of the trees below.

For the main building, which serves as the centrepiece of the drawing, the current colour palette does not sufficiently highlight its importance. To enhance its prominence, I adjust the roof colour to a vibrant orange, and transform the wooden frames to a rich dark brown. These changes will help the building stand out effectively while maintaining visual harmony within the overall scene.

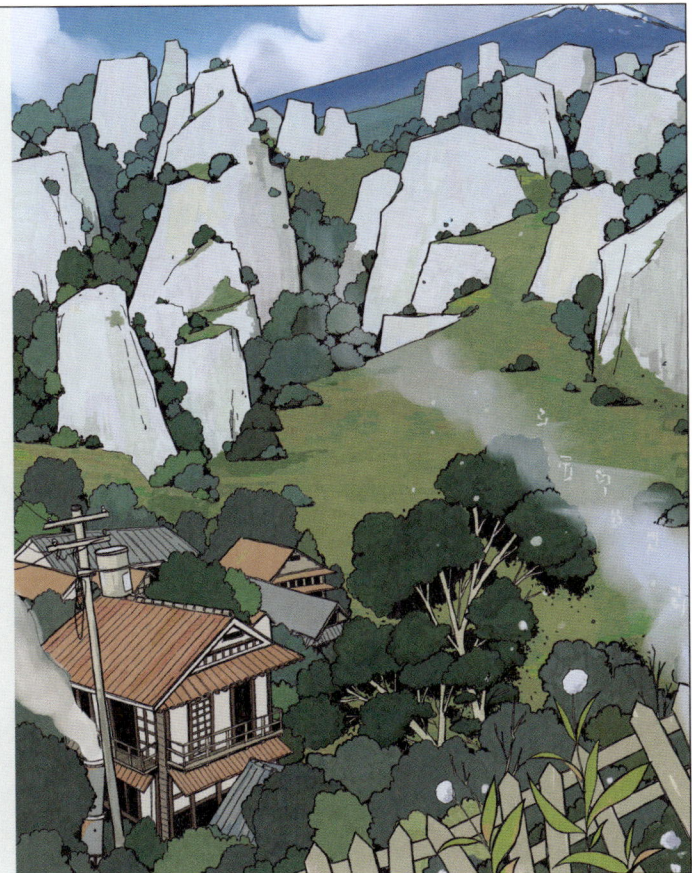

ADJUSTING BASE COLOURS TO ENHANCE FOCUS: DARKEN FENCE, BRIGHTEN ROOF, AND TRANSFORM WOODEN FRAMES

Angela Hao

13 SHADING

Shading and lighting are not only the final touches of my illustration, but also the most enchanting and enjoyable aspects of the process. To start the shading stage, I first establish the light source and its direction. In this case, the light source is the sun, positioned to the left, casting a warm, late-afternoon glow on the scene.

Once the light source is defined, I apply greyish-blue tones for the shadows on the building, and use a lighter greyish-blue for the darker areas around distant trees and bushes. I set the shadow layer to a Linear Burn blending mode, though Multiply can be used for similar effects. I adjust the layer's opacity as needed to achieve the desired depth and realism. Adding these shadows enhances the overall depth of the drawing, bringing the illustration to life.

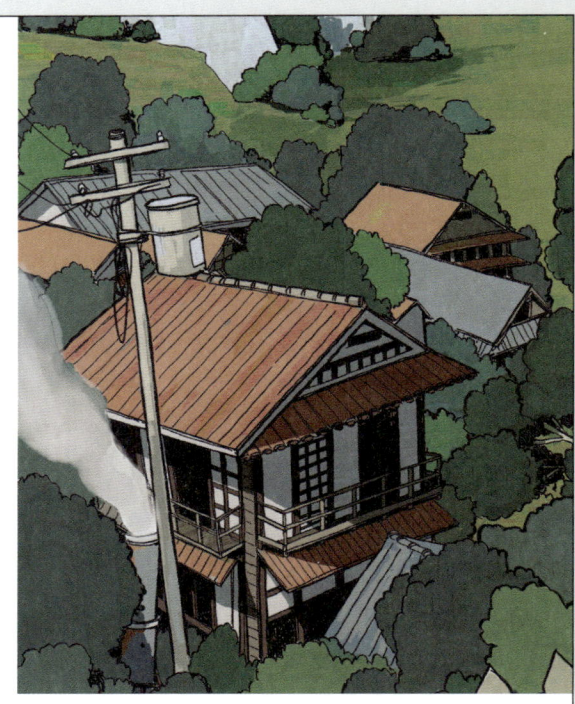

DEFINING THE LIGHT SOURCE, ADDING SHADOWS WITH BLUE TONES, AND ADJUSTING LAYER OPACITY FOR DEPTH

14 LIGHTING

One of the most frequent questions I receive about my artwork is how I achieve that warm, joyful atmosphere. The secret lies in the lighting stage. Warm lighting can create a magical ambience and infuse the illustration with life. To achieve this effect, I start by creating a new layer dedicated to lighting with the Overlay blending mode. Using a soft airbrush, I apply a vibrant, saturated orange-red colour to the areas illuminated by sunlight – focusing on the roof, walls, grassland, and rocks. I then adjust the layer's opacity to ensure a natural blend with the rest of the artwork. It's crucial to avoid overdoing the lighting, as too much can make the scene look artificial. Striking the right balance requires practice and patience.

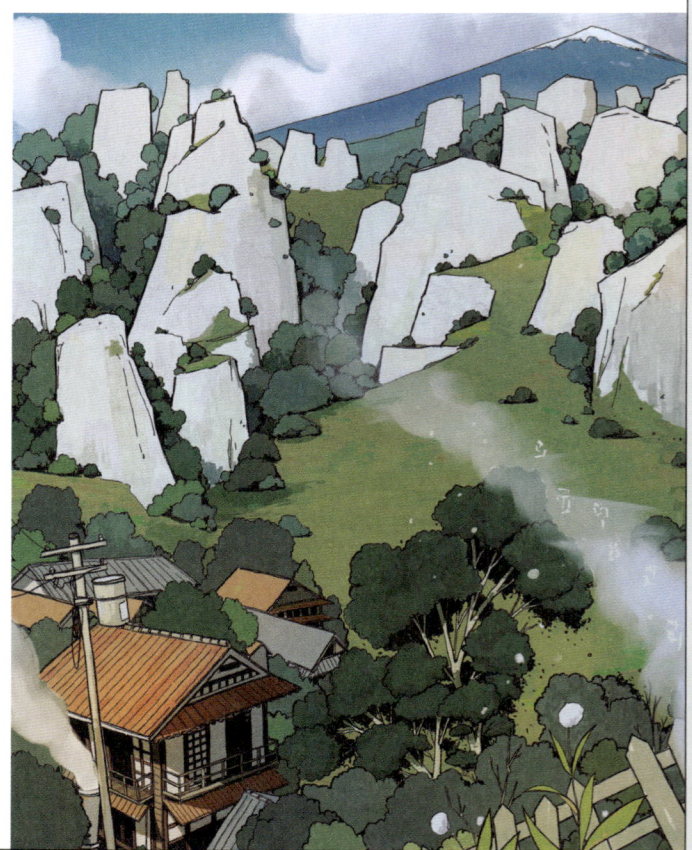

I CREATE A LIGHTING LAYER, APPLY BRIGHT ORANGE-RED WITH A SOFT BRUSH, AND ADJUST OPACITY

15 FINAL TOUCHES

Completing an illustration is like reading a novel filled with twists and turns that ultimately lead to a satisfying conclusion. The final touches resemble that last moment in reading the story. In the final stage of my painting process, there are two key elements I always address. First, I add shimmering, floating particles – sparkles, if you will – that give the illusion of movement and breathe life into the scene. In this piece, the sparkles appear to drift from the viewer's perspective towards the mountain, extending the visual path and drawing the eye deeper into the artwork. To achieve this, I create a new layer set to the Add blending mode and use a sparkling-pen brush to dot the canvas, following the principles of linear perspective. The closer the sparkles are to the viewer, the larger they appear, and vice versa.

Second, I emphasize the effects of light by altering the colour of the ink lines in areas directly hit by sunlight. I change these lines from black to a saturated orange-red, enhancing the warmth and glow. With these final touches, the illustration comes to life, bringing the story to its perfect conclusion.

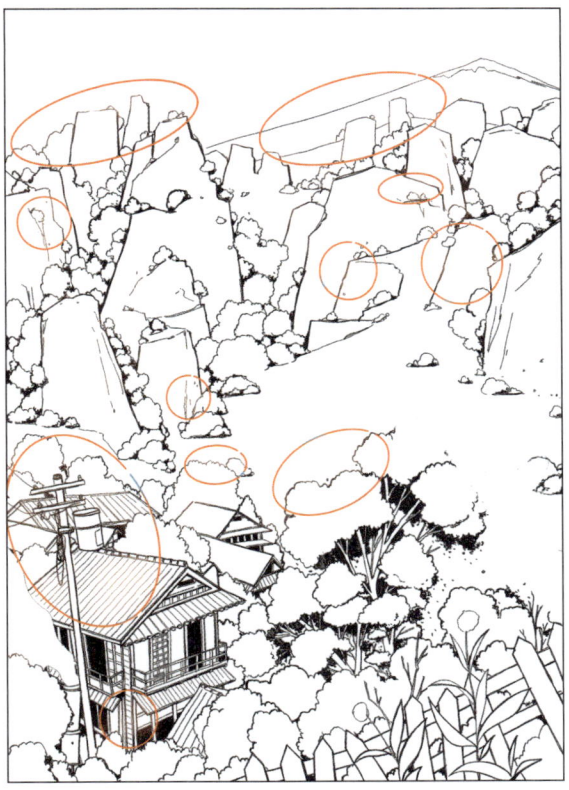

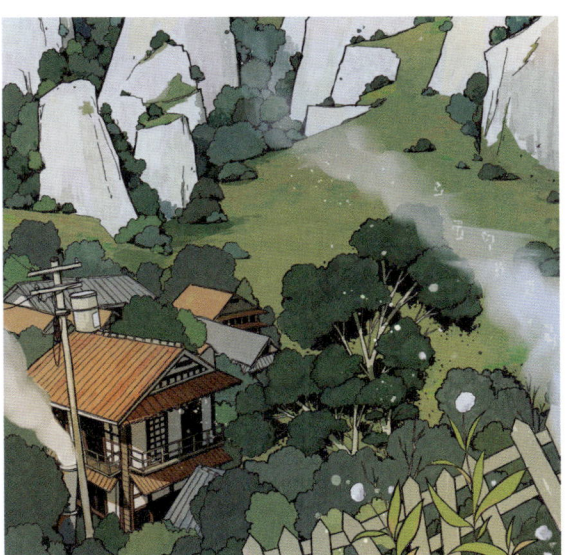

I ADD SHIMMERING SPARKLES WITH AN ADD LAYER TO CREATE MOVEMENT AND EXTEND VISUAL DEPTH

CONCLUSION

I'm quite pleased with how the final piece turned out, particularly the colour combination. The Ghibli-inspired greens and blues really bring out that fresh, countryside feel I was aiming for. While the composition stays similar to the original, the vibe has changed, adding a new warmth and energy. This project taught me a lot about how subtle shifts in colour and lighting can dramatically transform the mood of an illustration. There's always more to learn, but I'm happy with the progress made here.

Angela Hao

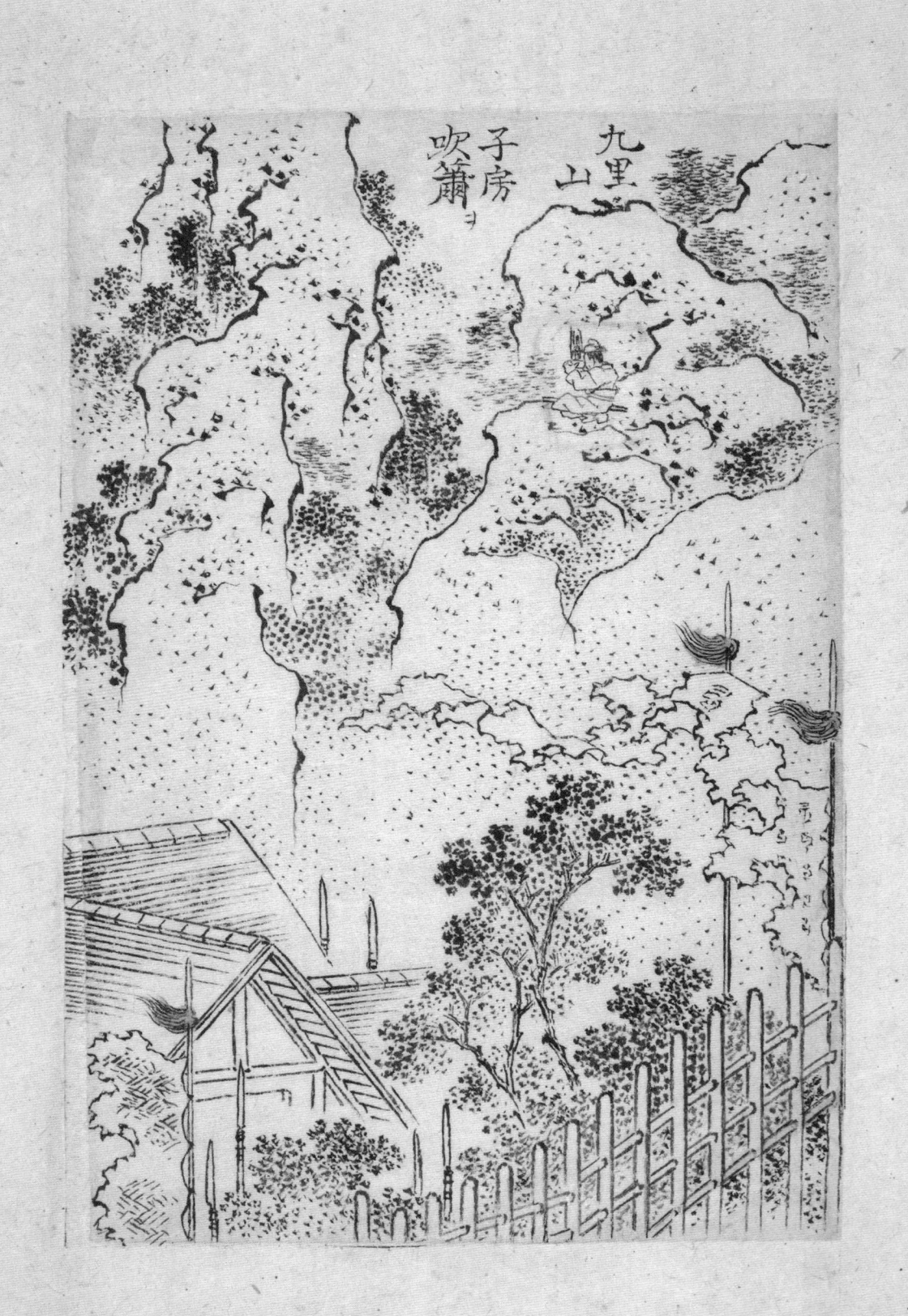

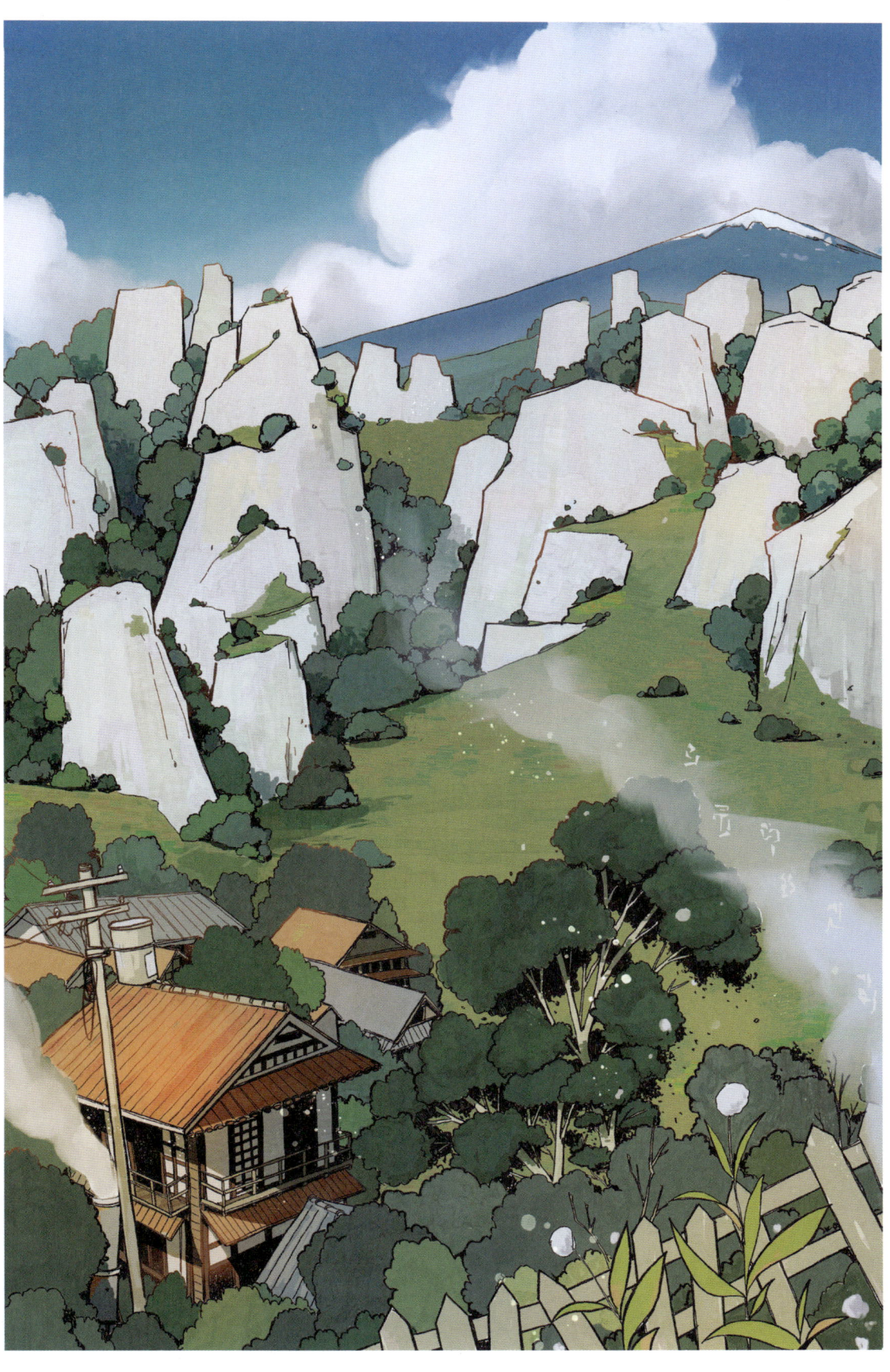

ON MT JIULI, ZIFANG DEMORALISES THE ENEMY BY PLAYING A MELANCHOLY TUNE

ANGELA HAO

BELOW: *The Convenience Store*
A quiet Japanese storefront, beneath a red sign's glow,
where time lingers with a humming vending machine
and silent power pole

OPPOSITE PAGE: *My Neighbor Mr Cat*
A countryside stillness. Antique store weathered by time,
where a curious girl watches the neighbour's cat at rest

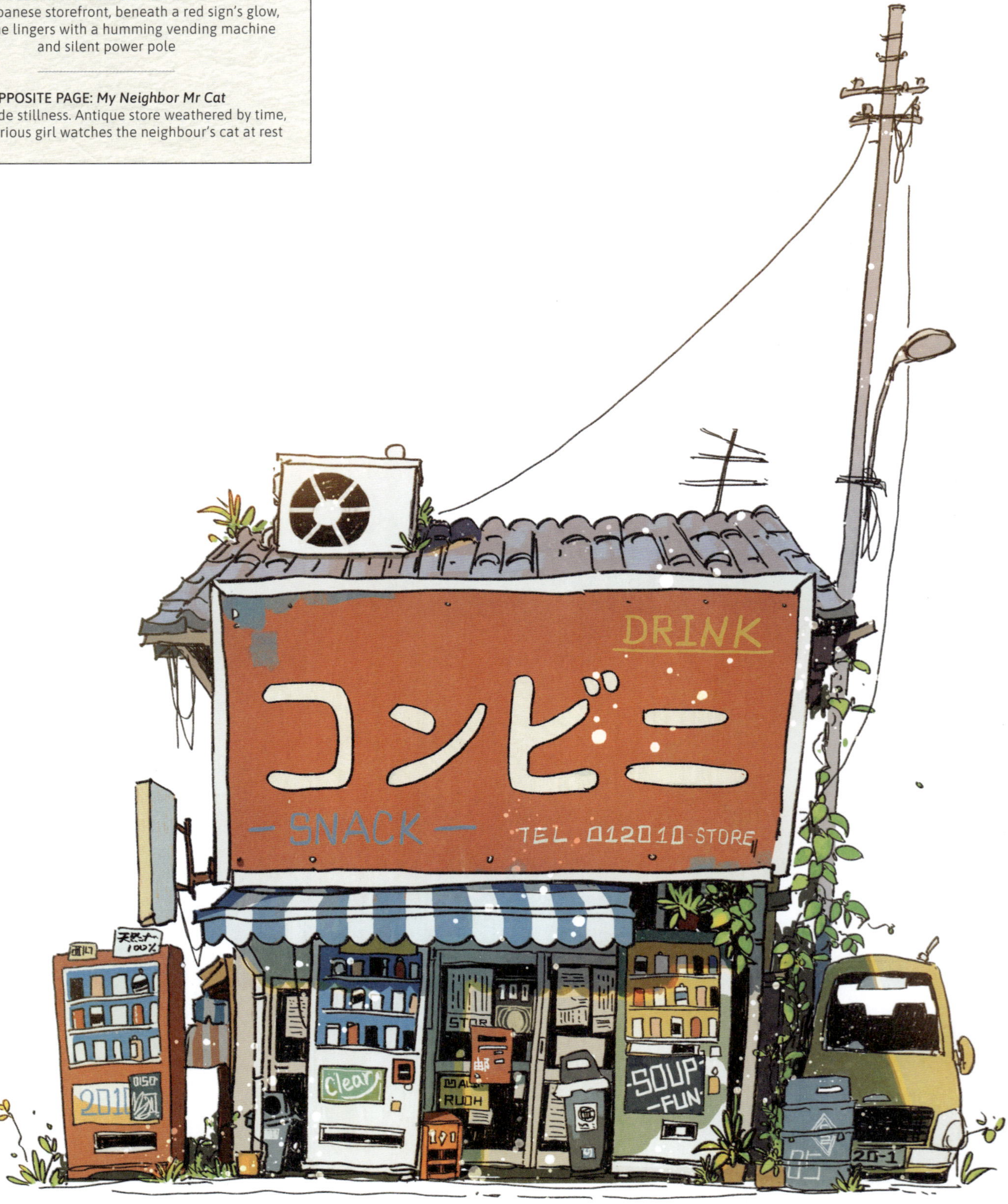

GALLERY: ANGELA HAO

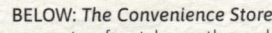

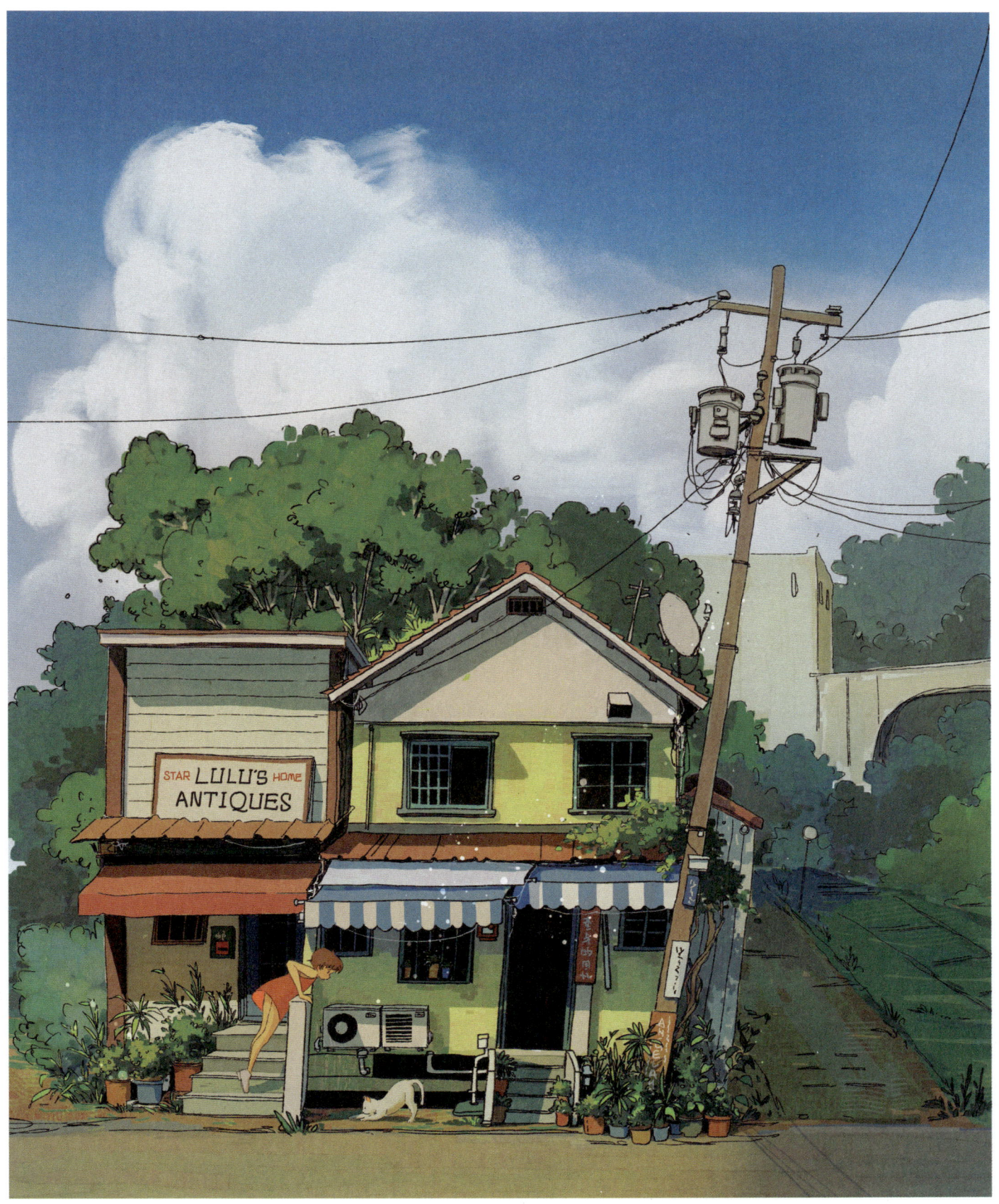

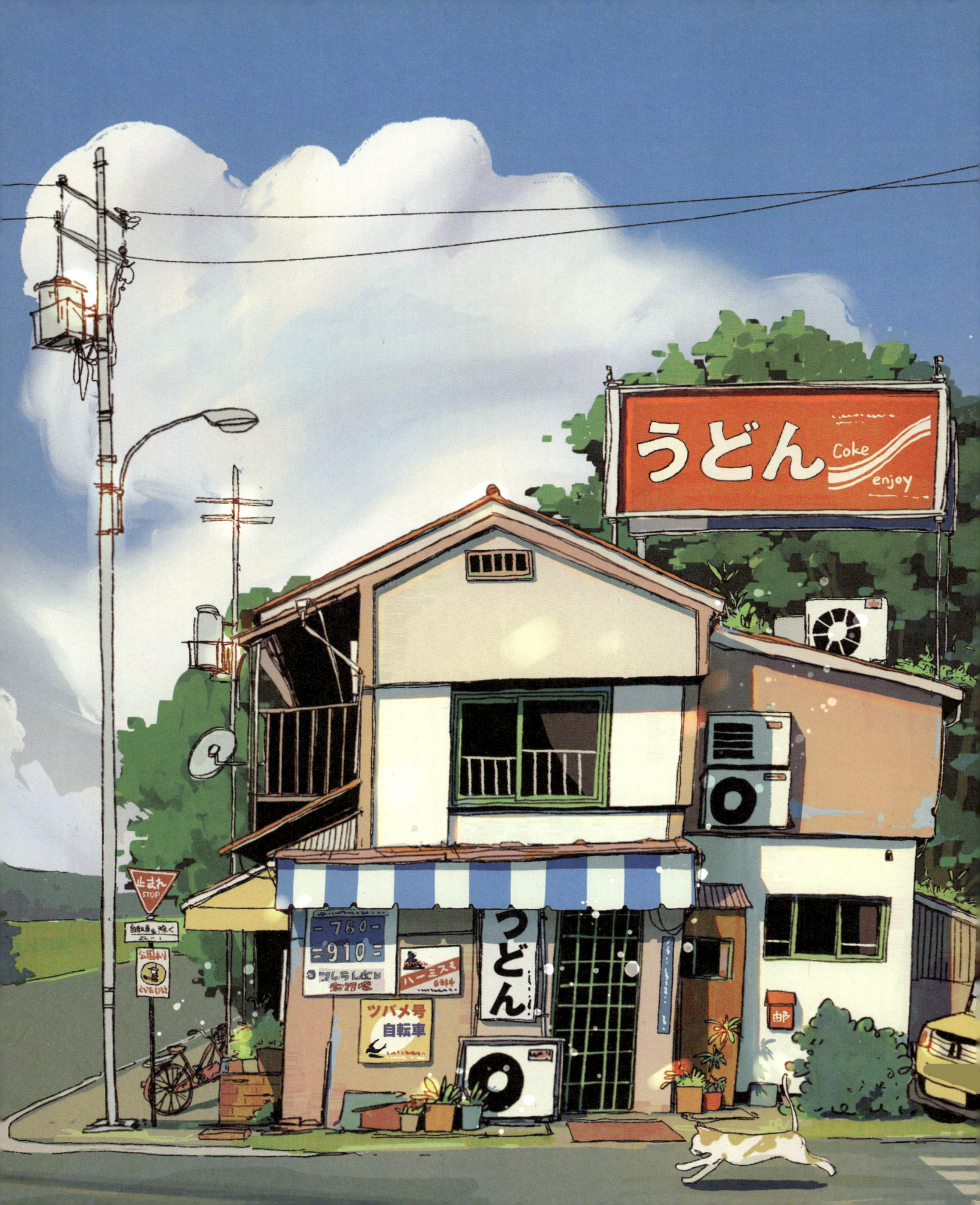

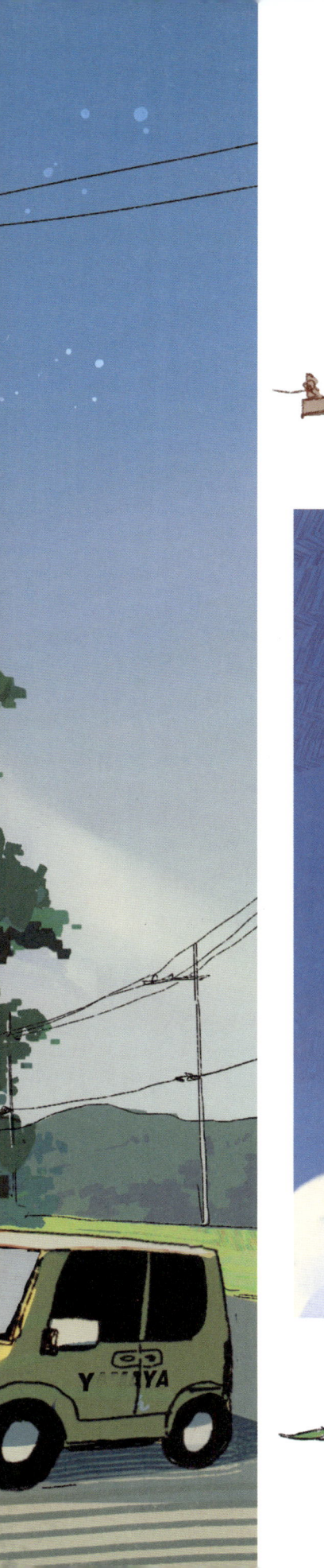

LEFT: *The Udon Shop*
A summer's breath at an udon shop – fields stretch, mountains loom, and a cat darts joyfully

---

BELOW: *An Old Building at Street Corner*
An old house bathed in vibrant, anime hues – whispers of warmth and nostalgia drift through its walls

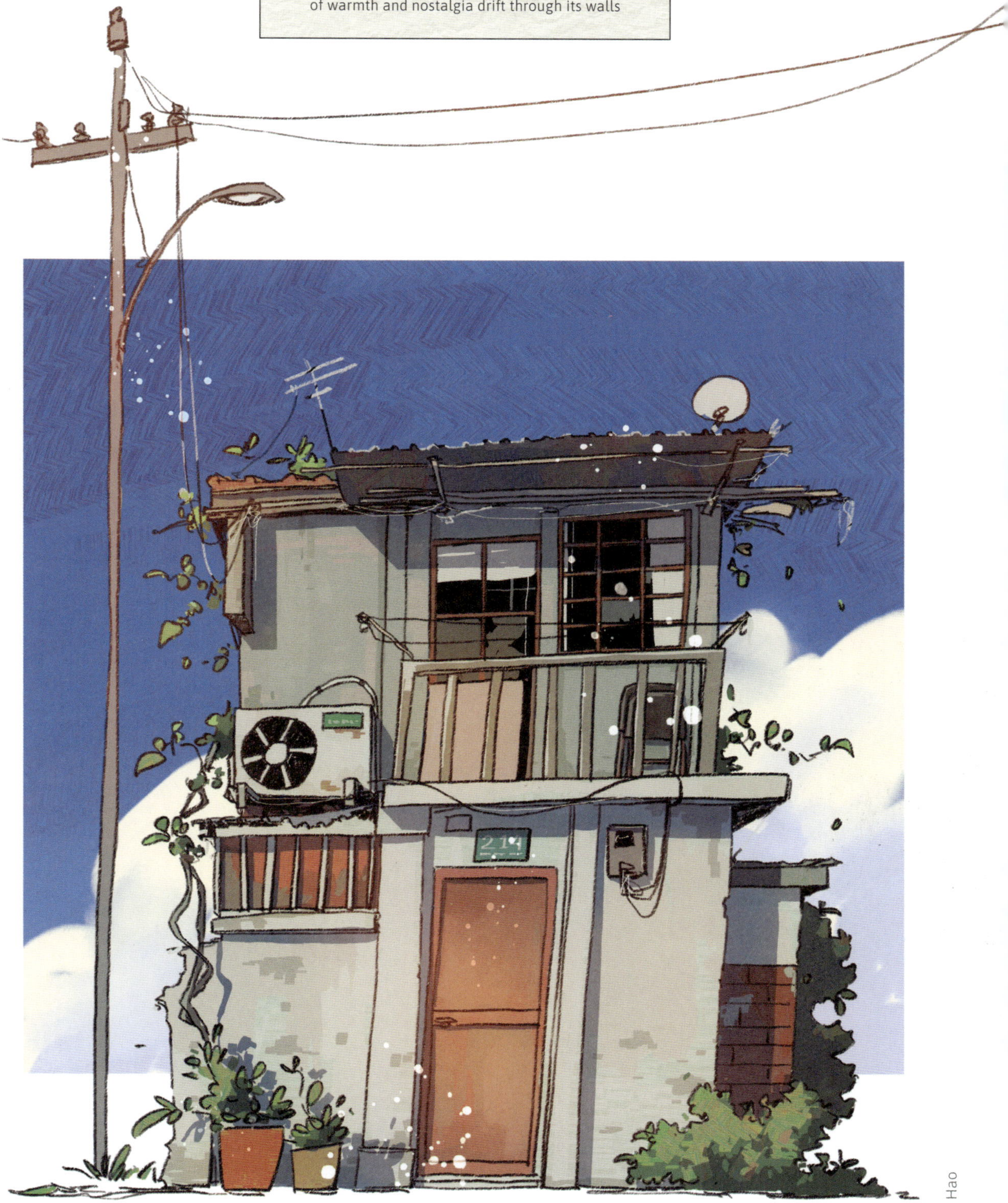

Angela Hao

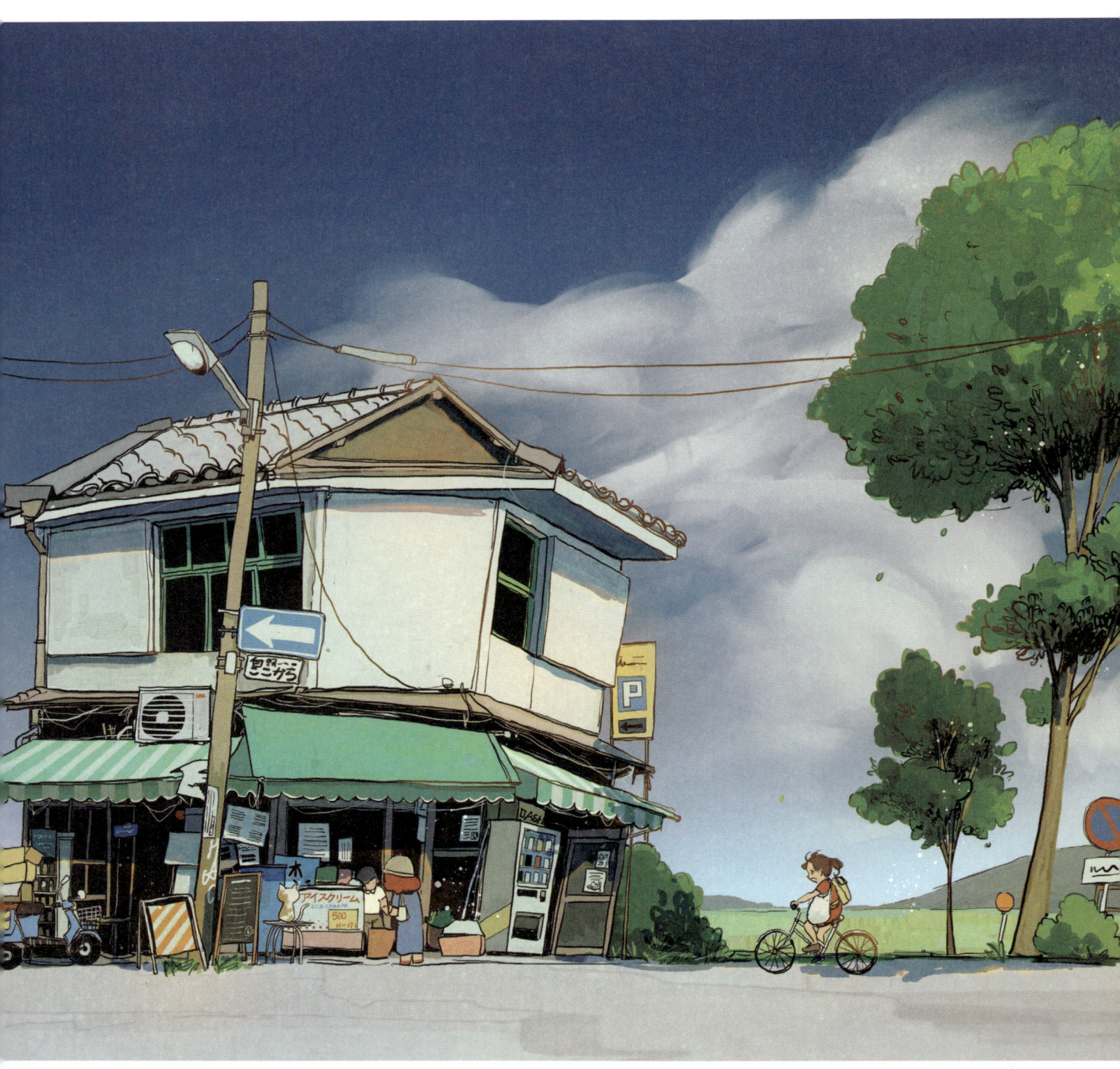

ABOVE: *The Grocery Store*
By the meadow's edge, a wobbly store – mom shops, while daughter rides home with bright news

---

RIGHT: *Secret Leaning Tower*
A broken-windowed building leans at sunset, drying clothes sway, a bunny toy hangs – whispers of mystery in the air

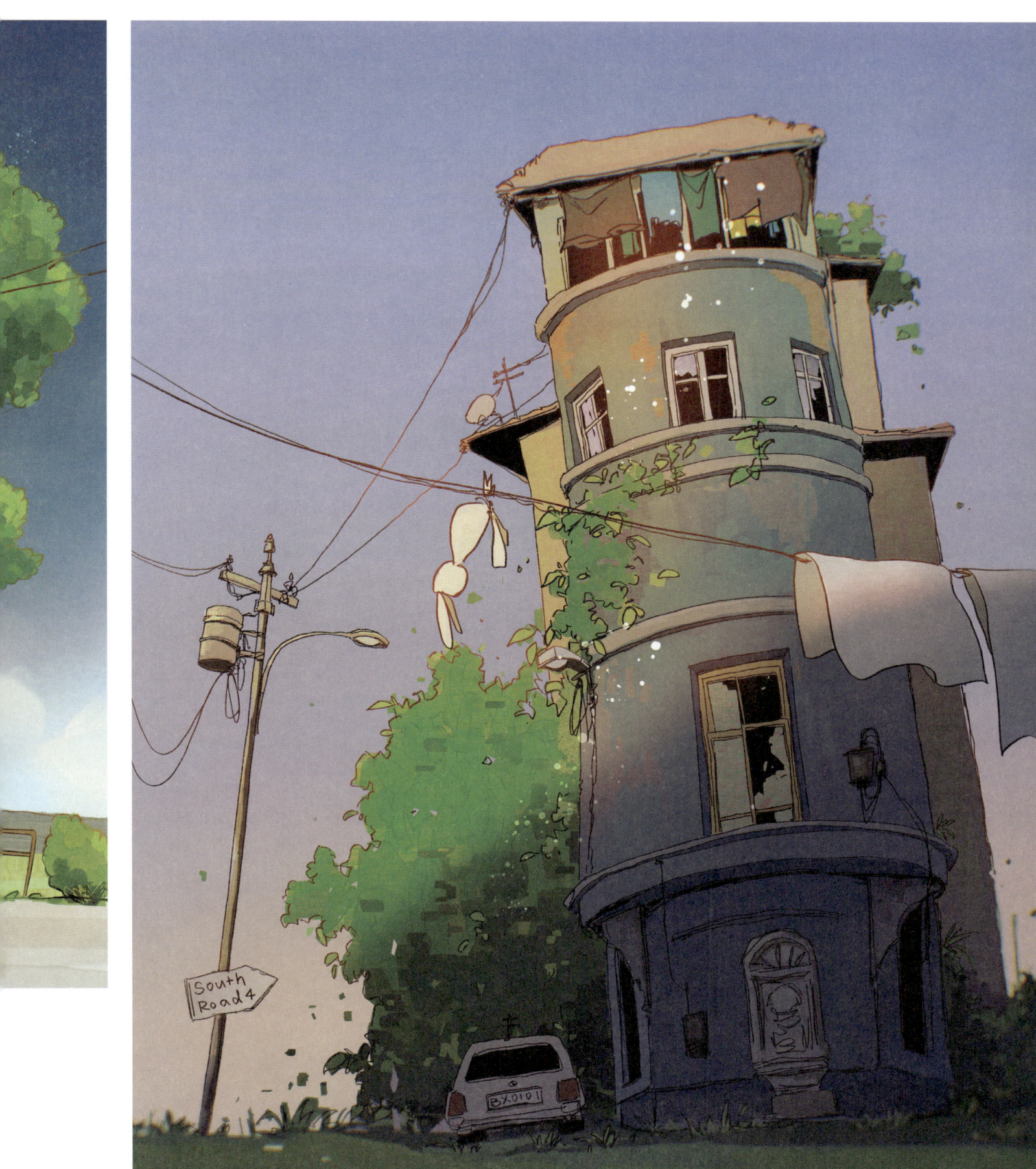

LIU BANG OF THE HAN B
WHITE SNAKE ON MT MA

BY PARAKID

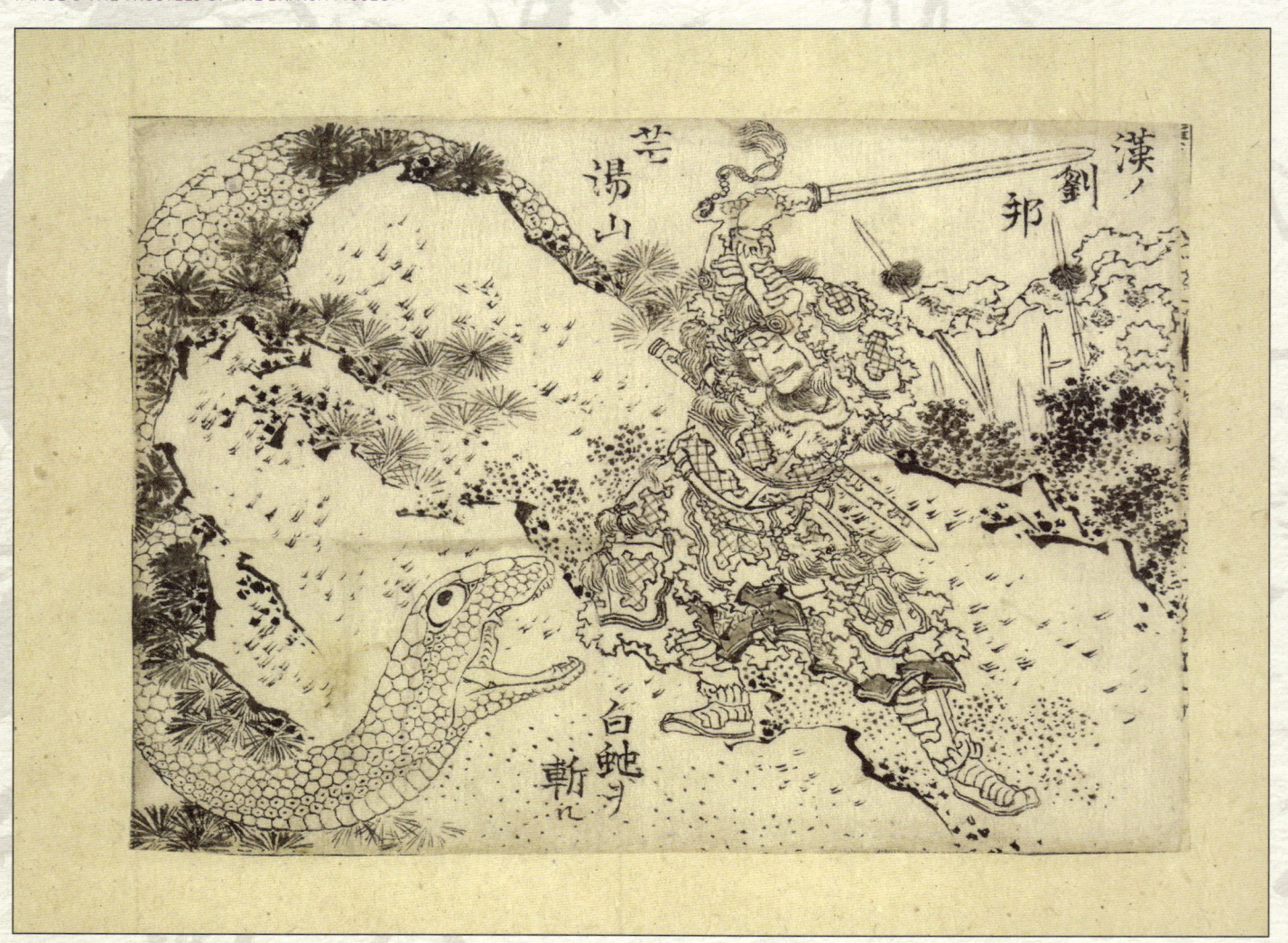

HEADS THE
NGDANG

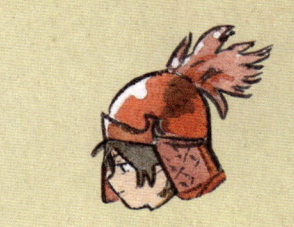

DISCOVERING
HOKUSAI

I have fond memories of drawing from a young age, primarily focusing on cartoon characters from my favourite television shows. Once I was exposed to anime at the end of middle school, I was strongly inspired to pursue a career in animation. It was only when I neared the end of my college journey that I found myself liking illustration more, so I followed that path instead. Throughout the years, my style has been shaped by many additional influences such as American comics and manga, as well as prolific artists such as Katsushika Hokusai and Carl Larsson, animated works like *Tekkonkinkreet,* and a mix of the simplicity that daily life can bring.

It was during my school years that I first encountered Hokusai's artwork. It opened my eyes to many other artists who have either drawn inspiration from his style or offered their unique interpretations of it. What draws me the most to Hokusai's style are the beautiful pops of colour and the depth present in his paintings. Some of his artworks use a limited colour palette, which is something that inspires me, too. In his own way, Hokusai masterfully blends elements of reality with fantasy. Even in his flatter paintings, the use of texture and detail elevates the work to the next level and creates a great sense of depth. These are just a few of the aspects I hope to achieve one day in my own paintings.

01 ROUGH EXPLORATION

I begin by creating a digital sketch based on the concept I have in mind. My intention is for the human character to be the main focal point; he wipes his sword clean following the defeat of the giant white snake. Though I start with a vertical composition as it shows the snake's entire body wrapped around the tree, I will later change it to a horizontal composition to match the original artwork's aspect. Creating the sketch digitally saves me time, allowing me to quickly resize the elements and make changes.

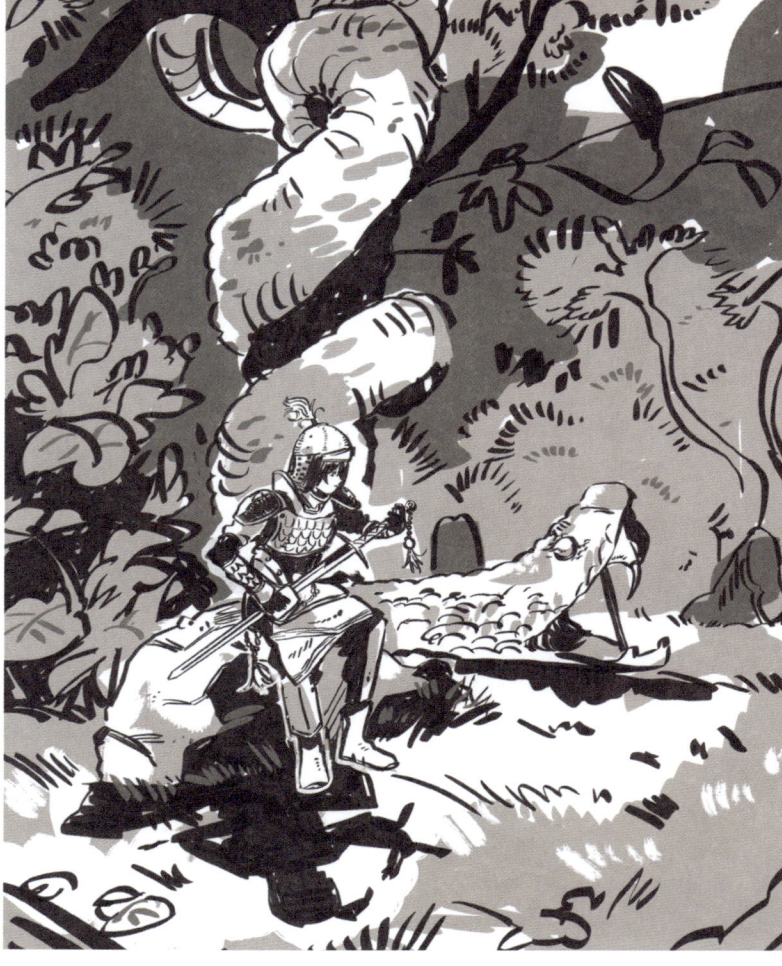

FIRST SKETCH DONE, REIMAGINED IN MY STYLE

02 SECOND ROUGH SKETCH

I take the initial sketch and make it horizontal. The elements in the foreground, middle ground, and background are positioned apart to make better use of the available space, while still keeping the primary focus on the character confronting the snake. I decide to keep the original lighting scheme, which is why I do not include any shadows in this version. This second sketch serves to bring further inspiration and ideas, guiding me towards what the final version should look like.

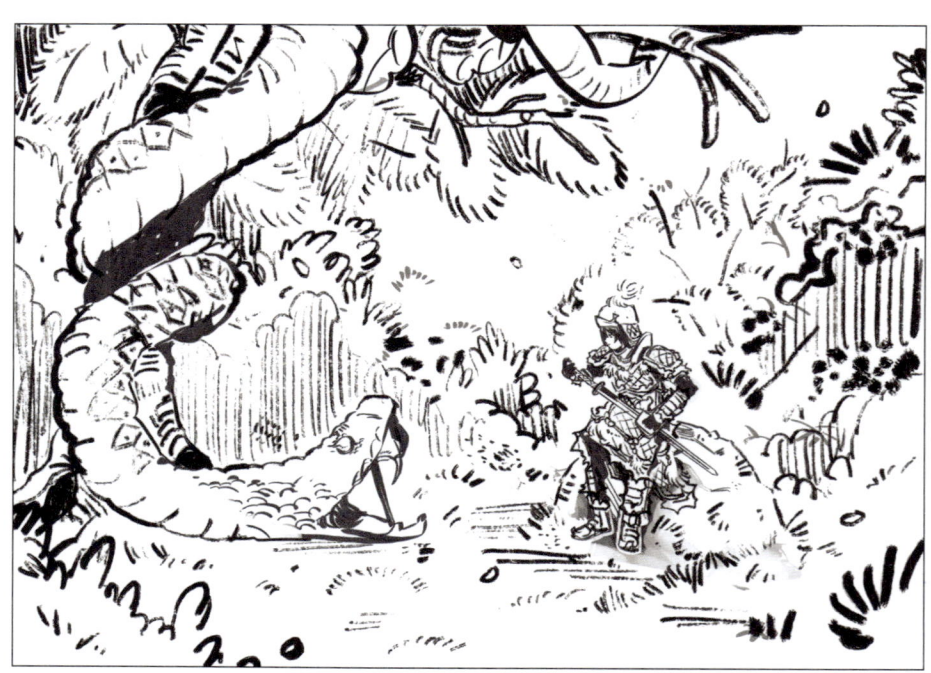

SKETCH IS UPDATED AFTER SWITCHING THE RATIO FROM VERTICAL TO HORIZONTAL

03 FINAL ROUGH SKETCH

In this last sketch, I centre the character and giant snake. In the previous version, there was too much empty space around the main characters, so I zoom in a bit more. I add a waterfall in the background, along with some rocks, then add giant boulders to the foreground and some tree foliage. I think a lot more about details in this final sketch; I want to have most of it sorted out before diving into the line work. I especially enjoy adding in little touches, such as the moss on the rocks.

MORE DEPTH AND DETAIL
ADDED TO THE FINAL SKETCH

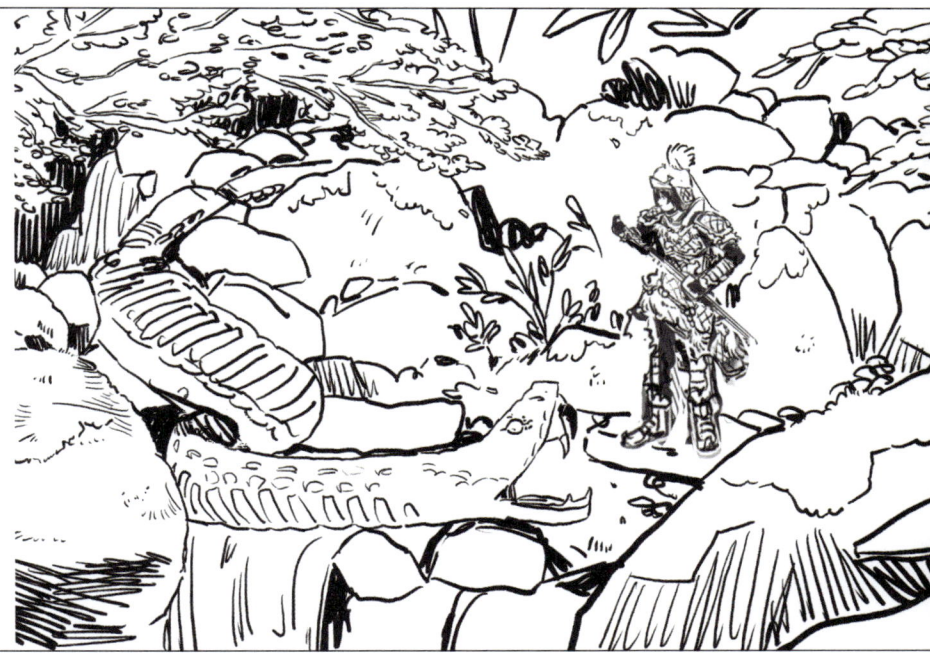

04 LIGHT & SHADOWS

Unlike the second sketch (where I skipped the lighting), I go into this step with a better idea of how to position the light. I use two values to represent the darker shadows versus the lighter ones. In this instance, I envision the shadows created by the surrounding trees becoming lighter as they extend towards the background and further away from the source of the waterfall.

SHADOWS AND LIGHTING
ARE ADDED, FINALIZING
THE CONCEPT

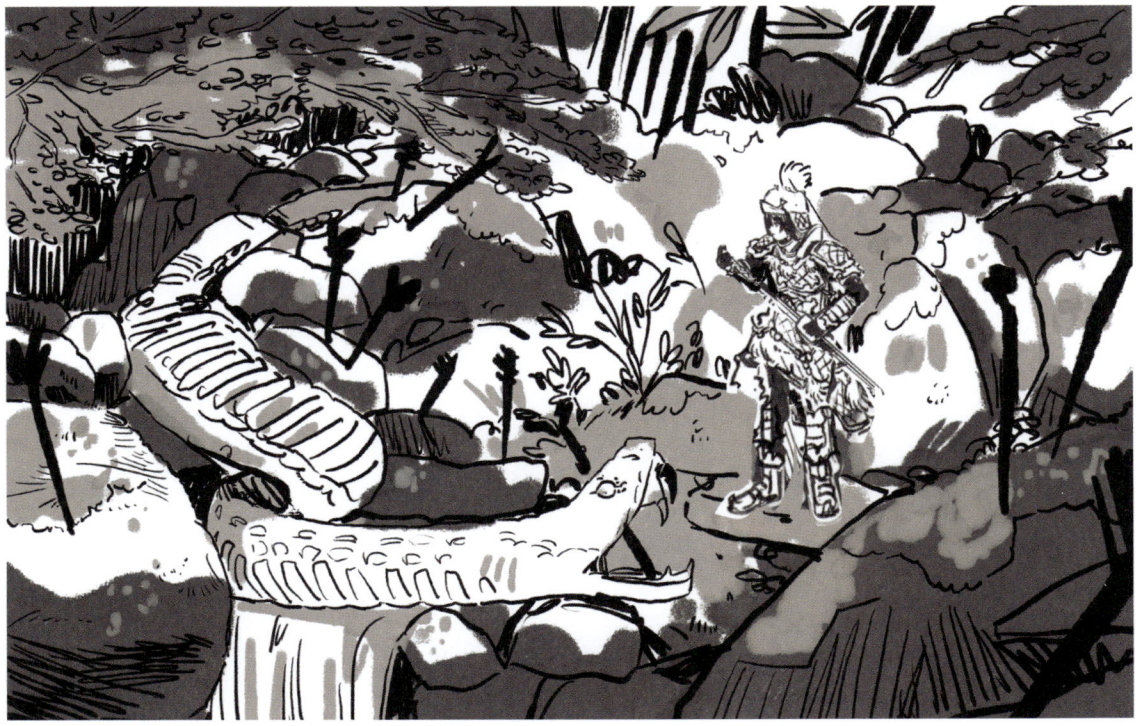

Parakid

05 EXPLORATION LINE WORK

In total, I finished three versions of this illustration. Initially, I used this version, so I will treat it as such and explain my line work and colour.

For this step, the digital sketch is printed and I use an ink brush, light box, and watercolour paper to transfer the line work. My idea is to experiment with a flatter style reminiscent of Hokusai's artwork. This means I must minimize the level of detail in both the foreground and background, compared to my usual approach.

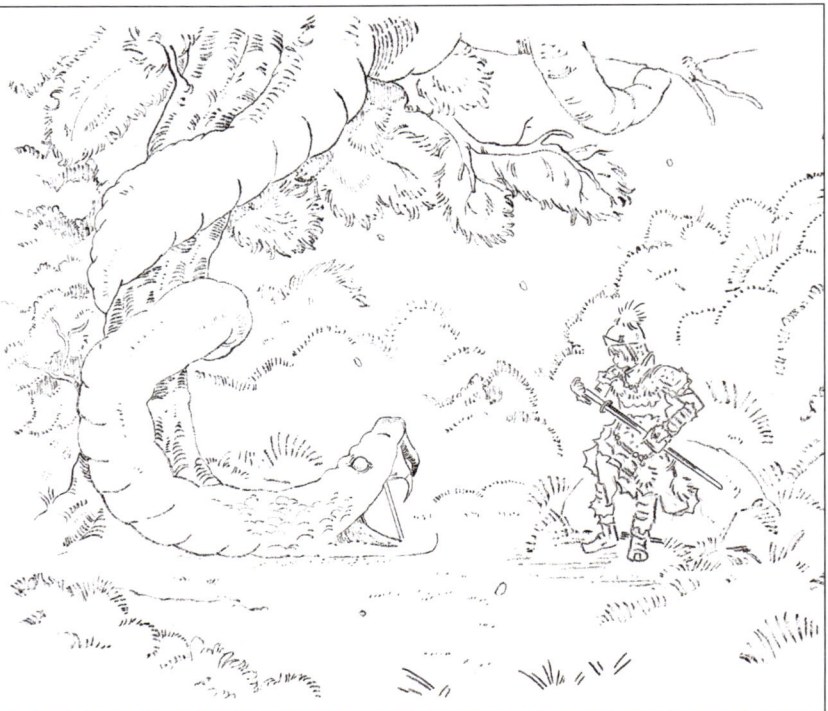

LINE WORK COMPLETED FOR THE
SECOND EXPLORATION SKETCH

06 LINE WORK CLOSE-UP

What really captivates me about Hokusai's work is the remarkable sense of depth without the need to add much detail. I spend a lot of time thinking about colour schemes and how I would approach this recreation to attain a similar feel. I tend to draw a lot of detail in my illustrations, so instead, I focus more on simplicity. What is the most effective method to enhance the artwork with colour?

CLOSE-UP VIEW OF
THE LINE WORK

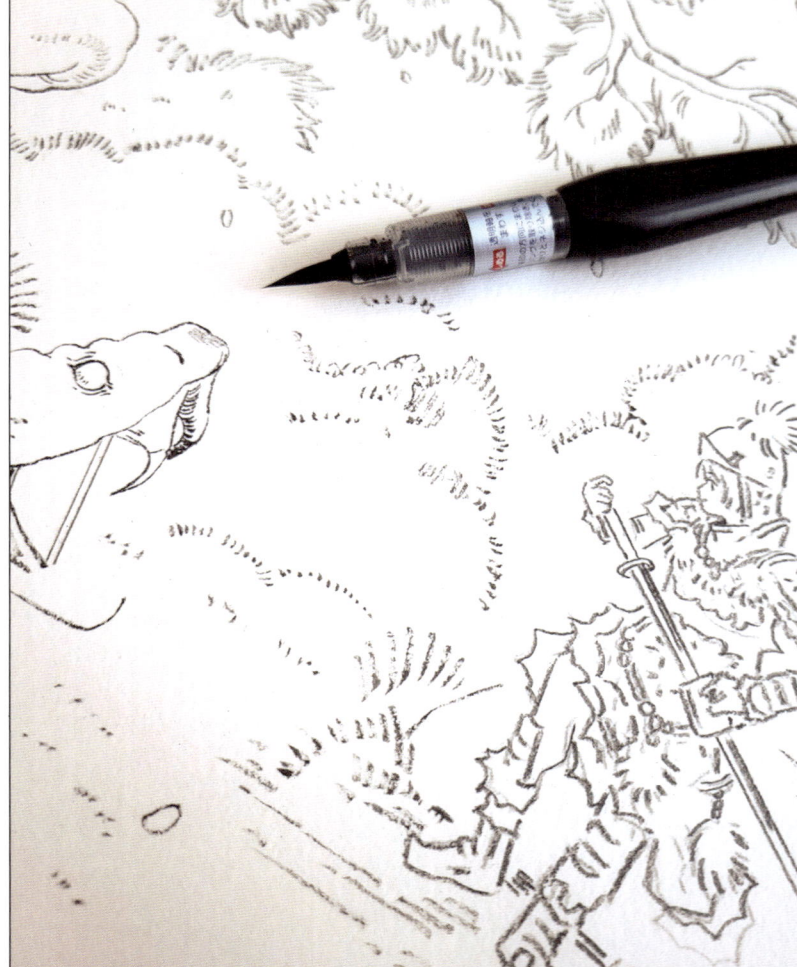

07 ADDING BASE COLOURS

In my approach to watercolour, I usually start by covering large areas with a base colour and, in some cases, I might cover the whole piece with the initial wash. For this version, I utilize shades of green and blue to represent the grass and the sky. Once these colours are down, I go back into these areas with deeper colours to create a distinction between the different elements and sections of the composition.

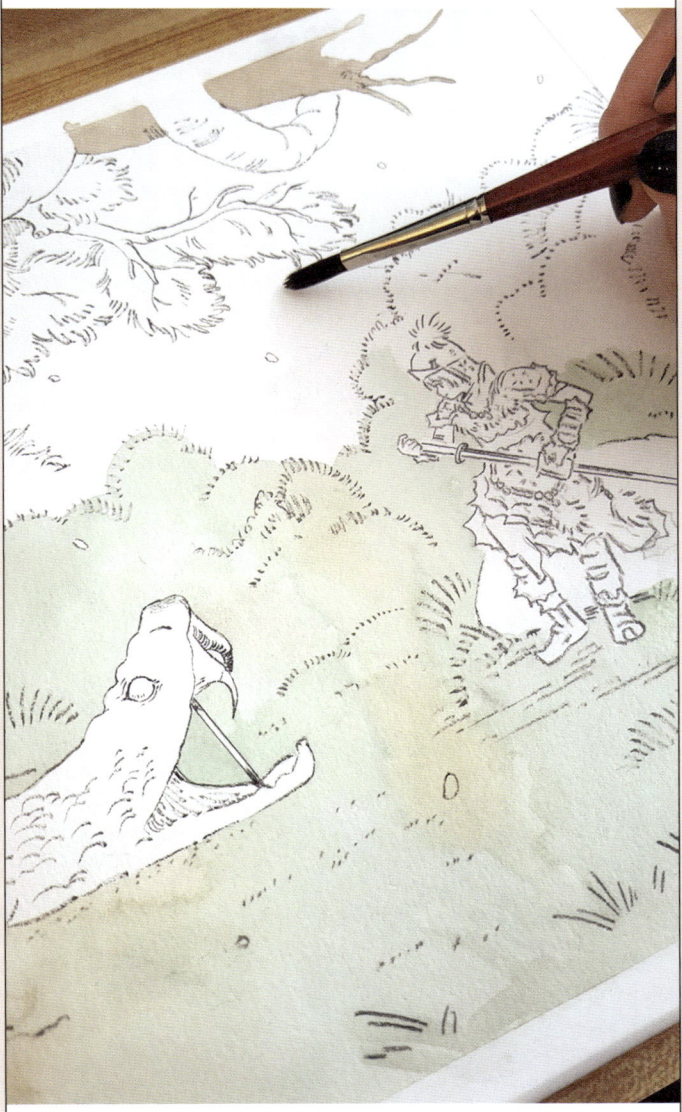

LAYING DOWN THE GREEN-GRASS BASE USING WATERCOLOUR

08 VERSION 2: FINAL COLOURS

This was one option for the colour palette, prior to my scanning of the artwork and making digital touch-ups. Ultimately, the finished appearance shows soft hues with little shadows, creating a gentle aesthetic. This version was not chosen in the end.

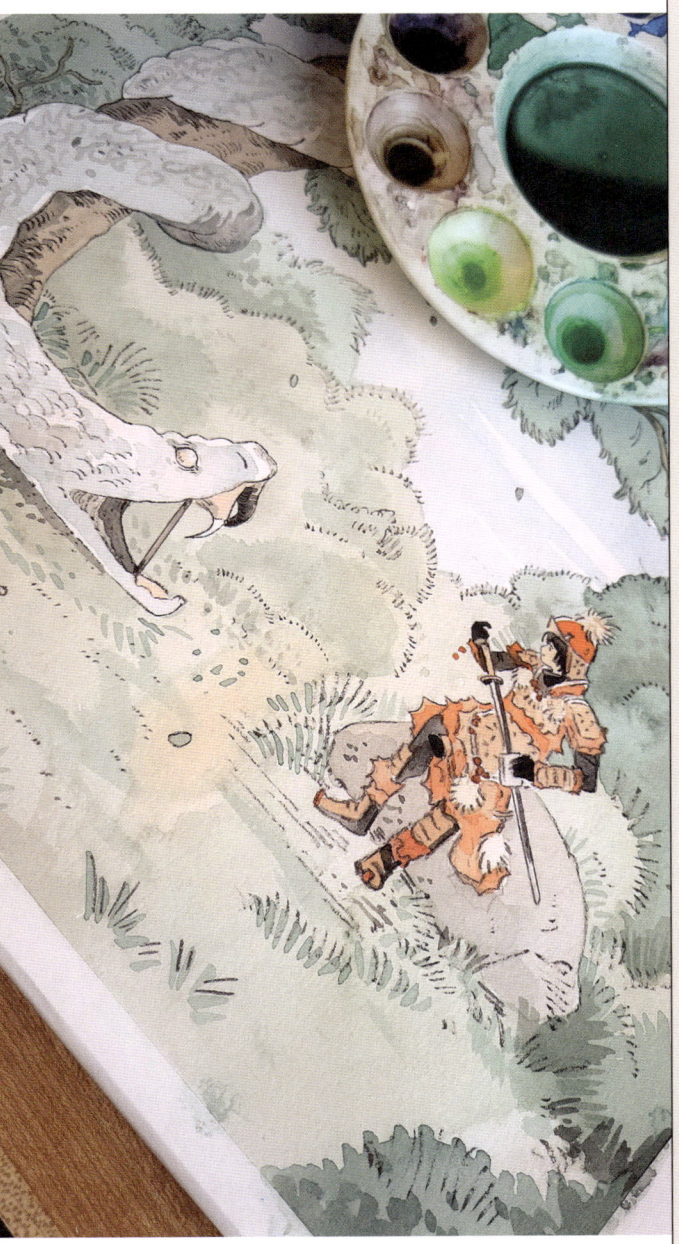

FINAL COLOURS FOR THE SECOND VERSION OF THE ARTWORK

09 REWORKING LINE & COLOUR

I move on to creating the third and final version. I add more of my usual style, focusing on details and line-work shadows before bringing in colour. I begin by adding colour to the background elements, including the stones near the waterfall.

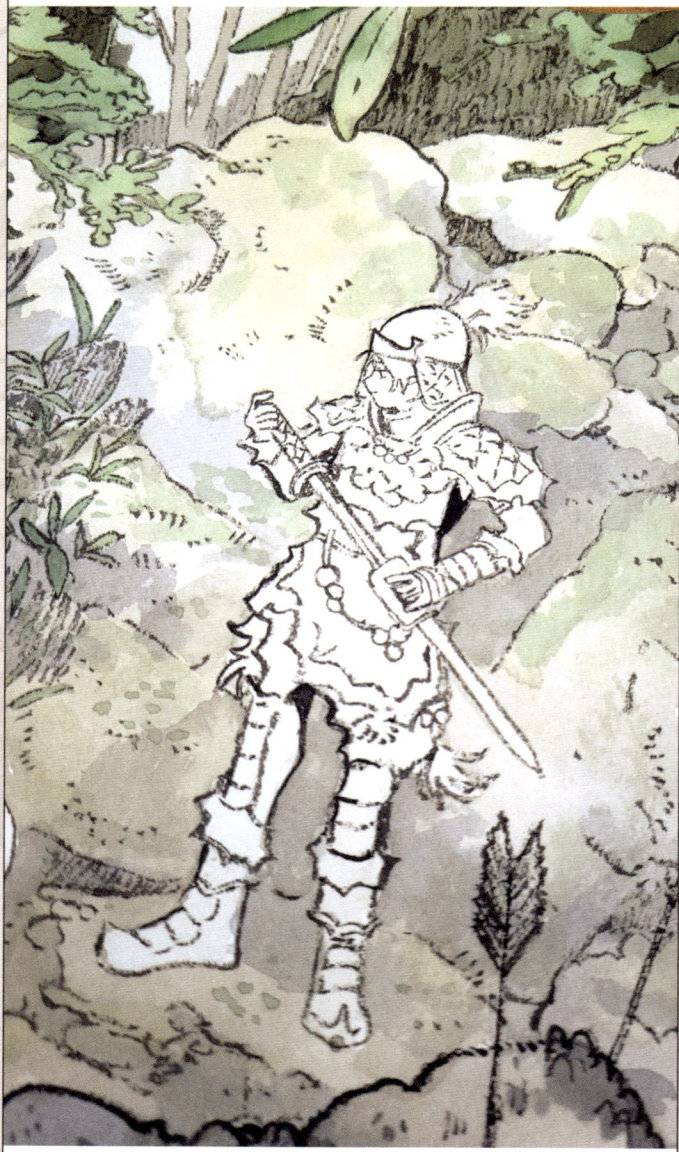

REWORKING THE IDEA AND LAYING
DOWN THE LINE WORK AND COLOURS

10 FOLIAGE & GREENERY

One subject I truly love to illustrate is the beauty of nature; every season and the variety of colour that nature brings. I find great joy in capturing the tree branches that frame the scene, as well as the delicate little plants that emerge from the rock crevices. It's important to spend time on the little details that bring a piece together.

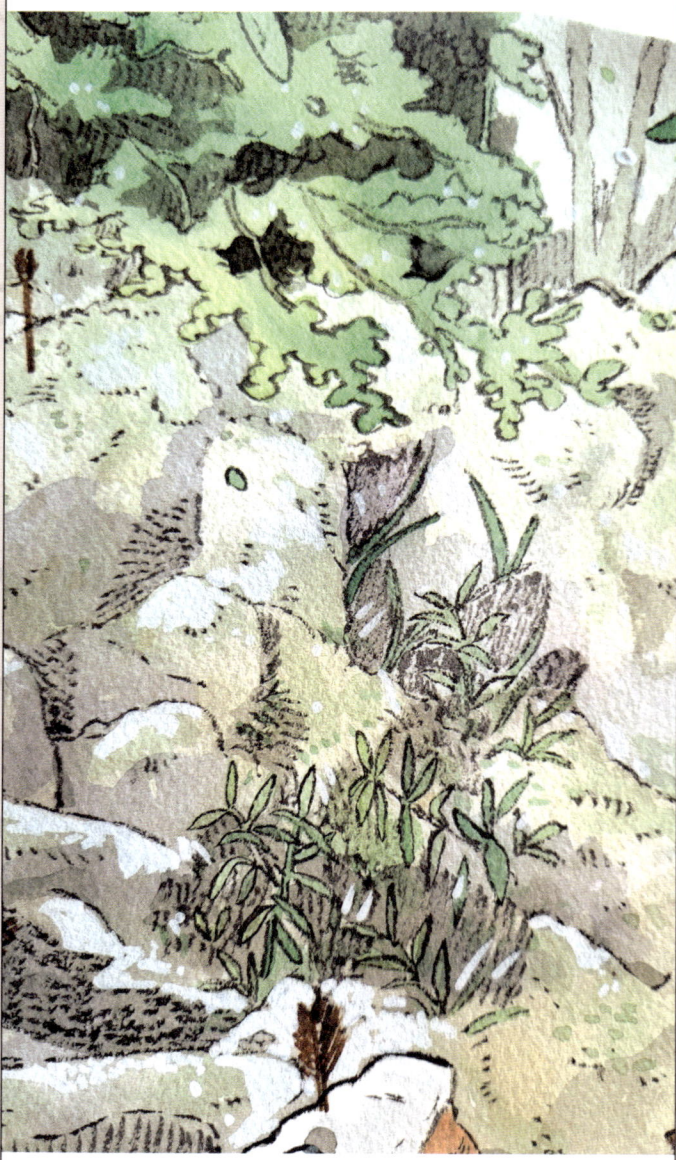

CLOSE-UP OF SOME GREEN PLANTS GROWING
AROUND THE WATERFALL AND BETWEEN THE STONES

11 SNAKE ON THE STREAM

Hokusai has masterfully illustrated multiple snakes, showcasing them with remarkable detail and in various styles. This inspired me to create my own illustration of the snake with a sense of volume and life. The scale of the giant snake in relation to a human figure was a fun concept to capture from the start. As I work on the details and the curves of the snake, I find the process to be both soothing and enjoyable, allowing me to get lost in the art of detailing.

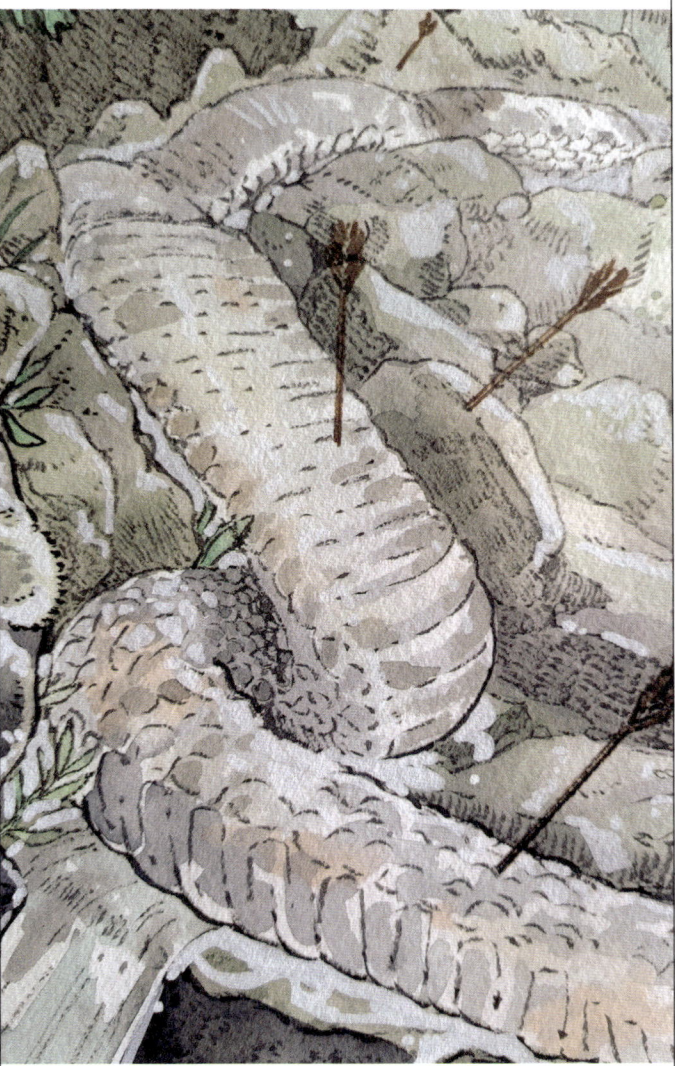

CLOSE-UP OF THE TWISTED SNAKE
BODY AS IT LIES ON THE STREAM PATH

12 SHARP FANGS

The idea of defeating such a powerful creature is truly inspiring; I can easily envision how terrifying it would be to stand so near to it, even after it has died, and I take care to communicate the feeling of danger. As finishing touches, I use paint markers to apply white highlights to the foreground and throughout the background, distinguishing the boulders in the front from the rest of the scene, highlighting important areas. The final adjustments are made digitally; some colours are subtly changed to create a clearer difference among selected elements.

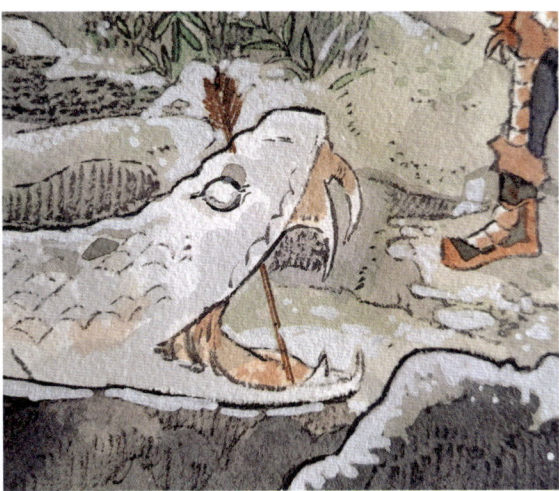

THE SNAKE'S BODY LIES NEAR THE END OF THE
WATERFALL, AN ARROW PIERCING THE HEAD

CONCLUSION

After a few variations, I am happy with the final version. In my personal work, I find joy in capturing the moments that occur between significant life events, and I feel like illustrating the tranquillity after a conflict brings a sense of peace. Hokusai's artistry continuously inspires me; I recognize that I have much to learn in understanding the elements that add to the beauty of his illustrations. The process of exploring and applying these techniques in my work is what makes the journey enjoyable.

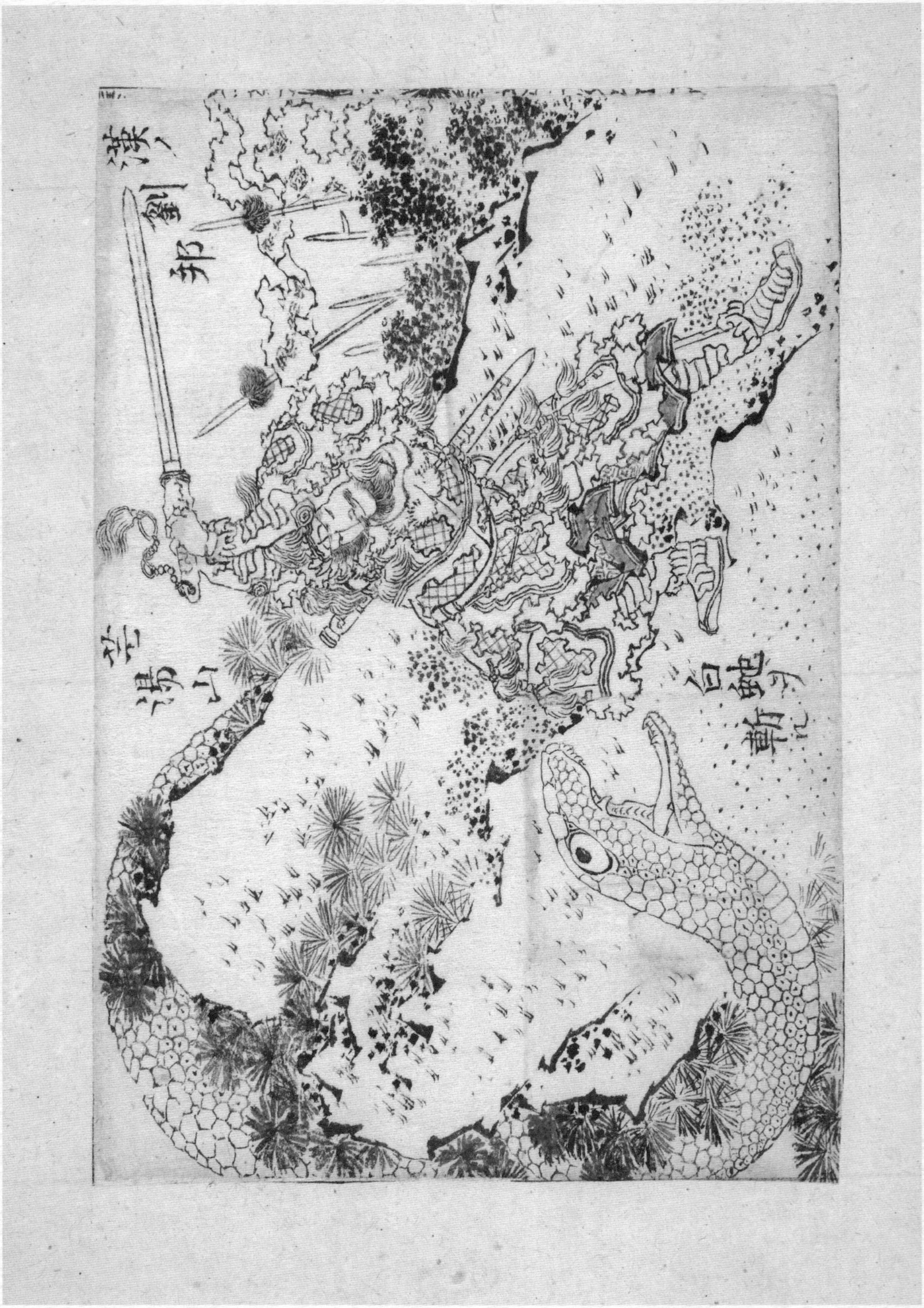
漢ノ劉邦
芒碭山
白蛇ヲ斬ル

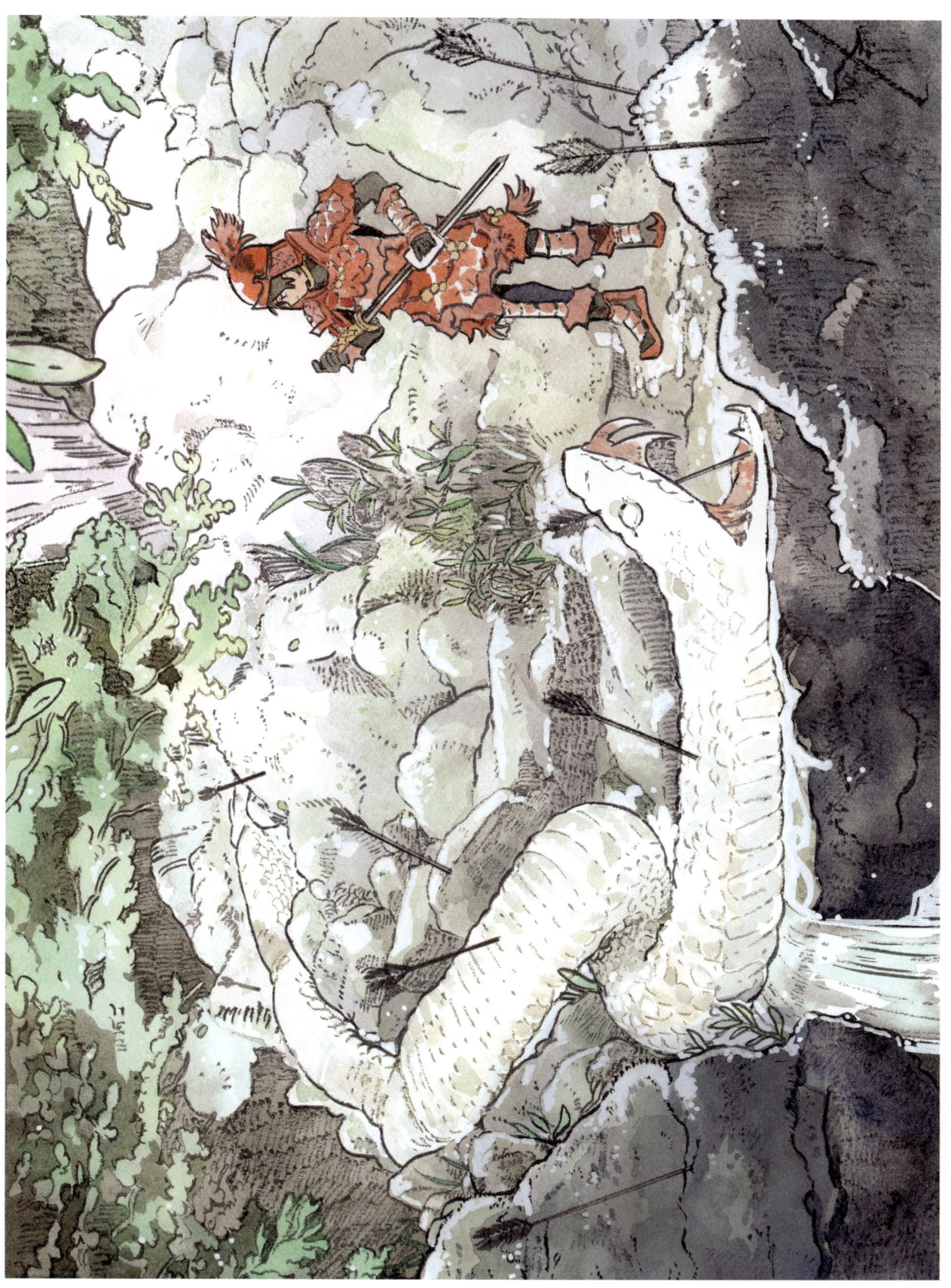

BELOW: *Beach Trip*
Girl holding her beach float on the sand, posing for a picture

RIGHT: *Morning Walk*
Characters walking down stone steps among cats and nature on a sunny day

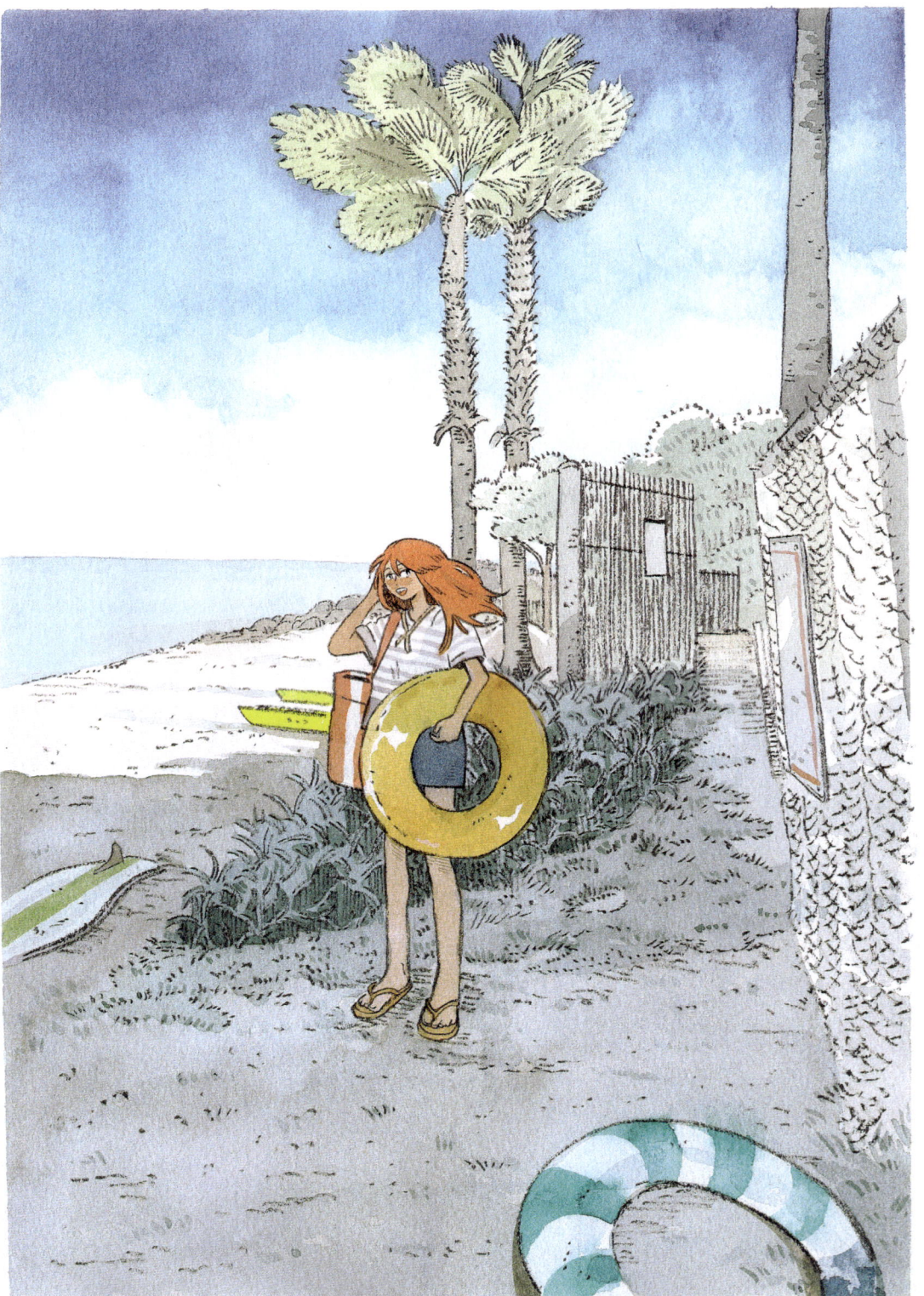

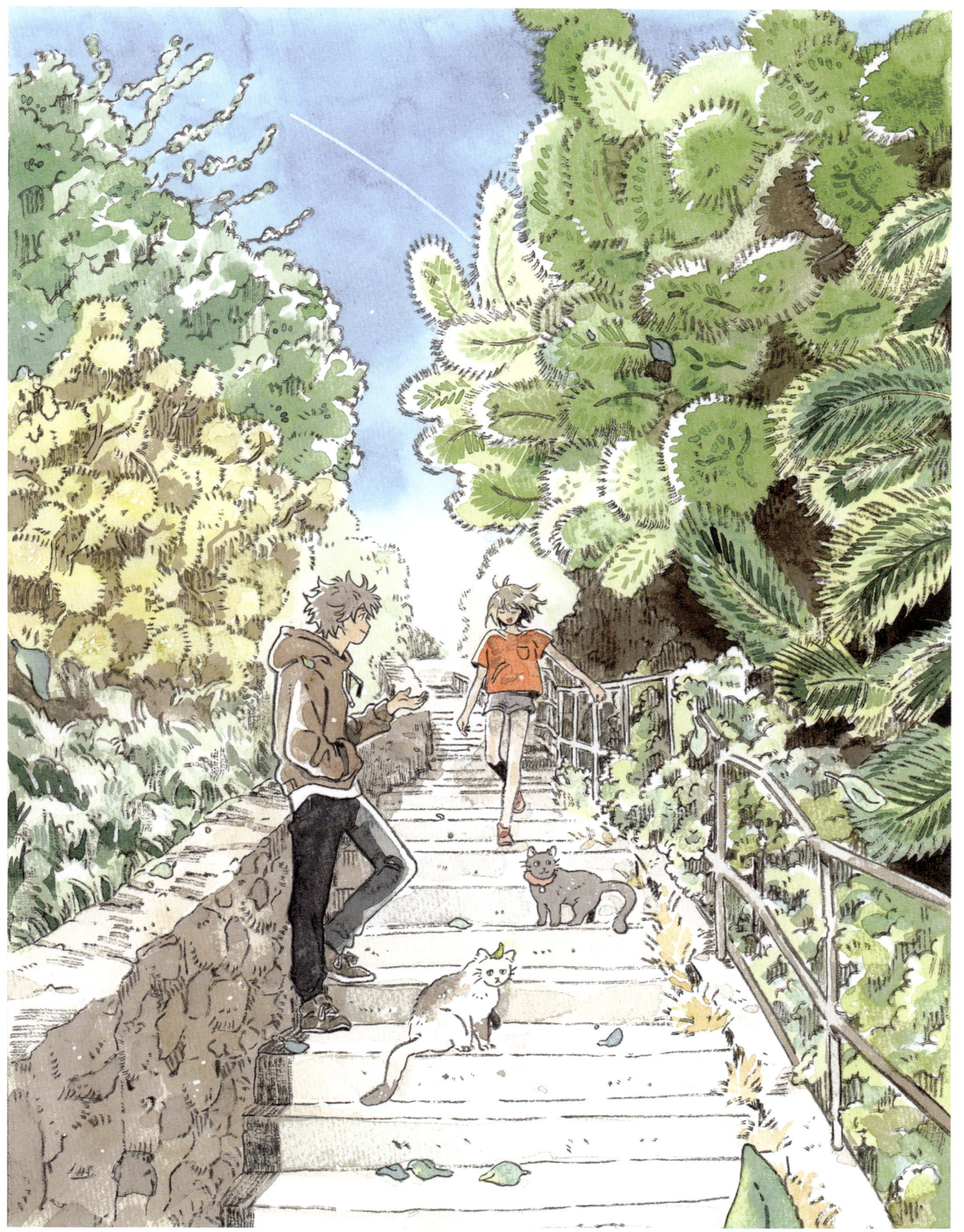

Parakid

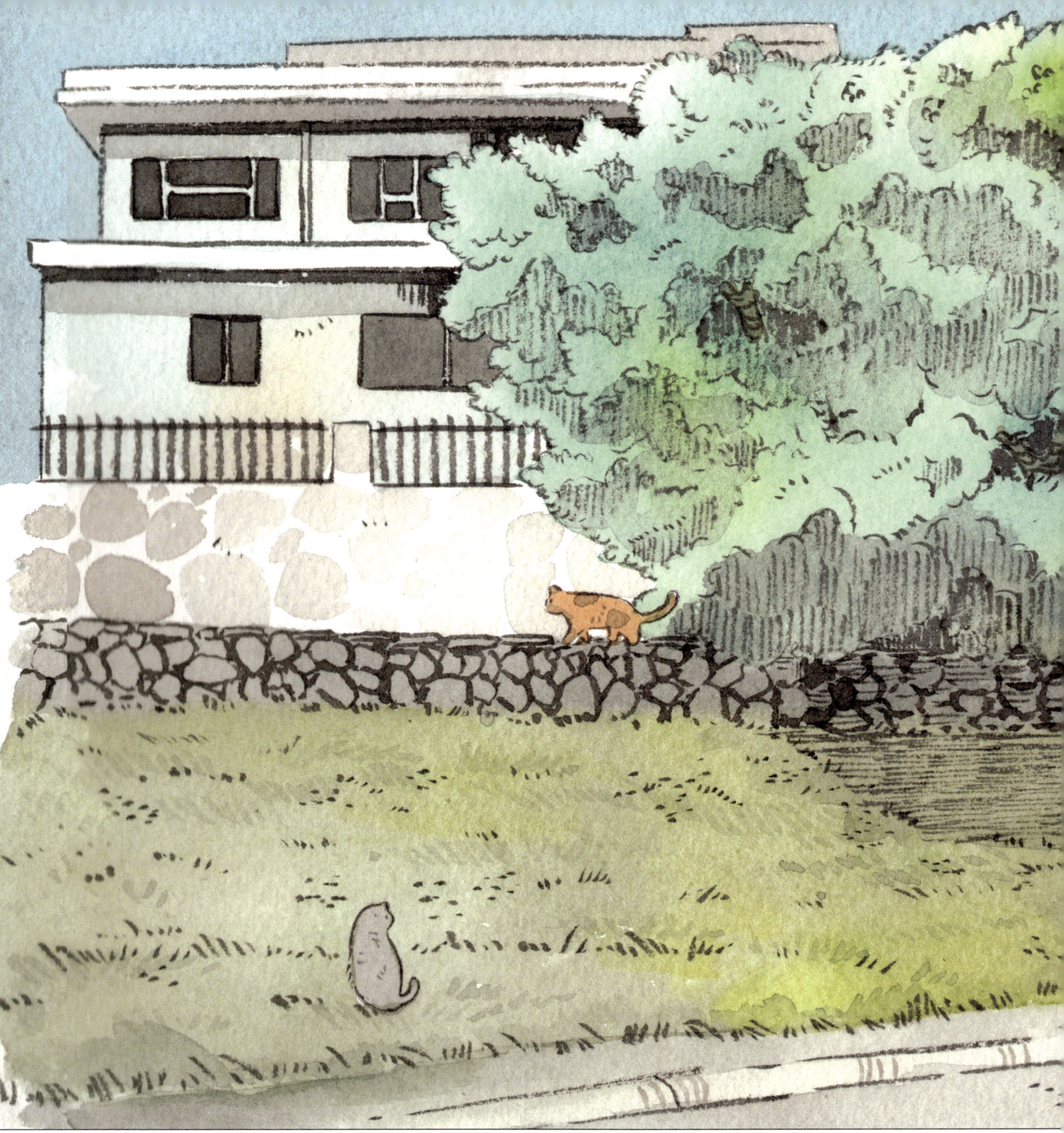

Strays
Sunny street where two characters
stop to pet a cat on the sidewalk

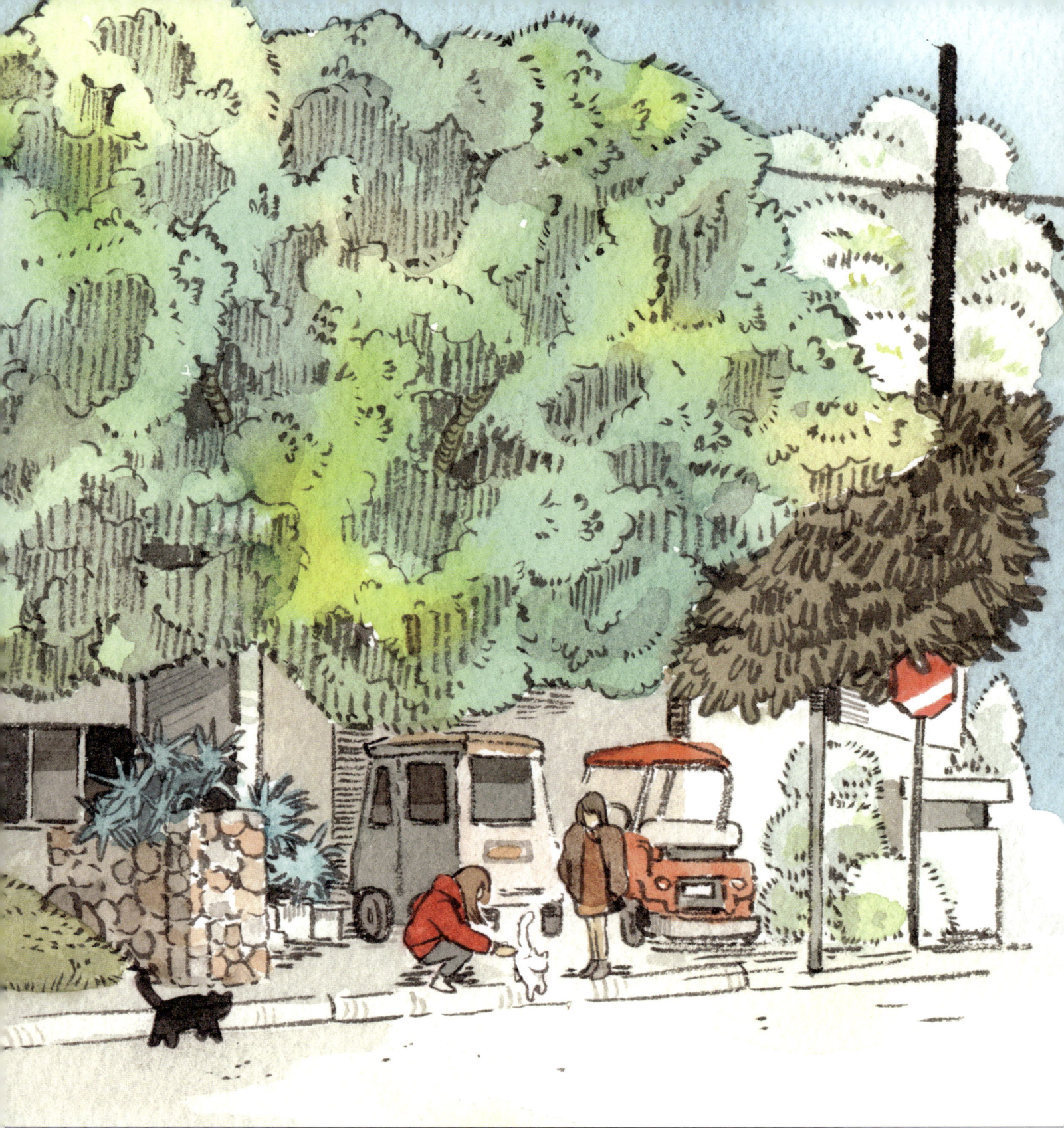

RIGHT: *Snow Fight*
Two friends having a
snowball fight

_____

OPPOSITE PAGE:
Apprentices
Two student witches holding
hands and running around
campus between classes

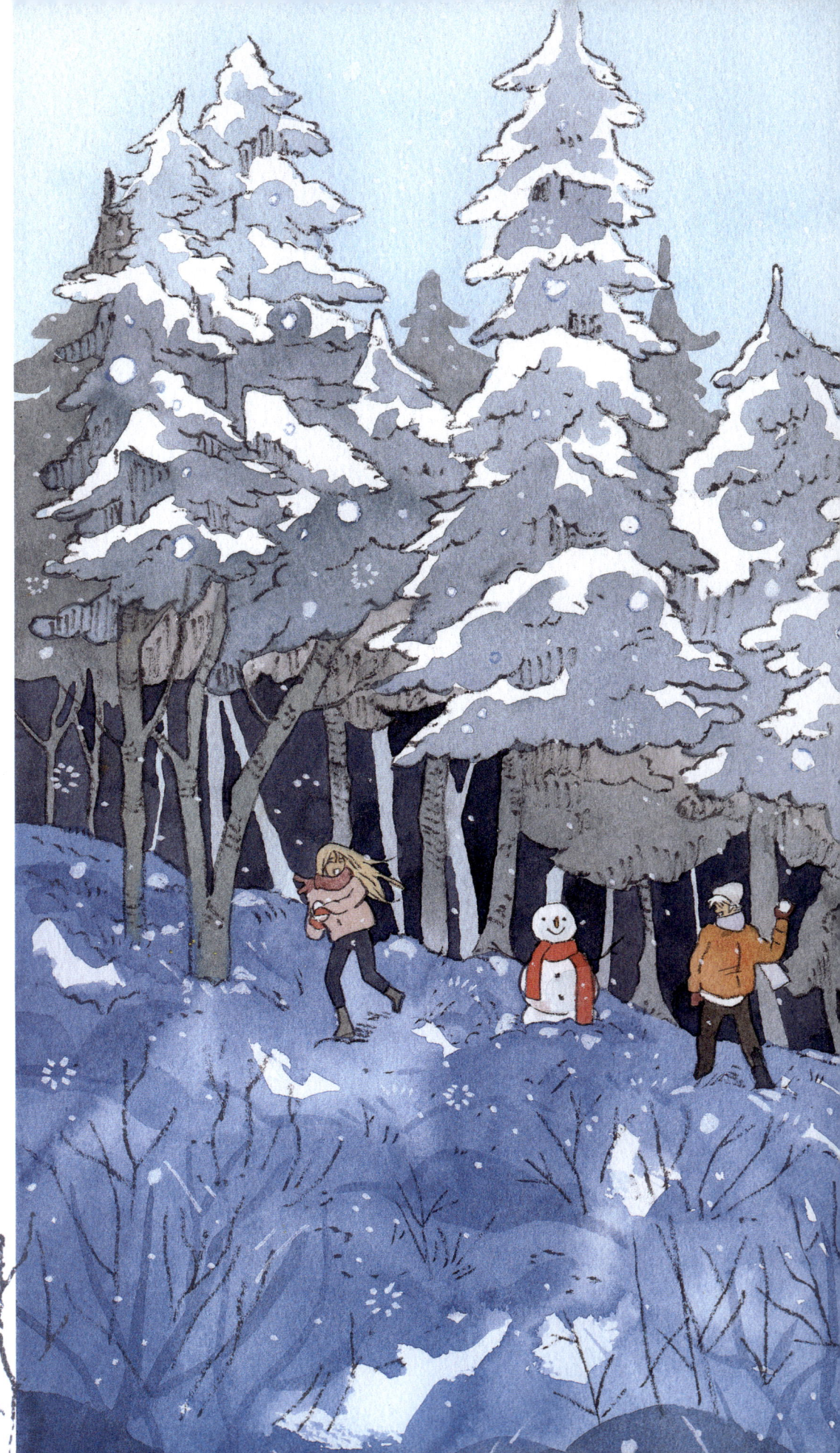

244

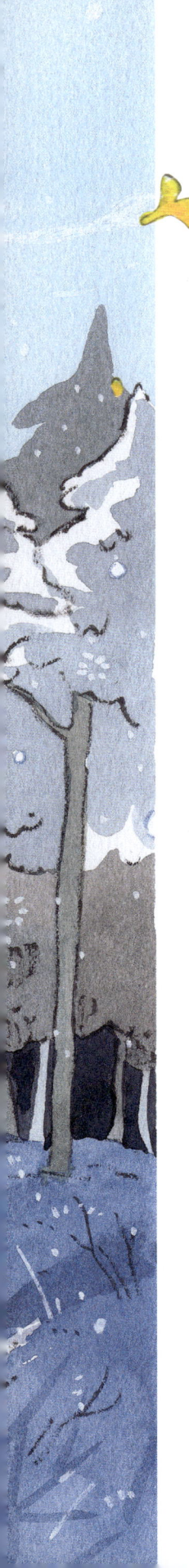

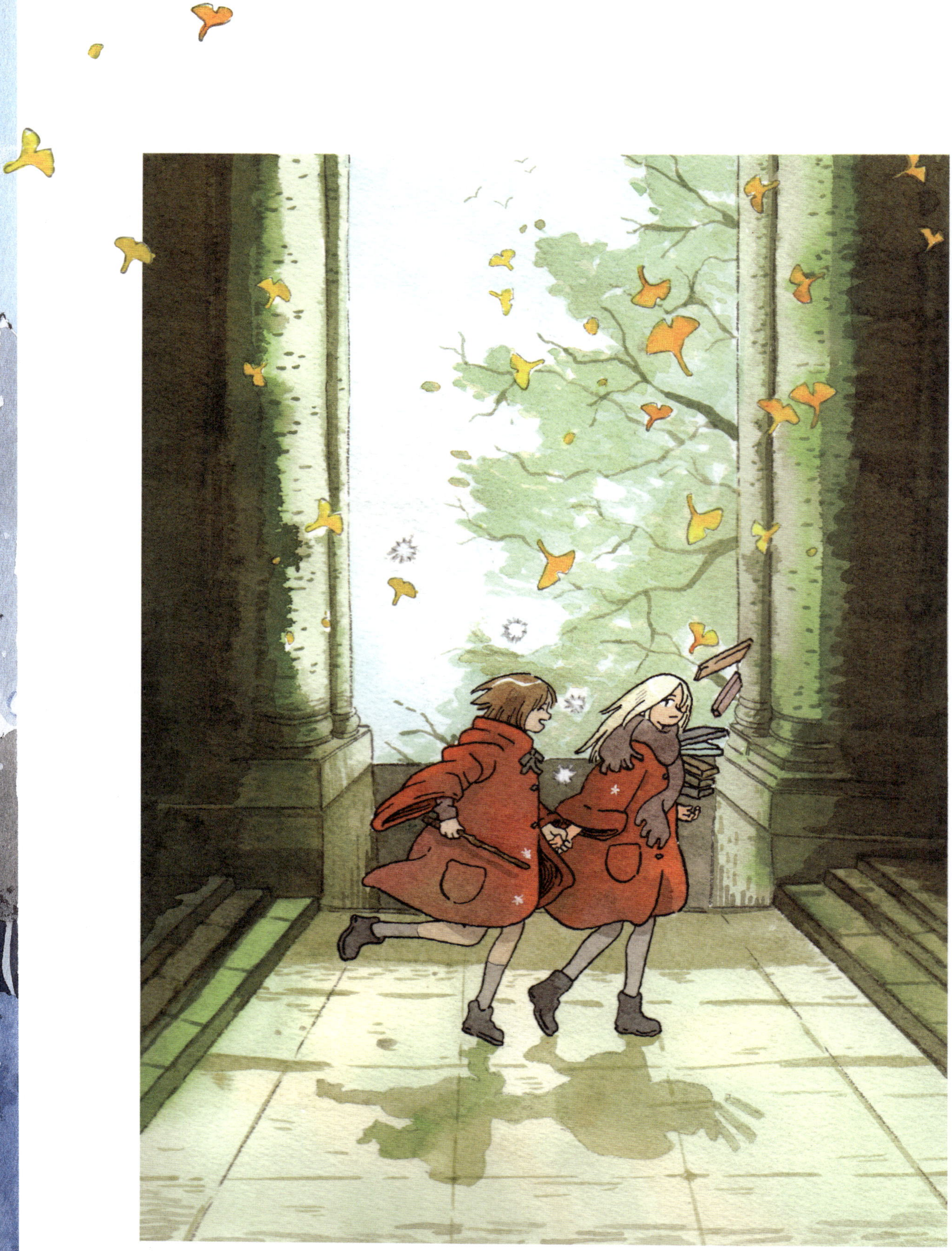

Parakid

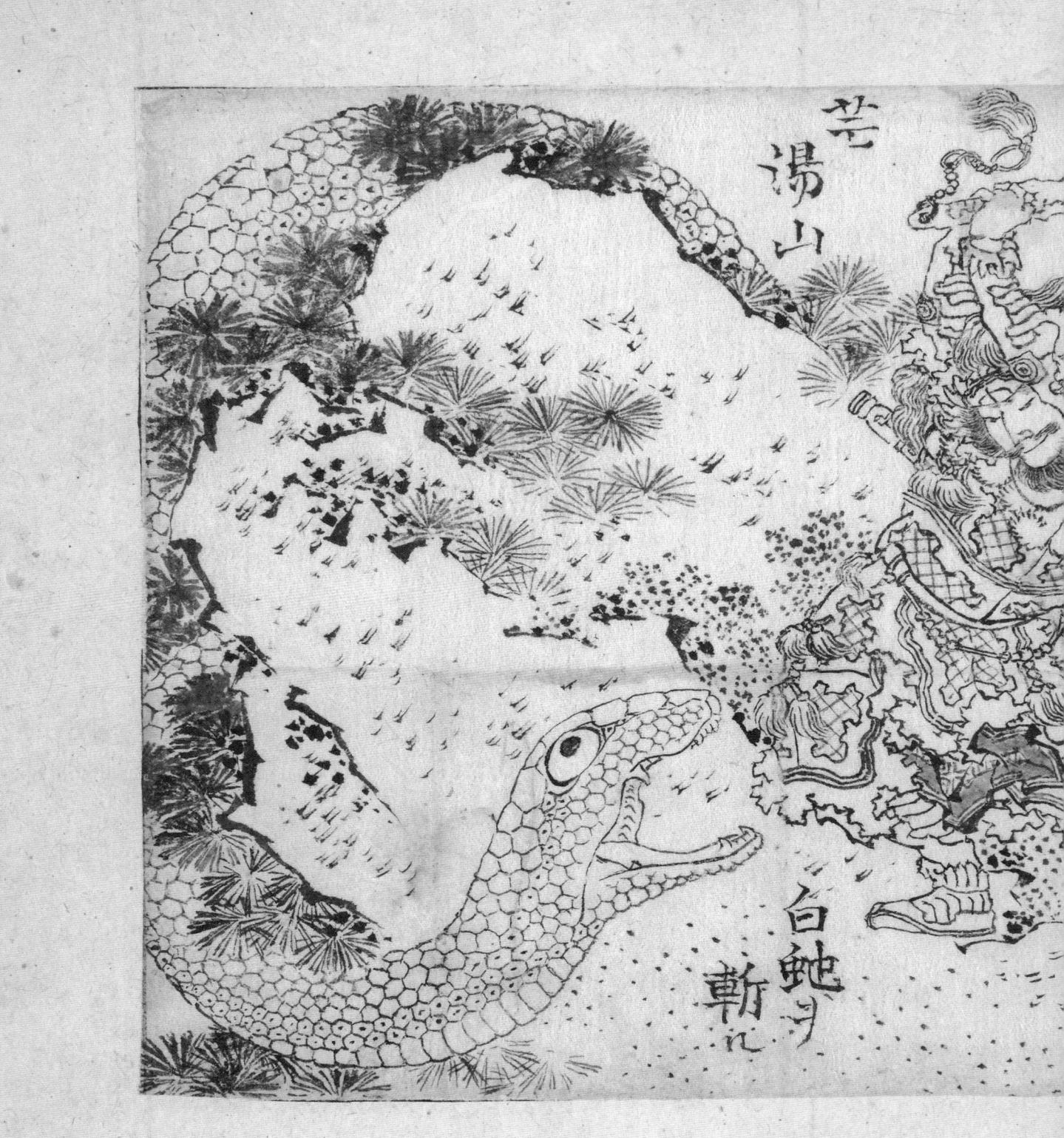

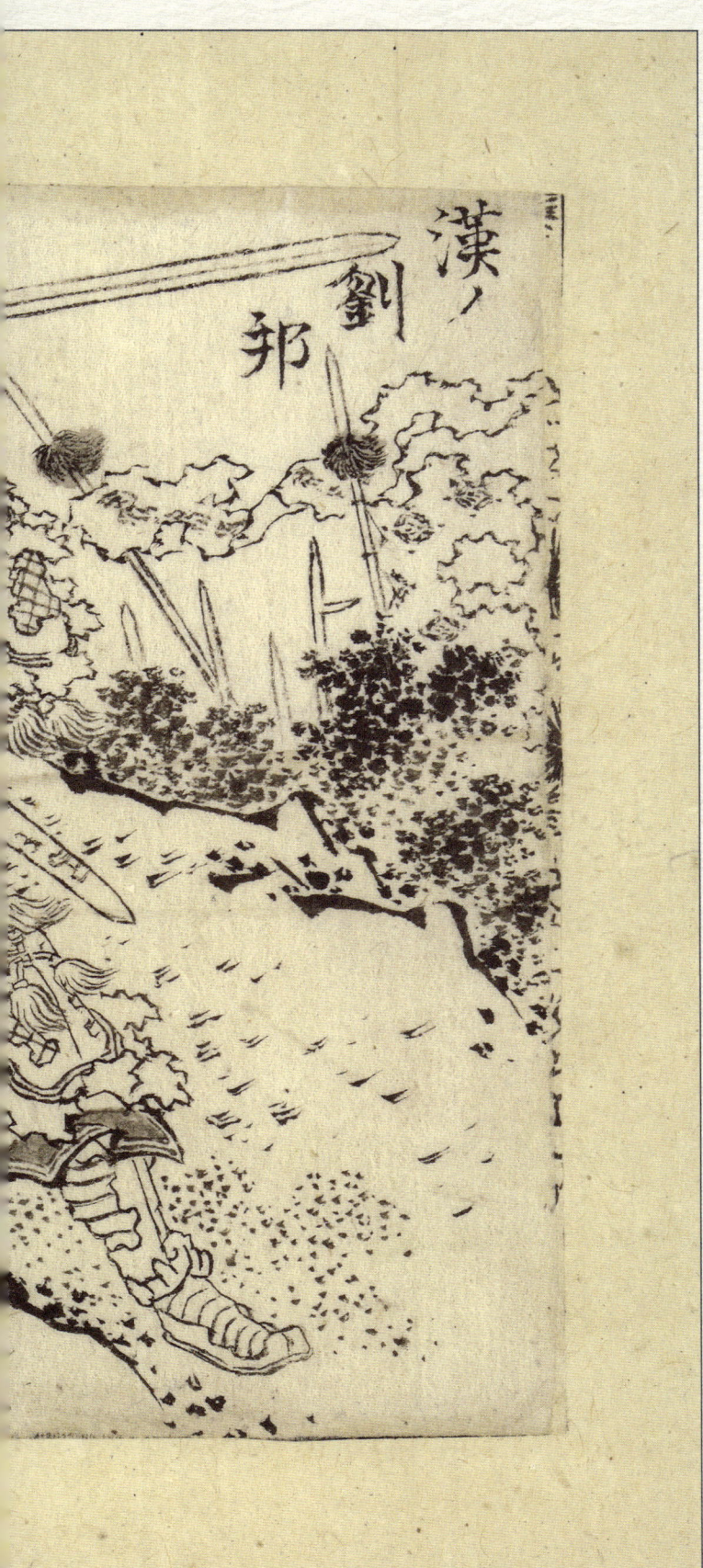

漢ノ
劉
邦

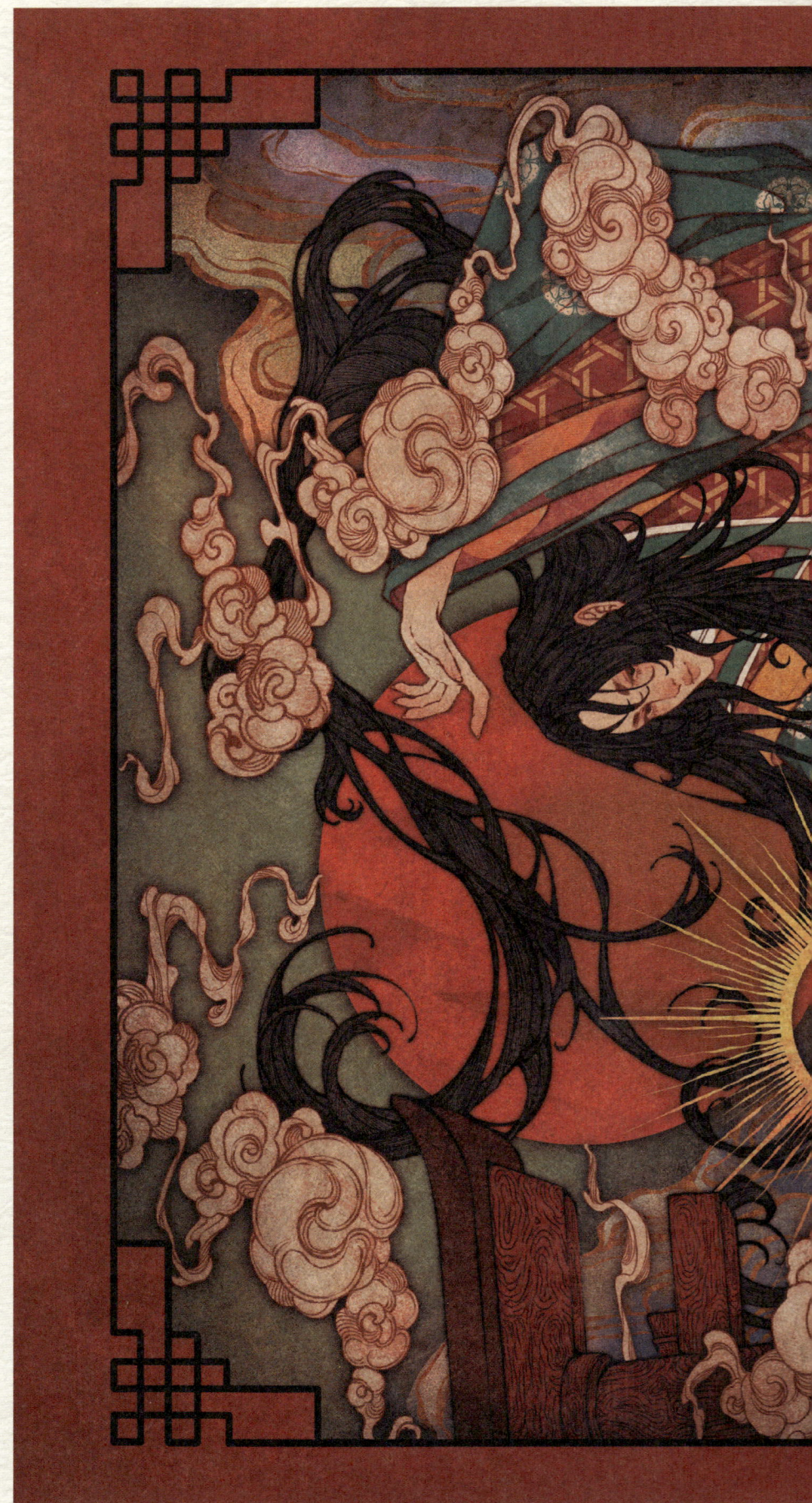

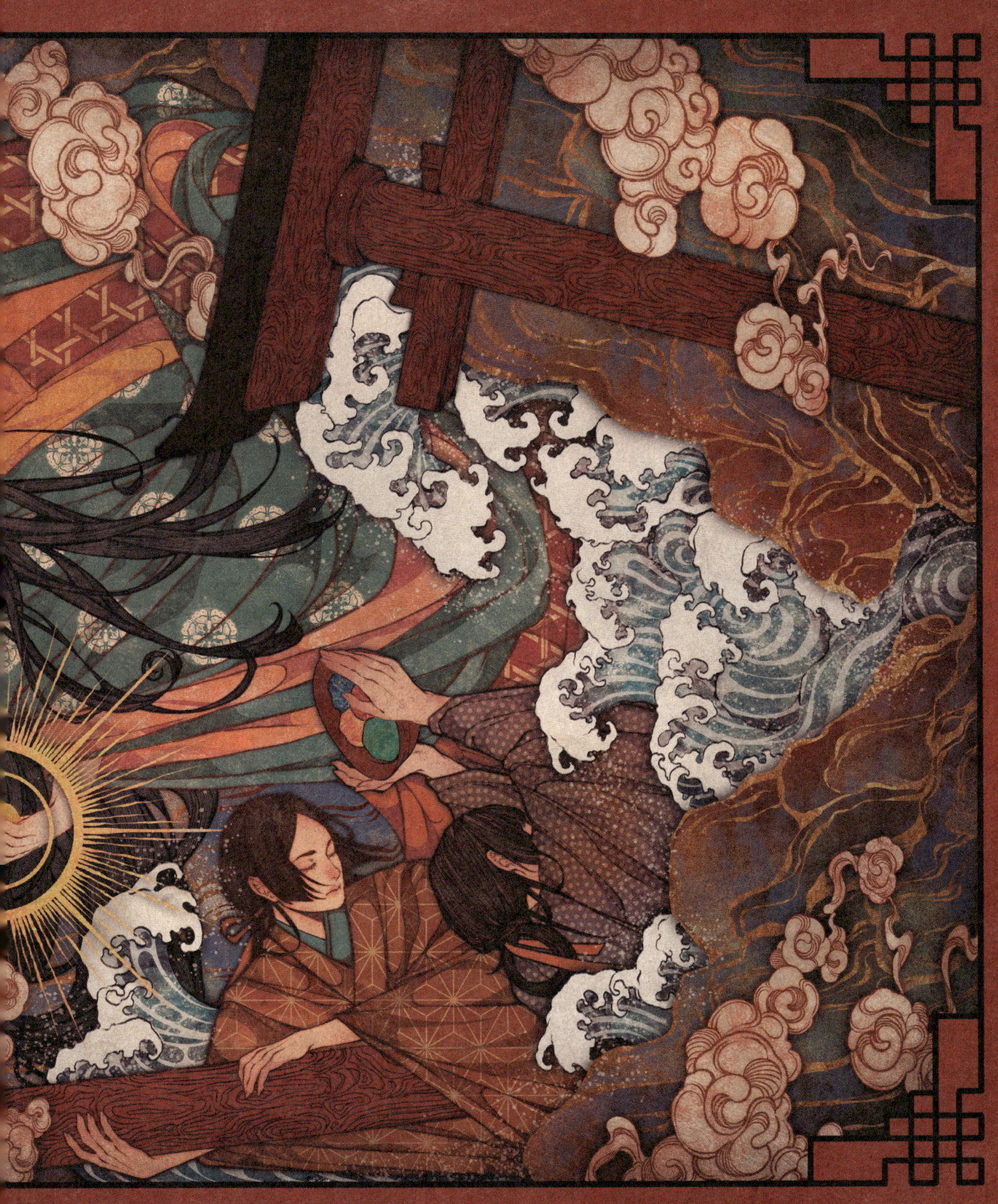

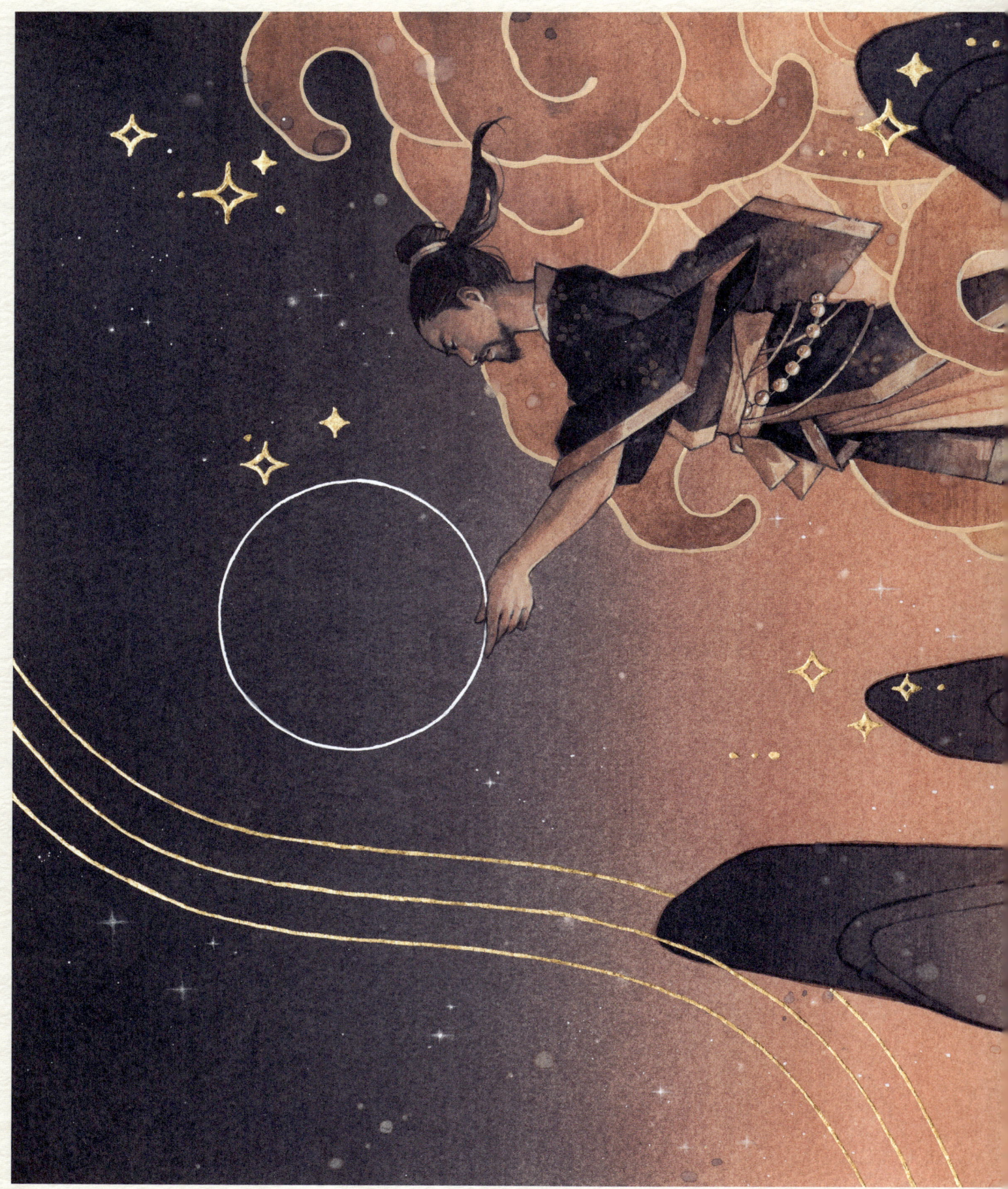

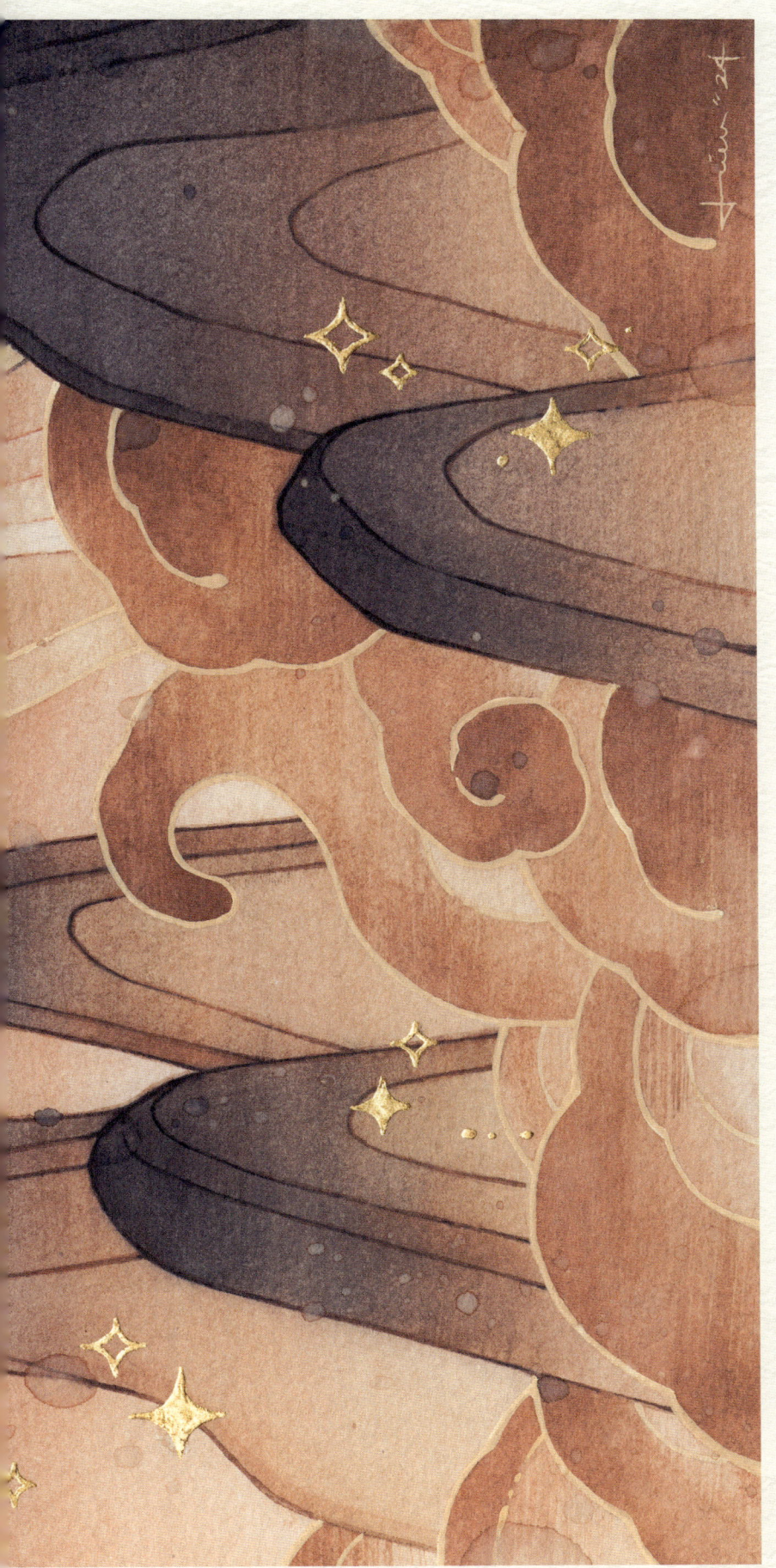

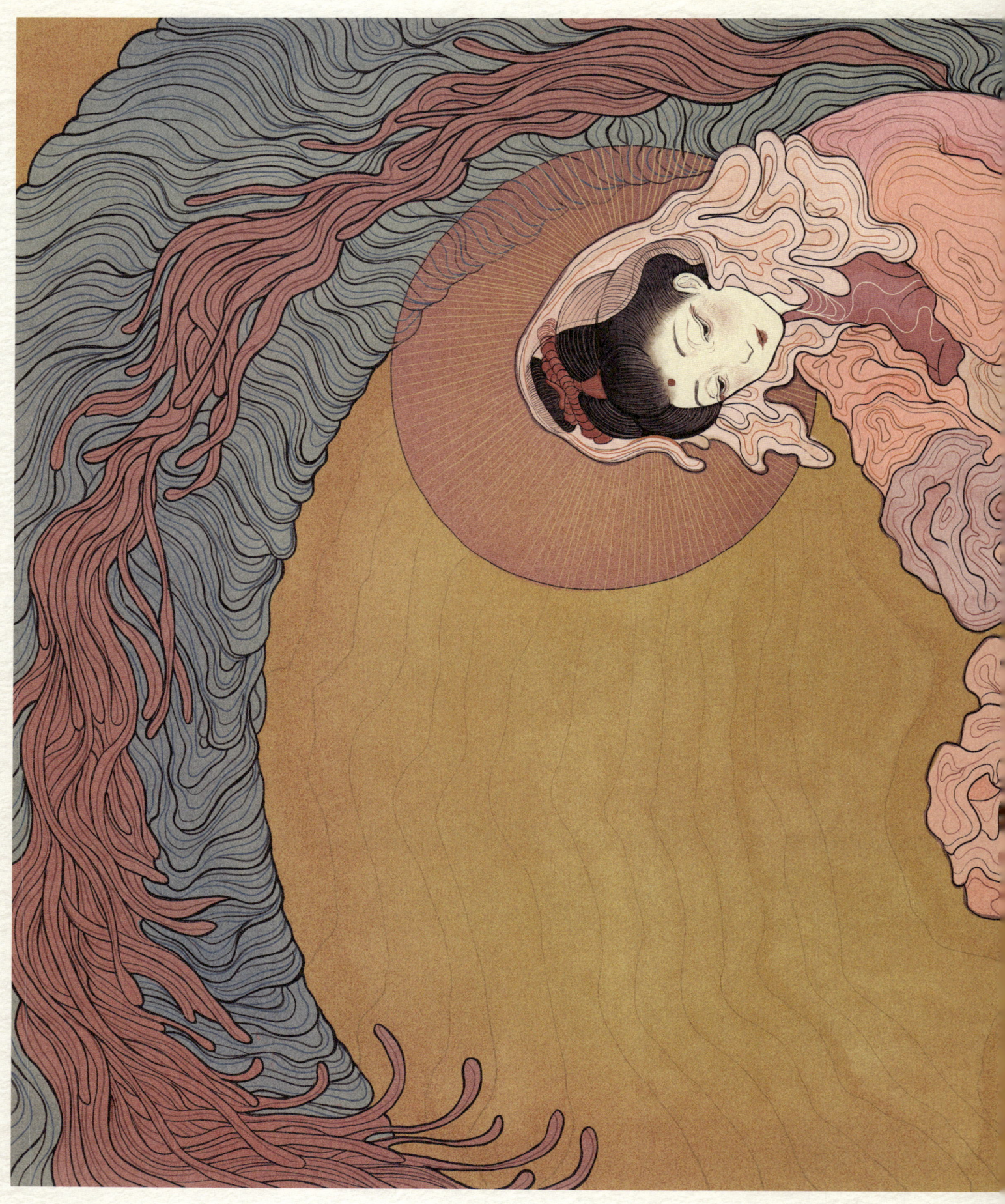

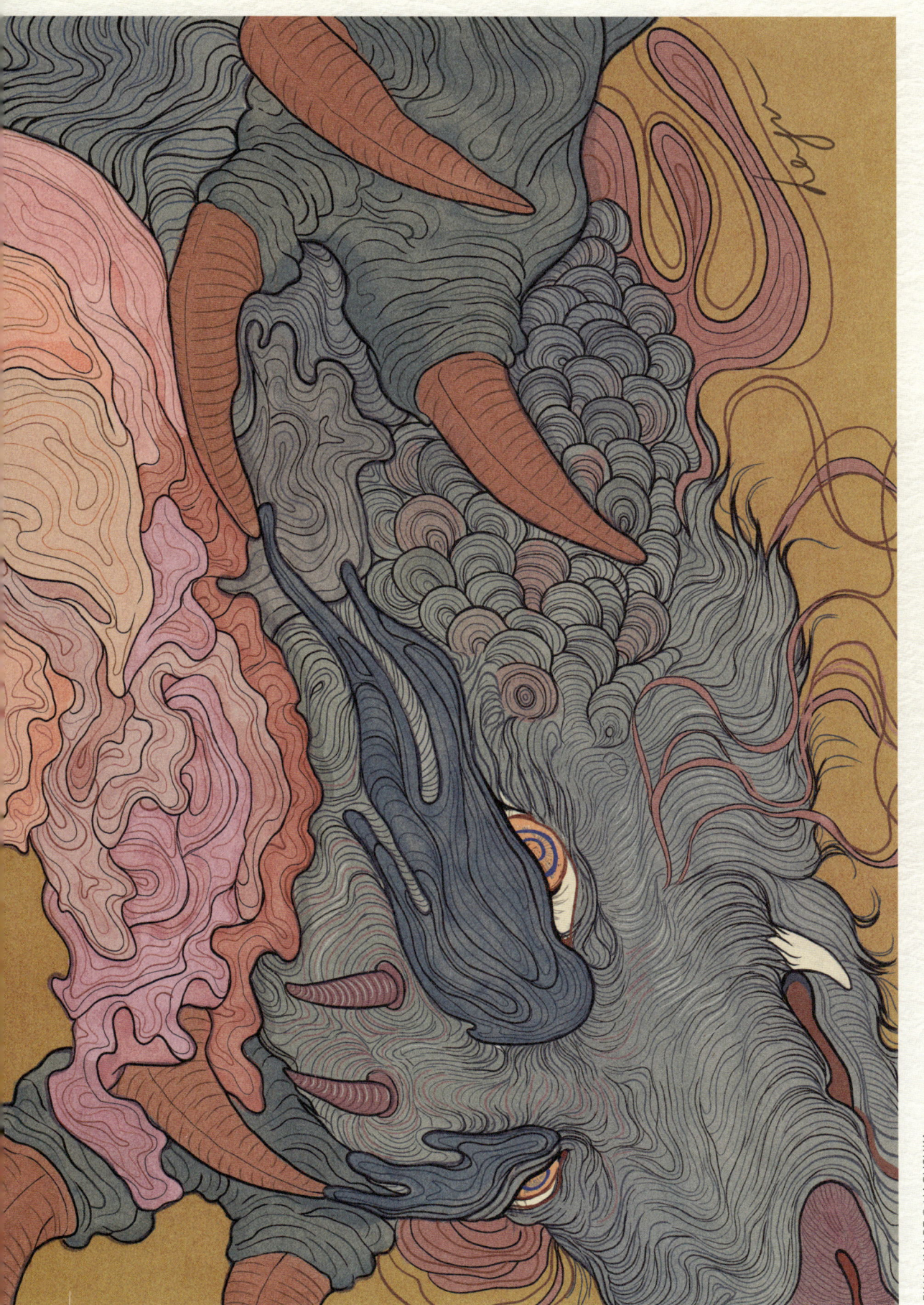

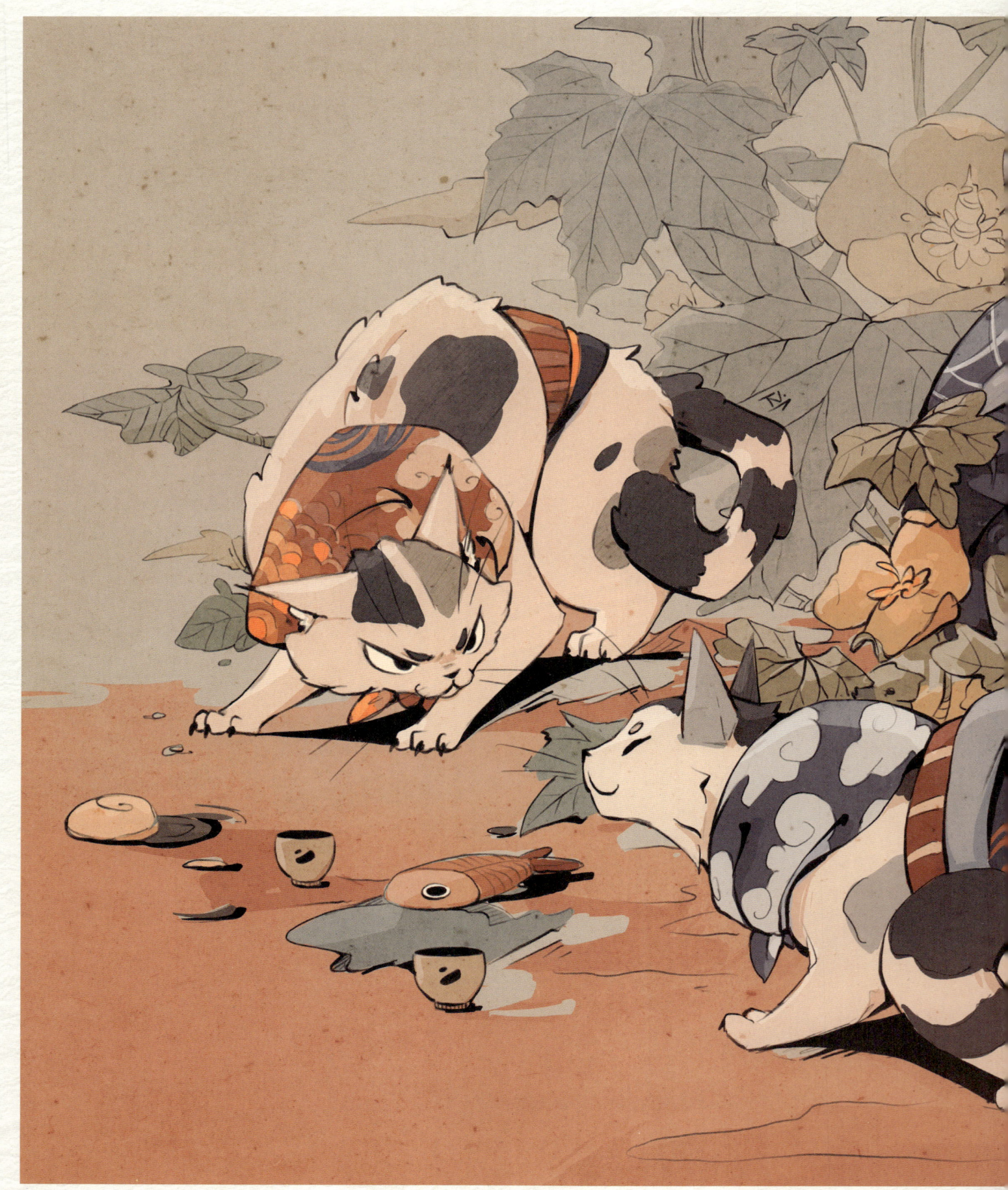

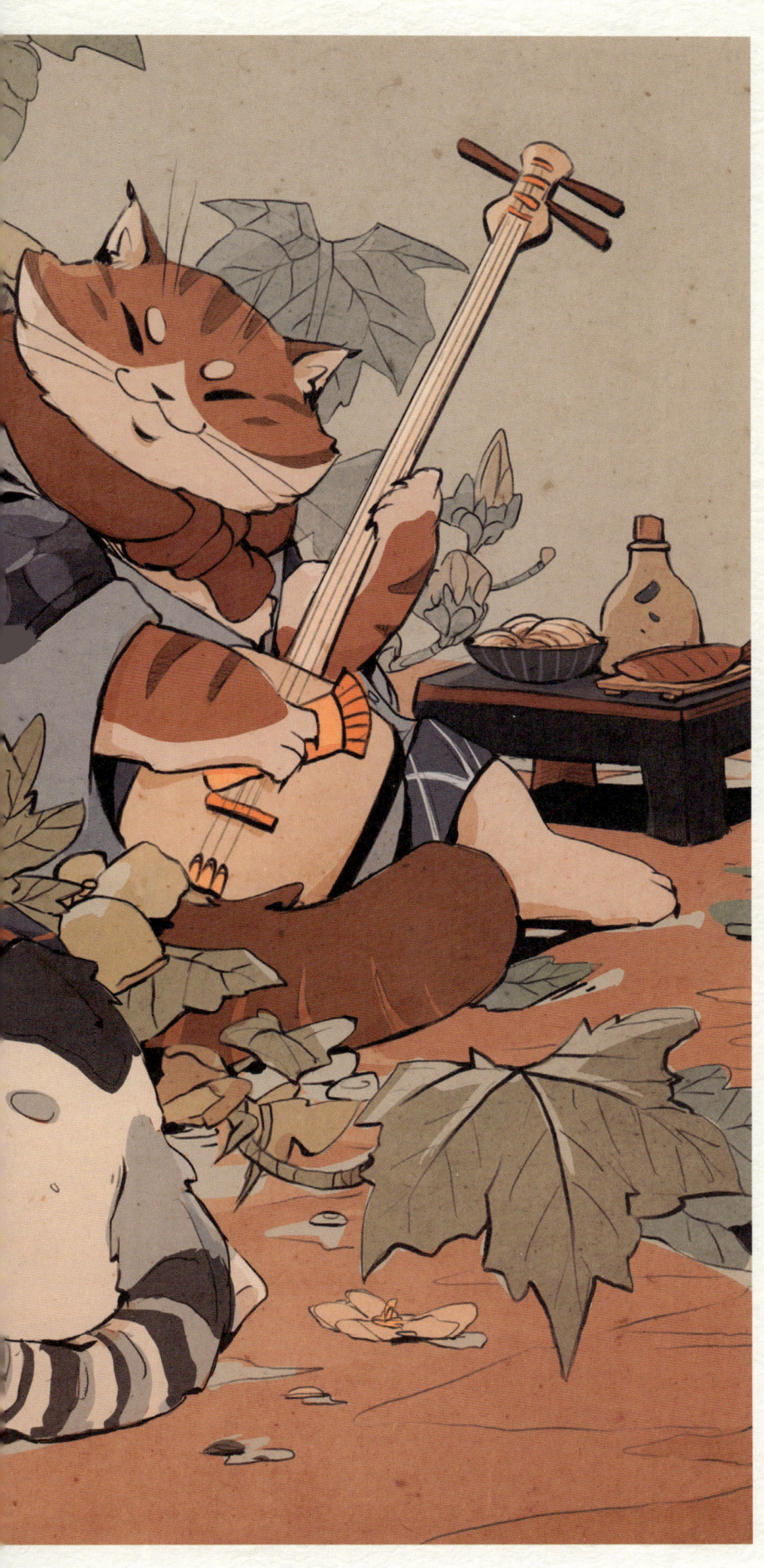

FINAL IMAGE © TESSA NELISSEN

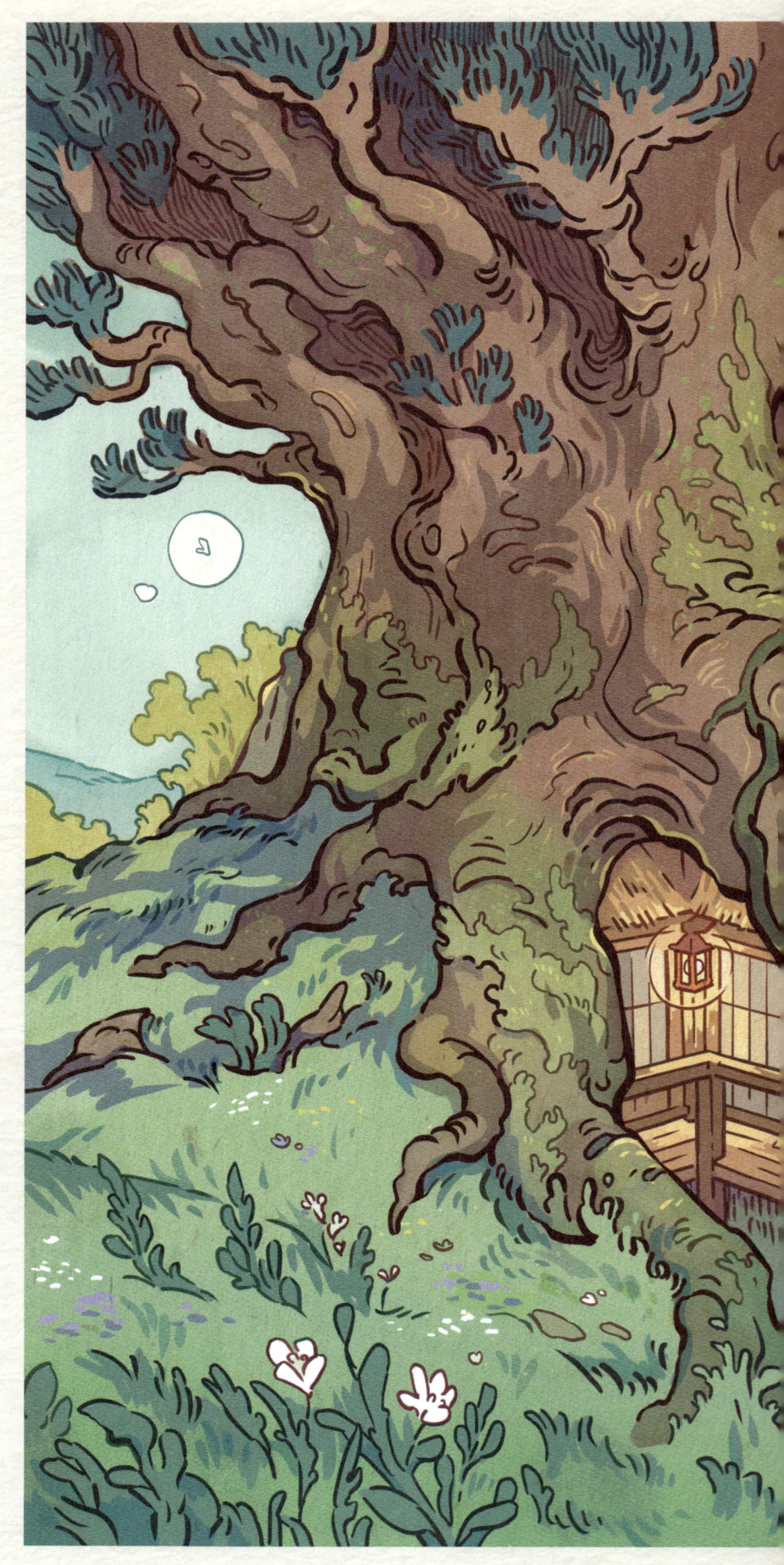

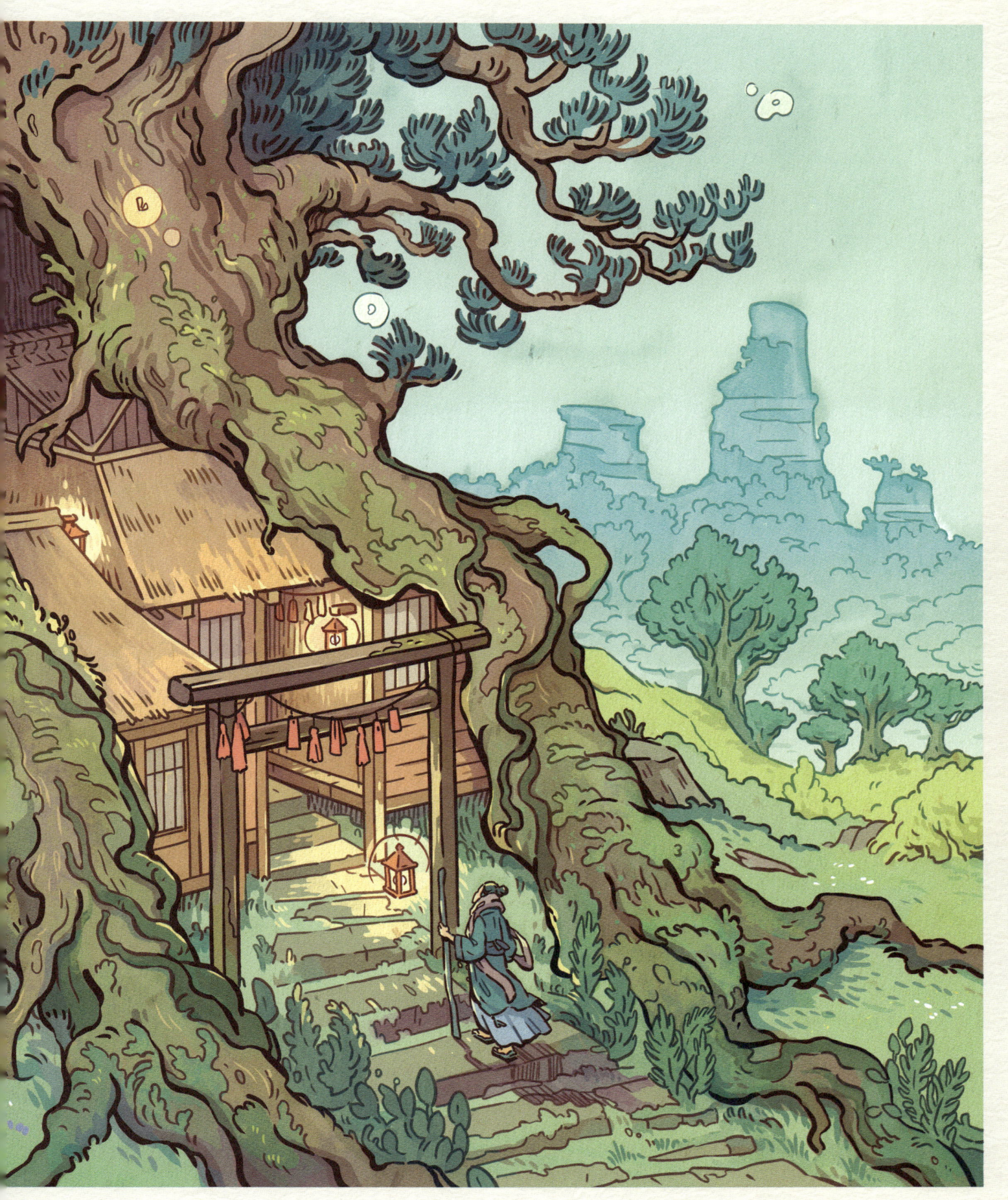

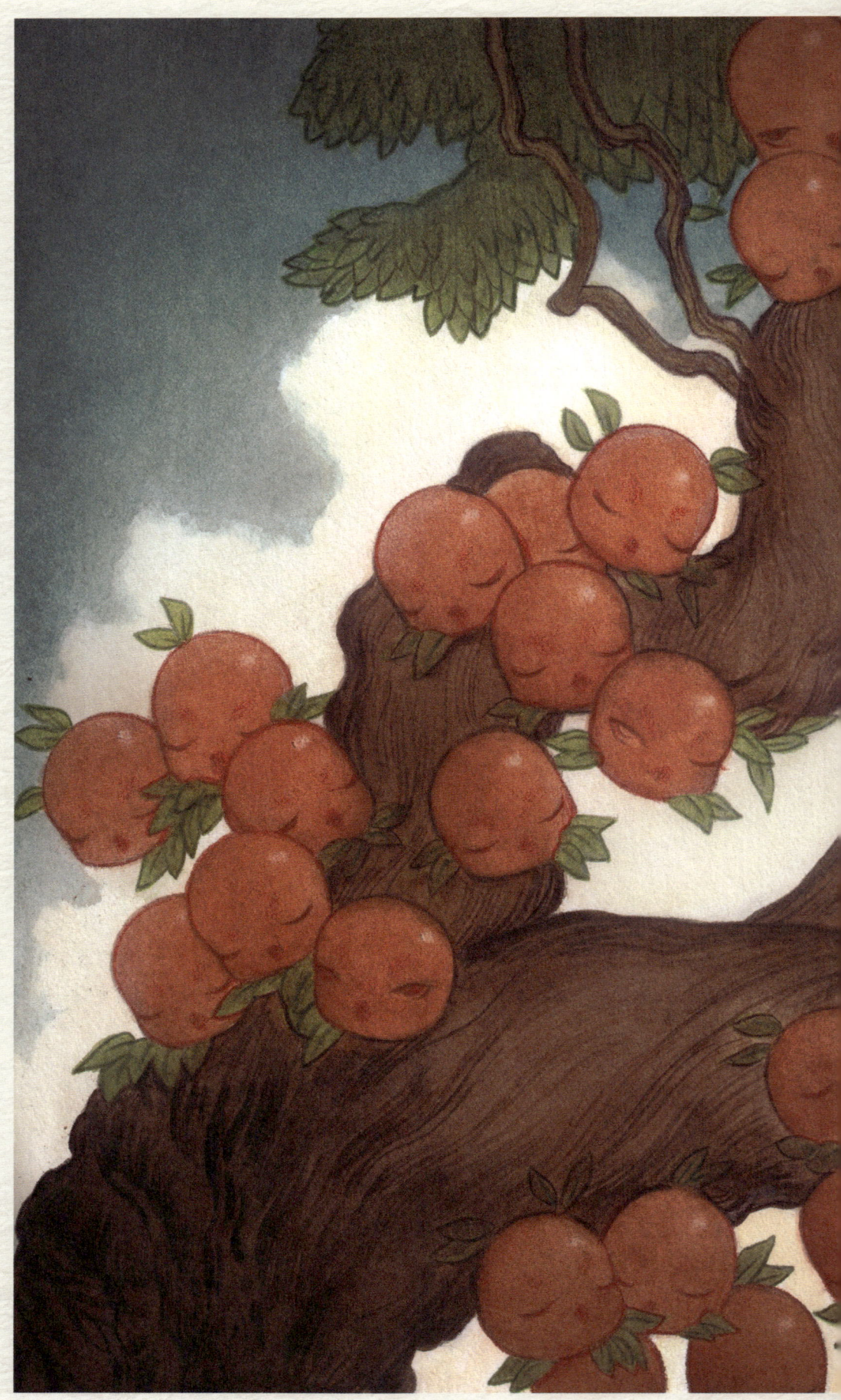

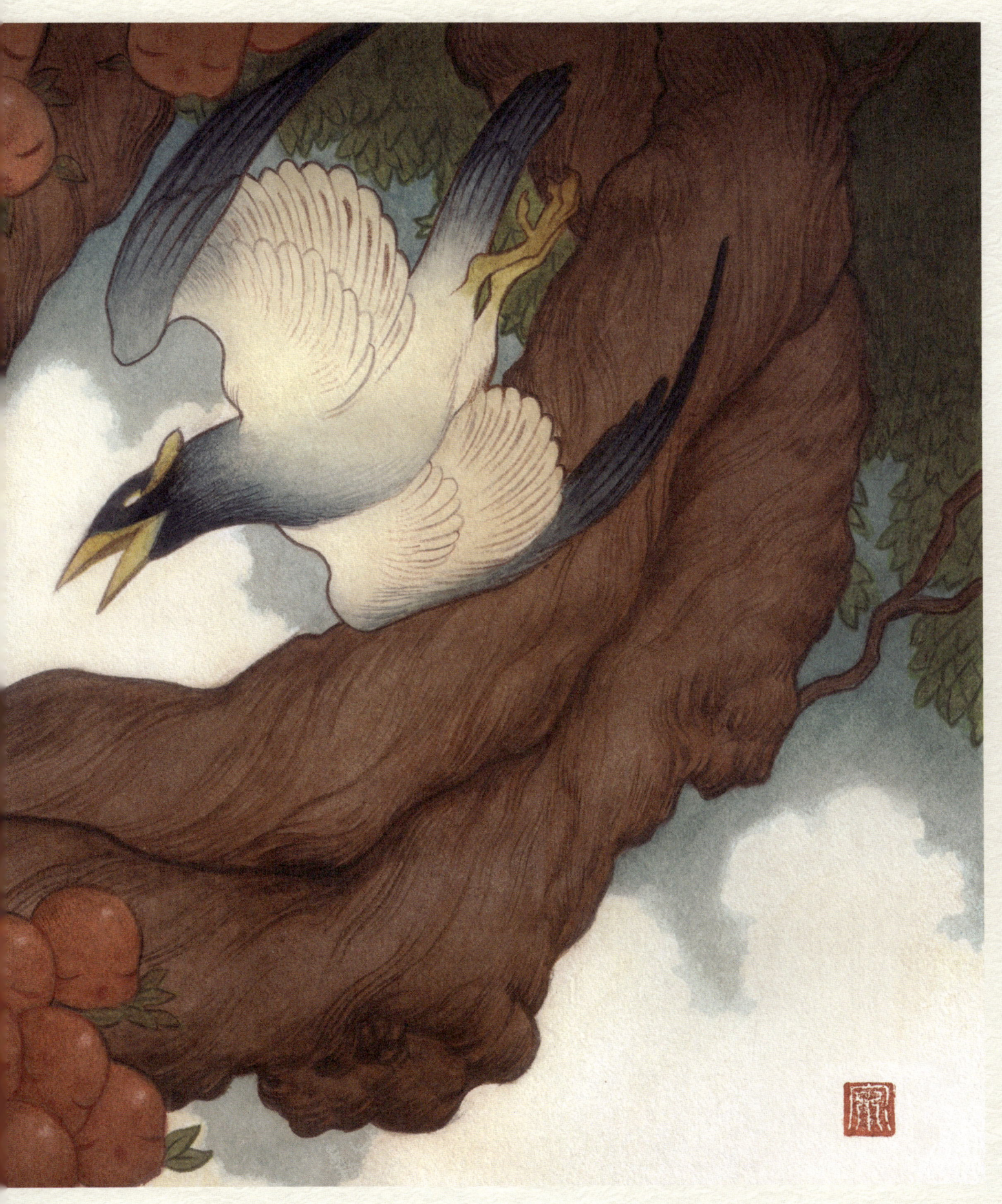

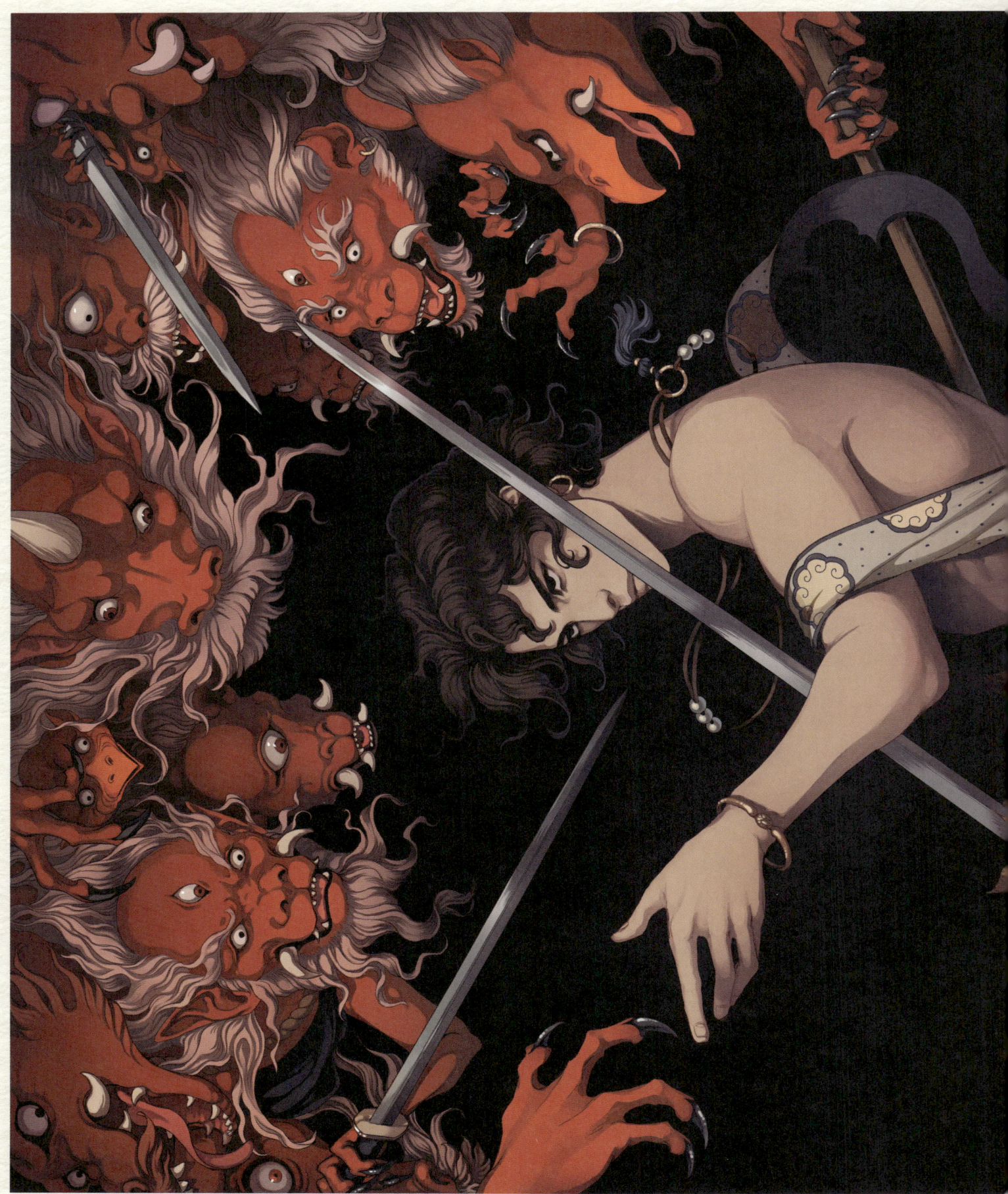

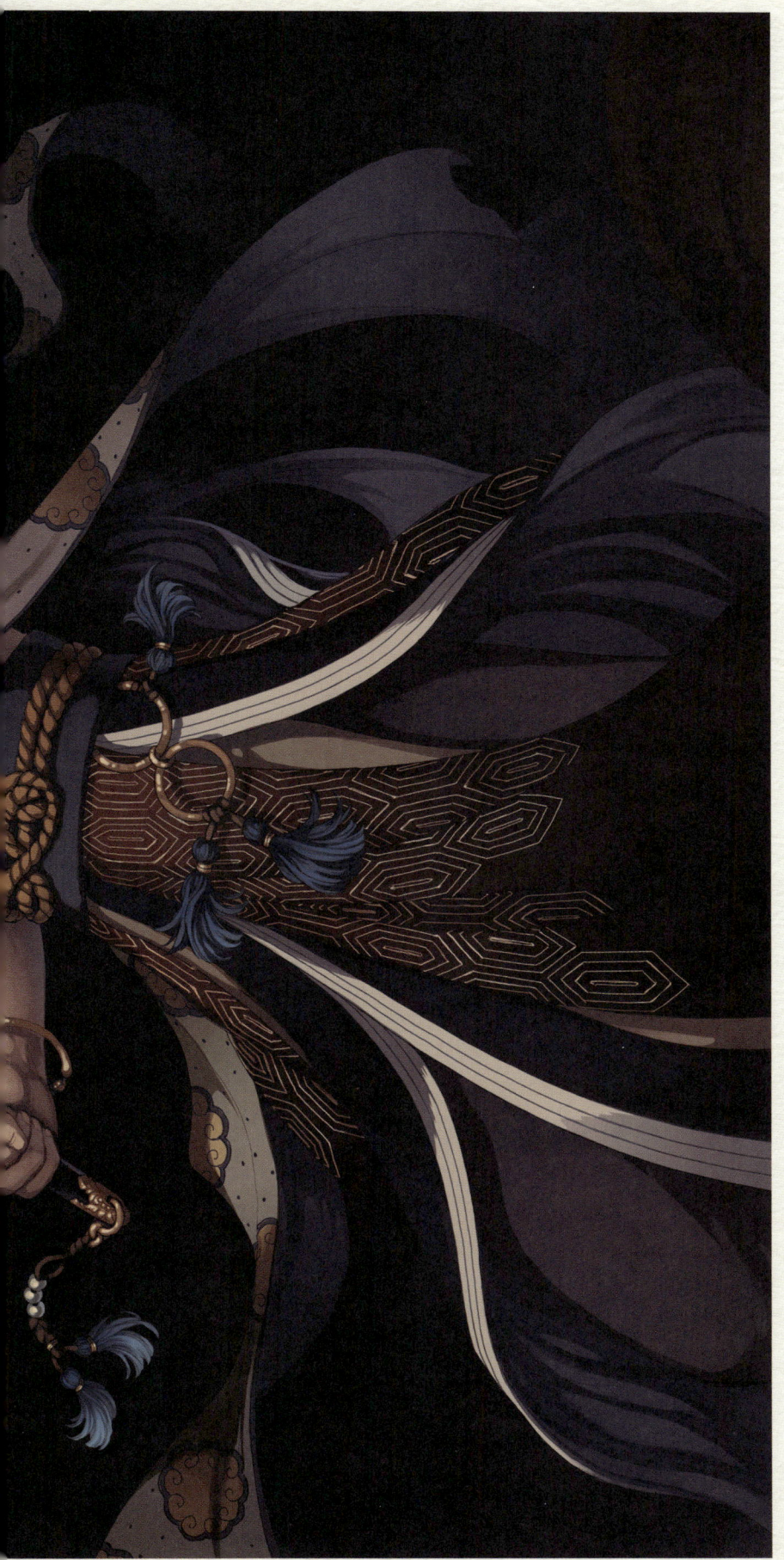

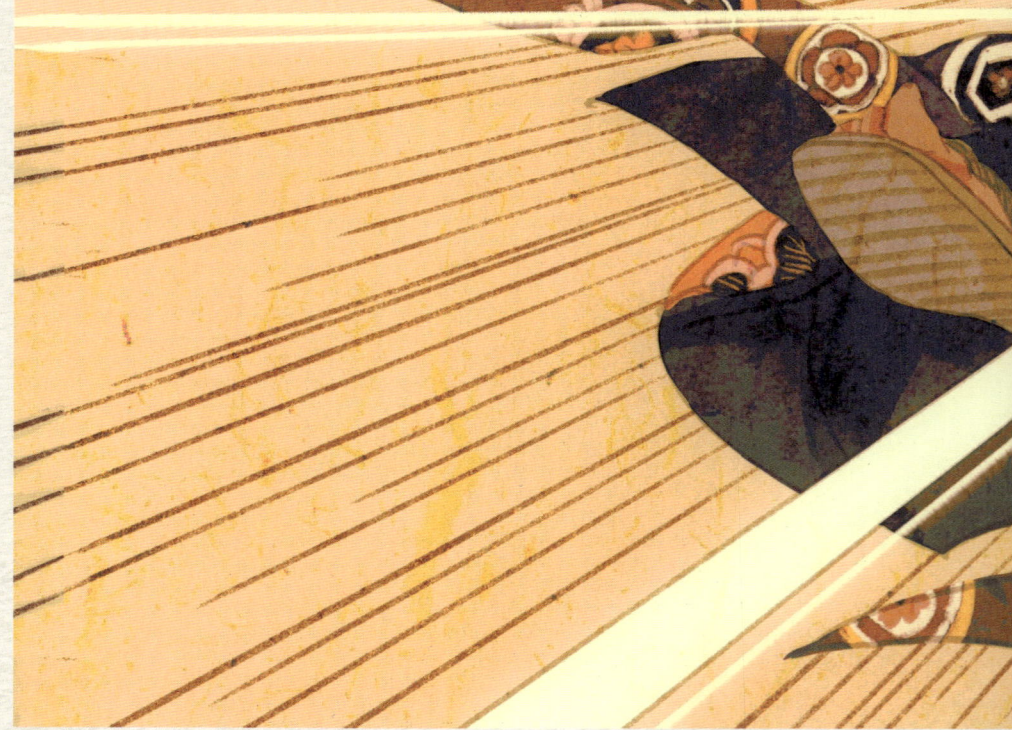

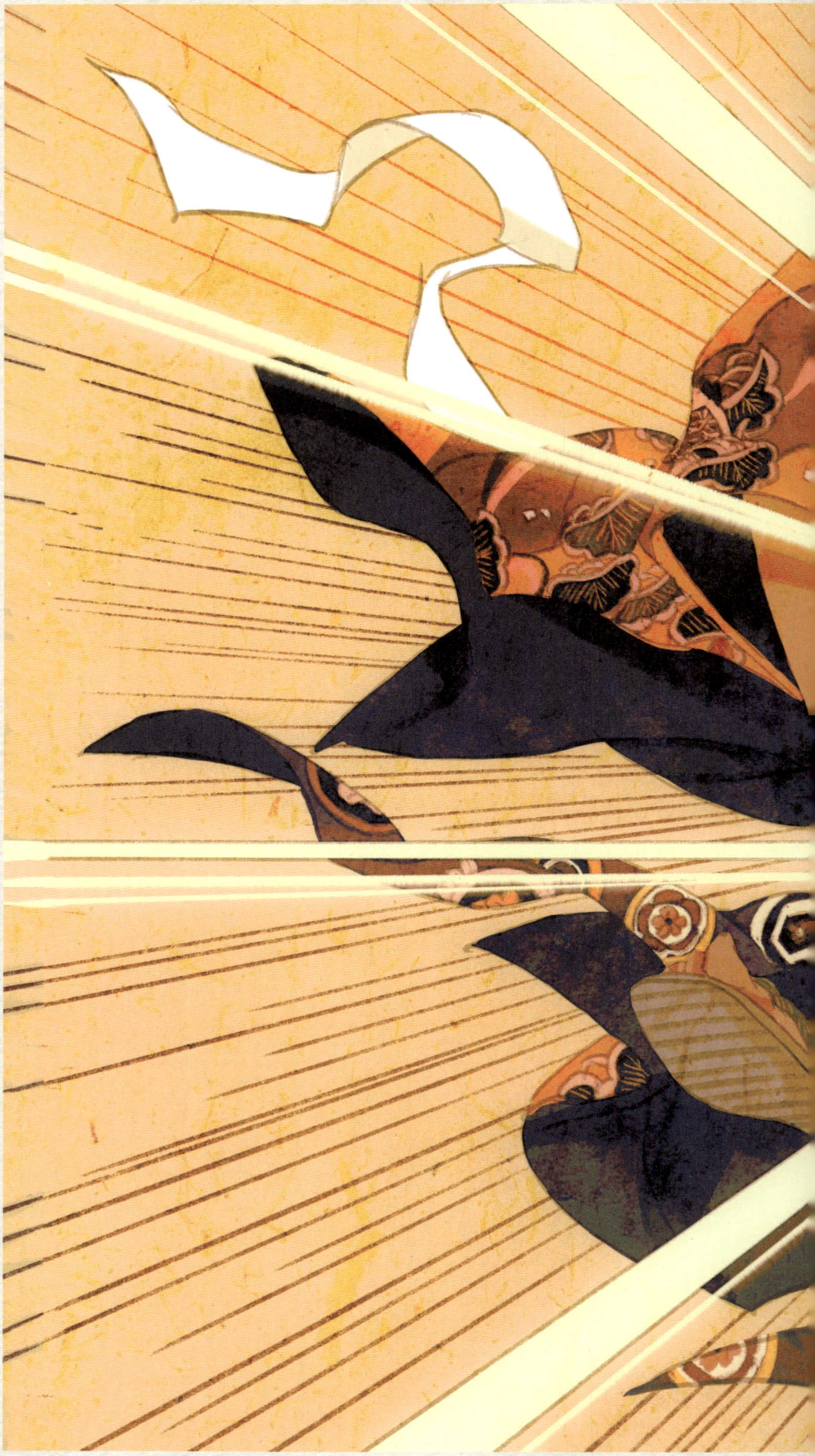

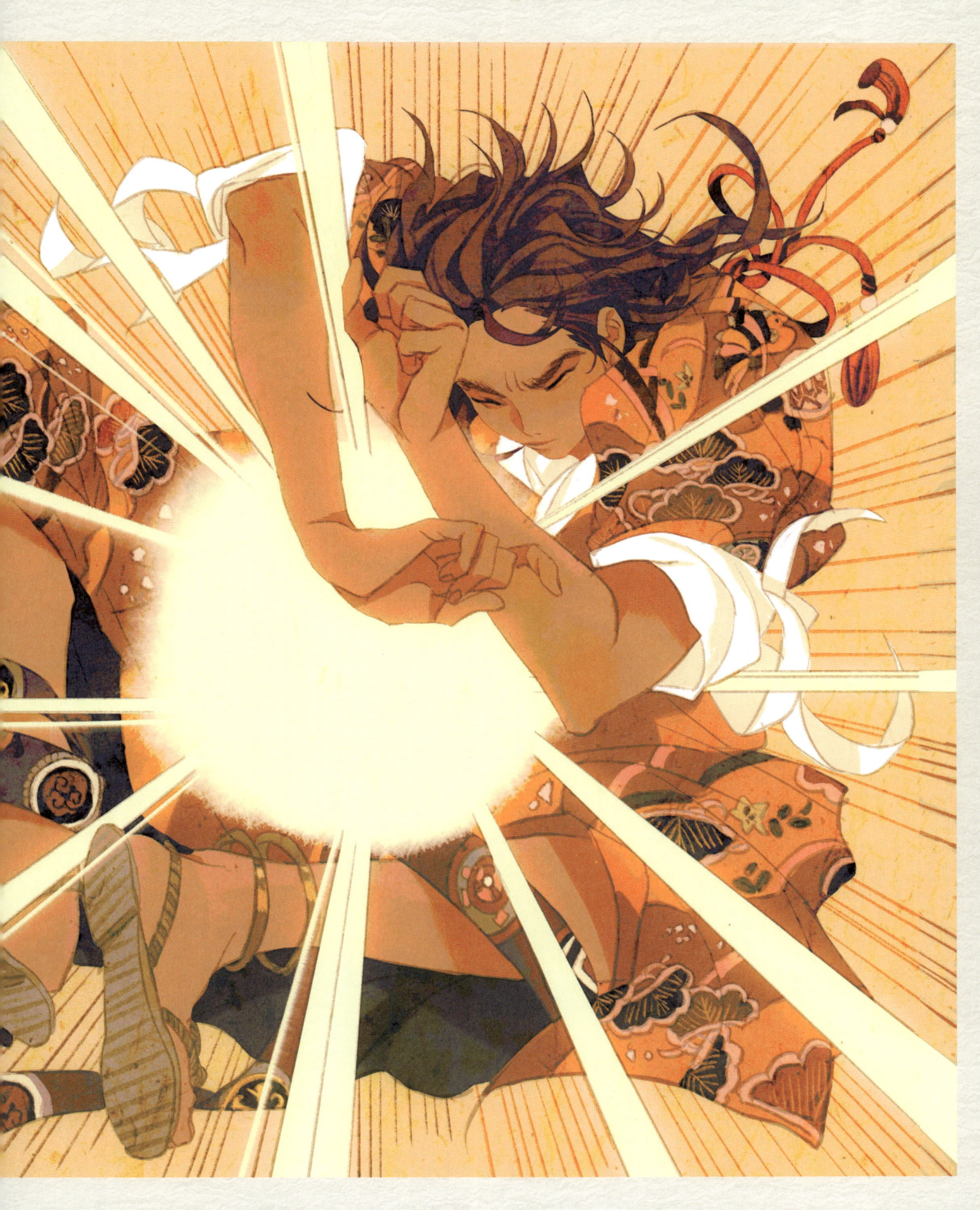

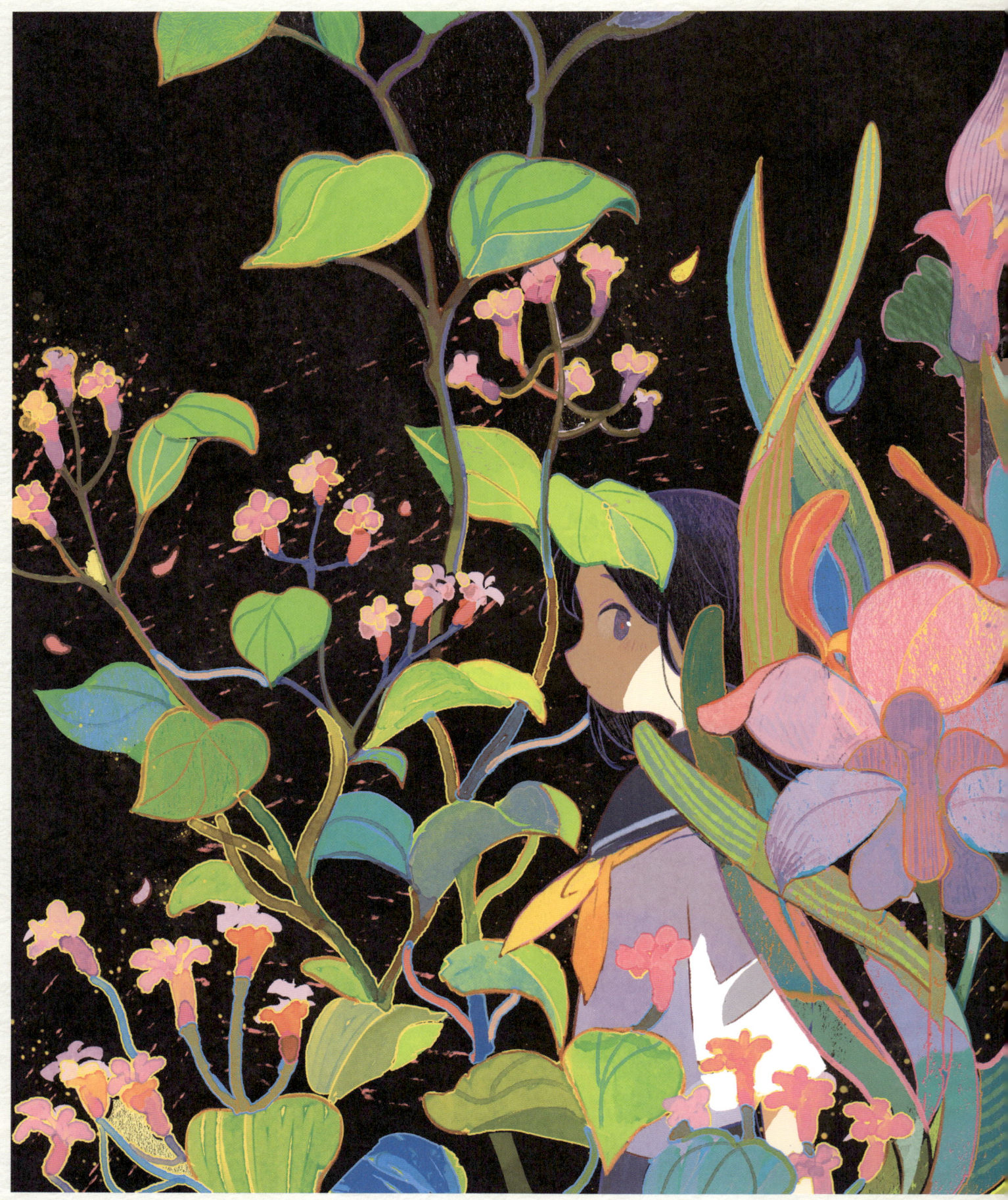

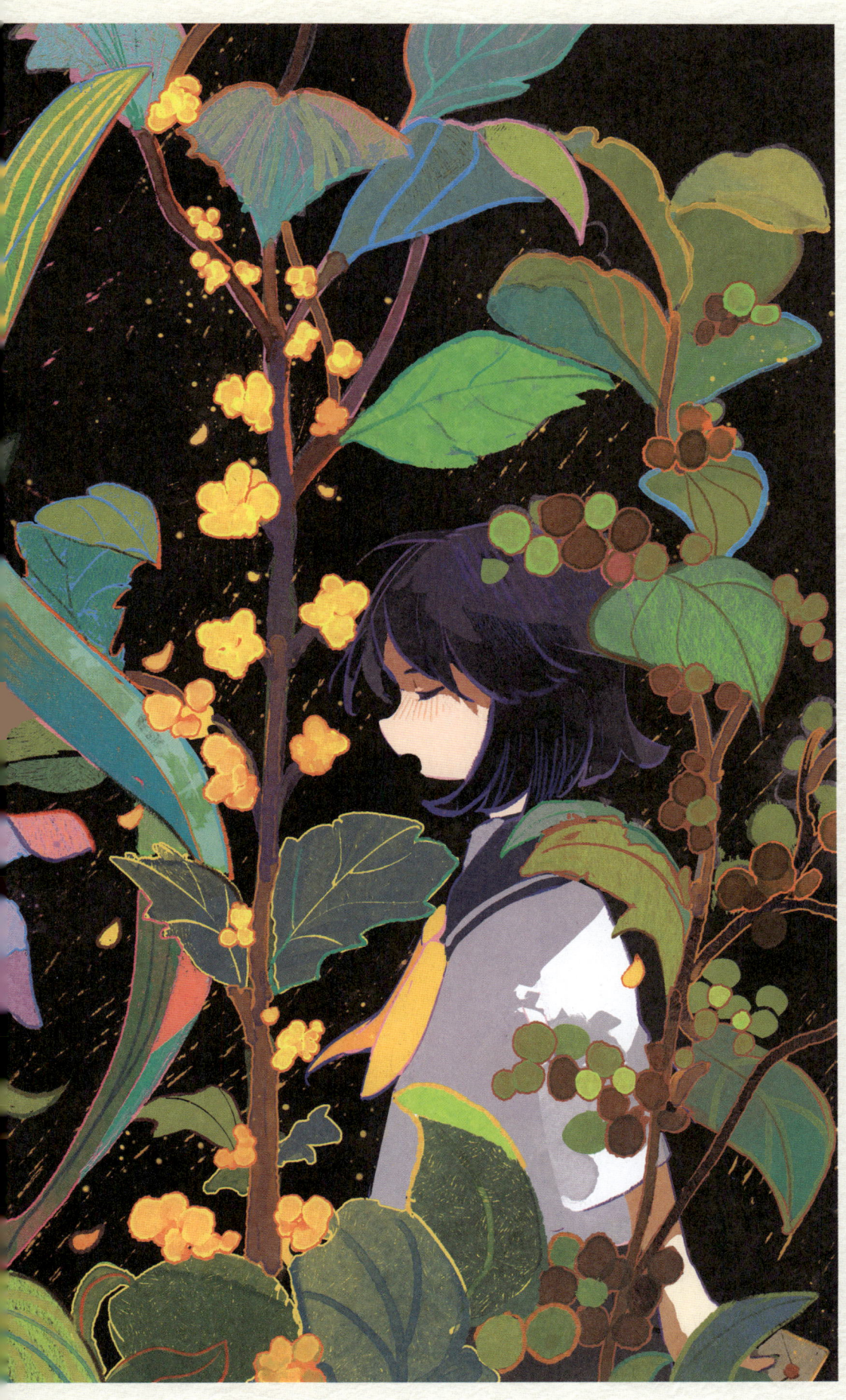

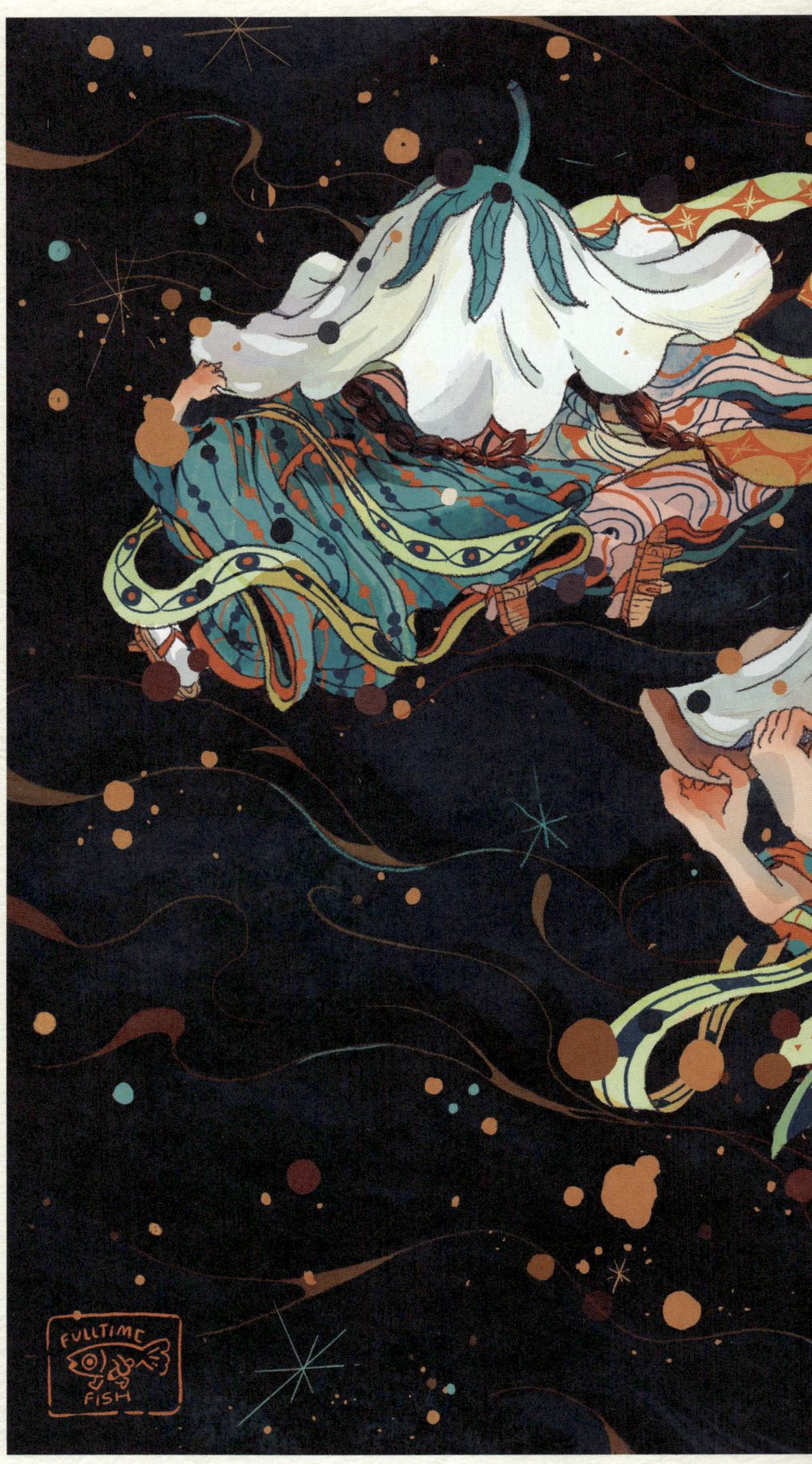

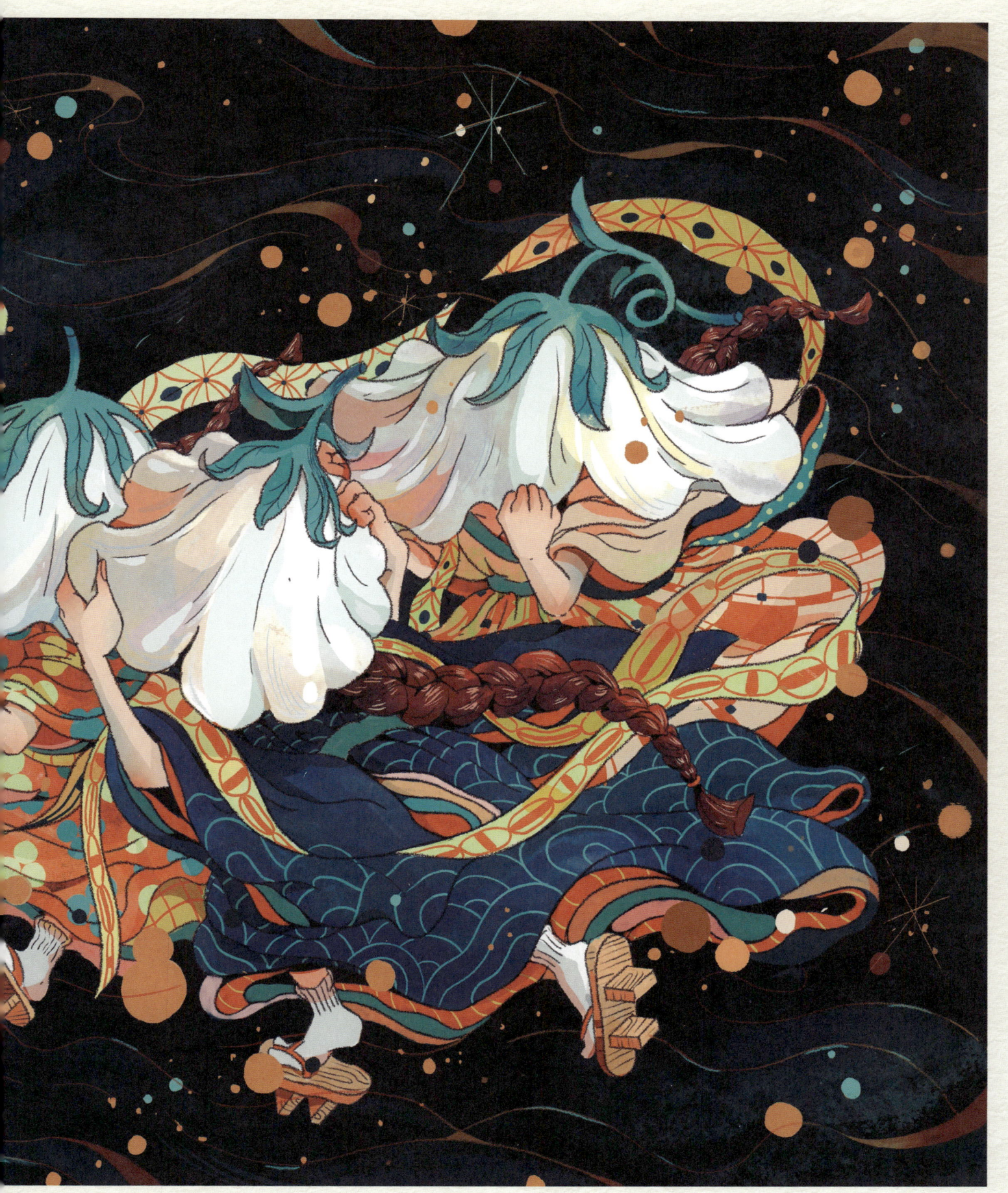

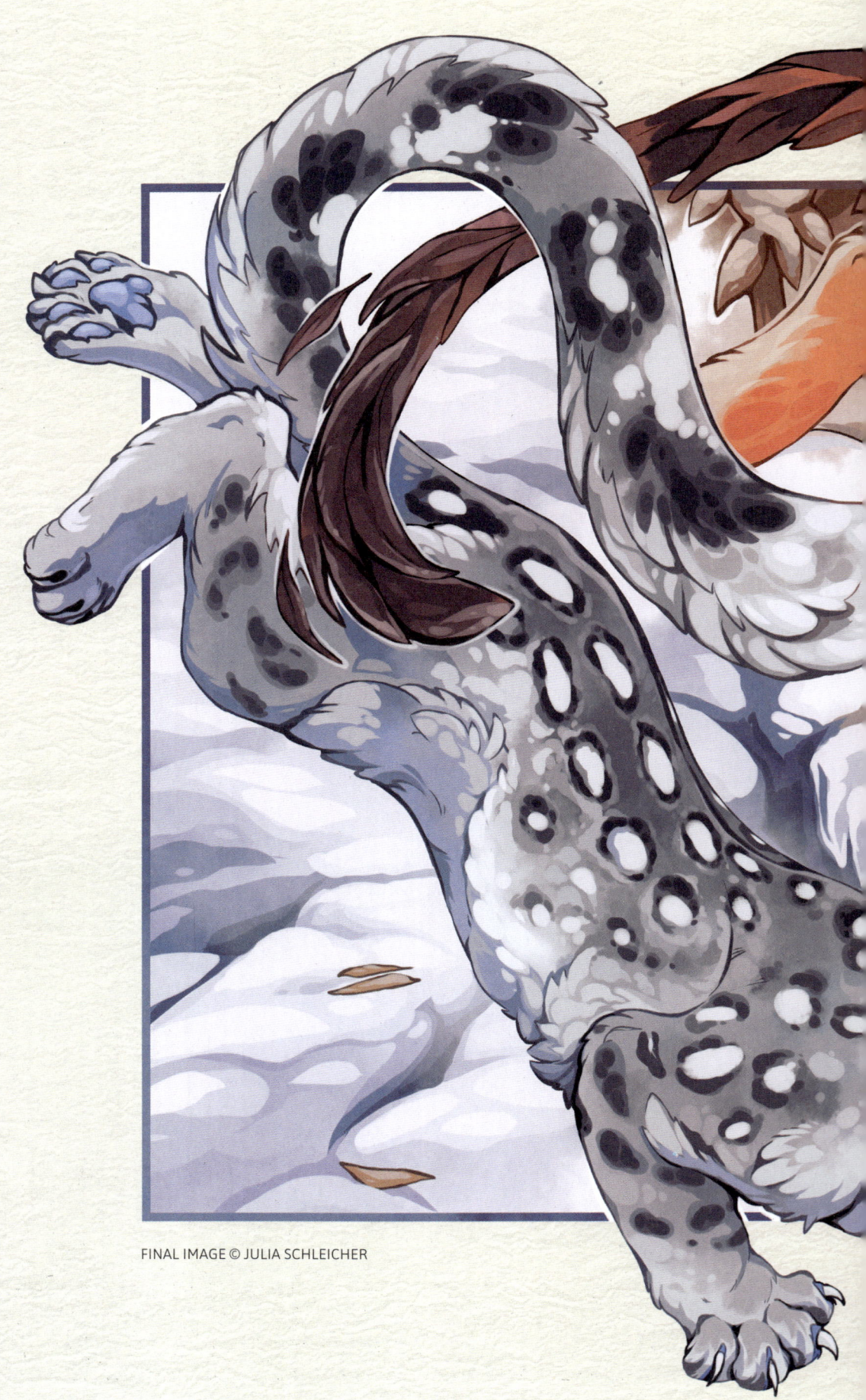

FINAL IMAGE © JULIA SCHLEICHER

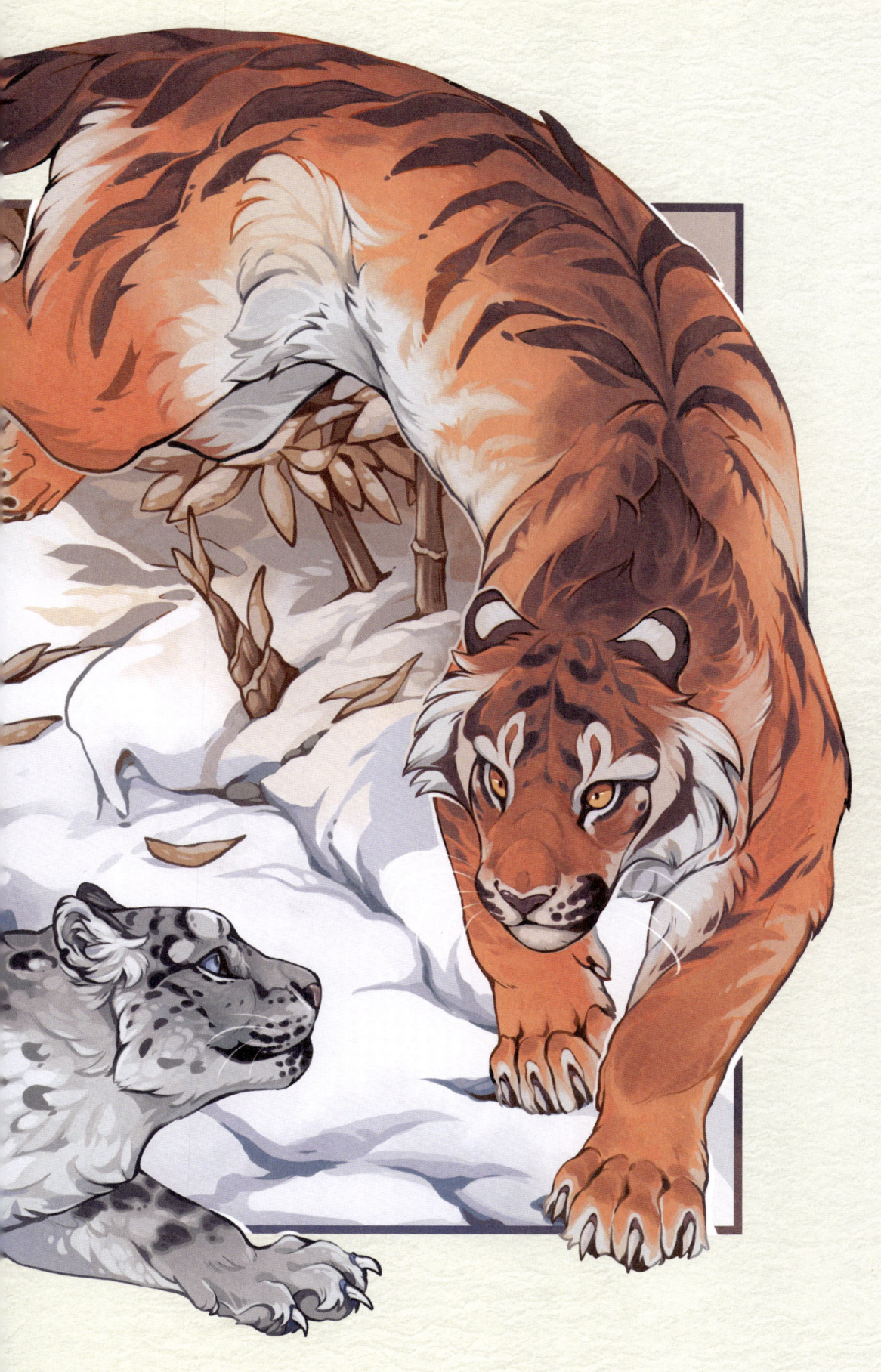

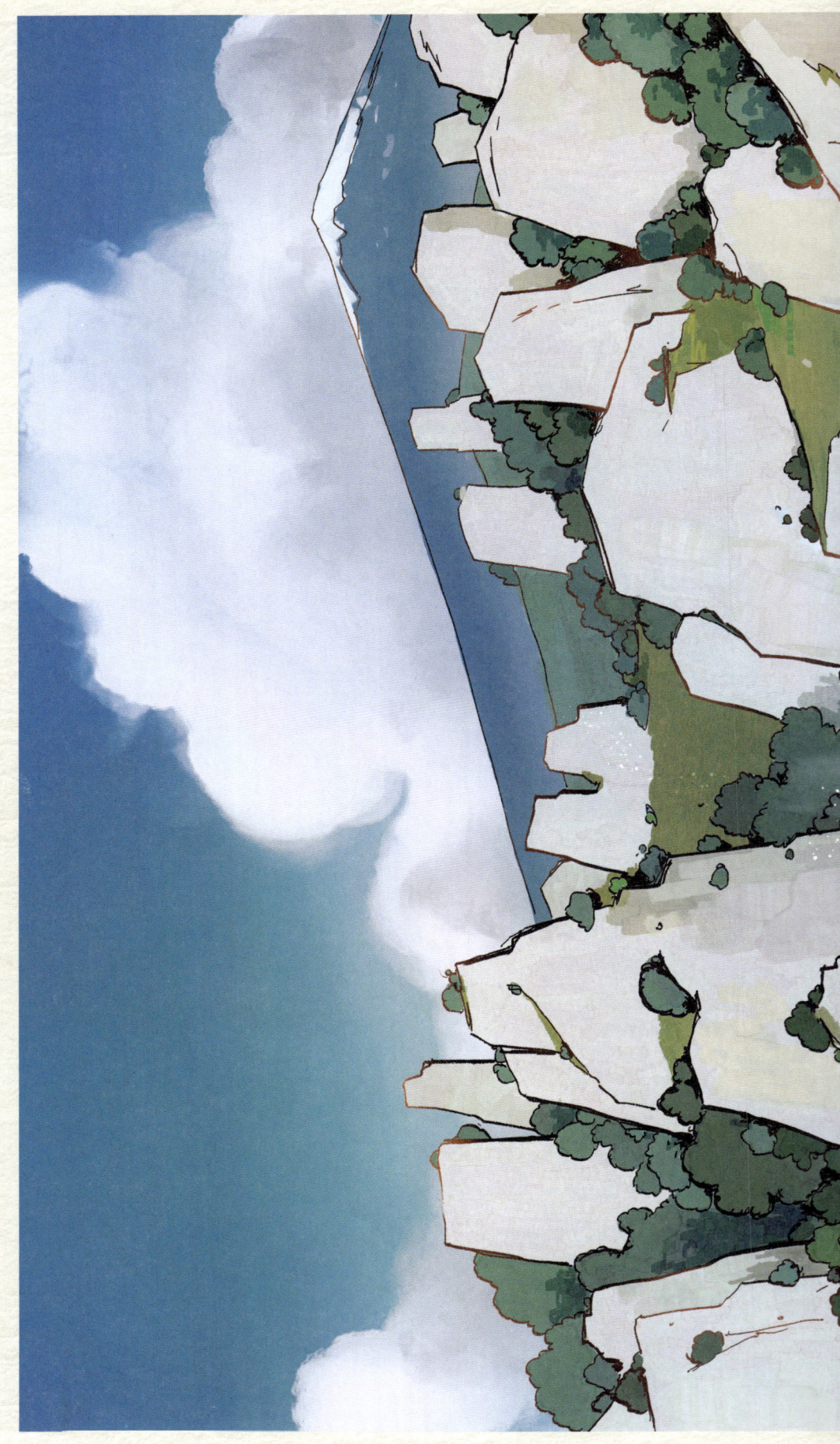

FINAL IMAGE © ANGELA HAO

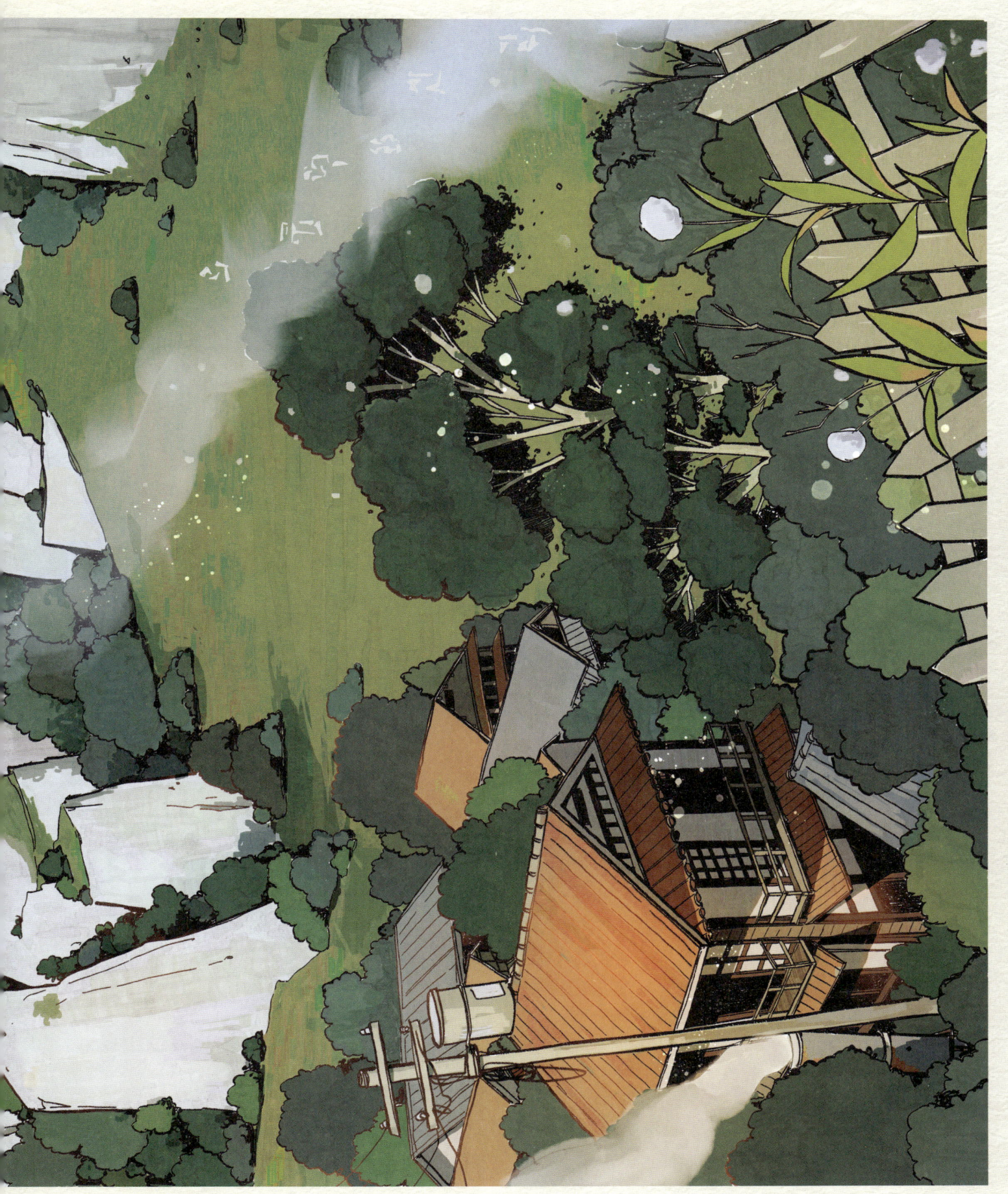

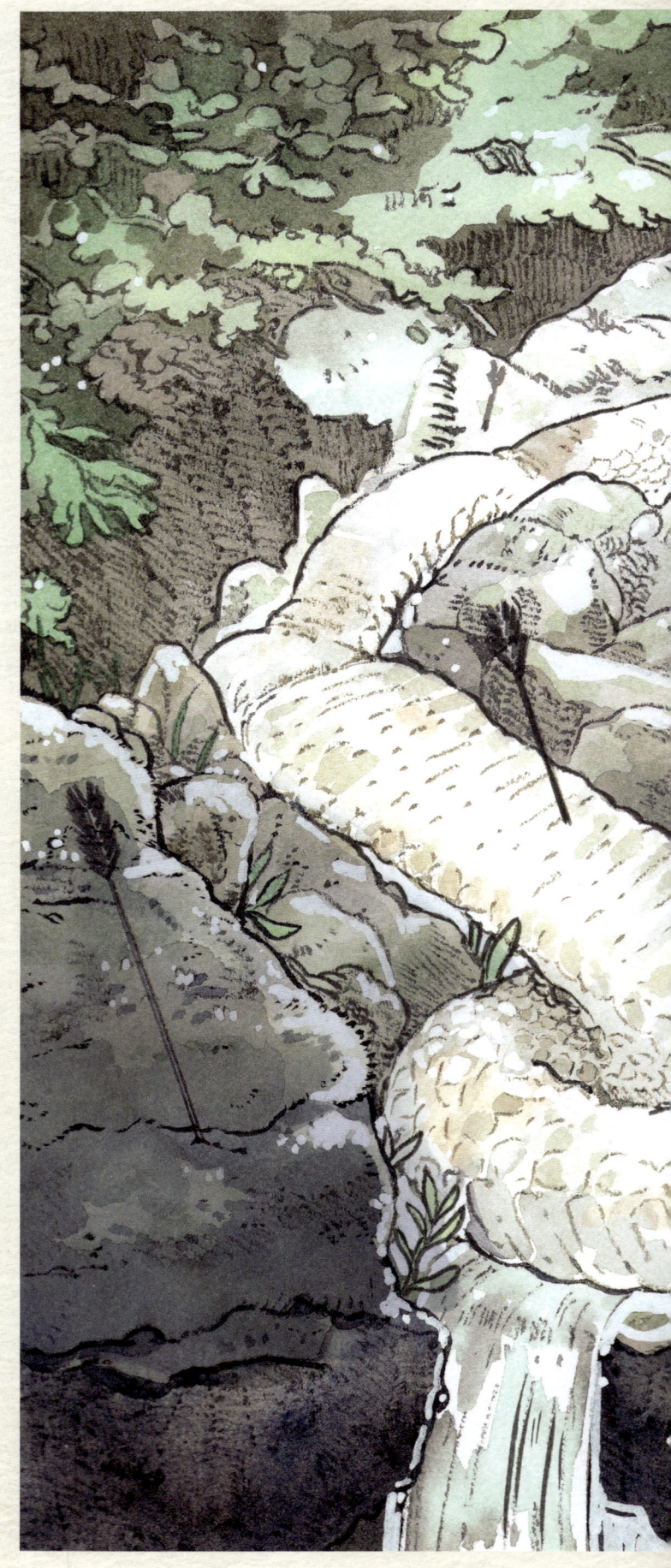

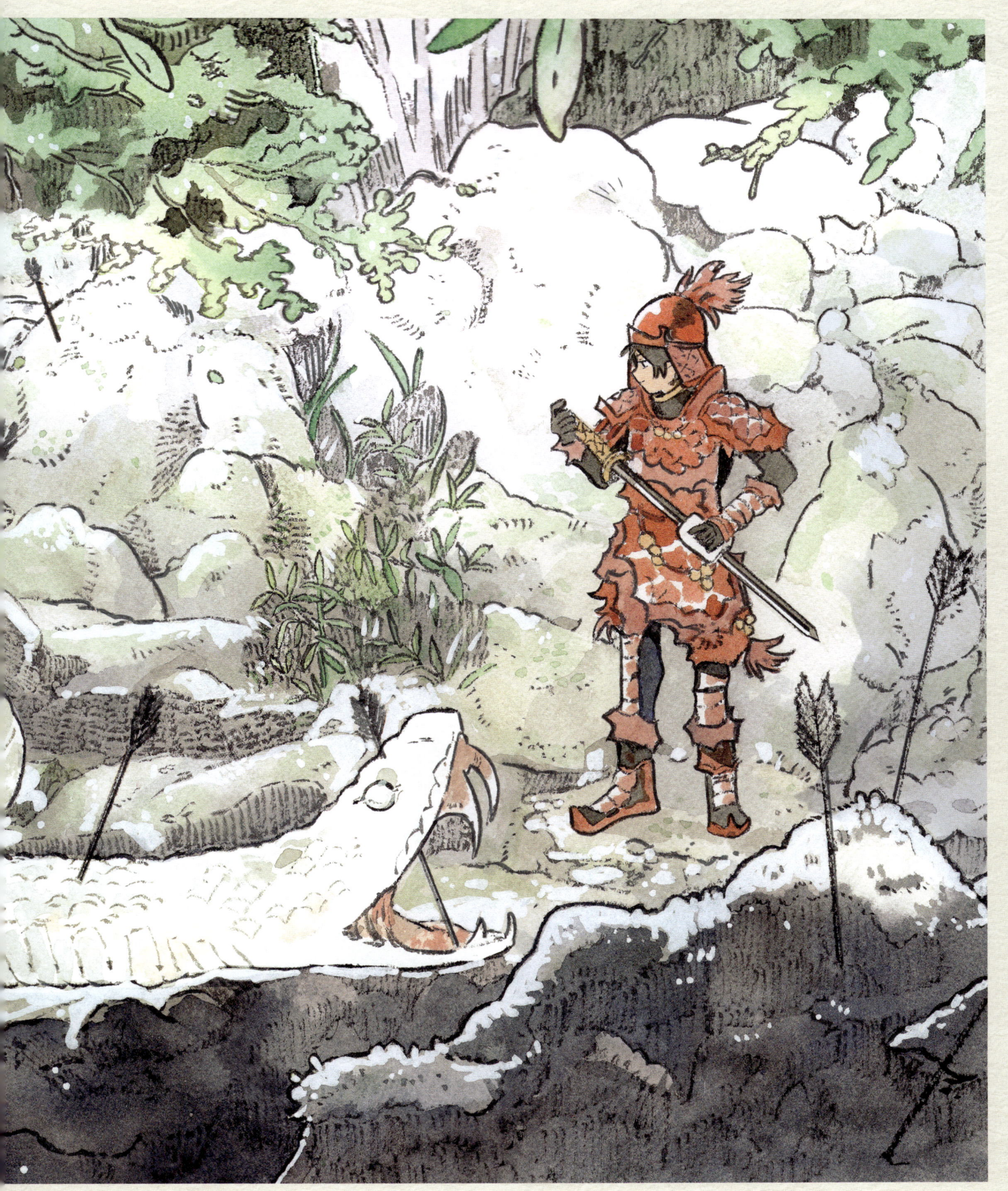

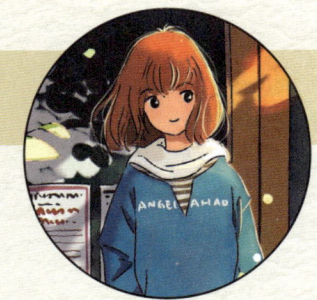

ANGELA HAO
instagram.com/angelahao_art

Angela Hao is a US-based digital illustrator with a passion for creating background art, architecture, and storefronts, drawing inspiration from nature, culture, and the world of manga and anime.

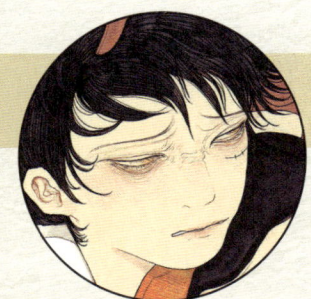

HAGUSHKA
x.com/hagushka

Hagushka is a freelance illustrator known for creating art that combines dark fantasies with soft lines.

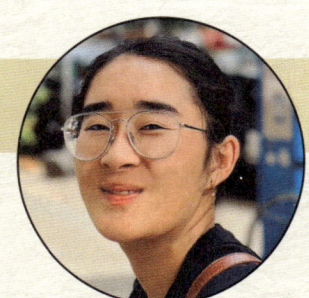

JAMIE CHEN
instagram.com/fulltimefish

Jamie Chen, also known as Fulltimefish, is an illustrator and graphic designer based in California. As a digital artist, her work focuses on fantastical and surreal themes inspired by manga, nature, and everyday moments.

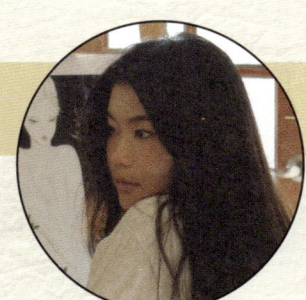

JANICE SUNG
janicesung.com

Janice Sung is a Canadian artist and painter. Drawing inspiration from Neoclassical, Baroque, and traditional Chinese and Japanese art, Janice blends human figures with natural elements to create ethereal and timeless pieces.

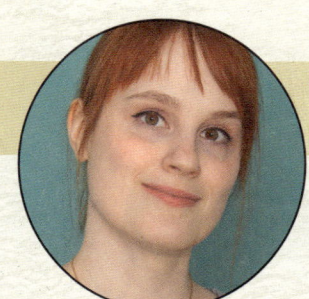

JOHANNA FORSTER
johannaforster.com

Johanna Forster is a German illustrator known for her drawings of blooming nature and adorable creatures, which she sells online and on commission for game and book projects.

IMAGE © ANGELA HAO

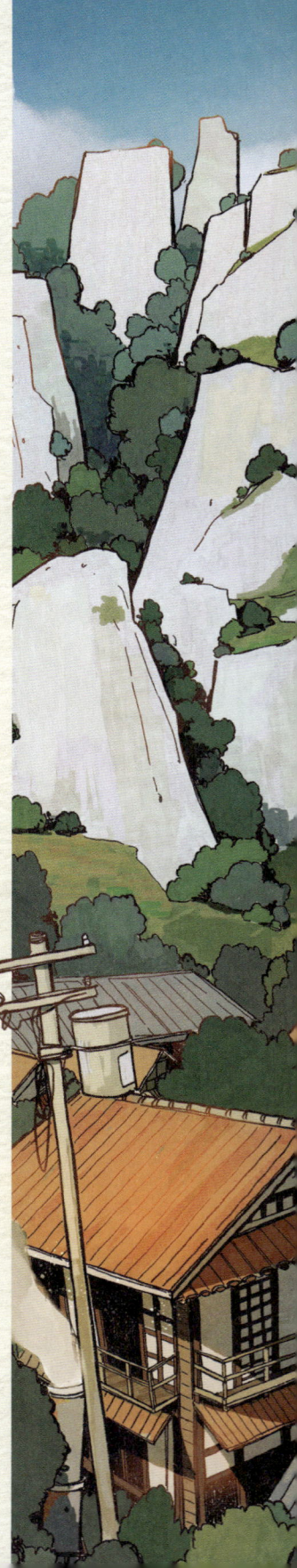

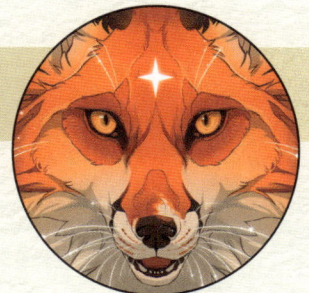

JULIA SCHLEICHER
instagram.com/juli_artwork

Julia Schleicher is a freelance artist based in Germany. She loves to combine animals with nature and draws inspiration for her personal and freelance art from anything that comes her way.

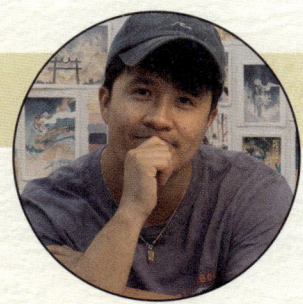

KELOGSLOOPS
kelogsloops.com

Hieu Nguyen is an Australian artist who goes by the name of Kelogsloops. He loves drawing mostly female portraiture, finding joy in experimenting with the world of watercolour to explore fantasy and surreal concepts.

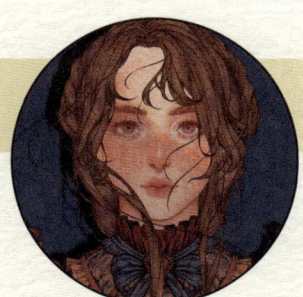

LOLLOCO
instagram.com/thelolloco

Lolloco is a self-taught freelance illustrator and digital artist who is deeply inspired by the elegance of Art Nouveau, the symbolic richness of ukiyo-e, and the meticulous brushstrokes found in the Gongbi painting style.

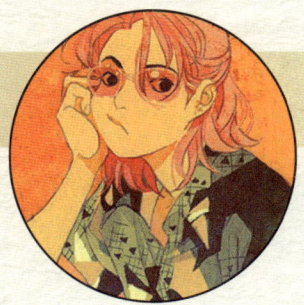

LUOMAN
instagram.com/luoman_art

Man Luo is a Chinese artist living in Paris, France, who specializes in drawing female characters.

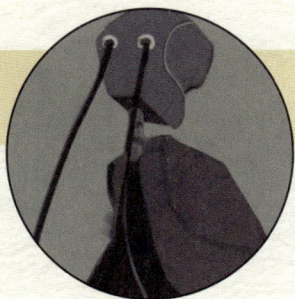

MENGXUAN LI
x.com/MengxuanLiArt

Mengxuan Li is a freelance illustrator and concept artist who loves to draw nature scenes and little characters.

CONTRIBUTORS

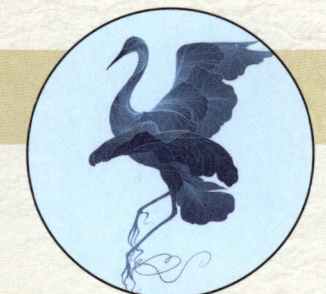

MONA FINDEN
monafinden.com

Mona Finden is a full-time digital artist who lives and works in Oslo, Norway. She specializes in character art that is often fantasy, and mostly works on book illustrations.

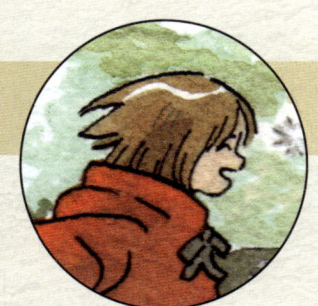

PARAKID
parakid.com

Aspiring to capture the feeling of a moment frozen in time through her watercolour and ink illustrations, Parakid primarily focuses on slice-of-life moments that bring a sense of nostalgia and peace.

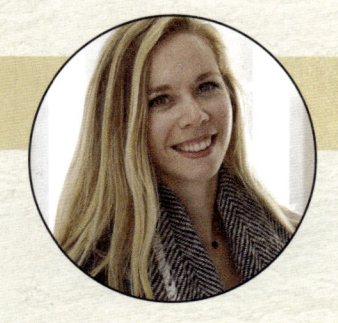

TESSA NELISSEN
instagram.com/jessali_tn

Tessa Nelissen is a Dutch illustrator residing in Norway. She mostly uses digital media to draw cute and colourful characters and scenery, often containing cats.

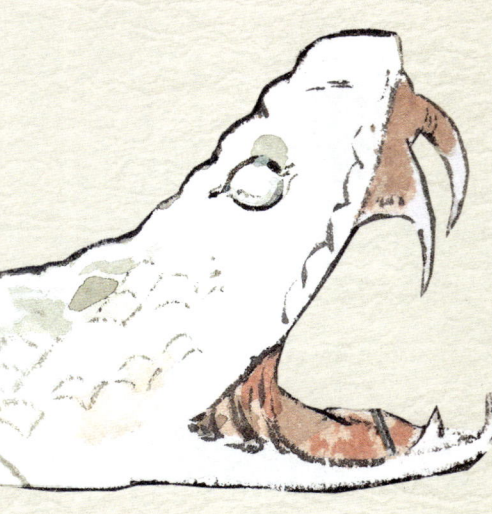

IMAGE © PARAKID

ACRYLIC
a water-based paint made from pigment and resin

ANIME
an animation, or style of animation,
that originates in Japan

BAROQUE
an elaborate style of art, popular across
Europe in the 17th and 18th centuries

BLOCKING
a technique that places bold colours next
to each other to create contrast

CEL SHADING
a technique used in animation and video games
to create a stylized, flat appearance

CHIBI
a Japanese art style that involves drawing heavily stylized
'cute' characters, often found in anime and manga

COMPOSITION
a way to describe how different elements
of an art piece are arranged

CONTOUR
a line that defines an object or element

EDO PERIOD
a time period in Japan lasting from 1603 to
1868, known widely as an era of creativity

GOUACHE
a water-based paint similar to watercolour,
but opaque instead of transparent

HEIAN PERIOD
a time period in Japan lasting from the late
8th century to the early 12th century

HUE
the basic colour of a pigment, regardless
of value (such as blue, red, or green)

MANGA
comics or graphic novels that originate in Japan

MOTIF
a repeated theme in a work of art

NEGATIVE SPACE
the empty space that surrounds an object
or element in a drawing or painting

NEOCLASSICAL
an art style that began in the mid-18th century inspired
by the artwork found in ancient Greece and Rome

NIHONGA
a traditional Japanese painting style using
ink or pigments on silk or paper

OPACITY
the degree of which an object or element blocks
light and visibility, or lack of transparency

PORTRAITURE
the art of drawing or painting a person's likeness

REALISM
an art style that depicts everyday life, made
popular in the mid-19th century

RENDERING
adding detail to an image

SHINTO
a traditional Japanese religion that revolves
around nature and natural spirits called kami

TEXTURE
using marking techniques to create the illusion of depth

UKIYO-E
a traditional Japanese art form involving the use of
woodblock printing to capture images of everyday life

WASHI PAPER
a traditional Japanese paper made from plant fibres

WOODBLOCK PRINTING
a printing technique that involves using carved blocks
to press patterns or images onto paper or textiles

GLOSSARY

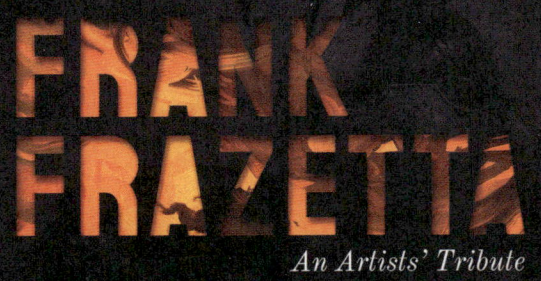

FRANK FRAZETTA

An Artists' Tribute

This book celebrates Frank Frazetta's enduring influence on artists working across the creative industry today, featuring professional illustrators, concept artists, painters, and sculptors who hold 'the godfather of fantasy art' among their biggest inspirations.

In step-by-step tutorials, eleven artists reveal how they create exclusive homages inspired by their favourite elements of Frazetta's work and style. Respected guests and industry legends – including Sara Frazetta, Robert Rodriguez, Allen Williams, Rafael Grassetti, and The Shiflett Brothers – also share their personal tales of Frazetta's influence on their lives and work, and discuss their favourites of his many iconic paintings.

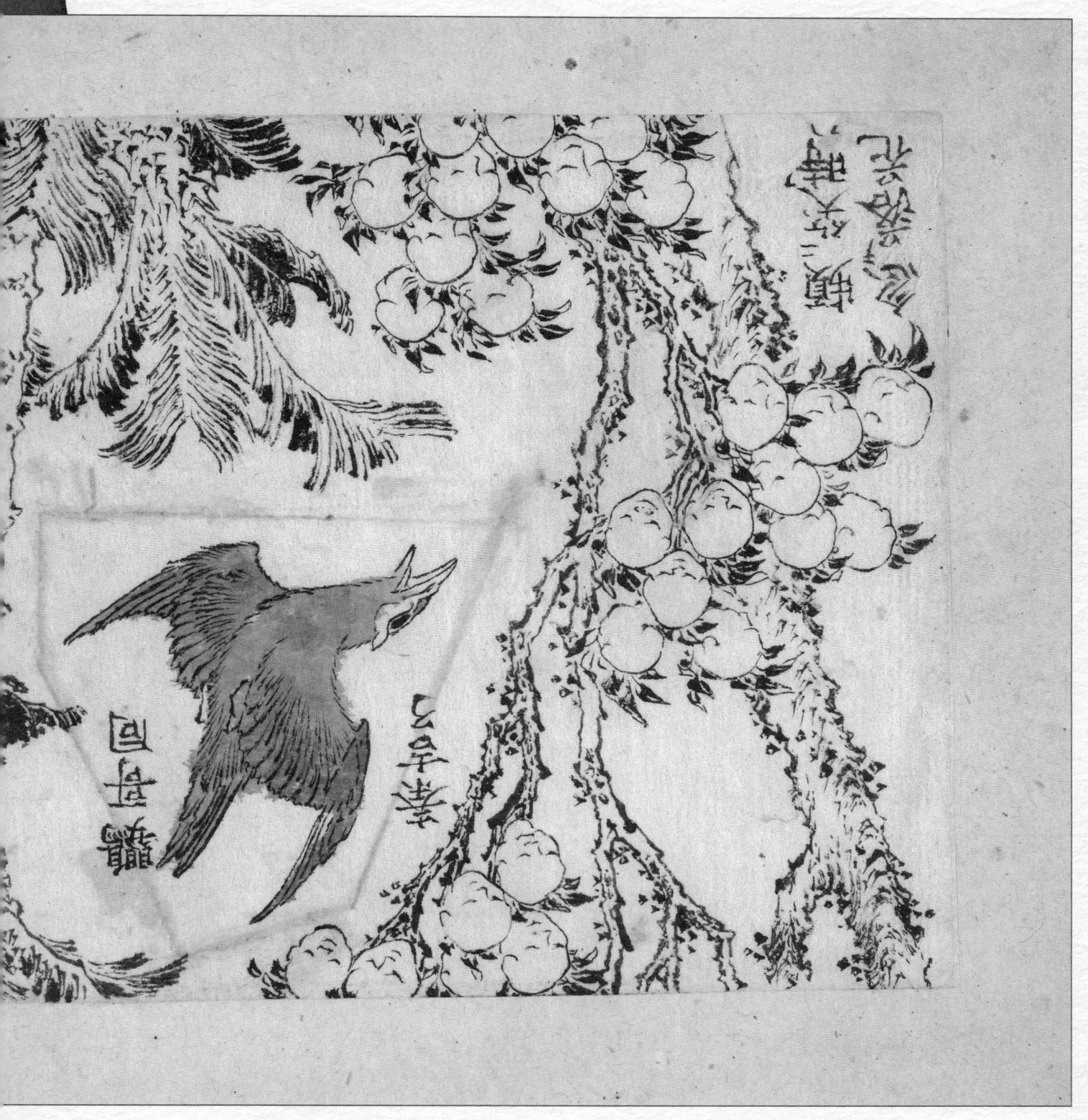

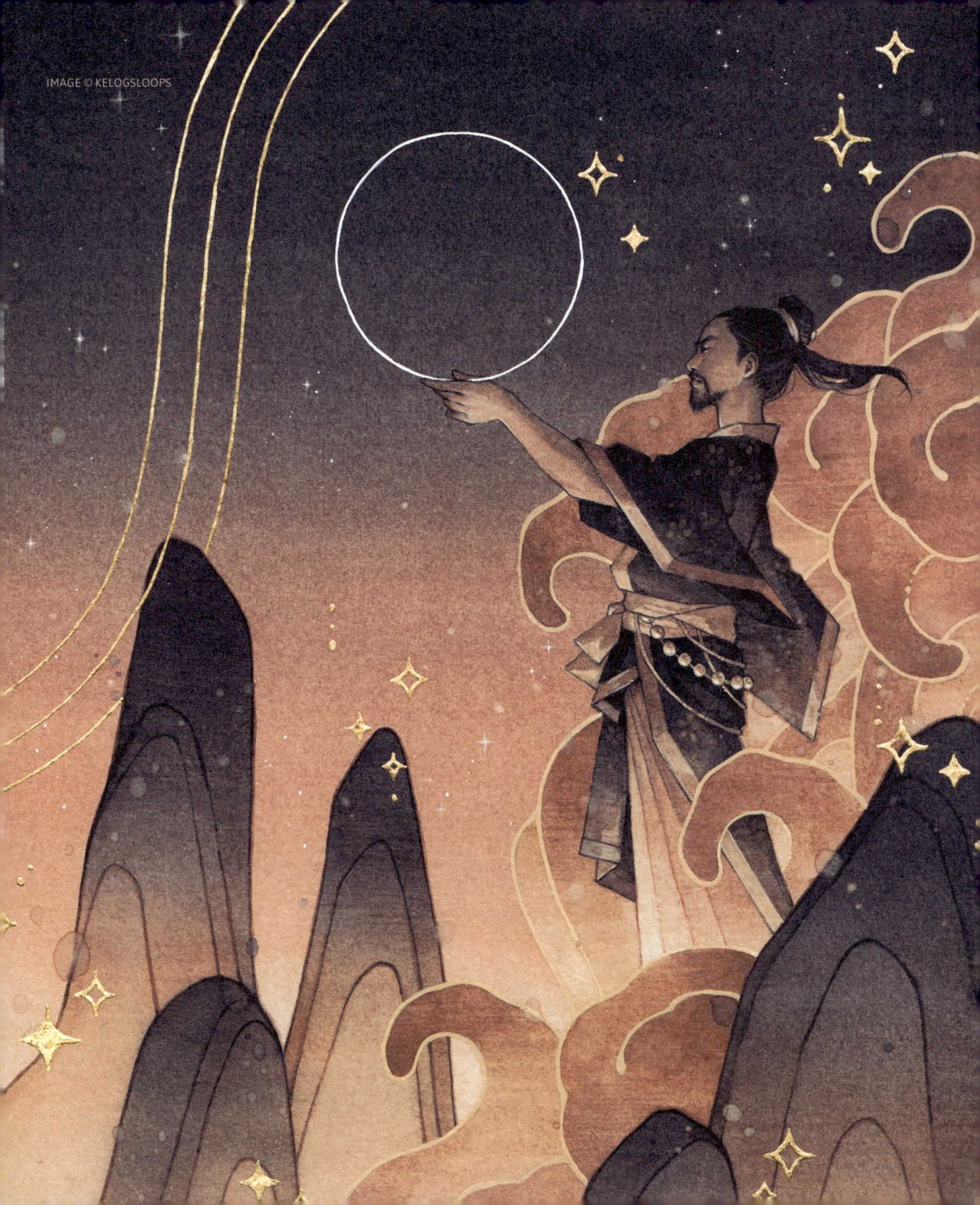

3dtotalPublishing

3DTOTAL PUBLISHING IS A TRAILBLAZING, CREATIVE PUBLISHER SPECIALIZING IN INSPIRATIONAL AND EDUCATIONAL RESOURCES FOR ARTISTS.

Our titles feature top industry professionals from around the globe who share their experience in skilfully written step-by-step tutorials and fascinating, detailed guides. Illustrated throughout with stunning artwork, these bestselling publications offer creative insight, expert advice, and essential motivation. Fans of digital art will enjoy our comprehensive volumes covering Adobe Photoshop, Procreate, and Blender, as well as our superb titles based around character design, including *Fundamentals of Character Design* and *Creating Characters for the Entertainment Industry*. The dedicated, high-quality blend of instruction and inspiration also extends to traditional art. Titles covering a range of techniques, genres, and abilities allow your creativity to flourish while building essential skills.

Well-established within the industry, we now offer over 100 titles and counting, many of which have been translated into multiple languages around the world. With something for every artist, we are proud to say that our books offer the 3dtotal package:

LEARN · CREATE · SHARE

VISIT US AT STORE.3DTOTAL.COM

3dtotal Publishing is part of 3dtotal.com, a leading website for CG artists founded by Tom Greenway in 1999.

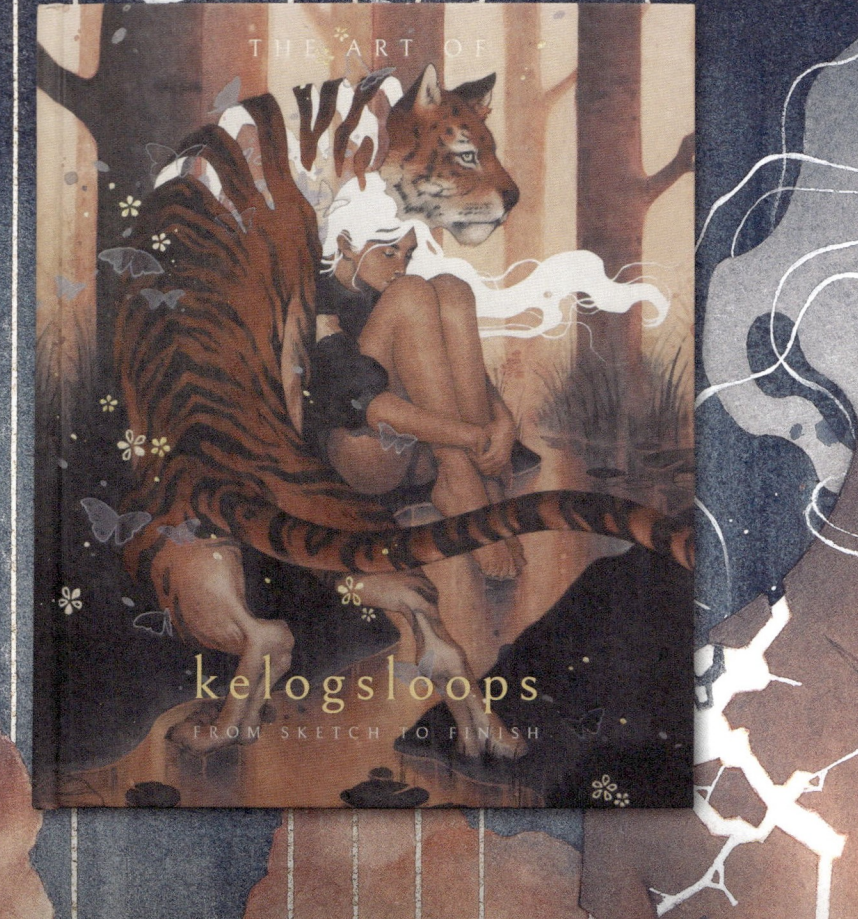

THE ART OF

kelogsloops

FROM SKETCH TO FINISH

kelogsloops

The Art of Kelogsloops: From Sketch to Finish is the artist's debut book where readers can discover more about his creative journey, including schooling, first professional steps, and how he came to work with studios such as Disney and Paramount Pictures, as well as popular card-game powerhouses like *Magic: The Gathering*. With its high-quality finish and exciting content, it is a keepsake readers will cherish for many years to come.

store.3dtotal.com